EMPLOYMENT COURT PRACTICE

AUSTRALIA
Law Book Co.
Sydney

CANADA AND USA
Carswell
Toronto

HONG KONG
Sweet & Maxwell Asia

NEW ZEALAND
Brookers
Wellington

SINGAPORE and MALAYSIA
Sweet & Maxwell Asia
Singapore and Kuala Lumpur

EMPLOYMENT COURT PRACTICE

2008

By

Jonathan Swift, First Treasury Counsel, Chancery

Chris Chapman, Solicitor and fee paid Employment Judge
Deputy Chairman of the Central Arbitration Committee
Member of the ACAS Panel of Arbitrators

John Macmillan, Regional Employment Judge, Employment Tribunals

Sarah Moore, Barrister and fee paid Employment Judge, Employment
Tribunals

Daniel Oudkerk, Barrister

Naomi Cunningham, Barrister

Hamish Cameron Blackie, Barlow Robbins LLP

Thomas Kibling, Barrister

LONDON
SWEET & MAXWELL
2008

EMPLOYMENT COURT PRACTICE 2008
Published in 2008 by
Sweet & Maxwell Limited of 100 Avenue Road,
http://www.sweetandmaxwell.co.uk
Typeset by LBJ Typesetting Ltd of Kingsclere
Printed in the UK by CPI William Clowes
Beccles NR34 7TL

No natural forests were destroyed to make this product;
only farmed timber was used and re-planted.

British Library Cataloguing in Publication Data

A CIP catalogue record for this book
is available from the British Library

ISBN 978-1-84703-709-1

FOREWORD TO 2007 EDITION

by Sir Patrick Elias
President of the Employment Appeal Tribunal

Some 40 years ago the Donovan Commission recommended the use of industrial tribunals (as they were) to deal with certain employment disputes. What they envisaged was the notion of a wise man dispensing justice under a palm tree (even before the advent of global warming), dealing largely with dismissal claims. The procedures would be quick, uncomplicated and readily accessible to the most unskilled employee.

The present system of employment tribunals bears as much relationship to that model as the computer does to the calculator. The jurisdiction of tribunals has grown massively. They now deal with law which is of very considerable complexity, as any litigant caught up in indirect discrimination claims quickly learns. The amounts of compensation are in many fields unlimited, and complex cases may take weeks to be heard. Yet tribunals are still expected to be sufficiently informal to enable litigants in person to pursue their claims. Chairing a tribunal is now a most arduous and responsible task, requiring an array of personal and legal skills.

Procedures have developed apace to match the burgeoning development of the substantive law. There is far greater emphasis placed on case management, considerations of efficiency have become more pronounced, and the rules on grievance and dismissal procedures in particular have created their own curious and complex area of jurisdiction.

This book is designed to assist litigants and their advisors through the complex maze of tribunal procedure, including the procedures dealing with appeals to the EAT and from the EAT to the Court of Appeal. It takes the form of commentary to the legislative material, which includes the primary statutes, the regulations and the various bodies of rules. The first half of the book is directed to employment litigation procedure in general, and the second deals with particular areas of interest and concern such as territorial jurisdiction, claims under EU law, and human rights.

There are now a very substantial number of appeals to the EAT which fall generally in the area of practice and procedure. Last year over a quarter of the appeals fell into this category, so judges regularly have to grapple with this difficult area. Some judges have become veritable anoraks in some of the more arcane areas of tribunal procedure! The rules and regulations provide a myriad of intellectual puzzles—a not altogether happy consequence of the increasing formalisation of the tribunal system. Sadly they are not all capable of resolution merely by the application of the overriding objective which requires the rules to be construed and discretions exercised in a way which ensures that cases are dealt with justly.

Jonathan Swift, recently appointed Chancery Treasury devil, and Chris Chapman, a Chairman of Employment Tribunals, have the overall editorial responsibility for the text. They have discharged it admirably. They have gathered together a team of experts who are steeped in the law and lore of tribunal procedures. There are practitioners on both sides of the profession, and also full time tribunal chairmen. As one would expect from such a distinguished team, the commentary is of the highest quality. One finds erudition and elucidation in equal measure. Anyone with a procedural problem will be greatly assisted to have available not only all the potentially relevant legal rules which bear upon the issue, but also the lucid and detailed commentary. I most warmly recommend this work.

Sir Patrick Elias
Employment Appeal Tribunal
23rd February 2007

PREFACE

Last year we made the rather bold claim that *Employment Court Practice* was intended to be a "White Book" for Employment lawyers. Slightly more than one year on, it is fair to say that we have not quite matched the metronomic regularity with which the White Book is published, but as everyone knows, Employment law tends to walk to the beat of its own drum. In 2008, our aim remains the same—to publish a guide to procedure before all the primary Employment law jurisdictions that is comprehensive, authoritative, and accessible.

Perhaps the single most significant event in this area of the law in the last 12 months remains a work in progress. In March 2007, the Government published the outcome of the independent review of the employment dispute resolution system undertaken by Michael Gibbons. To say that the dispute resolution legislation put in place by the Employment Act 2002 has not been wholly successful would be an understatement. The intention—to put in place practical measures to encourage employees and employers to resolve disputes without resort to the Employment Tribunals—was both pragmatic and commendable. The execution of this intention fell woefully short, and at least from the perspective of the legal system, gave rise only to an additional set of difficult "front-end" rules, a sense that litigants attempting to get to the Employment Tribunal were being unfairly impeded, and overall, yet a further cause for litigation. In the course of this year, the Employment Appeal Tribunal has stuck to the task of making sense out of the practical application of the dispute resolution measures, most notably in *Lawrence v HM Prison Service* ([2007] I.R.L.R. 468, charting the boundary between the application of the statutory grievance and disciplinary procedures), and *City of Bradford v Pratt* and *Highland Council v TGWU* ([2007] I.R.L.R. 192, and [2008] I.R.L.R. 198), both cases on the information to be provided when raising grievances under the statutory procedure). The Court of Appeal also weighed in with its decision in *Bainbridge v Redcar (No. 2)* ([2007] I.R.L.R. 494), making it clear that the powers to reduce and increase compensation for failures to follow the statutory procedures should not be applied when, even if the procedure had been followed to the letter, doing so would have been obviously futile.

For the future, the Gibbons Review, the consultation that followed, and the Employment Bill that has just emerged from consideration by a Grand Committee of the House of Lords, all point in a new direction. If enacted, the Bill will remove the relevant parts of the Employment Act 2002, and with it the statutory dismissal and grievance procedures. In its place, although there will be no new "front-end" deterrent to Employment Tribunal litigation, the present limits on ACAS' powers of conciliation will be removed. In addition there will be a new system of financial penalties, based on compliance (or rather non-compliance) with the statutory Codes of Practice. For the present it looks like these penalties will work in a way similar to the present provisions applicable to the uplift and reduction of compensatory awards. Needless to say, the Employment Act 2008, if that is what it becomes, will loom large in this work in 2009.

This year's commentary incorporates all the leading cases since February 2007. One clear feature of the past year has been the re-emergence of the "guideline" decision. There have been several areas where the Employment Appeal Tribunal has taken the opportunity to re-state general applicable principles. This has happened across a range of matters. In *Hamilton v GMB* ([2007] I.R.L.R. 391) apparent bias was addressed—and the challenging notion of "apparent sub-conscious bias" emerged; *Software 2000 Ltd v Andrews* [2007] I.R.L.R. 568 attempted a general rehearsal of the approach to *Polkey* compensation reductions; *Amey Services v Cardigan* [2008] I.R.L.R.

279 set out the extent of the jurisdiction of the Employment Appeal Tribunal when reviewing case management decisions of Employment Tribunals; and in *Secretary of State for Health v Rance* ([2007] I.R.L.R. 665) the circumstances in which new points of law could and could not be raised before the Employment Appeal Tribunal were set out in detail. In *Rance*, an opportunity to clear the decks was plainly missed. The EAT's approach to new points of law has always been oddly restrictive in comparison, for example, with the approach of the Court of Appeal in other areas. The decision in *Rance* not only underlines that position, but perhaps makes it worse by appearing unduly prescriptive.

Elsewhere, there are important decisions on many matters. On the admissibility of evidence of fact (*Digby v East Cambridgeshire CC* [2007] I.R.L.R. 585, *Amwell View School v Doherty* [2007] I.R.L.R. 198); the admission of expert evidence (*Hospice of St Mary of Furness v Howard* [2007] I.R.L.R. 944, *Middlesborough Borough Council v Surtees* [2007] I.R.L.R. 981); the admissibility of without prejudice communications (*Brunel University v Vaseghi* [2007] I.R.L.R. 592, *Framlington Group v Barnetson* [2007] I.R.L.R. 598); the power to strike out claims because they have no reasonable prospect of success (*Johns v Solent SD Ltd* [2008] I.R.L.R. 88, *North Glamorgan NHS Trust v Ezias* [2007] I.R.L.R. 603); the territorial jurisdiction of the Tribunal in respect of various causes of action (*Bleuse v MBT Transport Ltd* [2008] I.R.L.R. 264, *Williams v University of Nottingham* [2007] I.R.L.R. 660); damages for loss of a chance (*BMA v Chaudhary* [2007] I.R.L.R. 800); damages for the consequences of dismissal (*GAB Robins v Triggs* [2008] EWCA Civ. 17); the precedent value of Scottish decisions in England and Wales (*Airbus v Webb* [2008] EWCA Civ. 49); wasted costs orders (*Mitchells Solicitors v Funwerk Information Technologies York Ltd* [2008] UKEAT/0541/07)); and the effect of unless orders made by the Tribunal (*Chukwudebeluv v Chubb Security Personnel Ltd* [2008] EWCA Civ. 327). Finally—in terms of new developments—the Tribunals Courts and Enforcement Act 2007 has now given Chairmen of Employment Tribunals the new title of Employment Judges: a title we have adopted for this edition.

Our deepest thanks go again to our team of expert Editors. All are busy and successful practitioners or members of the tribunals judiciary and have given generously of their time despite the tight publication schedule. There are also two special awards this year: the first (for outstanding foresight) goes to HHJ McMullen QC, the first of the Employment Appeal Tribunal judges to admit in a judgment to having read this book; the second (for valour) is to Michael Reed, Legal Officer at the Free Representation Unit. Michael fought the good fight to establish the *Employment Court Practice* "wiki" which enables all our Editors to update this work collaboratively for new editions. In this work he was ably assisted by Naomi Cunningham, and together they put the IT back into employment law! We are considerably better informed for their efforts; we hope also wiser. Finally we thank Sweet & Maxwell who have also responded to the challenges of the deadlines and the innovative writing and editing development, in particular Alice Trouncer and Rebecca Freestone.

In *Hamling v Coxlease School*, the Employment Appeal Tribunal rightly said that rules and procedures are "no more than the vehicles to enable" substantive rights to be realised. But they are none the less important for that. We hope that the 2008 edition of *Employment Court Practice* will continue to assist all employment law practitioners in their day to day work on behalf of their clients. We are very grateful for those who have commented on the 2007 edition, and welcome all suggestions for the future. We have attempted to state the law as at April 25, 2008.

Jonathan Swift
11, King's Bench Walk,
Temple. EC4Y 7EQ.

Christopher Chapman
Sheffield
chapmc@chapmc.demon.co.uk

April 25, 2008

CONTENTS

TABLE OF ABBREVIATIONS

ACAS	Advisory, Conciliation and Arbitration Service
AR 2006	Employment Equality (Age) Regulations 2006
CAB	Citizens Advice Bureau
CAC	Central Arbitration Committee
CEHR	Commission for Equality and Human Rights
CITB	Construction Industry Training Board
CPR	Civil Procedure Rules
CRE	Commission for Racial Equality
DDA 1995	Disability Discrimination Act 1995
DDP	Statutory Dismissal and Disciplinary Procedure under Employment Act 2002 Sch.2 Pt 1
DPA	Data Protection Act 1998
DRC	Disability Rights Commission
DRR	Employment Act 2002 (Dispute Resolution) Regulations 2004
EA	Employment Act 2002
EAT	Employment Appeals Tribunal
EAT PD	Employment Appeal Tribunal Practice Direction
EAT Rules	Employment Appeal Tribunal Rules 1993
ECHR	European Convention on Human Rights
ECITB	Engineering Construction Industry Training Board
ECJ	European Court of Justice
ECtHR	European Court of Human Rights
EDT	Effective Date of Termination
EOC	Equal Opportunities Commission
EP(C)A 1978	Employment Protection (Consolidation) Act 1978
EqPA	Equal Pay Act 1970
ERA 1996	Employment Rights Act 1996
ET	Employment Tribunal
ETA	Employment Tribunals Act 1996
ETR	Employment Tribunal Rules
FH	Full Hearing
GP	Statutory Grievance Procedure under Employment Act 2002 Sch.2 Pt 2
NIRC	National Industrial Relations Court
PH	Preliminary Hearing
RBR 2003	Employment Equality (Religion or Belief) Regulations 2003
RRA 1976	Race Relations Act 1976
SDA1975	Sex Discrimination Act 1975
SERPS	State Earned Related Pension Scheme
SIAC	Special Immigration Appeal Commission
SOR 2003	Employment Equality (Sexual Orientation) Regulations 2003

TULR(C)A	Trade Union and Labour Relations (Consolidation) Act 1992
TUPE	Transfer of Undertakings (Protection of Employment) Regulations 2006
TURERA 1993	Trade Union Reform and Employment Rights Act 1993

TABLE OF STATUTES

References in bold indicate where legislation is reproduced in full

TABLE OF STATUTORY INSTRUMENTS

References in bold indicate where legislation is reproduced in full

TABLE OF EC SECONDARY LEGISLATION

References in bold indicate where legislation is reproduced in full

TABLE OF TREATIES AND CONVENTIONS

References in bold indicate where legislation is reproduced in full

TABLE OF CIVIL PROCEDURE RULES

References in bold indicate where legislation is reproduced in full

TABLE OF CASES

TABLE OF EUROPEAN COURT OF JUSTICE CASES

CHAPTER 1

INTRODUCTION

Tradition has it that the Employment Tribunal was intended to be a jurisdiction free of procedural niceties and pitfalls, designed to provide prompt resolution for problems arising in the workplace. If ever that was the position, that was a long time ago. The potential for complex claims and complex litigation is most evident in the field of discrimination—cases in the employment field have effectively led the development of anti-discrimination law in the United Kingdom. In the early and mid-1990s, claims under the Sex Discrimination Act 1975 by ex-servicewomen required to leave the armed forces when they became pregnant presented the Employment Tribunal system with the task of co-ordinating several thousand claims, and with challenges of adapting the then rather rudimentary procedural rules to deal with complex disclosure and evidential issues. The other fact rendering these claims significant was the Tribunals' unlimited financial jurisdiction in discrimination claims. High value discrimination claims are a continuing feature of Employment Tribunal litigation, most obviously the constant series of "sexism in the City" claims. The fact that the Employment Tribunal is the forum for these high value claims requires Tribunals to have sophisticated procedural tools.

The Employment Tribunals (Constitution and Rules of Procedure) Regulations 2004 now provide a detailed framework of procedures covering all the substantive jurisdictions of the Employment Tribunal. None of this should be seen as proceduralism for its own sake: it is simply a reflection of the need to handle important substantive claims. Employment Tribunals now enjoy extensive powers of case management comparable to those exercised by the High Court and the County Courts. Perhaps perversely, pursuit of the overriding requirement that claims should be dealt with justly has had the consequence that Tribunal litigation has become a much more formalised process. Case Management Discussions are commonplace, and the burdens on parties to formulate and then comply with case management orders are now no different to those in "mainstream" litigation.

This new focus on procedure is also the consequence of several other trends. First the fact that the substantive jurisdiction of Employment Tribunals is itself substantial. Regulation of the employment relationship remains a key aspect of social policy. Both employees and workers are protected by a significant body of statutory rights, and many of these are

1

the domain of the Employment Tribunal. Litigating employment disputes is increasingly regarded as the pursuit of industrial relations by other means, not just by trades unions but also by representative bodies (statutory and non-statutory) and individual employees of all levels of seniority. The fact that employment litigation often raises issues that are complex and hard-fought has meant that it is essential that the procedures available, particularly to Employment Tribunals must accommodate the needs of sophisticated claims as much as those that are straightforward. An approach based on the lowest common denominator will no longer do. Secondly, Employment Tribunals are, as are all other courts, subject to the demands of efficiency. A tighter and more prescriptive approach to process is seen as a key tool for the proper use of judicial resources. The 2004 Employment Tribunal Rules place a much greater emphasis on the powers of Tribunals themselves to take interlocutory steps to streamline the course of claims. They also provide more significant scope for Tribunals to sanction abuses of process or even simple failures to "play by the rules" through strike-out powers, powers to debar parties on specific points, and powers to make costs orders. Thirdly, employment litigation, like all other categories of litigation is now coloured by the influence of human rights. In procedural terms the impact is a heightened awareness of the formal requirements of fairness, a matter most explicitly seen in the present requirements as to the manner in which interlocutory applications must be made. This awareness goes further and has a more general impact on the approach to procedural requirements. One aspect of fairness is clarity: if the procedural rules themselves demonstrate the steps that will be taken, or if Employment Tribunals use the powers available to them to lay out what is required, the risk of unfair advantage diminishes. These considerations strongly influence Tribunals to use their procedural powers to their full extent.

It is trite law that both the Employment Tribunal and the Employment Appeal Tribunal are legislative creations, and in terms of the procedural as much as the substantive law these Tribunals only have the powers granted to them under primary and secondary legislation. Yet these statutory powers are replete with wide-ranging discretions. This fact is both a virtue and a vice. It is virtuous for the simple reason that Tribunals are able to take decisions that are the best fit to deal with the conduct of each case before them. Each claim has the potential to throw up its own peculiarities, and if Tribunals cannot react to these matters they cannot be resolved in a way that is just—one size fits all justice is not really any form of justice at all. The vice is equally obvious. The existence of an apparent sea of discretions can be bewildering for litigants and Tribunals alike. For litigants it can be difficult to know what orders in which form should be sought to pursue or defend claims to the full extent possible. For Tribunals, the danger is that the options available might tend to overwhelm. Although the discretions are potentially broad it is imperative that they are exercised in a principled way since the value of predictability of approach in matters procedural is as great as in the application of the substantive law. Conversely, if the options are various it is sometimes comforting to avoid real scrutiny of the specifics and use the same options in the same way on all occasions. Standard form directions orders (which are now more and more common) are a useful device: the challenge for Tribunals is to have the sense of discrimination required to know when a claim before them requires a different approach.

OVERVIEW OF THIS BOOK

The focus of this work is the procedural and jurisdictional rules applicable to Employment Tribunals and the Employment Appeal Tribunal: its aim is to be a Court Practice for employment practitioners, providing an authoritative source for the information necessary for the day to day handling of employment claims, when preparing for hearings, and when grappling with issues arising in the course of hearings themselves. This book seeks to meet the practical requirements of employment lawyers by providing this information side by side with the legislative provisions themselves.

1–003

Part One concerns the procedural rules that govern employment law litigation. It comprises full versions of the texts of the Employment Tribunals Act 1996, the Employment Tribunals (Constitution and Rules of Procedure) Regulations 2004, the Employment Appeal Tribunal Rules 1993 and the Employment Appeal Practice Direction, together with section by section, rule by rule commentary. Part One also contains the procedural rules applicable to appeals from the Employment Appeal Tribunal to the Court of Appeal. The material parts of CPR Part 52 and the Practice Direction under Part 52 are set out in full, and their practical application is explained.

Part Two is directed to areas that straddle the line between the procedural and the substantive. A point often made is that no absolute distinction can be drawn between the rules of substantive law and the rules of procedural law. In all instances the one affects the other. Firstly, attention is given to key jurisdictional matters. Jurisdiction can be an important area of attention arising at the interlocutory stages of Employment Tribunal claims. Jurisdictional points arise in various guises: time limits and the principles that govern the exercise of statutory discretions to extend time for the presentation of claims; the scope of the Tribunal's jurisdiction to determine contractual claims; the territorial jurisdiction of Employment Tribunals to consider and determine claims arising outside Great Britain. All these areas are specifically considered. For the present,

1–004

the most gnarled jurisdictional issues are those arising as a consequence of the introduction of statutory grievance and disciplinary procedures. Part Two contains the material provisions of the Employment Act 2002 (sections 29–33, and Schedules 2–4), and the provisions of the Employment Act 2002 (Dispute Resolution) Regulations 2004. Again, each section and each regulation is the subject of detailed commentary.

Next, Part Two covers the application of EU law in Tribunal claims, the use of the Employment Tribunal as a vehicle for claims based on EU legislation, and the impact on Tribunal proceedings of the Human Rights Act 1998. These are areas where, given the statutory nature of Employment Tribunals, procedural law jurisdictional provisions and substantive law converge. The final sections of Part Two concern the disposal of Employment Tribunal claims, dealing with remedies and with statutory and non-statutory compromise agreements. These areas represent the practical realisation of employment law claims.

PART 1

EMPLOYMENT LITIGATION PROCEDURE

CHAPTER 2

Employment Tribunals Act 1996

Contents

Sect.

PART I EMPLOYMENT TRIBUNALS

Introductory

Employment tribunals

2–001   **1.1—(1) The Secretary of State may by regulations make provision for the establishment of tribunals to be known as employment tribunals.**

8

(2) Regulations made wholly or partly under section 128(1) of the Employment Protection (Consolidation) Act 1978 and in force immediately before this Act comes into force shall, so far as made under that provision, continue to have effect (until revoked) as if made under subsection (1).

This legislation was previously entitled the Industrial Tribunals Act 1996. **2–002** "Employment Tribunal" was substituted for "Industrial Tribunal" by s.1 of the Employment Rights (Dispute Resolution) Act 1998.

Regulations made under Section 128

Section 128 of the Employment Protection (Consolidation) Act 1978 is repealed **2–003** by s.45 of the Employment Tribunals Act 1996. The regulations passed under that act, including the Constitution and Rules of Procedure Regulations 2001 continued to have effect by virtue of s.1(1) of this Act until the passing of the Employment Tribunals (Constitution and Rules of Procedure) Regulations 2004.

Status of the tribunal

Subsection 1 provides for the establishment of tribunals. Their status as tribunals **2–004** rather than courts has the effect that they are unable to make a declaration under s.4(2) of the Human Rights Act 1998 concerning the incompatibility of UK legislation. The same is true of the Employment Appeal Tribunal, notwithstanding s.20(3). See *Whittaker v P&D Watson (trading as P&M Watson Haulage)* [2002] I.C.R. 1244

By RSC Ord.52 the Employment Tribunal is an "inferior court". The Divisional Court has jurisdiction over the tribunal concerning contempt of court (*Peach Grey v Sommers* [1995] I.C.R. 549). By the Supreme Court Act 1981, s.42(1)(a), a person declared a vexatious litigant by the High Court may be required to seek leave of the High Court before commencing proceedings in the tribunal. However, the tribunal is within the definition of a Court under art.21 of the Brussels Convention on Jurisdiction and the Enforcement of Judgments in Civil and Commercial Matters 1968 (*Turner v Grovit* [1999] I.C.R. 1114).

Independence of the tribunal

Doubts over the independence of employment tribunals were expressed in the **2–005** case of *Scanfuture (UK) Ltd v Secretary of State for Trade and Industry* [2001] I.C.R. 1096, because the Secretary of State appointed and paid for the lay members who sat alongside the employment judge in the Employment Tribunal. Changes to the appointment regime were made in 1999 following the case in order that the tribunal now complies with art.6 of the European Convention on Human Rights.

Enactments conferring jurisdiction on employment tribunals

2. Employment tribunals shall exercise the jurisdiction conferred **2–006** **on them by or by virtue of this Act or any other Act, whether passed before or after this Act.**

Power to confer further jurisdiction on employment tribunals

3.—(1) The appropriate Minister may by order provide that pro- **2–007** **ceedings in respect of—**

(a) any claim to which this section applies, or

    (b) any claim to which this section applies and which is of a description specified in the order,

may, subject to such exceptions (if any) as may be so specified, be brought before an employment tribunal.

    (2) Subject to subsection (3), this section applies to—

    (a) a claim for damages for breach of a contract of employment or other contract connected with employment,

    (b) a claim for a sum due under such a contract, and

    (c) a claim for the recovery of a sum in pursuance of any enactment relating to the terms or performance of such a contract,

if the claim is such that a court in England and Wales or Scotland would under the law for the time being in force have jurisdiction to hear and determine an action in respect of the claim.

    (3) This section does not apply to a claim for damages, or for a sum due, in respect of personal injuries.

    (4) Any jurisdiction conferred on an employment tribunal by virtue of this section in respect of any claim is exercisable concurrently with any court in England and Wales or in Scotland which has jurisdiction to hear and determine an action in respect of the claim.

    (5) In this section—

"appropriate Minister", as respects a claim in respect of which an action could be heard and determined by a court in England and Wales, means the Lord Chancellor and, as respects a claim in respect of which an action could be heard and determined by a court in Scotland, means the Secretary of State, and

"personal injuries" includes any disease and any impairment of a person's physical or mental condition.

    (6) In this section a reference to breach of a contract includes a reference to breach of—

    (a) a term implied in a contract by or under any enactment or otherwise,

    (b) a term of a contract as modified by or under any enactment or otherwise, and

    (c) a term which, although not contained in a contract, is incorporated in the contract by another term of the contract.

Contract of employment

2–008   The term is defined under s.42 as a contract of service or apprenticeship, whether express of implied, and (if express) whether oral or in writing.

    The effect of this section is to give the appropriate Minister power to make regulations to give the tribunals jurisdiction to hear further claims beyond those for which jurisdiction has already been given. The provision substantially repeats the previous provisions of s.131 of the Employment Protection (Consolidation) Act 1978 which was the source for the Employment Tribunal Extension of Jurisdiction Orders of 1994 in respect of England and Wales, and separately for Scotland. These remain in force and govern the tribunal's jurisdiction to hear claims for breach of contract.

By s.8 an order under s.3 may provide a cap to the amount that the tribunal may award in relation to such a claim. Presently the amount specified is £25,000.

[3A Meaning of "Employment Judge"

A person who is a member of a panel of chairmen of employment tribunals which is appointed in accordance with regulations under s.1(1) may be referred to as an Employment Judge."

Amendment: Words in s.3A added by Sch.8 para.36 Tribunals Courts and Enforcement Act 2007, effective from December 1, 2007.

Employment Judges

The new nomenclature for the legally qualified member of the tribunal is in line **2–008/1** with changes previously seen in the civil courts where Registrars became referred to as "District Judges". The new terminology is not mandatory however; the expression "may be referred to. . . ." appears to indicate that there is an element of choice in the matter regarding whether to use the new terminology or not. Practice would appear to indicate that the correct form of address will continue to be "Sir" or "Madam", similar to the practice in the civil courts with District Judges. No change in terminology has been made in respect of the wing members of the tribunal, and there has been no change in respect of the equal status of each member of the tribunal panel in the decision making process. In practice, the chairman is now referred to as Employment Judge in judgments, orders, correspondence and Hearing lists.

MEMBERSHIP ETC.

Composition of a tribunal

4.—(1) Subject to the following provisions of this section and to **2–009** **section 7(3A) proceedings before an employment tribunal shall be heard by—**

(a) **the person who, in accordance with regulations made under section 1(1), is the chairman, and**

(b) **two other members, or (with the consent of the parties) one other member, selected as the other members (or member) in accordance with regulations so made.**

(2) Subject to subsection (5), the proceedings specified in subsection (3) shall be heard by the person mentioned in subsection (1)(a) alone.

(3) The proceedings referred to in subsection (2) are—

(a) **proceedings on an application under section 161, 165 or 166 of the Trade Union and Labour Relations**

(Consolidation) Act 1992,

(b) proceedings on a complaint under section 126 of the Pension Schemes Act 1993,

(c) proceedings on a reference under section 11, 163 or 170 of the Employment Rights Act 1996, on a complaint under section 23, 34 or 188 of that Act, on a complaint under section 70(1) of that Act relating to section 64 of that Act, on an application under section 128, 131 or 132 of that Act, or for an appointment under section 206(4) of that Act,

(ca) proceedings on a complaint under regulation 15(10) of the Transfer of Undertakings (Protection of Employment) Regulations 2006,

(cc) proceedings under a complaint under section 11 of the National Minimum Wage Act 1998;

(cd) proceedings on a complaint under section 19 or 22 of the National Minimum Wage Act 1998;

(d) proceedings in respect of which an employment tribunal has jurisdiction by virtue of section 3 of this Act,

(e) proceedings in which the parties have given their written consent to the proceedings being heard in accordance with subsection (2) (whether or not they have subsequently withdrawn it), and

(f) proceedings in which the person (or, where more than one, each of the persons) against whom the proceedings are brought does not, or has ceased to, contest the case.

(4) The Secretary of State may by order amend the provisions of subsection (3).

(5) Proceedings specified in subsection (3) shall be heard in accordance with subsection (1) if a person who, in accordance with regulations made under section 1(1), may be the chairman of an employment tribunal, having regard to—

(a) whether there is a likelihood of a dispute arising on the facts which makes it desirable for the proceedings to be heard in accordance with subsection (1),

(b) whether there is a likelihood of an issue of law arising which would make it desirable for the proceedings to be heard in accordance with subsection (2),

(c) any views of any of the parties as to whether or not the proceedings ought to be heard in accordance with either of those subsections, and

(d) whether there are other proceedings which might be heard concurrently but which are not proceedings specified in subsection (3), decides at any stage of the proceedings that the proceedings are to be heard in accordance with subsection (1).

(6) Where (in accordance with the following provisions of this Part) the Secretary of State makes employment tribunal procedure regulations, the regulations may provide that, any act required or authorised by the regulations to be done by an employment tribunal may be done by the person mentioned in subsection (1)(a) alone.

(6A) Subsection (6) in particular enables employment tribunal procedure regulations to provide that—

(a) the determination of proceedings in accordance with regulations under section 7(3A), (3B) or (3C)(a),

(b) the carrying-out of pre-hearing reviews in accordance with regulations under subsection (1) of section 9 (including the exercise of powers in connection with such reviews in accordance with regulations under paragraph (b) of that subsection), or

(c) the hearing and determination of a preliminary issue in accordance with regulations under section 9(4) (where it involves hearing witnesses other than the parties or their representatives as well as where, in accordance with regulations under section 7(3C)(b), it does not),

may be done by the person mentioned in subsection (1)(a) alone.

(6B) Employment tribunal procedure regulations may (subject to subsection (6C)) also provide that any act which—

(a) by virtue of subsection (6) may be done by the person mentioned in subsection (1)(a) alone, and

(b) is of a description specified by the regulations for the purposes of this subsection, may be done by a person appointed as a legal officer in accordance with regulations under section 1(1); and any act so done shall be treated as done by an employment tribunal.

(6C) But regulations under subsection (6B) may not specify—

(a) the determination of any proceedings, other than proceedings in which the parties have agreed the terms of the determination or in which the person bringing the proceedings has given notice of the withdrawal of the case, or

(b) the carrying-out of pre-hearing reviews in accordance with regulations under section 9(1).]

(7) . . .

The tribunal will ordinarily be composed of an employment judge and two lay **2–010** members. As to the process by which these individuals are chosen see reg.8 of the Employment Tribunals (Constitution and Rules of Procedure) Regulations 2004.

Employment judge sitting alone

2–011   By s.4(2), subject to s.4(5), certain types of hearing, set out in full in s.4(3), are reserved to be heard by an employment judge sitting alone. Cases where the respondent does not, or has ceased to, contest the proceedings and cases where the parties have consented to the hearing before the employment judge alone are suitable to be heard by an employment judge alone. The expression "the respondent does not contest the proceedings" will include the situation where a respondent is debarred from taking any part in the proceedings because of a failure to lodge form ET3 on time, *The Basingstoke Press Ltd v Clarke* [2007] I.R.L.R. 588.

Section 4(5) requires that if an employment judge of the employment tribunal so decides then a case that would otherwise be heard alone may be heard by a panel of three under s.4(1). The decision may be taken at any point in time after taking into account the likelihood of a dispute of fact, an issue of law which makes it desirable to be heard before a panel of three, the views of the parties, or the possibility that the s.4(3) proceedings may take place concurrently with proceedings that require a panel of three.

The language of s.4(3) is mandatory but subject to s.4(5). The power of the employment judge to hear cases alone will not be properly exercised if specific regard is not been taken of the matters set out in s.4(5) (*Sogbetun v Hackney LBC* [1998] I.C.R. 1264). Absent consideration of these matters, the decision is a nullity. In *Post Office v Howell* [2000] I.C.R. 913, the EAT held that a failure to expressly consider the facts under s.4(5) did not necessarily go to jurisdiction, but would amount to an irregularity.

The two apparently contradictory decisions were considered in *Morgan v Brith Gof Cyf* [2001] I.C.R. 978 where Lindsay J. preferred the approach in *Howell*. The result appears to follow the intention of the section that there is a presumption in favour of s.4(3) cases being heard alone subject to consideration of the s.4(5) factors, rather than a presumption that s.4(3) cases are improperly heard if the s.4(5) factors have not been considered (see *Gladwell v Secretary of Trade and Industry* [2007] I.C.R. 264, EAT).

The approach in *Howell* was also preferred in *Sterling Development (London) Ltd v Pagano* [2007] I.R.L.R. 471 where H.H. Peter Clarke set out the process to be followed in the case management of a case to determine whether a case should be heard before a tribunal or employment judge sitting alone:

". . . we think that the correct procedure . . . should be as follows:

(1) Listing is a judicial function. The question as to whether a hearing is to be before a Chairman alone or full panel in accordance with s4 ETA is a matter for judicial, not administrative, decision.

(2) Interim case management decisions will be dealt with by a Chairman alone (see rule 17(1)). In many cases a CMD will be held prior to the substantive hearing, as in this case. It should be routine for the Chairman conducting the CMD to inform the parties as to whether, in his opinion, the substantive hearing is to be before a full panel or a Chairman alone, applying s4(2) ETA read with s4(3) and inviting any submissions as to whether he should exercise his discretion under s4(5) for the hearing to take place before a full panel. A simple explanation of the respective merits of trial mode should be given to the parties, particularly unrepresented parties. If representations are made he should rule on the point, giving brief reasons for his ruling. The mode of trial, Chairman alone or full Tribunal, will then be recorded in the Chairman's CMD written order.

(3) Where no CMD has been held, a Chairman (if appropriate the Regional Chairman, by direction to the Secretary) must ensure that

the Notice of Hearing sent out under rule 27(1) and read with rule 26(2) states whether the hearing is to be before a full panel or Chairman alone; if the latter, parties should be expressly invited to make representations if they wish as to why the hearing should take place before a full panel, giving reasons, including those factors referred to in s4(5) ETA. That was the procedure followed in the Gladwell and present cases. Any such representations will then be considered, after obtaining the views of all parties, and a judicial decision, with Reasons, made by a Chairman.

(4) In either event, a judicial decision has been made which is susceptible to appeal. Absent any representations or appeal the mode of hearing is settled, subject to any change of circumstances which requires the hearing Chairman to revisit the question of composition. Absent any such point being raised, we see no reason why the final hearing should be susceptible to challenge on a point of law, the relevant judicial decision having been taken earlier, either at a CMD or in the form of standard directions."

Remuneration, fees and allowance

5.—(1) The Secretary of State may pay to— 2–012

   (a) the President of the Employment Tribunals (England and Wales),

   (b) the President of the Employment Tribunals (Scotland),

   (c) any person who is an Employment Judge on a full-time basis of a panel of chairmen of tribunals which is appointed in accordance with regulations made under section 1(1), and

   (d) any person who is a legal officer appointed in accordance with such regulations such remuneration as he may with the consent of the Treasury determine.

(2) The Secretary of State may pay to—

   (a) members of employment tribunals,

   (b) any assessors appointed for the purposes of proceedings before employment tribunals, and

   (c) any persons required for the purposes of section 2A(1)(b) of the Equal Pay Act 1970 to prepare reports, such fees and allowances as he may with the consent of the Treasury determine.

(3) The Secretary of State may pay to any other persons such allowances as he may with the consent of the Treasury determine for the purposes of, or in connection with, their attendance at employment tribunals.

PROCEDURE

Conduct of hearings

6.—(1) A person may appear before an employment tribunal in 2–013
person or be represented by

(a) counsel or a solicitor,

(b) a representative of a trade union or an employers' association, or

(c) any other person whom he desires to represent him.

(2) The Arbitration Act 1996 does not apply to any proceedings before an employment tribunal.

The right to representation

2–014   The right to representation under s.6(1) is unqualified. Even if, by reason of matters of professional conduct, a representative ought not to appear because of a conflict of interest, the tribunal has no power to interfere with the parties' choice of representative (*Dispatch Management Services v Douglas* [2002] I.R.L.R. 389). The employment tribunal has no power to interfere with the choice of representative of a party, though there is a clear distinction between the right of a party to select the person who is to represent him and the power of the tribunal to regulate the conduct of the representative in the performance of that task (*Bache v Essex CC* [2000] I.C.R. 313). In extreme cases a tribunal might have to consider striking out the claim or response on the grounds that the conduct of the representative makes it impossible for the tribunal to do justice between the parties (*Edmondson v BMI Healthcare* EAT/654/01). However, that course of action must only be considered as a last resort.

Employment Tribunal procedure regulations

2–015   7.—(1) The Secretary of State may by regulations ("employment tribunal procedure regulations") make such provision as appears to him to be necessary or expedient with respect to proceedings before employment tribunals.

(2) Proceedings before employment tribunals shall be instituted in accordance with employment tribunal procedure regulations.

(3) Employment tribunal procedure regulations may, in particular, include provision—

(a) for determining by which tribunal any proceedings are to be determined,

(b) for enabling an employment tribunal to hear and determine proceedings brought by virtue of section 3 concurrently with proceedings brought before the tribunal otherwise than by virtue of that section,

(c) for treating the Secretary of State (either generally or in such circumstances as may be prescribed by the regulations) as a party to any proceedings before an employment tribunal (where he would not otherwise be a party to them) and entitling him to appear and to be heard accordingly,

(d) for requiring persons to attend to give evidence and produce documents and for authorising the administration of oaths to witnesses,

(e) for enabling an employment tribunal, on the application of any party to the proceedings before it or of its own motion, to order—

      (i) in England and Wales, such discovery or inspection of documents, or the furnishing of such further particulars, as might be ordered by a county court on application by a party to proceedings before it, or

     (ii) in Scotland, such recovery or inspection of documents as might be ordered by a sheriff,

(f) for prescribing the procedure to be followed in any proceedings before an employment tribunal, including provision—

      (i) ... (ia) for postponing fixing a time and place for a hearing, for such period as may be determined in accordance with the regulations for the purpose of giving for the proceedings to be settled by way of conciliation and withdrawal, and

     (ii) for enabling an employment tribunal to review its decisions, and revoke or vary its orders and awards, in such circumstances as may be determined in accordance with the regulations,

(g) for the appointment of one or more assessors for the purposes of any proceedings before an employment tribunal, where the proceedings are brought under an enactment which provides for one or more assessors to be appointed,

(h) for authorising an employment tribunal to require persons to furnish information and produce documents to a person required for the purposes of section 2A(1)(b) of the Equal Pay Act 1970 to prepare a report, and

(j) for the registration and proof of decisions, orders and awards of employment tribunals.

(3ZA) Employment tribunal procedure regulations may—

(a) authorise the Secretary of State to prescribe, or prescribe requirements in relation to any form which is required by such regulations to be used for the purpose of instituting, or entering an appearance to, proceedings before employment tribunals,

(b) authorise the Secretary of State to prescribe requirements in relation to documents to be supplied with any such form, and

(c) make provision about the publication of anything prescribed under authority conferred by virtue of the subsection.

(3A) Employment tribunal procedure regulations may authorise the determination of proceedings without any hearing in such circumstances as the regulations may prescribe.

(3B) Employment tribunal procedure regulations may authorise the determination of proceedings without hearing anyone other than the person or persons by whom the proceedings are brought (or his or their representatives) where—

    (a) the person (or where more than one, each of the persons) against whom the proceedings are brought has done nothing to contest the case, or

    (b) it appears from the application made by the person (or where more than one, each of the persons) bringing the proceedings that he is not (or they are not) seeking any relief which an employment tribunal has power to give or that he is not (or they are not) entitled to any such relief.

(3C) Employment tribunal procedure regulations may authorise the determination of proceedings without hearing anyone other than the person or persons by whom, and the person or persons against whom, the proceedings are brought (or his or their representatives) where—

    (a) an employment tribunal is on undisputed facts bound by the decision of a court in another case to dismiss the case of the person or persons by whom, or of the person or persons against whom, the proceedings are brought, or

    (b) the proceedings relate only to a preliminary issue which may be heard and determined in accordance with regulations under section 9(4)

(4) A person who without reasonable excuse fails to comply with—

    (a) any requirement imposed by virtue of subsection (3)(d) or (h), or

    (b) any requirement with respect to the discovery, recovery or inspection of documents imposed by virtue of subsection (3)(e), or

    (c) any requirement imposed by virtue of employment tribunal procedure regulations to give written answers for the purpose of facilitating the determination of proceedings as mentioned in subsection (3A), (3B) or (3C) is guilty of an offence and liable on summary conviction to a fine not exceeding level 3 on the standard scale.

(5) Subject to any regulations under section 11(1)(a), employment tribunal procedure regulations may include provision authorising or requiring an employment tribunal, in circumstances specified in the regulations, to send notice or a copy of—

    (a) any document specified in the regulations which relates to any proceedings before the tribunal, or

(b) any decision, order or award of the tribunal,

to any government department or other person or body so specified.

(6) Where in accordance with employment tribunal procedure regulations an employment tribunal determines in the same proceedings—

(a) a complaint presented under section 111 of the Employment Rights Act 1996, and

(b) a question referred under section 163 of that Act,

subsection (2) of that section has no effect for the purposes of the proceedings in so far as they relate to the complaint under section 111.

This is the enabling provision under which the Secretary of State is given power **2–016** to introduce rules of procedure governing the conduct of matters in the tribunal. The current rules are found in the Employment Tribunals (Constitution and Rules of Procedure) Regulations 2004 (SI 2004/1861), as amended.

Practice Directions

7A.—(1) Employment tribunal procedure regulations may include **2–017** provision—

(a) enabling the President to make directions about the procedure of employment tribunals, including directions about the exercise by tribunals of powers under such regulations,

(b) for securing compliance with such directions, and

(c) about the publication of such directions.

(2) Employment tribunal procedure regulations may, instead of providing for any matter, refer to provision made or to be made about that matter by directions made by the President.

(3) In this section, references to the President are to a person appointed in accordance with regulations under section 1(1) as—

(a) President of the Employment Tribunals (England and Wales), or

(b) President of the Employment Tribunals (Scotland).

Under the Employment Tribunals Act as originally enacted, only the Employ- **2–018** ment Appeal Tribunal had power to issue Practice Directions under s.30. The power to issue practice directions was extended to the Employment Tribunal by s.27 of the Employment Act 2002 and came into force on July 9, 2004 following comments made in *Eurobell Holdings v Barker* [1998] I.C.R. 299 that it was undesirable for different directions to apply in practice in difference regions around the country.

The Tribunals, Courts and Enforcement Act 2007, not yet in force, proposes a new s.7B. The effect of the new section will be to enable regulations and practice directions for a mediation scheme, under which members of the Tribunal may act as mediators between the parties, see Sch.8, para.42 of the act. At the time of writing, the act has received the Royal Assent but no commencement date has been provided.

Procedure in contract cases

2–019 **8.—(1) Where in proceedings brought by virtue of section 3 an employment tribunal finds that the whole or part of a sum claimed in the proceedings is due, the tribunal shall order the respondent to the proceedings to pay the amount which it finds due.**

(2) An order under section 3 may provide that an employment tribunal shall not in proceedings in respect of a claim, or a number of claims relating to the same contract, order the payment of an amount exceeding such sum as may be specified in the order as the maximum amount which an employment tribunal may order to be paid in relation to a claim or in relation to a contract.

(3) An order under section 3 may include provisions—

> **(a) as to the manner in which and time within which proceedings are to be brought by virtue of that section, and**
>
> **(b) modifying any other enactment.**

(4) An order under that section may make different provision in relation to proceedings in respect of different descriptions of claims.

2–020 The sum presently specified as being the amount which the tribunal may order to be paid in relation to a claim is restricted to £25,000: see Employment Tribunals Extension of Jurisdiction (England and Wales) Order 1994 (SI 1994/1623), at para.13–016.

Pre-hearing reviews and preliminary matters

2–021 **9.—(1) Employment tribunal procedure regulations may include provision—**

> **(a) for authorising the carrying-out by an employment tribunal of a preliminary consideration of any proceedings before it (a "pre-hearing review"), and**
>
> **(b) for enabling such powers to be exercised in connection with a pre-hearing review as may be prescribed by the regulations.**

(2) Such regulations may in particular include provision—

> **(a) for authorising any tribunal carrying out a pre-hearing review under the regulations to make, in circumstances specified in the regulations, an order requiring a party to the proceedings in question, if he wishes to continue to participate in those proceedings, to pay a deposit of an amount not exceeding £500, and**
>
> **(b) for prescribing—**

    (i) the manner in which the amount of any such deposit is to be determined in any particular case,

    (ii) the consequences of non-payment of any such deposit, and

    (iii) the circumstances in which any such deposit, or any part of it, may be refunded to the party who paid it or be paid over to another party to the proceedings.

[(2A) Regulations under subsection (1)(b), so far as relating to striking out, may not provide for striking out on a ground which does not apply outside a pre-hearing review.]

(3) The Secretary of State may from time to time by order substitute for the sum specified in subsection (2)(a) such other sum as is specified in the order.

(4) Employment tribunal procedure regulations may also include provision for authorising an employment tribunal to hear and determine separately any preliminary issue of a description prescribed by the regulations which is raised by any case.

This is the enabling provision concerning the extent to which regulations may be issued to govern the conduct of pre-hearing reviews and the payment of deposits. **2–022**

National security

10.—(1) If on a complaint under—— **2–023**

    (a) section 145A, 145B or 146 of the Trade Union and Labour Relations (Consolidation) Act 1992 (inducements and detriments in respect of trade union membership etc), or

    (b) section 111 of the Employment Rights Act 1996 (unfair dismissal),
    it is shown that the action complained of was taken for the purpose of safeguarding national security, the employment tribunal shall dismiss the complaint.

(2) Employment tribunal procedure regulations may make provision about the composition of the tribunal (including provision disapplying or modifying section 4) for the purposes of proceedings in relation to which—

    (a) a direction is given under subsection (3), or

    (b) an order is made under subsection (4).

(3) A direction may be given under this subsection by a Minister of the Crown if—

    (a) it relates to particular Crown employment proceedings, and

(b) the Minister considers it expedient in the interests of national security.

(4) An order may be made under this subsection by the President or a Regional Chairman in relation to particular proceedings if he considers it expedient in the interests of national security.

(5) Employment tribunal procedure regulations may make provision enabling a Minister of the Crown, if he considers it expedient in the interests of national security—

(a) to direct a tribunal to sit in private for all or part of particular Crown employment proceedings;

(b) to direct a tribunal to exclude the applicant from all or part of particular Crown employment proceedings;

(c) to direct a tribunal to exclude the applicant's representatives from all or part of particular Crown employment proceedings;

(d) to direct a tribunal to take steps to conceal the identity of a particular witness in particular Crown employment proceedings;

(e) to direct a tribunal to take steps to keep secret all or part of the reasons for its decision in particular Crown employment proceedings.

(6) Employment tribunal procedure regulations may enable a tribunal, if it considers it expedient in the interests of national security, to do in relation to particular proceedings before it anything of a kind which, by virtue of subsection (5), employment tribunal procedure regulations may enable a Minister of the Crown to direct a tribunal to do in relation to particular Crown employment proceedings.

(7) In relation to cases where a person has been excluded by virtue of subsection (5)(b) or (c) or (6), employment tribunal procedure regulations may make provision—

(a) for the appointment by the Attorney General, or by the Advocate General for Scotland, of a person to represent the interests of the applicant;

(b) about the publication and registration of reasons for the tribunal's decision;

(c) permitting an excluded person to make a statement to the tribunal before the commencement of the proceedings, or the part of the proceedings, from which he is excluded.

(8) Proceedings are Crown employment proceedings for the purposes of this section if the employment to which the complaint relates—

(a) is Crown employment, or

    (b) is connected with the performance of functions on behalf of the Crown.

(9) The reference in subsection (4) to the President or a Regional Chairman is to a person appointed in accordance with regulations under section 1(1) as—

    (a) a Regional Chairman,

    (b) President of the Employment Tribunals (England and Wales), or

    (c) President of the Employment Tribunals (Scotland).

In *B v BAA* [2005] I.C.R. 1530 it was held that s.10(1) may be relied upon by **2–024** employers other than the Crown, however, the effect of this section was construed by reference to the interpretative requirement under s.3 of the Human Rights Act 1998, such that, despite the express language of the sub-section, the Tribunal was also required to consider the fairness of the decision to dismiss, as if s.98(4) of the Employment Rights Act 1998 applied.

The regulations made under s.10(5) are contained in Sch.2 to the Employment Tribunal (Constitution and Rules of Procedure) Regulations 2004.

[Confidential information]

10A.—(1) Employment tribunal procedure regulations may enable **2–025** **an employment tribunal to sit in private for the purpose of hearing evidence from any person which in the opinion of the tribunal is likely to consist of—**

    (a) **information which he could not disclose without contravening a prohibition imposed by or by virtue of any enactment,**

    (b) **information which has been communicated to him in confidence or which he has otherwise obtained in consequence of the confidence reposed in him by another person, or**

    (c) **information the disclosure of which would, for reasons other than its effect on negotiations with respect to any of the matters mentioned in section 178(2) of the Trade Union and Labour Relations (Consolidation) Act 1992, cause substantial injury to any undertaking of his or in which he works.**

(2) The reference in subsection (1)(c) to any undertaking of a person or in which he works shall be construed—

    (a) **in relation to a person in Crown employment, as a reference to the national interest,**

    (b) **in relation to a person who is a relevant member of the House of Lords staff, as a reference to the national interest or (if the case so requires) the interests of the House of Lords, and**

Employment Tribunals Act 1996

(c) in relation to a person who is a relevant member of the House of Commons staff, as a reference to the national interest or (if the case so requires) the interests of the House of Commons.]

2–026   The regulations made under this section are at para.16 of Sch.1 to the Employment Tribunal (Constitution and Rules of Procedure) Regulations 2004 (SI 2004/1861).

Restriction of publicity in cases involving sexual misconduct

2–027   **11.—(1) Employment tribunal procedure regulations may include provision—**

(a) **for cases involving allegations of the commission of sexual offences, for securing that the registration or other making available of documents or decisions shall be so effected as to prevent the identification of any person affected by or making the allegation, and**

(b) **for cases involving allegations of sexual misconduct, enabling an employment tribunal, on the application of any party to proceedings before it or of its own motion, to make a restricted reporting order having effect (if not revoked earlier) until the promulgation of the decision of the tribunal.**

(2) If any identifying matter is published or included in a relevant programme in contravention of a restricted reporting order—

(a) **in the case of publication in a newspaper or periodical, any proprietor, any editor and any publisher of the newspaper or periodical,**

(b) **in the case of publication in any other form, the person publishing the matter, and**

(c) **in the case of matter included in a relevant programme—**

(i) **any body corporate engaged in providing the service in which the programme is included, and**

(ii) **any person having functions in relation to the programme corresponding to those of an editor of a newspaper,**

shall be guilty of an offence and liable on summary conviction to a fine not exceeding level 5 on the standard scale.

(3) Where a person is charged with an offence under subsection (2) it is a defence to prove that at the time of the alleged offence he was not aware, and neither suspected nor had reason to suspect, that the publication or programme in question was of, or included, the matter in question.

(4) Where an offence under subsection (2) committed by a body corporate is proved to have been committed with the consent or connivance of, or to be attributable to any neglect on the part of—

(a) a director, manager, secretary or other similar officer of the body corporate, or

(b) a person purporting to act in any such capacity,
he as well as the body corporate is guilty of the offence and liable to be proceeded against and punished accordingly.

(5) In relation to a body corporate whose affairs are managed by its members "director", in subsection (4), means a member of the body corporate.

(6) In this section—

"identifying matter", in relation to a person, means any matter likely to lead members of the public to identify him as a person affected by, or as the person making, the allegation,

"relevant programme" has the same meaning as in the Sexual Offences(Amendment) Act 1992,

"restricted reporting order" means an order—

(a) made in exercise of a power conferred by regulations made by virtue of this section, and

(b) prohibiting the publication in Great Britain of identifying matter in a written publication available to the public or its inclusion in a relevant programme for reception in Great Britain,

"sexual misconduct" means the commission of a sexual offence, sexual harassment or other adverse conduct (of whatever nature) related to sex, and conduct is related to sex whether the relationship with sex lies in the character of the conduct or in its having reference to the sex or sexual orientation of the person at whom the conduct is directed,

"sexual offence" means any offence to which section 4 of the Sexual Offences (Amendment) Act 1976, the Sexual Offences (Amendment) Act 1992 or section 274(2) of the Criminal Procedure (Scotland) Act 1995 applies (offences under the Sexual Offences Act 1956, Part I of the Criminal Law (Consolidation)(Scotland) Act 1995 and certain other enactments), and

"written publication" has the same meaning as in the Sexual Offences (Amendment) Act 1992.

The regulations made under this section are at paras 49–50 of Sch.1 to the **2–028** Employment Tribunal (Constitution and Rules of Procedure) Regulations 2004 (SI 2004/1861).

Restriction of publicity in disability cases

2–029   12.—(1) This section applies to proceedings on a complaint under section 17A or 25(8) of the Disability Discrimination Act 1995 in which evidence of a personal nature is likely to be heard by the employment tribunal hearing the complaint.

(2) Employment tribunal procedure regulations may include provision in relation to proceedings to which this section applies for—

(a) enabling an employment tribunal, on the application of the complainant or of its own motion, to make a restricted reporting order having effect (if not revoked earlier) until the promulgation of the decision of the tribunal, and

(b) where a restricted reporting order is made in relation to a complaint which is being dealt with by the tribunal together with any other proceedings, enabling the tribunal to direct that the order is to apply also in relation to those other proceedings or such part of them as the tribunal may direct.

(3) If any identifying matter is published or included in a relevant programme in contravention of a restricted reporting order—

(a) in the case of publication in a newspaper or periodical, any proprietor, any editor and any publisher of the newspaper or periodical,

(b) in the case of publication in any other form, the person publishing the matter, and

(c) in the case of matter included in a relevant programme—

(i) any body corporate engaged in providing the service in which the programme is included, and

(ii) any person having functions in relation to the programme corresponding to those of an editor of a newspaper,

shall be guilty of an offence and liable on summary conviction to a fine not exceeding level 5 on the standard scale.

(4) Where a person is charged with an offence under subsection (3), it is a defence to prove that at the time of the alleged offence he was not aware, and neither suspected nor had reason to suspect, that the publication or programme in question was of, or included, the matter in question.

(5) Where an offence under subsection (3) committed by a body corporate is proved to have been committed with the consent or connivance of, or to be attributable to any neglect on the part of—

(a) a director, manager, secretary or other similar officer of the body corporate, or

(b) a person purporting to act in any such capacity,
he as well as the body corporate is guilty of the offence
and liable to be proceeded against and punished
accordingly.

(6) In relation to a body corporate whose affairs are managed by
its members "director", in subsection (5), means a member of the
body corporate.

(7) In this section—

"evidence of a personal nature" means any evidence of a medical,
or other intimate, nature which might reasonably be assumed to be
likely to cause significant embarrassment to the complainant if
reported,

"identifying matter" means any matter likely to lead members of
the public to identify the complainant or such other persons (if any)
as may be named in the order,

"promulgation" has such meaning as may be prescribed by regulations made by virtue of this section,

"relevant programme" means a programme included in a programme service, within the meaning of the Broadcasting Act 1990,

"restricted reporting order" means an order—

(a) made in exercise of a power conferred by regulations
made by virtue of this section, and
(b) prohibiting the publication in Great Britain of identifying matter in a written publication available to the public
or its inclusion in a relevant programme for reception in
Great Britain, and

"written publication" includes a film, a sound track and any other
record in permanent form but does not include an indictment or
other document prepared for use in particular legal proceedings.

The regulations made under this section are at para.50 of Sch.1 to the **2–030**
Employment Tribunal (Constitution and Rules of Procedure) Regulations 2004 (SI
2004/1861).

Costs and expenses

13.—(1) Employment tribunal procedure regulations may include **2–031**
provision—

(a) for the award of costs or expenses;
(b) for the award of any allowances payable under section
5(2)(c) or (3).

(1A) Regulations under subsection (1) may include provision
authorising an employment tribunal to have regard to a person's
ability to pay when considering the making of an award against him
under such regulations.

(1B) Employment tribunal procedure regulations may include provision for authorising an employment tribunal—

    (a) to disallow all or part of the costs or expenses of a representative of a party to proceedings before it by reason of that representative's conduct of the proceedings;

    (b) to order a representative of a party to proceedings before it to meet all or part of the costs or expenses incurred by a party by reason of the representative's conduct of the proceedings;

    (c) to order a representative of a party to proceedings before it to meet all or part of any allowances payable by the Secretary of State under section 5(2)(c) or (3) by reason of the representative's conduct of the proceedings.

(1C) Employment tribunal procedure regulations may also include provision for taxing or otherwise settling the costs or expenses referred to in subsection (1)(a) or (1B)(b) (and, in particular in England and Wales, for enabling the amount of such costs to be assessed by way of detailed assessment in a county court).

(2) In relation to proceedings under section 111 of the Employment Rights Act 1996—

    (a) where the employee has expressed a wish to be reinstated or re-engaged which has been communicated to the employer at least seven days before the hearing of the complaint, or

    employment tribunal procedure regulations shall include provision for requiring the employer to pay the costs or expenses of any postponement or adjournment of the hearing caused by his failure, without a special reason, to adduce reasonable evidence as to the availability of the job from which the complainant was dismissed or of comparable or suitable employment.

[13A Payments in respect of preparation time

2–032   (1) Employment tribunal procedure regulations may include provision for authorising an employment tribunal to order a party to proceedings before it to make a payment to any other party in respect of time spent in preparing that other party's case.

(2) Regulations under subsection (1) may include provision authorising an employment tribunal to have regard to a person's ability to pay when considering the making of an order against him under such regulations.

(3) If employment tribunal procedure regulations include—

    (a) provision of the kind mentioned in subsection (1), and

(b) provision of the kind mentioned in section 13(1)(a),

they shall also include provision to prevent an employment tribunal exercising its powers under both kinds of provision in favour of the same person in the same proceedings.]

The regulations made under this section are at paras 38–48 of Sch.1 to the **2–033** Employment Tribunal (Constitution and Rules of Procedure) Regulations 2004 (SI 2004/1861) and para.10 of Sch.4 to those Regulations.

Interest

14.—(1) The Secretary of State may by order made with the **2–034** approval of the Treasury provide that sums payable in pursuance of decisions of employment tribunals shall carry interest at such rate and between such times as may be prescribed by the order.

(2) Any interest due by virtue of such an order shall be recoverable as a sum payable in pursuance of the decision.

(3) The power conferred by subsection (1) includes power—

(a) to specify cases or circumstances in which interest is not payable,

(b) to provide that interest is payable only on sums exceeding a specified amount or falling between specified amounts,

(c) to make provision for the manner in which and the periods by reference to which interest is to be calculated and paid,

(d) to provide that any enactment—

(i) does or does not apply in relation to interest payable by virtue of subsection (1), or

(ii) applies to it with such modifications as may be specified in the order,

(e) to make provision for cases where sums are payable in pursuance of decisions or awards made on appeal from employment tribunals,

(f) to make such incidental or supplemental provision as the Secretary of State considers necessary.

(4) In particular, an order under subsection(1) may provide that the rate of interest shall be the rate specified in section 17 of the Judgments Act 1838 as that enactment has effect from time to time.

See the Employment Tribunals (Interest) Order 1990 (SI 1990/479) and the **2–035** Employment Tribunals (Interest on Awards in Discrimination Cases) Regulations 1996 (SI 1996/2803) at paras 17–052 and 17–068.

Enforcement

15.—(1) Any sum payable in pursuance of a decision of an employ- **2–036** ment tribunal in England and Wales which has been registered in accordance with employment tribunal procedure regulations shall, if a county court so orders, be recoverable by execution issued from the county court or otherwise as if it were payable under an order of that court.

(2) Any order for the payment of any sum made by an employment tribunal in Scotland (or any copy of such an order certified by the Secretary of the Tribunals) may be enforced as if it were an extract registered decree arbitral bearing a warrant for execution issued by the sheriff court of any sheriffdom in Scotland.

(3) In this section a reference to a decision or order of an employment tribunal—

(a) does not include a decision or order which, on being reviewed, has been revoked by the tribunal, and

(b) in relation to a decision or order which on being reviewed, has been varied by the tribunal, shall be construed as a reference to the decision or order as so varied.

2–037   The process by which a tribunal award may be enforced is set out in CPR r.70.5 and its associated practice direction. The application must be made to the court for the district where the person against whom the award was made resides or carries on business, unless the court otherwise orders. The application notice must be in the form and contain the information required by the relevant practice direction. The current form is N322A. A copy of the award must be filed with the application notice. The application may be dealt with by a court officer without a hearing. The costs allowed on such an application are on a sliding scale set out in CPR r.45.6.

The Tribunals, Courts and Enforcement Act 2007, not yet in force, proposes an amendment to s.5(1) (Enforcement of decisions of the tribunal in England and Wales), the effect of which will be to remove the need to register a decision of the Tribunal so that a litigant will be able to enforce a judgment through the County Court without registration similar to the position under s.15(2); see s.27 of the Act. At the time of writing, the Act has received the Royal Assent but no commencement date has been provided.

RECOUPMENT OF SOCIAL SECURITY BENEFITS

Power to provide for recoupment of benefits
2–038   16.—(1) This section applies to payments which are the subject of proceedings before employment tribunals and which are—

(a) payments of wages or compensation for loss of wages,

(b) payments by employers to employees under sections 146 to 151, sections 168 to 173 or section 192 of the Trade Union and Labour Relations (Consolidation) Act 1992,

(c) payments by employers to employees under—

    (i) Part III, V, VI or VII,

    (ii) section 93, or

    (iii) Part X,

of the Employment Rights Act 1996, or

> (d) payments by employers to employees of a nature similar to, or for a purpose corresponding to the purpose of, payments within paragraph (b) or (c),and to payments of remuneration under a protective award under section 189 of the Trade Union and Labour Relations (Consolidation) Act 1992.

(2) The Secretary of State may by regulations make with respect to payments to which this section applies provision for any or all of the purposes specified in subsection (3).

(3) The purposes referred to in subsection (2) are—

> (a) enabling the Secretary of State to recover from an employer, by way of total or partial recoupment of job-seeker's allowance or income support—
>
>> (i) a sum not exceeding the amount of the prescribed element of the monetary award, or
>> (ii) in the case of a protective award, the amount of the remuneration,
>
> (b) requiring or authorising an employment tribunal to order the payment of such a sum, by way of total or partial recoupment of either benefit, to the Secretary of State instead of to an employee, and
>
> (c) requiring an employment tribunal to order the payment to an employee of only the excess of the prescribed element of the monetary award over the amount of any jobseeker's allowance or income support shown to the tribunal to have been paid to the employee and enabling the Secretary of State to recover from the employer, by way of total or partial recoupment of the benefit, a sum not exceeding that amount.

(4) Regulations under this section may be framed—

> (a) so as to apply to all payments to which this section applies or to one or more classes of those payments, and
>
> (b) so as to apply to both jobseeker's allowance and income support, or to only jobseeker's allowance or income support.

(5) Regulations under this section may—

> (a) confer powers and impose duties on tribunals or other persons,
>
> (b) impose on an employer to whom a monetary award or protective award relates a duty—

> > > (i) to furnish particulars connected with the award, and
> > > (ii) to suspend payments in pursuance of the award during any period prescribed by the regulations,
> > (c) provide for an employer who pays a sum to the Secretary of State in pursuance of this section to be relieved from any liability to pay the sum to another person,
> > (cc) provide for the determination by the Secretary of State of any issue arising as to the total or partial recoupment in pursuance of the regulations of a jobseeker's allowance, unemployment benefit or income support,
> > (d) confer on an employee a right of appeal to an appeal tribunal constituted under Chapter 1 of Part 1 of the Social Security Act 1998 against any decision of the Secretary of State on any such issue and
> > (e) provide for the proof in proceedings before employment tribunals (whether by certificate or in any other manner) of any amount of jobseeker's allowance or income support paid to an employee.

(6) Regulations under this section may make different provision for different cases.

2–039 Regulations made under s.16(2): the Employment Protection (Recoupment of Jobseekers Allowance and Income Support) Regulations 1996 (SI 1996/2349).

[Recoupment: further provisions]

2–040 17.—(1) Where in pursuance of any regulations under section 16 a sum has been recovered by or paid to the Secretary of State by way of total or partial recoupment of jobseeker's allowance or income support—

> (a) no sum shall be recoverable under Part III or V of the Social Security Administration Act 1992, and
> (b) no abatement, payment or reduction shall be made by reference to the jobseeker's allowance or income support recouped.

(2) Any amount found to have been duly recovered by or paid to the Secretary of State in pursuance of regulations under section 16 by way of total or partial recoupment of jobseeker's allowance shall be paid into the National Insurance Fund.

(3) In section 16—

"monetary award" means the amount which is awarded, or ordered to be paid, to the employee by the tribunal or would be so awarded or ordered apart from any provision of regulations under that section, and "the prescribed element", in relation to any monetary award, means so much of that award as is attributable to such matters as may be prescribed by regulations under that section.

(4) In section 16 "income-based jobseeker's allowance" has the same meaning as in the Jobseekers Act 1995.

Conciliation

18.—(1) This section applies in the case of employment tribunal proceedings and claims which could be the subject of employment tribunal proceedings— 2–041

    (a) under—

        (i) section 2(1) of the Equal Pay Act 1970,

        (ii) section 63 of the Sex Discrimination Act 1975, or

        (iii) section 54 of the Race Relations Act 1976,

    (b) arising out of a contravention, or alleged contravention, of section 64, 68, 86 137, 138, 145A, 145B, 146, 168, 168A, 169, 170, 174, 188 or 190 of the Trade Union and Labour Relations (Consolidation) Act 1992,

    (c) under section 17A or 25(8) of the Disability Discrimination Act 1995,

    (d) arising out of a contravention, or alleged contravention, of section 8, 13, 15, 18(1), 21(1), 28, 80G(1), 80H(1)(b), 80(1), 92, or 135, or of Part V, VI, VII or X, of the Employment Rights Act 1996,

   (dd) under or by virtue of section 11, 18, 20(1)(a) or 24 of the National Minimum Wage Act 1998,

    (e) which are proceedings in respect of which a tribunal has jurisdiction by virtue of section 3 of this Act,

    (f) under or arising out of a contravention, or alleged contravention, of a provision specified by an order under subsection (8)(b) as a provision to which this paragraph applies,

   (ff) under regulation 30 of the Working Time Regulations 1998,

    (g) under regulation 27 or 32 of the Transnational Information and Consultation of Employees Regulations 1999,

    (h) arising out of a contravention, or alleged contravention of regulation 5(1) or 7(2) of the Part-time Workers (Prevention of Less Favourable Treatment) Regulations 2000,

    (i) arising out of a contravention, or alleged contravention of regulation 3 or 6(2) of the Fixed-term Employees (Prevention of Less Favourable Treatment) Regulations 2002,

   (j) under regulation 9 of those Regulations,

   (k) under regulation 28 of the Employment Equality (Sexual Orientation) Regulations 2003

   (l) under regulation 28 of the Employment Equality (Religion or Belief) Regulations 2003,

  (m) under regulation 18 of the Merchant Shipping (Working Time: Inland Waterways) Regulations 2003,

   (n) under regulation 41 or 45 of the European Public Limited-Liability Company Regulations 2004,

   (o) [under regulation 19 of the Fishing Vessels (Working Time: Sea-fishermen) Regulations 2004],

   (p) under regulation 29 or 33 of the Information and Consultation of Employees Regulations 2004,

   (q) under paragraph 4 or 8 of the Schedule to the Occupational and Personal Pension Schemes (Consultation by Employers and Miscellaneous Amendment) Regulations 2006,

   (r) under regulation 36 of the Employment Equality (Age) Regulations 2006, or

   (s) under regulation 30 or 34 of the European Cooperative Society (Involvement of Employees) Regulations 2006.

   (t) under regulations 45 or 51 of the Companies (Cross Boarder Mergers) Regulations 2007

(2) Where an application has been presented to an employment tribunal, and a copy of it has been sent to a conciliation officer, it is the duty of the conciliation officer—

   (a) if he is requested to do so by the person by whom and the person against whom the proceedings are brought, or

   (b) if, in the absence of any such request, the conciliation officer considers that he could act under this subsection with a reasonable prospect of success,

      to endeavour to promote a settlement of the proceedings without their being determined by an employment tribunal.

(2A) Where employment tribunal procedure regulations include provision postponing the fixing of a time and place for a hearing for the purpose of giving an opportunity for the proceedings to be settled by way of conciliation and withdrawn, subsection (2) shall have effect from the end of the postponement to confer a power on the conciliation officer, instead of imposing a duty.

(3) Where at any time—

   (a) a person claims that action has been taken in respect of which proceedings could be brought by him before an employment tribunal, but

(b) before any application relating to that action has been presented by him a request is made to a conciliation officer (whether by that person or by the person against whom the proceedings could be instituted) to make his services available to them,

the conciliation officer shall act in accordance with subsection (2) as if an application had been presented to an employment tribunal.

(4) Where a person who has presented a complaint to an employment tribunal under section 111 of the Employment Rights Act 1996 has ceased to be employed by the employer against whom the complaint was made, the conciliation officer shall (for the purpose of promoting a settlement of the complaint in accordance with subsection (2)) in particular—

(a) seek to promote the reinstatement or re-engagement of the complainant by the employer, or by a successor of the employer or by an associated employer, on terms appearing to the conciliation officer to be equitable, or

(b) where the complainant does not wish to be reinstated or re-engaged, or where reinstatement or re-engagement is not practicable, and the parties desire the conciliation officer to act, seek to promote agreement between them as to a sum by way of compensation to be paid by the employer to the complainant.

(5) Where at any time—

(a) a person claims that action has been taken in respect of which a complaint could be presented by him to an employment tribunal under section 111 of the Employment Rights Act 1996, but

(b) before any complaint relating to that action has been presented by him a request is made to a conciliation officer (whether by that person or by the employer) to make his services available to them,

the conciliation officer shall act in accordance with subsection (4) as if a complaint had been presented to an employment tribunal under section 111.

(6) In proceeding under this section a conciliation officer shall, where appropriate, have regard to the desirability of encouraging the use of other procedures available for the settlement of grievances.

(7) Anything communicated to a conciliation officer in connection with the performance of his functions under this section shall not be admissible in evidence in any proceedings before an employment tribunal, except with the consent of the person who communicated it to that officer.

(8) The Secretary of State may by order—

(a) direct that further provisions of the Employment Rights Act 1996 be added to the list in subsection (1)(d), or

(b) specify a provision of any other Act as a provision to which subsection (1)(f) applies.

Effect of conciliation

2–042   Section 203 of the Employment Rights Act, together with equivalent provisions within the Sex Discrimination Act 1975, the Race Relations Act 1976, the Employment Equality (Religion or Belief) Regulations 2003 (SI 2003/1660), the Employment Equality (Sexual Orientation) Regulations 2003, Trade Union and Labour Relations (Consolidation) Act 1992, the Working Time Regulations 1998 (SI 1998/1833), the Part Time Workers (Prevention of Less Favourable Treatment Regulations 2000 (SI 2000/1551), the Fixed-term Employees (Prevention of Less Favourable Treatment) Regulations 2002 (SI 2002/2034), and the Employment Equality (Age) Regulations 2006 (SI 2006/1031), provide that the parties to a claim before the tribunal cannot settle their claims before the tribunal unless specific conditions are satisfied. One of those conditions is contained within s.203(2)(e) which states that the general prohibition is excluded if agreement is reached between the parties to refrain from instituting or continuing proceedings where a conciliation officer, defined under s.42 but commonly referred to as an ACAS officer, has taken action under s.18 ETA.

Jurisdictions engaged

2–043   The requirement that claims before the tribunal should be conciliated relates to the list of jurisdictions set out in s.18(1).

Duty of conciliation officer

2–044   The duty of the conciliation officer is to promote the settlement of claims where they have been issued, either at the request of both parties, or where he considers that there is a reasonable prospect of success of settling the claim without their being determined by a tribunal: s.18(2). In the case of an existing claim of unfair dismissal under ERA 1996 s.111, or a potential claim where proceedings have not yet been issued, the conciliation officer is required to promote reinstatement or re-engagement on terms that are equitable. Where the conciliation officer regards this as being not practicable, or where the employee does not wish to be re-employed, but nevertheless the parties which the claim to be settled, the conciliation officer is required to promote agreement as to a sum of compensation to be paid by the employer: s.18(4) and (5).

In carrying out his duties, the conciliation officer is required, where appropriate, to have regard to the desirability of encouraging the use of other procedures available for the settlement of grievances under s.18(6). Use of the word grievance here pre-dates its use in the Employment Act 2002 and should be construed in a non-technical sense. Equally there is no definition provided of the expression "other procedures", and so again the ACAS officer is required to consider both formal schemes such as the ACAS Arbitration Scheme, and informal schemes such as mediation.

The duty of the ACAS officer is to be—and appear to be—impartial, and to promote the agreement. Per Kilner Brown J. in *Duport Furniture Products Ltd v Moore* [1979] I.C.R. 165: the conciliation officer should not get himself involved in the rightness or wrongness of the agreement. A conciliation officer should not be put in such a position that his role is misunderstood by one party or the other. A conciliation officer should never be put in such a position that one side of industry may take the view that ACAS is in favour of another section of industry, or the other side of industry may take the view that ACAS is in favour of the other section of industry.

In *Clarke v Redcar and Cleveland BC* [2006] I.R.L.R. 324, the EAT reaffirmed these principles in a detailed review of the relationship between the role of the ACAS conciliator and the purpose of the compromise agreement vehicle for the resolution of contentious proceedings. The function of the conciliator in respect of any settlement facilitated by the conciliator and contained within the COT3 resolving the proceedings is as follows:

(a) The ACAS officer has no responsibility to see that the terms of the settlement are fair on the employee;

(b) The expression "promote a settlement" must be given a liberal construction capable of covering whatever action by way of such promotion, as is applicable in the circumstances of the particular case;

(c) The ACAS officer must never advise as to the merits of the case. It would be quite wrong to say that the ACAS officer was obliged to go through the framework of the legislation. Indeed, it might defeat the officer's very function if she were obliged to tell a claimant, in effect, that they might receive considerably more money;

(d) It is not for the tribunal to consider whether the officer correctly interpreted her duties; it is sufficient that she intended and purported to act under the section; and

(e) If the ACAS officer was to act in bad faith or adopt unfair methods when promoting a settlement, the agreement might be set aside and might not operate to bar proceedings.

When the duty is engaged

The duty to act as described above is engaged as soon as a copy of the presented **2-045** application has been sent to the conciliation officer (s.18(2)), or, prior to the issue of proceedings, a person claims that action has been taken against him that could be brought before a tribunal and either side of the potential dispute requests the ACAS officer to make his services available to them (s.18(3)). Prior to the introduction of the Employment Tribunals (Constitution and Rules of Procedure) Regulations 2004 (SI 2004/1861), the duty continued until both liability and remedy had been determined (*Courage Take Home Trade Limited v Keys* [1986] I.C.R. 874). With the introduction of those rules, for certain cases, there was introduced a fixed period of conciliation (rr.22–24). Following the expiry of the conciliation period the duty as described above comes to an end, though the ACAS officer retains a power to settle such proceedings (s.18(2A)).

Admissibility of communications

Section 18(7) precludes any communication between a party and an ACAS officer **2-046** being introduced in evidence before an employment tribunal. The provision does not restrict itself to without prejudice communications, though without prejudice communications are intended to be protected as made clear in the statement of Sir John Donaldson, President of the National Industrial Relations Court in 1972, [1972] I.C.R. 1:

"Fears have been expressed that this court will require conciliation officers of the Department of Employment or of the Commission on Industrial Relations or others to reveal the content of confidential discussions into which the parties have entered bona fide with a view to settlement. Such fears are completely without foundation. The confidentiality of communications to statutory conciliation officers is protected by section [18] of the Act. Furthermore, the courts have for many years recognised that the public interest requires respect for the confidentiality of such discussions, whether directly between the parties or with independent third parties. This court will pursue the same policy."

Communication with the ACAS officer is an occasion of absolute privilege: *Freer v Glover* [2006] I.R.L.R. 521.

Settlement by conciliation

2–047   Because it is a requirement under s.203(2)(e) ERA 1996 that the ACAS officer has "taken action" under s.18 ETA, and as s.18 ETA requires the ACAS officer to "promote" a settlement, it is the position of ACAS that agreements that it has not promoted, but which it is asked to rubber stamp, are not an effective method to settle claims. In practice ACAS refuses to rubber stamp agreements that have previously been negotiated between the parties.

Effect of settlement

2–048   The claims settled by a COT3 agreement are only those claims in the contemplation of the parties at the time of settlement: *Livingstone v Hepworth Refractories Plc* [1992] I.C.R. 287; [1992] I.R.L.R. 63 per Wood J.: ". . . the agreement must relate to those matters which are within [the parties] presumed contemplation at the time". In that case, it was held that the words used in the settlement—"in full and final settlement of all claims which the applicant may have against the respondent arising from his employment with the respondent or out of its termination"—did not encompass claims made under the Sex Discrimination Act in respect of the employer's pension scheme. See and compare *University of East London v Hinton* [2005] I.C.R. 1261, CA for a similar approach in relation to statutory compromise agreements.

Parties will be at risk where general words of release, such as "in full and final settlement of all claims. . ." are used. There are no special rules of interpretation applicable to a general release, which is to be construed in the same way as any other contract. The issue is to ascertain the intention of the parties objectively in the context of the circumstances in which the release was entered into. In *BCCI v Ali* [2001] I.C.R. 337 it was held that when the employees' agreements had been entered into, neither party could realistically have supposed that a claim for damages in respect of disadvantage on the labour market was a possibility and that, accordingly, the parties could not be held to have intended the release to apply to such claims. Although it has been accepted that it is, in principle, possible to compromise future unknown claims, clear language to this effect is required (*Royal Orthopaedic Hospital Trust v Howard* [2002] I.R.L.R. 849).

Best practice for both conciliated agreements and compromise agreements is to set out the claims in the contemplation of the parties that are being settled and the jurisdictions of the tribunal that are being excluded from pursuit in the future.

Confidentiality of terms

2–049   Whilst the form COT3 is not open to public inspection, an order of an employment tribunal referring to the agreement contained in the form COT3 is. To preserve confidentiality, it is not uncommon for the form COT3 to record that the parties have agreed terms set out in an attached (but separate) document, recording the detail of the deal, similar to the practice in the High Court of recording settlement in a "Tomlin" order.

Form of settlement agreement

In contrast to the position under s.203 ERA and its parallel provisions found in **2–050**
the discrimination legislation, there is no requirement in the ETA that a conciliated agreement need be in writing. Once agreement to the terms has been
indicated by both sides to the ACAS officer, the agreement is binding on both
parties (see *Gilbert v Kembridge Fibres Ltd* [1984] I.C.R. 188). In that case, the
employee's subsequent refusal to sign a written agreement that recorded the terms
agreed orally, did not affect the validity of the compromise that had been reached.

Representative's authority

In accordance with normal common law principles the parties' solicitors or **2–051**
barristers have ostensible authority to bind their clients to conciliated agreements.
This was so even where the legal representative settled a claim without, or contrary
to, their client's instructions (*Times Newspapers Ltd v Fitt* [1981] I.C.R. 637). A CAB
adviser will similarly bind a claimant in negotiations if held out as having ostensible
authority, which will arise if named in the employee's originating application as the
representative (*Freeman v Sovereign Chicken Ltd* [1991] I.C.R. 853, EAT).

Finality of settlement

Where so requested, the tribunal has a duty to investigate whether an agreement **2–052**
purporting to settle a claim has complied with the formalities of settlement (*Duport
Furniture Products Ltd v Moore* [1982] I.C.R. 84). However, the tribunal has no
jurisdiction to set aside a consent order properly made on the basis of a conciliated
agreement.

In *Eden v Humphries & Glasgow Ltd* [1981] I.C.R. 183, an employee who had been
unfairly dismissed appealed against the amount of compensation awarded to him by
an employment tribunal. Before the appeal was heard, a conciliated agreement was
reached under which the employer would pay him an additional sum of money and
give him a testimonial. The appeal was withdrawn. Later, the employee changed his
mind and requested that the settlement be set aside, and that the appeal be listed
on the grounds that by the Employment Appeal Tribunal Rules 1976, r.20(1), the
appeal tribunal had power, of its own motion or on application, to review any order
it made, or to revoke or vary any order on the grounds that the interests of justice
required such review. The agreement had been compliant; the issue was whether
the appeal tribunal had jurisdiction to set aside a consent order properly made
because the interests of justice required it. Per Slynn J., at pp.185–186:

> "We have to remember that we are a body set up by statute with only the powers
> which the statute gives us. It does not seem to us that those powers do include
> jurisdiction to set aside an agreement which has been arrived at between the
> parties to compromise an appeal to this tribunal".

In *Larkfield of Chepstow Ltd v Milne* [1988] I.C.R. 1, the employment judge had
announced that the tribunal would reserve its decision, and invited the parties to
reach a settlement. The parties did so and recorded it in a COT3 form. That
settlement was subsequently approved by a different employment judge and the
originating application stayed by consent. Some months later, the parties were
informed that the tribunal had been minded to reach a decision in the applicant's
favour whereas the agreement reached was for equal apportionment of liability.
The claimant applied to set aside the consent order made by the second
employment judge. It was held that since there had been no decision or misrepresentation by the tribunal, there were no grounds for avoiding the settlement agreed
by the parties.

Whilst the statutory duty upon ACAS to promote settlement described above will have expired, the EAT may take such steps as it thinks fit to enable the parties to avail themselves of any opportunities for conciliation (EAT r.36—see 5–128). The EAT has now issued a conciliation protocol under which, during the paper sift, a direction may be given to require the parties to consider conciliation by ACAS.

Conciliation procedure

2–053   **19.—(1) Employment tribunal procedure regulations shall include in relation to employment tribunal proceedings in the case of which any enactment makes provision for conciliation—**

> **(a) provisions requiring a copy of the application by which the proceedings are instituted, and a copy of any notice relating to it which is lodged by or on behalf of the person against whom the proceedings are brought, to be sent to a conciliation officer, and**

> **(b) provisions securing that the applicant and the person against whom the proceedings are brought are notified that the services of a conciliation officer are available to them.**

2–054   Regulations made under this section are at paras 21–24 of Sch.1 to the Employment Tribunal (Constitution and Rules of Procedure) Regulations 2004 (SI 2004/1861).

The Tribunals, Courts and Enforcement Act 2007, not yet in force, proposes a new s.19A, see s.142 of the Act. The effect of the new provision will enable agreements conciliated through ACAS to be enforced directly through the County Courts, as though they were a decision of the Tribunal under the proposed amendment to s.15 ETA as described above. At the time of writing, the Act has received the Royal Assent, but no commencement date has been provided.

PART II THE EMPLOYMENT APPEAL TRIBUNAL

INTRODUCTORY

The Appeal Tribunal

2–055   **20.—(1) The Employment Appeal Tribunal ("the Appeal Tribunal") shall continue in existence.**

(2) The Appeal Tribunal shall have a central office in London but may sit at any time and in any place in Great Britain.

(3) The Appeal Tribunal shall be a superior court of record and shall have an official seal which shall be judicially noticed.

(4) Subsection (2) is subject to regulation 34 of the Transnational Information and Consultation of Employees Regulations [1999,] [regulation 46(1) of the European Public Limited-Liability Company Regulations] [2004,] regulation 36(1) of the Information and Consultation of Employees Regulations 2004 and regulation 37(1) of the European Cooperative Society (Involvement of Employees) Regu-

lations 2006 and Regulation 58(1) of the4 Companies (Cross Boarder Mergers) Regulations 2007.

Practice and procedure before the EAT is governed by the Employment Appeal **2–056** Tribunal Rules 1993 and the EAT Practice Direction. It may sit at any place in Great Britain. It routinely sits in London and in Edinburgh: the London EAT hearing appeals from tribunals in England and Wales, the Edinburgh EAT hearing appeals from tribunals in Scotland. As to the exercise of the discretion to sit outside London and Edinburgh, see *Williams v Cowell (t/a The Stables) (No.1)* [2000] I.C.R. 85 per Judge L.J.: the exercise of the discretion "involves examining not only the consequent advantage to those citizens who would benefit from the adoption of a new venue, but also any corresponding disadvantage to other citizens of the consequent reduction in resources available for the existing courts."

Where there are conflicting decisions of the Scottish Court of Session and the English Court of Appeal, the Scottish EAT may follow the Court of Session on a question of Scots law (*Brown v Rentokill Ltd* [1992] I.R.L.R. 302). See also *Marshalls Clay Products Ltd v Caulfield* [2004] I.C.R. 1502 per Lord Justice Laws, "as a matter of pragmatic good sense the ET and the EAT in either jurisdiction will ordinarily expect to follow decisions of the higher appeal court in the other jurisdiction (whether the Court of Session or the Court of Appeal) where the point confronting them is indistinguishable from what was decided there."

The EAT is not a "court" for the purposes of s.4(5) of the Human Rights Act 1998, and therefore cannot make a declaration of incompatibility under s.4(2) of that Act (*Whittaker v P&D Watson (t/a P & M Watson Haulage)* [2002] I.C.R. 1244, EAT).

Status of the Employment Appeal Tribunal

Whilst the Employment Tribunal is an inferior court (*Peach Grey & Co v Sommers* **2–057** [1995] I.C.R. 549), the Employment Appeal Tribunal is, by s.20(3) of the Employment Tribunals Act 1996 a "superior court of record". It is not part of the High Court, though it is undoubtedly "any court" for the purpose of s.42(1A)(b) of the Supreme Court Act 1981 (*Vidler v Unison* [1999] I.C.R. 746).

In relation to all matters incidental to the exercise of its jurisdiction it has the same rights, powers and privileges as the High Court (see s.29 below), however its power to hear and determine certain types of case are still limited by the ETA 1996 (*Refreshment Systems Ltd (t/a Northern Vending Services) v Wolstenholme, Times*, March 2, 2004, 2003 WL 23192314.).

Whilst the EAT is a superior court of record, the question of whether it has inherent jurisdiction to regulate its own affairs was expressly left in the balance in *X v Commissioner for Police* [2003] I.C.R. 1031, despite the contrary view expressed in the earlier decision in *Chief Constable of the West Yorkshire Police v A* [2001] I.C.R. 128. Whilst the High Court may regulate its own affairs through its long established inherent jurisdiction, the EAT is fettered by reference to the statutory framework in which it exists.

JURISDICTION

Jurisdiction of Appeal Tribunal

21.—(1) An appeal lies to the Appeal Tribunal on any question of 2–058 law arising from any decision of, or arising in any proceedings before, an employment tribunal under or by virtue of—

(a) the Equal Pay Act 1970,

(b) the Sex Discrimination Act 1975,

(c) the Race Relations Act 1976,

(d) the Trade Union and Labour Relations (Consolidation) Act 1992,

(e) the Disability Discrimination Act 1995, or

(f) the Employment Rights Act 1996.

(ff) . . .

(fg) . . .

(g) this Act,

(ga) the National Minimum Wage Act 1998,

(gb) the Employment Relations Act 1999,

(gc) the Equality Act 2006,

(h) the Working Time Regulations 1998, . . .

(i) the Transnational Information and Consultation of Employees Regulations 1999

(j) the Part-time Workers (Prevention of Less Favourable Treatment) Regulations 2000

(k) the Fixed-term Employees (Prevention of Less Favourable Treatment) Regulations 2002

(l) the Employment Equality (Sexual Orientation) Regulations 2003

(m) the Employment Equality (Religion or Belief) Regulations 2003

(n) the Merchant Shipping (Working Time: Inland Waterways) Regulations 2003

(o) the European Public Limited-Liability Company Regulations 2004

(p) the Fishing Vessels (Working Time: Sea-fishermen) Regulations 2004,

(q) the Information and Consultation of Employees Regulations 2004,

(r) the Schedule to the Occupational and Personal Pension Schemes (Consultation by Employers and Miscellaneous Amendment) Regulations 2006,

(s) the Employment Equality (Age) Regulations 2006, or

(t) the European Cooperative Society (Involvement of Employees) Regulations 2006

(u) the Companies (Cross Boarder Mergers) Regulations 2007

(2) No appeal shall lie except to the Appeal Tribunal from any decision of an employment tribunal under or by virtue of the Acts listed or the Regulations referred to in subsection (1).

(3) Subsection (1) does not affect any provision contained in, or made under, any Act which provides for an appeal to lie to the Appeal Tribunal (whether from an employment tribunal, the Certification

Officer or any other person or body) otherwise than on a question to which that subsection applies.

(4) The Appeal Tribunal also has any jurisdiction in respect of matters other than appeals which is conferred on it by or under—

> **(a) the Trade Union and Labour Relations (Consolidation) Act 1992,**
> **(b) this Act, or**
> **(c) any other Act.**

Appeal on a point of law only

The EAT only has jurisdiction to hear an appeal if the tribunal below has **2–059** misdirected itself in law. See, for example *British Telecommunications Plc v Sheridan* [1990] I.R.L.R. 27; *Secretary of State for Education and Employment v Bearman* [1998] I.R.L.R. 431; and *Eclipse Blinds Ltd v Wright* [1992] I.R.L.R. 133.

For the Appeal Tribunal to find that there has been a misdirection as to the law it must find that:

> (a) the tribunal below misdirected itself in law; or
> (b) where the appeal relates to a question of fact, the tribunal came to a conclusion that no reasonable tribunal could have come to on the facts (i.e. the decision was "perverse").

The Employment Appeal Tribunal is not entitled to review interlocutory decisions of the employment tribunal on their merits without regard to whether or not the directions were erroneous in law (*Balamoody v UKCCN* [2002] I.R.L.R. 288; *Medallion Holidays Ltd v Birch* [1985] I.R.L.R. 406; *Adams & Raynor v West Sussex CC* [1990] I.R.L.R. 215, disapproving *British Library v Palyza* [1984] I.R.L.R. 306).

The exercise of an administrative discretion is, however, capable of review by the EAT as a question of law, so that where a form ET1 was faxed by the claimant to the tribunal, and in the process was reduced in size so that it was rejected by the tribunal as not being in the prescribed form, this was an error of law: *Grant v In2Focus Sales Development Ltd* EATUK/0310/06/LA.

Function of the EAT

In disposing of the appeal, the EAT may not allow an appeal by consent without **2–060** itself considering whether the reasoned decision of an employment tribunal should be set aside: see *J Sainsbury Plc v Moger* [1994] I.C.R. 800, approved in *Dickie v Cathay Pacific Airways Ltd* [2004] I.C.R. 1733.

The EAT should not substitute its own view of a set of facts for that of the original tribunal. See *Retarded Children's Aid Society Ltd v Day* [1978] I.C.R. 437. The Employment Appeal Tribunal's function is to correct errors of law, the fact that its members would decide a case differently does not mean that they can overrule an industrial tribunal who have not misdirected themselves.

Accordingly, the EAT will not interfere with the employment tribunal's finding of fact on quantum (*Fougere v Phoenix Motor Co Ltd* [1976] I.C.R. 495, or on contribution, *Nelson v BBC* [1977] I.C.R. 649; *Hollier v Plysu* [1983] I.R.L.R. 260, CA).

Misuse of process

The appeal must be against the decision of the employment tribunal, rather than **2–061** its reasons, so, in *Harrod v Ministry of Defence* [1981] I.C.R. 8, the EAT dismissed an appeal *in limine* where the appellant had conceded that there had been no dismissal, but wished to appeal the decision because the Employment Tribunal had reached that decision for the wrong reasons.

It has been suggested that *IMI Yorkshire Imperial Ltd v Olender* [1982] I.C.R. 69 is authority for the proposition that subs(1) excludes the possibility of an appeal where there is no dispute between the parties, but one party is seeking to establish a point of principle for the future. The EAT made no reference to the section at all, but indicated only that it thought it was not "right", generally, to hear an appeal which no longer involved any practical results for one of the parties to the appeal, namely, the employees. Similarly, *Baker v Superite Tools Ltd* [1986] I.C.R. 189, made no reference to the section when an appeal was taken to the EAT concerning whether certain workers were employees or self-employed. Whilst both employer and worker were satisfied that the Tribunal had correctly determined that the workers were self employed, the employees wished to take the matter to the EAT in order that a more weighty decision be obtained which might assist the employees in their dealing with the Inland Revenue; per Peter Gibson J. "we regard it as a misuse of the appellate procedure laid down by Parliament".

Perversity

2–062   Any appeal on grounds of perversity must be fully particularised. Classically, findings of fact are only to be regarded as perverse if they are unsupported by any evidence (see *Piggott Brothers v Jackson* [1992] I.C.R. 85). In *Yeboah v Crofton* [2002] I.R.L.R. 634, the Court of Appeal concluded that an appeal on the grounds of perversity will only succeed if an overwhelming case has been shown. It is not permissible to interfere with a decision on the basis of the weight to be given to evidence, see *British Telecommunications Plc v Sheridan* [1990] I.R.L.R. 27; *Post Office v Lewis* (1997) 141 Sol. Jo. LB 105, CA; *Wade v Chief Constable of West Yorkshire Police, The Times*, September 9, 1998, CA. However, the distinction between what is a perverse decision and what is not is not always easy to determine, since the application of this concept is situation-specific, and to some extent, instinctive. Even though the bar is a high one, it can still be reached (see, for example *Anglian Home Improvements Ltd v Kelly* [2005] I.C.R. 242). In that case, in the face of an instruction not to do so, an employee recorded money as having been banked when it had not yet been received, resulting in a misleading record of the employer's cash at bank. By a majority the Tribunal concluded the dismissal to be unfair. The Court of Appeal concluded that this decision was perverse.

The notice of appeal

2–063   Under ordinary circumstances, it is not permissible at the appeal stage of the proceedings to introduce a point not taken at the initial hearing (*Kumchyk v Derby City Council* [1978] I.C.R. 1116, applied in *McLeod v Hellyer Bros Ltd* [1987] I.R.L.R. 232; *Fadipe v Reed Nursing Personnel* [2005] I.C.R. 1760, CA, and *Leicestershire CC v Unison* [2006] I.R.L.R. 810, CA). There is no error on the part of an employment judge if he does not assist the parties or their representatives in taking all the available arguments that appear on the merits of the case (see *Kumchyk* above).

As an exception to this rule, in *House v Emerson Electric Industrial Controls* [1980] I.C.R. 795, Talbot J. held that if a tribunal had accepted jurisdiction and made a finding in favour of an employee, where quite plainly it had no such jurisdiction to do so, what they did would have been a nullity and the appeal tribunal ought to say so. However in *Barber v Thames Television Plc* [1991] I.C.R. 253, the EAT made it clear that not all attacks upon jurisdiction would allow a new point to be taken. Each case was to be looked at on its merits. Neither the decision in *House* nor in *Barber* were referred to in the considered appeal in *Aziz v Embassy of Republic of Yemen* [2005] I.C.R. 1391, where the Court of Appeal considered that whilst the Employment Appeal Tribunal's discretion to allow a new point of law should only be exercised in exceptional circumstances, it could not override the right of a State to claim on appeal that it had not submitted to the jurisdiction.

The EAT retains a discretion to allow a new point of law, but it should be exercised only in exceptional circumstances, and for compelling reasons, especially if the result would be to open up issues of fact that were not sufficiently investigated before the employment tribunal because of the strong public interest in finality in litigation. The EAT should provide reasons for any decision on such a point, particularly if exercising its discretion in a "particularly unusual manner" (*Leicestershire CC v Unison* [2006] I.R.L.R. 810, CA; *Jones v Governing Body of Burdett Coutts School* [1998] I.R.L.R. 521, CA).

The EAT may exercise a discretion to allow a point to be taken on appeal that had been conceded before the tribunal, though such occasions will be rare. Held in *Secretary of State for Health v Rance* [2007] I.R.L.R. 665, the EAT should consider:

(1) the period of time that had passed since the judgment or concession;
(2) the reason for the change of position;
(3) whether attempts were made to raise the matter on review before the tribunal;
(4) the reason for the tribunal's refusal; and
(5) whether the judgement was one following a contested hearing or not.

See also the EAT Practice Direction 6–059.

MEMBERSHIP ETC.

Membership of Appeal Tribunal

22.—(1) The Appeal Tribunal shall consist of— **2–064**

    (a) **such number of judges as may be nominated from time to time by the Lord Chief Justice, after consulting the Lord Chancellor from the judges of the High Court and the Court of Appeal,**

    (b) **at least one judge of the Court of Session nominated from time to time by the Lord President of the Court of Session, and**

    (c) **such number of other members as may be appointed from time to time by Her Majesty on the joint recommendation of the Lord Chancellor and the Secretary of State ("appointed members").**

(2) **The appointed members shall be persons who appear to the Lord Chancellor and the Secretary of State to have special knowledge or experience of industrial relations either—**

    (a) **as representatives of employers, or**

    (b) **as representatives of workers (within the meaning of the Trade Union and Labour Relations (Consolidation) Act 1992).**

(3) **The Lord Chief Justice Chancellor shall appoint one of the judges nominated under subsection (1) to be the President of the Appeal Tribunal.**

Employment Tribunals Act 1996

(3A) The Lord Chief Justice must not make an appointment under subsection (3) unless—

(a) he has consulted the Lord Chancellor, and

(b) the Lord President of the Court of Session agrees.

(4) No judge shall be nominated a member of the Appeal Tribunal except with his consent.

(5) The Lord Chief Justice may nominate a judicial office holder (as defined in section 109(4) of the Constitutional Reform Act 2005) to exercise his functions under this section.

(6) The Lord President of the Court of Session may nominate a judge of the Court of Session who is a member of the First or Second Division of the Inner House of that Court to exercise his functions under subsection (3A)(b).

Membership of Appeal Tribunal

2–065   The decision in *Lawal v Northern Spirit Ltd* [2003] I.C.R. 856; [2003] I.R.L.R. 538 brought to an end the practice under which the Lord Chancellor appointed Recorders, to sit as part-time judicial members of the EAT.

Temporary membership

2–066   23.—(1) At any time when—

(a) the office of President of the Appeal Tribunal is vacant, or

(b) the person holding that office is temporarily absent or otherwise unable to act as the President of the Appeal Tribunal,

the Lord Chief Justice may nominate another judge nominated under section 22(1)(a) to act temporarily in his place.

(2) At any time when a judge of the Appeal Tribunal nominated under paragraph (a) or (b) of subsection (1) of section 22 is temporarily absent or otherwise unable to act as a member of the Appeal Tribunal—

(a) in the case of a judge nominated under paragraph (a) of that subsection, the Lord Chief Justice may nominate another judge who is qualified to be nominated under that paragraph to act temporarily in his place, and

(b) in the case of a judge nominated under paragraph (b) of that subsection, the Lord President of the Court of Session may nominate another judge who is qualified to be nominated under that paragraph to act temporarily in his place.

(3) At any time when an appointed member of the Appeal Tribunal is temporarily absent or otherwise unable to act as a member of the

Appeal Tribunal, the Lord Chancellor and the Secretary of State may jointly appoint a person appearing to them to have the qualifications for appointment as an appointed member to act temporarily in his place.

(4) A person nominated or appointed to act temporarily in place of the President or any other member of the Appeal Tribunal, when so acting, has all the functions of the person in whose place he acts.

(5) No judge shall be nominated to act temporarily as a member of the Appeal Tribunal except with his consent.

(6) The functions conferred on the Lord Chief Justice by the preceding provisions of this section may be exercised only after consulting the Lord Chancellor.

(7) The functions conferred on the Lord Chancellor by subsection (3) may be exercised only after consultation with the Lord Chief Justice.

(8) The Lord Chief Justice may nominate a judicial office holder (as defined in section 109(4) of the Constitutional Reform Act 2005) to exercise his functions under this section.

Temporary additional judicial membership

24.—(1) This section applies if both of the following conditions are met— **2-067**

(a) the Lord Chancellor thinks that it is expedient, after consulting the Lord Chief Justice, for a qualified person to be appointed to be a temporary additional judge of the Appeal Tribunal in order to facilitate in England and Wales the disposal of business in the Appeal Tribunal;

(b) the Lord Chancellor requests the Lord Chief Justice to make such an appointment.

(1A) The Lord Chief Justice may, after consulting the Lord Chancellor, appoint a qualified person as mentioned in subsection (1)(a).

(1B) An appointment under this section is—

(a) for such period, or

(b) on such occasions,

as the Lord Chief Justice determines, after consulting the Lord Chancellor.

(2) In this section "qualified person" means a person who—

(a) is qualified for appointment as a judge of the High Court under section 10 of the Senior Courts Act 1981, or

(b) has held office as a judge of the High Court or the Court of Appeal.

(3) A person appointed to be a temporary additional judge of the Appeal Tribunal has all the functions of a judge nominated under section 22(1)(a).

(4) The Lord Chief Justice may nominate a judicial office holder (as defined in section 109(4) of the Constitutional Reform Act 2005) to exercise his functions under this section.

Tenure of appointed members

2–068   25.—(1) Subject to subsections (2) to (4), an appointed member shall hold and vacate office in accordance with the terms of his appointment.

(2) An appointed member—

(a) may at any time resign his membership by notice in writing addressed to the Lord Chancellor and the Secretary of State, and

(b) shall vacate his office on the day on which he attains the age of seventy.

(3) Subsection (2)(b) is subject to section 26(4) to (6) of the Judicial Pensions and Retirement Act 1993 (Lord Chancellor's power to authorise continuance of office up to the age of seventy-five).

(4) If the Lord Chancellor, after consultation with the Secretary of State, is satisfied that an appointed member—

(a) has been absent from sittings of the Appeal Tribunal for a period longer than six consecutive months without the permission of the President of the Appeal Tribunal,

(b) has become bankrupt or made an arrangement with his creditors, or has had his estate sequestrated or made a trust deed for behoof of his creditors or a composition contract,

(c) is incapacitated by physical or mental illness, or

(d) is otherwise unable or unfit to discharge the functions of a member,

the Lord Chancellor may declare his office as a member to be vacant and shall notify the declaration in such manner as the Lord Chancellor thinks fit; and when the Lord Chancellor does so, the office becomes vacant.

(5) The Lord Chancellor may declare an appointed member's office vacant under subsection (4) only with the concurrence of the appropriate senior judge.

(6) The appropriate senior judge is the Lord Chief Justice of England and Wales, unless the member whose office is to be declared vacant exercises functions wholly or mainly in Scotland, in which case it is the Lord President of the Court of Session.

Staff

2–069   26. The Secretary of State may appoint such officers and servants of the Appeal Tribunal as he may determine, subject to the approval of the Minister for the Civil Service as to numbers and terms and conditions of service.

Remuneration, pensions and allowances

27.—(1) The Secretary of State shall pay—

    (a) the appointed members,

    (b) any person appointed to act temporarily in the place of an appointed member, and

    (c) the officers and servants of the Appeal Tribunal,

such remuneration and such travelling and other allowances as he may, with the relevant approval, determine; and for this purpose the relevant approval is that of the Treasury in the case of persons within paragraph (a) or (b) and the Minister for the Civil Service in the case of persons within paragraph (c).

(2) A person appointed to be a temporary additional judge of the Appeal Tribunal shall be paid such remuneration and allowances as the Lord Chancellor may, with the approval of the Treasury, determine.

(3) If the Secretary of State determines, with the approval of the Treasury, that this subsection applies in the case of an appointed member, the Secretary of State shall—

    (a) pay such pension, allowance or gratuity to or in respect of that person on his retirement or death, or

    (b) make to the member such payments towards the provision of a pension, allowance or gratuity for his retirement or death,

as the Secretary of State may, with the approval of the Treasury, determine.

(4) Where—

    (a) a person ceases to be an appointed member otherwise than on his retirement or death, and

    (b) it appears to the Secretary of State that there are special circumstances which make it right for him to receive compensation,

the Secretary of State may make to him a payment of such amount as the Secretary of State may, with the approval of the Treasury, determine.

Composition of Appeal Tribunal

28.—(1) The Appeal Tribunal may sit, in accordance with directions given by the President of the Appeal Tribunal, either as a single tribunal or in two or more divisions concurrently.

(2) Subject to subsections (3) to (5), proceedings before the Appeal Tribunal shall be heard by a judge and either two or four appointed members, so that in either case there is an equal number—

2–070

2–071

Employment Tribunals Act 1996

(a) of persons whose knowledge or experience of relations is as representatives of employers, and

(b) of persons whose knowledge or experience of relations is as representatives of workers.

(3) With the consent of the parties, proceedings before the Appeal Tribunal may be heard by a judge and one appointed member or by a judge and three appointed members.

(4) Proceedings on an appeal on a question arising from any decision of, or arising in any proceedings before, an tribunal consisting of the person mentioned in section 4(1)(a) alone shall be heard by a judge alone unless a judge directs that the proceedings shall be heard in accordance with subsections (2) and (3).

Composition of Appeal Tribunal

2–072   Except where the Employment Appeal Tribunal is hearing an appeal from an employment judge sitting alone (where the appeal will be conducted by a judge sitting alone), the EAT will consist of a panel of three (or very exceptionally five), i.e. a judge and a balance of lay members with knowledge or experience in industrial relations on both sides of the employer/employee equation. However, with the consent of both parties, the judge and only one of the lay members may sit. Where, however, the consent of the parties is sought, the parties are to be told whether the remaining representative is drawn from the panel of lay members with knowledge or experience in industrial relations as a representative of employers or employees (*de Haney v Brent Mind* [2004] I.C.R. 348).

PROCEDURE

Conduct of hearings

2–073   29.—(1) A person may appear before the Appeal Tribunal in person or be represented by—

(a) counsel or a solicitor,

(b) a representative of a trade union or an employers' association, or

(c) any other person whom he desires to represent him.

(2) The Appeal Tribunal has in relation to—

(a) the attendance and examination of witnesses,

(b) the production and inspection of documents, and

(c) all other matters incidental to its jurisdiction,

the same powers, rights, privileges and authority (in England and Wales) as the High Court and (in Scotland) as the Court of Session.

2–074   The provisions of subs.(1) are identical to the equivalent provisions concerning representation before the employment tribunal: see para.2–013. As to the rules concerning the attendance of witnesses and the production of documents, see EAT Rules 1993, r.27.

Appeal Tribunal procedure rules

30.—(1) The Lord Chancellor, after consultation with the Lord **2–075** President of the Court of Session, shall make rules ("Appeal Tribunal procedure rules") with respect to proceedings before the Appeal Tribunal.

(2) Appeal Tribunal procedure rules may, in particular, include provision—

(a) with respect to the manner in which, and the time within which, an appeal may be brought,

(b) with respect to the manner in which any application or complaint to the Appeal Tribunal may be made,

(c) for requiring persons to attend to give evidence and produce documents and for authorising the administration of oaths to witnesses,

(d) for requiring or enabling the Appeal Tribunal to sit in private in circumstances in which an employment tribunal is required or empowered to sit in private by virtue of section 10A of this Act,

(e) [ ]

(f) for interlocutory matters arising on any appeal or application to the Appeal Tribunal to be dealt with otherwise than in accordance with section 28(2) to (5) of this Act.

(2A) Appeal Tribunal procedure rules may make provision of a kind which may be made by employment tribunal procedure regulations under section 10(2), (5), (6) or (7).

(2B) For the purposes of subsection (2A)—

(a) the reference in section 10(2) to section 4 shall be treated as a reference to section 28, and

(b) the reference in section 10(4) to the President or a Regional Chairman shall be treated as a reference to a judge of the Appeal Tribunal.

(2C) Section 10B shall have effect in relation to a direction to or determination of the Appeal Tribunal as it has effect in relation to a direction to or determination of an employment tribunal.

(3) Subject to Appeal Tribunal procedure rules, the Appeal Tribunal has power to regulate its own procedure.

The rules referred to are the Employment Appeal Tribunal Rules 1993, as **2–076** amended by the Employment Appeal Tribunal (Amendment) Rules 2001 (SI 2001/1128), the Employment Appeal Tribunal (Amendment) Rules 2004 (SI 2004/2526), and the Employment Appeal Tribunal (Amendment) Rules 2005 (SI 2005/1871).

The Appeal Tribunal has power to regulate its own affairs under s.30(3), and has issued practice directions from time to time. The practice direction presently in force is Practice Direction (EAT: Procedure) 2004.

Contempt of the Appeal Tribunal is punishable only by or with the consent of a judge—see s.36 below, para.2–087.

Restriction of publicity in cases involving sexual misconduct

2–077   31.—(1) Appeal Tribunal procedure rules may, as respects proceedings to which this section applies, include provision—

    (a) for cases involving allegations of the commission of sexual offences, for securing that the registration or other making available of documents or decisions shall be so effected as to prevent the identification of any person affected by or making the allegation, and

    (b) for cases involving allegations of sexual misconduct, enabling the Appeal Tribunal, on the application of any party to the proceedings before it or of its own motion, to make a restricted reporting order having effect (if not revoked earlier) until the promulgation of the decision of the Appeal Tribunal.

(2) This section applies to—

    (a) proceedings on an appeal against a decision of an employment tribunal to make, or not to make, a restricted reporting order, and

    (b) proceedings on an appeal against any interlocutory decision of an employment tribunal in proceedings in which the employment tribunal has made a restricted reporting order which it has not revoked.

(3) If any identifying matter is published or included in a relevant programme in contravention of a restricted reporting order—

    (a) in the case of publication in a newspaper or periodical, any proprietor, any editor and any publisher of the newspaper or periodical,

    (b) in the case of publication in any other form, the person publishing the matter, and

    (c) in the case of matter included in a relevant programme—

        (i) any body corporate engaged in providing the service in which the programme is included, and

        (ii) any person having functions in relation to the programme corresponding to those of an editor of a newspaper,

shall be guilty of an offence and liable on summary conviction to a fine not exceeding level 5 on the standard scale.

(4) Where a person is charged with an offence under subsection (3) it is a defence to prove that at the time of the alleged offence he

was not aware, and neither suspected nor had reason to suspect, that the publication or programme in question was of, or included, the matter in question.

(5) Where an offence under subsection (3) committed by a body corporate is proved to have been committed with the consent or connivance of, or to be attributable to any neglect on the part of—

    (a) a director, manager, secretary or other similar officer of the body corporate, or

    (b) a person purporting to act in any such capacity,

he as well as the body corporate is guilty of the offence and liable to be proceeded against and punished accordingly.

(6) In relation to a body corporate whose affairs are managed by its members "director", in subsection (5), means a member of the body corporate.

(7) "Restricted reporting order" means—

    (a) in subsections (1) and (3), an order—

        (i) made in exercise of a power conferred by rules made by virtue of this section, and

       (ii) prohibiting the publication in Great Britain of identifying matter in a written publication available to the public or its inclusion in a relevant programme for reception in Great Britain, and

    (b) in subsection (2), an order which is a restricted reporting order for the purposes of section 11.

(8) In this section—

"identifying matter", in relation to a person, means any matter likely to lead members of the public to identify him as a person affected by, or as the person making, the allegation,

"relevant programme" has the same meaning as in the Sexual Offences (Amendment) Act 1992,

"sexual misconduct" means the commission of a sexual offence, sexual harassment or other adverse conduct (of whatever nature) related to sex, and conduct is related to sex whether the relationship with sex lies in the character of the conduct or in its having reference to the sex or sexual orientation of the person at whom the conduct is directed,

"sexual offence" means any offence to which section 4 of the Sexual Offences (Amendment) Act 1976, the Sexual Offences (Amendment) Act 1992 or section 274(2) of the Criminal Procedure (Scotland) Act 1995 applies (offences under the Sexual Offences Act 1956, Part I of the Criminal Law (Consolidation)(Scotland) Act 1995 and certain other enactments), and

53

"written publication" has the same meaning as in the Sexual Offences (Amendment) Act 1992.

2–078   Similar to the powers of an employment tribunal, the Employment Appeal Tribunal has powers to restrict the reporting of matters, up to the promulgation of the final decision, which might lead members of the public to identify any person making or affected by an allegation of sexual misconduct or the commission of sexual offences. For a full discussion of the rules see EAT Rules 1993, r.23.

Restriction of publicity in disability cases

2–079   32.—(1) This section applies to proceedings—

    (a) on an appeal against a decision of an employment tribunal to make, or not to make, a restricted reporting order, or

    (b) on an appeal against any interlocutory decision of an employment tribunal in proceedings in which the employment tribunal has made a restricted reporting order which it has not revoked.

(2) Appeal Tribunal procedure rules may, as respects proceedings to which this section applies, include provision for—

    (a) enabling the Appeal Tribunal, on the application of the complainant or of its own motion, to make a restricted reporting order having effect (if not revoked earlier) until the promulgation of the decision of the Appeal Tribunal, and

    (b) where a restricted reporting order is made in relation to an appeal which is being dealt with by the Appeal Tribunal together with any other proceedings, enabling the Appeal Tribunal to direct that the order is to apply also in relation to those other proceedings or such part of them as the Appeal Tribunal may direct.

(3) If any identifying matter is published or included in a relevant programme in contravention of a restricted reporting order—

    (a) in the case of publication in a newspaper or periodical, any proprietor, any editor and any publisher of the newspaper or periodical,

    (b) in the case of publication in any other form, the person publishing the matter, and

    (c) in the case of matter included in a relevant programme—

        (i) any body corporate engaged in providing the service in which the programme is included, and

        (ii) any person having functions in relation to the programme corresponding to those of an editor of a newspaper, shall be guilty of an offence and liable on summary conviction to a fine not exceeding level 5 on the standard scale.

(4) Where a person is charged with an offence under subsection (3), it is a defence to prove that at the time of the alleged offence he was not aware, and neither suspected nor had reason to suspect, that the publication or programme in question was of, or included, the matter in question.

(5) Where an offence under subsection (3) committed by a body corporate is proved to have been committed with the consent or connivance of, or to be attributable to any neglect on the part of—

(a) a director, manager, secretary or other similar officer of the body corporate, or

(b) a person purporting to act in any such capacity,

he as well as the body corporate is guilty of the offence and liable to be proceeded against and punished accordingly.

(6) In relation to a body corporate whose affairs are managed by its members "director", in subsection (5), means a member of the body corporate.

(7) "Restricted reporting order" means—

(a) in subsection (1), an order which is a restricted reporting order for the purposes of section 12, and

(b) in subsections (2) and(3), an order—

(i) made in exercise of a power conferred by rules made by virtue of this section, and

(ii) prohibiting the publication in Great Britain of identifying matter in a written publication available to the public or its inclusion in a relevant programme for reception in Great Britain.

(8) In this section—

"complainant" means the person who made the complaint to which the proceedings before the Appeal Tribunal relate,

"identifying matter" means any matter likely to lead members of the public to identify the complainant or such other persons (if any) as may be named in the order,

"promulgation" has such meaning as may be prescribed by rules made by virtue of this section,

"relevant programme" means a programme included in a programme service, within the meaning of the Broadcasting Act 1990, and

"written publication" includes a film, a sound track and any other record in permanent form but does not include an indictment or other document prepared for use in particular legal proceedings.

2–080   As with cases involving allegations of sexual misconduct, the Employment Appeal Tribunal has powers to restrict the reporting of matters, up to the promulgation of the final decision, which might lead members of the public to identify any person named in the order. For a full discussion of the rules see EAT Rules 1993, r.23A.

Restriction of vexatious proceedings

2–081   33.—(1) If, on an application made by the Attorney General or the Lord Advocate under this section, the Appeal Tribunal is satisfied that a person has habitually and persistently and without any reasonable ground—

> (a) instituted vexatious proceedings, whether before the Certification Officer, in an employment tribunal or before the Appeal Tribunal, and whether against the same person or against different persons, or
>
> (b) made vexatious applications in any proceedings, whether before the Certification Officer, in an employment tribunal or before the Appeal Tribunal,

the Appeal Tribunal may, after hearing the person or giving him an opportunity of being heard, make a restriction of proceedings order.

(2) A "restriction of proceedings order" is an order that—

> (a) no proceedings shall without the leave of the Appeal Tribunal be instituted before the Certification Officer, in any employment tribunal or before the Appeal Tribunal by the person against whom the order is made,
>
> (b) any proceedings instituted by him before the Certification Officer, in any employment tribunal or before the Appeal Tribunal before the making of the order shall not be continued by him without the leave of the Appeal Tribunal, and
>
> (c) no application (other than one for leave under this section) is to be made by him in any proceedings before the Certification Officer, in any employment tribunal or before the Appeal Tribunal without the leave of the Appeal Tribunal.

(3) A restriction of proceedings order may provide that it is to cease to have effect at the end of a specified period, but otherwise it remains in force indefinitely.

(4) Leave for the institution or continuance of, or for the making of an application in, any proceedings before the Certification Officer, in an employment tribunal or before the Appeal Tribunal by a person who is the subject of a restriction of proceedings order shall not be given unless the Appeal Tribunal is satisfied—

> (a) that the proceedings or application are not an abuse of the process of the tribunal in question, and

    (b) that there are reasonable grounds for the proceedings or application.

(5) A copy of a restriction of proceedings order shall be published in the London Gazette and the Edinburgh Gazette.

Similar to the power contained within s.42 of the Supreme Court Act 1981 in relation to civil proceedings, the Appeal Tribunal has power to prevent a vexatious litigant from instituting proceedings before either the employment tribunal or the EAT. The application is made by the Attorney General, or in Scotland the Lord Advocate. The guidance on the definition of vexatious proceedings given by Lord Bingham in *Att-Gen v Barker* [2000] 1 F.L.R. 759 (a family law case) was adopted in *Att-Gen v Wheen* [2001] I.R.L.R. 91, CA. In *Wheen*, the claimant had made thirteen applications to the tribunal, each of which was unsuccessful, and appealed five decisions to the EAT, each of which was described as an abuse of process. The Court of Appeal emphasised that when considering a s.33 application it is not open to the party to re-argue the points that he has lost in the Court previously, and that even if the party currently has an appeal pending, the Court may take into account the decision of the Court below. **2–082**

Held in *Her Majesty's Att-Gen v Deman* UKEAT/0113/06/RN, the reference in s.33(1)(a) to the institution of proceedings in the employment appeal tribunal is not restricted to the institution of proceedings under its originating jurisdictions, but refers also to the commencement of appeals under its appellate jurisdiction. Obiter, the distinction in s.33(1) between the institution of proceedings and the making of applications is artificial, and as far as possible, the provisions should be interpreted to give a power to restrain the bringing of proceedings where the claimant has been guilty of vexatious conduct of any kind in connection with proceedings.

Costs and expenses

34.—(1) Appeal Tribunal procedure rules may include provision for the award of costs or expenses. **2–083**

(2) Rules under subsection (1) may include provision authorising the Appeal Tribunal to have regard to a person's ability to pay when considering the making of an award against him under such rules.

(3) Appeal Tribunal procedure rules may include provision for authorising the Appeal Tribunal—

    (a) to disallow all or part of the costs or expenses of a representative of a party to proceedings before it by reason of that representative's conduct of the proceedings;

    (b) to order a representative of a party to proceedings before it to meet all or part of the costs or expenses incurred by a party by reason of the representative's conduct of the proceedings.

(4) Appeal Tribunal procedure rules may also include provision for taxing or otherwise settling the costs or expenses referred to in subsection (1) or (3)(b) (and, in particular in England and Wales, for enabling the amount of such costs to be assessed by way of detailed assessment in the High Court).

2–084   The new rules on costs, which came into effect from October 1, 2004 were introduced by Employment Appeal Tribunal (Amendment) Rules 2004 and are set out in EAT Rules 1993, rr.34–34D. By the Employment Appeal Tribunal (Amendment) Rules 2004, r.21 the new rules, with the exception of r.34C apply irrespective of when the appeal tribunal proceedings were commenced.

DECISIONS AND FURTHER APPEALS

Powers of Appeal Tribunal

2–085   **35.—(1) For the purpose of disposing of an appeal, the Appeal Tribunal may—**

> **(a) exercise any of the powers of the body or officer from whom the appeal was brought, or**
> **(b) remit the case to that body or officer.**

(2) Any decision or award of the Appeal Tribunal on an appeal has the same effect, and may be enforced in the same manner, as a decision or award of the body or officer from whom the appeal was brought.

2–086   For the power of disposal of an appeal by consent, for which consent is required, see para.15 of the Practice Direction.

Where an appeal is pursued on the grounds of the inadequacy of the reasons given by the employment tribunal, the EAT may refer the case back to the original tribunal for amplification or clarification of the decision under challenge. Whilst the power of the EAT to do this was questioned in an obiter passage by the Court of Appeal in *Tran v Greenwich Vietnam Community Project* [2002] I.R.L.R. 735, the EAT confirmed that it had such power in *Burns v Consignia* (No. 2) [2004] I.R.L.R. 425 following the decision in *English v Emery Reinbold & Strick Ltd* [2003] I.R.L.R. 710. The Court of Appeal has subsequently approved the process in *Barke v SEETEC Business Technology Centre Ltd* [2005] I.R.L.R. 633. In *Barke*, Dyson L.J. identified the source of the EAT's power to refer a case back to the employment tribunal as deriving from r.30(3) of Sch.1 to the employment tribunal (Constitution and Rules of Procedure) Regulations 2004, and s.30(3) of the ETA. Rule 30(3) has since been amended (by SI 2005/1865). In its amended form, r.30(3) only permits reasons to be sought when the decision of the employment tribunal was given orally. This amendment may also affect the extent of the EAT's residual power under s.30(3) ETA.

In all other cases, the power of the Appeal Tribunal to correct errors that have occurred below can be categorised into three forms of order. It may substitute its own decision for that of the tribunal below, or it may remit the case to the same tribunal in order that it may readdress the case with the benefit of the EAT's decision on the law, or it may remit the case to a newly constituted tribunal.

Where the EAT finds that the employment tribunal has misdirected itself in law, it should remit the case for rehearing unless it is satisfied that, notwithstanding the error, the conclusion of the employment tribunal was unarguably right (*Dobie v Burns International Security Services (UK) Ltd* [1984] I.C.R. 812; [1984] I.R.L.R. 329; *Bache v Essex CC* [2000] I.C.R. 313; [2000] I.R.L.R. 251; *O'Kelly v Trust House Forte* [1983] I.C.R. 728; *Wilson v Post Office* [2000] I.R.L.R. 834). The EAT should remit the decision back to the employment tribunal as it should not usurp the fact finding role of the employment tribunal (*Morgan v Electrolux Ltd* [1991] I.C.R. 369; [1991] I.R.L.R. 89).

Where the case is remitted, the employment tribunal can only deal with the remitted aspects of the case, even though the parties might have agreed that some other aspect of the case should be heard (*Aparau v Iceland Frozen Foods Ltd No. 2* [2000] I.C.R. 341).

In determining whether to remit a case back to the originally constituted tribunal or a newly constituted one, the EAT ought to take into account the six factors identified by Burton J. in *Sinclair Roche & Temperley v Heard* [2004] I.R.L.R. 763, approved by the Court of Appeal in *Barke v SEETEC Business Technology Centre Ltd* [2005] I.R.L.R. 633.

(a) *proportionality*—whether the cost of remitting to a newly constituted tribunal could be justified given the sums of money at stake, along with the distress and inconvenience to the parties are matters properly taken into account;

(b) *passage of time*—if there has been such a passage of time that there is a real risk that the original tribunal will have forgotten the details of the case then the case should not be remitted to the same tribunal;

(c) *bias/partiality*—where there is a risk of bias the case ought not be referred back to the original tribunal, even where an allegation of bias did not form the basis of the appeal;

(d) *totally flawed decision*—where the original decision was wholly flawed, or the case was completely mishandled;

(e) *second bite*—the appellate tribunal ought only to remit a case back to the original tribunal if it is confident that the latter will be prepared to look at matters afresh, and at matters that it had not considered before and be willing to reach a different conclusion following the guidance of the EAT;

(f) *tribunal professionalism*—in the absence of any indication to the contrary the appellate tribunal ought to consider that the original tribunal will approach its duties with a professional approach.

On an appeal against a purely interlocutory decision where no further factual investigations are required, the EAT has power to allow an amendment to a pleading that has been refused below. Section 35(1)(a) should be considered alongside the overriding objective contained in the Employment Appeal Tribunal Rules 1993 r.2A. *Transport and General Workers Union v Safeway Stores Ltd* UKEAT/0092/07/LA; *SKS Ltd v Brown* EAT/0245/07/JOJ

Enforcement of decisions etc.

36.—(1)–(3) . . .   2–087

(4) No person shall be punished for contempt of the Appeal Tribunal except by, or with the consent of, a judge.

(5) A magistrates' court shall not remit the whole or part of a fine imposed by the Appeal Tribunal unless it has the consent of a judge who is a member of the Appeal Tribunal.

Subsection (1)–(5) repealed by s.57 of the Employment Relations Act 2004.   2–088

Appeals from Appeal Tribunal

37.—(1) Subject to subsection (3), an appeal on any question of law lies from any decision or order of the Appeal Tribunal to the relevant appeal court with the leave of the Appeal Tribunal or of the relevant appeal court.   2–089

(2) In subsection (1) the "relevant appeal court" means—

(a) in the case of proceedings in England and Wales, the Court of Appeal, and

(b) in the case of proceedings in Scotland, the Court of Session.

(3) No appeal lies from a decision of the Appeal Tribunal refusing leave for the institution or continuance of, or for the making of an application in, proceedings by a person who is the subject of a restriction of proceedings order made under section 33.

(4) This section is without prejudice to section 13 of the Administration of Justice Act 1960 (appeal in case of contempt of court).

2–090
In England and Wales, appeals from a decision of the Employment Appeal Tribunal lie on a point of law to the Court of Appeal. Permission of either the EAT, or, the Court of Appeal, is required. The rules governing the time limits for seeking leave to appeal are set out in para.21 of the EAT Practice Statement. The rules concerning appeals to the Court of Appeal are set out in CPR r.52 and the practice direction thereto.

Traditionally, it has been accepted that on an appeal, the Court of Appeal is concerned with the correctness of the original employment tribunal decision (see *Vento v Chief Constable for West Yorkshire Police* (No. 2) [2003] I.C.R. 318; *Yeboah v Crofton* [2002] I.R.L.R. 634). However, for a contrary view, that the question is whether the EAT's judgment is sustainable in law, see *Balfour Beatty Power Networks Ltd v Wilcox* [2007] I.R.L.R. 63; *Gover v Propertycare Ltd* [2006] I.C.R. 1073.

If the EAT dismisses an appeal following a preliminary hearing, that decision may be the subject of an appeal to the Court of Appeal. Ordinarily, the Court of Appeal draws a distinction between appeals following a preliminary hearing at the EAT, and those following a final hearing (see *Lambe v 186K Ltd* [2005] I.C.R. 307). For the power of the Appeal Tribunal to review, revoke or vary its own decisions see r.33(1).

PART III SUPPLEMENTARY

CROWN EMPLOYMENT AND PARLIAMENTARY STAFF

Crown employment
2–091
38.—(1) This Act has effect in relation to Crown employment and persons in Crown employment as it has effect in relation to other employment and other employees.

(2) In this Act "Crown employment" means employment under or for the purposes of a government department or any officer or body exercising on behalf of the Crown functions conferred by a statutory provision.

(3) For the purposes of the application of this Act in relation to Crown employment in accordance with subsection (1)—

(a) references to an employee shall be construed as references to a person in Crown employment, and

(b) references to a contract of employment shall be construed as references to the terms of employment of a person in Crown employment.

(4) Subsection (1) applies to—

(a) service as a member of the naval, military or air forces of the Crown, and

(b) employment by an association established for the purposes of Part XI of the Reserve Forces Act 1996;
but Her Majesty may by Order in Council make any provision of this Act apply to service as a member of the naval, military or air forces of the Crown subject to such exceptions and modifications as may be specified in the Order in Council.

Parliamentary staff

39.—(1) This Act has effect in relation to employment as a relevant member of the House of Lords staff or a relevant member of the House of Commons staff as it has effect in relation to other employment.

(2) Nothing in any rule of law or the law or practice of Parliament prevents a relevant member of the House of Lords staff or a relevant member of the House of Commons staff from bringing before an employment tribunal proceedings of any description which could be brought before such a tribunal by a person who is not a relevant member of the House of Lords staff or a relevant member of the House of Commons staff.

(3) For the purposes of the application of this Act in relation to a relevant member of the House of Commons staff—

(a) references to an employee shall be construed as references to a relevant member of the House of Commons staff, and

(b) references to a contract of employment shall be construed as including references to the terms of employment of a relevant member of the House of Commons staff.

(4) In this Act "relevant member of the House of Lords staff" means any person who is employed under a contract of employment with the Corporate Officer of the House of Lords.

(5) In this Act "relevant member of the House of Commons staff" has the same meaning as in section 195 of the Employment Rights Act 1996; and (subject to an Order in Council under subsection (12) of that section)—

(a) subsections (6) and (7) of that section have effect for determining who is the employer of a relevant member of

2–092

Employment Tribunals
Act 1996

the House of Commons staff for the purposes of this Act, and

(b) subsection (8) of that section applies in relation to proceedings brought by virtue of this section.

GENERAL

Power to amend Act

2–093   40.—(1) The Secretary of State may by order—

(a) provide that any provision of this Act to which this section applies and which is specified in the order shall not apply to persons, or to employments, of such classes as may be prescribed in the order, or

(b) provide that any provision of this Act to which this section applies shall apply to persons or employments of such classes as may be prescribed in the order subject to such exceptions and modifications as may be so prescribed.

(2) This section applies to sections 3, 8, 16 and 17 and to section 18 so far as deriving from section 133 of the Employment Protection (Consolidation) Act 1978.

Orders, regulations and rules

2–094   41.—(1) Any power conferred by this Act on a Minister of the Crown to make an order, and any power conferred by this Act to make regulations or rules, is exercisable by statutory instrument.

(2) No recommendation shall be made to Her Majesty to make an Order in Council under section 38(4), and no order shall be made under section 3, 4(4) or 40, unless a draft of the Order in Council or order has been laid before Parliament and approved by a resolution of each House of Parliament.

(3) A statutory instrument containing—

(a) an order made by a Minister of the Crown under any other provision of this Act except Part II of Schedule 2, or

(b) regulations or rules made under this Act,

is subject to annulment in pursuance of a resolution of either House of Parliament.

(4) Any power conferred by this Act which is exercisable by statutory instrument includes power to make such incidental, supplementary or transitional provision as appears to the Minister exercising the power to be necessary or expedient.

Interpretation

2–095   42.—(1) In this Act—

"the Appeal Tribunal" means the Employment Appeal Tribunal,
"Appeal Tribunal procedure rules" shall be construed in accordance
with section 30(1),

"appointed member" shall be construed in accordance with section
22(1)(c),

"Certification Officer" shall be construed in accordance with
section 254 of the Trade Union and Labour Relations (Consolidation) Act 1992

"conciliation officer" means an officer designated by the Advisory,
Conciliation and Arbitration Service under section 211 of the Trade
Union and Labour Relations (Consolidation) Act 1992,

"contract of employment" means a contract of service or apprenticeship, whether express or implied, and (if it is express) whether
oral or in writing,

"employee" means an individual who has entered into or works
under (or, where the employment has ceased, worked under) a
contract of employment,

"employer", in relation to an employee, means the person by whom
the employee is (or, where the employment has ceased, was)
employed,

"employers' association" has the same meaning as in the Trade
Union and Labour Relations (Consolidation) Act 1992,

"employment" means employment under a contract of employment
and "employed" shall be construed accordingly,

"employment tribunal procedure regulations" shall be construed
in accordance with section 7(1),

"statutory provision" means a provision, whether of a general or a
special nature, contained in, or in any document made or issued
under, any Act, whether of a general or special nature,

"successor", in relation to the employer of an employee, means
(subject to subsection (2)) a person who in consequence of a change
occurring (whether by virtue of a sale or other disposition or by
operation of law) in the ownership of the undertaking, or of the part
of the undertaking, for the purposes of which the employee was
employed, has become the owner of the undertaking or part, and

"trade union" has the meaning given by section 1 of the Trade
Union and Labour Relations (Consolidation) Act 1992.

(2) The definition of "successor" in subsection (1) has effect
(subject to the necessary modifications) in relation to a case where—

    (a) the person by whom an undertaking or part of an undertaking is owned immediately before a change is one of the
persons by whom (whether as partners, trustees or otherwise) it is owned immediately after the change, or

    (b) the persons by whom an undertaking or part of an
undertaking is owned immediately before a change

> (whether as partners, trustees or otherwise) include the persons by whom, or include one or more of the persons by whom, it is owned immediately after the change,

as it has effect where the previous owner and the new owner are wholly different persons.

(3) For the purposes of this Act any two employers shall be treated as associated if—

> (a) one is a company of which the other (directly or indirectly) has control, or
>
> (b) both are companies of which a third person (directly or indirectly) has control;

and "associated employer" shall be construed accordingly.

FINAL PROVISIONS

Consequential amendments

2-096   43. Schedule 1 (consequential amendments) shall have effect.

Transitionals, savings and transitory provisions

2-097   44. Schedule 2 (transitional provisions, savings and transitory provisions) shall have effect.

Repeals and revocations

2-098   45. The enactments specified in Part I of Schedule 3 are repealed, and the instruments specified in Part II of that Schedule are revoked, to the extent specified in the third column of that Schedule.

Commencement

2-099   46. This Act shall come into force at the end of the period of three months beginning with the day on which it is passed.

Extent

2-100   47. This Act does not extend to Northern Ireland.

Short title

2-101   48. This Act may be cited as the Employment Tribunals Act 1996.
2-102

SCHEDULE 2

Transitional Provisions, Savings and Transitory Provisions

9.—(1) If section 31 of the Trade Union Reform and Employment Rights Act 1993 has not come into force before the commencement of this Act, section 38 shall have effect until the relevant commencement date as if for subsection (4) there were substituted—

"(4) Subsection (1)—

(a) does not apply to service as a member of the naval, military or air forces of the Crown, but

(b) does apply to employment by an association established for the purposes of Part XI of the Reserve Forces Act 1996."

(2) The reference in sub-paragraph (1) to the relevant commencement date is a reference—

(a) if an order has been made before the commencement of this Act appointing a day after that commencement as the day on which section 31 of the Trade Untion Reform and Employment Rights Act 1993 is to come into force, to the day so appointed, and

(b) otherwise, to such day as the Secretary of State may by order appoint.

There are three Schedules to the ETA. Paragraph 9 of Sch.2 is the only part of **2–103** those Schedules that is now material. The remaining parts of the Schedules are either incorporated elsewhere, are beyond the scope of this work, or comprise transitional provisions that have now lapsed.

Employment Tribunals Act 1996

CHAPTER 3

EMPLOYMENT TRIBUNALS (CONSTITUTION AND RULES OF PROCEDURE) REGULATIONS 2004

2004 No. 1861

Contents

REGS

General Editorial Introduction

In July 2001 the Government, through the Department of Trade and Industry **3–001** published a consultation paper entitled "Routes to Resolution" because of its concern that the annual number of claims to employment tribunals was increasing alarmingly, and because of its perception that parties were having recourse to litigation before attempting to resolve their differences in the workplace. In November 2001 it published its response to that consultation and at the same time the Employment Tribunals System Task Force was set up to review the operation of the employment tribunals system. Its terms of reference were to identify ways of improving operational efficiency; to advise on the need for new investment; to consider how to improve liaison between all those involved in the system; and to examine possible improvements to the management of case flow and case management. Its report: "Moving Forward" was published in July 2002 and contained 61 recommendations for the improvement of tribunal proceedings. Publication in

March 2001 of the Leggatt Report (Tribunals for Users: One system, one service), paved the way for the integration in April 2006 of the Employment Tribunals Services and the Employment Appeal Tribunal in an integrated Tribunals Service under the umbrella of the Department for Constitutional Affairs, now the Ministry of Justice the successor to the Lord Chancellor's department.

At the time of introduction of the Dispute Resolution Regulations, the government indicated that it would review their operation in 2006–7. A committee, set up by the Department of Trade and Industry (now the Department for Business, Enterprise, and Regulatory Reform), and chaired by Michael Gibbons reported in March 2007. The report, entitled "Better Dispute Resolution: A review of employment dispute resolution in Great Britain", contained a total of 17 recommendations. Its headline recommendation was the complete repeal of the statutory dispute resolution procedures set out in the 2004 Regulations. The government immediately announced that it accepted the recommendations in their entirety and published a consultation paper entitled "Success at work: Resolving disputes in the workplace". In the letter accompanying the review the employment judge identified the driving intention of the recommendations as being:

(1) Reduction of the complexity of the current system;
(2) To reduce costs to businesses and employees, whilst:

    (a) Upholding and preserving all existing employee rights;
    (b) Ensuring access to justice; and
    (c) Ensuring that the policy intention of the 2004 Regulations is not undermined by unnecessary complexity.

Besides the radical but inevitable recommendation that the 2004 Regulations should be repealed in their entirety, and a different solution adopted for resolving employment disputes and reducing the number of tribunal claims, the review also made these key recommendations:

(1) Giving tribunals a discretion to reflect unreasonable behaviour (by respondents) and procedures in awards of either compensation or costs;
(2) Introduction of a simpler process for resolving money disputes (claims for wages and breach of contract) without the need for a hearing;
(3) Ensuring the availability of quality advice to claimants and respondents through an adequately resourced helpline; and
(4) Offering a free early dispute resolution service, including, where appropriate, mediation.

In July 2007, the government announced that legislation to enact the necessary changes would be contained in an Employment Simplification Bill to be introduced in the 2007/8 parliamentary session. The Employment Bill 2007 introduced in the House of Lords in December 2007 will go part of the way to implement those changes. Clause 1 repeals the relevant provisions in the Employment Act 2002 which make provision for the statutory dispute resolution procedures: ss.29–33 and Sch.24. Clause 2 repeals s.98A of the Employment Rights Act 1996 (procedural unfairness). Clause 3 will insert a new s.207A (Effect of failure to comply with Code: adjustment of awards) into the Trade Union and Labour Relations (Consolidation) Act 1992. The new section will enable employment tribunals, in respect of the jurisdictions listed in a new Sch.A2, to increase an award of compensation by no more than 25 per cent if it considers it just and equitable to do so. To do so it must be satisfied that: (a) the claim to which the proceedings relate concerns a matter to which a relevant Code of Practice applies; (b) the employer has failed to comply with that Code in relation to that matter; and (c) that failure was unreasonable. In anticipation of this legislative change ACAS will be preparing for parliamentary approval a revised Code of Practice dealing with disciplinary and grievance issues. Clause 4 will amend s.7 of the Employment Tribunals Act 1996 to permit certain proceedings to be determined without a Hearing. Clause 6 will effectively repeal the relevant provisions of s.18 of the Employment Tribunals Act 1996 introducing fixed periods of conciliation in relation to the relevant jurisdictions: see commentary at 2–041 and 4–196. It is unlikely that the measures will be enacted before April 2009. The other recommendations arising from the review will be adopted in new Regulations and Rules or in statutory instruments.

Part 2 of the Employment Act 2002 covered employment tribunal reform and included the power in s.27 for the President of the employment tribunals to issue Practice Directions. It also included the enabling provisions that laid the basis for the Regulations introduced in 2004, by amending the relevant sections of the Employment Tribunals Act 1996. Part 3 established a framework for the encouragement of the resolution of employment disputes in the workplace by introducing a requirement for employers and employees to follow compulsory discipline and grievance procedures. The Government published for consultation in December 2003 draft Employment Tribunal Regulations and Rules, partly to adopt the recommendations of the Employment Tribunals System Task Force and at the same time to introduce regulations and rules to enable the tribunals to identify claims to which the new dispute resolution framework might apply. It published its response to that consultation in July 2004. The Employment Tribunal Regulations 2004 (SI 2004/1861) came into effect on October 1, 2004. They replace SIs 2001/1170 and 1171 (the Employment Tribunal Regulations for England, Wales, and Scotland). They have been amended by SI 2004/2351 which added Sch.6 (equal value claims) to the Regulations; by SI 2005/435 (which delayed until October 1, 2005 compulsory use of the prescribed forms); by SI 2005/1865 (which primarily amended drafting errors in the original Regulations); and by SI 2006/680 (which dealt with the necessary amendments required by the transfer of responsibility for the Employment Tribunals Service to the Department for Constitutional Affairs).

The Secretary of State, in exercise of the powers conferred on her by section 24(2) of the Health and Safety at Work etc. Act 1974, sections 1(1), 4(6), and (6A), 7(1), (3), (3ZA), (3A), and (5), 7A(1) and (2), 9(1), (2) and (4), 10(2), (5), (6) and (7), 10A(1), 11(1), 12(2), 13, 13A(1) and (2), 19 and 41(4) of the Employment Tribunals Act 1996 and paragraph 36 of Schedule 8 to the Government of Wales Act 1998, and paragraph 37 of Schedule 6 to the Scotland Act 1998, and after consultation with the Council of Tribunals, in accordance with section 8(1) of the Tribunals and Inquiries Act 1992, hereby makes the following Regulations:—   **3–002**

The Secretary of State for these purposes was the Secretary of State for Trade   **3–003**
and Industry. The Employment Tribunals Service and the Employment Appeal Tribunal came under the responsibility of the Department for Constitutional Affairs on April 6, 2006 with the creation of the unified Tribunals Service. It is now part of the Ministry of Justice. Further changes were contained in the Tribunals, Court and Enforcement Act 2007, and will come into effect on the appointed dates.

Citation, commencement and revocation

3–004   **1.—(1) These Regulations may be cited as the Employment Tribunals (Constitution and Rules of Procedure) Regulations 2004 and the Rules of Procedure contained in Schedules 1, 2, 3, 4, 5 and [6] to these Regulations may be referred to, respectively, as—**

> (a) **the Employment Tribunals Rules of Procedure [2004];**
> (b) **the Employment Tribunals (National Security) Rules of Procedure [2004];**
> (c) **the Employment Tribunals (Levy Appeals) Rules of Procedure [2004];**
> (d) **the Employment Tribunals (Health and Safety—Appeals against Improvement and Prohibition Notices) Rules of Procedure [2004];**
> (e) **the Employment Tribunals (Non-Discrimination Notices Appeals) Rules of Procedure [2004]; and**
> (f) **the Employment Tribunals (Equal Value) Rules of Procedure [2004].**

(2) These Regulations shall come into force on 1 October 2004.

(3) Subject to the savings in regulation 20, the Employment Tribunals (Constitution and Rules of Procedure) Regulations 2001 and the Employment Tribunals (Constitution and Rules of Procedure) (Scotland) Regulations 2001 are revoked.

Commentary

3–005   *Regulation 1(1).* The number (6) in square brackets in reg.1(1) was added by reg.2(2) of the Employment Tribunals (Constitution and Rules of Procedure) (Amendment) Regulations 2004 (SI 2004/2351). The Regulations, as originally drafted and introduced into Parliament in July 2004, did not contain Sch.6 dealing with the conduct of equal pay claims. Schedule 6 was introduced by SI 2004/2351, which was made on September 7, 2004 and came into force on October 1, 2004. All the references to the date (2004) enclosed in the square brackets in regs 1(1)(a) to (f) were added by reg.2(2) of the Employment Tribunals (Constitution and Rules of Procedure) (Amendment) (No.2) Regulations 2005 (SI 2005/1865) with effect from October 1, 2005.

Paragraph 1(1)(f). Paragraph 1(1)(f) was added by SI 2004/2351. The same Regulations added a new Sch.6 to the original Rules and dealt with equal value claims and the procedure for handling them in the employment tribunals.

Application of the regulations

3–006   The Regulations apply to England, Wales, and Scotland. They do not apply to Northern Ireland. The 2001 Regulations and Rules had separate versions for Scotland and England and Wales. The previous rules in respect of the two jurisdictions are revoked save in respect of the transitional provisions set out in reg.20.

The original Regulations made on July 19, and which came into force on October 1, 2004 contained only five schedules. The Employment Tribunals (Constitution and Rules of Procedure) (Amendment) Regulations 2004 (SI 2004/2351) added a new

Sch.6 to the Rules dealing with equal value claims and made consequential amendments to the Regulations and to the Rules consequential to the addition of Sch.6.

Regulation 1(2)—Commencement date. Although the original Rules came into force in **3–007** October 2004, the original published version did not incorporate Sch.6, and that omission was remedied by SI 2004/2351. The original Regulations envisaged, however, that the use by claimants and respondents of the prescribed forms for commencing proceedings and responding to those proceedings would be compulsory after April 6, 2005, but this was subsequently changed to October 1, 2005.

Interpretation

2. In these Regulations and in Schedules 1, 2, 3, 4, 5 and 6:— **3–008**

"ACAS" means the Advisory, Conciliation and Arbitration Service referred to in section 247 of TULR(C)A;

"appointing office holder" means, in England and Wales, the Lord Chancellor, and in Scotland, the Lord President;

"chairman" means the President or a member of the panel of chairmen appointed in accordance with regulation 8(3)(a), or, for the purposes of national security proceedings, a member of the panel referred to in regulation 10 selected in accordance with regulation 11(a), and in relation to particular proceedings it means the chairman to whom the proceedings have been referred by the President, Vice President or a Regional Chairman;

"compromise agreement" means an agreement to refrain from continuing proceedings where the agreement meets the conditions in section 203(3) of the Employment Rights Act;

"constructive dismissal" has the meaning set out in section 95(1)(c) of the Employment Rights Act;

"Disability Discrimination Act" means the Disability Discrimination Act 1995;

"electronic communication" has the meaning given to it by section 15(1) of the Electronic Communications Act 2000;

"Employment Act" means the Employment Act 2002;

"Employment Rights Act" means the Employment Rights Act 1996;

"Employment Tribunals Act" means the Employment Tribunals Act 1996;

"Employment Tribunal Office" means any office which has been established for any area in either England & Wales or Scotland specified by the President and which carries out administrative functions in support of functions being carried out by a tribunal or chairman, and in relation to particular proceedings it is the office notified to the parties in accordance with rule 61(3) of Schedule 1;

"enactment" includes an enactment comprised in, or in an instrument made under, an Act of the Scottish Parliament;

"Equal Pay Act" means the Equal Pay Act 1970;

"excluded person" means, in relation to any proceedings, a person who has been excluded from all or part of the proceedings by virtue of:-

    (a) a direction of a Minister of the Crown under rule 54(1)(b) or (c) of Schedule 1, or

    (b) an order of the tribunal under rule 54(2)(a) read with 54(1)(b) or

    (c) of Schedule 1;

"hearing" means a case management discussion, pre-hearing review, review hearing or Hearing (as those terms are defined in Schedule 1) or a sitting of a chairman or a tribunal duly constituted for the purpose of receiving evidence, hearing addresses and witnesses or doing anything lawful to enable the chairman or tribunal to reach a decision on any question;

"legally represented" has the meaning set out in rule 38(5) of Schedule 1;

"Lord President" means the Lord President of the Court of Session;

"misconceived" includes having no reasonable prospect of success;

"national security proceedings" means proceedings in relation to which a direction is given under rule 54(1) of Schedule 1, or an order is made under rule 54(2) of that Schedule;

"old (England & Wales) regulations" means the Employment Tribunals (Constitution and Rules of Procedure) [Scotland] Regulations 2001;

"old (Scotland) regulations" means the Employment Tribunals (Constitution and Rules of Procedure)[Scotland] Regulations 2001;

"panel of chairmen" means a panel referred to in regulation 8(3)(a);

"President" means, in England and Wales, the person appointed or nominated by the Lord Chancellor to discharge for the time being the functions of the President of Employment Tribunals (England and Wales), and, in Scotland, the person appointed or nominated by the Lord President to discharge for the time being the functions of the President of Employment Tribunals (Scotland);

"Race Relations Act" means the Race Relations Act 1976;

"Regional Chairman" means a member of the panel of chairmen who has been appointed to the position of Regional Chairman in accordance with regulation 6 or who has been nominated to discharge the functions of a Regional Chairman in accordance with regulation 6;

"Register" means the Register of judgments and written reasons kept in accordance with regulation 17;

"Secretary" means a person for the time being appointed to act as the Secretary of employment tribunals either in England and Wales or in Scotland;

"Sex Discrimination Act" means the Sex Discrimination Act 1975;

"special advocate" means a person appointed in accordance with rule 8 of Schedule 2;

"tribunal" means an employment tribunal established in accordance with regulation 5, and in relation to any proceedings means the tribunal to which the proceedings have been referred by the President, Vice President or a Regional Chairman;

"TULR(C)A" means the Trade Union and Labour Relations (Consolidation) Act 1992;

"Vice President" means a person who has been appointed to the position of Vice President in accordance with regulation 7 or who has been nominated to discharge the functions of the Vice President in accordance with that regulation;

"writing" includes writing delivered by means of electronic communication.

Regulation 2—Interpretation

Electronic communication

An "electronic communication" is defined by s.15(1) of the Electronic Communications Act 2000 as a communication transmitted (whether from one person to another, from one device to another or from a person to a device or vice versa)—(a) by means of a telecommunication system (within the meaning of the Telecommunications Act 1984); or (b) by other means but while in an electronic form. **3–009**

Employment tribunal office

These Regulations changed the organisation of employment tribunals by abolishing the central office for both England and Wales and Scotland, and the regional offices in England and Wales. As a consequence although internal administration of tribunals may be conducted on a regional basis as before, this will not affect the parties, who will deal with a particular office, as directed by the Secretary. The change avoids the consequences of the problem highlighted in Scotland where, prior to the 2004 Regulations, a claim had to be presented to the central office in Glasgow for it to be a valid presentation (see *Matheson v Mazars Solutions Ltd* [2003] UKEAT 0048/03/1612 EAT). The position is now regularised throughout England and Wales and Scotland so that a claim may validly be presented to any tribunal office within the appropriate jurisdiction. There are 22 employment tribunal offices in England and Wales, and four in Scotland, which have been established for areas specified by the President. All of these have the same powers and perform the same functions, each dealing with the registration of claims, and the disposal of all matters up to and including the hearing, and each having an authorised person performing the statutory functions of the Secretary of the tribunals (see Appendix 1 for a list of all tribunal offices in England, Wales, and Scotland). **3–010**

Misconceived

The definition given is non-exhaustive—i.e. the phrase includes "having no reasonable prospect of success". For these purposes "reasonable" is synonymous with "realistic" (see *Balamoody v United Kingdom Central Council for Nursing* [2002] **3–011**

I.R.L.R. 288; *ED&F Man Liquid Products Ltd v Patel* [2003] EWCA Civ 472; and *Ezsias v North Glamorgan NHS Trust* [2006] UKEAT 705), and this is a matter that is to be assessed objectively (compare *Scott v Commissioners of Inland Revenue* [2004] I.R.L.R. 713; [2004] I.C.R. 1410, considering "misconceived" in the context of the tribunal's costs jurisdiction).

Register

3–012   The Register is maintained by the Secretary of Tribunals in accordance with the requirements of reg.17 (see below). Prior to 2004, the obligation to maintain a register of judgments and reasons contained in reg.12 of the Employment Tribunals (Constitution and Rules of Procedure) Regulations 2001 extended to a duty to include the names and addresses of the parties, and the nature of the claim, as well as the document recording the decision of the tribunal. The requirement is now more limited.

Old (England and Wales) regulations.

3–013   Regulation 2(3) of the Employment Tribunals (Constitution and Rules of Procedure) (Amendment) (No.2) Regulations 2005 (SI 2005/1865) amended the provisions by deleting "Scotland" from this provision and inserting it in the next. It was a typographical error in the original regulations.

Overriding objective

3–014   **3.—(1) The overriding objective of these regulations and the rules in Schedules 1, 2, 3, 4, 5 and [6] is to enable tribunals and chairmen to deal with cases justly.**

(2) Dealing with a case justly includes, so far as practicable:—

(a) **ensuring that the parties are on an equal footing;**
(b) **dealing with the case in ways which are proportionate to the complexity or importance of the issues;**
(c) **ensuring that it is dealt with expeditiously and fairly; and**
(d) **saving expense.**

(3) A tribunal or chairman shall seek to give effect to the overriding objective when it or he:—

(a) **exercises any power given to it or him by these regulations or the rules in Schedules 1, 2, 3, 4 , 5 and [6]; or**
(b) **interprets these regulations or any rule in Schedules 1, 2, 3, 4, 5 and [6].**

(4) The parties shall assist the tribunal or the chairman to further the overriding objective.

The overriding objective. . . to deal with cases justly.

3–015   The concept of the overriding objective was first introduced into the Regulations by reg.10 of the Employment Tribunals (Constitution and Rules of Procedure) Regulations 2001 (SI 2001/1171). It is a principle adopted from the Civil Procedure

Rules 1998 (CPR) which itself borrowed from the statement of the general principles of arbitration law contained in the Arbitration Act 1996, s.1, which provides that the object of arbitration is to obtain the fair resolution of disputes by an impartial tribunal without unnecessary delay or expense.

In the CPR the statement of the overriding objective that courts should be able to deal with cases justly envisages five principles as opposed to the four in the Regulations. The only principle not carried over from the CPR into the Regulations is that of allocation of resources, as no fees are paid in the employment tribunal, whether at the commencement of proceedings or on listing a case for hearing, and there is no costs regime whereby the unsuccessful litigant normally pays the costs of the proceedings.

The relevance of the CPR to interpretation of the Regulations and Rules

The CPR is not specifically referred to in the Regulations or Rules. Nevertheless **3–016** many of the principles and some of the terminology of the CPR occur in the Regulations and the Rules and the appellate courts have had recourse to the CPR when interpreting the Rules since 2001. As early as 2002 the Court of Appeal laid down clear guidelines for tribunals applying rules for determining time limit issues where documents were posted by a party, having recourse to CPR r.6.7, and applying the presumptions in that rule with regard to the service of documents by post (see *Consignia Plc v Sealy* [2002] I.R.L.R. 624, CA; [2002] I.C.R. 1193).

However, such "borrowing" from the CPR has its limits and must always be consistent with the provisions of the Rules themselves. In *Lehman Brothers Ltd v Smith* UKEAT/0486/05 the EAT held that tribunals were not obliged to follow the model of the CPR when determining whether to allow an application to amend a claim outside the limitation period. The EAT concluded that whereas under CPR r.17.4 that can only be done where the new claim arises out of the same facts, the tribunal's power under r.10(2)(q) (leave to amend a claim or response) required the tribunal to apply the balance of hardship and prejudice test laid down in cases preceding introduction of principles from the CPR into tribunal regulations and rules rather than the prescribed and narrower test under the CPR. (See r.10(2)(q) for the tribunal's powers to amend a claim or response.)

In *Goldman Sachs Services Ltd v Montali* [2002] I.C.R. 1251 the EAT stated that, when exercising any power under the Rules, the employment tribunal should follow the same general principles as underlie the CPR. In that case this meant that a tribunal should not reverse any earlier interlocutory order, which has dictated the parties' preparation of their cases, in the absence of a material change in circumstances. However, the overriding objective is an inherently flexible tool, and there is no general rule that case management orders may be revoked only if there has been some material change of circumstances see (*Onwuka v Spherion Technology UK Ltd* [2005] I.C.R. 563 and *Hart v English Heritage* [2006] I.C.R. 655). What is important is whether there is good reason to revisit an order that has been made.

The EAT has held that the tribunal must take into account all the factors listed in CPR r.3.9 (relief from sanctions) when determining, for example whether to strike out for failure to comply with an order (*Maresca v The Motor Insurance Repair Research Centre* [2005] I.C.R. 197), or whether to review a decision not to permit a party to take part in the proceedings under r.9 (*British School of Motoring v Fowler* UKEAT/0059/06). CPR r.3.9 lists nine matters the court must take into account when considering an application for relief from the consequences of a procedural sanction: the interests of the administration of justice; the promptness of the application; whether the failure to comply was intentional; whether there is a good explanation for non-compliance; the extent if any of compliance with other orders; whether the failure was that of the party or an adviser; whether the hearing date can still be met; the effect of the failure on both parties; the effect of granting relief on both parties. In the BSM case the EAT concluded that the matters listed in CPR r.3.9 applied equally to the employment tribunal, with the emphasis on the respective prejudice to the parties.

Significance of the overriding objective

3–017   In *Williams v Ferrosan Ltd* [2004] I.R.L.R. 607 Hooper J. expressed the view that the introduction of the CPR enabled the appellate courts to look afresh at rules that prior to the CPR had become "encrusted" by numerous cases. That view was cited with approval by H.H. Judge Clark in *Sodexho v Gibbons* [2005] I.R.L.R. 836; [2005] I.C.R. 1647 where in a case on the case management powers of the employment tribunal, the judge expressed the view that the case of *Williams v Ferrosan* required more prominence than before. This points to the conclusion that decisions that preceded the existence of the overriding objective will not in all instances be regarded as conclusive. They may require reconsideration in this new context. The overriding objective to deal with cases justly requires the tribunal to see the Rules not as a "trap for the unwary, but a procedure designed to do justice between the parties." Introduction of the overriding objective coupled with the extensive powers for proactive case management of proceedings is designed to enable employment judges to "exercise their independent judgment to ensure fairness between the parties" (*per* Judge Clark in *Sodexho* above).

Instances where the overriding objective has been relied on to justify the course of action taken include: ordering that the employment tribunal had power to accept a claim despite the fact that the claimant had ostensibly failed to provide all the required information under r.1 (*Grimmer v KLM Cityhopper UK* [2005] I.R.L.R. 596; *Richardson v U Mole Ltd* [2005] I.R.L.R. 668; [2005] I.C.R. 1664); to justify the power of an employment tribunal to review a decision not to accept an employer's response received out of time notwithstanding the strict requirements of r.4 and the apparent absence of a power to review such a decision in the Rules (*Moroak t/a Blake Envelopes v Cromie* [2005] I.R.L.R. 535; [2005] I.C.R. 1226); to review a decision on other broader grounds (*Pendragon Plc t/a C D Bramall Bradford v Copus* [2005] I.C.R. 1671; *Sodexho Ltd v Gibbons* [2005] I.R.L.R. 836; [2005] I.C.R. 1647); and to permit a respondent debarred from taking any part in the proceedings to seek reasons for the purpose of a review under r.33 but not to appeal (*NSM Music Ltd v Leefe* [2006] I.C.R. 450).

The most obvious situations where the tribunal must have regard to the overriding objective are when considering extensions of time to take procedural steps, where relief is being sought from procedural sanctions, and when discharging its case management powers: see and compare *Cobbold v London Borough of Greenwich* unreported, August 9, 1999, CA, where the Court of Appeal emphasised that the requirement to deal with cases justly required not merely dealing with them expeditiously, but rather that cases should be dealt with fairly. Although not relying on the overriding objective for justification the Court of Appeal has affirmed that the "first object of any system of justice is to get triable cases tried" (*Blockbuster Entertainment Ltd v James* [2006] I.R.L.R. 630, *per* Sedley L.J. at [18]). For that reason it will be rare that an employment tribunal will be justified in striking out a party for non-compliance with procedural directions and orders where it is still possible to have a fair hearing.

Regulation 3(2)

3–018   As pointed out in the introduction, the Regulations specify four as opposed to five examples of the features of the overriding objective compared to CPR r.1.1. However, the language used is identical in three of those situations: ensuring that the parties are on an equal footing; saving expense; and ensuring that the case is dealt with expeditiously and fairly. Proportionality is defined less extensively, and the tribunal is not expressly required to have regard to the requirement to allot to a case an appropriate share of the tribunal's resources, while taking into account the need to allot resources to other cases. Nevertheless the tribunal will when exercising its case management powers at either the stage of issuing standard directions or at a case management conference, attempt to define the issues, and limit the number of witnesses and documents, to ensure that hearings do not take a disproportionate amount of time. In that respect the parties and their representatives are expected to co-operate by excluding unnecessary documents and witnesses and agreeing undisputed facts where possible.

Regulation 3(2)(a)—Ensuring that the parties are on an equal footing

In the CPR the obligation to respect the principle of proportionality specifically **3–019** requires the court to consider the financial position of each party (CPR r.1.(2)(c)(iv)). The civil justice reports that preceded introduction of the CPR identified a lack of equality between the powerful wealthy litigant and the under-resourced litigant as one of the problems endemic in the administration of the civil justice system. One of the specific objectives of the reforms was to establish an equality of arms to ensure that there should be a level playing field between litigants of unequal financial or other resources. No such principle exists in the Regulations. The imperative to have regard to unequal financial resources is not so acute when costs orders are the exception rather than the norm. What the tribunal must do when, for example setting time limits, ordering preparation of witness statements and setting deadlines for the exchange of information is respect the difficulties of the unrepresented litigant. The tribunal cannot correct an imbalance in the level of representation by, for example, assuming the role of representative for the unrepresented party. Nevertheless it must ensure that the issues are explored. Compare *Pascoe v First Secretary of State* [2006] EWHC 2356 (Admin) where the "essence" of equality of arms was stated to be the reasonable opportunity for a party to present its case.

Regulation 3(2)(b)—Dealing with the case in ways which are proportionate to the complexity or importance of the issues

The principle of proportionality was critical to the new approach to civil **3–020** procedure brought in by the CPR at a time when there was concern about delay and the cost of civil justice. That was not the same concern when the overriding objective was introduced into the Tribunal Regulations in 2001 and the wording of the Regulations reflects that. The wording of the Regulations is significantly different from that of CPR r.1.1(2)(c). In the latter dealing with cases in ways which are proportionate requires the court to consider proportionality in relation to the amount of money involved, the importance of the case, the complexity of the issues, and to the financial position of each party. The wording of the Regulations omits any reference to the amount of money involved or the financial position of each party. The rationale for this must be a combination of many factors. Primarily it is because the parties do not pay fees either to commence proceedings or to have the claim determined. The costs regime is different: costs are not awarded to the successful party as a matter of course; the claimant may be seeking the recovery of a small sum of money in objective terms; for some claims the only remedy sought may be a declaration and no financial remedy is sought at all. As a consequence tribunals are reluctant to impose too stringent a time limit on the length of a hearing or to limit evidence; nevertheless the introduction of fixed periods of conciliation, standard case management orders, allocation of mainly money claims to a fast-track procedure where the parties are given standard directions and a provisional hearing date before the response is received are an indication that tribunals are willing to impose time restraints on the length of hearings in cases

ET(CRP) Regs 2004

that on the face of it do not involve large sums claimed or complex factual or legal issues. Use by parties of the new claim and response forms which hold more detail have facilitated the earlier identification of issues. This enables the tribunal acting on its own initiative to issue case management orders and to set a timetable for the hearing at the outset rather than leaving it to the parties to determine the pace of the litigation.

Regulation 3(2)(c)—Expeditiously and fairly

3–021   There may be a tension between the concept of expedition and fairness. For example it might be necessary to permit an application to amend a claim or response to ensure that the real issues in a case are explored, notwithstanding that may lead to delay or the vacation of a hearing date already fixed. However, absent factors strongly pointing in the opposite direction, the need for a fair hearing ought usually to prevail over the desire for a fast one (see and compare *Cobbold v London Borough of Greenwich*, unreported, August 9, 1999, CA).

Regulation 3(2)(d)—Saving expense

3–022   This is just one example of the principle of proportionality. It must be taken into account when a decision is taken with regard to disclosure and other case management orders, and especially when considering whether to adjourn a hearing, when the application is made either late in the day or at the actual hearing itself.

Regulation 3(3)

3–023   The only difference between the wording of reg.3(3) and its equivalent in CPR r.1.2 is that in the latter the court is enjoined that it "must" seek to give effect to the overriding objective, whereas in the Regulations the employment judge or tribunal "shall" seek to give effect to it. For all practical purposes it is difficult to see that this minor difference in language is evidence of any material difference in purpose. There is no equivalent in the Regulations of CPR r.1.4 which refers to the court's duty to manage cases.

CPR r.1.4 goes on to define active case management as including, for example at CPR r.1.4(2)(e): encouraging the parties to use an alternative dispute resolution procedure, or at CPR r.1.4(2)(f) helping the parties to settle the whole or part of the case. As yet no such equivalent obligation is imposed on tribunals, primarily because of the availability of conciliation to the parties and the fact that so many parties before the tribunals are not legally represented. That is not to say that tribunals, using their powers under rr.10 (general power to manage proceedings) and 17 (case management discussions) do not use the equivalent powers under CPR r.1.4 to identify issues at an early stage, fix timetables, or give directions to ensure that claims are determined efficiently.

Despite the lack of an equivalent Regulation corresponding to CPR r.1.4, and the absence of an express obligation to manage cases, the better view is that tribunals do have the ability to employ each of the tools referred to at CPR r.1.4(2)(a) to (l) when considering orders under r.10 and at case management conferences under r.17, and also when controlling the progress of a hearing, by, for example, setting time limits for cross-examination and submissions. It is likely that a decision made by a tribunal that is consistent with the ambit of powers set out in CPR r.1.4 would be endorsed on appeal, despite the fact that the obligation of the tribunal is couched in slightly different language. The Court of Appeal has stated that case management decisions ought normally to be respected by higher courts. In *Powell v Pallisers of Hereford Ltd* [2002] EWCA Civ 959; unreported, July 1, 2003, CA, Chadwick L.J. said (at [32]) that reported cases and the overriding objective require that the Court of Appeal should "exercise a proper degree of self-discipline by respecting case management decisions made by judges in cases which they are to try".

Regulation 3(4)

The parties are required to assist the tribunal or the employment judge to **3–024** further the overriding objective. In that respect the position is no different to that under CPR r.3.1 where the obligation is expressed as a requirement to help the court to further the overriding objective.

Rule 11(4) in Sch.1 of the Rules provides one specific example of an instance where the obligation under reg.3(4) is actually prescribed in a particular situation. A party making any application for an order in the course of proceedings is required by r.11(4) to give an explanation, at the time of making the application, of how the order will assist the tribunal or employment judge in dealing with the proceedings efficiently and fairly. That requirement must be complied with before the tribunal will consider the application on the merits. That is the only specific instance in the rules outside the obligation to serve a response within a time limit and the obligation to give reasons when making an application to review. The duty to assist may also be seen as requiring parties to co-operate with the listing process by giving accurate information about the availability of witnesses and the expected length of the hearing.

The absence of any specific "sanction" linked to reg.3(4) is compensated for by the tribunal's powers to make orders under rr.10 and 11, backed up if necessary with the option to impose sanctions (including costs).

President of Employment Tribunals

4.—**(1) There shall be a President of Employment Tribunals 3–025 (England and Wales), responsible for the administration of justice by tribunals and chairmen in England and Wales, who shall be appointed by the Lord Chancellor and shall be a person described in paragraph (3).**

(2) There shall be a President of Employment Tribunals (Scotland), responsible for the administration of justice by tribunals and chairmen in Scotland, who shall be appointed by the Lord President and shall be a person described in paragraph (3).

(3) A President shall be a person:—

> **(a) having a seven year general qualification within the meaning of section 71 of the Courts and Legal Services Act 1990;**
>
> **(b) being an advocate or solicitor admitted in Scotland of at least seven years standing; or**
>
> **(c) being a member of the Bar of Northern Ireland or solicitor of the Supreme Court of Northern Ireland of at least seven years standing.**

(4) A President may resign his office by notice in writing to the appointing office holder.

(5) If the appointing office holder is satisfied that the President is incapacitated by infirmity of mind or body from discharging the duties of his office, or the President is adjudged to be bankrupt or makes a composition or arrangement with his creditors, the appointing office holder may revoke his appointment.

ET(CRP) Regs 2004

(6) The functions of President under these Regulations may, if he is for any reason unable to act or during any vacancy in his office, be discharged by a person nominated for that purpose by the appointing office holder.

The President of employment tribunals

3–026   Notwithstanding that there is now a common system for the administration of tribunals in England, Wales and Scotland there is a President of the Employment Tribunals, who has overall responsibility for the administration of justice by tribunals and employment judge in both of the respective jurisdictions. In England and Wales, the President is appointed by the Lord Chancellor, and in Scotland, he is appointed by the Lord President.

The functions of the President include responsibility for determining the number of tribunals to be established; giving directions as to when and where they shall sit; selecting employment judges and lay members for hearings; selecting panels of employment judges and lay members to hear national security cases; specifying the areas for which particular regional employment judges are to be responsible; making Practice Directions; and sitting as an employment judge himself. As far as selecting the panel to hear particular cases is concerned that function is discharged in practice by the regional employment judge and Regional Secretary for the particular region. Rule 35 (Preliminary consideration of application for review) specifically provides that the President, along with a regional employment judge, the Vice-President, or an employment judge nominated by the regional employment judge or Vice-President may consider an application for review where it is not practicable for the original employment judge who heard the case to consider it. Similarly under r.31 the President is again along with the Vice-President or regional employment judge one of the individuals who is competent to sign a judgment, order or reasons where the employment judge is unable to do so due to death, incapacity or absence.

Establishment of employment tribunals

3–027   **5.—(1) Each President shall, in relation to that part of Great Britain for which he has responsibility, from time to time determine the number of tribunals to be established for the purposes of determining proceedings.**

(2) The President, a Regional Chairman or the Vice President shall determine, in relation to the area specified in relation to him, at what times and in what places in that area tribunals and chairmen shall sit.

3–028   At present employment tribunals mainly sit in the major hearing centres located in the major regional towns and cities. There is a complete list of the addresses and telephone numbers of all the tribunals in Great Britain in Appendix 1. From time to time, particularly in rural areas a tribunal may be required to sit in a town that does not have a permanent hearing centre and in that case the panel and parties will attend the location selected. Among the recommendations of the Leggatt committee on the administration and organisation of administrative tribunals was greater sharing of facilities and resources including hearing centres. The Tribunals Service is now actively encouraging the use of shared tribunal hearing rooms. In the larger Hearing centres, it will entail use of employment tribunal Hearing rooms by the Criminal Injuries Compensation Appeal panel and other tribunals. In time, the secretariat of the Tribunals Service will be providing assistance to all first tier tribunals.

Regional Chairmen

6.—(1) The Lord Chancellor may from time to time appoint **3–029** Regional Chairmen from the panel of full-time chairmen and each Regional Chairman shall be responsible to the President (England and Wales) for the administration of justice by tribunals and chairmen in the area specified by the President (England and Wales) in relation to him.

(2) The President (England and Wales) or the Regional Chairman for an area may from time to time nominate a member of the panel of full time chairmen to discharge for the time being the functions of the Regional Chairman for that area.

The regional employment judge is responsible for the administration of justice in **3–030** the region for which he or she is responsible. Responsibility for the quality of the service in respect of users is that of the Regional Secretary. All regional employment judges meet regularly with the President to discuss training and judicial standards and factors affecting the administration of justice as far as it does not interfere with judicial independence. The regional employment judge is also responsible for reporting to the President annually on the performance of fee-paid employment judge with a view to ensuring their sitting commitments are satisfied and providing evidence as to the suitability of a fee-paid employment judge for promotion to a salaried appointment. The regional employment judge also has responsibility for the investigation and disposal of complaints about judicial conduct, referring the matter to the President if the complaint justifies further action.

Vice President

7.—(1) The Lord President may from time to time appoint a Vice **3–031** President from the panel of full time chairmen and the Vice President shall be responsible to the President (Scotland) for the administration of justice by tribunals and chairmen in Scotland.

(2) The President (Scotland) or the Vice President may from time to time nominate a member of the panel of full time chairmen to discharge for the time being the functions of the Vice President.

There are no regional employment judges in Scotland: the role is discharged by **3–032** the Vice-President. Regulation 7 therefore only applies to Scotland.

Panels of members of tribunals—general

8.—(1) There shall be three panels of members of Employment **3–033** Tribunals (England and Wales), as set out in paragraph (3).

(2) There shall be three panels of members of Employment Tribunals (Scotland), as set out in paragraph (3).

(3) The panels referred to in paragraphs (1) and (2) are:—

    (a) a panel of full-time and part-time chairmen appointed by the appointing office holder consisting of persons—

        (i) having a seven year general qualification within the meaning of section 71 of the Courts and Legal Services Act 1990;

ET(CRP) Regs 2004

        (ii) **being an advocate or solicitor admitted in Scotland of at least seven years standing; or**

        (iii) **being a member of the Bar of Northern Ireland or solicitor of the Supreme Court of Northern Ireland of at least seven years standing;**

(b) **a panel of persons appointed by the Secretary of State after consultation with such organisations or associations of organisations representative of employees as she sees fit; and**

(c) **a panel of persons appointed by the Secretary of State after consultation with such organisations or associations of organisations representative of employers as she sees fit.**

(4) Members of the panels constituted under these Regulations shall hold and vacate office under the terms of the instrument under which they are appointed but may resign their office by notice in writing, in the case of a member of the panel of chairmen, to the appointing office holder and, in any other case, to the Secretary of State; and any such member who ceases to hold office shall be eligible for reappointment.

(5) The President may establish further specialist panels of chairmen and persons referred to in paragraphs (3)(b) and (c) and may select persons from such specialist panels in order to deal with proceedings in which particular specialist knowledge would be beneficial.

Panels of members of tribunals

3–034   Prior to 1999 trade unions and employers' associations nominated candidates for appointment to the respective panels. Appointment now to the respective panels as with appointment to the position of fee-paid employment judge (the only route to appointment to a position of salaried employment judge) is by open competition. Reappointment is automatic every three years unless a member has misconducted himself or failed without reasonable excuse to fulfil the minimum sittings requirement. Although prior to 1999 employment tribunals were not "independent and impartial" within the meaning of Art.6 of the European Convention on Human Rights, when determining claims in which the Secretary of State was a party, the new arrangements for appointment and removal satisfied the test of whether a fair-minded and informed observer would consider the tribunal members to be independent and impartial (see *Scanfuture UK Ltd v Secretary of State for Trade and Industry* [2001] I.R.L.R. 416; [2001] I.C.R. 1096). The test laid down by the House of Lords (in *Porter v Magill* [2002] 2 A.C. 357, HL) and subsequently reaffirmed by their Lordships (in *Lawal v Northern Spirit* [2003] I.R.L.R. 538; [2003] I.C.R. 856, HL) is whether a fair-minded and informed observer, having considered the given facts, would conclude that there was a real possibility that the tribunal was biased. The key to this test is the public's perception of the possibility of unconscious bias: see the commentary below in respect of reg.9. See also Ch.15, below.

Regulation 8(3)(a), (b) and (c)

The combined effect of s.48(1) and paras 35–39, Sch.8 of the Tribunals Courts **3–035** and Enforcement Act 2007, which introduced a new s.3A into the Employment Tribunals Act 1996, is that with effect from December 1, 2007, the employment judge is referred to in all judgments, correspondence and lists as an Employment Judge. (The Tribunals Courts and Enforcement Act 2007 (Commencement No. 1) Order 2007, SI 2007/2709). Despite the wording of the Regulation the practice is now to appoint members of the employment tribunal following open competition rather than nomination, to ensure wider representation on the panels from younger people, women and ethnic minorities. Once appointed, however, that person must be allocated to one or other of the respective panels.

Regulation 8(5)—Specialist panels

This is a power in the Regulations that was introduced only in 2004, but has not **3–036** yet been exercised. There have been suggestions from commentators that specialist panels might be appointed, for example, to determine claims under the Equal Pay Act 1970, in view of the complex legal and factual issues. In the explanatory notes published by the Government in 2004 at the time the Regulations were approved the only indication that was given was that the President might appoint a specialist panel to hear a case where a "specialist knowledge would be beneficial in determining the case". The power to appoint a specialist panel is not to be confused with the practice whereby in cases under the Race Relations Act 1976 it has been the practice since 1976 for at least one lay member hearing a race discrimination case to have "special knowledge or experience of relations between people of different racial groups in the employment field" as a result of a commitment given by a government Minister in the House of Lords during a debate on the Bill.

Composition of tribunals—general

9.—(1) For each hearing, the President, Vice President or the **3–037** Regional Chairman shall select a chairman, who shall, subject to regulation 11, be a member of the panel of chairmen, and the President, Vice President or the Regional Chairman may select himself.

(2) In any proceedings which are to be determined by a tribunal comprising a chairman and two other members, the President, Regional Chairman or Vice President shall, subject to regulation 11, select one of those other members from the panel of persons appointed by the Secretary of State under regulation 8(3)(b) and the other from the panel of persons appointed under regulation 8(3)(c).

(3) In any proceedings which are to be determined by a tribunal whose composition is described in paragraph (2) or, as the case may be, regulation 11(b), those proceedings may, with the consent of the parties, be heard and determined in the absence of any one member other than the chairman.

(4) The President, Vice President, or a Regional Chairman may at any time select from the appropriate panel another person in substitution for the chairman or other member of the tribunal previously selected to hear any proceedings before a tribunal or chairman.

Regulation 9(2)—A properly constituted panel

3–038   It is the responsibility of the ETS staff and the employment judge to ensure that the panel is correctly constituted. A claim determined before a tribunal panel that was incorrectly constituted (by, for example, containing both members drawn from the "employer's panel") is a nullity as the tribunal would have no jurisdiction to determine the claim: compare the judgment of the Court of Appeal in *Storer v British Gas Plc* [2000] I.R.L.R. 495, CA; [2001] I.C.R. 603. Although that case involved interpretation of what was then r.8(2) of the 1993 Rules (the requirement for hearings to be in public) it was held by the Court of Appeal to be a jurisdictional question, rather than a procedural irregularity which might not have invalidated the decision. By analogy a tribunal constituted other than in accordance with reg.9(2) is improperly constituted and lacks jurisdiction.

Regulation 9(2)—A properly constituted panel—bias

3–039   See also Ch.15, below. The jurisprudence of the European Court of Human Rights has established that there are three criteria whereby the independence and impartiality of a tribunal can be determined under Art.6 of the ECHR: (a) in the manner of appointment and tenure of its members; (b) in the existence of guarantees of the absence of outside pressures on the decision-making process; and (c) whether the body conducts itself in a way that demonstrates the appearance of independence. The first question has been addressed in the commentary on reg.8. The second issue concerns the question of whether the members of the tribunal might be guilty of actual or perceived bias due to some connection with the parties or their representatives. The third addresses the conduct of the members of the panel during the hearing itself. The two types of bias or potential bias can be described as "interest bias" and "conduct bias".

Interest bias

3–040   An employment judge or member is disqualified from hearing any case in which he has a personal interest in the outcome of the case or there is a real danger or possibility of bias. The question is whether the outcome of the case could realistically affect the members' interest (see *Medicaments and Related Classes of Goods (No. 2), Re* [2001] I.C.R. 564 CA). The Court of Appeal has attempted to give guidance on what relationships or connections might or might not suggest that members of a tribunal should consider recusing themselves from hearing a case (*Locabail (UK) Ltd v Bayfield Properties Ltd* [2000] I.R.L.R. 96). The following examples drawn from the judgment are not exhaustive. It would be rare for any objection to be taken to religion, ethnic or national origin, gender, age, class, means or sexual orientation. Ordinarily the same would apply to a range of other situations: the social, educational, service or employment background of members of the panel; or of the family of panel members; similarly previous political associations, membership of social, sporting or charitable bodies; Masonic associations (the previous Lord Chancellor Lord Irvine did ask tribunal employment judges to voluntarily disclose membership of the Masons, a practice still in operation); previous judicial decisions (although see the cases below where the employment judge was the subject of outstanding complaints); previous articles or speeches; previous instructions to act for a party in the proceedings; or membership of the same set of barristers' chambers. The judgment contains an extensive list of potential situations where the tribunal should consider the potential of an appearance of bias: the list is not meant to be exhaustive, nor can it be suggested that none of the previous situations will never support an allegation of bias. In contrast the following are situations that are likely to create a real danger of bias: personal friendship or animosity between the panel and any person involved in the litigation; close acquaintanceship of any member of the panel with any person involved in the case especially if credibility was to be an issue; if the employment judge had rejected the evidence of a party or witness in a previous case in terms that might suggest a predisposition to reject the witness' evidence as reliable; or if there were real grounds to doubt the panel's ability to ignore extraneous considerations, prejudices and predilections and bring an objective judgment to bear on the case.

In *Hamilton v GMB (Northern Region)* [2007] I.R.L.R. 391, the EAT concluded that a member of the tribunal—who was an official of another trade union, engaged in a similar equal pay campaign to the respondent union involved in the litigation— ought to have recused herself on the grounds of apparent bias. An application for recusal was refused by the tribunal after the initial five day hearing, but before submissions. In the same appeal, the EAT advised that lay members with any concerns about the propriety of sitting on a case should raise the issue with the employment judge as soon as possible, thereby enabling the employment judge to explore the extent of any potential bias before the hearing. It is important to stress that the reviewing court will neither cross-examine the members of the tribunal beyond seeking their views on any affidavit supplied in the case (see EAT Practice Direction—Procedure 2004, 11), nor pay attention to any comments of the panel on the impact of any knowledge on them. The EAT Practice Direction warns litigants that unsuccessful allegations of bias or improper conduct will attract the possibility of a costs order.

In practical terms shareholdings present the greatest difficulty: the panel may be unaware if their pension funds are invested in the particular company; the shareholding may be small. The question of previous connections was explored in a case where the husband of the tribunal employment judge had previously been instructed by one of the parties: that did not raise the presumption of bias, as the relationship was too remote and the claimant had waived the right to object when the relationship was disclosed (*Jones v DAS Legal Expenses Insurance Co Ltd* [2004] I.R.L.R. 218).

Where the allegation of bias is that the employment judge has previously commented on a witness or a representative it should not without more sustain an allegation of bias: that is an important principle in the administration of justice (*Lodwick v LB of Southwark* UKEAT/0116/05). However, it is no answer to an allegation of bias on the part of the employment judge that he is only one of a three person panel with an equal vote (*Lodwick v LB of Southwark* [2004] I.R.L.R. 554; [2004] I.C.R. 884). If the employment judge's conduct in a previous matter is the subject matter of an outstanding complaint of bias or improper conduct involving a party or a potential witness then the employment judge, should normally recuse himself from the proceedings. The mere fact of a complaint however could not give rise to an automatic decision to recuse. The substance of the allegations had to be addressed and analysed (*Breeze Benton Solicitors v Waddell* [2004] All E.R. 41; *Ansar v Lloyds Bank TSB Plc* [2006] ICR 1565).

In the context of an appeal where the issue was whether there was a presumption **3–040/1** of bias, where the employment judge on a pre-hearing review hearing was to be the same employment judge who had previously made findings adverse to the claimant, the Court of Appeal reaffirmed the following propositions outlined by Burton J. in the EAT below:

(a) The test to be applied as stated by Lord Hope in *Porter v Magill* [2002] 2 A.C. 357, at [103] and recited by Pill L.J. in *Lodwick v London Borough of Southwark* [2004] I.R.L.R. 554 CA at [18] in determining bias is: whether the fair-minded and informed observer, having considered the facts, would conclude that there was a real possibility that the Tribunal was biased;

(b) If an objection of bias is then made, it will be the duty of the employment judge to consider the objection and exercise his judgment upon it. He would be as wrong to yield to a tenuous or frivolous objection as he would to ignore an objection of substance: *Locabail* at [21];

(c) Although it is important that justice must be seen to be done, it is equally important that judicial officers discharge their duty to sit and do not, by acceding too readily to suggestions of appearance of bias, encourage parties to believe that by seeking the disqualification of a judge, they will have their case tried by someone thought to be more likely to decide the case in their favour: *Re JRL ex parte CJL* [1986] 161 C.L.R. 342 at 352, per Mason J., High Court of Australia recited in *Locabail* at [22];

(d) It is the duty of a judicial officer to hear and determine the cases allocated to him or her by their head of jurisdiction. Subject to certain limited exceptions, a judge should not accede to an unfounded disqualification application: *Clenae Pty Ud v Australia & New Zealand Banking Group Ltd* [1999] VSCA 35, cited in *Locabail* at [24];

(e) The EAT should test the Employment Tribunal's decision as to recusal and also consider the proceedings before the Tribunal as a whole and decide whether a perception of bias had arisen: Pill L.J. in *Lodwick*, at [18];

(f) The mere fact that a judge, earlier in the same case, or in a previous case, had commented adversely on a party or witness, or found the evidence of a party or witness to be unreliable, would not, without something more, find a sustainable objection: *Locabail* at [25];

(g) Parties cannot assume or expect that findings adverse to a party in one case entitle that party to a different judge or tribunal in a later case. Something more must be shown: Pill L.J. in *Lodwick* above, at [21], recited by Cox J. in *Breeze Benton Solicitors (A Partnership) v Weddell* [2004] All E.R. (D) at [41];

(h) Courts and tribunals need to have broad backs, especially in a time when some litigants and their representatives are well aware that to provoke actual or ostensible bias against themselves can achieve what an application for adjournment (or stay) cannot: Sedley L.J. in Bennett at [19];

(i) There should be no underestimation of the value, both in the formal English judicial system as well as in the more informal Employment Tribunal hearings, of the dialogue which frequently takes place between the judge or Tribunal and a party or representative. No doubt should be cast on the right of the Tribunal, as master of its own procedure, to seek to control prolixity and irrelevancies: Peter Gibson J in *Peter Simper & Co Ltd v Cooke* [1986] I.R.L.R. 19 EAT at [17];

(j) In any case where there is real ground for doubt, that doubt should be resolved in favour of recusal: *Locabail* at para.25; and

(k) Whilst recognising that each case must be carefully considered on its own facts, a real danger of bias might well be thought to arise (*Locabail* at [25]) if:

    (i) there were personal friendship or animosity between the judge and any member of the public involved in the case;

    (ii) the judge were closely acquainted with any member of the public involved in the case, particularly if the credibility of that individual could be significant in the decision of the case;

    (iii) in a case where the credibility of any individual were an issue to be decided by the judge, the judge had in a previous case rejected the evidence of that person in such outspoken terms as to throw doubt on his ability to approach such person's evidence with an open mind on any later occasion;

    (iv) on any question at issue in the proceedings before him the judge had expressed views, particularly in the course of the hearing, in such extreme and unbalanced terms as to throw doubt on their ability to try the issue with an objective judicial mind; or

    (v) for any other reason, there were real grounds for doubting the ability of the judge to ignore extraneous considerations, prejudices and predilections and bring an objective judgment to bear on the issues. (*Ansar v Lloyds TSB Bank Plc* [2007] I.R.L.R. 211, CA).

Conduct bias

Conduct bias may manifest itself in a number of ways: the panel may by the way **3–041** it intervenes or asks questions interfere with the right of the parties to present their case, subject to the obligations on the tribunal and the parties under the overriding objective; the tribunal may indicate that it has formed a view of the case and the likelihood of success before all the evidence has been heard; a member of the panel may appear not to have been taking an active role in the course of the hearing. In the first instance the test will be whether the fair minded observer would take the view that the interventions of the employment judge (in most instances) gave the impression of partiality to one side or the other (*Peter Simper & Co v Cooke* [1986] I.R.L.R. 19; *Locabail (UK) Ltd v Bayfield Properties Ltd* [2000] I.R.L.R. 96, at [25]). It is no bar to a challenge that the parties raised no objection during the hearing (*Lodwick v LB of Southwark* [2004] I.R.L.R. 554, CA; [2004] I.C.R. 884, *per* Pill L.J. at [20]; *Stansbury v Datapulse Plc* [2004] I.R.L.R. 466, CA; [2004] I.C.R. 523).

Whilst a tribunal may in the course of evidence or argument express views or opinions about the strength or weakness of an element of the evidence or a party's argument it must not do so in a manner that either indicates that it has formed a view before all the evidence has been heard or in a manner that influences a party to abandon a point or withdraw a claim or response (*Ellis v Ministry of Defence* [1985] I.C.R. 257, cited in *Chris Project v Hutt* UKEATS/0065/05; *Jiminez v London Borough of Southwark* [2003] I.R.L.R. 477; [2003] I.C.R. 1176, CA). The Court of Appeal in *Jiminez* drew a distinction between the premature expression of a concluded view (which is not permissible) and the preliminary expression of a strongly held view, which can be a helpful way of encouraging the parties to resolve the matter. Where an employment judge on an application under r.20 that a claimant should be ordered to pay a deposit had expressed the view that the claimant's claims had no reasonable prospect of success (the test under r.18), as opposed to little prospect of success (the test under r.20), that employment judge's subsequent decision to strike out the claimant's whistle blowing claim at a subsequent hearing gave the appearance of bias. (*North Glamorgan NHS Trust v Ezsias* [2007] I.R.L.R. 603). Parties raising an allegation of bias are required to comply with the provisions of the EAT Practice Direction in relation to costs and the obligations of the tribunal in respect of case management decisions (EAT P.D. 2004, para.11).

Excessive intervention by a tribunal may, but will not always provide the basis for a claim of bias. It is necessary to apply the "fair-minded and informed observer" standard, and also to assess whether the interventions are in fact an indication of bias, rather than, for example, merely over-eager attempts to understand the evidence or otherwise properly to control the hearing process (*Luis Roberto DeMarco Almeida v Opportunity Equity Partners Ltd* [2006] UKPC 44).

As far as sleeping members are concerned, the position has been considered twice by the appellate courts (in *Stansbury v Datapulse Plc* [2004] I.R.L.R. 466, CA; [2004] I.C.R. 523; *Fordyce v Hammersmith and Fulham Conservative Association* UKEAT/0390/05). A number of principles emerge from these judgments and the unreported authorities referred to in the judgments: it is the duty of the employment tribunal to be alert throughout the hearing; if a member of the tribunal is unable due to the effects of alcohol or tiredness to give full attention to the evidence and the proceedings, the hearing is flawed and the case must be heard before a fresh tribunal; it is no bar to an appeal that no objection is raised at the time; or that the decision was reserved or unanimous; or that the decision discloses no arguable defect of law or reasoning. In the event of a dispute as to what actually occurred the task of the EAT is to resolve that dispute, on any affidavits and the comments of the tribunal panel, notwithstanding that it will not call the actual members of the panel to give evidence or to be cross-examined. The principle derives from art.6(1) of the ECHR and the principles governing whether a tribunal hearing is flawed where there is an allegation that a member has not given the proceedings the full attention deserved is analogous with the principles in relation to bias (*Fordyce* at [8], and the authorities there cited). It does not offend the principle either that parties are being permitted a "second bite at the cherry", although the courts must be wary of the increasing prevalence of allegations of bias (see Rimer J. in *London Borough of Hackney v Sagnia* UKEAT/0600/03 and UKEAT/0135/04 at [63]).

Practical guidance and waiver of the right to object

3–042   Tribunals, parties and advocates are given practical guidance in observations drawn from the authorities cited above on what to do in a situation where the reality or possibility of bias may arise:

(a) In any case involving automatic disqualification, the tribunal member should recuse himself at the earliest opportunity and preferably before an objection is taken (*Locabail*).

(b) If for any reason a panel member would feel personally embarrassed hearing a case the same applies (*Locabail*).

(c) There must be a real as opposed to a fanciful chance of objection (*Jones*).

(d) Courts and tribunals need to have broad backs, especially in a time when some litigants and their representatives are well aware that to provoke actual or ostensible bias against themselves can achieve what an application for adjournment (or stay) cannot (*per* Sedley L.J. in *Bennett v London Borough of Southwark* [2002] I.R.L.R. 407, at [19]).

(e) The first step the tribunal can take is to establish whether another employment judge or member can hear the case (*Jones*).

(f) In any other case once the tribunal becomes aware of any matter which could give rise to a real danger of bias, it is desirable that full disclosure is given to the parties as soon as possible (*Locabail*). The tribunal panel should make every effort in the time available to clarify the full nature of the interest which might give rise to the conflict of interest and the possibility of bias (*Jones*).

(g) Whatever explanation is to be given to the parties should be recorded or noted, to avoid controversy later (*Jones*). The explanation must be full, and the reasons for late disclosure given and the parties told if an alternative employment judge or member is available and when (*Jones*).

(h) The options open to the parties must be explained: to consent to the employment judge or member continuing to sit and the possibility of losing the right to object; the right to make an application for the employment judge or member to recuse himself; and the opportunity to apply for an adjournment if no alternative member or employment judge can be found with an indication of the likely hearing date; in such a situation the parties must have sufficient time to consider the options (*Jones*).

(i) The employment judge must still consider any objection from either party on its merits, as it would be as wrong to accede to a frivolous objection as to ignore an objection of substance (*Locabail* and *Bennett*).

(j) The factors to take into account if an application to recuse is made are: the nature of the conflict; whether the parties are willing for the case to continue if no alternative tribunal can be found; if the case has already started, how long it has been going on and how far it still has to go; the cost implications of the adjournment; how the public would perceive the situation if the panel member did not withdraw (*Locabail*).

(k) A party can waive the right to object to a case of interest bias, but not to conduct bias, but if the waiver is to be effective it must be clear and unequivocal; be made with full knowledge of the facts; where one party wants to continue it is the tribunal's duty to decide but in any case of doubt the tribunal should opt for recusal (*Locabail*).

Regulation 9(3)—Sittings with only one member

In a number of situations the problem may arise that the tribunal cannot be **3–043** constituted as a full tribunal. The hearing may continue with one member but for that to be permissible both parties must consent. Consent cannot be presumed if one party does not attend the hearing, having chosen instead to send written representations. A respondent debarred by r.9 from taking part in the proceedings is not a party and therefore their consent is not required (*Comber v Harmony Inns Ltd* [1993] I.C.R. 15). Conversely a respondent against whom a default judgment has been issued under r.8, is not thereby debarred from taking part in the proceedings and their consent would be needed. (On the difference between a default judgment under r.8 and an order debarring the respondent from taking part in the proceedings under r.9, see *NSM Music Ltd v Leefe* [2006] I.C.R. 450.) In addition before a party can give consent to the claim being heard before anything other than a full tribunal, there must be informed consent. The parties are entitled to know from which panel the remaining member is drawn (see *Rabahallah v BT Group Plc* [2005] I.R.L.R. 184; [2005] I.C.R. 440, following *de Haney v Brent Mind* [2004] I.C.R. 348, which held that the same applied to the Employment Appeal Tribunal). In practice the tribunal should follow the advice of the then President of the EAT, Burton J., in *Rabahallah*, that a form should be signed not only giving consent but identifying the employment judge and panel and the relevant panel from which the member is drawn.

Regulation 9(4)—Substitution of an employment judge or member

The power to substitute cannot be exercised once the hearing has commenced, **3–044** for example because of the illness or death of a member of the tribunal: in those circumstances the only way to proceed is for the parties to consent to the hearing proceeding before a two person tribunal (although not if it is the employment judge who is incapacitated) or for the hearing to start again with a replacement member. Arguably in those circumstances it might be appropriate to replace the entire panel. However, where there has been a hearing on liability, it would not be objectionable to appoint a replacement member if a member is incapacitated, or if the EAT or the Court of Appeal has sent a case back to the original panel for further consideration (see *Montfort International Plc v McKenzie*, EAT 0155/06 February 6, 2007). Whereas there is an obligation to obtain the consent of the parties under reg.9(3) there is no requirement to seek the parties' consent under reg.9(4).

Panels of members of tribunals – national security proceedings

10. In relation to national security proceedings, the President **3–045** shall:—

> (a) select a panel of persons from the panel of chairmen to act as chairmen in such cases; and

ET(CRP) Regs 2004

      (b) **select:—**

          (i) **a panel of persons from the panel referred to in regulation 8(3)(b) as persons suitable to act as members in such cases; and**

          (ii) **a panel of persons from the panel referred to in regulation 8(3)(c) as persons suitable to act as members in such cases.**

National security proceedings

3–046   National security proceedings are proceedings in respect of which the relevant direction or order has been made under s.10 of the Employment Tribunals Act 1996. Under s.10 of the Employment Tribunals Act 1996 either a Minister of the Crown may give a direction (s.3(b)) or the President or a regional employment judge (under s.3(4)) may make an order if it is expedient in the interests of national security in respect of proceedings before the employment tribunal. Once such an order has been made the panel to determine the case is selected in accordance with reg.10(a) to (c). The hearing itself before the tribunal selected to determine the claim is then conducted in accordance with r.54 which, by virtue of reg.2 applies to proceedings in respect of which a direction has been given under r.54(1) or an order under r.(2) in Sch.1. Once proceedings are "national security proceedings" they are subject to this provision which gives the tribunal a discretionary power to sit in private, exclude witnesses and representatives, and conceal the identity of witnesses pursuant to the power delegated by s.10 of the Employment Tribunals Act 1996. Where proceedings before an employment tribunal become by virtue of r.54(3) national security proceedings, the provisions of Sch.2 of the Regulations apply rather than Sch.1, and in the case of any conflict the provisions of Sch.2 apply.

Panel of persons

3–047   Regulation 10(b) then provides that Regulations may make provision for the composition of any tribunal convened for the purposes of determining any claim in respect of which a reg.10 direction or order has been given.

   The President may create the necessary specialist panels to hear these cases from within the panels already constituted to hear cases under reg.8. Regulation 11 then sets out how that is done in respect of any specific case.

Composition of tribunals – national security proceedings

3–048   **11. In relation to national security proceedings:—**

      (a) **the President, the Regional Chairman or the Vice President shall select a chairman, who shall be a member of the panel selected in accordance with regulation 10(a), and the President, Regional Chairman or Vice President may select himself; and**

      (b) **in any such proceedings which are to be determined by a tribunal comprising a chairman and two other members, the President, Regional Chairman or Vice President shall select one of those other members from the panel selected in accordance with regulation 10(b)(i) and the** other from the panel selected in accordance with regulation 10(b)(ii).

All that this Regulation does is prescribe the procedure for selection of the actual **3–049** panel to determine an individual case involving national security from within the panels of chairman and members already nominated under reg.10. For these purposes the President, Vice-President, or relevant regional employment judge may select himself to be the employment judge. To that extent reg.11 mirrors reg.9, with one important exception: there is no provision corresponding to reg.9(3): the power of the parties to consent to the tribunal sitting with only one member, so the tribunal must be a full tribunal.

Modification of section 4 of the Employment Tribunals Act (national security proceedings)

12.—(1) For the purposes of national security proceedings section **3–050** 4 of the Employment Tribunals Act shall be modified as follows.

(2) In section 4(1)(a), for the words "in accordance with regulations made under section 1(1)" substitute the words "in accordance with regulation 11(a) of the Employment Tribunals (Constitution and Rules of Procedure) Regulations 2004".

(3) In section 4(1)(b), for the words "in accordance with regulations so made" substitute the words "in accordance with regulation 11(b) of those Regulations".

(4) In section 4(5), for the words "in accordance with Regulations made under section 1(1)" substitute the words "in accordance with regulation 10(a) of the Employment Tribunals (Constitution and Rules of Procedure) Regulations 2004".

This Regulation makes the necessary amendments to s.4 of the Employment **3–051** Tribunals Act 1996, consequent on regs 10 and 11. Section 4 provides that a tribunal shall comprise either a full tribunal or a employment judge sitting alone in respect of the jurisdictions listed at s.4(2) to (5). The four amendments to s.4 introduced by reg.12 make it clear that in respect of national security proceedings, regs 10 and 11 supersede the Regulations in relation to the composition of the tribunal appointed to determine the proceedings.

Practice directions

13.—(1) The President may make practice directions about the **3–052** procedure of employment tribunals in the area for which he is responsible, including practice directions about the exercise by tribunals or chairmen of powers under these Regulations or the Schedules to them.

(2) The power of the President to make practice directions under paragraph (1) includes power:—

(a) to vary or revoke practice directions;

(b) to make different provision for different cases or different areas, including different provision for specific types of proceedings.

(3) The President shall publish a practice direction made under paragraph (1), and any revocation or variation of it, in such manner as he considers appropriate for bringing it to the attention of the persons to whom it is addressed.

The President may make practice directions

3–053   Section 27 of the Employment Act 2002 amended the Employment Tribunals Act 1996 by introducing a new s.7A to enable Regulations to be made giving the President power to issue practice directions. Prior to the 2004 Regulations the President had no power to make practice directions. In the recommendations of the Employment Tribunals Task Force (at para.6.36) the introduction of this power was welcomed, although it recommended that it should not be at the expense of flexibility or the introduction of innovative changes. The absence of a power in the previous regulations and the undesirability of employment tribunals following different practices and procedures in different regions had been identified by a former President of the Employment Appeal Tribunal, Morison J. in *Eurobell Holdings Plc v Barker* [1998] I.C.R. 299. He concluded that it was desirable that tribunals should seek to agree on what is the best practice from the point of view of the judicial management of proceedings, and that it was desirable that a statutory power be given to the President of Employment Tribunals to make practice directions to apply country wide. This Regulation contains that statutory power.

So far although the President has given guidance to tribunals, for example, in relation to whether witness statements should be read or taken as read, he has not issued any practice directions since being given the power in October 2004. He has however, issued two directions, which together with the practice directions issued by the President in Scotland, appear on the Employment Tribunals service website. The first stays all proceedings in the Employment Tribunal in which an issue has arisen under reg.30 of the Employment Equality (Age) Regulations 2006, (dismissal at age 65). The second imposes a similar stay in respect of proceedings where the employment status of agency workers employed by government bodies is in issue. As and when it is invoked the provisions of reg.13(2) give the President a wide discretion, without any obligation to consult interested parties, to make practice directions in respect of any aspect of the tribunal's jurisdiction.

In December 2006 the President of Employment Tribunals in Scotland issued three practice directions in respect of claims in Scotland dealing with respectively lists of documents (PD1), sisting (staying) proceedings to enable meditation to take place (PD2), and most importantly specifying the procedure to be followed in respect of counterclaims (PD3).

PD1 requires legally represented parties, but limited to legally represented parties, to disclose their list of documents to the other parties 14 days before the Hearing. PD2 enables tribunals to sist (stay) proceedings to enable mediation to take place where all parties wish it. PD 3 will require the respondent to a counterclaim to specify the amount claimed in its claim in addition to supplying the required information under r.7 and will require the claimant (the respondent to the counterclaim) to indicate within 28 days (or any extended period ordered by the tribunal) of being sent the claim whether it is resisted and the reasons for resistance. Notes attached to each of the Practice Directions explain the reasons for issuing them. At this stage it is unclear whether the President in England and Wales intends to follow suit.

Power to prescribe

3–054   **14.—(1) The Secretary of State may prescribe—**

(a) one or more versions of a form, one of which shall be used by all claimants for the purpose of commencing

proceedings in an employment tribunal ("claim form") except any claim or proceedings listed in paragraph (3);

(b) one or more versions of a form, one of which shall be used by all respondents to a claim for the purpose of responding to a claim before an employment tribunal ("response form") except respondents to a claim or proceedings listed in paragraph (3); and

(c) that the provision of certain information and answering of certain questions in a claim form or in a response form is mandatory in all proceedings save those listed in paragraph (3).

(2) The Secretary of State shall publish the forms and matters prescribed pursuant to paragraph (1) in such manner as she considers appropriate in order to bring them to the attention of potential claimants, respondents and their advisers.

(3) The proceedings referred to in paragraph (1) are:—

(a) those referred to an employment tribunal by a court;

(b) proceedings to which any of Schedules 3 to 5 apply; or

(c) proceedings brought under any of the following enactments:-

  (i) sections 19, 20 or 22 of the National Minimum Wage Act 1998;

  (ii) section 11 of the Employment Rights Act where the proceedings are brought by the employer.

Regulation 14(1)—Power to prescribe

Section 25 of the Employment Act 2002 inserted into s.7 of the Employment **3–055** Tribunals Act 1996 a new s.7(3ZA) providing that Regulations may be introduced enabling the Secretary of State to (a) prescribe forms to be used when instituting or responding to proceedings; (b) prescribe the information to be supplied in such forms; and (c) prescribe the documentation to be supplied with such forms. Prior to 2004 there was no obligation to use any prescribed form, as long as the required information was supplied. All that r.1 required was a document in writing giving the name of the applicant, his address, the name and address of the person against whom relief was sought, and the grounds, supported by particulars, on which relief was sought. An applicant could do this in a letter and many did, although in practice parties used the two page printed forms of IT1 (application) and IT3 (notice of appearance). The 2004 Rules provided that with effect from October 2004, more information was required on lodging a claim, but use of the prescribed form would not be compulsory until April 6, 2005, a date subsequently extended to October 1, 2005 (by SI 2005/435).

Regulation 14(1)(a) and (b)—Prescribed claim and response forms

There are two forms for use in the employment tribunal: the ET1 (claim to an **3–056** employment tribunal), and the ET3 (response to an employment tribunal claim). Each document is available in printed form, or it can be downloaded from the ETS

ET(CRP) Regs 2004

web site, and then either completed online or sent by email, posted or faxed. There is now a facility on the ETS website to save a partially completed form for completion at a later date. The ET3 advises the respondent of the time limit for service of the response (28 days) and advises the respondent of the last possible date for service, and the two potential consequences of a failure to respond.

The ETS has indicated that it will not accept any in-house or commercial version of either document. It has been held that a decision by the ETS Secretary not to accept a claim or response as it was not in accordance with the prescribed form (the information had not scanned into the computer) is a decision within the meaning of the Rules, notwithstanding that it is not taken by an employment judge, and is therefore capable of review under r.34 (*Butlins Skyline Ltd v Beynon* [2007] I.C.R. 121. In *Grant v In 2 Focus Sales Development Services Ltd* (UKEAT/0310/06/LA/ UKEAT/0311/06/LA), the Tribunal Secretary refused to accept a complaint on the grounds that it was not on a form prescribed in accordance with reg.14. Since the appropriate form had been filled in and faxed to the Tribunal, the reason that it did not comply was not self evident, and the Secretary gave no further explanation. The parties had inferred that it was because it was reduced in size as a consequence of the faxing process. The respondent contended that the Secretary was entitled to refuse the form on the grounds that size was an essential feature of the prescribed form, and that in any event the EAT did not have jurisdiction to hear an appeal from what was simply the administrative act of the Secretary. The EAT, following *Butlins v Beynon* held that it did have jurisdiction to hear the appeal, and that the Secretary had erred in law in refusing to accept the form. The form was still a prescribed form, notwithstanding the reduction in size. Furthermore it was incumbent on the Secretary under r.3(1) to explain why a claim (or response) was not being accepted.

Regulation 14(1)(c)—Provision of mandatory information

3–057   Rule 1(4)(a) to (i) set out the basis for the requirement for the provision of the mandatory information required of a claimant, and r.4(3)(a) to (d) the mandatory information required of the respondent. The language used in the Regulations is "mandatory"; rr.1 and 4 refer to the "required information". The meaning is the same. It is not clear why different language is used in the Rules compared to the Regulations.

Regulation 14(1) and Regulation 14(3)—Exempt provisions

3–058   The obligation to use the prescribed forms does not apply to five categories of proceedings:

(a) Where a case has been referred to the tribunal by a court;
(b) Where the case has been brought under Sch.3 (levy appeals);
(c) Where the case involves a non-discrimination notice under Sch.5;
(d) Claims brought under the provisions of ss.19 (power to issue enforcement notice), 20 (claim for non-compliance with an enforcement notice), or 22 (appeals against penalty notices) of the National Minimum Wage Act 1998;
(e) References by an employer under s.11 of the Employment Rights Act 1996 (questions relating to a statement under ss.1 and 4 of the Employment Rights Act 1996).

Regulation 14(2)—Published forms

3–059   The forms are available in three formats: as printed forms; as downloadable forms in pdf. format from the ETS website, or as forms that can be completed online on the same site.

Calculation of time limits

15.—[(1) Any period of time for doing any act required or permit- **3–060**
ted to be done under any of the rules in Schedules 1, 2, 3, 4, 5 and 6,
or under any decision, order or judgment of a tribunal or a chairman, shall be calculated in accordance with paragraphs (2) to (6).]

(2) Where any act must or may be done within a certain number of
days of or from an event, the date of that event shall not be included
in the calculation. For example, a respondent is sent a copy of a claim
on 1st October. He must present a response to the Employment
Tribunal Office [within 28 days of the date on which] he was sent the
copy. The last day for presentation of the response is 29th October.

(3) Where any act must or may be done not less than a certain
number of days before or after an event, the date of that event shall
not be included in the calculation. For example, if a party wishes to
submit representations in writing for consideration by a tribunal at a
hearing, he must submit them not less than 7 days before the
hearing. If the hearing is fixed for 8th October, the representations
must be submitted no later than 1st October.

(4) Where the tribunal or a chairman gives any decision, order or
judgment which imposes a time limit for doing any act, the last date
for compliance shall, wherever practicable, be expressed as a calendar date.

(5) In rule 14(4) of Schedule 1 the requirement to send the notice
of hearing to the parties not less than 14 days before the date fixed
for the hearing shall not be construed as a requirement for service of
the notice to have been effected not less than 14 days before the
hearing date, but as a requirement for the notice to have been placed
in the post not less than 14 days before that date. For example, a
hearing is fixed for 15th October. The last day on which the notice
may be placed in the post is 1st October.

(6) Where any act must or may have been done within a certain
number of days of a document being sent to a person by the
Secretary, the date when the document was sent shall, unless the
contrary is proved, be regarded as the date on the letter from the
Secretary which accompanied the document. For example, a respondent must present his response to a claim to the Employment Tribunal
Office [within 28 days of the date on which] he was sent a copy of the
claim. If the letter from the Secretary sending him a copy of the
claim is dated 1st October, the last day for presentation of the
response is 29th October.

Regulation 15(1)

The whole of this paragraph in square brackets was substituted for the original **3–061**
paragraph by para.2(6)(a) of SI 2004/2351 with effect from October 1, 2004. The
amendment was necessary to reflect the addition of Sch.6 to the Rules, and merely
added the number "6" to the list of numbered schedules in the Regulation.

Regulation 15(2) and (6)

3–062   The wording in square brackets was an amendment effected by para.2(6)(b) of SI 2004/2351 with effect from October 1, 2004. The amendment merely substituted the wording "within 28 days of which" for "within 28 days on which", a typographical error in the original Regulations.

Regulation 15(2) and (3)

3–063   This is one of the few situations where the parliamentary draftsman has actually indicated in legislation a practical example of how to calculate the relevant time limit. The period and the relevant date is printed on the front page of the response form sent to the respondent on service of the claim. All six schedules contain examples of time limits. Whenever the Rules or an order of the tribunal specifies that an event or action must take place within a specified number of days from a particular date or before a specified date, the actual date of that event or day is not included in the calculation. In both instances the Regulation gives a practical example.

Regulation 15(4)

3–064   Wherever an employment judge or tribunal sets out a timetable for compliance by the parties with specified procedural requirements, for example, disclosure of documents, exchange of witness statements, the practice is always to specify the date and time for compliance, rather than the number of days for compliance. Standard documentation used by tribunals where an employment judge has made orders on paper rather than at a case management discussion contain a table of dates for compliance with standard case management orders. The exceptions will be where the time limit is expressed as a specified number of days before the hearing, when the date for the hearing has not been fixed. In that event, for example, where an order is made for exchange of witness statements 42 days before the hearing, then reg.15(2) and (3) will apply and the date of the hearing is excluded from the calculation.

In an appeal concerned with the requirements of s.32(3) of the Employment Act and r.1(4) of the Employment Tribunals (Procedure) Regulations, (the obligation to lodge a grievance and wait 28 days before submitting the claim), the EAT has held that in the absence of a specific rule on time the tribunal should have recourse to CPR 2.8 for guidance on how to compute time: *Basingstoke Press Ltd (in administration) v Clarke* [2007] I.C.R. 1284, [2007] I.R.L.R. 588. See also commentary at 10–037.

Application of Schedules 1–5 to proceedings

3–065   **16.—(1) Subject to paragraphs (2) (3) [and (4),] the rules in Schedule 1 shall apply in relation to all proceedings before an employment tribunal except where separate rules of procedure made under the provisions of any enactment are applicable.**

(2) In proceedings to which the rules in Schedule 1 apply and in which any power conferred on the Minister, the tribunal or a chairman by rule 54 (national security proceedings) of Schedule 1 is exercised, Schedule 1 shall be modified in accordance with Schedule 2.

(3) The rules in Schedules 3, 4 and 5 shall apply to modify the rules in Schedule 1 in relation to proceedings which consist, respectively, in:—

(a) an appeal by a person assessed to levy imposed under a levy order made under section 12 of the Industrial Training Act 1982;

(b) an appeal against an improvement or prohibition notice under section 24 of the Health and Safety at Work etc Act 1974; and

(c) an appeal against a non-discrimination notice under section 68 of the Sex Discrimination Act, section 59 of the Race Relations Act or paragraph 10 of Schedule 3 to the Disability Rights Commission Act 1999.

[(4) In proceedings which involve an equal value claim (as defined in Rule 2 of Schedule 6) Schedule 1 shall be modified in accordance with Schedule 6.]

Regulation 16

Regulation 16 provides that Sch.1 of the Rules applies to all proceedings before an employment tribunal unless the proceedings are governed by the provisions of legislation to which the remaining five schedules apply. In other words if the proceedings are national security proceedings (Sch.1, r.54), the provisions of Sch.2 apply; if it is a levy appeal under s.12 of the Industrial Training Act 1982, Sch.3 applies; if it is an appeal against an improvement or prohibition notice under s.24 of the Health and Safety at Work Act 1974, Sch.4 applies; if it is an appeal against a non-discrimination notice Sch.5 applies; and finally if the claim is an equal value claim as defined by Sch.6, Sch.6 applies.

3–066

Regulation 16(1)

The wording in square brackets was an amendment effected by para.2(7)(a) of SI 2004/2351 with effect from October 1, 2004. It was introduced to reflect the amendment to reg.16 as the result of the addition of a new para.16(4) by para.2(7)(b) of SI 2004/2351 with effect from October 1, 2004.

3–067

Regulation 16(4)

This entire paragraph between the square brackets was an amendment to the Regulation introduced by para.2(7)(b) of SI 2004/2351 with effect from October 1, 2004. It was another consequential change to the original Regulations necessitated by the introduction of Sch.6.

3–068

Register

17.—(1) The Secretary shall maintain a Register which shall be open to the inspection of any person without charge at all reasonable hours.

3–069

(2) The Register shall contain a copy of all judgments and any written reasons issued by any tribunal or chairman which are required to be entered in the Register in accordance with the rules in Schedules 1 to 5.

(3) The Register, or any part of it, may be kept by means of a computer.

Regulation 17(1)—A Register

Regulation 17 represents a major change in response to criticism that the Register was being exploited to enable claims handling organisations to obtain details of claimants and respondents to enable those organisations to offer their

3–070

ET(CRP) Regs 2004

representation services. Under the 2001 Regulations (reg.12) the Secretary was obliged to maintain a Register which contained details of all originating applications, and appeals against the various orders now covered by Schs 3, 4, and 5 of the 2004 Rules; in addition the Register had to contain decisions and reasons for decisions. The new Regulations only require the maintenance of a register of decisions and written reasons, where supplied.

Proof of decisions of tribunals

3–071   **18. The production in any proceedings in any court of a document purporting to be certified by the Secretary to be a true copy of an entry of a judgment in the Register shall, unless the contrary is proved, be sufficient evidence of the document and of the facts stated therein.**

3–072   All judgments sent to parties by the tribunal contain a printed endorsement at the foot of the document indicating the date that the judgment was entered in the Register, and was sent to the parties. It will bear the signature of a member of the tribunal staff. If the document contains that information it satisfies the requirements of reg.18.

Jurisdiction of tribunals in Scotland and in England & Wales

3–073   **19.—(1) An employment tribunal in England or Wales shall only have jurisdiction to deal with proceedings (referred to as "English and Welsh proceedings") where—**

> **(a) the respondent or one of the respondents resides or carries on business in England and Wales;**
>
> **(b) had the remedy been by way of action in the county court, the cause of action would have arisen wholly or partly in England and Wales;**
>
> **(c) the proceedings are to determine a question which has been referred to the tribunal by a court in England and Wales; or**
>
> **(d) in the case of proceedings to which Schedule 3, 4 or 5 applies, the proceedings relate to matters arising in England and Wales.**

(2) An employment tribunal in Scotland shall only have jurisdiction to deal with proceedings (referred to as "Scottish proceedings") where—

> **(a) the respondent or one of the respondents resides or carries on business in Scotland;**
>
> **(b) the proceedings relate to a contract of employment the place of execution or performance of which is in Scotland;**
>
> **(c) the proceedings are to determine a question which has been referred to the tribunal by a sheriff in Scotland; or**

(d) **in the case of proceedings to which Schedule 3, 4 or 5 applies, the proceedings relate to matters arising in Scotland.**

Regulation 19(1)—Proceedings in England and Wales

The issue of where the claim will be dealt with is entirely separate from the **3–074** question of whether the tribunal has any jurisdiction in the claim at all, for example if the work is carried out abroad or the employer does not carry on business at all in Great Britain. Whether or not the employment has a sufficient connection with Great Britain has to be resolved in accordance with the guidance of the House of Lords (*Lawson v Serco Ltd* [2006] I.R.L.R. 289, HL; [2006] I.C.R. 250; *Lawson* dealt with the jurisdiction of employment tribunals to determine claims for unfair dismissal). For further examples of the application of the *Serco* guidance, see *Burke v British Council*, UKEAT/0125/06, 14.12.2006. For discrimination and breach of contract see *Saggar v Ministry of Defence* [2005] I.R.L.R. 618, CA; [2005] I.C.R. 1073.

Notwithstanding that there is now a common procedure in respect of proceedings in England, Wales, and Scotland, employment tribunals in England and Wales deal with "English and Welsh cases", employment tribunals in Scotland with "Scottish cases". An employment tribunal in England and Wales will deal with the case in these four circumstances:

(a) The respondent (or one of them) resides or carries on business in England and Wales;
(b) If the parties had been seeking a remedy in the county court, did the cause of action arise wholly or partly in England and Wales;
(c) If the proceedings are to determine a question referred to the tribunal by a court in England and Wales; or
(d) in respect of levy appeals, appeals against improvement or prohibition notices, and appeals against non-discrimination notices, the proceedings relate to matters arising in England and Wales.

Subject to compliance with the requirements of the Rules, proceedings commenced in either England and Wales or Scotland may be transferred from England and Wales to Scotland or vice versa in accordance with Sch.1, r.57 (see para.4–345). However, the power to transfer applies only to a claim properly commenced in the correct jurisdiction in the first place: the power to transfer cannot apply to correct a defect of jurisdiction in the original claim.

Transitional provisions

20.—(1) [These Regulations and Schedules 1 to 6] to them shall 3–075 apply in relation to all proceedings to which they relate where those proceedings were commenced on or after 1 October 2004.

(2) These Regulations and Schedules 1 and 2 to them (with the exception of rules 1 to 3 and 38 to 48 of Schedule 1) shall apply to proceedings:—

(a) **which were commenced prior to 1 October 2004; and**
(b) **to which Schedule 1 to either the old (England & Wales) regulations or the old (Scotland) regulations applied; provided that a copy of the originating application was not sent to the respondent prior to 1 October 2004.**

(3) In relation to the proceedings described in paragraph (2), the following provisions of Schedule 1 to the old (England & Wales) regulations or the old (Scotland) regulations (as the case may be) shall continue to apply:—

    (a) rule 1 (originating application);

    (b) rule 2 (action upon receipt of originating application) with the exception of paragraphs (2), (4) and (5) of that rule; and

    (c) rule 14 (costs).

(4) In relation to proceedings described in paragraph (2) but where a copy of the originating application was sent to the respondent prior to 1 October 2004, Schedules 1 and 2 to these Regulations shall apply with the exception of rules 1 to 9, 21 to 24, 33 and 38 to 48 of Schedule 1 and rules 2, 3 and 4 of Schedule 2.

(5) In relation to proceedings described in paragraph (4), the following provisions of the old (England & Wales) regulations or the old (Scotland) regulations (as the case may be) shall continue to apply:—

    (a) in Schedule 1:—

        (i) rule 1 (originating application);

        (ii) rule 2 (action upon receipt of originating application) with the exception of paragraphs (2), (4) and (5) of that rule;

        (iii) rule 3 (appearance by respondent);

        (iv) rule 8 (national security);

        (v) rule 14 (costs); and

    (b) rule 1 of Schedule 2.

(6) In relation to proceedings commenced prior to 1 October 2004 and to which Schedule 4, 5 or 6 to the old (England & Wales) regulations or the old (Scotland) regulations (as the case may be) applied, the provisions of those schedules shall continue to apply to such proceedings.

[(7) In relation to proceedings:—

    (i) which were commenced prior to 1 October 2004;

    (ii) to which schedule 3 to either the old (England and Wales) regulations or the old (Scotland) regulations applied; and

    (iii) in which the tribunal has not, prior to 1 October 2004, required a member of the panel of independent experts to prepare a report under section 2A(1)(b) of the Equal Pay Act;

these Regulations and rules 1 to 13 of Schedule 6, with the exception of rule 4(3)(a) shall apply.

(8) In relation to proceedings:—

   (i) which were commenced prior to 1 October 2004

  (ii) to which Schedule 3 to either the old (England & Wales) regulations or the old (Scotland) regulations applied; and

 (iii) in which the tribunal has, prior to 1 October 2004, required a member of the panel of independent experts to prepare a report under section 2A(1)(b) of the Schedule 3 to either the old (England & Wales) regulations or the old (Scotland) regulations (as the case may be) shall continue to apply.

(9) In relation to proceedings described in paragraph (8), the following rules of Schedule 6 shall also apply and shall take precedence over any conflicting provision in Schedule 3 to either the old (England & Wales) regulations or the old (Scotland) regulations, namely:

   – rules 3, 11(2), 11(4), 12, 13(1) and 13(3).

(10) Rule 14 of Schedule 6 shall apply to all proceedings to which, in accordance with this regulation, rule 10 of Schedule 2 applies.".]

Regulation 20(1)

Regulation 20(1) was amended by para.2(8)(a) of SI 2004/2351 with effect from October 1, 2004 to reflect the addition of Sch.6 to the Regulations. **3–076**

Regulation 20(7) to (10)

The Regulation was amended by the addition of paras (7) to (10) inclusive by para.2(8)(b) of SI 2004/2351 with effect from October 1, 2004 to set out the transitional provisions in respect of equal value claims. The majority of the transitional provisions are now only of historical significance. **3–077**

Regulation 20(1) to (6)

The combined effect of reg.20(1) to (6) is as follows in respect of the transitional provisions set out in reg.20: **3–078**

  (a) if proceedings were commenced after October 1, 2004 all the provisions of respectively Schs 1 to 6 apply to those proceedings, irrespective of when the cause of action arose; (reg.20(1));

  (b) if the proceedings were proceedings to which the old Sch.1 applied, and were commenced prior to October 1, 2004, but the originating application (now a claim) had not been served on the respondent prior to October 1, 2004, then the Regulations, Schs 1 and 2 (the general Rules and national security rules) will apply with the exception of—

    (i) rr.1 to 3 (acceptance of claims) and;

(ii) rr.38 to 48 (costs).
(Regulation 20(2))

(c) if the proceedings are proceedings described in (b) above, the following provisions of the old Rules (Employment Tribunals (Constitution and Rules of Procedure Regulations 2001 SI 2001/1171) continue to apply to those proceedings—

(i) r.1 (originating application);
(ii) r.2 (action on receipt of an originating application) with the exception of paras (2), (4) and (5) (which deal with the contents of the Register, and are now overruled by reg.17 in these Regulations);
(iii) r.14 (costs).
(Regulation 20(3))

(d) if the proceedings were proceedings as described in (b) above, but had been served on the respondent prior to October 1, 2004 then the provisions of Sch.1 of these Regulations will apply to those proceedings with the exception of the following—

(i) rr.1 to 9 (acceptance of claims, responses, counterclaims, default judgments and debarring from taking part in the proceedings);
(ii) rr.21 to 24 (conciliation rules);
(iii) rr.33 and 38 to 48 (review of default judgments and costs).
(Regulation 20(4))

(e) if the proceedings were proceedings as described in (b) above, (and are national security proceedings) but had been served on the respondent prior to October 1, 2004 then the provisions of Sch.2 of these Regulations will apply to those proceedings with the exception of the following—

(i) r.2 (notification of proceedings);
(ii) r.3 (responding to the claim);
(iii) r.4 (service of documents by the Secretary).
(Regulation 20(4))

(f) if the proceedings are proceedings in respect of which the preceding paras (d) and (e) apply then the following provisions of the old Rules (Employment Tribunals (Constitution and Rules of Procedure Regulations 2001 SI 2001/1171) continue to apply to those proceedings—

(1) In Sch.1—

(i) r.1 (originating application);
(ii) r.2 (action on receipt of an originating application), with the exception of r.2(2), (4) and (5);
(iii) r.3 (appearance by a respondent);
(iv) r.8 (national security);
(v) r.14 (costs).
In Sch.2—

(2) r.1 of Sch.2 (service of response).
(Regulation 20(5))

(g) if the proceedings were commenced prior to October 1, 2004 and were either levy proceedings (Sch.4), appeals in respect of an improvement or prohibition notice (Sch.5), or appeals against a non-discrimination notice (Sch.6) under the old Regulations and Rules, then the old provisions of the respective schedules continue to apply.

Regulation 20(7) to (9)

Equal value claims: If the claim is an equal value claim and is commenced after **3–079** October 1, 2004 Sch.6 applies in its entirety. In respect of proceedings in respect of an equal value claim commenced before that date the position depends on whether or not the tribunal has commissioned a report from a member of the independent panel of experts. Depending therefore on appointment the position can be summarised as follows:

(a) No Expert appointed—The Regulations, and rr.1 to 13 of Sch.6 apply with the exception of r.4(3)(a) (striking out at the stage 1 hearing); Regulation 20(7)
(b) Expert appointed—the old Sch.3 continues to apply, together with rr.3 (case management); 11(2) (expert's duty to assist tribunal); 11(4) (disclosure of expert's report and use of other expert evidence); 12 (written questions to the expert); 13(1) and 13(3) of Sch.6 (procedural matters); in the event of any conflict the new Rules apply; Regulation 20(8) and (9).

Regulation 20(10)

If the equal value claim is also a "national security" claim under Sch.2, then if **3–080** r.10 in Sch.2 (reasons) applies then r.14 also in Sch.6 applies so that the tribunal must treat the independent expert's report in the same way as reasons are dealt with under r.10.

CHAPTER 4

Employment Tribunals Rules of Procedure

Contents
Para.

SCHEDULE I

HOW TO BRING A CLAIM

ACCEPTANCE OF CLAIM PROCEDURE

RESPONSE

ACCEPTANCE OF RESPONSE PROCEDURE

CONSEQUENCES OF A RESPONSE NOT BEING PRESENTED OR ACCEPTED

CASE MANAGEMENT

DIFFERENT TYPES OF HEARING

CASE MANAGEMENT DISCUSSIONS

SCHEDULE 4

THE EMPLOYMENT TRIBUNALS (HEALTH AND SAFETY-APPEALS AGAINST IMPROVEMENT AND PROHIBITION NOTICES) RULES OF PROCEDURE

SCHEDULE 5

THE EMPLOYMENT TRIBUNALS (NON-DISCRIMINATION NOTICES APPEALS) RULES OF PROCEDURE

SCHEDULE 6

THE EMPLOYMENT TRIBUNALS (EQUAL VALUE) RULES OF PROCEDURE

108

SCHEDULE 1

Regulation 16

The Employment Tribunals Rules of Procedure

HOW TO BRING A CLAIM

Starting a claim

1.—(1) A claim shall be brought before an employment tribunal by **4–001**
the claimant presenting to an Employment Tribunal Office the
details of the claim in writing. Those details must include all the
relevant required information (subject to paragraph (5) of this rule
and to rule 53 (Employment Agencies Act 1973)).

(2) The claim may only be presented to an Employment Tribunal
Office in England and Wales if it relates to English and Welsh
proceedings (defined in regulation 19(1)). The claim may only be
presented to an Employment Tribunal Office in Scotland if it relates
to Scottish proceedings (defined in regulation 19(2)).

(3) Unless it is a claim in proceedings described in regulation
14(3), a claim which is presented on or after 1st October 2005 must
be presented on a claim form which has been prescribed by the
Secretary of State in accordance with regulation 14.

(4) Subject to paragraph (5) and to rule 53, the required information in relation to the claim is—

(a) each claimant's name;
(b) each claimant's address;
(c) the name of each person against whom the claim is made
("the respondent");
(d) each respondent's address;
(e) details of the claim;
(f) whether or not the claimant is or was an employee of the
respondent;
(g) whether or not the claim includes a complaint that the
respondent has dismissed the claimant or has contemplated doing so;

(h) whether or not the claimant has raised the subject matter of the claim with the respondent in writing at least 28 days prior to presenting the claim to an Employment Tribunal Office;

(i) if the claimant has not done as described in (h), why he has not done so.

(5) In the following circumstances the required information identified below is not required to be provided in relation to that claim—

(a) if the claimant is not or was not an employee of the respondent, the information in paragraphs (4)(g) to (i) is not required;

(b) if the claimant was an employee of the respondent and the claim consists only of a complaint that the respondent has dismissed the claimant or has contemplated doing so, the information in paragraphs (4)(h) and (i) is not required;

(c) if the claimant was an employee of the respondent and the claim does not relate to the claimant being dismissed or a contemplated dismissal by the respondent, and the claimant has raised the subject matter of the claim with the respondent as described in paragraph (4)(h), the information in paragraph (4)(i) is not required.

(6) References in this rule to being dismissed or a dismissal by the respondent do not include references to constructive dismissal.

(7) Two or more claimants may present their claims in the same document if their claims arise out of the same set of facts.

(8) When section 32 of the Employment Act applies to the claim or part of one and a chairman considers in accordance with subsection (6) of section 32 that there has been a breach of subsections (2) to (4) of that section, neither a chairman nor a tribunal shall consider the substance of the claim (or the relevant part of it) until such time as those subsections have been complied with in relation to the claim or the relevant part of it.

Commencement

4–002 October 1, 2004. The date in para.(3) was originally "6 April" but was amended to "1st October" by reg.2 of the Employment Tribunals (Constitution and Rules of Procedure) (Amendment) Regulations 2005 (SI 2005/435).

Para.(1)—Presenting a claim

4–003 "Presenting" is a different concept from "service by post" and s.7 of the Interpretation Act 1978 therefore does not apply. Thus a claim form sent to a tribunal office by prepaid post which does not arrive is not "presented". A claim form is not presented until it actually arrives at the tribunal office or reaches a third party held out by the tribunal as able to receive claims on its behalf (see *Lang v Devon General Ltd* [1987] I.C.R. 4, EAT and *Tyne & Wear Autistic Society v Smith* [2005] I.R.L.R. 336; [2005] I.C.R. 663, EAT).

Employment tribunals now routinely accept claims presented by fax, email and through the internet as well as by post and hand delivery. The old cases were concerned only with postal and hand delivery of claims and issues like the absence of letter boxes after office hours. The extent to which cases such as *Ford v Stakis Hotels & Inns Ltd* [1988] I.R.L.R. 46; [1987] I.C.R. 943, EAT (which held that where the last day for presentation fell on a day when the Regional Office was closed and there was no letter box, that day was a dies non), still represent the law now that out of hours online presentation is available, is unclear.

Presentation occurs by email when the claim form is successfully submitted to the tribunal's website, even if it is not subsequently forwarded to the tribunal by the website host. As the tribunal holds out the website as a means by which claims can be presented, presentation to the site is presentation to the tribunal (*Tyne & Wear Autistic Society v Smith* (above) at [26] (which did not refer to *Mossman v Bray Management Ltd* UK/EAT/0477/04 which had previously held to the contrary)).

Mere delivery is sufficient. Thus putting a claim form in the tribunal office letter box after office hours on the last day was held to be presentation, as intervention by a clerk, for example, by date stamping the document, is not required (*Post Office v Moore* [1981] I.C.R. 623, EAT). A claim may therefore be presented on a day when the office is closed (*Swainston v Hetton Victory Club Ltd* [1983] I.R.L.R. 164, CA). The old cases should however be read in the light of the new regime of acceptance and rejection of claims and responses for which see rr.2(1), 3(1), 5(1) and 6(1). Although the Rules do not expressly say so, it is clearly the intention and almost certainly the effect of rr.1(1) to (4) and 3(1) and (2) that a claim has not been presented unless it is subsequently accepted, although the date of presentation will be the date of receipt, not the date of acceptance if later.

Presenting a claim—place of presentation and inter-regional transfers

See also reg.19 and the commentary to para.(2) at para.3–073.   **4–004**

The rules only require presentation at "an" office of the employment tribunal which means any permanently staffed office, not necessarily a regional office. Proceedings may be transferred to another office or region for hearing or case management or both. An application to transfer a claim should be made under r.11. However, a claim will not be transferred unless the regional employment judge (or in Scotland, the Vice President, see reg.7, at para.3–031) of the importing region agrees to accept it. There is power to transfer claims between England and Wales and Scotland (but see commentary on para.(2) below) but not to or from Northern Ireland (in consequence of s.47 of the Employment Tribunals Act 1996).

Presentation and rejection

There is as yet no authority under the new Rules on the relationship between   **4–005** presentation and either acceptance or rejection. In *Barry v Caledonian International Book Manufacturing Ltd* EAT/685/99, a case under the 1993 Rules of Procedure, the Secretary declined to register the originally presented claim because it did not contain sufficient information—the details of the complaint were missing—and the re-presented claim was out of time. The EAT held that presentation was different from registration and the original, rejected claim had been "presented" as it complied substantially with the provisions of r.1. Under the 2004 Rules it seems that this could not be the case unless there had first been a successful application to review or appeal the decision to reject the original claim form (see r.3(7)).

Para.(1)—"rule 53 (Employment Agencies Act 1973)"

See para.4–332. The only relevant information which is not required in such an   **4–006** application is the name and address of the respondent, being the Secretary of State.

Para.(2)—Transfers between England and Scotland

4–007   Claims brought in the wrong jurisdiction, e.g. in England against a respondent whose sole place of business is in Scotland, will not be transferred but will be rejected for want of jurisdiction.

For transfers after a claim has been accepted, see para.(1) above

Para.(4)—"required information"

4–008   This has the appearance of being mandatory. However, this requirement must be read subject to the overriding objective of dealing with cases fairly and justly (see *Grimmer v KLM Cityhoppers Ltd* [2005] I.R.L.R. 596, EAT; and *Richardson v U Mole Ltd* [2005] I.R.L.R. 668, EAT; and *Hamling v Coxlease School* [2007] I.R.L.R. 8; [2007] I.C.R. 108, EAT). In respect of the 1993 Rules of Procedure it was said in *Burns International Security Services Ltd v Butt* [1983] I.R.L.R. 438; [1983] I.C.R. 547, EAT that the only requirement which was mandatory was that the claim be in writing, the rest was merely directory. The judgment appears to remain good law, at least so far as the provision of the required information is concerned. Compare also, the approach of the ECtHR as to the extent to which rigid application of technical requirements is consistent with the requirements of ECHR art.6 (*Sotiris and Nikos Koutras Attee S.A. v Greece* 36 E.H.R.R. 24). For whether there has been a failure to provide relevant required information such as to justify rejection of the claim form, see r.3(3), (4) and (5).

An error in the required information may be corrected by amendment, and does not make the claim a nullity. On considering an application to amend the required information, the Employment Judge must have regard to the usual considerations including any prejudice suffered by the respondent as a result of the error: *Cummings v Compass Group UK t/a Scolarest* UKEAT/0625/06

"Required Information"

Para.(4)(a)—Claimant's name

—bankrupt claimants

4–009   A bankrupt may bring proceedings in his own name only where the claim is personal to the claimant. Claims for unfair dismissal (*Grady v Prison Service* [2003] I.R.L.R. 474; [2003] I.C.R. 753, EAT and *Khan v Trident Safeguards Ltd* [2004] I.R.L.R 961; [2004] I.C.R. 1591, CA) and, if restricted to claims for a declaration and compensation for injury to feelings, complaints of discrimination (*Khan*), are personal to the claimant. A discrimination complaint which includes a claim for loss of earnings is a hybrid claim and as such vests in the bankrupt's trustee (Insolvency Act 1986, s.306) and may not be pursued by the claimant.

—deceased claimants

4–010   Where the claimant has died before the proceedings were commenced, the claim may be presented by, and the proceedings instituted in the name of, a personal representative where the claim is brought under either the Employment Rights Act 1996, s.206(3) (ERA 1996) or the Trade Union and Labour Relations (Consolidation) Act 1992, s.292(2) (TULR(C)A). For discrimination claims see *Harris (personal representative of Andrews dec'd) v Lewisham & Guy's Mental Health NHS Trust* [2000] I.R.L.R. 320, CA and the Law Reform (Miscellaneous Provisions) Act 1934, s.1(1). Where there is no personal representative and the claim is brought under either ERA 1996 or TULR(C)A, the tribunal has power to appoint a representative for the purposes of the claim only (ERA 1996, s.206(4); TULR(C)A, s.292(3)). The power to appoint a representative can be exercised on application before a claim is presented although it is more usual to treat a claim presented on behalf of a deceased person as including such an application. If a personal representative has already been appointed, the claimant should be named in the claim form as "Mary Jane Doe (personal representative of John Joseph Doe deceased)". Where there has been no appointment the claim should be brought in the name of the deceased claimant.

Para.4(b)—Claimant's address

The employment tribunal has a discretion to accept a claim form that does not **4–011** contain this information if the omission is neither relevant nor material (see *Hamling v Coxlease School* [2007] I.R.L.R. 8; [2007] I.C.R. 108, EAT).

Para.(4)(c)—Respondent's name

—deceased respondent

Where it is known that the respondent has died, this should be indicated by **4–012** adding "(deceased)" after their name. If the identity of the respondent's executors or, (if Letters of Administration have been issued) personal representatives are known, they should be named as respondents in that capacity, i.e. Mary Jane Doe and Abraham Doe as personal representatives of John Joseph Doe deceased".

—insolvent respondents: claims for insolvency and related payments

Where the complaint is that the Secretary of State has refused to make an **4–013** employers payment under Ch.VI of Pt XI of the ERA 1996 the correct respondent is the Secretary of State not the former employer (*Jones v Secretary of State for Employment* [1982] I.C.R. 389, EAT). Where the former employer is not insolvent as defined by s.166 ERA 1996 and the Secretary of State has refused to make a redundancy payment to the claimant, the correct respondent is the former employer, not the Secretary of State.

—insolvent respondents: other claims

Employment tribunal proceedings may not be commenced against a company in **4–014** administration or compulsory liquidation or against an undischarged bankrupt without the leave of the administrator or the court overseeing the administration, winding up or bankruptcy proceedings: ss.11(3), 130(2) and 285(3)(b) of and para.43 of Sch.1B to the Insolvency Act 1986 as amended by the Enterprise Act 2002. Members and creditors voluntary liquidations and administrative receivership have no effect on proceedings. If the respondent is a partnership, proceedings may be commenced without leave unless all of the partners have been declared bankrupt.

Para.(4)(d)—Respondent's address for service

See also the commentary to r.3(3), (4) and (5). **4–015**

—address not in the UK

There is no express requirement in the Rules that the address for service should **4–016** be in the United Kingdom (see r.61(4)(h)(i)). Although the wording of r.61(4)(h)(ii) is ambiguous, it appears that the regional employment judge's consent is not required before service can be effected outside the United Kingdom unless such an address is put forward as an alternative address after attempts to send the claim form to the original address have failed.

—overseas companies

See ss.695 and 695A of the Companies Act 1985. **4–017**

—H.M. Forces and USAF personnel

4–018   See CPR PD6 para.5.

Para.(4)(e)—Details of the claim—meaning of "details."

4–019

"The test is whether it can be discerned from the claim as presented that the complainant is complaining of an alleged breach of an employment right which falls within the jurisdiction of the employment tribunal. . . There is no scope for . . . interpreting 'details of the claim' as 'particulars of the claim" (*Grimmer v KLM Cityhopper UK Ltd* [2005] I.R.L.R. 596, EAT).

And see also the commentary to r.3(3), (4) and (5).

Para.(7)—Multiple claimants—same facts, different causes of action

4–020   A single claim form may be used even if the grounds of complaint are different, e.g. arising out of a large scale redundancy exercise some claimants complain of unfair dismissal, breach of contract and for a redundancy payment while others, because of shortness of service, can only complain on one or two of those grounds.

Para.(8)—Meaning of "chairman"

4–020/1   The permissive form of s.3A of the Employment Tribunals Act ("[a] person who is a member of a panel of chairmen of employment tribunals which is appointed in accordance with regulations under section 1(1) may be referred to as an Employment Judge") means that no consequential amendment to the rules has been necessary: the term "chairman" is still used throughout.

Para.(8)—Shall not consider the claim

4–021   There are problems with interpreting para.(8) as the words ". . . shall [not] consider the substance of the claim. . . until such time as. . ." can be read as meaning that a claim may be stayed to allow any non-compliance with s.32(2) to (4) of the Employment Act 2002 (EA) (para.10–031) to be rectified, whereupon the claim could then be heard. However, such an interpretation is contrary to the clear requirement of r.3(2)(c) that in those circumstances, the claim is to be rejected. This interpretation was adopted in *Hounslow LBC v Miller* UKEAT/0645/06, which held that there was no power to stay a claim in such circumstances: the claim form had to be rejected. It is possible that the paragraph is directed at claims presented in breach of one of the provisions of s.32(2) to (4), but erroneously accepted with the breach only being identified some time after acceptance, and requires them to be stayed rather than struck out to allow the breach to be rectified. This remains a possible interpretation particularly in cases where the late rejection or striking out of the claim would leave the claimant without a remedy because of time limit issues.

ACCEPTANCE OF CLAIM PROCEDURE

What the tribunal does after receiving the claim

4–022   **2.—(1) On receiving the claim the Secretary shall consider whether the claim or part of it should be accepted in accordance with rule 3. If a claim or part of one is not accepted the tribunal shall not proceed to deal with any part which has not been accepted (unless it is accepted at a later date). If no part of a claim is accepted the claim shall not be copied to the respondent.**

(2) If the Secretary accepts the claim or part of it, he shall—

   (a) send a copy of the claim to each respondent and record in writing the date on which it was sent;

   (b) inform the parties in writing of the case number of the claim (which must from then on be referred to in all correspondence relating to the claim) and the address to which notices and other communications to the Employment Tribunal Office must be sent;

   (c) inform the respondent in writing about how to present a response to the claim, the time limit for doing so, what may happen if a response is not entered within the time limit and that the respondent has a right to receive a copy of any judgment disposing of the claim;

   (d) when any enactment relevant to the claim provides for conciliation, notify the parties that the services of a conciliation officer are available to them;

   (e) when rule 22 (fixed period for conciliation) applies, notify the parties of the date on which the conciliation officer's duty to conciliate ends and that after that date the services of a conciliation officer shall be available to them only in limited circumstances; and

   (f) if only part of the claim has been accepted, inform the claimant and any respondent which parts of the claim have not been accepted and that the tribunal shall not proceed to deal with those parts unless they are accepted at a later date.

Para.(1)

The Secretary's powers under the Rules in connection with the administration of cases, including the power to accept and reject claims, are delegated to the Regional Secretaries and Office Managers. The vetting of claim and response forms is further delegated by the Regional Secretaries to specially trained clerks. **4–023**

Para.(1)—". . . shall not proceed to deal with. . . "

In the case of a claim form rejected in its entirety, the practice is to return it to the claimant. Where a claim is rejected only in part, a photocopy of the claim form is returned. The rejected claim or part claim is given a pre-acceptance number for use in correspondence and to enable any resubmitted claim to be linked to it. Where a claim is only partially accepted because the statutory grievance procedure has not been complied with in respect of some heads of complaint, the rejected claims can be added subsequently by way of amendment once the procedure has been complied with: *Mackay v Hanna t/a Blakes Newsagents* UKEAT/0181/07. **4–024**

Para.(2)—Informing the parties

Where the subparagraphs require the Secretary to inform or notify the parties of something, this is done by way of a standard letter which includes all of the required information. **4–025**

Para.(2)(a)—Sending the claim

—effect on the statutory grievance procedure

4–025/1   Where some complaints on a claim form are accepted and some rejected because no written statement of grievance had been sent to the respondent, the sending of the claim form to the respondent does not amount to the sending of a written statement of grievance in respect of the rejected claims. The claimant must send an independent Step 1 statement: *Gibbs t/a Jarlands Financial Services v Harris* UKEAT/0023/07.

—address for service

4–026   For address for service see r.61(4)(h)(i). The tribunal will not check that an address for service given in the claim form is correct.

For overseas companies, HM Forces and USAF personnel, and where the address for service is outside the UK, see commentary to r.1(4)(d). For substituted service see r.61(6).

Foreign sovereign states

4–027   Section 12 of the State Immunity Act 1978 provides special rules for the service of proceeding against foreign sovereign states. The judgment in *Bone v Fabcon Projects Ltd* (below) and in consequence para.(2)(a) are in direct conflict with s.12(1) of the State Immunity Act 1978 which provides:

> "Any writ or other document required to be served for instituting proceedings against a State shall be served by being transmitted through the Foreign and Commonwealth Office to the Ministry of Foreign affairs of the State, and service shall be deemed to have been effected when the writ or document is received at the Ministry".

It is submitted that as these provision are the codification of customary international law by primary legislation. They cannot be circumvented merely by the substitution in the Rules of Procedure of the concept of "sending" to the respondent for the concept of "service" on the respondent.

—date and proof of receipt

4–028   In practice claims are always sent by first class post although r.61(1) permits sending by fax "or other electronic means" or personal delivery. The requirement to send the claim to the respondent is not to be equated with the more technical concept of service and therefore neither CPR 6.7, nor s.7 of the Interpretation Act 1978 apply (*Bone v Fabcon Projects Ltd* [2006] I.R.L.R. 908; [2006] I.C.R. 1421, EAT). This is because the last date for entering a response, which is stated on the documents sent to the respondent, is calculated by reference to the date of sending the claim, not the date of actual or deemed receipt (see reg.15(2) at para.3–060 for how the date for entering a response is to be calculated). No proof of receipt is required, as this is deemed by r.61(2).

The time for presenting the response to a claim runs from the date when the claim form is first sent to the respondent, even if the respondent informs the tribunal that it has not been received. There is no power under the rules to "re-send" the claim form so as to make the date of *re-sending* the date from which the time for *entering* the response is to be calculated (*Bone v Fabcon Projects Ltd* above). Therefore, if the respondent informs the tribunal that a claim form sent to them under para.(2)(a) has not been received, and the tribunal sends a fresh copy of the claim form, the time for entering the response must still be calculated by reference to the date when the first copy of the claim form was sent. If the 28 day period has not expired, the respondent should apply for an extension of time to enter the response. If it has expired, the respondent must either submit the response out of time and apply for the inevitable decision to reject it to be reviewed (*Moroak t/a Blake Envelopes v Cromie* [2005] I.R.L.R. 536; [2005] I.C.R. 1226, EAT), or apply to have the default judgment set aside under r.33 (for which see para.4–244), when the burden would be on the respondent to satisfy the tribunal that the first copy of the claim form had not been received.

If, through the error of the tribunal staff, the claim form was not originally sent to the address for the respondent given on the form, it is submitted that para.(2)(a) would not have been complied with, and the date of the sending of the second copy of the claim form would be the date from which the time for entering the response is to be calculated. If the claimant has incorrectly stated the address on the claim form but the claim is not returned by Royal Mail, the accepted interpretation of r.61(4)(h)(i) (see para.4–357) would suggest that para.(2)(a) has been complied with, and a default judgment could be entered in due course. However, in *Bone v Fabcon Projects Ltd* (above), the original claim form was correctly addressed and its application to cases where that was *not* the case must be doubtful. This is because para.(2)(a) requires that the claim form be sent to the respondent, and not merely sent to the respondent at the address given on the claim form. In the case of a respondent who complains before a default judgment has been issued that it has learned of proceedings which it has not received, and who claims that they are no longer (or never have been) at the address given on the claim form, para.(2)(a) would appear not to have been complied with in respect of the sending of the first claim form, and time for entering the response should run from the date the second copy of the claim is sent.

—nominated addresses

Although the rules are silent on the specific point, and the practice is officially **4–029** frowned upon because r.61(4)(h)(i) is said to require that the claim form is sent to the respondent's address specified therein (although it is at least arguable that the rule is only about a party's own address for service), a local arrangement sanctioned by the regional employment judge whereby all claims made, for example, against a local authority or large employer are to be sent to a central address rather than the address on the claim form, would appear to be in accordance with the overriding objective (reg.3, see para.3–014) and the regional employment judge's powers to order substituted service "in any case he considers appropriate" (r.61(6) see para.4–357). Moreover, if the nominated address was that of the solicitor to the authority, or the solicitors retained by the large employer, and the solicitors had notified the tribunal in writing that they were prepared to accept service of all tribunal proceedings, by analogy with CPR r.6.4(1), then the claim form should be sent to that address.

—when the claim is to be copied to the Secretary of State

Where the claim may result in a payment out of the National Insurance Fund, it **4–030** is to be copied to the Secretary of State: r.61(7). The Secretary of State is not required to enter a response, as this action does not make him or her a party to the proceedings although he may intervene by entering a response.

Para.(2)(d)—Enactments providing for conciliation

For the enactments which provide for conciliation, see s.18 of the Employment **4–031** Tribunals Act 1996 (ETA).

Para.(2)(e)—Conciliation

—fixed conciliation periods

4–032   For fixed conciliation periods and the circumstances in which they can be extended or abridged, see rr.22–24.

—ACAS involvement after conciliation period has expired

4–033   This is entirely a matter of internal ACAS policy. Under s.18(2) and (2A), ETA a conciliation officer has a duty to conciliate in short and standard conciliation period cases during the fixed conciliation period only. After the expiration of the fixed conciliation period, the duty to conciliate is replaced by a power to conciliate. ACAS appears to start from the premise that conciliation will not be offered after the expiration of the fixed conciliation period, but may be offered at the discretion of the conciliation officer on application by a party in exceptional circumstances which have "prevented any meaningful attempts to settle" within the fixed periods (ACAS Annual Report 2005). Examples of circumstances in which conciliation has been offered after the expiration of the fixed periods given in the Annual Report include: severe communication difficulties because of the number of unrepresented claimants or respondents; delays in receiving key paperwork from the tribunal; conciliation not previously possible pending the outcome of a judicial intervention or a relevant internal procedure; and the incapacity of a party due to serious illness.

When the claim will not be accepted by the Secretary

4–034   **3.—(1) When a claim is required by rule 1(3) to be presented using a prescribed form, but the prescribed form has not been used, the Secretary shall not accept the claim and shall return it to the claimant with an explanation of why the claim has been rejected and provide a prescribed claim form.**

(2) The Secretary shall not accept the claim (or a relevant part of one) if it is clear to him that one or more of the following circumstances applies—

(a) the claim does not include all the relevant required information;

(b) the tribunal does not have power to consider the claim (or that relevant part of it); or

(c) section 32 of the Employment Act (complaints about grievances) applies to the claim or part of it and the claim has been presented to the tribunal in breach of subsections (2) to (4) of section 32.

(3) If the Secretary decides not to accept a claim or part of one for any of the reasons in paragraph (2), he shall refer the claim together with a statement of his reasons for not accepting it to a chairman. The chairman shall decide in accordance with the criteria in paragraph (2) whether the claim or part of it should be accepted and allowed to proceed.

(4) If the chairman decides that the claim or part of one should be accepted he shall inform the Secretary in writing and the Secretary shall accept the relevant part of the claim and then proceed to deal with it in accordance with rule 2(2).

(5) **If the chairman decides that the claim or part of it should not be accepted he shall record his decision together with the reasons for it in writing in a document signed by him. The Secretary shall as soon as is reasonably practicable inform the claimant of that decision and the reasons for it in writing together with information on how that decision may be reviewed or appealed.**

(6) **Where a claim or part of one has been presented to the tribunal in breach of subsections (2) to (4) of section 32 of the Employment Act, the Secretary shall notify the claimant of the time limit which applies to the claim or the part of it concerned and shall inform the claimant of the consequences of not complying with section 32 of that Act.**

(7) **Except for the purposes of paragraph (6) and (8) or any appeal to the Employment Appeal Tribunal, where a chairman has decided that a claim or part of one should not be accepted such a claim (or the relevant part of it) is to be treated as if it had not been received by the Secretary on that occasion.**

(8) **Any decision by a chairman not to accept a claim or part of one may be reviewed in accordance with rules 34 to 36. If the result of such review is that any parts of the claim should have been accepted, then paragraph (7) shall not apply to the relevant parts of that claim and the Secretary shall then accept such parts and proceed to deal with it as described in rule 2(2).**

(9) **A decision to accept or not to accept a claim or part of one shall not bind any future tribunal or chairman where any of the issues listed in paragraph (2) fall to be determined later in the proceedings.**

(10) **Except in rule 34 (review of other judgments and decisions), all references to a claim in the remainder of these rules are to be read as references to only the part of the claim which has been accepted.**

Transitional provisions

The rule applies to claims commenced before October 1, 2004, provided that a **4–035** copy of the claim form was not sent to the respondent prior to that date; see reg.20(4) and (5), at para.3–075. There are likely to be some claims, principally part-time worker pension claims, where the claim form was sent to the respondent prior to October 1, 2004 to which rr.1–9 of the 2004 Rules of Procedure do not apply, but which are governed by the corresponding provision (r.3(1)) of the 2001 Rules of Procedure (SI 2001/1171). In such a case therefore, the respondent is required to enter an appearance rather than to present a response. The prescribed form does not apply, and time for entering the appearance may be extended after it has expired.

Para.(1)—Prescribed form

For the power to prescribe the form, see reg.14.   **4–036**

For the tribunal's powers in respect of the prescribed form, see commentary to r.1(3).

Rejecting claims not on the prescribed form: role of the Secretary

4–037   The Secretary is required by the Rules to reject the claim if it is not on the prescribed form, and has no discretion to exercise. The only forms which will be accepted are those which have been published by the employment tribunals themselves. Thus forms which correspond exactly to the prescribed form, but have been published by commercial law stationers, or are held on solicitors' IT systems as blank documents, will not be accepted. If a claim is rejected, the Secretary must state reasons for the decision that enable the claimant to know what must be put right in any resubmitted claim (see *Grant v In 2 Focus Sales Development Services Ltd* UKEAT/0310/06, January 30, 2007).

Rejecting claims not on the prescribed form: role of the employment judge

4–038   A decision of the Secretary to reject a claim form is not subject to confirmation by the employment judge under para.(3), and para.(8) only provides for a review of a decision of an employment judge to accept or reject a claim form. In *Butlins Skyline Ltd (1) Smith (2) v Beynon* [2007] I.C.R. 121 (note) it was held that a decision by the Secretary to reject a response said not to be on the prescribed form was a "decision made by a tribunal" for the purposes of r.34(1) (para.4–247), and therefore reviewable by the employment judge and also subject to the right of appeal to the EAT although the review option should be pursued first. In *Grant v In 2 Focus Sales Development Services Ltd* UKEAT/0310/06, January 30, 2007, the EAT concluded that a right of appeal did exist since the decision of the Secretary was a question arising in the proceedings for the purposes of s.21 of the ETA.

Para.(2)(a)—"Relevant required information"

4–039   The expression "required information" means so much of the information required by para.(4) as remains relevant in the circumstances of a particular claim having regard to para.(5).

Para.(2)(b)—No power to consider the claim

4–040   A claim which appears to be, or even one which is admitted to be, out of time is not a claim which the tribunal has no power to consider, and should therefore not be rejected where the relevant statutory provisions allow the tribunal to extend time for presentation in certain circumstances. Even for those jurisdictions where there is no power to extend time, the claim should be accepted, sent to the respondents and the claimant should be required to give the reasons that the claim should not be struck out under r.18(7)(a).

The Secretary will not reject a complaint of unfair dismissal brought by an employee with less than 12 months service. The claim will be accepted, served on the respondent who will be told that they are not required to enter a response, and the claimant will be required to give the reasons that the claim should not be struck out under r.18(7)(a).

Paras (3), (4) and (5)—Rejecting the claim—role of the employment judge

4–041   The employment judge's decision must be made "in accordance with the criteria in paragraph (2)", one of which is that the failure to provide the required information must be "clear to him". Thus, it is not sufficient grounds for rejecting the claim that there is room for doubt as to whether one of the circumstances in subpara.(a)-(c) applies. Generally, the requirements relating to the acceptance of a claim should be applied in light of the overriding objective (see *Grimmer v KLM Cityhopper UK Ltd* [2005] I.R.L.R. 596, EAT; *Richardson v U Mole Ltd* [2005] I.R.L.R. 668; [2005] I.C.R.1664, EAT; and *Burns International Security Services Ltd v Butt* [1983] I.R.L.R. 438; [1983] I.C.R. 547, EAT).

Paras (3), (4) and (5)—Employment judge's decision: general principles

The majority of cases under the new rules draw on three basic principles: the **4–042** relevance of the omitted information; the materiality of the omission; and proportionality. It is clear that, if possible, the rules should be interpreted so as to admit the claim (see *Hamling v Coxlease School* [2007] I.C.R. 108; [2007] I.R.L.R. 8; *Butlins Skyline Ltd v Beynon* [2007] I.C.R. 121 (note); and *Grant v In 2 Focus Sales Development Services Ltd* UKEAT/0310/06, January 30, 2007).

Paras (3), (4) and (5)—Required information—employment judge's decision: specific examples

Rule 1(4)(b) Claimants address: the claim was valid where the claimant supplied **4–043** only a telephone number (*Gosport Working Men's Club Ltd v Taylor* (1978) 13 I.T.R. 321, EAT), and only the claimant's solicitors name and address were provided (*Hamling v Coxlease School* [2007] I.C.R. 108; [2007] I.R.L.R. 8, EAT).

Rule 1(4)(d) Respondents address: " . . . to hold that [a claim form] should be **4–044** considered bad merely because it does not give the address of an organisation as well known as the RAC, would be mere pedantry" (*Smith v Automobile Proprietary Ltd* [1973] I.C.R. 306; (1973) 8 I.T.R. 247, NIRC). The same reasoning would apply to any employer well known within a region such as a local authority or a large manufacturer.

Rule 1(4)(e) Details of the claim: **4–045**

"The test is whether it can be discerned from the claim as presented that the complainant is complaining of an alleged breach of an employment right which falls within the jurisdiction of the employment tribunal. . . There is no scope for . . . interpreting 'details of the claim' as 'particulars of the claim'" (*Grimmer v KLM Cityhopper UK Ltd* [2005] I.R.L.R. 596, EAT).

Thus in Grimmer the claimant had put only "flexible working" as the details of her claim, but EAT held that the claim form should have been accepted. Similarly "unfair dismissal" was held to be sufficient in *Burns International Security Services Ltd v Butt* (see above) and "Sex Discrimination Act or the Race Discrimination Act" was held to be sufficient in *Dodd v British Telecommunications Plc* [1988] I.R.L.R. 16; [1988] I.C.R. 116, EAT.

Rule 1(4)(f) Whether claimant an employee: the failure by a claimant to state **4–046** specifically that he was an employee did not permit the claim to be rejected, when it was clear from the nature of the claim and other information in the claim form that he was asserting that he was an employee (*Richardson v U Mole Ltd* [2005] I.R.L.R. 668; [2005] I.C.R. 1664, EAT). Even if there had been a failure to provide the required information, the rejection of the claim should have been reviewed on the grounds that the omission was immaterial as the point was not in dispute. Although this case concerned the old claim form there is no reason to suppose that the principle would not apply to cases where the prescribed form is used.

Rule 1(4)(h) Whether written grievance sent to respondent: the claimant failed to **4–047** state specifically that she had raised the subject matter of the claim with the Respondent, but the details of the claim made it clear that she had in fact done so and had waited 28 days, and therefore the claim should have been accepted (*Mark Warner Ltd v Aspland* [2006] I.R.L.R. 87, EAT). This is an old form case, but again there is no reason to suppose that the same principle would not apply if the prescribed form had been used.

Para.(5)—"as soon as reasonably practicable"—meaning of

4–048   The administrative target is three working days including both the days of receipt and return.

Para.(6)—Automatic extensions of time

4–049   For s.32 of the Employment Act 2002 (EA) see para.10–031.

The phrase "the time limit concerned. . . " is a reference to the automatic extension of the original time limit for bringing proceedings to which one of the statutory grievance procedures applies by reg.15(1) and (3) of the Employment Act 2002 (Dispute Resolution) Regulations 2004 (SI 2004/752) (DRR) (see para.11–065). Regulation 15 of the DRR automatically extends time if the claimant has either previously sent their step 1 letter to the respondent or, if they have not done so, because the claim form has been presented before that requirement has been complied with and in consequence is rejected.

Para.(7)—". . . as if it had not been received by the Secretary. . ."

4–050   That is, had not been presented. The words ". . . except for the purposes of paragraph (6) . . ." —claims rejected for non-compliance with ss.32(2) to (4) EA— should not be taken as implying that such a claim may still be regarded as having been presented on the original date of presentation. The words are intended to reflect no more than that para.(6) requires the Secretary to take some action in connection with the form which, for those purposes but no others, has to be treated as having been received.

Para.(8)—Review of decisions to reject—date of presentation

4–051   The claim is treated as though it had been presented on the date of receipt, not the date of final acceptance.

Para.(9)—Wrongly accepted claims

4–052   A respondent wishing to challenge the acceptance of a claim, or part of one, should apply to strike out the claim or part under r.18(7)(a) (see para.4–169) on the grounds that the claimant is not entitled to bring the proceedings having failed to comply with one of the requirements of para.(2).

RESPONSE

Responding to the claim

4–053   **4.—(1) If the respondent wishes to respond to the claim made against him he must present his response to the Employment Tribunal Office within 28 days of the date on which he was sent a copy of the claim. The response must include all the relevant required information. The time limit for the respondent to present his response may be extended in accordance with paragraph (4).**

(2) Unless it is a response in proceedings described in regulation 14(3), any response presented on or after 1st October 2005 must be on a response form prescribed by the Secretary of State pursuant to regulation 14.

(3) The required information in relation to the response is—

(a) the respondent's full name;

(b) the respondent's address;

(c) whether or not the respondent wishes to resist the claim in whole or in part; and

(d) if the respondent wishes to so resist, on what grounds.

(4) The respondent may apply under rule 11 for an extension of the time limit within which he is to present his response. The application must be presented to the Employment Tribunal Office within 28 days of the date on which the respondent was sent a copy of the claim (unless the application is made under rule 33(1)) and must explain why the respondent cannot comply with the time limit. Subject to rule 33, the chairman shall only extend the time within which a response may be presented if he is satisfied that it is just and equitable to do so.

(5) A single document may include the response to more than one claim if the relief claimed arises out of the same set of facts, provided that in respect of each of the claims to which the single response relates—

(a) the respondent intends to resist all the claims and the grounds for doing so are the same in relation to each claim; or

(b) the respondent does not intend to resist any of the claims.

(6) A single document may include the response of more than one respondent to a single claim provided that—

(a) each respondent intends to resist the claim and the grounds for doing so are the same for each respondent; or

(b) none of the respondents intends to resist the claim.

Commencement

October 1, 2004 but subject to transitional provisions which may still be relevant **4–054** to a small number of cases. The date in para.(2) was originally "6 April" [sic] but was amended to "1st October" by reg.2 of the Employment Tribunals (Constitution and Rules of Procedure) (Amendment) Regulations 2005 (SI 2005/435).

Transitional provisions

The rule applies to claims commenced before October 1, 2004 provided that a **4–055** copy of the claim form was not sent to the respondent prior to that date; see reg.20(4) and (5) at para.3–075. There are likely to be some claims, principally part-time worker pension claims, where the claim form was sent to the respondent prior to October 1, 2004 to which rr.1–9 of the 2004 Rules of Procedure do not apply, but which are governed by the corresponding provision (r.3(1)) of the 2001 Rules of Procedure (SI 2001/1171). In such a case, therefore, the respondent is required to enter an appearance rather than present a response, the prescribed form does not apply and time for entering the appearance may be extended after it has expired.

Para.(1)—Time for entering the response

4–056   The date by which the response is to be received by the tribunal is stated on the documents sent with the claim form. It is calculated in accordance with reg.15(2) (see para.3–060), and may be challenged by the respondent if it appears to be incorrect. Regulation 15(2) requires that 28 days be added to the date on which the claim is sent to the respondent, e.g. a claim sent on the 2nd of the month requires a response by the 30th which appears to be within 29 days of the date on which "he was sent a copy of the claim", rather than 28.

Presenting the response

4–057   What is said about claim forms in connection with the meaning of presentation, and methods and time of presentation therefore now seem to apply to responses. As with claim forms, a response is not presented unless it is actually received by the tribunal office.

Foreign Sovereign States

4–058   Section 12(2) of the State Immunity Act 1978 provides special rules for the entering of appearances by foreign sovereign states. The time for entering a response in such a case would only begin to run two months after the claim form was received at the Ministry of Foreign Affairs of the respondent state.

Para.(3)—"required information"—rejecting the response

4–059   As to the approach to this, see the commentary on rr.1 and 3 above.

Para.3(a)—"required information"—respondent's full name

—deceased respondents

4–060   In proceedings brought under the Trade Union and Labour Relations (Consolidation) Act 1992 (TULR(C)A), or the Employment Rights Act 1996 (ERA 1996), s.292(2) of the former and s.206(1) of the latter provide for proceedings to be defended by a deceased respondent's personal representative. The right to defend the claim almost certainly exists at common law independently of the statutory provisions and unquestionably does so in respect of the statutory torts of discrimination. However, unlike the position with deceased claimants, there is no provision in either Act for the tribunal to appoint a representative solely for the purpose of defending the claim in the absence of a legal personal representative. Where neither a personal representative nor an executor has been appointed or is likely to be appointed before the time for entering a response expires, the prudent course is to ask for the proceedings to be stayed to allow an appointment to be made. A stay has the double effect of stopping time running for the purposes of the 28 day time limit for responding to the claim and also for calculating the length of the conciliation period in short and standard track cases (see r.24, para.4–207), as well as avoiding any risk that by entering a response a person who is not the deceased's executor or personal representative will make themselves executor de son tort. In the event of reluctance (or unreasonable delay) on the part of the deceased's beneficiaries to make an appointment, the better course would be to join one or more of them personally as a respondent to the proceedings under r.10(2)(k) (see para.4–106).

Para.(4)—Applications for extension of time—when to be made

4–061   An application to extend the time for presenting the response must be made ". . . within 28 days . . ." which means before the end of the day on which the tribunal has informed the respondent that it must present its response by, or if that has been incorrectly calculated, the end of the day which is the last day by virtue of reg.15(2) (see para.3–060). The rule does not require that the application for an extension of time be granted within 28 days and so an application made by fax, email or in writing and hand delivered after office hours on the last day, would, subject to proof of time of delivery if required by the tribunal, be in time. Contrary to the position under all previous Rules of Procedure, subject expressly only to r.33, the time for presenting the response cannot be extended after it has expired. Rule 10(2) contains a list of examples of case management orders which may be made. Rule 10(2)(e) (see para.4–106) which is an order "extending any time limit, whether or not expired. . ." is expressed to be subject to r.4(4). Although both para.(4) and r.10(2)(e) are silent on the point, it would appear that any application for a second or subsequent extension of time must similarly be made before the expiration of the existing extension. There are two exceptions to the prohibition on post hoc extensions of time. If the tribunal issues a default judgment, r.33 requires the application for a review to include an application to extend time, this being the only express exception to para.(4). Although there is no scope for interpreting para.(4) read with r.10(2)(e) so as to allow late applications either on the grounds that the interests of justice require it or on any other ground, in *Moroak t/a Blake Envelopes v Cromie* [2005] I.R.L.R. 536; [2005] I.C.R. 1226, EAT, it was held that there is also an exception where an employment judge reviews a decision not to accept a response presented after the time limit had expired which, if granted, necessarily requires that time be extended after the event.

Granting applications for extension of time—principles to be applied

For the principles to be followed by an employment judge in exercising his or her discretion whether to extend time for entering a response see *Kwik Save Stores Ltd v Swain* [1997] I.C.R. 49, EAT which continues to be applicable under the new Rules of Procedure (*Moroak* at [30]). **4–062**

Para.(5)—Multiple claimants

Multiple claimants may use the same form if their claims arise out of the same set of facts. There is an added requirement in the case of respondents; that the grounds of resistance must be the same in each case. **4–063**

Para.(6)—Multiple respondents—discrimination claims

In discrimination claims where there is an individual respondent as well as the employer, separate responses will be required if the employing respondent is not accepting responsibility for the individual respondent's actions, even if this is only pleaded in the alternative. **4–064**

ACCEPTANCE OF RESPONSE PROCEDURE

What the tribunal does after receiving the response

5.—(1) On receiving the response the Secretary shall consider whether the response should be accepted in accordance with rule 6. If the response is not accepted it shall be returned to the respondent and (subject to paragraphs (5) and (6) of rule 6) the claim shall be dealt with as if no response to the claim had been presented. 4–065

(2) If the Secretary accepts the response he shall send a copy of it to all other parties and record in writing the date on which he does so.

Commencement

4–066   October 1, 2004 but subject to transitional provisions which may still be relevant to a small number of cases.

Transitional provisions

4–067   The rule applies to claims commenced before October 1, 2004 provided that a copy of the claim form was not sent to the respondent prior to that date; see reg.20(4) and (5), see para.3–075.

Para.(1)—Rejecting the response—informing the parties

4–068   When the form is returned to the respondent, a letter is sent to them explaining the reason for the rejection of the response and, if the reason was that it was not on the prescribed form, a copy of the prescribed form is also sent. The letter of rejection is not copied to the claimant and they are not sent a separate letter until the 28 day period has expired when they are informed that the respondent has failed to enter a response.

When the response will not be accepted by the Secretary

4–069   **6.—(1) Where a response is required to be presented using a prescribed form by rule 4(2), but the prescribed form has not been used, the Secretary shall not accept the response and shall return it to the respondent with an explanation of why the response has been rejected and provide a prescribed response form.**

(2) The Secretary shall not accept the response if it is clear to him that any of the following circumstances apply—

> **(a) the response does not include all the required information (defined in rule 4(3));**
>
> **(b) the response has not been presented within the relevant time limit.**

(3) If the Secretary decides not to accept a response for either of the reasons in paragraph (2), he shall refer the response together with a statement of his reasons for not accepting the response to a chairman. The chairman shall decide in accordance with the criteria in paragraph (2) whether the response should be accepted.

(4) If the chairman decides that the response should be accepted he shall inform the Secretary in writing and the Secretary shall accept the response and then deal with it in accordance with rule 5(2).

(5) If the chairman decides that the response should not be accepted he shall record his decision together with the reasons for it in writing in a document signed by him. The Secretary shall inform both the claimant and the respondent of that decision and the reasons for it. The Secretary shall also inform the respondent of the consequences for the respondent of that decision and how it may be reviewed or appealed.

(6) Any decision by a chairman not to accept a response may be reviewed in accordance with rules 34 to 36. If the result of such a

review is that the response should have been accepted, then the Secretary shall accept the response and proceed to deal with the response as described in rule 5(2).

Commencement

October 1, 2004 but subject to transitional provisions which may still be relevant to a small number of cases. **4–070**

Transitional provisions

The rule applies to claims commenced before October 1, 2004 provided that a copy of the claim form was not sent to the respondent prior to that date; see regs.20(4) and (5), see para.3–075. **4–071**

General

For the approach to the exercise of the powers under this rule, see the commentary to r.3, in particular at paras 4–037, 4–038 and 4–042. **4–072**

Consequences of rejection

Rule 9 applies automatically once a response is rejected and the 28 day period has expired. **4–073**

Paras (3), (4) and (5)—Out of time responses—employment judge's decision

An employment judge's decision not to accept a response presented out of time can be reviewed under r.34(3)(e) (para.4–247) on the grounds that the interests of justice require it (*Moroak t/a Blake Envelopes v Cromie* [2005] I.R.L.R. 536; [2005] I.C.R. 1226, EAT). For the principles to be followed by an employment judge in exercising her discretion whether to extend time for entering a response see *Kwik Save Stores Ltd v Swain* [1997] I.C.R. 49, EAT which continues to be applicable under the new Rules of Procedure (*Moroak* at [30]). In connection with an application to review a default judgment it was held in *Pendragon Plc t/a C D Bramall Ltd v Copus* [2005] I.C.R. 1671, EAT that although the reason for the delay must be considered, the absence of a good reason is not fatal, provided there is shown to be merit in the proposed response. The employment judge's discretion is a broad, just and equitable one. It would appear to be appropriate to apply this approach in this context too, as a failure to review the decision to reject the response would be likely to lead to a default judgment which could then be reviewed on the principles of *Copus*. **4–074**

When hearing an application to review a decision to reject a response submitted out of time, an Employment Judge was wrong to refuse the application where the respondent appeared to have a good, arguable defence but had deliberately misled the tribunal over the reasons for the late presentation of the response form for which in fact there was no legitimate excuse: *Compass Group UK and Ireland Ltd t/a/ Scolarest v Wilson* UKEAT/0203/07.

"Punishment clearly is not the purpose of these sanctions: see the observations of Chadwick LJ in *Hussein v Birmingham CC* [2005] EWCA Civ. 1570, CA at [36] dealing with similar provisiions in the CPR. As Chadwick LJ there pointed out ultimately all discretions should be exercised so as to achieve the overriding objective, which is to deal with cases justly. Moreover as the judgment of Mummery LJ in *Kwik Save* [1997] I.C.R. 49 shows, an important consideration will be the extent of any prejudice to the parties". *D and H Travel v Foster* [2006] I.C.R. 1537 at [62], per Elias P.

Para.(6)—Accepting the response—claimant's right to challenge

4–075   By providing only for a review of a decision not to accept the response, para.(6) seems to exclude by implication the right of the claimant to apply for a review of a decision to accept the response. However, r.18(7)(a) permits a claimant to apply for the response to be struck out on the grounds that the respondent is not entitled to contest the proceedings because one of the circumstances in para.(2) applied and therefore the response should not have been accepted.

Counterclaims

4–076

7.—(1) When a respondent wishes to present a claim against the claimant ("a counterclaim") in accordance with article 4 of the Employment Tribunals Extension of Jurisdiction (England and Wales) Order 1994 or as the case may be, article 4 of the Employment Tribunals Extension of Jurisdiction (Scotland) Order 1994, he must present the details of his counterclaim to the Employment Tribunal Office in writing. Those details must include—

(a) **the respondent's name;**

(b) **the respondent's address;**

(c) **the name of each claimant whom the counterclaim is made against;**

(d) **the claimant's address;**

(e) **details of the counterclaim.**

(2) A chairman may in relation to particular proceedings by order made under rule 10(1) establish the procedure which shall be followed by the respondent making the counterclaim and any claimant responding to the counterclaim.

(3) The President may by a practice direction made under regulation 13 make provision for the procedure which is to apply to counterclaims generally.

Commencement

4–077   October 1, 2004 but subject to transitional provisions which may still be relevant to a small number of cases.

Generally

4–078   There were no provisions corresponding to r.7 in the 2001 Rules of Procedure although counterclaims have been permitted since 1994. Rule 7 reflects the previous practice with regard to counterclaims. For the Employment Tribunals Extension of Jurisdiction (England and Wales) Order 1994 (SI 1994/1623) see Ch.13. The Employment Tribunals Extension of Jurisdiction (Scotland) Order is SI 1994/1624. For further comment on the effect of the Extension of Jurisdiction Order, see Ch.13 below.

Respondent who has not entered a response

4–079   There is nothing in r.7 which requires the respondent to have entered a response as a pre-condition for raising a counterclaim, and art.4 of the Orders refers to "a claim of an employer" not a counterclaim by a respondent. The right to bring a counterclaim is therefore not dependent on the employer's status as a respondent. Moreover, as a counterclaim is allocated its own case number and file (the tribunal continues to have jurisdiction to determine the counterclaim even if the claim is subsequently withdrawn), it appears to be fresh proceedings and not "the proceedings" in r.9(1) which a respondent who has not entered a response is barred from defending. Therefore, where a response which includes a counterclaim is rejected for whatever reason, the counterclaim is unaffected by the rejection and should be accepted, allocated a case number and served on the claimant.

Presenting a counterclaim

A counterclaim is not a claim for the purposes of rr.1–3 and is therefore not **4–080** required to be made on the prescribed form. There is no form prescribed for counterclaims and reg.14 (see para.3–054) does not give the Secretary of State power to prescribe one. The employment tribunals have a counterclaim form which is available on request.

Para.(1)(a) to (d)—Details of the counterclaim

The details which must be included in the counterclaim are not described as **4–081** required information, and therefore do not have the same status as the equivalent provisions in r.1(4), and the rule does not give the Secretary power not to accept a counterclaim where the information is not provided.

Para.(2)—Response to counterclaim

As the counterclaim is not a claim for the purposes of rr.1–3 the consequences **4–082** attendant upon the service of a claim do not arise in the absence of an order by the employment judge under r.10(1), thus the claimant is not required to enter a response to the counterclaim unless an employment judge so orders or a Practice Direction applies (see below). The response to a counterclaim can be in any form, including by letter. A failure to enter a response to the counterclaim, even if ordered, does not by itself debar the claimant from defending the counterclaim, and the default judgment procedure under r.8 does not apply. A claimant who has failed to comply with an order to respond to the counterclaim can only be debarred from defending the counterclaim as the result of an order made at a Hearing or pre-hearing review (r.13(1)), or the original requirement to enter the response was the subject of an "unless" order under r.13(2) (for r.13 see para.4–137).

Para.(3)—Practice Directions

The President (England and Wales) has not yet made any Practice Directions **4–083** under reg.13 in respect of counterclaims. The President (Scotland) made the following Practice Direction on February 14, 2007:

"(a) Where a respondent wishes to present a claim against the claimant ("a counter claim") in accordance with Article 4 of the Employment Tribunals (Extension of Jurisdiction) (Scotland) Order 1994 they should (if reasonably practicable) specify the amount claimed as part of the detail of the counter claim along with the other information provided for in regulation 7 of the Employment Tribunals (Rules of Procedure) Regulations 2004.
(b) When a claimant receives notice of a counter claim the claimant will indicate to the Tribunal Office if it is intended to resist the counter claim and the reasons for so resisting within a period of 28 days from the date on which he or she was sent a copy of the counter claim, unless an order of the Tribunal is granted extending that period."

CONSEQUENCES OF A RESPONSE NOT BEING PRESENTED OR ACCEPTED

Default judgments

4–084

8.—(1) In any proceedings if the relevant time limit for presenting a response has passed, a chairman may, in the circumstances listed in paragraph (2), issue a default judgment to determine the claim without a hearing if he considers it appropriate to do so.

(2) Those circumstances are when either—

(a) no response in those proceedings has been presented to the Employment Tribunal Office within the relevant time limit;

(b) a response has been so presented, but a decision has been made not to accept the response either by the Secretary under rule 6(1) or by a chairman under rule 6(3), and the Employment Tribunal Office has not received an application under rule 34 to have that decision reviewed; or

(c) a response has been accepted in those proceedings, but the respondent has stated in the response that he does not intend to resist the claim.

(3) A default judgment may determine liability only or it may determine liability and remedy. If a default judgment determines remedy it shall be such remedy as it appears to the chairman that the claimant is entitled to on the basis of the information before him.

(4) Any default judgment issued by a chairman under this rule shall be recorded in writing and shall be signed by him. The Secretary shall send a copy of that judgment to the parties, to ACAS, and, if the proceedings were referred to the tribunal by a court, to that court. The Secretary shall also inform the parties of their right to have the default judgment reviewed under rule 33. The Secretary shall put a copy of the default judgment on the Register (subject to rule 49 (sexual offences and the Register)).

(5) The claimant or respondent may apply to have the default judgment reviewed in accordance with rule 33.

(6) If the parties settle the proceedings (either by means of a compromise agreement (as defined in rule 23(2)) or through ACAS) before or on the date on which a default judgment in those proceedings is issued, the default judgment shall have no effect.

(7) When paragraph (6) applies, either party may apply under rule 33 to have the default judgment revoked.

Commencement

4–085
October 1, 2004 but subject to transitional provisions which may still be relevant to a small number of cases. Paragraph (2) was substituted for the words in the Regulations as originally laid before Parliament by the Employment Tribunals

(Constitution and Rules of Procedure) (Amendment) Regulations 2004 (SI 2004/2351) also with effect from October 1, 2004.

Transitional provisions

The rule applies to claims commenced before October 1, 2004 provided that a **4–086** copy of the claim form was not sent to the respondent prior to that date; see reg.20(4) and (5) at para.3–075. There was no power to issue judgment by default under the 2001 Rules of Procedure.

Generally

Unlike the corresponding provisions of the CPR, which provide for a default **4–087** judgment to be issued by a purely administrative process, a default judgment can only be issued in the employment tribunal as the result of a judicial decision. That decision is made on the employment judge's own initiative and without seeking the views of either party. There is no provision in the rules to allow a claimant to apply for a default judgment, although if it appeared that the respondent's failure to enter a response had been overlooked by the tribunal there could be no objection in principle to such an application. As the claimant would be seeking a judgment rather than an order, r.11 would not apply to the application but it would nonetheless be prudent for the application to explain why a default judgment was desirable. The application need not be copied to the respondent by the claimant as a respondent who has not entered a response is not a party to the proceedings (r.9). However, the tribunal will copy the application to the respondent in the same way as other routine correspondence.

"relevant time limit" means either the original time limit of 28 days prescribed by r.4(1) or any extension of that time granted by an employment judge.

Employment judge's discretion

The exercise of judicial discretion inevitably involves a balancing of the compet- **4–088** ing injustices which would arise from either making or withholding a decision. Merely because the respondent is not a party to the proceedings by virtue of its own default, does not entitle the employment judge to discount its interests. The amendment of r.9(b) by the Employment Tribunals (Constitution and Rules of Procedure) (Amendment) Regulations 2004 (SI 2004/2351), which added the requirements of the interests of justice (r.34(3)(e) see para.4–247) to the grounds on which a respondent who has not entered a response can apply for the review of a judgment other than a default judgment, largely eliminates the perceived tactical advantage previously said to be gained by claimants who objected to a default judgment being issued. However, r.34(3)(e) is still potentially narrower in its scope than r.33 (Review of Default Judgments) (see para.4–247), which imposes no restrictions on the grounds on which a decision can be reviewed, and accordingly an employment judge should carefully consider the consequences of a decision not to issue a default judgment given the impact of r.9 on the respondent's right to participate further in the proceedings (*NSM Music Ltd v Leefe* [2006] I.C.R. 450, EAT). A decision not to issue a default judgment is not reviewable under r.34 (see r.34(1)), nor can the employment judge be required to give reasons for not issuing a default judgment as neither r.30(1)(a) or (b) apply (see para.4–233).

When not "appropriate"

Paragraph (1) clearly contemplates the possibility that a default judgment will **4–089** not be issued as the result of the exercise of the employment judge's discretion, but gives no guidance as to the circumstances in which that might be appropriate. Some parallels can be drawn with CPR rr.12.9 and 12.10, which suggest that an employment judge should not issue a default judgment in the following circumstances without either taking the action identified or seeking further information or clarification from the claimant either by way of letter or a Case Management Discussion:

- if there is doubt as to the correct identity of the respondent, in particular whether the named respondent is a legal entity, (e.g. the name given on the claim form is only a trading name), or may not have been the claimant's employer, (e.g. the claimant has named their manager as the respondent to an unfair dismissal claim rather than the company which employed them);
- where the claim form has been returned by Royal Mail undelivered (thus rebutting the presumption of receipt in r.61(2) (para.4–357)) unless either the reason for the non-delivery is that the claimant has refused to accept it or, the respondent is a limited company and the claim was sent to its registered office (Companies Act 1985, s.725(1));
- where the respondent is a limited company and the address to which the claim form was sent is not the registered office (Companies Act 1985, s.725(1));
- if there appears to be a jurisdictional issue such as the claim being out of time or non-compliance with the statutory grievance procedure (see para.10–031). The case should be listed for pre-hearing review under r.18(7)(a) (see para.4–169). However a default judgment should not be withheld only because the claim appears to be weak or lacks particulars;
- if the claimant has notified the tribunal that they object to a default judgment being issued. The original wording of para.(2) prescribed as one of the circumstances in which a default judgment could be issued that the claimant had not informed the tribunal in writing that he did not wish a default judgment to be issued. As this provision no longer appears in the rule, such an objection can now only be a factor which the employment judge should take into account, but if sufficient reason is provided it would seem to be wrong in principle to override the objection. The claim should be listed for Hearing (see r.26 at para.4–213);
- where the respondent is the Crown (CPR r.12.4(4)) or a foreign sovereign state (State Immunity Act 1978, s.12(4)) unless the employment judge is satisfied that the proceedings have been properly served;
- granting reinstatement or re-engagement as a remedy (by analogy with CPR r.12.4(2)(a)). The default judgment should be for liability only with the remedy listed for hearing before a full tribunal;
- for costs or preparation time with or without another remedy, even if the tests of rr.40 or 44 appear to be satisfied (see paras 4–277 and 4–296). See *Sutton v The Ranch Ltd* [2006] I.C.R. 1179, EAT and the commentary to r.9 "Taking part in proceedings—costs and preparation time";
- where the respondent is or may be a diplomatic agent who enjoys diplomatic immunity (CRP r.12.10(b)(iii) and (iv)); and
- where a respondent who has entered a response might be vicariously or jointly liable for any award made against the respondent in default. The respondent who has entered the response would appear to have no standing in the proceedings against the respondent in default, and could therefore neither apply for a default judgment against that respondent to be set aside nor be heard on the question of remedy against them. The automatic barring provisions of r.9 which operate whether or not a default judgment is issued, would normally be sufficient in such a case.

Para.(2)—Circumstances in which default judgment may be issued

4–090   The employment judge does not require to be satisfied that the claim form was received by the respondent as this is deemed to have occurred "unless the contrary is proved" by r.61(2).

Subparagraph (b) must be read as including at the end the words "and the time for entering a response has expired" (see para.(1)).

Subparagraph (c) would permit a default judgment to be issued on liability only if, for example, the only dispute was about length of service or rate of pay. There is no power to enter a default judgment if the response appears to have no reasonable prospect of success or even if it is scandalous or vexatious. In such circumstances the claimant should apply for a pre-hearing review to consider whether the response should be struck out under r.18(7)(b) which, if successful, would allow a default judgment to be entered.

Para.(3)—Effect on conciliation period

Where the default judgment deals with both liability and remedy, the conciliation **4–091** period ends on the date of the default judgment (r.23(1)(a)). Where the default judgment deals only with remedy the conciliation period ends on the date which is 14 days after the date of the default judgment (r.23(1)(b)). For r.23 see para.4–205.

Para.(3)—Remedy

If the claimant is seeking a non-monetary remedy such as reinstatement, the **4–092** default judgment should be confined to liability with the remedy listed for Hearing before a full tribunal. Despite the wording of the rule, an employment judge is entitled to seek clarification from the claimant about the amount being claimed before issuing a default judgment: "the information before him" does not mean "on the face of the claim form".

Paras (6) and (7)—Settlement prior to default judgment

The reference to r.23(2) appears to be wrong. The reference should be to **4–093** r.23(1)(f).

For compromise agreements generally see the Employment Rights Act 1996, s.203.

For the ACAS Arbitration Scheme see the ACAS Arbitration Scheme (Great Britain) Order 2004 (SI 2004/753).

For r.33 see para.4–244. The default judgment must be revoked in these circumstances: r.33(5).

Taking no further part in the proceedings

9. A respondent who has not presented a response to a claim or **4–094**
whose response has not been accepted shall not be entitled to take
any part in the proceedings except to—

(a) **make an application under rule 33 (review of default judgments);**

(b) **make an application under rule 35 (preliminary consideration of application for review) in respect of rule 34(3)(a), (b) or (e);**

(c) **be called as a witness by another person; or**

(d) **be sent a copy of a document or corrected entry in accordance with rule 8(4), 29(2) or 37;**

and in these rules the word "party" or "respondent" includes a respondent only in relation to his entitlement to take such a part in the proceedings, and in relation to any such part which he takes.

Commencement

4–095   October 1, 2004 but subject to transitional provisions which may still be relevant to a small number of cases. In para.(b) the words "or (e)" were first added by reg.2(9)(b) of the Employment Tribunals (Constitution and Rules of Procedure) (Amendment) Regulations 2004 (SI 2004/2351) with effect also from October 1, 2004, but the amendment contained a typographical error (the omission of "(3)") which was corrected by reg.2(4)(a) of the Employment Tribunals (Constitution and Rules of Procedure) (Amendment) (No. 2) Regulations 2005 (SI 2005/1865). There is no reason however to suppose that the first amendment was ineffective.

"Respondent who has not presented a response"

4–096   The restrictions imposed by r.9 only apply after the time for entering a response has expired. Until the time for entering a response has expired, whether it be the original 28 day period or any extension thereof, the respondent is therefore a "party" and is able to participate in the proceedings to any extent necessary.

Challenging the effect of the rule

—applications for review

4–097   The rule is automatic in its effect and does not require or envisage the making of a decision by an employment judge. Any purported attempt to review the application of the rule and to vary its consequences is therefore of no effect (*Butlins Skyline Ltd (1) Smith (2) v Beynon* [2007] I.C.R. 121, EAT (note) (unopposed appeal)).

—appeals

4–098   The respondent is only debarred from participating in the employment tribunal proceedings, not from appealing or responding to an appeal to the Employment Appeal Tribunal (*Atos Origin IT Services UK Ltd v Haddock* [2005] I.R.L.R. 20; [2005] ICR 277, EAT).

—respondent attending the hearing

4–099   In *Tull v Severin* [1998] I.C.R. 1037, EAT, a respondent who had failed to enter an appearance [response] attended the hearing but the employment judge declined to allow them to take part. On appeal, it was held that the respondent's attendance at the hearing amounted to an application for an extension of time for entering a response and called for the employment judge of her own motion to consider extending the time limit, and exercising her discretion in accordance with the principles in *Kwik Save Stores Ltd v Swain* [1997] I.C.R. 49, EAT, to allow a late application. In view of r.4(4) (application for an extension of time to enter a response can only be made before the time limit expires), this approach is no longer possible, but the decision in *Tull* does suggest that if a respondent who has not entered a response appears at a hearing, whether it be a default judgment remedy hearing or a full hearing where a default judgment has not been issued, and seeks to be heard, the employment judge should consider whether they are or should be, seeking permission to apply to have the default judgment set aside, adjourn the hearing to allow them to comply with the requirements of r.33(2) and extend the time limit imposed by r.33(1) to enable them to do so. However, the employment judge has no power to entertain and in consequence, to dismiss, an application to set aside a default judgment made orally at a hearing (*B.S.M. v Fowler* UK/ EAT/0059/06).

For r.33 see para.4–244.

—counterclaims

4–100   For the ability of a respondent who is barred from defending the claim to bring a counterclaim, see the commentary to r.7(1) at para.4–079.

Taking part in the proceedings

The rule does not, in fact, exhaustively define the extent to which a respondent **4–101** who has not entered a response may or may not take part in the proceedings.

—costs and preparation time

A costs order may be made both in favour of and against a respondent who has **4–102** not had a response accepted (r.38(4) see para.4–266), but a preparation time order can only be made against such a respondent (r.42(4) see para.4–291). In *Sutton v The Ranch Ltd* [2006] I.C.R. 1170, EAT it was held, in the case of a respondent who had taken no part in the proceedings at all, that costs could only be awarded against a respondent who had not presented a response if the respondent had taken one or more of the steps permitted by r.9. The power to award costs must also arise when a respondent takes one of the steps previously expressly permitted by r.3(3)(a) and (b) of the 2001 Rules of Procedure and now, as discussed above (see para.4–069), by implication r.9, as well as any other step of a similar nature actually taken by the respondent. The same reasoning supports the view that a wasted costs order (r.48) can only be made in favour of a respondent or against their representative if the respondent was a "party" at the material time.

—request for reasons

A request for reasons for a judgment or order falls within r.9(b), if the reason for **4–103** the request is expressly stated to be with a view to making an application for a review under r.35. A request for reasons with a view to appealing does not fall within the exception in r.9 but reasons can be required by EAT at any time (r.30(3)(b)). A request for reasons which does not explain why they are required also does not come within the exceptions in r.9 (*NSM Music Ltd v Leefe* [2006] I.C.R. 450, EAT).

—composition of the tribunal

A respondent who has not entered a response is not a party whose consent is **4–104** required under reg.9(3) to a tribunal comprising an employment judge and one lay member (*Comber v Harmony Inns Ltd* [1993] I.C.R. 15, EAT) nor, presumably, to an employment judge sitting alone under s.4(3)(a) of the Employment Tribunals Act 1996.

Remedy hearings

A respondent who has unsuccessfully applied for a default judgment to be set **4–105** aside on review under r.33 may be permitted to participate in a subsequent remedy hearing. The employment judge's decision to reject the application for review under r.33 necessarily includes the rejection of an application to extend time for the presentation of a response. As there has been no default judgment in respect of the remedy, a respondent who wishes to be heard on the question of remedy should apply under r.34 for a review of the notional decision not to extend time for entering a response (*D & H Travel Ltd (1) Anderson (2) v Foster* [2006] I.C.R. 1537, EAT). In the absence of this "tortuous and highly artificial route" [55], there would be a real question whether r.9 might be incompatible with art.6(1) ECHR [63].

CASE MANAGEMENT

General power to manage proceedings

10.—(1) Subject to the following rules, the chairman may at any **4–106** **time either on the application of a party or on his own initiative make an order in relation to any matter which appears to him to be**

appropriate. Such orders may be any of those listed in paragraph (2) or such other orders as he thinks fit. Subject to the following rules, orders may be issued as a result of a chairman considering the papers before him in the absence of the parties, or at a hearing (see regulation 2 for the definition of "hearing").

(2) Examples of orders which may be made under paragraph (1) are orders—

(a) as to the manner in which the proceedings are to be conducted, including any time limit to be observed;

(b) that a party provide additional information;

(c) requiring the attendance of any person in Great Britain either to give evidence or to produce documents or information;

(d) requiring any person in Great Britain to disclose documents or information to a party to allow a party to inspect such material as might be ordered by a County Court (or in Scotland, by a sheriff);

(e) extending any time limit, whether or not expired (subject to rules 4(4), 11(2), 25(5), 30(5), 33(1), 35(1), 38(7) and 42(5) of this Schedule, and to rule 3(4) of Schedule 2);

(f) requiring the provision of written answers to questions put by the tribunal or chairman;

(g) that, subject to rule 22(8), a short conciliation period be extended into a standard conciliation period;

(h) staying (in Scotland, sisting) the whole or part of any proceedings;

(i) that part of the proceedings be dealt with separately;

(j) that different claims be considered together;

(k) that any person who the chairman or tribunal considers may be liable for the remedy claimed should be made a respondent in the proceedings;

(l) dismissing the claim against a respondent who is no longer directly interested in the claim;

(m) postponing or adjourning any hearing;

(n) varying or revoking other orders;

(o) giving notice to the parties of a pre-hearing review or the Hearing;

(p) giving notice under rule 19;

(q) giving leave to amend a claim or response;

(r) that any person who the chairman or tribunal considers has an interest in the outcome of the proceedings may be joined as a party to the proceedings;

(s) that a witness statement be prepared or exchanged; or

(t) as to the use of experts or interpreters in the proceedings.

(3) An order may specify the time at or within which and the place at which any act is required to be done. An order may also impose conditions and it shall inform the parties of the potential consequences of non-compliance set out in rule 13.

(4) When a requirement has been imposed under paragraph (1) the person subject to the requirement may make an application under rule 11 (applications in proceedings) for the order to be varied or revoked.

(5) An order described in [either] paragraph (2)(d) which requires a person other than a party to grant disclosure or inspection of material may be made only when the disclosure sought is necessary in order to dispose fairly of the claim or to save expense.

(6) Any order containing a requirement described in either sub-paragraph (2)(c) or (d) shall state that under section 7(4) of the Employment Tribunals Act, any person who without reasonable excuse fails to comply with the requirement shall be liable on summary conviction to a fine, and the document shall also state the amount of the maximum fine.

(7) An order as described in paragraph (2)(j) may be made only if all relevant parties have been given notice that such an order may be made and they have been given the opportunity to make oral or written representations as to why such an order should or should not be made.

(8) Any order made under this rule shall be recorded in writing and signed by the chairman and the Secretary shall inform all parties to the proceedings of any order made as soon as is reasonably practicable.

Rule 10(1) and (4)—General power to manage proceedings

Rule 4 in the 2001 Rules (Case management) gave the employment tribunal a **4–107** general power to give such directions on any matter arising in connection with the proceedings. Rule 10 develops that, by in particular listing a number of the particular powers in relation to case management that can be exercised. The list contains a non-exhaustive list of twenty examples. Rule 10 has to be read in conjunction with: (a) r.17(2) which states that an employment judge may deal at a case management discussion with any of the matters listed at r.10(12); and (b) r.11 which enables the parties to apply for an order to be issued (under but not limited to r.10), varied, or revoked, or to apply for a case management discussion. Under r.10 the employment judge can act on his own initiative or in response to an application (under r.11). He can make an order in relation to any matter which seems to him appropriate. An order can relate to any of the matters listed in r.10(2) or such other orders as he thinks fit. Orders can be made on paper in the absence of the parties, subject to rr.10(7), 12(2), or 18(7) (see the commentary on r.10(7)), or at a hearing conducted in accordance with r.14(4) (see the commentary at para.4–154). In acting on his own initiative or in responding to an application from the parties, the employment judge must have regard to the overriding objective and in particular reg.3(3) (see the commentary at paras 3–014 to 3–024). Once a full tribunal has been convened the employment judge may not take case management decisions in the course of the proceedings independently of the members, if those decisions are taken during the course of the actual Hearing (*Magenta Security Services v Wilkinson*, EAT 0385/06). This does not prevent the employment judge making orders for example between a Hearing on liability and a further Hearing to determine remedy. Because it is implicit in r.10 that the employment judge can and will act on his own initiative, without having the observations on any proposed order being considered r.10(4) specifically provides that a party or any other person on whom a requirement has been imposed, may apply, under r.11, for the order to be varied or revoked (see the commentary at paras 4–247 to 4–255 on the difference between reviewing an order under r.34 and revisiting an order under these provisions, and the relevant authorities).

Rule 10(2)—Examples of orders

4–108   The list is extensive but not exclusive and the employment judge may issue orders in relation to any aspect of the proceedings in accordance with the overriding objective and subject to the rules.

Rule 10(2)(a)—Orders as to the manner in which the proceedings are to be conducted

4–109   This gives the employment judge an overall power to manage the proceedings. It is neither as extensive nor as prescriptive as CPR r. 1.4. (the court's duty to manage cases). Nevertheless an employment judge can have regard to CPR r.1.4, both in its general statement of the overriding objective under the CPR to manage cases, and more specifically, in relation to the specific examples of active case management listed at CPR r.1.4(2). Similarly the employment judge issuing orders either on paper when the respondent has served a response, or at a hearing, or case management discussion could have regard to the following examples of what amounts to active case management under the CPR r.1.4(2):

(i)   Encouraging the parties to co-operate with each other in the conduct of the proceedings (CPR r.1.4(2)(a) and reg.3(4));
(ii)   identifying the issues at an early stage (CPR r.1.4(2)(b));
(iii) fixing timetables or otherwise controlling the progress of the case (CPR r.1.4(2)(g));
(iv)   considering whether the likely benefits of taking a particular step justify the cost of taking it (CPR r.1.4(2)(h) and reg.3(2)(b));
(v)   dealing with as many aspects of the case as it can on the same occasion (CPR r.1.4(2)(i));
(vi)   dealing with the case without the parties needing to attend court (CPR r.1.4(2)(j);
(vii) making use of technology (CPR r.1.4(2)(k)).

The second part of the Rule enables the employment judge to impose time limits. It has to be read with r.10(2)(e), which enables the employment judge generally to extend time limits, with the exception of those listed in the sub-paragraph and including any time limits set under the powers in this Rule.

Rule 10(2)(b)—Orders for the provision of information

4–110   Previous rules referred to the provision of further and better particulars of the claim or response. The revised requirements of the rules and the new claim and response forms have eliminated some of the necessity for the provision of further information by a party. An order under this rule should only be made if it is necessary for the just disposal of the proceedings in line with the overriding objective. Orders should be made where they would serve to clarify the issues in a claim, and where they are necessary to provide reasonable details of complaints and allegations that are to be pursued at a hearing (see *White v University of Manchester* [1976] I.C.R. 419, and *International Computers Ltd v Whitley* [1978] I.R.L.R. 318), but an order should not be made if it would be oppressive (*Byrne v Financial Times* [1991] I.R.L.R. 417). The provisions of CPR r.18 are also instructive. CPR r.18.1 enables the court to order a party to: (a) clarify any matter which is in dispute; or (b) give additional information in relation to any such matter. Further clarification is given in CPR PD 18 and the following features of the practice direction are likely to be applied by the tribunal: (a) the party seeking information should first make a written request for the information within a specified timescale; and (b) the request should be concise and strictly confined to matters which are reasonably necessary and proportionate to enable the party to know and respond to the case.

Rule 10(2)(c) and (6)—Witness orders

The tribunal may compel the attendance of a witness either to give evidence, or **4–111** produce documents or information. A tribunal will only grant an application for a witness order if satisfied that the witness is likely to give relevant evidence, that the witness will only attend if compelled to do so, and that other methods of introducing the evidence have been considered (see *Wilcox v Humphreys and Glasgow Ltd* [1976] I.C.R. 306, and *Eagle Star v Hayward* [1981] I.C.R. 860). The discretion to make such an order will usually only be reviewed by the EAT on the basis of error of law, or Wednesbury unreasonableness (see *Noorani v Merseyside TEC Ltd* [1999] I.R.L.R. 184).

The requirement in r.11(4) where the party making the application is legally represented, to provide the necessary information under r.11(4)(a) to (c), does not apply to applications for witness orders under r.10(2)(c), so the previous practice of not alerting the other party to the fact that the application has been made is maintained. The Rule does not clarify what is to happen if the application is made by a party who is not legally represented. In that case, r.11(5) obliges the tribunal Secretary to notify the other party of the required information under r.11(4). Logically r.11(5) for these purposes should be read subject to the exclusion in r.11(4), in respect of applications for witness orders. Otherwise, there is no comparability of treatment of represented or unrepresented parties, but the wording of r.11(5) does not make that clear. If, however, the construction of r.11(4) is read on the basis that an application for a witness order prevents r.11 from ever applying, the problem disappears. The effect of r.11(5) is to make what, under r.11(4) is the obligation of the party or its representative become the responsibility of the Secretary. As, however, the requirements of r.11(4) can never apply in respect of applications for witness orders, the implied pre-condition of there being an application for a witness order is satisfied in both instances, so that in neither case is there any obligation to comply with r.11(4).

There are provisions in the CPR dealing with witnesses and witness orders (CPR r.34), but the situations are not sufficiently analogous in the two jurisdictions to indicate that any assistance may be derived from the CPR.

It is the responsibility of the person securing the order to serve it on the witness and make arrangements for their attendance. Rule 10(6) then provides that the order must notify the person on whom the witness order is served that if they fail to attend, they are liable to a fine on conviction and the specified maximum amount of that fine (currently £1,000), pursuant to the provisions of s.7(4) of the Employment Tribunals Act 1996 (see para.2–015). Rule 11 permits the person on whom the witness order is served to apply for it to be revoked, usually on the basis that they are not in a position to provide relevant evidence.

Rule 10(2)(d) and (6)—Disclosure of documents or information

4–112   Under r.4 of the 2001 Rules the position in relation to disclosure of documents was more specific. It provided:

> "A tribunal may, on the application of a party or of its own motion . . . (b) require one party to grant to another such disclosure or inspection (including the taking of copies) of documents as might be granted by a court under rule 31 of the Civil Procedure Rules 1998(a)."

Despite the change to the wording, and in particular the absence of any reference to CPR r.31 in r.10, it is clear that the effect of this Rule is to apply to the Rules on disclosure the provisions of CPR r.31, and in particular CPR r.31.5 which limits the duty of disclosure to standard disclosure, which is by virtue of CPR r.31.6 disclosure of the following:

    (a) the documents on which the party intends to rely;
    (b) the documents which adversely affect his own case;
    (c) the documents which adversely affect another party's case; or
    (d) any documents which support another party's case.

A party is further obliged by CPR r.31.7 to make a reasonable search for documents falling within r.31.6. Factors relevant to deciding the reasonableness of the search include:

    (a) the number of documents involved;
    (b) the nature and complexity of the proceedings;
    (c) the ease and expense of retrieval; and
    (d) the significance of any document which is likely to be located during the search.

CPR r.31.8 further refines the duty of disclosure to documents in the control of the party in question, which for these purposes are documents:

    (a) in or previously in the party's possession;
    (b) where the party had a right to possession; or
    (c) where the party had a right to inspection or to take copies.

The procedure for disclosure is laid out in CPR r.31.10, and it is important to stress that the obligation is a continuing obligation until the conclusion of the litigation. (CPR r.31.11).

It also incorporates CPR r.31.12 which enables the tribunal, subject where appropriate to r.11(3), to make an order for specific disclosure, that is of a particular document or class of documents.

Rule 10(2)(d) and (5)—Disclosure by non-parties—"requiring any person"

4–113   Most importantly, the wording of the Rule, which extends to any person in Great Britain, not just the parties, enables the tribunal to utilise CPR r.31.17 and order disclosure of documents in the possession of third parties. Rule 10(5) limits the power of the tribunal to order disclosure by a third party to disclosure which is "necessary in order to dispose fairly of the claim or to save expense". An application for such an order must comply with both r.11, and the requirements of CPR r.31.17. The application must be supported by evidence, and the tribunal can only make an order under r.11 if the documents are likely to support the case of the claimant or adversely affect the case of any other party to the claim, and disclosure is necessary to dispose fairly of the claim or to save costs.

The EAT has ruled that while CPR r.31 is clearly applicable in the employment tribunal by virtue of r.10(2)(d), it was not persuaded that the Practice Direction was necessarily binding on the tribunal. Nonetheless the principle in the Practice Direction that it is preferable to adopt a step by step approach to disclosure did apply (*South Tyneside District Council v Anderson* UKEAT/0002/05).

A power to order disclosure of a document includes a power to order disclosure initially to the tribunal, before disclosure to the other party of a document to enable the tribunal to determine after examination whether to order disclosure with redaction of part of the document (e.g., to prevent the revelation of a person's identity). In the case in question, the proper course for the tribunal to have adopted would have been to disclose to the tribunal the original unamended documents (in that case witness statements obtained in the employer's investigation), to consider the respondents' suggestions for redaction, to enable the tribunal to decide the best way to proceed. The tribunal should then suggest its own redactions subject to a further opportunity for the respondents to comment (*Asda Stores Ltd v Thompson* [2004] I.R.L.R. 598; applying *Science Research Council v Nasse* [1979] I.C.R. 921; [1979] I.R.L.R. 465, HL).

The claimant alleging unfair selection for redundancy is not generally entitled to disclosure of the assessment forms (as opposed to the overall score sheets of all employees) of those not selected for redundancy: the claimant is not entitled to say the selection was unfair, I cannot indicate why, but I need to see the assessments to say why, as that would be to invite the tribunal to do its own scoring and selection. Where the employer was carrying out large scale redundancies, it would only be in rare and exceptional cases that the assessments of other employees would be relevant (*British Aerospace v Green* [1995] I.R.L.R. 433; [1995] I.C.R. 1006, CA). The EAT has expressed a different view (which is inconsistent with Green) that unless the tribunal and therefore the claimant sees the other assessments it cannot tell whether the employer's assertion that the process was carried out and applied fairly is correct (*FDR Ltd v Holloway* [1995] I.R.L.R. 400). The Court of Session has indicated that the two judgments are inconsistent, and that tribunals should follow the Court of Appeal in Green (In *King v Eaton Ltd* [1996] I.R.L.R. 199). Arguably, there is no inconsistency if the issue is in fact the way in which the assessment was applied supported by a specific allegation, rather than the general request in *Green* to see if there was evidence that the assessments were unfairly made or applied.

As far as confidential documents are concerned, the correct approach for the tribunal to adopt when dealing with the issue of the disclosure of a document claimed to be confidential is to weigh up the conflicting interests of the parties, and to decide whether disclosure is necessary for a fair trial of the action. The EAT will usually be reluctant to interfere with case management decisions within the scope of an employment judge's discretionary powers (*National Probation Service (Teesside) v Devon* UKEAT/0419). In determining whether the contents of a statement given in confidence to the employer during an investigation should be disclosed, that confidentiality is only one factor to be taken into account. Relevance was also important, but the compelling consideration for the tribunal is whether disclosure is necessary for the fair disposal of the proceedings. (*Arqiva Ltd v Sagoo* UKEAT 0135/07)

A party seeking to withhold documents on the basis that they were written "without prejudice" in an attempt to resolve potential litigation must demonstrate that they came into existence as a genuine attempt to resolve an extant grievance. The fact that a person had invoked a grievance procedure, and by implication the statutory grievance procedure, did not of itself attach to the material in question the benefit of the "without prejudice" rule. (*BNP Paribas v Mezzotero* [2004] I.R.L.R. 508). There, the claimant had raised allegations of discrimination, and reference was made to the "public interest in ensuring that issues in such cases are fully explored", but the principles ought to be equally applicable to all cases.

In *Brunel University v Webster & Vaseghi* ([2007] I.R.L.R. 592 CA), and again in *Framlington Group Ltd v Barnetson* ([2007] I.R.L.R. 598) the Court of Appeal has examined the parameters of the "without prejudice" rule, and without expressly overruling the judgment in *BNP Paribas v Mezzotero* has cast some doubt on its continuing validity. The first case involved the publication by the employer of a document asserting that the employees had demanded unreasonable amounts of compensation in an ongoing discrimination claim. The employees claimed victimisation, asserting they had been subjected to a detriment (i.e. effectively ridiculed), because they had brought a discrimination claim in good faith. The employer sought to argue that the employees could not rely on the without prejudice communications to progress their victimisation claims. The Court of Appeal held:

- where both parties referred to "without prejudice" communications in the ET1 and ET3, that was sufficient to waive privilege (at 41);
- where an employer sets up an impartial enquiry involving a fact-finding exercise as to what happened during a "without prejudice" meeting, that will also amount to a waiver of privilege (note: the facts were quite unusual—(at 25);
- the Court of Appeal declined to comment on the correctness of the controversial decision in *BNP Paribas v Mezzotero*, save to comment that (at [32]):
  - ○ it might sometimes be difficult to prove victimisation if employees are never allowed to rely on "without prejudice" communications; and
  - ○ the *BNP Paribas v Mezzotero* exception to the sanctity of "without prejudice" communications should only arise if one of the parties has made it clear at an appropriate stage that it seeks to exclude any reference to "without prejudice" discussions

In *Framlington* the Court reaffirmed that there has to be a "dispute" between the parties for the rule to be engaged, but that there is a dispute where it can reasonably be inferred that the parties contemplated or could reasonably have been expected to have contemplated litigation if the dispute could not have been resolved.

Where a party alleges that disclosure of information or a document might potentially involve the respondent being compelled to disclose a document, that would be inadmissible by reason of the prohibitions at s.18 of the Regulation of Investigatory Powers Act 2000 , the tribunal should not make orders for disclosure at the interim stage but leave it to the tribunal determining the substantive claim to deal with the situation if and when it arises in the course of evidence (*Barracks v Commissioner of Police for the Metropolis* [2006] EWCA Civ. 1041,CA).

Legal professional privilege which attaches to communications between a party and his professional advisers does not extend to other types of representatives such as trade unions or claims handling consultants (*New Victoria Hospital v Ryan* [1993] I.C.R. 201; [1993] I.R.L.R. 202).

Disclosure and public interest immunity

4–114   Where the Crown is the respondent and claims public interest immunity from disclosure, there are a number of principles to be applied: the party seeking disclosure must satisfy the tribunal that the documents were likely to give substantial support to his contentions in respect of an issue in the case (*Air Canada v Secretary of State for Trade and Industry* [1983] 2 W.L.R. 494); that hurdle must be overcome before the court or tribunal looks at the disputed documents (*Air Canada*); the power to inspect should be used with extreme care and not until the respondent has had an opportunity to appeal (*Halford v Sharples* [1992] I.C.R. 146). Thereafter, any claim of public interest immunity will fall to be considered in accordance with the relevant general principles, see *R v Chief Constable of West Midlands ex parte Wiley* [1995] 1 A.C. 274, and *R v H* [2004] 2 A.C. 134.

Rule 10(2)(e)—power to extend time

This rule retains the tribunal's overall power to extend any time limit to perform **4–115** any action under the rules subject to the following exceptions and qualifications in specific rules:

(i) the tribunal has a power (under r.11) to extend the time for serving a response under r.4(4), but only if the respondent applies for an extension of time within the period of 28 days from service of the claim. Rule 10(2)(e) gives the tribunal no power to extend that period of 28 days for making that application, and the power to extend the time limit for compliance is subject to that application being made within the 28 day period (see para.4–061). There is nothing in the rules to prevent a subsequent application to extend time as long as it is made before the expiry of the 28 days;

(ii) under r.11(2), any application for an order must be made no less than ten days before the hearing at which the application is to be made, subject to the tribunal's power to abridge that ten day period if in the interests of justice (see para.4–131);

(iii) an application by a respondent to have a withdrawn claim dismissed (under r.25) must be made within 28 days of notice of withdrawal, but r.25(5) permits an employment judge to extend that 28 day period if it is just and equitable to do so (see para.4–209);

(iv) a request for written reasons under r.30(5) must be made within 28 days of the date that the judgment was sent to the parties, subject to the power of the employment judge under r.30(5) to extend that period if it is just and equitable to do so (see para.4–233);

(v) a party wishing to set aside a default judgment under r.33(1) must apply within 14 days of the date that the judgment was sent to the parties, subject to the power of the employment judge under r.33(1) to extend that period if it is just and equitable to do so;

(vi) a party applying to review a decision under r.34 must make that application within 14 days of the date that the judgment was sent to the parties, subject to the power of the employment judge under r.35(1) to extend that period if it is just and equitable to do so;

(vii) an application for a costs order under r.38(7) must be made no later than 28 days of the date the judgment determining the claim was issued, subject to the power of the employment judge under r.38(7) to extend that period if it is just and equitable to do so;

(viii) an application for a preparation time order under r.42(5) must be made no later than 28 days of the date the judgment determining the claim was issued, subject to the power of the employment judge under r.38(7) to extend that period if it is just and equitable to do so; and

(ix) Rule 3(4) of Sch.2 permits the employment judge to extend time limits for responding to a claim where it is just and equitable to do so (see para.4–364).

Rule 10(2)(f)—Requiring the provision of written answers to questions

4–116   The precise parameters of this rule are unclear. It will not for example permit the employment judge or tribunal to order a party to provide answers to questions designed to elicit information that constitutes required information under either r.1(4) or r.4(3). It will enable the employment judge to order a party to answer questions rather than to supply information under r.10(2)(b). Arguably, the tribunal should first consider whether such an order will be consistent with the overriding objective and secondly ought to have regard to the same considerations as are applicable to orders for the provision of further information (see the commentary on r.10(2)(b)).

Rule 10(2)(g)—Power to extend conciliation periods

4–117   The regime of statutory conciliation was profoundly altered by the 2004 Regulations, and commentary on the new fixed and standard period is dealt with under r.22. This provision enables the tribunal employment judge to extend a short to a standard conciliation period. He can only do so if the conditions in r.22(8) are satisfied:

(a) the short period must not have ended;

(b) the employment judge must consider that a standard conciliation period would be more appropriate based on the complexity of the proceedings; and

(c) the employment judge must make an order notifying the parties and ACAS.

Rule 10(2)(h)—Staying or sisting proceedings

4–118   The most common reasons for wishing to stay proceedings (in effect putting them on hold and not making case management orders or listing the claim for hearing) are:

(i) The respondent is involved in insolvency proceedings where the consent of the court is required for the claim to proceed (if the respondent is subject to an administration order);

(ii) the outcome of the litigation may depend on a ruling from an appellate court or the ECJ on a legal issue that will determine the outcome of the claim;

(iii) there are pending civil or criminal proceedings which might affect the outcome of the claim or prejudice either party if a hearing took place (*Carter v Credit Change Ltd* [1979] I.C.R. 908, CA; *Bowater Plc v Charlwood* [1991] I.C.R. 798); and

(iv) the parties are still involved in an internal disciplinary or grievance procedure. The tribunal's discretion is a wide one, but must be exercised judicially (see *Jacobs v Norsalta* [1977] I.C.R. 189).

Rule 10(2)(i)—Dealing with parts of proceedings separately

4–119   This rule should be read with r.18(2)(a), which permits the employment judge to deal with any preliminary matter. Care must be taken to ensure that it is possible to identify preliminary issues in relation to, for example, limitation or whether there has been a dismissal separately from the main issues in the claim (see *Wellcome Foundation v Darby* [1996] I.R.L.R. 538, EAT; *Lindsay v Ironsides Ray & Vials* [1994] I.R.L.R. 318, EAT; *J Sainsbury Plc v Moger* [1994] I.C.R. 800; and *Arthur v London Eastern Railway Ltd* [2007] I.C.R. 193).

Rule 10(2)(j) and (7)—Consolidating claims

4–120   Before exercising this power the tribunal must give all parties the opportunity of objecting under r.10(7).

Rule 10(2)(k)—Adding respondents

The tribunal of its own volition may add a respondent, notwithstanding that a **4–121** relevant time limit may have elapsed (subject to the respondent's right to object and to apply under r.11(1) to vary or revoke the order, or to seek a pre-hearing review to determine whether r.18(7) applies). The same principles apply to a decision to add a respondent, as to whether to permit an amendment to a claim (*Cocking v Sandhurst (Stationers) Ltd* [1974] I.C.R. 650, and see also below commentary on r.10(q)).

CPR rr.19.2 and 19.5 may also be of relevance and assistance. Under the CPR the court may add a party if (a) it is desirable so that the court can resolve all the matters in dispute in the proceedings; or (b) there is an issue involving the new party and an existing party which is connected to the matters in dispute, and it is desirable to add the new party so that the court can resolve the issue. The court can substitute a new party for an existing one under CPR r.19.2(4) if the existing party's interest or liability has passed to the new party, and it is desirable to substitute the new party so that the court can resolve the issues in the case. This power cannot be used once there has been judgment. CPR r.19.5 deals with the difficulty of adding a proposed new respondent where the primary limitation period has expired. Under CPR r.19.5 a new party can only be added after expiry of the original primary limitation period if the original proceedings were commenced when the relevant limitation period was current, and it is necessary to add the respondent. Under CPR r.19.5(3) adding an additional respondent is only necessary if the original respondent was named by mistake; the claim cannot be properly carried on without adding the respondent, or; the original respondent has died or been made bankrupt. Because of the relatively short periods for commencing proceedings in the employment tribunal and the existence of exceptions to those periods, and taking into account the need in the context of the overriding objective to balance the respective prejudice, it is submitted that while tribunals should act in accordance with CPR r.19.2, the provisions of r.19.5 are not consistent with tribunal practice in respect of amendments, and should not be followed.

Rule 10(2)(m)—Postponements and adjournments

The following seven principles should be considered when deciding whether or **4–122** not to grant an adjournment:

   (i) the importance of the proceedings and their likely consequences to the party seeking the adjournment;

  (ii) the risk of the party being prejudiced if the application is refused;

 (iii) the risk of prejudice or other disadvantage to the other party if the adjournment is granted;

 (iv) the convenience of the court;

  (v) the interests of justice generally (including, but not limited to the efficient dispatch of court business);

 (vi) the desirability of not delaying future litigants by adjourning early; and

 (vii) the extent to which the party applying for the adjournment had been responsible for creating the difficulty which led to the application.

(*R v Kingston-upon-Thames Justices* [1994] IMM A.R. 172, CA).

Although the employment judge's discretion to adjourn is broad, it must be exercised judicially. The exercise of the discretion requires the balancing of all material considerations including the fairness of granting any adjournment, both to the claimant and the respondent (*Teinaz v LB of Wandsworth* [2002] I.C.R. 1471, CA). In *Andreou v Lord Chancellor's Department* [2002] I.R.L.R. 728, the Court of Appeal provided guidance as to the steps to be taken if an adjournment is sought on medical grounds. The fact sensitive nature of the exercise is demonstrated by *Eastwood v Winckworth Sherwood* UKEAT/0174/05, where a Tribunal had declined to allow an adjournment of a pre-hearing review following late disclosure by the respondent. The Appeal Tribunal concluded that the Tribunal ought to have considered a number of factors:

(i) the complexity of the issue;
(ii) the agreement of the respondent to the request for an adjournment;
(iii) the fact that the parties had reached agreement in relation to other procedural steps in relation to exchange of statements, and other steps that would assist the tribunal in dealing with the case fairly;
(iv) the fact that the respondent's late disclosure did impede the claimant's preparation for the hearing;
(v) the fact that there had been no prior delay; and
(vi) the fact that the parties had received adequate notice of the hearing had to be set against the fact that there had been late disclosure which had prevented the claimant dealing with his preparation.

Rule 10(2)(n)—Varying or revoking other orders

4–123   This rule needs to be read in conjunction with r.11(1), which also permits a party to apply for an order to be issued, varied or revoked, and r.12 which enables the employment judge to make an order on his own initiative. The relationship between these rules and r.34 (review of other judgments and decisions), which does not permit an order to be reviewed unless it is a judgment or decision within the meaning of r.34 has been considered in the context of two appeals against a refusal by an employment judge to consider applications for a review of a case management order made under r.10. First by the EAT in *Onwuka v Spherion Technology UK Ltd* [2005] I.C.R. 567, where it was concluded that the Tribunal has a residual power to vary or revoke, and therefore to "review" under rr.10 (general power to manage proceedings), 11 (applications in proceedings), 12 (employment judge's power to make an order on his own initiative), or 33 (power to review a default judgment). Secondly by the EAT in *Hart v English Heritage* [2006] I.C.R. 655 where it was held that (i) a tribunal decision which was not a judgment or decision falling within r.33 or r.34 of the 2004 Regulations could not be reviewed, but (ii) it could be reconsidered under r.10 even though that provision referred to an order rather than a decision. The term "order" in r.10, and particularly in r.10(2), despite the unsatisfactory nature of the language used, should be construed so as to cover all decisions taken by a tribunal in the proper exercise of its case management powers, save where those decisions were subject to the review procedure in rr.33 and 34. In theory, there is no limit to the number of times that a tribunal could reconsider a previous case management decision. While a tribunal therefore had jurisdiction to revisit case management decisions, it should not ordinarily do so, unless there had been a material change in circumstances, or there was a point of substance that needed to be considered even where there had been no change of circumstances, but merely a previous failure to argue the point (*Onwuka v Spherion Technology UK Ltd* [2005] I.C.R. 567 and *Montali v Goldman Sachs Services Ltd* [2002] I.C.R. 1251).

Rule 10(2)(o)—Giving notice of a pre-hearing review or the hearing

4–124   This permits the tribunal to order a pre-hearing review on its own initiative or in response to an application under r.11(1). In addition the tribunal will usually fix the date for the hearing at either the conclusion of a case management discussion or at a pre-hearing review.

Rule 10(2)(p)—Giving notice under r.19

4–125   This permits the tribunal to give the parties the requisite notice of its intention under r.19 to make one or other of the orders envisaged by r.18(7) (see para.4–169 and notes thereon).

Rule 10(2)(q)—Leave to amend a claim or response

Rule 10(2)(q) confers on the tribunal a far wider discretion than obtained under **4–126** the corresponding provisions in the CPR, where the purpose of any proposed amendment would be to allow a claim in particular to be pursued where the original time limit to bring proceedings may have expired. Under CPR r.17.4(2), an amendment will not be allowed to permit a new claim out of time unless it arises out of the same or substantially the same facts. All the historical authorities on allowing amendments to claims (and responses), where the effect might be to add an additional claim after expiry of the time limit for commencing proceedings, were reviewed in *Lehman Brothers Ltd v Smith* [2005] UKEAT/0486/05. Here, the EAT approved the proposition that the tribunal must assess the respective prejudice of allowing or not allowing the particular amendment. In distinct contrast to the position under the CPR, the fact that the potential new claim may be out of time is only one of the factors to be taken into consideration.

Amendment may be permitted in order to add a claim that was not available when the claim form was first presented (see *BMA v Chaudhary* [2003] I.C.R. 1510; and *Prakash v Wolverhampton City Council* UKEAT/0140/06, September 6, 2006). As such it is possible to "present" a claim (for example, for the purposes of s.111 of the Employment Rights Act) by amendment.

Whether or not an application to amend should be allowed is judged on the basis of whether it would be just and equitable to allow the amendment (*Ali v Office of National Statistics* [2005] I.R.L.R. 201, CA). In the same case it was held that whether or not the proposed amendment represents a new claim or a clarification of an existing claim requires an examination of the entire claim form: usually it cannot be presumed that a claim alleging direct discrimination encompassed a claim based on indirect discrimination. The factors to be taken into account by the tribunal when considering whether or not to allow an amendment remain those set out in *Selkent Bus Co Ltd v Moore* [1996] I.C.R. 836; [1996] I.R.L.R. 661.

(a) The nature of the amendment: does it add a new cause of action or is it the addition of or amendment to a cause of action on the basis of facts already pleaded?
(b) The applicability of any relevant time limit: the tribunal must consider whether the new claim is out of time and whether the time limit should be extended under the applicable statutory procedure.
(c) The timing and manner of the application: an application should not be refused solely on the grounds of delay, as the paramount factor is the relative injustice and hardship involved.

Arguably another relevant factor to be taken into account must be the fact that the claimant and the employer may not have followed the relevant provisions of the Dispute Regulations, if applicable and the requirements of s.32 of the Employment Act 2002.

An application to amend should not be refused simply because the consequence of allowing the application will be an adjournment of a hearing (*Cobbold v London Borough of Greenwich* August 9, 1999, CA). The over-riding objective is that cases should be dealt with justly. That includes not only that the case is dealt with expeditiously, but also that it is dealt with fairly.

Rule 10(2)(r)—Joining respondents with an interest in the outcome

This rule was introduced to overcome the problem highlighted by the case of **4–127** *Rutherford v Secretary of State for Trade and Industry* [2001] I.R.L.R. 599; [2001] I.C.R. 123. The claimant in the case argued that the statutory age limit that prevented either claims for unfair dismissal or redundancy payments in respect of employees over the age of 65 was indirectly discriminatory against men. As the government was not originally a party to the proceedings against the employer, the tribunal was hampered in its need to have access to the arguments objectively justifying the limit and the statistics on the impact of the cut off. By consent, the Secretary of State was made a party to the proceedings to facilitate argument on the point. Rule 10(2)(q) now formalises that power in an appropriate case.

Rule 10(2)(s)—Witness statements

4–128   It is standard practice in all discrimination claims, and usually in all claims for unfair dismissal, for the tribunal to order the preparation and exchange of typed witness statements in respect of all witnesses, including, where relevant, the parties, irrespective of whether the parties are represented. The order will usually provide for simultaneous exchange on a given date, in accordance with r.10(3). The tribunal has the power to order sequential exchange of witness statements.

Rule 10(2)(t)—Orders as to the use of experts

4–129   In light of CPR rr.35.1–35.14 (experts and assessors) and the associated PD 35, and the Guide for experts and those instructing them, the EAT has given guidelines to parties and tribunals on the use of expert evidence pending the introduction of more formal rules and provisions, particularly in relation to costs (in *de Keyser Ltd v Wilson* [2001] I.R.L.R. 324). Although the judgment was given in relation to the 2001 rules, it remains valid after the introduction of r.10(2):

   (i) It by no means follows that just because a party wishes to use expert evidence that it will be admitted (see *Whitehouse v Jordan* [1981] 1 W.L.R. 246, HL; *Midland Bank v Hett, Stubbs & Kemp* [1979] 1 Ch 384; *M & R (minors), Re* [1996] 1 All E.R. 239, CA). It is for the tribunal to decide if it needs the evidence, a prudent party will first explore with the tribunal in correspondence or at a case management discussion whether in principle expert will be admitted.

   (ii) Except where one side is already committed to a particular expert, joint instruction should be the norm.

   (iii) The terms of the instructions and the expert's fees should be agreed in advance;

   (iv) If the means available to one side or another are such that in its view it cannot agree to share or to risk any exposure to the expert's fees or expenses, or if, irrespective of its means, a party refuses to pay or share such costs, the other party or parties can be expected reasonably to prefer to require their own expert. But even in such a case, the weight to be attached to that expert's evidence (a matter entirely for the tribunal to judge) may be found to have been increased if the terms of his instruction shall have been submitted to the other side, if not for agreement then for comment, ahead of their being finalised for sending to the expert.

   (v) If a joint expert is to be used, tribunals, lest the parties dally, may fix a period within which the parties are to seek to agree the identity of the expert and the terms of a joint letter of instruction, and the tribunal may fix a date by which the joint experts' report is to be made available.

   (vi) Any letter of instruction should specify in as much detail as can be given any particular questions the expert is to be invited to answer, and all more general subjects which he is to be asked to address.

   (vii) Such instructions are as far as possible to avoid partisanship. Insofar as the expert is asked to make assumptions of fact, they are to be spelled out. It will be wise if the letter emphasises that in preparing his evidence, the expert's principal and overriding duty is to the tribunal rather than to any party.

(viii) Where a joint expert is to be used, the tribunal may specify, if his identity or instructions shall not have been agreed between the parties by a specified date, that the matter is to be restored to the tribunal, which may then assist the parties to settle that identity and those instructions.

(ix) In relation to the issues to which an expert is or is not to address himself (whether or not he is a joint expert), the tribunal may give formal directions as it does generally, in relation to the issues to be dealt with at the main hearing.

(x) Where there is no joint expert, the tribunal should, in the absence of appropriate agreement between the parties, specify a timetable for disclosure or exchange of experts' reports and, where there are two or more experts, for meetings (see below).

(xi) Any timetable may provide for the raising of supplementary questions with the expert or experts (whether there is a joint expert or not); and for the disclosure or exchange of the answers in good time before the hearing.

(xii) in the event of separate experts being instructed, the tribunal should encourage arrangements for them to meet on a without prejudice basis with a view to their seeking to resolve any conflict between them and, where possible, to their producing and disclosing a Schedule of agreed issues and of points of dispute between them.

(xiii) if a party fails, without good reason, to follow these guidelines, and if in consequence another party or parties suffer delay or are put to expense which a due performance of the guidelines would have been likely to avoid, then the tribunal may wish to consider whether, on that party's part, there has been unreasonable conduct within the meaning of [r.12(1) (as to costs)] (now r.38).

These guidelines build on previous advice from Morison J., in *Buxton v Equinox Design Ltd* [1999] I.C.R. 269; [1999] I.R.L.R. 158.

Where there has been an order for the instructions and use of a joint expert, it may still nevertheless be necessary to permit the respondent to instruct its own expert if either there is ambiguity as to whether the alleged impairment is mental or physical, or if there is an issue as to whether the alleged impairment is genuine. (*Hospice of St Mary of Furness v Howard* [2007] I.R.L.R. 944; compare also *Mid-Devon District Council v Stevenson* EAT/0196/07)

Use of Electronic Communications

Rule 10(8)

Any order must be recorded in writing and signed by the employment judge, but **4–130** it is the responsibility of the tribunal staff to ensure that the parties are informed of any order as soon as is reasonably practicable. Normally this is in writing and by post but as there is the possibility of an order requiring a party to take action within a short timescale the regulations permit and the overriding objective encourages the use of electronic communications, for example fax or email.

Applications in proceedings

11.—(1) At any stage of the proceedings a party may apply for an **4–131** **order to be issued, varied or revoked or for a case management discussion or pre-hearing review to be held.**

(2) An application for an order must be made not less than 10 days before the date of the hearing at which it is to be considered (if any)

unless it is not reasonably practicable to do so, or the chairman or tribunal considers it in the interests of justice that shorter notice be allowed. The application must (unless a chairman orders otherwise) be in writing to the Employment Tribunal Office and include the case number for the proceedings and the reasons for the request. If the application is for a case management discussion or a pre-hearing review to be held, it must identify any orders sought.

(3) An application for an order must include an explanation of how the order would assist the tribunal or chairman in dealing with the proceedings efficiently and fairly.

(4) When a party is legally represented in relation to the application (except where the application is for a witness order described in rule 10(2)(c) only), that party or his representative must, at the same time as the application is sent to the Employment Tribunal Office, provide all other parties with the following information in writing—

(a) details of the application and the reasons why it is sought;

(b) notification that any objection to the application must be sent to the Employment Tribunal Office within 7 days of receiving the application, or before the date of the hearing (whichever date is the earlier);

(c) that any objection to the application must be copied to both the Employment Tribunal Office and all other parties; and the party or his representative must confirm in writing to the Employment Tribunal Office that this rule has been complied with.

(5) Where a party is not legally represented in relation to the application, the Secretary shall inform all other parties of the matters listed in paragraphs (4)(a) to (c).

(6) A chairman may refuse a party's application and if he does so the Secretary shall inform the parties in writing of such refusal unless the application is refused at a hearing.

Rule 11(1)—Applications for orders

4–132   Rule 10 sets out the case management powers of the tribunal. Rule 12 permits the employment judge or tribunal to act on its own initiative. Rule 11 retains the power of the parties to seek an order, to vary or revoke an existing order, to ask for a case management discussion under r.17, or to ask for a pre-hearing review under r.18.

Rule 11(1)—Applications to vary or revoke orders

4–133   See commentary to r.10(2) above at paras 4–108 et seq.

Rule 11(6)—Powers of the employment judge on the application

4–134   Any application made under this rule may be refused by the employment judge, but although the parties are to be informed of the refusal, neither r.11 nor r.30 requires the employment judge to give reasons for such refusal. There is no obligation in r.11 to give reasons for refusing an application, and r.30 only creates an obligation to give reasons for judgments or orders, which for these purposes can only be the limited types of orders envisaged in r.28(1)(b). A decision of the employment judge rejecting an application under r.11 is neither a r.28 order nor a r.10 order (see the commentary on rr.28 to 30 at paras 4–226 to 4–233). However, there is nothing in the rules to prevent a party making a further application or repeating the application.

Chairman acting on his own initiative

4–135

12.—(1) Subject to paragraph (2) and to rules 10(7) and 18(7), a chairman may make an order on his own initiative with or without hearing the parties or giving them an opportunity to make written or oral representations. He may also decide to hold a case management discussion or pre-hearing review on his own initiative.

(2) Where a chairman makes an order without giving the parties the opportunity to make representations—

> **(a) the Secretary must send to the party affected by such order a copy of the order and a statement explaining the right to make an application under paragraph (2)(b); and**

> **(b) a party affected by the order may apply to have it varied or revoked.**

(3) An application under paragraph (2)(b) must (subject to rule 10(2)(e)) be made before the time at which, or the expiry of the period within which, the order was to be complied with. Such an application must (unless a chairman orders otherwise) be made in writing to an Employment Tribunal Office and it must include the reasons for the application. Paragraphs (4) and (5) of rule 11 apply in relation to informing the other parties of the application.

Rule 12(1) and (2)—Power of the employment judge to act on his own initiative

An employment judge acting on his own initiative and without either hearing the parties or giving them an opportunity to make oral or written representations, may issue orders, decide to hold a case management discussion, or pre-hearing review. That power is subject to a general qualification under r.12(2). Additionally the power is subject to two exceptions under r.10(7) (power to consolidate claims) (see para.4–106), and r.18(7) (striking out claims and determining jurisdiction issues) (see para.4–169), where the rules specifically provide that notice must be given, to enable a party to show cause.

Where the employment judge has made such an order without hearing the parties, r.12(2) preserves their right to apply to vary or revoke the order, as long as the application, supported by reasons, is made before expiry of the time specified for compliance in the original order (r.12(3)). An application under r.10(2)(e) can be made for an extension of time in which to make that application and/or to extend the time for compliance with the original order (r.12(3)).

4–136

Compliance with orders and practice directions

13.—(1) If a party does not comply with an order made under these rules, under rule 8 of Schedule 3, rule 7 of Schedule 4 or a practice direction, a chairman or tribunal—

4–137

(a) **may make an order in respect of costs or preparation time under rules 38 to 46; or**

(b) **may (subject to paragraph (2) and rule 19) at a pre-hearing review or a Hearing make an order to strike out the whole or part of the claim or, as the case may be, the response and, where appropriate, order that a respondent be debarred from responding to the claim altogether.**

(2) An order may also provide that unless the order is complied with, the claim or, as the case may be, the response shall be struck out on the date of non-compliance without further consideration of the proceedings or the need to give notice under rule 19 or hold a pre-hearing review or Hearing.

(3) Chairmen and tribunals shall comply with any practice directions issued under regulation 13.

Rule 13(1)(a)

4–138   For commentary on the difference between costs orders and preparation time orders, see para.4–291.

Rule 13(1)(b)

4–139   See the commentary at para.4–094 for the effect of an order under r.9.

Rule 13(2)—Compliance with unless orders

4–140   The rule provides for an automatic strike-out without more in the event of a party's non-compliance. An "unless order" takes effect on expiry of the term specified for compliance without the need for a further order, as it is a conditional order which becomes effective on non-compliance (*Chukwudebelor v Chubb Security Personnel Ltd* [2008] EWCA Civ. 827 [at 38]). In practice, the tribunal will write and inform the parties that it has done so. Where the tribunal strikes out the claim or response because of non-compliance with an unless order (under r.13(2)) it is a decision open to review under r.34, as it is in effect a conditional judgment, which becomes final on non-compliance with the order. In addition the tribunal retains a role to review the strike-out order coupled with an application for an extension of time for compliance with the original order: it does not become functus officio on issuing the order (*Uyanya-Odu v Schools Offices Services Ltd* UKEAT/0294/05). A material change in circumstances would be among the grounds for such an application.

Rule 13(3)

4–141   See the commentary at para.3–053 on reg.13. No practice directions have yet been issued. In December 2006 the President of Employment Tribunals in Scotland issued three Practice Directions in respect of claims in Scotland dealing with respectively lists of documents (PD1), sisting (staying) proceedings to enable meditation to take place (PD2), and most importantly specifying the procedure to be followed in respect of counterclaims (PD3).

DIFFERENT TYPES OF HEARING

Hearings—general

4–142   **14.—(1) A chairman or a tribunal (depending on the relevant rule) may hold the following types of hearing—**

(a) a case management discussion under rule 17;

(b) a pre-hearing review under rule 18;

(c) a Hearing under rule 26; or

(d) a review hearing under rule 33 or 36.

(2) So far as it appears appropriate to do so, the chairman or tribunal shall seek to avoid formality in his or its proceedings and shall not be bound by any enactment or rule of law relating to the admissibility of evidence in proceedings before the courts.

(3) The chairman or tribunal (as the case may be) shall make such enquiries of persons appearing before him or it and of witnesses as he or it considers appropriate and shall otherwise conduct the hearing in such manner as he or it considers most appropriate for the clarification of the issues and generally for the just handling of the proceedings.

(4) Unless the parties agree to shorter notice, the Secretary shall send notice of any hearing (other than a case management discussion) to every party not less than 14 days before the date fixed for the hearing and shall inform them that they have the opportunity to submit written representations and to advance oral argument. The Secretary shall give the parties reasonable notice before a case management discussion is held.

(5) If a party wishes to submit written representations for consideration at a hearing (other than a case management discussion) he shall present them to the Employment Tribunal Office not less than 7 days before the hearing and shall at the same time send a copy to all other parties.

(6) The tribunal or chairman may, if it or he considers it appropriate, consider representations in writing which have been submitted otherwise than in accordance with paragraph (5).

Rule 14(1)—The following types of hearing

The Rules use the capital letter to denote a hearing that represents a final **4–143** determination of the claim either on liability, remedy or both. All other types of hearing adopt the lower case. As is clear from the wording of this Rule and the provisions of rr.17, 18, 26, and 33, only a hearing can dispose of the claim of the claimant. All other types of "hearings" are, with the exception of a review hearing under either rr.33 and 36, interim hearings that must be either (a) case management discussions under r.17; or (b) pre-hearing reviews under r.18, or possibly the final category of hearing identified in reg.2 of the Regulations ("a sitting of an employment judge or a tribunal duly constituted for the purpose of receiving evidence, hearing addresses and witnesses or doing anything lawful to enable the employment judge or tribunal to reach a decision on any question.").

Rule 14(1)(a)—A case management discussion

These have replaced the directions hearings that used to be heard under the **4–144** provisions of r.4 (case management) under the 2001 Rules, and are dealt with fully at paras 4–162 to 4–168.

Rule 14(1)(b)—A pre-hearing review

4–145   Pre-hearing reviews held under the 2001 Rules were limited to determining under r.7 whether a party (invariably the applicant) should be ordered to pay a deposit. They were distinct from hearings held under the provisions of r.6 (entitlement to bring or contest proceedings). These were conventionally known as preliminary hearings, and were usually held before a full tribunal to determine such issues as whether the applicant was an employee, had sufficient continuity of employment to bring a claim, or whether the claim to the tribunal had been brought in time. Pre-hearing reviews now can be held to resolve all those issues previously dealt with under rr.6 and 7, in addition to those matters set out in r.18, which is dealt with more fully at para.4–169.

Rule 14(1)(c)—A Hearing

4–146   This is a hearing for the purposes of disposing of the claim, and will deal with both liability and where possible remedy. For the detailed discussion of r.26 see para.4–214 et seq.

Rule 14(1)(d)—A review hearing under rule 33 or rule 36

4–147   For a detailed discussion of review hearings see paras 4–244 et seq.

Rule 14(2)

4–148   Rule 14 has to be treated with respect: informality can go too far (*Aberdeen Steak Houses Group Plc v Ibrahim* [1988] I.R.L.R. 420; [1988] I.C.R. 550, EAT). The discretion must be exercised judicially; the parties must know which rules are to be applied with regard to the order of proceedings; total informality and the absence of generally recognised rules of procedure may be counter-productive and lead to the necessary conclusion that the parties did not receive a fair hearing. In normal circumstances, this will involve the party opening the case presenting all of their evidence, not delaying cross-examination for tactical reasons, parties putting their case in full to avoid the need to recall witnesses and then if so, ensuring that the other party is permitted to ask questions. Although the tribunal is not a court in practice, its procedure mirrors civil court procedure and is primarily adversarial rather than inquisitorial. However, the principle that the employment judge or the tribunal can regulate its own procedure, subject to the rules or any Practice Direction, that has been a feature of the rules since their inception is still retained, though now it is less conspicuous, being located in r.60, entitled "Powers."

Admissibility of evidence

4–149   Evidence is only admissible if it is relevant to an issue between the parties and probative of a disputed issue (*XXX v YYY* [2004] I.R.L.R. 471, CA; exclusion of video recording by tribunal). That is essentially the only rule in relation to the admissibility of evidence that is observed. The converse also applies: tribunals cannot generally refuse to admit evidence that is relevant and probative (*Rosedale Mountings v Sibley* [1980] I.C.R. 816). In practice parties often rely on hearsay, and submit unsigned witness statements from witnesses unable to attend the hearing. It is tribunal practice to admit such evidence, whilst at the same time advising parties that its overall weight must reflect the fact that the witness cannot be cross-examined. The one exception to the rule that the rules of evidence do not apply is the rule in relation to without prejudice remarks and correspondence. Such evidence can only be excluded if there was a dispute between the parties at the time the communication took place, to which the rule is alleged to attach. A claimant or respondent may therefore seek to admit evidence of alleged without prejudice communications (*BNP Paribas v Mezzotero* [2004] I.R.L.R. 508, EAT). In

Brunel University v Vaseghi UKEAT/0307/06 evidence of without prejudice discussions aimed at compromising discrimination claims was admitted in the context of a subsequent claim of victimisation. Approved at [2007] I.R.L.R. 592 CA; and compare *Framlington Group Ltd v Barnetson* [2007] I.R.L.R. 598 CA.

Such situations apart, the rule will operate to exclude all evidence of negotiations between the parties attempting to achieve a settlement of the dispute, even if the without prejudice formula is not referred to in the correspondence unless justice demands that the material is considered. It is permissible to reserve the position of the parties in relation to costs, and where this is done the correspondence may be looked at after conclusion of the proceedings for the purposes of any application for costs. Use of the formula does not prevent the tribunal from looking at the document(s) to see whether it does apply but if the documents are privileged the rule will attach to all the documents involved in the process of the negotiation, even if they do not expressly contain offers to settle (*Rush & Tomkins Ltd v Greater London Council* [1989] A.C. 1289, H.L.; *Cutts v Head* [1984] 1 A.E.R. 597, CA; *South Shropshire District Council v Amos* [1986] 1 W.L.R. 1271, CA). Evidence may also be excluded on the basis of wider public policy considerations (Amwell School Governors v Dogherty [2007] I.C.R. 135). In that case, an application based on ECHR art.8 to exclude a tape recording of deliberations following a disciplinary hearing (the recording having been made secretly by the employee) was refused. However the recording was deemed inadmissible on the basis that the employee had consented to the disciplinary panel deliberating in private, and admitting the recording would be contrary to the public interest in frank discussion in the course of such deliberation.

Rule 14(3)—Shall make such enquiries of persons appearing . . . and of witnesses as he or it considers appropriate

Rules 14(2) and 14(3) were previously one composite rule (r.11(1) in the 2001 rules). The provision that now appears as r.14(3) in these rules was added to the 1993 Regulations, (SI 1993/2687, replacing SI 1985/16), specifically to enable tribunals to give assistance to unrepresented parties. The practice of tribunals giving assistance to unrepresented parties in the formulation and presentation of the case was given judicial approval by the Court of Appeal (*Divine-Bortey v London Borough of Brent* [1998] I.R.L.R. 525; [1998] I.C.R. 886, CA, approving *Dimtsu v Westminster City Council* [1991] I.R.L.R. 450). This paragraph seemingly places an obligation on the tribunal to take a proactive role in establishing the real issues and ensuring that the facts relevant are established, if necessary suggesting that the claim or response might require amendment, and if necessary an adjournment. However as stressed by the Court of Appeal in *Divine-Bortey*, it must be left to the judgment of the tribunal, and it is not an obligation such that a failure to do so gives rise to an error of law. In addition, the tribunal must avoid assuming the role of advocate for either party. In a case decided under the Disability Discrimination Act 1995, the Court of Appeal observed that the employment tribunal is not a service provider within the meaning of s.21(1) of the Disability Discrimination Act 1995 and is also not obliged to adopt a more interventionist and inquisitorial approach by virtue of the duty in the 1995 Act to make reasonable adjustments to accommodate persons with a disability (*Woodrup v London Borough of Southwark* [2003] I.R.L.R. 111).

What the tribunal must not do is find in favour of a party on the basis of something not raised by that party in the claim and raised late in the course of proceedings. Although employment judges are able to assist unrepresented parties in formulating and presenting their cases, such assistance must be balanced against the need to ensure fairness to the other party. In the case in question the issue was raised by the tribunal of its own motion and the respondents were prevented from

4–150

calling witnesses or addressing the issue fully in submissions (*Birmingham City Council v Laws* EAT/0360/06).

Rule 14(3)—. . . shall otherwise conduct the hearing in such manner as he or it considers most appropriate for the clarification of the issues and generally for the just handling of the proceedings

4–151   Rule 14(3) mirrors r.60(1) which provides that the employment judge or tribunal may regulate its own procedure, subject to the Rules and any Practice Direction. There is no hard and fast rule to determine who should call their evidence first (*Gill v Harold Andrews Ltd* [1974] I.C.R. 294; *Oxford v DHSS* [1977] I.C.R. 884). Usually, if there is a burden of proof in the relevant legislation, it is the party on whom that burden lies to commence. For that reason, in a claim for unfair dismissal, if the dismissal is admitted, the employer commences, as the burden of proof to prove the reason for dismissal—and that it is a potentially fair reason for dismissal—is on the employer. In a discrimination case, notwithstanding the burden of proof placed on employers by the various discrimination jurisdictions, it is still for the claimant to prove facts from which the tribunal could draw an inference of discrimination, in the absence of a cogent explanation from the respondent (*King v Great Britain China Centre* [1991] I.R.L.R. 513; [1992] I.C.R. 516, CA; reaffirmed in *Igen Ltd v Wong* [2005] I.R.L.R. 258; [2005] I.C.R. 931). In respect of claims for breach of contract (under respectively the Employment Tribunals Extension of Jurisdiction (England and Wales) and the Employment Tribunals Extension of Jurisdiction (Scotland) Orders 1994 (SI 1994/1623 and SI 1994/1624), and for wages (under s.23 of the Employment Rights Act 1996), the practice is for the claimant to present his evidence first.

A decision taken on the basis of a material judicial decision to which the parties were not alerted and allowed to comment on is not necessarily a breach of the rules of natural justice, and a denial of the right to a fair hearing. The question is whether the failure is seriously irregular and unfair. For it to be so, the authority must be sufficient to alter or affect the way that the issues have been addressed to a significant extent, so that it truly can be said by a fair-minded observer that the case was decided in a way which could not have been anticipated by a party fixed with such knowledge of the law and procedure as it would be reasonable to attribute to him in all the circumstances. The hearing must have led to a material injustice and produced substantial prejudice (*Stanley Cole (Wainfleet) Ltd v Sheridan* [2003] I.R.L.R. 885; [2003] I.C.R. 1449, CA).

A failure by an employment tribunal to allow parties to make legal representations about findings of fact for which neither party had contended does *not* amount to a procedural irregularity sufficient to render a hearing unfair. As a general rule, tribunals should be careful to ensure that parties have an opportunity to make submissions on any matter that might affect the outcome of the case, either in closing submissions if the point is identified early enough, or by giving the parties a further opportunity to make either written or oral submissions. It was pointed out that the Regulations and Rules give the tribunal a wide discretion in relation to procedural matters (*Judge v Crown Leisure Ltd* [2005] I.R.L.R. 823, CA).

The notice of hearing sent to the parties will alert them to the fact that the hearing will, subject to time considerations, endeavour to address the question of remedy at the conclusion of the hearing on liability. It is incumbent on the tribunal at the hearing to clarify at the outset how it intends to deal with the question of remedy in the hearing, including whether it will hear evidence from the claimant during evidence on liability or separately after dealing with liability. Even if the question of quantum has to be adjourned to a subsequent hearing there is nothing to prevent the tribunal giving a preliminary indication on quantum even though it may subsequently be required to take a different view (*Chaplin v H J Rawlinson Ltd* [1991] I.C.R. 553, EAT).

A tribunal should be cautious in deciding whether to resolve preliminary issues as **4–152** opposed to issues that are appropriate for resolution at a pre-hearing review, and which were previously dealt with at preliminary hearings: for example, is the claim in time, or does the claimant have sufficient service to bring a claim for unfair dismissal? What may seem to be a short cut might cause more delay and costs than if the tribunal had heard all the evidence, found all the facts, and then decided the discreet issue of fact or law in the context of all the findings (*NUT v Governing Body of St Mary's School* [1995] I.R.L.R. 317, EAT, approved [1997] I.R.L.R. 242; *Secretary of State for Education & Science v Birchall* [1994] I.R.L.R. 630, EAT). The proper way to resolve preliminary matters that may dispose of the claim is at a pre-hearing review. For example, the tribunal might be asked to resolve the preliminary issue of whether there was a dismissal. In such instances the preferable route might be to determine that question in an overall decision on whether there was a dismissal, the reason for that dismissal and whether it was fair. Such a finding may reduce the risk that on a successful appeal the matter has to be remitted.

A number of propositions in relation to the conduct of hearings still remain valid despite the fact that the 2004 Regulations introduce an entirely new framework for the conduct of tribunal claims because they remain consistent with the overriding objective. The tribunal must endeavour to ensure that the volume of documents is kept within reasonable bounds, that witnesses are limited to the relevant issues, and that the estimated hearing duration is kept to, to avoid adjournments and part-heard cases (*Inner London Education Authority v Lloyd* [1981] I.R.L.R. 394, CA; on delay and adjournments see *Kwamin v Abbey National Plc* [2004] I.R.L.R. 516; [2004] I.C.R. 84, sub nom. *Bangs v Connex South Eastern Ltd* [2005] I.R.L.R. 389; [2005] I.C.R. 763). Whilst the tribunal may not impose arbitrary time limits on cross-examination and closing submissions, an attempt to agree a timetable for the cross-examination of the claimant and witnesses to ensure, where practicable, that the hearing is completed within the agreed time estimate is consistent with reg.3(2)(c) and (4), duty to conduct a case expeditiously and fairly and the duty of the parties to assist the tribunal in furthering the overriding objective (*Zurich Insurance Co v Gulson* UKEAT/747/97). A tribunal has a discretion to prevent lengthy cross-examination but in doing so must not disable itself from receiving relevant and significant evidence).

It is the duty of the employment judge to make a note of the proceedings to assist the appellate court in the event of an appeal, even though the EAT will only call for production of the employment judge's notes or relevant extracts in the circumstances specified in the EAT's Practice Direction 2004, at para.7 (*Houston v Lightwater Farms Ltd* [1990] I.R.L.R. 469; [1990] I.C.R. 502, EAT). Evidence before the tribunal is still absolutely privileged for defamation purposes (*Trapp v Mackie* [1979] 1 All E.R. 489; [1979] 1 W.L.R. 377, HL). Hearsay evidence is admissible at the discretion of the tribunal if it is relevant. It is for the tribunal to determine what weight to attach to that evidence: for example in a case where the allegation is harassment, it is rare for there to be direct eye-witness evidence, so evidence of a complaint to another person that the incident occurred may be corroborative, despite being hearsay (*Lawrence v London Borough of Newham*, unreported, 1978). The tribunal has no discretion to refuse to admit evidence which is admissible as being relevant to and probative of issues before the tribunal (*Rosedale Mouldings Ltd v Sibley* [1980] I.R.L.R. 387; [1980] I.C.R. 816, EAT; *ALM Medical Services Ltd v Bladon* [2002] I.R.L.R. 807; [2002] I.C.R. 1444, CA).

Whilst the tribunal "has a discretion, in accordance with the overriding objective" to exclude relevant evidence which is unnecessarily repetitive, or of only "marginal relevance in the interests of proper, modern case management", that "discretion must be exercised judicially". (per H.H.J. Clark in *Digby v East Cambridgeshire District Council* [2007] I.R.L.R. 585, at [12]).

That principle did not, however, extend to the opinion of an employment consultant as opposed to a medical consultant that the claimant he had interviewed lacked motivation (*Larby v Thurgood* [1993] I.C.R. 66, HC).

4-153 The tribunal may use its own specialist knowledge and experience to assess and interpret the evidence, but is not entitled to substitute it for the evidence. If the tribunal intends to rely on the specialist knowledge of one of its members, it must tell the parties that one of its members has that expertise so that they may comment on the facts known to and adverted to by that member (*Hammington v Berker Sportcraft Ltd* [1980] I.C.R. 248).

The power to conduct the hearing in the manner most appropriate to clarification of the issues—and generally for the just handling of the proceedings—will not normally extend to the tribunal either encouraging or not preventing a submission at the close of the first party's evidence that there is no claim to answer, however attractive that course of action may be from the cost perspective. It would be rare for a submission of no case to answer to be made to an employment tribunal, and even more rare for that submission to succeed. The principles governing a submission of that nature can be summarised as follows:

(a) there is no inflexible rule of law and practice that a tribunal must hear both sides, but it should normally do so;

(b) the power to stop a case at "half-time" must be exercised with caution;

(c) it may be a complete waste of time to call on the other party in a hopeless case;

(d) even where there is an onus of proof on a party, as in a discrimination case, it will only be in an exceptional or frivolous case that it would be right to take such a course; and

(e) where there is no burden of proof, for example under s.98(4) of the Employment Rights Act 1996, it will be difficult to envisage arguable cases where it is appropriate to take that step (*Clarke v Watford Borough Council*, unreported, May 4, 2000, EAT; cited with approval in *Logan v Commissioners of Customs and Excise* [2004] I.R.L.R. 64; [2004] I.C.R 1, CA).

The EAT has reaffirmed that the principles established in *Logan v Commissioners of Customs and Excise*, which were laid down in relation to the 2001 Rules, are equally applicable to the 2004 Rules, notwithstanding the increased powers to strike out claims that have no reasonable prospects of success (*Wiggan v R N Wooler and Co Ltd* [2007] UKEAT/0542/06).

The Court of Appeal made it clear in Logan that the fourth proposition also applied to claims for constructive dismissal. In *Boulding v Land Securities Trillium (Media Services) Ltd* UKEAT/0023/06/RN, the principle was further extended to "whistleblowing" cases, on the basis that they are tantamount to discrimination claims. The rules on conciliation recognise that, assigning them to the category of claims in which there is no fixed period for conciliation. The fourth proposition must now be read subject to the guidance of the Court of Appeal, on the approach to the burden of proof in discrimination cases. The claimant must still prove facts from which the tribunal could conclude, in the absence of an explanation from the respondent, that there has been discrimination, but the burden will pass to the employer at that point. If anything the provisions on the burden of proof reinforce the fourth proposition set out in *Clarke* (*Igen Ltd v Wong* [2005] I.R.L.R. 258; [2005] I.C.R. 931, CA).

Rule 14(4)

4-154 The time limit of 14 days is calculated in accordance with reg.15, so that the date of the hearing is not included in the calculation. Therefore if the hearing is to take place on June 15, the notice of hearing must be sent no later than June 1, unless both parties waive the requirement and agree to shorter notice. However the obligation is to send the notice, it is not a requirement that the notice of hearing be received no less than 14 days before the hearing. The requirement for 14 days notice, subject to any agreement to a shorter period, applies to all hearings with the exception of case management discussions. However under r.17 there is no minimum period of notice laid down in the rules, which enables the employment judge at a pre-hearing review to determine at the conclusion of a pre-hearing review under r.18 or at a hearing under r.26, where the hearing is to be adjourned for example, that an immediate case management discussion takes place. Rule 14(4) does provide that parties must be given reasonable notice before any other type of case management discussion is to be held. There is no guidance in the rules as to what is reasonable. However where for example a case has been listed for hearing and an issue arises, which could properly be resolved at a case management conference, then it might be appropriate to give the parties less than two days notice for example, rather than risk the hearing having to be adjourned. In such situations the overriding objective would engage to avoid the risks of an application for an adjournment.

Rule 14(5) and (6)

A party can submit written representations for consideration at any hearing, but **4–155** if he does so he must present them to the tribunal not less than seven days prior to the hearing. Again reg.15 applies: if the hearing is on June 8, the representations must be physically in the hands of the tribunal no later than June 1. To comply, the documents must be faxed, emailed, or handed in on that date or posted at least two days prior to that date. As far as the other parties are concerned, the obligation is only to send them to all other parties at the same time so that the other party may only see the representations in question less than seven days before the hearing. The EAT has observed, prior to the 2004 rules, that where an employment tribunal has ordered written submissions, as opposed to a party deciding to submit them, then it must allow sufficient time for them to be prepared, and in particular to be assimilated by the other party and the tribunal before any oral submissions (*Sinclair Roche & Temperley v Heard* (No 1) [2004] I.R.L.R. 763). However even if either party has submitted representations other than in accordance with r.14(5) the employment judge or tribunal may still take them into account if it is appropriate to do so.

Use of Electronic Communications

15.—(1) A hearing (other than those mentioned in sub-paragraphs **4–156** **(c) and (d) of rule 14(1)) may be conducted by use of electronic communications provided that the chairman or tribunal conducting the hearing considers it just and equitable to do so.**

(2) Where a hearing is required by these rules to be held in public and it is to be conducted by use of electronic communications in accordance with this rule then, subject to rule 16, it must be held in a place to which the public has access and using equipment so that the public is able to hear all parties to the communication.

Rule 15(1)

This Rule was prompted by a suggestion that emerged from the recommenda- **4–157** tions of the Employment Tribunals System Taskforce, as a means of saving time and cost. It permits the tribunal where either a case management hearing or a pre-hearing review is being conducted, to conduct that hearing primarily by the means of a telephone conference call without the need for the parties to attend. Before deciding whether or not to conduct the hearing in that manner, the employment judge or tribunal must consider both whether it is just and equitable to do so, and whether to do so is in accordance with the overriding objective. As and when video phones, and computer software permitting video conferencing over the internet are used more extensively by parties and tribunals greater advantage will be taken of this facility. "Electronic communications" are defined in reg.2.

Rule 15(2)—Hearings required to be held in public

4–158   As a case management discussion is now required by reg.17(1) to be held in private, as a result of the change to the Rules, the practical effect of r.15(2) is to limit the applicability of r.15(2) to pre-hearing reviews. Essentially, therefore, a pre-hearing review conducted electronically must be held in a tribunal hearing room.

Hearings which may be held in private

4–159   **16.—(1) A hearing or part of one may be conducted in private for the purpose of hearing from any person evidence or representations which in the opinion of the tribunal or chairman is likely to consist of information—**

(a) **which he could not disclose without contravening a prohibition imposed by or by virtue of any enactment;**

(b) **which has been communicated to him in confidence, or which he has otherwise obtained in consequence of the confidence placed in him by another person; or**

(c) **the disclosure of which would, for reasons other than its effect on negotiations with respect to any of the matters mentioned in section 178(2) of TULR(C)A, cause substantial injury to any undertaking of his or any undertaking in which he works.**

(2) Where a tribunal or chairman decides to hold a hearing or part of one in private, it or he shall give reasons for doing so. A member of the Council on Tribunals (in Scotland, a member of the Council on Tribunals or its Scottish Committee) shall be entitled to attend any Hearing or pre-hearing review taking place in private in his capacity as a member.

Rule 16(1)

4–160   It is suggested that the application to sit in private should itself be made to the tribunal sitting in private. It has been held in the criminal jurisdiction that such an application should be dealt with in camera, although the reasons should be announced orally in public in accordance with r.17(2) and r.30, unless reasons are reserved (*R. v Ealing Justices, Ex parte Weafer* [1982] 74 Cr.App. R 204, DC). By analogy, unless the application is heard in private, it cannot enable the party making the application to give full reasons in support without prejudicing the very privacy the application is seeking to achieve by the application. The application should be made either at a case management discussion under rr.10 and 17, or by way of an application under r.11, or at the substantive hearing. The tribunal does not, however, have power, except under this rule, to exclude either members of the public or the press from any part of the hearing, on the grounds that the evidence to be given might be salacious or sensitive. The tribunal in the case in question, recognising that it had no power to sit in private under the rule that then applied (r.8 of the 1993 Regulations), instead relied on its general power to manage the proceedings under the equivalent of what is now r.14(3). It purported to make an order excluding the press and members of the public from hearing some of the evidence. On an application by newspapers for judicial review, the High Court ruled that the only powers open to the tribunal in a case of this nature were either an order that the proceedings be conducted in private under the rule then in force, or a restricted reporting order under what is now r.50 (the tribunal in that case had made such an order which the respondent contended had been breached by a newspaper) (see *R v Southampton Industrial Tribunal, Ex parte Ins News Group Ltd and Express Newspapers Plc* [1995] I.R.L.R. 247, HC).

Rule 16(2)

As the tribunal or employment judge is obliged to give reasons for the decision, the question arises as to whether this is a judgment under r.28(1)(a) or an order under r.28(1)(b). Arguably it cannot be an order as it does not order a person to do or not to do something, except in the limited sense that the Secretary and the full tribunal conducting the r.26 Hearing are impliedly being required to disregard r.26(3), which provides that any hearing of a claim shall take place in public, subject to r.16. However it does not constitute a judgment, as it does not constitute a final determination of the proceedings, or a particular issue in the proceedings, except in the limited sense that the decision determines the particular issue of whether the hearing should be held other than in accordance with r.26(3). It is only if the decision is a judgment that it is capable of review under r.34, because r.34 provides that orders and decisions that are not expressly covered by r.34 cannot be reviewed under these rules. As r.34 only permits the tribunal to review judgments and decisions and not to accept claims, responses, or counterclaims, then a party seeking to set the decision aside on review would have to bring itself within r.34(1). Alternatively there may be a power not to review but to ask the tribunal to revisit the decision (see *Hart v English Heritage* [2006] I.C.R. 655).

4–161

CASE MANAGEMENT DISCUSSIONS

Conduct of case management discussions

17.—(1) Case management discussions are interim hearings, and may deal with matters of procedure and management of the proceedings and they [shall] be held in private. Case management discussions shall be conducted by a chairman.

(2) Any determination of a person's civil rights or obligations shall not be dealt with in a case management discussion. The matters listed in rule 10(2) are examples of matters which may be dealt with at case management discussions. Orders and judgments listed in rule 18(7) may not be made at a case management discussion.

4–162

Rule 17(1)

The word "shall" in square brackets was substituted for the word "may" by para.2(4)(c) of the Employment Tribunals (Constitution and Rules of Procedure) (Amendment) (No. 2) Regulations 2005 (SI 2005/1835) with effect from October 1,

4–163

2005). The explanatory note which accompanied the regulations indicated that the main purpose of the amendments was to correct minor clarifications to and correct drafting errors in the original regulations and to implement s.36 of the Employment Relations Act 2004 which deals with national security proceedings. The original regulation left the decision whether or not to hold a case management discussion in private to the discretion of the employment judge: the amendment removes that discretion and requires a private hearing. Daily case lists and notices on the door of the tribunal emphasise the private nature of the hearing.

At a case management discussion it is often necessary for the employment judge to ensure that matters are dealt with expeditiously, that time is not spent unreasonably and that proper progress is made. It is from time to time necessary for an employment judge to be robust, to abbreviate discussion and to move forward (*EB v BA* UKEAT/0227/07/ at [65])

Rule 17(1)—Interim hearings. . .

4–164   A hearing is defined by reg.2 as a case management discussion, pre-hearing review, review hearing or Hearing. Rule 4 in Sch.1 defines each type of hearing or Hearing for these purposes. There is no definition of what constitutes an interim hearing, except that both case management discussions and pre-hearing reviews are described as interim hearings in the Rules. Clearly, an interim hearing cannot be the final hearing under r.26, which is held for the purposes of disposing of the proceedings, though it might be a hearing under r.26 held for the purposes of deciding any outstanding procedural or substantive issues. By default therefore, an interim hearing is any hearing that does not amount to a hearing held to finally dispose of the proceedings under r.26, but is either a case management discussion, a pre-hearing review or a hearing under reg.2 which is a "sitting of an employment judge or a tribunal duly constituted for the purpose of receiving evidence, hearing addresses and witnesses or doing anything lawful to enable the employment judge or tribunal to reach a decision on any question", other than a hearing that disposes of the proceedings under r.26.

Rule 17(1)—Matters of procedure and management of the proceedings

4–165   Case management discussions are, according to the explanatory guidance that accompanied publication of the Rules, intended as a means of ensuring the smooth running of a case through the tribunal system. Under the previous provisions of r.4, which was entitled "case management" the tribunal had the power to give such directions as appeared appropriate on any matter arising in connection with the proceedings. It could do so on its own initiative or on the application of either party. It became the practice, particularly in the case of discrimination claims, and very much at the suggestion of the courts, to hold directions hearings, the purpose being to define the issues between the parties, deal with disclosure and witness statements, and fix hearing dates with the agreement of the parties. Rule 17 formalises the practice of holding directions hearings. The tribunal may still elect to give directions on paper without the need for a hearing, or it may hold the hearing but conduct it by means of a telephone conference call in accordance with r.15. Rule 11(1) permits any party to apply at any time for a case management discussion to be held (subject to r.11(3) (the need to identify where an order is being sought, how the proposed order will assist the employment judge or tribunal in dealing with the proceedings efficiently and fairly). The tribunal can also decide under r.12 to hold a case management discussion of its own initiative. The employment judge has available to him all the powers in r.10, but may also make any further order except an order of the kind listed in r.18(7). In other words, he cannot strike out the claim or response or determine any preliminary issue in relation to whether or not the claimant is entitled to bring the proceedings in question. It seems that although an employment judge has express power at a pre-hearing review to do anything that may be done at a case management discussion (under r.18(2)(b)), there is no reciprocal power for the employment judge at a case management discussion to do anything that is permitted at an pre-hearing review, unless expressly excluded under r.17(2). For example the employment judge may neither (despite the fact that case management discussions and pre-hearing reviews are both interim hearings) make an order for payment of a deposit under r.18(2)(c) and 20, nor deal with an application for interim relief under r.18(2)(e).

Rule 17(2)—"Any determination of a person's civil rights or obligations"

The function of the case management discussion is to manage the proceedings: it **4–166** cannot dispose of the proceedings. In particular, issues such as whether the tribunal has jurisdiction to hear the claim are outside the scope of a case management discussion. In addition, the tribunal has no power to make a restricted reporting order, or to strike out a claim at a case management discussion. These are expressly excluded by the final sentence of r.17(2). Essentially a case management discussion replaces and extends the ambit of what used to be a hearing for directions, and now more closely follows the scope of Pt 3 of the CPR.

Rule 10(2)

Rule 10 contains the majority of the tribunal's powers of case management (see **4–167** the notes at para.4–106 et seq.).

Rule 18(7)

Rule 18(7) sets out the power of the tribunal to hold a hearing to determine the **4–168** types of issues previously dealt with by tribunals at preliminary hearings held under r.6 of the 2001 Regulations.

PRE-HEARING REVIEWS

Conduct of pre-hearing reviews

18.—(1) Pre-hearing reviews are interim hearings and shall be 4–169 conducted by a chairman unless the circumstances in paragraph (3) are applicable. Subject to rule 16, they shall take place in public.

(2) At a pre-hearing review the chairman may carry out a preliminary consideration of the proceedings and he may—

(a) **determine any interim or preliminary matter relating to the proceedings;**

(b) **issue any order in accordance with rule 10 or do anything else which may be done at a case management discussion;**

(c) **order that a deposit be paid in accordance with rule 20 without hearing evidence;**

(d) **consider any oral or written representations or evidence;**

(e) **deal with an application for interim relief made under section 161 of TULR(C)A or section 128 of the Employment Rights Act.**

(3) Pre-hearing reviews shall be conducted by a tribunal composed in accordance with section 4(1) and (2) of the Employment Tribunals Act if—

       (a) a party has made a request in writing not less than 10 days before the date on which the pre-hearing review is due to take place that the pre-hearing review be conducted by a tribunal instead of a chairman; and

       (b) a chairman considers that one or more substantive issues of fact are likely to be determined at the pre-hearing review, that it would be desirable for the pre-hearing review to be conducted by a tribunal and he has issued an order that the pre-hearing review be conducted by a tribunal.

(4) If an order is made under paragraph (3), any reference to a chairman in relation to a pre-hearing review shall be read as a reference to a tribunal.

(5) Notwithstanding the preliminary or interim nature of a pre-hearing review, at a pre-hearing review the chairman may give judgment on any preliminary issue of substance relating to the proceedings. Judgments or orders made at a pre-hearing review may result in the proceedings being struck out or dismissed or otherwise determined with the result that a Hearing is no longer necessary in those proceedings.

(6) Before a judgment or order listed in paragraph (7) is made, notice must be given in accordance with rule 19. The judgments or [orders] listed in (7) must be made at a pre-hearing review or a Hearing if one of the parties has so requested. If no such request has been made such judgments or [orders] may be made in the absence of the parties.

(7) Subject to paragraph (6), a chairman or tribunal may make a judgment or order—

       (a) as to the entitlement of any party to bring or contest particular proceedings;

       (b) striking out or amending all or part of any claim or response on the grounds that it is scandalous, or vexatious or has no reasonable prospect of success;

       (c) striking out any claim or response (or part of one) on the grounds that the manner in which the proceedings have been conducted by or on behalf of the claimant or the respondent (as the case may be) has been scandalous, unreasonable or vexatious;

       (d) striking out a claim which has not been actively pursued;

       (e) striking out a claim or response (or part of one) for non-compliance with an order or practice direction;

       (f) striking out a claim where the chairman or tribunal considers that it is no longer possible to have a fair Hearing in those proceedings;

(g) making a restricted reporting order (subject to rule 50).

(8) A claim or response or any part of one may be struck out under these rules only on the grounds stated in sub-paragraphs (7)(b) to (f).

(9) If at a pre-hearing review a requirement to pay a deposit under rule 20 has been considered, the chairman who conducted that pre-hearing review shall not be a member of the tribunal at the Hearing in relation to those proceedings.

Pre-hearing reviews

Under the 2004 Rules what used to be pre-hearing reviews conducted under r.7 **4–170** and preliminary hearings held under r.6 (entitlement to bring or contest proceedings) have been combined in one composite rule. At the same time the requirement for a full tribunal to sit to determine a number of preliminary issues has been removed. Pre-hearing reviews are, like case management discussions, interim hearings, but unlike case management discussions which deal with matters of procedure and management, a pre-hearing review can as well as doing anything that can be done at the case management discussion, also determine any interim or preliminary matter relating to the proceedings.

Rule 18(1)

Unless an employment judge determines that the hearing should take place in **4–171** private pursuant to r.16, the hearing must take place in public. The hearing takes place before an employment judge sitting alone unless the provisions of r.18(3) apply.

Rule 18(2)

A pre-hearing review is a preliminary consideration of the proceedings, and **4–172** therefore the employment judge cannot finally dispose of the proceedings; however this proposition has to be read subject to r.18(5) which provides that an employment judge may give judgment on a preliminary issue of substance relating to the proceedings, which may result in the proceedings being struck out or dismissed or otherwise disposed of in such a way that a hearing (under r.26) is no longer necessary. The issue is more fully discussed in the commentary on r.18(5) and (7). In addition, the employment judge can exercise all the powers available to him under rr.17 and 10 to give directions and issue case management orders. In connection with his powers under r.18, the employment judge may consider oral or written representations or hear evidence (r.18(2)(d)), whereas if he is considering whether or not to order a deposit to be paid under r.20, he may do so without hearing evidence (r.18(2)(c)).

Rule 18(3)—Composition of the tribunal

The effect of this provision is to require a pre-hearing review to be conducted by **4–173** an employment judge sitting alone unless:

(a) Any party has made a request in writing not less than ten days before the pre-hearing review for it to be conducted by a full tribunal; and

(b) an employment judge considers that one or more substantive issues of fact are likely to be determined; that it would be desirable for the hearing to be conducted before a full tribunal; and he has issued an order to that effect.

It is clear that both of these requirements must be satisfied. It is not sufficient for a party to make the request in writing, indicating that these three considerations apply, because the employment judge must also take the view that the three conditions are established. The rule contains no express power to extend the ten day time limit, and the ten day period is calculated in accordance with reg.15, so that if the hearing is to take place on June 11, the request must be made (not received) on June 1. It is not the task of the employment judge to alert parties to the fact that the Rule requires them to take the initiative in seeking a full tribunal at the pre-hearing review. Although r.18(3) refers to s.4(1) and (2) of the Employment Tribunals Act 1996 (on the composition of the tribunal), it makes no reference to s.4(5) of the Act which requires an employment judge to determine at all stages whether to hold a hearing before a full tribunal. In those circumstances there is no obligation on the employment judge, in the absence of any indication in r.18(3) that the employment judge must have regard to the provisions of s.4(5), to inform the parties of their right to ask for a full tribunal. The overriding objective does not compel the employment judge to establish whether either party is aware of the requirements of r.18(3), even if one or other or both is unrepresented. Not only that, but if the pre-hearing review has actually been convened, it is difficult to see how either party, or the employment judge for that matter, can overcome the prescriptive requirements of r.18(3)(a) in relation to the time limit of ten days in which to make the application. The only basis on which the tribunal could act to waive that requirement would be under the general power contained in r.10. Rule 10(2)(e), which enables the tribunal to give notice of a pre-hearing review gives the tribunal a power to make an order extending any time limit, even if the period has expired, and the list of exclusions from that power does not extend to cover r.18. Therefore, although the employment judge is not required to be proactive and draw the parties' attention to the facility to seek an order for the pre-hearing review to be before a full tribunal, he may accede to such an application at the actual hearing, and overcome the difficulty in r.18(3) about the period of ten days by relying on r.10(2)(e) to extend the time for that application. In the event that the application is granted, the hearing would have to be adjourned, unless the parties waive the requirements of r.14(4). If they do, and assuming that there are members available, there seems no reason in the rules as to why the pre-hearing review could not take place the same day, before the reconstituted full tribunal, thereby avoiding an adjournment. Arguably there is no need to give a further notice of the pre-hearing review, as it is still the originally convened hearing that is taking place, but the tribunal is differently constituted. That leaves open the question of whether the parties should assist the tribunal in furthering the overriding objective by waiving any objection to the need to give notice of the proposed hearing date.

Rule 18(5)—Judgment on preliminary issues of substance

4–174   This provision read in conjunction with r.18(2)(a) and 18(7) makes it clear that the tribunal may consider a range of preliminary issues, which if decided against, the claimant will result in the proceedings being dismissed. Apart from the orders which can be made under r.18(7)(b)-(f) striking out the proceedings, the combined effect of r.18(2)(a), 18(5) and 18(7)(a) is that the tribunal may determine a number of fundamental issues, some of them going to the question of the jurisdiction of the tribunal to hear and determine the claim. Obvious examples include but are not limited to:

    (i) determining whether the claim is in time;
    (ii) determining the claimant's employment status and length of service;
    (iii) determining whether the claimant has complied with the requirements of s.32 of the Employment Act 2002 before bringing the claim; and
    (iv) determining in the context of a potential claim whether there has been a relevant transfer under TUPE.

As to the need for caution when considering whether a preliminary issue is suitable for early detemination, see the cases at para.4–119 above.

Rule 18(6)

In the original rule, the word "order" was used in the singular. It was amended to read in the plural with the substitution of orders in the square brackets by para.2(4)(d) of the Employment Tribunals (Constitution and Rules of Procedure) (Amendment) (No. 2) Regulations 2005 SI 2005/1835, with effect from October 1, 2005. It is purely a tidying up exercise of the drafting of the original rule.

4–175

Rule 18(7)(a)—Entitlement to bring or contest proceedings

This provision coupled with r.18(2)(a) and r.18(5) gives the tribunal the power to resolve all preliminary issues affecting the jurisdiction of the employment tribunal (see the commentary on r.18(5)).

4–176

Rule 18(7)(b)—Striking out claims and responses

The corresponding provision in r.15(2)(c) of the 2001 Rules used the formula "scandalous, misconceived or vexatious". Prior to that, the phrase used was "scandalous, vexatious or frivolous." A frivolous application was one that was "bound to fail" (See *Jiad v Byford* [2003] I.R.L.R. 232 CA; *Anyanwu v South Bank Students' Union & South Bank University* [2001] I.R.L.R. 305). The 2001 Rules replaced "frivolous" with "misconceived", and in 2004 the change effectively substituted the definition of misconceived from the Regulations for the phrase itself. For these purposes "reasonable" is synonymous with "realistic" (see *Balamoody v United Kingdom Central Council for Nursing* [2002] I.R.L.R. 288; *ED&F Man Liquid Products Ltd v Patel* [2003] EWCA Civ. 472; and *Ezsias v North Glamorgan NHS Trust* [2006] UKEAT 705), and this is a matter that is to be assessed objectively.

4–177

The EAT considered the application of r.18 of the Tribunal Rules in *Ezsias v North Glamorgan NHS Trust* [2006] UKEAT 705 ([56]-[65]). The substance of that judgment may be summarised as follows. As regards the application of the criterion of "no reasonable prospect of success" the test is that stated in *Balamoody*—i.e. realistic, rather than fanciful ([56]). A "classic situation" where the power under r.18 may be used is where the tribunal concludes that even on the facts advanced by the claimant the case "has no prospect of success as a matter of law" ([57]). Where facts are in issue "it can only be in the most extreme case" that a tribunal could conclude "that the disputed facts will inevitably or almost inevitably be resolved against the claimant" [58]. Where there are material disputes of fact, it is in principle possible for a tribunal "in a clear case" to conclude that a claimant has no chance of establishing the facts alleged [64]. In the same case, on appeal to the Court of Appeal, the court gave an example where the power might be exercised of a situation where the facts sought to be advanced by the claimant were "totally and inexplicably inconsistent with undisputed contemporaneous documentation" [2007] I.R.L.R. 603 at [29]. However, in a situation where the claim of unfair dismissal includes a dispute between the parties as to the reason/primary reason for dismissal the primary factual basis on which the tribunal concludes that the dismissal, must have been for the reason advanced by the employer must itself be undisputed [64].

In light of the decision in *Ezsias*, the following points are made. Firstly, the Appeal Tribunal's reference to the "classic situation" where r.18 would apply should not be regarded as the only situation in which a tribunal may strike out a claim under r.18. The classic situation identified by the Appeal Tribunal is in fact one in which the claim could properly be regarded as frivolous or vexatious (see *Balamoody* above). The power under r.18 to deal summarily with claims that have no

4–178

reasonable prospect of success may well therefore extend beyond the circumstances identified by the EAT. Secondly, the observations made by the EAT in *Ezsias* as to the extent to which the existence of disputed points of fact is fatal to an application under r.18 must be considered in light of the judgment of the Court of Appeal in *ED&F Man* (which was not cited to the Appeal Tribunal). Although it is not open to a tribunal under r.18 to conduct a "mini-trial" of substantial issues of fact, the mere existence of a dispute of fact may not be fatal to an application under r.18. Before this point is reached the disputed point must both be material to the possible resolution of the claim being pursued by the claimant (i.e. something which if resolved in the claimant's favour is realistically capable of being material to the outcome of the claim), and also the disputed point itself must be one on which the claimant's position is something better than "merely arguable". Thirdly, the overall approach of caution favoured by the EAT to applications under r.18 must be applied in a way that is sensitive to the actual issues that arise in each case, and the specific context of each case. For example, on a r.18 hearing, a tribunal may be much better placed to determine an issue directed to the reasonableness of an employer's actions than to determine a straight dispute of fact on an issue central to a claim.

It is important to recognise that it is not open to the EAT to approach the matter on an appeal as if it was a tribunal of first instance. In principle a decision under r.18 is a matter for the discretion of the Employment Tribunal: an appeal can only succeed if the decision is perverse or based on a misdirection of law: see *Balamoody* (above) per Ward L.J. at [49]-[50]. See also on this point, *Medallion Holidays v Birch* [1985] I.C.R. 578. In this case the EAT specifically rejected the argument that an appeal against a decision to strike out should be treated as a re-hearing of the application, see per *Waite J.* at pp.580H-581H, and 583H-584E.

The phraseology used here is to be compared with that in r.20 which talks about "little reasonable prospects of success" in the context of the tribunal's power to order the payment of a deposit as a condition of being allowed to continue where the claim has only limited prospects of success.

A party wishing to seek an order striking out a claim or response under r.18(7)(b) would be well advised to seek an order under r.20 in the alternative. The sanction under r.20, in the event of non-payment of the deposit is more immediate, as the tribunal is not required under r.20 to consider whether a fair hearing is still possible.

Rule 18(7)(c)—Striking out claims on the basis of the manner conducted

4–179   This provision is aimed at the conduct of a party and their representative as opposed to the merits of the claim or response. In *Bolch v Chipman* [2004] I.R.L.R. 140 a case under the previous r.15(2)(d), which though differently worded used the same formula of "scandalous, unreasonable or vexatious" conduct, the EAT held that what is required of the tribunal before such an order is made is a four stage enquiry. First there must be not only a conclusion that the party has behaved scandalously, unreasonably or vexatiously, but secondly that the proceedings have been conducted in that way. The tribunal must then go on to consider whether a fair trial is still possible, because ordinarily a strike-out order should not be seen as a punishment. This is despite the fact that there is a separate provision to that effect in r.18(7)(f). Finally, even then the tribunal must still (in accordance with the overriding objective) determine that an order striking out the proceedings is a proportionate response to the conduct in question. An order for costs might suffice. Alternatively, for example, it might be permissible to allow the respondent who by virtue of the rule is treated as never having put in a response, still to take part in the proceedings on the question of remedy (see also *NSM Music Ltd v Leefe* [2006] I.C.R. 450 on the consequences of an order under r.9, and also the commentary at para.4–094).

Rule 18(7)(d)—Striking out a claim not actively pursued

Despite the fact that the Rules contain ample powers to ensure that claims reach **4–180**
a hearing date within a reasonable timescale, there is retained in this rule a power
to strike out a claim that has not been actively pursued. That power should be
exercised in accordance with the common law principles laid down by the House of
Lords in *Birkett v James* [1978] A.C. 297.

The court, or in this case, the tribunal, should only strike out a case that has not
been actively pursued where:

(a) Any default of the part of the claimant, by for example failing to reply to
correspondence from the tribunal or to comply with orders has been
intentional or contumelious (contemptuous); or

(b) where there has been inordinate or inexcusable delay on the part of the
claimant or his representative, such that there is no longer any prospect of
a fair trial or there is substantial prejudice to the respondent.

The tribunal may still be able in either of these situations to rely in any event on
the provisions of either r.18(7)(e) or r.18(7)(f). Arguably, before acting under this
rule, the tribunal ought first to consider making an order requiring the claimant to
take action before a specified date or risk the claim being struck out, and secondly
ought still to take into account whether there is still the possibility of a fair hearing
and whether an order striking out the claim is a proportionate response.

Unless orders

Where the tribunal strikes out the claim or response because of non-compliance **4–181**
with an unless order (under r.13(2)) it is a decision open to review under r.34, as it
is in effect a conditional judgment, which becomes final on non-compliance with the
order. In addition the tribunal retains a role to review the strike-out order or an
application for an extension of time: it does not become functus officio on issuing
the order (*Uyanya-Odu v Schools Offices Services Ltd* UKEAT/0294/05). For the effect of
"unless orders" and whether a further order is required, see commentary at 4–140.

Rule 18(7)(e)

Notwithstanding the prescriptive nature of the rule, it is clear that the mere fact **4–182**
of non-compliance with an order of the tribunal, even an unless order, will not of
itself justify the tribunal striking out the claim or response on this ground. The
EAT has made it clear that the starting point is that the employment tribunal must
be able to impose a sanction where there has been wilful disobedience by a party of
an order (see *Weir Valves & Controls (UK) Ltd v Armitage* [2004] I.C.R. 371, EAT,
citing with approval *De Keyser Ltd v Wilson* [2001] I.R.L.R. 324 at [25], and *Bolch v
Chipman* [2004] I.R.L.R. 140, EAT). However, it does not follow that a striking out
order or other sanction should always be the result of disobedience to an order. The
guiding consideration is the overriding objective. This requires justice to be done
between the parties. The tribunal should consider all the circumstances. It should
consider the magnitude of the default, whether the default is the responsibility of
the solicitor or the party, what disruption, unfairness or prejudice has been caused,
and whether a fair hearing is still possible. It should consider whether striking out
or some lesser remedy would be an appropriate response to the disobedience. The
EAT went on to draw on the provisions of CPR r.3.9 where there is a checklist to be
considered upon an application for relief from a sanction. Although the rules
contain no equivalent provision to CPR r.3.9, the overriding objective requires a
broadly similar approach. Subsequently in *Blockbuster Entertainment Ltd v James*
[2006] I.R.L.R. 630 the Court of Appeal, approving the approach articulated in

Bolch, and *Weir Valves*, stressed the various factors the tribunal must take into account (per Sedley L.J. at [5] and [21]).

"This power, as the employment tribunal reminded itself, is a Draconic power, not to be readily exercised. It comes into being if, as in the judgment of the tribunal had happened here, a party has been conducting its side of the proceedings unreasonably. The two cardinal conditions for its exercise are either that the unreasonable conduct has taken the form of deliberate and persistent disregard of required procedural steps, or that it has made a fair trial impossible. If these conditions are fulfilled, it becomes necessary to consider whether, even so, striking out is a proportionate response. The principles are more fully spelt out in the decisions of this court in *Arrow Nominees v Blackledge* [2000] 2 B.C.L.C. 167 and of the EAT in *De Keyser v Wilson* [2001] I.R.L.R. 324, *Bolch v Chipman* [2004] I.R.L.R. 140 and *Weir Valves v Armitage* [2004] I.C.R. 371, but they do not require elaboration here since they are not disputed. It will, however, be necessary to return to the question of proportionality before parting with this appeal. (at para.5)

It is not only by reason of the Convention right to a fair hearing vouchsafed by article 6 that striking out, even if otherwise warranted, must be a proportionate response. The common law, as Mr James has reminded us, has for a long time taken a similar stance: see *Re Jokai Tea Holdings* [1992] 1 W.L.R. 1196, especially at 1202E-H. What the jurisprudence of the European Court of Human Rights has contributed to the principle is the need for a structured examination. The particular question in a case such as the present is whether there is a less drastic means to the end for which the strike-out power exists. The answer has to take into account the fact—if it is a fact—that the tribunal is ready to try the claims; or—as the case may be—that there is still time in which orderly preparation can be made. It must not, of course, ignore either the duration or the character of the unreasonable conduct without which the question of proportionality would not have arisen; but it must even so keep in mind the purpose for which it and its procedures exist. If a straightforward refusal to admit late material or applications will enable the hearing to go ahead, or if, albeit late, they can be accommodated without unfairness, it can only be in a wholly exceptional case that a history of unreasonable conduct which has not until that point caused the claim to be struck out will now justify its summary termination. Proportionality, in other words, is not simply a corollary or function of the existence of the other conditions for striking out. It is an important check, in the overall interests of justice, upon their consequences".

In *Ridsdill v D Smith & Nephew Medical* [2006] UKEAT/0704/05, the EAT considered the approach to be adopted where the tribunal is faced with parties who had failed to comply with case management orders. It concluded that it was incumbent on the tribunal to consider an adjournment, even where one was not requested, to remedy the non-compliance, and if necessary coupling that with unless orders. The EAT emphasised that the tribunal must adopt a structured approach to the issue of whether the claim should be struck out, demonstrating a transparent process of enquiry, assessing all the issues rather than concentrating on "a fixed moment of fairness." The tribunal is effectively by these judgments compelled to intervene to issue a strike out order only at the point of no return: the mere fact of non-compliance alone will not justify the order unless the tribunal has considered the proportionality of the sanction, whether a fair trial is still possible, and the respective prejudice to the parties. It will usually first have issued unless orders, but even then the tribunal must still consider firstly whether there has been either a failure to pursue the claim, or wilful disregard of orders, such that a fair trial is no longer possible.

It was justifiable to strike out a respondent who had deliberately and persistently disregarded orders of the tribunal: equally it was a proportionate response to allow the respondent to be heard on the question of remedy (*Premium Care Homes Ltd v Osborne* UKEAT/0077/06).

Rule 18(7)(f)

Although this power to strike out exists in the rules as a separate ground, its **4-183** significance is diminished because the tribunal is required by the authorities previously quoted in the commentary always to ask the question whether it is still possible to have a fair hearing.

Rule 18(7)(g)

This rule enables the tribunal to make a restricted reporting order at a pre- **4-184** hearing review instead of at the full hearing. Where doing so the employment judge must observe the requirements of r.50 (see para.4–319).

Notice requirements

19.—(1) Before a chairman or a tribunal makes a judgment or 4-185 order described in rule 18(7), except where the order is one described in rule 13(2) or it is a temporary restricted reporting order made in accordance with rule 50, the Secretary shall send notice to the party against whom it is proposed that the order or judgment should be made. The notice shall inform him of the order or judgment to be considered and give him the opportunity to give reasons why the order or judgment should not be made. This paragraph shall not be taken to require the Secretary to send such notice to that party if that party has been given an opportunity to give reasons orally to the chairman or the tribunal as to why the order should not be made. (2) Where a notice required by paragraph (1) is sent in relation to an order to strike out a claim which has not been actively pursued, unless the contrary is proved, the notice shall be treated as if it were received by the addressee if it has been sent to the address specified in the claim as the address to which notices are to be sent (or to any subsequent replacement for that address which has been notified to the Employment Tribunal Office).

This Rule needs to be read in conjunction with r.61 which lays down the **4-186** requirements to be followed for service of notices and documents under the rules (see para.4–357).

PAYMENT OF A DEPOSIT

Requirement to pay a deposit in order to continue with proceedings

20.—(1) At a pre-hearing review if a chairman considers that the 4-187 contentions put forward by any party in relation to a matter required to be determined by a tribunal have little reasonable prospect of success, the chairman may make an order against that party requir-

ing the party to pay a deposit of an amount not exceeding £500 as a condition of being permitted to continue to take part in the proceedings relating to that matter.

(2) No order shall be made under this rule unless the chairman has taken reasonable steps to ascertain the ability of the party against whom it is proposed to make the order to comply with such an order, and has taken account of any information so ascertained in determining the amount of the deposit.

(3) An order made under this rule, and the chairman's grounds for making such an order, shall be recorded in a document signed by the chairman. A copy of that document shall be sent to each of the parties and shall be accompanied by a note explaining that if the party against whom the order is made persists in making those contentions relating to the matter to which the order relates, he may have an award of costs or preparation time made against him and could lose his deposit.

(4) If a party against whom an order has been made does not pay the amount specified in the order to the Secretary either:—

    (a) within the period of 21 days of the day on which the document recording the making of the order is sent to him; or

    (b) within such further period, not exceeding 14 days, as the chairman may allow in the light of representations made by that party within the period of 21 days; a chairman shall strike out the claim or response of that party or, as the case may be, the part of it to which the order relates.

(5) The deposit paid by a party under an order made under this rule shall be refunded to him in full except where rule 47 applies.

Rule 20(1)—Contentions put forward by a party at a pre-hearing review

4–188   Rule 18(2)(c) provides that an employment judge may make an order under r.20 without hearing evidence. Under the old r.7(1) and 7(4) consideration of whether or not to order payment of a deposit was limited to an examination of the contents of the originating application and notice of appearance, written representations, and oral argument. The new rule is less prescriptive and refers to the "contentions" put forward by a party. Rule 18(2)(d) however, which must be read with r.20 and r.18(2)(c), enables the employment judge to consider any oral or written representations, or evidence—i.e. including any witness statement or documentary evidence, as long as the employment judge is not invited to hear that evidence and permit cross-examination. To that extent, it is a substantial shift from the practice before 2004. Where an Employment Tribunal made a deposit order under r.20 against the Appellant on the grounds that her claims had little prospect of success, and she failed to pay the deposit by the date specified, and her claims were struck out, the EAT held that the employment judge could have regard to the likelihood of the facts being established when making a deposit order. The EAT did not on the facts of that case need to resolve the question whether rule 20(4) was compatible with ECHR art.6: *Van Rensburg v Kingston on Thames* UKEAT/0096/07. In principle there is no reason why r.20(4) should not be regarded as a reasonable and proportionate limitation on the right of access to a court, and as such consistent with the requirements of ECHR art.6.

Rule 20(1)—Little reasonable prospect of success

Rule 7(4) of the 2001 rules used the phrase "no reasonable prospects of success." **4–189** Under the 2001 rules the tribunal had power under r.15(2)(c) to strike out an originating application or notice of appearance if it was "misconceived". As the term "misconceived" included having "no reasonable prospects of success", it was held that the concept had the same meaning in r.7 as in r.15. That meant that the tribunal could, if it concluded that the applicant's claim had no reasonable prospects of success, either strike out the claim, or make an order requiring a deposit to be paid (*H M Prison Service v Dolby* [2003] I.R.L.R. 694, EAT). Now orders for deposit payments are governed by a different test. At the pre-hearing review, assuming that a respondent is seeking orders in the alternative, the tribunal must first determine whether the claim has no reasonable prospect of success under r.18(7)(b), and if so it can strike out under that rule. If not satisfied that the claim has no reasonable prospects of success, it must then determine whether the claim has little reasonable prospect of success (a lower threshold). If so satisfied it can, subject to the rest of the provisions of r.20, order the claimant to pay a deposit. If no application is made under r.18, then the tribunal proceeds to determine the questions raised under r.20.

Rule 20(1)—Order to pay a deposit

An order that a party should pay a deposit is not capable of review because it is **4–190** not a judgment for the purposes of r.28(1) because (a) it is not a final determination of the proceedings: it is an order under r.28(1) and (b) because it is an order in relation to interim matters and orders a person to do something, it therefore cannot be reviewed under r.34(1)(b), because r.34(1) makes it clear that only those decisions set out in r.34(1)(a) to (c) are capable of being reviewed under r.34. It is however an order that can be revoked or varied under r.10(2)(a). In addition the time for payment can be extended notwithstanding that the time for payment has expired (r.10(2)(e)). If, however, the party fails to make the payment and the claim is struck out under r.20(4), that is then a judgment which can be reviewed under r.34 (*Sodexho v Gibbons* [2005] I.R.L.R. 836; [2005] I.C.R. 1647, EAT).

Rule 20(2)—Ability to comply

The enquiry is not an enquiry as to the means of the party, as might be envisaged **4–191** under r.41(2). It is an enquiry limited to the capacity of the party to comply with the terms of the order, which involves a consideration of the ability of the party to realise the necessary assets within the limited timescale of 21 days of the order, in the context of the enquiry carried out when determining the amount of the deposit.

The wording of this paragraph replicates the wording in r.7(5) of the 2001 rules. It is different to the wording of r.41(2) in relation to costs orders where the tribunal may, not must, have regard to ability to pay. Order 20(2) is mandatory and assumes an obligation on the tribunal or employment judge to make enquiries as to the ability to pay the deposit rather than an investigation into the means of the party in question. In that respect the party ought to provide some evidence of income, capital and capacity to pay. Whether or not the tribunal should adjourn the hearing to enable the necessary enquiries to be made must depend on the overriding objective.

Rule 20(3)

Although the rule refers to the employment judge's grounds for making the **4–192** order, it is clear that for these purposes grounds are the equivalent of reasons in r.30. The only apparent justification for the different terminology is the fact that a decision under r.20 cannot be reviewed. The order must also contain a note that alerts the party to the risk of a subsequent order for costs. By virtue of r.18(9) if an order is made under r.20, the employment judge making the order is not permitted to conduct the hearing of the complaint under r.26.

Rule 20(3) and (4)—Sent to the party

4–193   Under the 2001 rules there was an issue as to whether the date of service of the order was to be interpreted in accordance with s.7 of the Interpretation Act 1978 so that the period of 21 days would commence on the date of deemed service. The conflict in the authorities was resolved by the Court of Appeal in 2004 in a case involving the EAT rules, but which is of relevance to interpretation in any situation where the tribunal has to determine when a document was sent: a document is sent on the date that the document is posted by the employment tribunal (*Gdynia American Shipping Lines (London) Ltd v Chelminski* [2004] I.R.L.R. 725; [2004] I.C.R. 1523). The position is now governed by the provisions of the new reg.15 in the 2004 Regulations on the calculation of time limits, which makes it clear that all time limits in the rules are to be calculated in accordance with reg.15. Regulation 15 was not referred to in *Sodexho*, however, it appears to set out in legislative form the conclusion reached in *Chelminsky*. Consequently if the order is sent on October 1, the payment must be made to the Secretary no later than October 22, in accordance with reg.15(2), and that date must be included in the letter from the tribunal accompanying the order.

Rule 20(4)—Strike out the claim

4–194   The obligation to strike out for failure to pay the deposit is mandatory and the tribunal is not obliged to consider whether to take into account the overriding objective and in particular the factors set out in CPR r.3.9. Under the 2001 rules, an order under r.7(7) striking out an application for non-payment of a deposit was not a decision within the meaning of the then reg.2(2) that was capable of review under the old r.11 (*Kuttapan v Croydon London Borough Council* [1999] I.R.L.R. 349, EAT). However the distinction in the old rules between an order striking out for non-payment of a deposit and on the grounds that the claim was misconceived is not maintained in the new rules. If an order striking out a claim or response for non-payment of a deposit is a judgment it is reviewable under r.34(1)(b). In *Sodexho* (see notes to r.20(1) above), it was held that the order striking out under r.20(4) is a judicial determination rather than an administrative act; that it constitutes a final determination of the proceedings for the purposes of r.28(1)(a); and as it is therefore a judgment, it is capable of review under r.34(1)(b) (*Sodexho v Gibbons* [2005] I.R.L.R. 836; [2005] I.C.R. 1647, EAT).

Rule 20(5)—Refund of the deposit

4–195   Rule 47 envisages an initial three stage enquiry. It assumes first a r.20 payment of a deposit, secondly, failure in the proceedings by the party against whom the deposit order was made, and thirdly, no decision by the tribunal to make a costs or preparation time order against that party. If those three conditions are met the tribunal may make a costs or preparation time order if:

(i) after a consideration of the document recording the r.20 order that the tribunal considers that the grounds for finding against that party were substantially the same as the grounds for ordering the deposit; and

(ii) the claimant has conducted the proceedings unreasonably in persisting in having the matter determined.

CONCILIATION

General

Prior to the introduction of the 2004 rules, the services of an ACAS conciliator **4–196** were available to the parties throughout the proceedings. It was considered by the government in its consultation paper paving the way for the reforms in 2004, Routes to Resolution, that the facility was both expensive to fund and tended to encourage late rather than early settlement of claims. The 2004 rules introduce the concept of fixed periods of conciliation of either seven or thirteen weeks, with a limited power of extension. The unlimited period of conciliation remains for discrimination claims and whistle-blowing claims.

The proposals were dismissed by the Labour peer and lawyer Lord Wedderburn QC, in the parliamentary debate in the House of Lords, as the "product of a tiny but inexperienced mind". ACAS made it clear in its consultation paper in February 2004 that it did not intend to give the parties any assistance at all after the expiry of the fixed period for consultation or any extension, except in exceptional circumstances. Those were identified in the consultation paper as: serious illness of one of the parties; significant delay in receipt by ACAS of the papers from the ETS; extreme communication difficulties; significant complexities in a case dealing with a large number of unrepresented claimants; and a significant and unforeseeable change of circumstances. The evidence so far, including an ACAS discussion paper published in April 2006, assessing the impact of both the 2004 rules and the Dispute Resolution Regulations, indicates that the introduction of fixed periods of conciliation has failed to achieve the purpose of encouraging the earlier settlement of cases in the tribunal, and has hampered the attempts of parties to conclude a settlement after the services of the ACAS conciliator are no longer available. In such situations the only option open to the parties, assuming that they are represented, is a compromise agreement.

The ACAS duty to conciliate in individual disputes derives from s.18 of the Employment Tribunals Act 1996. It is the duty of the conciliator "to endeavour to promote a settlement of the proceedings without their being determined by an employment tribunal." The duty relates to both actual and potential complaints to an employment tribunal. The duty to assist the parties to resolve their differences requires the conciliator to attempt to help the parties see the strengths and weaknesses of their respective positions. The conciliator must not express an opinion on those respective positions, or express views on the merits of the case or the likely outcome. In *Clarke v Redcar* and *Cleveland Borough Council* [2006] I.R.L.R. 324; [2006] I.C.R. 897, the EAT reaffirmed that principle in a detailed review of the relationship between the role of the ACAS conciliator and the purpose of the compromise agreement vehicle for the resolution of contentious proceedings. The function of the conciliator in respect of any settlement facilitated by the conciliator and contained within the COT3 resolving the proceedings is as follows:

(a) The ACAS officer has no responsibility to see that the terms of the settlement are fair on the employee;

(b) The expression "promote a settlement" must be given a liberal construction capable of covering whatever action by way of such promotion as is applicable in the circumstances of the particular case;

(c) The ACAS officer must never advise as to the merits of the case. It would be quite wrong to say that the ACAS officer was obliged to go through the framework of the legislation. Indeed, it might defeat the officer's very function if she were obliged to tell a claimant, in effect, that they might receive considerably more money;

(d) It is not for the tribunal to consider whether the officer correctly interpreted her duties; it is sufficient that she intended and purported to act under the section; and

(e) If the ACAS officer was to act in bad faith or adopt unfair methods when promoting a settlement the agreement might be set aside and might not operate to bar proceedings.

Documents to be sent to conciliators

4–197   **21. In proceedings brought under the provisions of any enactment providing for conciliation, the Secretary shall send copies of all documents, orders, judgments, written reasons and notices to an ACAS conciliation officer except where the Secretary and ACAS have agreed otherwise.**

Rule 21—In proceedings brought under any enactment providing for conciliation

4–198   The full list of the legislative measures which provide for the services of conciliation officers and the duty to endeavour to promote a settlement is set out in s.18 of the Employment Tribunals Act 1996, as amended.

Fixed period for conciliation

4–199   **22.—(1) This rule and rules 23 and 24 apply to all proceedings before a tribunal which are brought under any enactment which provides for conciliation except national security proceedings and proceedings which include a claim made under one or more of the following enactments—**

   (a) **the Equal Pay Act, section 2(1);**
   (b) **the Sex Discrimination Act, Part II, section 63;**
   (c) **the Race Relations Act, Part II, section 54;**
   (d) **the Disability Discrimination Act, Part II, section 17A or 25(8);**
   (e) **the Employment Equality (Sexual Orientation) Regulations 2003;**
   (f) **the Employment Equality (Religion or Belief) Regulations 2003;**
   (g) **Employment Rights Act, sections 47B, 103A and 105(6A); and**
   (h) **the Employment Equality (Age) Regulations 2006**

(2) In all proceedings to which this rule applies there shall be a conciliation period to give a time limited opportunity for the parties to reach an ACAS conciliated settlement (the "conciliation period"). In proceedings in which there is more than one respondent there shall be a conciliation period in relation to each respondent.

(3) In any proceedings to which this rule applies a Hearing shall not take place during a conciliation period and where the time and place of a Hearing has been fixed to take place during a conciliation period, such Hearing shall be postponed until after the end of any

conciliation period. The fixing of the time and place for the Hearing may take place during a conciliation period. Pre-hearing reviews and case management discussions may take place during a conciliation period.

(4) In relation to each respondent the conciliation period commences on [the day following] the date on which the Secretary sends a copy of the claim to that respondent. The duration of the conciliation period shall be determined in accordance with the following paragraphs and rule 23.

(5) In any proceedings which consist of claims under any of the following enactments (but no other enactments) the conciliation period is seven weeks (the "short conciliation period")—

(a) Employment Tribunals Act, section 3 (breach of contract);

(b) the following provisions of the Employment Rights Act—

   (i) sections 13 to 27 (failure to pay wages or an unauthorised deduction of wages);
   (ii) section 28 (right to a guarantee payment);
   (iii) section 50 (right to time off for public duties);
   (iv) section 52 (right to time off to look for work or arrange training);
   (v) section 53 (right to remuneration for time off under section 52);
   (vi) section 55 (right to time off for ante-natal care);
   (vii) section 56 (right to remuneration for time off under section 55);
   (viii) section 64 (failure to pay remuneration whilst suspended for medical reasons);
   (ix) section 68 (right to remuneration whilst suspended on maternity grounds);
   (x) sections 163 or 164 (failure to pay a redundancy payment);

(c) the following provisions of TULR(C)A—

   (i) section 68 (right not to suffer deduction of unauthorised subscriptions)
   (ii) section 168 (time off for carrying out trade union duties);
   (iii) section 169 (payment for time off under section 168);
   (iv) section 170 (time off for trade union activities);
   (v) section 192 (failure to pay remuneration under a protective award);

(d) regulation 15(10) of the Transfer of Undertakings (Protection of Employment) Regulations 2006 (failure to pay compensation following failure to inform or consult).

[(e) regulations 13, 14(2) or 16(1) of the Working Time Regulations 1998 (right to paid annual leave)]

(6) In all other proceedings to which this rule applies the conciliation period is thirteen weeks (the "standard conciliation period").

(7) In proceedings to which the standard conciliation period applies, that period shall be extended by a period of a further two weeks if ACAS notifies the Secretary in writing that all of the following circumstances apply before the expiry of the standard conciliation period—

> (a) all parties to the proceedings agree to the extension of any relevant conciliation period;
>
> (b) a proposal for settling the proceedings has been made by a party and is under consideration by the other parties to the proceedings; and
>
> (c) ACAS considers it probable that the proceedings will be settled during the further extended conciliation period.

(8) A short conciliation period in any proceedings may, if that period has not already ended, be extended into a standard conciliation period if a chairman considers on the basis of the complexity of the proceedings that a standard conciliation period would be more appropriate. Where a chairman makes an order extending the conciliation period in such circumstances, the Secretary shall inform the parties to the proceedings and ACAS in writing as soon as is reasonably practicable.

Rule 22(1)

4–200   The entirety of this paragraph retains the unlimited power of the conciliation officer to conciliate in national security proceedings, and in all claims involving claims for equal pay, discrimination claims, and claims under the "whistleblowing" provisions of the Employment Rights Act 1996. By virtue of the Employment Equality (Age) (Consequential Amendments) Regulations 2007 SI 2007/825, which came into effect on April 6, 2007 a new r.22(1)(h) adds claims under those regulations to the list of claims in respect of which there is no fixed period for conciliation. The necessary consequential amendments are also made to s.105 of the Employment Rights Act 1996, so that a dismissal will be unfair if the reason for dismissal is the employee exercising, or seeking to exercise, his or her right to be accompanied, or to accompany another, at a meeting to request working beyond the intended date retirement under para.9 of Sch.6 to the Employment Equality (Age) Regulations 2006; to Regs 7(3) and 14(2) of the Employment Act 2002 (Dispute Resolution) Regulations 2004 SI 2004/752, so that complaints of age discrimination are treated in the same way as complaints under any other discrimination legislation; and the addition of the Employment Equality (Age) Regulations 2006 to the list in para.22(1) of Sch.1 to the Employment Tribunals (Constitution and Rules of Procedure) Regulations 2004 SI 2004/1861, which will exempt age discrimination claims from the requirement for a fixed conciliation period of 13 weeks. This particular change is likely to be of little practical effect, since ACAS has been treating age claims as if they were already included in the list.

Rule 22(3)

No hearing within the meaning of r.26 may take place during either of the fixed **4–201** periods of conciliation. Query whether if a hearing has taken place any decision given at a hearing during the fixed period would be a nullity (compare *Storer v British Gas Plc* [2000] I.R.L.R. 495; [2000] I.C.R. 603). Any hearing already listed during that period must be postponed. It is permissible to list a case for a Hearing during that period. Other types of hearing such as a pre-hearing review under r.18, or a case management discussion under r.17 is permissible.

Rule 22(4)

The words in square brackets were added to the original rule by virtue of **4–202** para.2(4)(e) of the Employment Tribunals (Constitution and Rules of Procedure) (Amendment) (No. 2) Regulations 2005 (SI 2005/1865) with effect from October 1, 2005.

Rule 22(5) and (8)

The whole of this provision between the square brackets was added by **4–203** para.2(4)(f) of the Employment Tribunals (Constitution and Rules of Procedure) (Amendment) (No. 2) Regulations 2005 (SI 2005/1835) with effect from October 1, 2005. It creates a period of seven weeks for conciliation (the "short conciliation period") in what are essentially claims for unpaid wages or the equivalent. An employment judge has power under r.22(8) to convert the "short period" into a "standard period" as long as the "short period" has not expired. He can only do so if he considers that the standard period would be more appropriate. The secretary must notify both ACAS and the parties of the decision as soon as is reasonably practicable, but seemingly the employment judge is not obliged to but may choose to give reasons for that decision.

Rule 22(5)(d)

Rule 22(5)(d) was amended by reg.3 of the Transfer of Undertakings (Protection **4–204** of Employment) (Consequential Amendments) Regulations 2006 (SI 2006/2405) with effect from October 1, 2006. The words "regulation 11(5) of the Transfer of Undertakings (Protection of Employment) Regulations 1981" were replaced by the words "regulation 15(10) of the Transfer of Undertakings (Protection of Employment) Regulations 2006". There are transitional arrangements in reg.5.

EARLY TERMINATION OF CONCILIATION PERIOD

23.—(1) Should one of the following circumstances arise during a **4–205 conciliation period (be it short or standard) which relates to a particular respondent (referred to in this rule as the relevant respondent), that conciliation period shall terminate early on the relevant date specified (and if more than one circumstance or date listed below is applicable to any conciliation period, that conciliation period shall terminate on the earliest of those dates)—**

> **(a) where a default judgment is issued against the relevant respondent which determines both liability and remedy, the date on which the default judgment is signed;**
>
> **(b) where a default judgment is issued against the relevant respondent which determines liability only, the date**

which is 14 days after the date on which the default judgment is signed;

(c) where either the claim or the response entered by the relevant respondent is struck out, the date on which the judgment to strike out is signed;

(d) where the claim is withdrawn, the date of receipt by the Employment Tribunal Office of the notice of withdrawal;

(e) where the claimant or the relevant respondent has informed ACAS in writing that they do not wish to proceed with attempting to conciliate in relation to those proceedings, the date on which ACAS sends notice of such circumstances to the parties and to the Employment Tribunal Office;

(f) where the claimant and the relevant respondent have reached a settlement by way of a compromise agreement (including a compromise agreement to refer proceedings to arbitration), the date on which the Employment Tribunal Office receives notice from both of those parties to that effect;

(g) where the claimant and the relevant respondent have reached a settlement through a conciliation officer (including a settlement to refer the proceedings to arbitration), the date of the settlement;

(h) where no response presented by the relevant respondent has been accepted in the proceedings and no default judgment has been issued against that respondent, the date which is 14 days after the expiry of the time limit for presenting the response to the Secretary.

(2) Where a chairman or tribunal makes an order which re-establishes the relevant respondent's right to respond to the claim (for example, revoking a default judgment) and when that order is made, the conciliation period in relation to that respondent has terminated early under paragraph (1) or has otherwise expired, the chairman or tribunal may order that a further conciliation period shall apply in relation to that respondent if they consider it appropriate to do so.

(3) When an order is made under paragraph (2), the further conciliation period commences on the date of that order and the duration of that period shall be determined in accordance with paragraphs (5) to (8) of rule 22 and paragraph (1) of this rule as if the earlier conciliation period in relation to that respondent had not taken place.

Rule 23

4–206   This rule does no more than set out the circumstances in which the fixed conciliation periods are either terminated early or re-instated after certain specified events.

EFFECT OF STAYING OR SISTING PROCEEDINGS ON THE CONCILIATION PERIOD

24. Where during a conciliation period an order is made to stay (or **4–207** **in Scotland, sist) the proceedings, that order has the effect of suspending any conciliation period in those proceedings. Any unexpired portion of a conciliation period takes effect from the date on which the stay comes to an end (or in Scotland, the sist is recalled) and continues for the duration of the unexpired portion of that conciliation period or two weeks (whichever is the greater).**

Rule 24

This rule again merely deals with the effect of a "stay" or "sist" on the **4–208** conciliation period. (For commentary on the general power to stay proceedings see commentary on r.10(2)(h) at para.4–118).
Withdrawal of Proceedings

RIGHT TO WITHDRAW PROCEEDINGS

25.—(1) A claimant may withdraw all or part of his claim at any **4–209** **time-this may be done either orally at a hearing or in writing in accordance with paragraph (2).**

(2) To withdraw a claim or part of one in writing the claimant must inform the Employment Tribunal Office of the claim or the parts of it which are to be withdrawn. Where there is more than one respondent the notification must specify against which respondents the claim is being withdrawn.

(3) The Secretary shall inform all other parties of the withdrawal. Withdrawal takes effect on the date on which the Employment Tribunal Office (in the case of written notifications) or the tribunal (in the case of oral notification) receives notice of it and where the whole claim is withdrawn, subject to paragraph (4), proceedings are brought to an end against the relevant respondent on that date. Withdrawal does not affect proceedings as to costs, preparation time or wasted costs.

(4) Where a claim has been withdrawn, a respondent may make an application to have the proceedings against him dismissed. Such an application must be made by the respondent in writing to the Employment Tribunal Office within 28 days of the notice of the withdrawal being sent to the respondent. If the respondent's application is granted and the proceedings are dismissed those proceedings cannot be continued by the claimant (unless the decision to dismiss is successfully reviewed or appealed).

(5) The time limit in paragraph (4) may be extended by a chairman if he considers it just and equitable to do so.

Rule 25 was a new rule introduced in 2004 to address the problem identified by **4–210** the Court of Appeal in *Ako v Rothschild Asset Management Ltd* [2002] I.C.R. 348, CA. In that case Mummery L.J. explained that in civil proceedings mere discontinuance of a claim without dismissal will not prevent the claimant commencing fresh proceedings, though the permission of the court might be required (CPR r.38.7). At the time r.15(2)(a) of the 2001 rules provided that the only way to formally bring a claim to an end was to dismiss it. Rule 25 is an attempt to address that problem. Rule 25(1) enables the claimant to withdraw all or part of the claim at any time in accordance with r.25(3). The respondent may then apply under r.25(4) to have the claim dismissed. Those proceedings then cannot be continued by the claimant unless that decision is reviewed or appealed. That raises two questions. Can a notice of withdrawal be set aside, and can the claimant commence fresh proceedings for the same claim or claims? The first question was answered in the negative in *Khan v Heywood & Middleton Primary Care Trust* [2006] I.R.L.R. 345 and also in *Ellis v Yansen* UKEAT/0132/06. For such a power to exist there would have to be an express provision in the rules. Despite the reference in r.25(4) to "those proceedings", once a claim was withdrawn and then dismissed on an application by the respondent the claimant was precluded from commencing any fresh proceedings based on the same cause of action, whereas that would not be the case if the claim was merely withdrawn (on which see *Verdin v Harrods Ltd* [2006] I.R.L.R. 339, EAT). In describing the drafting of the rule as both "lamentable" and "remarkable", the EAT accepted that the drafting of the rule does not expressly make it clear that the claimant cannot commence a fresh claim, which is the intention of r.25(4). The claimant appealed to the Court of Appeal, who upheld the judgment of the EAT ([2006] I.R.L.R. 345) Wall L.J. delivering the judgment of the court adopted the description of the drafting of rule as "lamentable", adding also that the rule was "ambiguous" and "poorly drafted" and suggesting that the rule be revised. He accepted that there was an apparent contradiction between paras (3) and (4) but concluded that the intention and effect of para.(4), despite the poor drafting, was to prevent the claimant from commencing fresh proceedings on the same facts where the claim had been dismissed as opposed to merely withdrawn. First there is an absence of an express power in the rules to commence fresh proceedings (one had existed in the original draft rules sent out for consultation); secondly the conclusion that para.(4) had been introduced to resolve the dilemma in *Ako*, by closing the apparent lacuna identified in the difference between withdrawal and dismissal of a claim (the view taken in *Verdin*); and thirdly the proposed construction of the Rule was consistent with CPR r.38.7 (Discontinuance and subsequent proceedings).

The sensible course of action for respondents wishing to prevent the risk of further proceedings, following this judgment, is always to apply within 28 days for the claim to be dismissed, because the claimant is not automatically precluded by the rule from commencing fresh proceedings if the claim is merely withdrawn under r.25(2) and (3): see *Khan* at [74]. Whether those subsequent proceedings would amount to an abuse of process would require the tribunal to address the questions raised in *Ako*: what was the reason for withdrawal of the original claim and in particular was it to commence proceedings in another forum? It is the practice in many regions always to seek the views of the claimant before automatically issuing an order under para.(4) to ensure that the claimant is not precluded from commencing proceedings either in the tribunal or elsewhere.

Rule 10(1) does not permit an employment judge to amend a notice of withdrawal and thereby revoke it; equally the notice of withdrawal takes effect immediately not at the end of the day, thereby preventing the withdrawal itself from being withdrawn at any time during that day, and finally, r.25(3) does not require the notice to state reasons for it to be effective (*Silva-Douglas v London School of Economics* EAT/0075/07).

4–211   In *Verdin v Harrods Ltd* (above), the EAT emphasised that an employment tribunal was wrong not to permit a claimant to withdraw her claim under r.25(3) without at the same time dismissing it under r.25(4), so as to enable her to commence proceedings in the High Court. It was stressed that withdrawal does not require the consent of the tribunal or the respondent. Withdrawal can be of the whole or part of the proceedings. There is no question of cause of action estoppel as there is no order under r.25(4), although it is implicit in the rule that withdrawal brings "the proceedings" to an end. A respondent wishing to ensure the final disposal of the proceedings was advised therefore to make an application under r.25(4) and would normally be entitled to that order if the claimant had no intention of litigating the issue further. However if the claimant's intention is to withdraw the proceedings for the purpose of pursuing litigation in another forum then the questions for the tribunal are whether the party withdrawing is intending to abandon the claim, and whether there is an abuse of process if the claimant is intending to resurrect the claim in fresh proceedings. If the answer to either of those questions is in the affirmative, then the respondent will normally be entitled to an order under r.25(4) but not if the answer to both the questions is no.

There is a clear distinction between an oral and written withdrawal of a claim and to be effective the written withdrawal must clearly identify which claim or part of the claim is being withdrawn (*Tamborrino v Kuypers* UKEAT0483/05 EAT).

The claimant who consents to an order under r.25(4) dismissing the claim without appreciating that this will prevent the commencement of fresh proceedings may have the option of seeking an order reviewing the order dismissing the claim. The order is a judgment under r.28(1) and therefore susceptible to review under r.34(1)(b) (per H.H.J. Richardson in *BASC v Cokayne* [2008] I.C.R. 185 at [36])

Rule 25(4)—Respondent's application to dismiss the proceedings

A respondent intending to apply to dismiss the proceedings under r.25(4) must also comply with r.11(4) if he is legally represented. (see the commentary at para.4–131).

4–212

THE HEARING

Hearings

26.—(1) A Hearing is held for the purpose of determining outstanding procedural or substantive issues or disposing of the proceedings. In any proceedings there may be more than one Hearing and there may be different categories of Hearing, such as a Hearing on liability, remedies, costs (in Scotland, expenses) or preparation time.

4–213

(2) Any Hearing of a claim shall be heard by a tribunal composed in accordance with section 4(1) and (2) of the Employment Tribunals Act. (3) Any Hearing of a claim shall take place in public, subject to rule 16.

(3) Any hearing of a claim shall take place in public, subject to rule 16.

General

Rule 14 is the general Rule which specifies the types of hearing that may take place during the progress of a claim through the tribunal. A hearing under r.26 is generally the final hearing to dispose of the claim, but will include all hearings on the questions of liability, remedy, costs or expenses, or preparation time orders.

4–214

Rule 26(2)—Composition of the tribunal

4–215   The Employment Tribunals Act 1996 provides in s.4 that a tribunal shall comprise an employment judge and two members drawn from the respective panels constituted in accordance with regs 5, 8, and 9, except where under s.4(2) an employment judge may sit alone.

Rule 26(3)—Shall take place in public

4–216   An employment tribunal may not hold a hearing in a room to which the public does not have access, such as the office of the regional employment judge, even if no hearing room is available and the reasons for the judgment disclose no error of law (*Storer v British Gas Plc* [2000] I.R.L.R. 495; [2000] I.C.R. 603, CA).

Rule 26(3)—Subject to rule 16

4–217   Rule 16 sets out the circumstances in which a tribunal may sit in private for part or the whole of the proceedings (see at para.4–159).

What happens at the Hearing

4–218   **27.—(1) The President, Vice President or a Regional Chairman shall fix the date, time and place of the Hearing and the Secretary shall send to each party a notice of the Hearing together with information and guidance as to procedure at the Hearing.**

(2) Subject to rule 14(3), at the Hearing a party shall be entitled to give evidence, to call witnesses, to question witnesses and to address the tribunal.

(3) The tribunal shall require parties and witnesses who attend the Hearing to give their evidence on oath or affirmation.

(4) The tribunal may exclude from the Hearing any person who is to appear as a witness in the proceedings until such time as they give evidence if it considers it in the interests of justice to do so.

(5) If a party fails to attend or to be represented (for the purpose of conducting the party's case at the Hearing) at the time and place fixed for the Hearing, the tribunal may dismiss or dispose of the proceedings in the absence of that party or may adjourn the Hearing to a later date.

(6) If the tribunal wishes to dismiss or dispose of proceedings in the circumstances described in paragraph (5), it shall first consider any information in its possession which has been made available to it by the parties.

(7) At a Hearing a tribunal may exercise any powers which may be exercised by a chairman under these rules.

Rule 27(1)—Notice of the hearing

4–219   In practice, the date, time and venue of the hearing is fixed either at:

(a) the end of or during a case management discussion;
(b) following on from determination of a preliminary issue at a pre-hearing review;
(c) when standard case management orders are made in fast-track cases; or

(d) by the appropriate officer in the listing section of the regional office, after discussion with the regional employment judge.

Rule 27(2)—Subject to Rule 14(3)

Rule 14(3) empowers the tribunal to question witnesses and to conduct the **4–220** hearing in such manner as it considers appropriate. Although this permits the tribunal to limit the length of questioning and to set timetables for the witnesses and the length of cross-examination, as well as to ask questions and limit the issues, it cannot prevent the parties from calling evidence, and neither can the tribunal dictate the order in which witnesses are called. Nevertheless the tribunal may encourage, for example, in a claim for unfair dismissal, calling the dismissing officer and the person who conducted the appeal, while at the same time suggesting that it may not be necessary for any other witnesses in the investigatory process to be called.

Rule 27(2)—Entitlement to address the tribunal—submissions of no case

It would be rare for a submission of no case to answer to be made to an **4–221** employment tribunal, and even more rare for that submission to succeed. The principles governing a submission of that nature can be summarised as follows:

(a) There is no inflexible rule of law and practice that a tribunal must hear both sides, but it should normally do so;
(b) The power to stop a case at "half-time" must be exercised with caution;
(c) It may be a complete waste of time to call on the other party in a hopeless case;
(d) Even where there is an onus of proof on a party, as in a discrimination case, it will only be in an exceptional or frivolous case that it would be right to take such a course; and
(e) Where there is no burden of proof, for example under s.98(4) of the Employment Rights Act 1996, it will be difficult to envisage arguable cases where it is appropriate to take that step (*Clarke v Watford Borough Council*, unreported, May 4, 2000, EAT; cited with approval in Logan v Commissioners of Customs and Excise [2004] I.R.L.R. 64; [2004] I.C.R., CA). Compare also *Wiggan v RN Wooler and Co Ltd* [2007] UKEAT/0542/06.

The Court of Appeal has made it clear in *Logan* that the fourth proposition also applies to claims for constructive dismissal. Subsequently in *Boulding v Land Securities Trillium (Media Services) Ltd* UKEAT/0023/06/RN, the principle was extended to "whistleblowing" cases. The fourth proposition must now be read subject to the guidance of the Court of Appeal on the approach to the burden of proof in discrimination cases (*Igen Ltd v Wong* [2005] I.R.L.R. 258; [2005] I.C.R. 931, CA).

Rule 27(2)—Entitlement to address the tribunal—written submissions

An employment tribunal may, particularly if the case raises complex issues or to **4–222** avoid a claim going part heard, order the parties to prepare written rather than oral submissions. Where it does so it must allow sufficient time for them to be prepared, consider and assimilated by the tribunal and the other parties, especially if they are to be followed by oral submissions (*Sinclair Roche & Temperley v Heard* (No. 1) [2004] I.R.L.R. 763). The EAT has laid down the following guidelines in relation to the use of written submissions, and this remains good practice still after the 2004 Rules.

(a) Written submissions should only be used where the parties agree.

(b) It is the responsibility of the employment judge that the procedure for the exchange and use of written submissions is in accordance with the rules of natural justice.

(c) Once written submissions have been received the tribunal should serve them on the other party.

(d) The parties should be given the opportunity to comment on the respective submission within a defined timescale.

(e) Only after that should the tribunal meet to reach its decision.
(*London Borough of Barking v Oguoko* [2000] I.R.L.R. 179, EAT).

Rule 27(4)—Exclusion of witnesses

4–223   This power was usually the practice in Scotland prior to the 2004 Rules. It is now a power given to all tribunals. At present there is no evidence to indicate that it is a power that has been grasped by tribunals in England and Wales. It does, however, indicate that there is now a presumption in Scotland that witnesses would not be excluded unless the tribunal exercised its discretion under r.27(4).

Rule 27(5)—Failure to attend

4–224   In every case, where a party fails to attend a scheduled hearing the tribunal must consider whether to make enquiries by telephone to ascertain the party's where-abouts. It does not have to be done in every case but the option must be considered (*Cooke v Glenrose Fish Company* [2004] I.R.L.R. 866; [2004] I.C.R. 1188, EAT). The current guidance issued to tribunal panels by the President of the Employment Tribunals, which is not a Practice Direction, advises that panels should proceed under r.27(5) after first satisfying themselves that that there are no special circumstances that justify contacting the missing party, on the basis that any error can be corrected on review. That guidance seems to run counter to the suggestion in *Cooke* that the tribunal ought normally consider whether or not to make the telephone call.

Once the tribunal has taken steps to ascertain the reason for the non-appearance of the claimant, it must then take one or other of the steps set out in the Rules: it can dispose of the claim, dismiss the claim, or adjourn. There is no requirement for the claimant to attend the hearing. Should the tribunal require the respondent to give evidence, for example, of the reason for dismissal, where there is a burden of proof on the respondent under s.98(2) of the Employment Rights Act 1996? The Court of Appeal has held in a case decided on the differently worded r.9(3) of the 1993 Regulations (which, however, did not differ in relation to the options available to the tribunal) that the tribunal has a wide discretion under what is now r.27(5) and it is entitled either to require the employer to prove the reason for dismissal, or dismiss the claim without further enquiry after carrying out the exercise now required under r.27(5) which goes further than its predecessor under both the 1993 and 2001 Rules as it now also requires the tribunal to consider any information, not just the claim and the response (*Roberts v Skelmersdale College* [2004] I.R.L.R. 69; [2003] I.C.R. 1127, CA).

Rule 27(6)—Procedure to be followed if a party fails to attend

4–225   Under r.9 of the 2001 Rules the tribunal was only required to consider the originating application and the notice of appearance. Rule 27(6) permits the tribunal to consider any information made available by the parties, including written representations, correspondence and statements and documents. The Rule obliges the tribunal to consider that information, and it has no discretion in that matter. Any judgment dismissing the claim must indicate that the tribunal has first considered any information in accordance with r.27(6).

Orders and judgments

28.—(1) Chairmen or tribunals may issue the following— **4–226**

(a) a "judgment", which is a final determination of the proceedings or of a particular issue in those proceedings; it may include an award of compensation, a declaration or recommendation and it may also include orders for costs, preparation time or wasted costs;

(b) an "order", which may be issued in relation to interim matters and it will require a person to do or not to do something.

(2) If the parties agree in writing upon the terms of any order or judgment a chairman or tribunal may, if he or it thinks fit, make such order or judgment.

(3) At the end of a hearing the chairman (or, as the case may be, the tribunal) shall either issue any order or judgment orally or shall reserve the judgment or order to be given in writing at a later date.

(4) Where a tribunal is composed of three persons any order or judgment may be made or issued by a majority; and if a tribunal is composed of two persons only, the chairman has a second or casting vote.

Rule 28(1)—Judgments and orders

The definition of a judgment presents no difficulty. It is to all intents and **4–227** purposes what constituted a decision for the purposes of r.12 of the 2001 Rules. Rule 12 of the 2001 Rules also dealt with reasons and the difference between summary and extended reasons. Reasons, the circumstances in which they are given and whether orally or in writing, and when written reasons are to be supplied, is now dealt with in a new r.30. A judgment will now be given in most instances where previously a decision was issued. Essentially they will be given in all instances where the claim is finally disposed of by the tribunal on the question of liability, quantum and costs, or where the tribunal has disposed of an interim issue, in the main at a pre-hearing review. Orders will be given in all other situations, and in the main they will relate to preliminary matters, such as those set out in r.10. The difficulty is that rr.10 and 11 both contemplate the issuing by an employment judge or a tribunal of a range of orders, many of them listed in r.10(2) that cannot be defined as something that will in the wording of r.28(1)(b) "require a person to do something." It is clear that an order may be an order for the purposes of r.10, but not an order for the purposes of r.28 (see *Onwuka v Spherion Technology UK Ltd* [2005] I.C.R. 567, at [28]; and *Hart v English Heritage* [2006] I.C.R. 655 at [29]). The difficulty of distinguishing between the limited power to review an order under r.34 and the power to revoke or revisit an order under r.10 was resolved in both *Onwuka* and *Hart*. The issue yet to be resolved is whether the requirement in r.30(1)(b) to give either oral or written reasons when requested, applies only to those orders to which r.28(1)(b) applies or extends to all the orders contemplated by rr.10 and 11 (see below in the commentary on r.28(3) and r.30(1)(b)).

Rule 28(1)(a)—A judgment . . . is a final determination

An order striking out a party for failure to pay a deposit ordered under r.20(4) is **4–228** a judgment for the purposes of this Rule and also r.34(1)(b) (*Sodexho Ltd v Gibbons* [2005] I.R.L.R. 836; [2005] I.C.R. 1647). However the order for payment of the deposit is not a judgment for these purposes, but an order under r.28(1)(b) but it is not one that may be reviewed under r.34(1).

Rule 28(3)—Oral decisions

4–229   The employment judge or the tribunal must either issue its judgment or order orally at the end of the hearing or reserve it to be given in writing at a later date. In the event that the judgment or order is announced orally, the employment judge or tribunal must give its reasons. Whether the tribunal is obliged to give reasons for all orders or only those in respect of which r.28(1)(b) applies, is considered in the commentary on r.28(1). The likely construction is that the combined effect of rr.28 and 30 raises a presumption that reasons must be given for all judgments, given at either a hearing or a r.26 Hearing, and reasons must be given in respect of all orders made at the conclusion of any other hearing, because the wording of r.30(1)(b) refers to "the hearing at which the order is made." That envisages that if the order is made on paper, that the employment judge or tribunal is not obliged to supply reasons but may choose to do so.

Rule 28(4)—Majority decisions

4–230   The Court of Appeal has expressed the view that it is undesirable on the whole for tribunals to reach split decisions. It might be inevitable in some cases but it is preferable, if possible, for the panel to attempt to reach a unanimous decision. Unanimity is more likely if time is given after an initial disagreement for everybody to consider the position. If, at the conclusion of the hearing, members are unable to agree on what the result of their complaint should be, it is preferable for the employment judge to reserve the decision so that he can write it up and circulate it to the other members. If it is the two lay members in the majority and are disagreeing with the employment judge, it is preferable to give the two lay members not only an opportunity to see that their views are correctly expressed in the decision document drafted by the employment judge, but also an opportunity to reflect on the grounds on which they are disagreeing with the employment judge about the outcome of the hearing (*Anglian Home Improvements Ltd v Kelly* [2004] I.R.L.R. 793; [2005] I.C.R. 242, CA). The practical difficulty that is likely to occur is that this suggestion that the members take time to reflect could potentially conflict with the aim of avoiding delay in the promulgation of decisions that may give rise to an appeal and is in conflict with r.30 which envisages judgments supported by oral reasons being given at the conclusion of the hearing.

Form and content of judgments

4–231   **29.—(1) When judgment is reserved a written judgment shall be sent to the parties as soon as practicable. All judgments (whether issued orally or in writing) shall be recorded in writing and signed by the chairman.**

(2) The Secretary shall provide a copy of the judgment to each of the parties and, where the proceedings were referred to the tribunal by a court, to that court. The Secretary shall include guidance to the parties on how the judgment may be reviewed or appealed.

(3) Where the judgment includes an award of compensation or a determination that one party is required to pay a sum to another (excluding an order for costs, expenses, allowances, preparation time or wasted costs), the document shall also contain a statement of the amount of compensation awarded, or of the sum required to be paid.

Rule 29(1)

Following the judgment of the EAT in *Kwamin v Abbey National Plc* [2004] I.R.L.R. **4–232** 516; [2004] I.C.R. 841, EAT tribunals were advised that it should be the norm in most instances to endeavour to ensure that the administrative target of ensuring that the parties received the written judgment within four weeks of the hearing was a judicial target as well. If the tribunal was forced to reserve its decision it should aim to achieve the target of reaching the decision on the case and sending the parties the reserved judgment within three and a half months. The parties were to be told when the chambers meeting was to take place so that they could remind the tribunal in the event of any delay. Although the Court of Appeal in the same case subsequently held that delay was not of itself a ground for appeal the practice has been maintained in the tribunals (see *Bangs v Connex South Eastern Ltd* [2005] I.R.L.R. 389; [2005] I.C.R. 763, CA, and the commentary on r.30 below).

Reasons

30.—(1) A tribunal or chairman must give reasons (either oral or **4–233** written) for any—

(a) **judgment; or**

(b) **order, if a request for reasons is made before or at the hearing at which the order is made.**

(2) Reasons may be given orally at the time of issuing the judgment or order or they may be reserved to be given in writing at a later date. If reasons are reserved, they shall be signed by the chairman and sent to the parties by the Secretary.

(3) [Where oral reasons have been provided] written reasons shall only be provided:—

(a) **in relation to judgments if requested by one of the parties within the time limit set out in paragraph (5); or**

(b) **in relation to any judgment or order if requested by the Employment Appeal Tribunal at any time.**

(4) When written reasons are provided, the Secretary shall send a copy of the reasons to all parties to the proceedings and record the date on which the reasons were sent. Written reasons shall be signed by the chairman.

(5) A request for written reasons for a judgment must be made by a party either orally at the hearing (if the judgment is issued at a hearing), or in writing within 14 days of the date on which the judgment was sent to the parties. This time limit may be extended by a chairman where he considers it just and equitable to do so.

(6) Written reasons for a judgment shall include the following information—

(a) **the issues which the tribunal or chairman has identified as being relevant to the claim;**

(b) **if some identified issues were not determined, what those issues were and why they were not determined;**

   (c) **findings of fact relevant to the issues which have been determined;**

   (d) **a concise statement of the applicable law;**

   (e) **how the relevant findings of fact and applicable law have been applied in order to determine the issues; and**

   (f) **where the judgment includes an award of compensation or a determination that one party make a payment to the other, a table showing how the amount or sum has been calculated or a description of the manner in which it has been calculated.**

Rule 30(1)(b)—Reasons to be provided for judgments and orders

4–234   As discussed in the commentary on r.28, this provision is not clearly drafted. The power to ask the tribunal for oral or written reasons is subject to an application for reasons, either before or at the hearing at which the order is made. There is no time limit as far as the period before the hearing is concerned, and presumably the parties will normally indicate if reasons are required in the application for an order or orally at the hearing. The issue that is not clear is whether the power to ask for reasons but more importantly the obligation to supply them applies only to orders to which r.28 applies or also to orders to which rr.10 and 11 apply. Although r.34 only gives the parties the power to apply to review a limited range of orders (see *Onwuka v Spherion Technology UK Ltd* [2005] I.C.R. 567 and *Hart v English Heritage* [2006] I.C.R. 655), a party can appeal any decision, but will require reasons for the purposes of an appeal unless the tribunal is requested to supply them by the EAT under r.30(3)(b), so it is important to know to which orders r.30(1)(b) applies. The narrower view is that the obligation under r.30 to supply reasons applies only in respect of orders to which r.28(1)(b) applies, because of the compulsive element contained in that Rule, rather than to the broader non-compulsive orders, that could be envisaged under r.10. The difficulty is that a party may well wish to appeal a decision by an employment judge not to grant leave to amend a claim or response under r.10(2)(q). Such a decision is not a judgment, as it does not dispose of the proceedings, nor does it dispose of an issue in the proceedings; it is not a r.28 order as it does not require either party to do or not do something without a tortuously semantic distortion of language; though it must be an order refusing leave to amend for the purposes of r.10 or r.11. Since this is just the type of decision that a party might wish to appeal r.30(1)(b) should apply, entailing the conclusion that the rule applies to all case management decisions made by a tribunal at any time at a hearing, although not to orders made in writing.

Rule 30(2)—At a later date

4–235   The Rules anticipate that the tribunal will normally announce its decision and the reasons for that decision at the close of the hearing. The Rules retain the option of the tribunal reserving its judgment and giving reasons at a later date. The ETS has an administrative target of endeavouring to ensure that judgments supported by reasons where given in writing are sent to the parties within four weeks of the hearing. Where reasons are reserved the practice in employment tribunals is to ensure that the date for the meeting(s) in chambers for the tribunal to reach its conclusions is fixed before the parties leave, and in most instances the tribunal will provisionally fix a date for the remedy hearing if required. The EAT has stated that after allowing for the need for the panel to meet and reach its conclusions, three and a half months should be the maximum time needed for preparation of all but the most complicated and lengthy judgments (*Kwamin v Abbey*

National Plc [2004] 516; [2004] I.C.R. 841, EAT). Although the judgment was overruled by the Court of Appeal that timescale remains the advisory practice in the employment tribunals, so that parties experiencing delay in promulgation of a reserved judgment should contact the tribunal office near the expiry of that period. Subject to that the Court of Appeal held in the same case (sub nom *Bangs v Connex South Eastern Ltd* [2005] I.R.L.R. 389; [2005] I.C.R. 763, CA) that appeals from an employment tribunal on the grounds of excessive delay in the promulgation of judgments are governed by the following principles.

(a) An appeal is confined to a question of law and there is no independent ground that the tribunal made erroneous findings of fact; it is not the function of the appellate body to weigh the evidence and correct erroneous findings of fact as the tribunal is the final arbiter on fact.

(b) There is no question of law based on the contention that there was unreasonable delay in promulgation. Delay is a question of fact not law although an unreasonable delay may sustain an argument under art.6 of the ECHR entitling the victim to compensation from the State. It does not however give rise to a question of law.

(c) There is no independent ground of appeal based on the ground that the delay has led to material factual errors and omissions which render the decision unsafe.

(d) The only basis of challenge to the facts must be on the grounds of perversity: it must be established that either the overall decision or individual findings are perverse due to the delay.

(e) There is no incompatibility with Art.6 of the ECHR for domestic legislation to limit appeals from employment tribunals to questions of law.

(f) Even if it was incompatible it is not possible to use s.3(1) of the Human Rights Act 1998 or s.21(1) of the Employment Tribunals Act 1996 to expand the right to appeal on a question of law into a right to appeal issues of fact.

(g) In exceptional cases unreasonable delay by the tribunal could properly be treated as a procedural error or material irregularity giving rise to a question of law in respect of the "proceedings" for the purposes of s.21(1) of the ETA 1996. The basis of that point of law would be that the unreasonable delay had deprived the party of the right to a fair trial within the meaning of art.6 of the ECHR.

Rule 30(3) and (5)—Provision of written reasons

The words in square brackets in r.30(3) have been amended on two separate occasions since their introduction in October 2004. Paragraph (3) originally read "written reasons shall only be provided". That was amended by para.2(9)(c) of SI 2004/2351, with effect from October 1, 2004 to include the rider "subject to para.(1). A further revision was made by SI 2005/1865 which by virtue of para.2(4)(h) deleted that rider and replaced it with "Where oral reasons have been provided." The effect of the various amendments is that a party is only entitled to written reasons in the following situations: **4–236**

(a) Where judgment is reserved. (r.30(2));

(b) Where judgment is given orally but the provision of reasons is reserved (r.30(2));

(c) Where the judgment and reasons are given orally but a party requests the provision of written reasons either orally at the hearing at which the judgment is given or in writing within 14 days of the date the judgment is sent to the parties (r.30(5)); and

(d) Where the judgment and reasons are given orally but a party requests the provision of written reasons either orally at the hearing at which the judgment is given or in writing more than 14 days from the date the judgment is sent to the parties, but the employment judge has extended time for requesting reasons on the basis he considers it just and equitable to do so. (r.30(5)).

Rule 30(3)(b)—Written reasons requested by the EAT

4–237   The EAT has held that where an employment tribunal has given no reasons, or no adequate reasons, or has failed to deal with an issue at all, then the EAT can invite the tribunal to clarify, supplement, or give its written reasons before proceeding to dispose of the appeal (*Burns v Consignia* (No. 2) [2004] I.R.L.R. 425; [2004] I.C.R. 1103, EAT). The lawfulness of what came to be known as the Burns procedure has been examined by the Court of Appeal in *Barke v Seetec Business Technology Centre Ltd* [2005] I.R.L.R. 633; [2005] I.C.R. 1373, CA. From that judgment the following principles are laid down in relation to the provision of reasons when requested by the EAT:

(a) The EAT has power to invite the employment tribunal to amplify its reasons in accordance with the Burns procedure as subsequently incorporated in the 2004 EAT Practice Direction.

(b) The procedure is of considerable benefit and should be upheld.

(c) The power derives not from s.35(1) of the Employment Tribunals Act 1996 (as found in *Burns*), but from r.30(3)(b) of the 2004 Rules. There is nothing in that rule to prevent the EAT asking for further reasons even if the tribunal has already provided reasons for its judgment.

(d) The tribunal is not functus officio on promulgation of its judgment and is not prevented from receiving and responding to questions.

(e) Under the rules there are several important functions which the employment tribunal can perform after its judgment and reasons have been entered in their register, including responding to a request for notes, and reviewing the decision, and therefore there is no reason why it should not respond to a request for further information.

(f) Rule 30(1) provides that the employment tribunal must give reasons. If it has failed to comply with that duty either because it has not supplied reasons at all or because its reasons are inadequate it cannot be said to be functus officio.

(g) Even if there was no power in the Rules, the EAT would be acting lawfully in requesting reasons because s.30(3) of the ETA 1996 allows the EAT to regulate its own procedure. The *Burns* procedure codified in the 2004 Practice Direction is an example of that regulation and is a discretionary power in the exercise of case management.

(h) It is not a procedure to be exercised with considerable caution and only in tightly defined circumstances. The overriding objective of dealing with cases justly would be frustrated by an unduly restrictive application of the *Burns* procedure.

(i) Whilst there are dangers in asking the original tribunal for further reasons where the ground of appeal is the inadequacy of reasons, in that the tribunal may wish to tailor its reasons to remedy the defect or have a second bite at the cherry, there is a greater danger that on remission to the original tribunal, the tribunal will subconsciously wish to reach the same conclusion. The EAT will have to make a judgment on how serious those dangers are.

(j) The *Burns* procedure will not be appropriate where the inadequacy of the reasoning is on the face of the decision so fundamental that there is a real risk that supplementary reasons will be reconstructions of proper reasons rather than the unexpressed actual reasons. The procedure will also not be appropriate where there are allegations of bias.

In *Barke*, Dyson L.J. identified the source of the EAT's power to refer a case back to the Employment Tribunal as deriving from r.30(3) of Sch.1 to the Employment Tribunals (Constitution and Rules of Procedure) Regulations 2004, and s.30(3) of the ETA. Rule 30(3) has since been amended (by SI 2005/1865). In its amended form r.30(3) only permits reasons to be sought when the decision of the Employment Tribunal was given orally. This amendment may also affect the extent of the EAT's residual power under s.30(3) ETA.

Rule 30(6)—Content of written reasons

Until the changes to the Rules in 2004 there was no statutory requirement **4–238** prescribed for the structure and content of written reasons. Prior to that the overriding consideration was that reasons provided by an employment tribunal should be "Meek compliant", following the judgment of the Court of Appeal in that case. (*Meek v Birmingham DC* [1987] I.R.L.R. 250). For a tribunal judgment to be *Meek* compliant, it had to outline the evidence given and indicate the tribunal's factual findings and contain a statement of the reasons leading to the tribunal's conclusion. An appellate court should be able to determine from the decision whether a question of law arose. Rule 30(6) attempts to give statutory force to the judgment in that case and expands on it. The EAT has held that whilst r.30(6) does not supersede the judgment in *Meek*, it nevertheless sets out what is required of a tribunal's reasons for it to be *Meek* compliant, so that a tribunal "which complies fully and properly with Rule 30(6) can be assured that its decision (in the absence of bias or incompetence) will be found to be Meek compliant" (*Fisher v Hoopoe Finance Ltd* UKEAT/0043/05 [21]). Subsequently the Court of Appeal has upheld this approach without expressly referring to the judgment in Fisher which was not cited to it (*Balfour Beatty Power Networks Ltd v Wilcox* [2007] I.R.L.R. 63, CA). Tribunals are advised (at [25] of the judgment), to recite the terms of r.30(5) and to indicate how their decision fulfils its requirements. Provided it can be reasonably spelled out from the judgment and reasons that what r.30(5) requires has been provided by the tribunal, then no error of law will have been committed.

Appellate courts have stressed repeatedly that tribunal judgment are not statutes; that parties and especially their lawyers are not expected to trawl through the conclusions of the tribunal line by line in an attempt to locate a slight gap in the reasoning, or a minor factual error, in an attempt to attack the decision on either a point of law or on the basis of perversity. The parties are however entitled to know why they have won or lost. There is no duty to deal with every argument advanced, but the reasons must identify the issues which were vital to the conclusion and how they were resolved and where evidence is rejected the reasons should identify the reasons for rejecting that evidence (*English v Emery Riembold & Strick Ltd* [2003] I.R.L.R. 710). In general tribunals ought to avoid using such phrase as "we preferred the evidence", or "faced with a conflict we preferred the evidence of a particular witness", without explaining why that evidence was preferred (see *Anya v University of Oxford* [2001] I.R.L.R. 377; [2001] I.C.R. 847, CA). Arguably, as suggested by the EAT in *Fisher*, r.30(6) effectively codifies what appellate courts have been indicating since *Meek* to be the essential requirements of any written reasons supplied by an employment tribunal.

Rule 30(6)(a)—The issues identified as relevant

The issues to be resolved in the hearing are more than a statement of the various **4–239** claims. In a complicated claim involving allegations of direct and indirect discrimination, which also involved questions of whether claims were in time, a list of issues identified by the respective counsel for the parties had been rejected by the tribunal in its judgment which had only listed the separate claims. The EAT commended the use by tribunals, in a decision handed down before adoption of the 2004 Rules, of a summary of the central issues in a claim, as a means of dealing with the situation where issues change in the course of a hearing, and issues appearing for the first time in closing submissions (*Sinclair Roche & Temperley v Heard* (No. 1) [2004] I.R.L.R. 763).

Absence of chairman

4–240   **31. Where it is not possible for a judgment, order or reasons to be signed by the chairman due to death, incapacity or absence—**

> **(a) if the chairman has dealt with the proceedings alone the document shall be signed by the Regional Chairman, Vice President or President when it is practicable for him to do so; and**

> **(b) if the proceedings have been dealt with by a tribunal composed of two or three persons, the document shall be signed by the other person or persons; and any person who signs the document shall certify that the chairman is unable to sign.**

Rule 31—Absence of the chairman

4–241   Rule 31 provides a simple mechanism to enable the parties to receive a judgment that can be enforced if for any reason the employment judge is unable to sign, due to death, incapacity or absence. Many employment judge leave a signed copy of the handwritten judgment on the file to cover this eventuality. Such a judgment would comply with r.29(1) as it would be both recorded in writing and signed by the employment judge.

The Register

4–242   **32.—(1) Subject to rule 49, the Secretary shall enter a copy of the following documents in the Register—**

> **(a) any judgment (including any costs, expenses, preparation time or wasted costs order); and**

> **(b) any written reasons provided in accordance with rule 30 in relation to any judgment.**

(2) Written reasons for judgments shall be omitted from the Register in any case in which evidence has been heard in private and the tribunal or chairman so orders. In such a case the Secretary shall send the reasons to each of the parties and where there are proceedings before a superior court relating to the judgment in question, he shall send the reasons to that court, together with a copy of the entry in the Register of the judgment to which the reasons relate.

Rule 32

4–243   Rule 49 relates to proceedings involving allegations of a sexual offence. For commentary on r.49 see para.4–316 and for commentary on r.16 (hearings which may be held in private) see para.4–159.

Review of default judgments

4–244

33.—(1) A party may apply to have a default judgment against or in favour of him reviewed. An application must be made in writing and presented to the Employment Tribunal Office within 14 days of the date on which the default judgment was sent to the parties. The 14 day time limit may be extended by a chairman if he considers that it is just and equitable to do so.

(2) The application must state the reasons why the default judgment should be varied or revoked. When it is the respondent applying to have the default judgment reviewed, the application must include with it the respondent's proposed response to the claim, an application for an extension of the time limit for presenting the response and an explanation of why rules 4(1) and (4) were not complied with.

(3) A review of a default judgment shall be conducted by a chairman in public. Notice of the hearing and a copy of the application shall be sent by the Secretary to all other parties.

(4) The chairman may—

    (a) refuse the application for a review;

    (b) vary the default judgment;

    (c) revoke all or part of the default judgment;

    (d) confirm the default judgment; and all parties to the proceedings shall be informed by the Secretary in writing of the chairman's judgment on the application.

(5) A default judgment must be revoked if the whole of the claim was satisfied before the judgment was issued or if rule 8(6) applies. A chairman may revoke or vary all or part of a default judgment if the respondent has a reasonable prospect of successfully responding to the claim or part of it.

(6) In considering the application for a review of a default judgment the chairman must have regard to whether there was good reason for the response not having been presented within the applicable time limit.

(7) If the chairman decides that the default judgment should be varied or revoked and that the respondent should be allowed to respond to the claim the Secretary shall accept the response and proceed in accordance with rule 5(2).

Rule 33(1)

The obligation to make the application for review of a default judgment in writing stating the grounds is mandatory. An oral application, even where made at a hearing to assess compensation and on the last day for making such an application, in default of an extension of time on the just and equitable principle, was defective (*Direct Timber Ltd v Hayward* UKEAT/0646/05).

4–245

Rule 33(2), (5) and (6)

4–246   The application for review must both explain the reason for the failure to comply with the obligation to serve the response in time, and indicate the nature of the proposed response. Ideally, the application should be accompanied by the proposed response or the actual response if served late, and rejected by the tribunal. On the application for review, the employment judge must consider not only the reason for the delay, but whether the respondent has grounds for defending the claim. The provision in r.33(6) is not the overriding consideration in r.33, so that failure by the respondent(s) to provide a good reason for the late response must defeat the application. The fact that r.33(6) states that the employment judge must consider whether there is a good reason for the late response, whereas r.33(5) only states that he may revoke all or part of the judgment if the respondent has a reasonable prospect of defending the claim, does not give r.33(6) more importance than r.33(5). The absence of any reference to the need to consider the length of the delay after the judgment before the application was made, the question of prejudice if the respondent is allowed to defend the claim, and the question of costs, does not preclude consideration of those factors. The discretion to review under r.33 was one to be exercised in accordance with broad just and equitable principles, notwithstanding the absence of any reference to that principle in r.33, beyond that in r.33(1). The overriding objective applied to enable the tribunal to weigh all the factors, including any explanation for the delay, and the tribunal was able to take into account the same principles as were applicable under CPR r.13.3(1) The proposition laid down under the previous rules by Mummery J. in *Kwik Save Stores Ltd v Swain* [1997] I.C.R. 49, at p.56 remained good law:

> ". . . it was incumbent on a respondent applying for an extension of tine for serving a notice of appearance [. . .] to put before the industrial tribunal all relevant documents and other factual material in order to explain [. . .] both the non-compliance and [. . .] the basis on which it was sought to defend the case on its merits; that an industrial tribunal chairman in exercising the discretion to grant an extension of time to enter a notice of appearance had to take account of all relevant factors, including the explanation or lack of explanation for the delay and the merits of the defence, weighing and balancing them one against the other, and to reach a conclusion which was objectively justified on the grounds of reason and justice; that it was important when doing so to balance the possible prejudice to each party . . . ".

These broad propositions were laid down in *Pendragon Plc t/a C D Bramall (Bradford) v Copus* [2005] I.C.R. 1671 at [18]. There support for the approach was derived from CPR r.13.3 (setting aside judgments). Generally it was stated that the provisions of the CPR were especially relevant, particularly in the event of any uncertainty or ambiguity in the Rules.

The respondent is required to demonstrate a reason for the delay to satisfy r.33(6), but although that is a mandatory factor it is not the significant factor. Ultimately, the tribunal is required to look at the balance of prejudice to the parties in allowing the application. Whether or not the respondent has an arguable defence to the claim, and can therefore bring the application within r.33(5) was described by the EAT as the "gateway to the discretion" (in *The Pestle and Mortar v Turner*, UKEAT/0652/05).

Review of other judgments and decisions

4–247

34.—(1) Parties may apply to have certain judgments and decisions made by a tribunal or a chairman reviewed under rules 34 to 36. Those judgments and decisions are—

(a) a decision not to accept a claim, response or counterclaim;

(b) a judgment (other than a default judgment but including an order for costs, expenses, preparation time or wasted costs); and

(c) a decision made under rule 6(3) of Schedule 4; and references to "decision" in rules 34 to 37 are references to the above judgments and decisions only. Other decisions or orders may not be reviewed under these rules.

(2) In relation to a decision not to accept a claim or response, only the party against whom the decision is made may apply to have the decision reviewed.

(3) Subject to paragraph

(4), decisions may be reviewed on the following grounds only—

(a) the decision was wrongly made as a result of an administrative error;

(b) a party did not receive notice of the proceedings leading to the decision;

(c) the decision was made in the absence of a party;

(d) new evidence has become available since the conclusion of the hearing to which the decision relates, provided that its existence could not have been reasonably known of or foreseen at that time; or

(e) the interests of justice require such a review.

(4) A decision not to accept a claim or response may only be reviewed on the grounds listed in paragraphs (3)(a) and (e).

(5) A tribunal or chairman may on its or his own initiative review a decision made by it or him on the grounds listed in paragraphs (3) or (4).

Rule 34(1)(a)—Review of a decision not to accept a claim, response or counterclaim

A judge has the power to review a decision not to accept a response where either **4–248** the claim has been rejected under r.6(2)(a) (failure to include the required information under r.4(3)) or under r.6(2)(b) (failure to present the response in time). That power is expressly contained in r.34(1)(a) and may be exercised in accordance with the broad power to review where it is just and equitable to do so under r.34(3)(e) (where the interests of justice require such a review). It is in accordance with the overriding objective to exercise that power because of the draconian effect of r.8 (default judgments), and more importantly r.9 (debar from taking any further part in the proceedings.) The same principles as were applicable to an application under r.33(2) for an extension of time to serve a late response, following the issue of a default judgment (under r.8), were relevant to an application under r.34 to review a decision not to accept a late or defective response (*Moroak t/a Blake Envelopes v Cromie* [2005] I.R.L.R. 353; [2005] I.C.R. 1226, EAT).

The tribunal must look at the reasons for late service, or failure to supply the required information, consider whether the respondents do have a defence to the claim, and then balance the respective prejudice to the parties in not allowing the response to stand. Problems arise if the tribunal has not made an order for a default judgment under r.8, either in relation to liability or liability and remedy, as the respondent is still debarred under r.9 from contesting compensation unless he first applies under this rule to review the decision not to accept the response. The EAT itself acknowledged that this was a "highly artificial" manner of circumventing the effect of r.9. (compare *D and H Travel Ltd v Foster* [2006] ICR 1537 and *Terry Ballard & Co (a firm) v Stonestreet* EAT 0568/06, and see also 4–105)

Rule 34(1)—Other decisions or orders may not be reviewed under these rules

4–249   This apparent restriction on the power of the tribunal to review or reconsider previous case management orders, as they do not come within the scope of r.34, "except under r.34" was considered in *Onwuka v Spherion Technology UK Ltd* [2005] I.C.R. 567, where it was concluded that the tribunal has power to vary or revoke, and therefore to review other orders under rr.10 (general power to manage proceedings), 11 (applications in proceedings), 12 (employment judge's power to make an order on his own initiative), or 33 (power to review a default judgment). That view was approved in *Hart v English Heritage* [2006] I.C.R. 655, where it was held that a tribunal decision which was not a judgment or decision falling within r.33 or r.34 of the 2004 Regulations could not be reviewed, but it could be reconsidered under r.10, even though that provision referred to an order rather than a decision. The term "order" in r.10, despite the unsatisfactory nature of the language used, should be construed so as to cover all decisions taken by a tribunal in the proper exercise of its case management powers, save where those decisions were subject to the review procedure in rr.33 and 34. In theory there is no limit to the number of times that a tribunal could reconsider a previous case management decision. While a tribunal, therefore, had jurisdiction to revisit case management decisions, it would not ordinarily do so unless there had been a material change in circumstances, or there was a point of substance that needed to be considered even where there had been no change of circumstances, but merely a previous failure to argue the point (*Onwuka v Spherion Technology UK Ltd* [2005] I.C.R. 567 and *Montali v Goldman Sachs Services Ltd* [2002] I.C.R. 1251 applied).

Rule 34(3)

4–250   Apart from a minor amendment to r.34(3)(a) (see below) the review power in the Rules is couched in identical terms to its predecessor in the 2001 Rules and therefore, subject to the amendment to the provisions of that sub-paragraph and the guidance on r.34(3)(e) in *Williams v Ferrosan* (see below) on the wider discretion now available to tribunals when deciding whether or not to review on just and equitable grounds, the old appellate authorities are probably still relevant.

Rule 34(3)(a)—Decision wrongly made as a result of an administrative error

4–251   Under both r.11(1) of the 1993 Rules, and r.13(1) of the 2001 Rules the phrase for this ground of review referred only to "an error on the part of the tribunal staff." The new formulation is "significantly different" (per Clark J. in *Sodexho*, at para.40). It can extend to an error on the part of the parties as well as tribunal staff (in the instant case by a party sending a document to the wrong address) (*Sodexho Ltd v Gibbons* [2005] I.C.R. 1647; [2005] I.R.L.R. 836).

Rule 34(3)(c)

4–252   Although the Rule does not make it explicit, it is not the fact of absence itself which will invoke this provision; the absent party must give a cogent and acceptable explanation for non-attendance. A party is expected to inform the tribunal of any change of address for example.

Rule 34(3)(d)

Fresh evidence will only be admitted if it is credible, if it might have had a **4–253**
decisive bearing on the tribunal's decision, and finally if there is a reasonable
explanation for the failure to make it available at the hearing (*Bagga v Heavy
Electricals (India) Ltd* [1972] I.C.R. 118; [1972] 7 I.T.R. 70, NIRC). It is imperative
that the party wishing to introduce the evidence lodges a copy of the statement with
the application for review (*Vauxhall Motors Ltd v Henry* [1978] 13 I.T.R. 332, EAT).
Where, however, the party has made a deliberate choice not to use a certain
category of evidence, he cannot then argue that had a different choice been made,
that the evidence could not have been obtained with due diligence (*Bingham v
Hobourn Engineering Ltd* [1992] I.R.L.R. 298, EAT).

Rule 34(3)(e)—The interests of justice require a review

Prior to the introduction of the overriding objective in the 2001 Rules, this **4–254**
ground of review was interpreted narrowly and in practice was limited to situations
where there had been either a procedural mishap or where the tribunal's decision
had been overtaken by subsequent events. That narrow approach is now too
restrictive and is inconsistent with the overriding objective which is to approach the
question of whether to grant the application justly. There is no principle that there
is an "exceptionality hurdle" for the power to be invoked (*Williams v Ferrosan Ltd*
[2004] I.R.L.R. 607, cited with approval in *Sodexho Ltd v Gibbons* [2005] I.C.R. 1647;
[2005] I.R.L.R. 836). This requires a balancing of the respective parties' interests.
The factors to be taken into account are similar to those to be considered on an
application to amend the claim or response (*Selkent Bus Co Ltd v Moore* [1996]
I.R.L.R. 661; [1996] I.C.R. 836). The Rules should be seen "not as a trap for the
unwary but a procedure designed to do justice between the parties" (*Sodexho Ltd v
Gibbons* [2005] I.C.R. 1647; [2005] I.R.L.R. 836, per Clark J. at [84]).

Instances where it was held that a review should have been granted in the
interests of justice include the following:

(a) Compensation assessed on an assumption that the claimant would be
    unemployed for ten months; obtained employment three days before
    promulgation at a reduced salary: review should have been granted (*Studio
    Press (Birmingham) Ltd v Davies* [1977] 11 I.T.R. 93); and

(b) The employment tribunal held that the employee had been unfairly
    dismissed, and a month later he was convicted for doing what he had been
    dismissed for: a review was refused. The EAT allowed the review and
    ordered a finding of 100 per cent contribution (*Ladup Ltd v Barnes* [1982]
    I.R.L.R. 7; [1982 I.C.R. 107).

Instances where it was held that a review should not have been granted in the
interests of justice included the following:

(a) Where the claimant had obtained a job at a higher rate of salary than
    envisaged in the assessment of compensation, a review was refused and the
    National Industrial Relations Court ruled that the tribunal should ask itself
    whether the forecasts which were the basis for the decision had changed to
    such an extent and in such a short time frame as to require a review in the
    interests of justice (*Yorkshire Engineering & Welding Co Ltd v Burnham* [1973]);
    and

(b) A failing on the part of the party's representative, professional or otherwise
    will rarely constitute a ground for review, as it would be a dangerous path to
    follow (*Lindsay v Ironsides Ray & Vials* [1994] I.C.R. 384; [1994] I.R.L.R. 318,

EAT). These examples illustrate how prior to the 2001 Rules it was very difficult to persuade the employment tribunal to review. The cases would not necessarily be decided the same way now. If the approach to be adopted is similar to that set out in the *Selkent* case then the relevant considerations must be the following:

(i) Any reason for not pursuing the point or issue at the original hearing;
(ii) Whether it is likely to have a material impact on the original decision in the sense that the point is arguable and has substance; and
(iii) There must be a consideration of the likely hardship and prejudice to both parties of not allowing the application.

Rule 34(5)

4–255   The power of the tribunal to review of its own motion is preserved by r.34(5). The employment judge may be invited to consider acting under this power, where the EAT has received a notice of appeal and is considering inviting the tribunal to adopt that course of action prior to a consideration of the appeal on the merits. The employment judge may also act under this provision on sight of a party's notice of appeal that suggests that a review might obviate the need for an appeal. As the time limit will probably have expired he will also have to extend time under r.35(1). He must then proceed under r.36(2). Under r.36(2) he is obliged to send a notice to the parties informing them that he proposes to review the decision, summarising the grounds on which he intends to do so, and giving them the opportunity to object. Usually a time limit will be set for that response. The notice must be sent within 14 days of the date the original decision was sent to the parties, subject to the power of the employment judge to extend that period under r.35(1).

Preliminary consideration of application for review

4–256

35.—(1) An application under rule 34 to have a decision reviewed must be made to the Employment Tribunal Office within 14 days of the date on which the decision was sent to the parties. The 14 day time limit may be extended by a chairman if he considers that it is just and equitable to do so.

(2) The application must be in writing and must identify the grounds of the application in accordance with rule 34(3), but if the decision to be reviewed was made at a hearing, an application may be made orally at that hearing.

(3) The application to have a decision reviewed shall be considered (without the need to hold a hearing) by the chairman of the tribunal which made the decision or, if that is not practicable, by—

(a) a Regional Chairman or the Vice President;

(b) any chairman nominated by a Regional Chairman or the Vice President; or

(c) the President; and that person shall refuse the application if he considers that there are no grounds for the decision to be reviewed under rule 34(3) or there is no reasonable prospect of the decision being varied or revoked.

(4) If an application for a review is refused after such preliminary consideration the Secretary shall inform the party making the appli-

cation in writing of the chairman's decision and his reasons for it. If the application for a review is not refused the decision shall be reviewed under rule 36.

Rule 35(2)—The application. . . must identify the grounds

An application will be properly constituted as long as the grounds under r.34(3) can be identified from the document containing the application; if in doubt the employment judge or the other party can seek additional information (under rr.10(2)(b) and 11) (*Sodexho Ltd v Gibbons* [2005] I.C.R. 1647; [2005] I.R.L.R. 836).

4–257

Rule 35(3)—Preliminary consideration of the application

Rule 35(3) clarifies what was an apparent ambiguity in the 2001 Rules. It was implicit in r.13 of the 2001 Rules that the employment judge was obliged by r.13(5) and (6) to in effect carry out a preliminary consideration of the application to determine if it had merit. If on that preliminary consideration, he took the view that the application had no reasonable prospect of success, he could refuse it, and the practice was to issue a decision to that effect supported by reasons. What the employment judge could not do was grant the application. If he took the view that the application was not one to which r.13(5) applied so that he did not dismiss it, he was obliged to convene a full hearing to consider the application and then to review the decision. The tribunal could then either confirm, vary or revoke the decision under r.13(7).

4–258

That preliminary nature of the review function is expressly spelled out in the heading to r.35. The employment judge of the tribunal, or one of the other possible individuals listed in r.35(3) considers the application and determines firstly whether the grounds for the review are covered by r.34(3). If not he can refuse the application, or seek further information to enable him to determine whether the application comes within r.34(3). Having determined whether the application satisfies r.34(3) he must then determine whether the application has no reasonable prospects of success. If so he may refuse it under r.35(3). If on that preliminary consideration the employment judge concludes that the application has been made for an admissible reason, and that it should not be dismissed on the basis that it has no reasonable prospect of success, then he must then proceed under r.36. Where the application is refused r.35(4) applies.

Rule 35(4)—Refusal of the application

If the employment judge concludes that the application should be refused either on the basis that there is no admissible ground for review or that the application, though admissible, has no reasonable prospects of success, he notifies the party making the application in writing, through the Secretary of that decision and the reasons for that decision. It would seem from the wording of the Rule that it is permissible to notify the party in writing in a letter and that it is not a requirement to issue a judgment supported by reasons. The letter notifying the party of the refusal of the application must however contain those reasons. That decision can be appealed in the same way as the original decision which the party is seeking to review.

4–259

The review

36.—(1) When a party has applied for a review and the application has not been refused after the preliminary consideration above, the decision shall be reviewed by the chairman or tribunal who made the original decision. If that is not practicable a different chairman or

4–260

tribunal (as the case may be) shall be appointed by a Regional Chairman, the Vice President or the President.

(2) Where no application has been made by a party and the decision is being reviewed on the initiative of the tribunal or chairman, the review must be carried out by the same tribunal or chairman who made the original decision and—

    (a) a notice must be sent to each of the parties explaining in summary the grounds upon which it is proposed to review the decision and giving them an opportunity to give reasons why there should be no review; and

    (b) such notice must be sent before the expiry of 14 days from the date on which the original decision was sent to the parties.

(3) A tribunal or chairman who reviews a decision under paragraph (1) or (2) may confirm, vary or revoke the decision. If the decision is revoked, the tribunal or chairman must order the decision to be taken again. When an order is made that the original decision be taken again, if the original decision was taken by a chairman without a hearing, the new decision may be taken without hearing the parties and if the original decision was taken at a hearing, a new hearing must be held.

Rule 36(1)

4–261   Assuming the application for a review has survived the initial preliminary consideration under r.34, there has to be a hearing, before the original tribunal or the employment judge if he sat alone. If that is not practicable there is power for the President, Vice-President, or regional employment judge to appoint a replacement employment judge or tribunal.

Rule 36(2)

4–262   Where the employment judge is acting on his own initiative he must comply with the two requirements of this Rule, which is explained in the commentary on r.34(5) above.

Rule 36(3)

4–263   The employment judge or tribunal retains the options under the previous rules to confirm, vary, or revoke the original decision. If the decision is revoked there is re-hearing of the claim. If the original decision was taken without a hearing that hearing can be on the same basis. If the original decision was taken at hearing, there must be another hearing. That hearing can be before the original employment judge or tribunal and in practice, it can take place immediately after the determination of the application for review. The parties are normally informed how the tribunal or employment judge intends to proceed. As it is a complete rehearing the tribunal may come to the same decision. Although the Rules do not spell it out it is open to the tribunal or employment judge considering the application for review to revoke the original decision and order the claim to be heard before a new employment judge or tribunal, in which case it will be at a later date and the employment judge or tribunal may then make any appropriate orders under r.10 for the management of those proceedings.

Correction of judgments, decisions or reasons

37.—**(1) Clerical mistakes in any order, judgment, decision or reasons, or errors arising in those documents from an accidental slip or omission, may at any time be corrected by certificate by the chairman, Regional Chairman, Vice President or President.**

4–264

(2) If a document is corrected by certificate under paragraph (1), or if a decision is revoked or varied under rules 33 or 36 or altered in any way by order of a superior court, the Secretary shall alter any entry in the Register which is so affected to conform with the certificate or order and send a copy of any entry so altered to each of the parties and, if the proceedings have been referred to the tribunal by a court, to that court.

(3) Where a document omitted from the Register under rules 32 or 49 is corrected by certificate under this rule, the Secretary shall send a copy of the corrected document to the parties; and where there are proceedings before any superior court relating to the decision or reasons in question, he shall send a copy to that court together with a copy of the entry in the Register of the decision, if it has been altered under this rule.

(4) In Scotland, the references in paragraphs (2) and (3) to superior courts shall be read as referring to appellate courts.

Rule 37–Power to correct judgments, orders or reasons

Rule 37 is the equivalent of the slip rule in civil proceedings. CPR r.40.12 enables the court to correct accidental slips or omissions in judgments and orders. It cannot be used to correct errors of law. See for example, *R & V Versicherung AG v Risk Insurance & Reinsurance Solutions AG* [2007] EWHC 79 (Comm), per Gloster J. at [23] and following. In that situation there must be an appeal under CPR r.52, subject to the judge's power where the order or judgment has not been sealed to review under CPR r.40.3(1). The Rule mirrors the CPR in its reference to accidental slips and omissions and the power is a power to correct clerical mistakes or errors. The usual examples are errors in the description of the parties, errors of arithmetic in the calculation of compensation, or errors in dates that may have an impact on that calculation. In practice, the tribunal will also normally correct calculations where the arithmetic is correct but the wrong dates have been used to calculate basic awards or redundancy payments, the wrong multiplier has been used in similar calculations, or the incorrect figure has been adopted for the purposes of calculating the figure for a week's pay. It will not be used where the tribunal has omitted an item from the calculation because the item was not referred to by the parties

Where an Employment Tribunal, instead of issuing a correction in respect of one error in its Judgment, withdrew the Reasons in their entirety and reissued them it was held by the EAT that time for the purposes of either an application for review or an appeal ran from the date of the fresh promulgation, or at least the Appellant (otherwise one day out of time) was entitled so to conclude. If the "correction" is so substantial as to merit withdrawal of the original Reasons, then it may amount to a Review under Rule 34(5). (*Aziz-Mir v Sainsbury's Plc* UKEATPA/0537/06/JOJ EAT December 15, 2006 (unreported)

The tribunal is not however permitted by this rule to use the certificate of correction to add additional findings of fact or to supplement its findings. (*Mayor & Burgesses of the London Borough of Newham v Bone* [2007] UKEAT 0243/07)

4–265

General power to make costs and expenses orders

4–266

38.—(1) Subject to paragraph (2) and in the circumstances listed in rules 39, 40 and 47 a tribunal or chairman may make an order ("a costs order") that—

    (a) a party ("the paying party") make a payment in respect of the costs incurred by another party ("the receiving party");

    (b) the paying party pay to the Secretary of State, in whole or in part, any allowances (other than allowances paid to members of tribunals) paid by the Secretary of State under section 5(2) or (3) of the Employment Tribunals Act to any person for the purposes of, or in connection with, that person's attendance at the tribunal.

(2) A costs order may be made under rules 39, 40 and 47 only where the receiving party has been legally represented at the Hearing or, in proceedings which are determined without a Hearing, if the receiving party is legally represented when the proceedings are determined. If the receiving party has not been so legally represented a tribunal [or Chairman] may make a preparation time order (subject to rules 42 to 45). (See rule 46 on the restriction on making a costs order and a preparation time order in the same proceedings.)

(3) For the purposes of these rules "costs" shall mean fees, charges, disbursements or expenses incurred by or on behalf of a party, in relation to the proceedings. In Scotland all references to costs (except when used in the expression "wasted costs") or costs orders shall be read as references to expenses or orders for expenses.

(4) A costs order may be made against or in favour of a respondent who has not had a response accepted in the proceedings in relation to the conduct of any part which he has taken in the proceedings.

(5) In these rules legally represented means having the assistance of a person (including where that person is the receiving party's employee) who—

    (a) has a general qualification within the meaning of section 71 of the Courts and Legal Services Act 1990

    (b) is an advocate or solicitor in Scotland; or

    (c) is a member of the Bar of Northern Ireland or a solicitor of the Supreme Court of Northern Ireland.

(6) Any costs order made under rules 39, 40 or 47 shall be payable by the paying party and not his representative.

(7) A party may apply for a costs order to be made at any time during the proceedings. An application may be made at the end of a hearing, or in writing to the Employment Tribunal Office. An application for costs which is received by the Employment Tribunal Office later than 28 days from the issuing of the judgment determining the claim shall not be accepted or considered by a tribunal or chairman unless it or he considers that it is in the interests of justice to do so.

(8) In paragraph (7), the date of issuing of the judgment determining the claim shall be either—

    (a) the date of the Hearing if the judgment was issued orally; or

    (b) if the judgment was reserved, the date on which the written judgment was sent to the parties.

(9) No costs order shall be made unless the Secretary has sent notice to the party against whom the order may be made giving him the opportunity to give reasons why the order should not be made. This paragraph shall not be taken to require the Secretary to send notice to that party if the party has been given an opportunity to give reasons orally to the chairman or tribunal as to why the order should not be made.

(10) Where a tribunal or chairman makes a costs order it or he shall provide written reasons for doing so if a request for written reasons is made within 14 days of the date of the costs order. The Secretary shall send a copy of the written reasons to all parties to the proceedings.

Commencement

October 1, 2004. Words in square brackets added by the Employment Tribunals (Constitution and Rules of Procedure) (Amendment) (No. 2) Regulations 2005 (2005 No. 1865).

Definitions

For "chairman", "Employment Tribunals Act", "Employment Tribunal Office", **4–267**
"hearing", "legally represented", "Secretary", "tribunal", "writing" see reg.2; for "chairman".

General

These Rules include a major overhaul of the provisions as to costs that were **4–268**
previously contained in r.14 of the 2001 Rules. The main substantive changes introduced are the provisions as to preparation time orders and wasted costs orders. A small but significant adjustment is the power (reversing the effect of *Kovacs v Queen Mary & Westfield* [2002] I.C.R. 919; [2002] I.R.L.R. 414) to take the means of the paying party into account when deciding both whether to make a costs or preparation time order and when determining the amount of any order.

To accommodate these changes the provisions as to costs have expanded from a single rule with 8 subparagraphs to 11 rules with a total of 50 subparagraphs. Much of the explanation for the increased length lies in repetition: rr.38–41 deal with costs or expenses orders, in terms very little different in substance from the 2001 Rules, while rr.42–45 deal in closely parallel terms with preparation time orders. Rule 46, dealing with the choice between a costs order and a preparation time order is of course wholly new, but r.47 deals in terms very little different from the 2001 Rules with the situation where a deposit has been ordered. Rule 48 contains the new wasted costs provisions.

As at March 2008, there is still fairly scant appellate authority interpreting the 2004 costs provisions. Because the basic conditions for the existence and exercise of the power are substantially unchanged, a large proportion of the pre-2004 case law remains authoritative. In *Khan v Kirklees Metropolitan Council* [2007] EWCA Civ. 1342, the employment tribunal had made a substantial costs order against the claimant, mistakenly referring to the 2004 rules instead of the 2001 rules. The Court of Appeal confirmed that there was no material difference between the general power to award costs conferred by r.40 paras (2) and (3) of the 2004 rules and that provided by r.14 of the 2001 rules.

Transitional arrangements

4–269   Transitional provisions at reg.20 apply most of the Rules, with only 38 to 48 and 1 to 3 excepted, to proceedings commenced before October 1, 2004 where the originating application (sic: the term "claim" is used in the Rules themselves) was not sent to the respondent before October 1, 2004. Rules 38–48 simply apply to all proceedings commenced on or after October 1, 2004. The result is that for the small category of cases commenced before October 1, 2004 where the claim was sent to the respondent on or after that date, most of the new rules applied alongside the old costs provisions. In *Criddle v Epcot Leisure Ltd* UKEAT/0275/05, June 24, 2005 the EAT held that the new "unless order" power at r.13(2) did not have the effect of permitting an unless order to be attached to a costs order made under the old costs power, r.14 of the 2001 Rules.

Rule 38(2)—Legally represented

4–270   Because the recoverability of costs in a case which goes to a hearing depends on the receiving party being legally represented at "the hearing", a party who has incurred legal costs in preparation for the hearing but has not had legal representation at the hearing itself cannot recover the costs incurred in the course of preparation. A preparation time order under r.42 may be available in respect of the time spent by legal advisers, but at a modest fixed hourly rate, currently £26.

"the hearing"

4–271   The rule does not deal expressly with the case where the receiving party is represented at one or more hearings, but not all. Reading this rule together with rr.40(2) and 46(2), the position appears to be as follows. Where the question falls to be decided at the conclusion of proceedings, the choice between a costs order and a preparation time order is determined by the nature of the receiving party's representation at that time. Where an order is made before the conclusion of the case, the tribunal or employment judge has by virtue of r.46(2) a free choice whether to make a costs order or preparation time order.

Rule 38(3)—The meaning of costs

4–272   Although by r.38(2) legal representation at the hearing or at the time when proceedings are determined is required to open the door to a costs order, the definition of "costs" is not restricted to fees incurred in respect of legal representation. It would seem, therefore, that a party who is represented by an unqualified consultant throughout the preparatory and interlocutory stages of a claim but instructs a barrister or solicitor for the substantive hearing will be able to recover not only the lawyer's fees but also the consultant's as "costs."

Rule 38(4)—Costs orders in respect of non-participating respondents

Rule 38(4) permits a costs order against a respondent that has either not **4–273** presented a response, or presented one and not had it accepted. However, since a costs order may only be made in accordance with r.40(3) in respect of the paying party's conduct in bringing or conducting the proceedings, a respondent cannot be made liable for costs incurred in any aspect of the proceedings in which it took no part: *Sutton v The Ranch Ltd* [2006] I.C.R. 1170, EAT. Rule 38(4) defines the only circumstances in which a respondent which has not had a notice of appearance accepted may be the subject of a costs order.

Rule 38(6)—"payable by the paying party and not his representative"

Costs may be made payable by a representative by virtue of the wasted costs **4–274** power under r.48. In *Royal Mail Group Plc v Sharma* UKEAT 0839/04, February 22, 2005 the EAT expressed the hope that the representatives would provide their clients with the wherewithal to meet the costs order made under the old Rules. In *Cooke v Glenrose Fish Co* [2004] I.R.L.R. 866, the solicitors had negligently failed to tell their client of the hearing date or attend themselves. The employment tribunal refused a review application and dismissed the claim, partly on the grounds of the availability of a remedy against the solicitors. On appeal, the EAT took into account the solicitors' undertaking to pay the costs thrown away in ordering that the decision should be set aside on review and the claim heard. This was a decision under the old rules, but it is suggested that r.38(6) would not preclude a similar course being taken under these Rules in a case where a representative is at fault but the stringent conditions for a wasted costs order are not met—or indeed where the representative wishes by offering an undertaking to avoid finding out whether they are thought to have been met.

Rule 38(7)—Timing of application

The general permission to apply for costs "at any time during the proceedings" **4–275** appears to trump the implication of the following sentence that an application made at a hearing may only be made at the end of the hearing. A party that has budgeted for a hearing of a given length may wish to make an application for costs during the course of the hearing if the unreasonable conduct of the other party has caused the case to be adjourned part-heard, particularly if its ability to continue to pay for representation depends on the outcome of the application.

When a costs or expenses order must be made

39.—(1) Subject to rule 38(2), a tribunal [or Chairman] must **4–276**
make a costs order against a respondent where in proceedings for
unfair dismissal a Hearing has been postponed or adjourned and—

> **(a) the claimant has expressed a wish to be reinstated or re-**
> **engaged which has been communicated to the respondent**
> **not less than 7 days before the Hearing; and**
> **(b) the postponement or adjournment of that Hearing has**
> **been caused by the respondent's failure, without a special**
> **reason, to adduce reasonable evidence as to the avail-**
> **ability of the job from which the claimant was dismissed,**
> **or of comparable or suitable employment.**

(2) A costs order made under paragraph (1) shall relate to any costs incurred as a result of the postponement or adjournment of the Hearing.

Commencement

October 1, 2004. Words in square brackets added by the Employment Tribunals (Constitution and Rules of Procedure) (Amendment) (No. 2) Regulations 2005 (2005 No. 1865).

When a costs or expenses order may be made

4–277   **40.—(1)** A tribunal or chairman may make a costs order when on the application of a party it has postponed the day or time fixed for or adjourned a Hearing or pre-hearing review. The costs order may be against or, as the case may require, in favour of that party as respects any costs incurred or any allowances paid as a result of the postponement or adjournment.

(2) A tribunal or chairman shall consider making a costs order against a paying party where, in the opinion of the tribunal or chairman (as the case may be), any of the circumstances in paragraph (3) apply. Having so considered, the tribunal or chairman may make a costs order against the paying party if it or he considers it appropriate to do so.

(3) The circumstances referred to in paragraph (2) are where the paying party has in bringing the proceedings, or he or his representative has in conducting the proceedings, acted vexatiously, abusively, disruptively or otherwise unreasonably, or the bringing or conducting of the proceedings by the paying party has been misconceived.

(4) A tribunal or chairman may make a costs order against a party who has not complied with an order or practice direction.

Commencement

October 1, 2004.

Rule 40(1)—Postponement or adjournment

4–278   The only condition for a costs order under r.40(1) is that there should have been postponement or adjournment of the hearing on the application of a party; in puzzling contrast to the general power to award costs under r.40(2) and (3), there is no express requirement of blameworthy conduct. If the condition that there has been an adjournment or postponement is satisfied, the door is opened to an award of costs against either party. The discretion must be exercised on some rational basis, and in practice the presence of blameworthy conduct of the kind envisaged in r.40(3) is likely in most if not all cases to be the chief consideration. The EAT's judgment in *Dutt v Kingston University*, unreported, UKEAT/0351/06, upholding a tribunal's award of part of the costs of an adjournment against a claimant states that blameworthy conduct is not necessary for an exercise of the discretion, but sheds no light on what factors might, in the absence of blameworthy conduct, form a proper basis for such an award. With respect, it must be doubted whether this decision is correct.

Costs awarded under this paragraph are expressly limited to the costs paid or expenses incurred as a result of the postponement or adjournment. Contrast the position under r.40(3), below.

Rule 40(2)—"shall consider making"

In practice tribunals rarely give this question any discernable consideration **4–279** unless an application for costs is made. However, if the tribunal does make an order it must decide, before doing so, not only that the party has "misconducted" himself in one of the ways described at r.40(3), but also, under r.40(2), that it is appropriate to make an order. The reasons must demonstrate that both stages of the enquiry have been carried out (*Beat v Devon CC*, UKEAT/0534/05).

Causation

There is no requirement that, once the conditions for the power to award costs **4–280** are established, the amount of costs awarded must be limited to the costs occasioned by the vexatious, abusive, disruptive or unreasonable conduct of the paying party (*McPherson v BNP Paribas* [2004] I.R.L.R. 558, CA). The judgment in *J Essien v JJ Joyce & Son Ltd* unreported UKEAT/0137/06 suggests that it is incumbent on the tribunal to explain how it arrives at the sum awarded by way of costs, and to make it clear what proportion of the award is attributable to costs occasioned by the unreasonable (etc.) behaviour. These were both decisions under the 2001 Rules, but there is nothing in the 2004 rules to suggest a different approach.

However, in *Roadbeach Ltd v Werner* unreported UKEAT/0304/07, the EAT upheld the tribunal's award of £1,500 for the costs of a hearing day thrown away by reason of the respondent's failure to present a response to the claim, but set aside its award of a further £1,500 on the grounds that there was no additional unreasonable conduct on the part of the respondent beyond its initial failure (corrected promptly after the abortive hearing) to present a response. Implicitly, therefore, this judgment proceeds on the basis that costs should be limited to the costs occasioned by the unreasonable (etc). conduct. *McPherson v BNP Paribas* does not appear to have been cited.

Conduct of proceedings

Costs cannot be awarded in respect of a party's conduct before proceedings **4–281** began: it is only the bringing of proceedings or the manner in which they are conducted that can attract a costs order (*Davidson v John Calder (Publishers) Ltd* [1985] I.C.R. 143; [1985] I.R.L.R. 97, EAT).

"vexatiously"

A claimant acts vexatiously if he brings "a hopeless case not with any expectation **4–282** of recovering compensation but out of spite to harass his employers or for some other improper motive" (*ET Marler Ltd v Robertson* [1974] I.C.R. 72, NIRC). See also *Beynon v Scadden* [1999] I.R.L.R. 700 and the cases cited at the notes to r.18(7)(b) and (c).

"misconceived"

The "misconceived" ground for a costs order [1974] I.C.R. 72, NIRC was added **4–283** by the 2001 Rules. By reg.2(2), "misconceived" includes having no reasonable prospect of success." This ground therefore requires the tribunal to decide, after the case has been decided, whether at some unspecified point in the past either party's contentions had "no reasonable prospect of success." As Sedley L.J. pointed out in *Lodwick v London Borough of Southwark* [2004] I.R.L.R. 554 at para.35, this is "not an easy concept, even for lawyers." The caution of Sir Hugh Griffiths in *ET Marler v Robertson* [1974] I.C.R. 72, NIRC remains pertinent: "Ordinary experience in life frequently teaches us that that which is plain for all to see once the dust of battle has subsided was far from clear to the contestants when they took up arms". The test for whether a case is "misconceived" for the purposes of the costs jurisdiction is the same as the test for striking out a claim under r.18(7)(b) on the grounds that it "has no reasonable prospect of success" (*HM Prison Service v Dolby* [2003] I.R.L.R. 694). See also the commentary under r.18(7), above. A party can be misconceived in bringing proceedings even if they believed they had a claim as the test is not whether the party against whom costs were sought believed they were in the right, but whether they had reasonable grounds for believing they were in the right (per Sedley L.J. in *Scott v Commissioners for Inland Revenue* [2004] I.R.L.R. 713, at 43 to 46).

"unreasonable"

4–284   Any conduct that is capable of being regarded as "vexatious" is almost certainly also "unreasonable," but the latter is a larger category, being capable of encompassing mere folly without any requirement of improper motive or bad faith. It was held under the old Rules not to amount to unreasonable conduct, without more, for a claimant to reject an offer of settlement which was more than the tribunal's final award (*Kopel v Safeway Stores* [2003] I.R.L.R. 753). Where the offer is merely not to pursue the claimant for costs if he withdraws his claim, the claim will need to be misconceived before it can be said to have been unreasonable to refuse the offer; see for example *Lake v Arco Grating* (UK) Ltd, UKEAT/0511/04, November 3, 2004.

Exceptional nature of the costs jurisdiction

4–285   It has been pointed out by the Court of Appeal in *Gee v Shell UK Ltd* [2003] I.R.L.R. 82, CA, at para.22, and in *Lodwick v London Borough of Southwark* [2004] I.R.L.R. 554 that an award of costs in the employment tribunal is exceptional. *Gee* was decided before the "misconceived" ground was added, *Lodwick* was decided after. These observations were explained by Burton P. in *Royal Mail Group Plc v Sharma* UKEAT/0839/04, February 22, 2005: "Insofar as there are references in cases, and indeed in the Court of Appeal, to the use of the costs jurisdiction being rare, it is rare because it is, fortunately, infrequent that there is conduct which can be characterised as unreasonable, such as to justify the operation of Rule 14." Burton P. made similar comments in *Salinas v (1) Bear Stearns International Holdings Inc (2) Chamberlain* [2005] I.C.R. 1117, EAT. Nevertheless, the decision to award costs does not flow automatically from the existence of the conditions specified at r.40(2). If the tribunal chooses to exercise the discretion, it must give reasons for so doing (*Criddle v Epcott Leisure Ltd* UKEAT/0275/05 and 0276/05, unreported, June 24, 2005).

The amount of a costs or expenses order

4–286   **41.—(1) The amount of a costs order against the paying party shall be determined in any of the following ways—**

(a) **the tribunal may specify the sum which the paying party must pay to the receiving party, provided that sum does not exceed £10,000;**

(b) **the parties may agree on a sum to be paid by the paying party to the receiving party and if they do so the costs order shall be for the sum so agreed;**

(c) **the tribunal may order the paying party to pay the receiving party the whole or a specified part of the costs of the receiving party with the amount to be paid being determined by way of detailed assessment in a County**

Court in accordance with the Civil Procedure Rules 1998 or, in Scotland, as taxed according to such part of the table of fees prescribed for proceedings in the sheriff court as shall be directed by the order.

(2) The tribunal or chairman may have regard to the paying party's ability to pay when considering whether it or he shall make a costs order or how much that order should be.

(3) For the avoidance of doubt, the amount of a costs order made under paragraphs (1)(b) or (c) may exceed £10,000.

Commencement
October 1, 2004.

General
The tribunal's written reasons for a costs order need to explain not only the fact **4–287** of the award, but also its amount, at any rate where the amount awarded falls very far short of the receiving party's expenditure (*Hugh Bryant and Reginald Bench t/a Bryant Hamilton & Co v Weir* UKEAT/0253/04, July 21, 2004).

Rule 41(1)(a)—Provided that sum does not exceed £10,000
Separate costs orders specifying sums totalling more than £10,000 are permiss- **4–288** ible, provided that they relate to different stages of the proceedings involving separate legal work and no individual order exceeds £10,000 (*James v Blockbuster Entertainment Ltd* UKEAT/0601/05, August 18, 2006).

Rule 41(1)(b) and (c)
Compare r.45(2) which imposes an absolute limit of £10,000 on the amount of a **4–289** preparation time order.

Rule 41(2)—ability to pay
In the absence of this express power under the earlier Rules, the Court of Appeal **4–290** had held in *Kovacs v Queen Mary and Westfield College* [2002] I.R.L.R. 414, that it was impermissible to have regard to the paying party's means. The consultation draft of the rules required the tribunal to have regard to the paying party's means; "may" was substituted for "shall" in the final version. It is suggested that this does not mean that the tribunal is entitled to disregard any evidence or submissions that it receives on the subject of the paying party's means; merely that it is under no obligation to make its own inquiries where no such material is volunteered.

The tribunal must state, if making a costs order, whether it has taken a party's means into account, and if so how it has done so, and this is true whether the tribunal assesses costs itself or orders detailed assessment in the county court (*Jiley v Birmingham & Solihull Mentel Health NHS Trust*, unreported, UKEAT/0584/06 and UKEAT/0155/07).

PREPARATION TIME ORDERS

General power to make preparation time orders

42.—(1) Subject to paragraph (2) and in the circumstances **4–291** described in rules 43, 44 and 47 a tribunal or chairman may make an order ("a preparation time order") that a party ("the paying party") make a payment in respect of the preparation time of another party ("the receiving party").

(2) A preparation time order may be made under rules 43, 44 or 47 only where the receiving party has not been legally represented at a Hearing or, in proceedings which are determined without a Hearing, if the receiving party has not been legally represented when the proceedings are determined. (See: rules 38 to 41 on when a costs order may be made; rule 38(5) for the definition of legally represented; and rule 46 on the restriction on making a costs order and a preparation time order in the same proceedings).

(3) For the purposes of these rules preparation time shall mean time spent by—

(a) the receiving party or his employees carrying out preparatory work directly relating to the proceedings; and

(b) the receiving party's legal or other advisers relating to the conduct of the proceedings; up to but not including time spent at any Hearing.

(4) A preparation time order may be made against a respondent who has not had a response accepted in the proceedings in relation to the conduct of any part which he has taken in the proceedings.

(5) A party may apply to the tribunal for a preparation time order to be made at any time during the proceedings. An application may be made at the end of a hearing or in writing to the Secretary. An application for preparation time which is received by the Employment Tribunal Office later than 28 days from the issuing of the judgment determining the claim shall not be accepted or considered by a tribunal or chairman unless they consider that it is in the interests of justice to do so.

(6) In paragraph (5) the date of issuing of the judgment determining the claim shall be either—

(a) the date of the Hearing if the judgment was issued orally; or,

(b) if the judgment was reserved, the date on which the written judgment was sent to the parties.

(7) No preparation time order shall be made unless the Secretary has sent notice to the party against whom the order may be made giving him the opportunity to give reasons why the order should not be made. This paragraph shall not be taken to require the Secretary to send notice to that party if the party has been given an opportunity to give reasons orally to the chairman or tribunal as to why the order should not be made.

(8) Where a tribunal or chairman makes a preparation time order it or he shall provide written reasons for doing so if a request for

written reasons is made within 14 days of the date of the preparation time order. The Secretary shall send a copy of the written reasons to all parties to the proceedings.

Commencement
October 1, 2004.

Rule 42(2)
See notes to r.38(2) above. The choice of the indefinite article ("a hearing") here, **4–292** contrasting with the definite article of 38(2) is obscure. It is not thought that it is intended to restrict the availability of preparation time orders to cases where the receiving party has not been legally represented at any hearing. That choice is determined by the nature of the receiving party's representation at the conclusion of the case, or, where r.46(2) applies, is at the tribunal's or employment judge's discretion; see further the notes to r.46(2) at para.4–306.

Rule 42(4)
See notes to r.38(4) at para.4–273. **4–293**

Rule 42(5)
See notes to r.38(7) at para.4–275. **4–294**

"When a preparation time order must be made"

43.—(1) Subject to rule 42(2), a tribunal [or Chairman] must **4–295** make a preparation time order against a respondent where in proceedings for unfair dismissal a Hearing has been postponed or adjourned and—

   (a) the claimant has expressed a wish to be reinstated or re-engaged which has been communicated to the respondent not less than 7 days before the Hearing; and

   (b) the postponement or adjournment of that Hearing has been caused by the respondent's failure, without a special reason, to adduce reasonable evidence as to the availability of the job from which the claimant was dismissed, or of comparable or suitable employment.

(2) A preparation time order made under paragraph (1) shall relate to any preparation time spent as a result of the postponement or adjournment of the Hearing.

Commencement
October 1, 2004. Words in square brackets added by the Employment Tribunals (Constitution and Rules of Procedure) (Amendment) (No. 2) Regulations 2005 (2005 No. 1865).

"When a preparation time order may be made"

44.—(1) A tribunal or chairman may make a preparation time **4–296** order when on the application of a party it has postponed the day or time fixed for or adjourned a Hearing or a pre-hearing review. The preparation time order may be against or, as the case may require, in favour of that party as respects any preparation time spent as a result of the postponement or adjournment.

(2) A tribunal or chairman shall consider making a preparation time order against a party (the paying party) where, in' the opinion of the tribunal or the chairman (as the case may be), any of the circumstances in paragraph (3) apply. Having so considered the tribunal or chairman may make a preparation time order against that party if it considers it appropriate to do so.

(3) The circumstances described in paragraph (2) are where the paying party has in bringing the proceedings, or he or his representative has in conducting the proceedings, acted vexatiously, abusively, disruptively or otherwise unreasonably, or the bringing or conducting of the proceedings by the paying party has been misconceived.

(4) A tribunal or chairman may make a preparation time order against a party who has not complied with an order or practice direction.

Commencement
October 1, 2004.

Rule 44(1)—Postponement or adjournment
4–297   See the notes to r.40(1) at para.4–278.

Rule 44(2)—"shall consider making"
4–298   See the notes to r.40(2) at para.4–279.

"Vexatiously"
4–299   See the notes under this heading above at para.4–282.

"Misconceived"
4–300   See the notes under this heading above at para.4–283.

"Unreasonable"
4–301   See the notes under this heading above at para.4–284.

Exceptional nature of the costs jurisdiction
4–302   See the notes under this heading above at para.4–285; there is no reason to expect that the power to make preparation time orders will be exercised on any different basis.

Calculation of a preparation time order

4–303   45.—(1) In order to calculate the amount of preparation time the tribunal or chairman shall make an assessment of the number of hours spent on preparation time on the basis of—

(a) information on time spent provided by the receiving party; and

(b) the tribunal or chairman's own assessment of what it or he considers to be a reasonable and proportionate amount of time to spend on such preparatory work and with reference to, for example, matters such as the complexity of the proceedings, the number of witnesses and documentation required.

(2) Once the tribunal or chairman has assessed the number of hours spent on preparation time in accordance with paragraph (1), it or he shall calculate the amount of the award to be paid to the receiving party by applying an hourly rate of £25.00 to that figure (or such other figure calculated in accordance with paragraph (4)). No preparation time order made under these rules may exceed the sum of £10,000.

(3) The tribunal or chairman may have regard to the paying party's ability to pay when considering whether it or he shall make a preparation time order or how much that order should be.

(4) For the year commencing on 6th April 2006, the hourly rate of £25 shall be increased by the sum of £1.00 and for each subsequent year commencing on 6 April, the hourly rate for the previous year shall also be increased by the sum of £1.00.

Commencement
October 1, 2004.

Rule 45(2)—Limit on the amount of a preparation time order
Compare r.41(1)(b) and (c) which permits an unlimited sum to be awarded by way of costs if the amount is assessed in the County Court or agreed.　**4–304**

Restriction on making costs or expenses orders and preparation time orders

46.—(1) A tribunal or chairman may not make a preparation time　**4–305** order and a costs order in favour of the same party in the same proceedings. However where a preparation time order is made in favour of a party in proceedings, the tribunal or chairman may make a costs order in favour of another party or in favour of the Secretary of State under rule 38(1)(b) in the same proceedings.

(2) If a tribunal or a chairman wishes to make either a costs order or a preparation time order in proceedings, before the claim has been determined, it or he may make an order that either costs or preparation time be awarded to the receiving party. In such circumstances a tribunal or chairman may decide whether the award should be for costs or preparation time after the proceedings have been determined.

Commencement
October 1, 2004.

Rule 46(2)—Restrictions on making preparation time orders

4-306   As noted under r.38(2) above at para.4–271, this provision appears to confer on the tribunal or employment judge an unfettered discretion whether to make a costs or a preparation time order in circumstances where it or he wishes to make an order before the claim has been determined. The second sentence of the paragraph permits the decision as to which kind of order to make to be postponed until the claim has been determined, but it does not require that the decision must be so postponed or provide that if it is it must be determined by the nature of the receiving party's representation at that time.

Costs, expenses or preparation time orders when a deposit has been taken

4-307   47.—(1) When:—

(a) a party has been ordered under rule 20 to pay a deposit as a condition of being permitted to continue to participate in proceedings relating to a matter;

(b) in respect of that matter, the tribunal or chairman has found against that party in its or his judgment; and

(c) no award of costs or preparation time has been made against that party arising out of the proceedings on the matter; the tribunal or chairman shall consider whether to make a costs or preparation time order against that party on the ground that he conducted the proceedings relating to the matter unreasonably in persisting in having the matter determined; but the tribunal or chairman shall not make a costs or preparation time order on that ground unless it has considered the document recording the order under rule 20 and is of the opinion that the grounds which caused the tribunal or chairman to find against the party in its judgment were substantially the same as the grounds recorded in that document for considering that the contentions of the party had little reasonable prospect of success.

(2) When a costs or preparation time order is made against a party who has had an order under r.20 made against him (whether the award arises out of the proceedings relating to the matter in respect of which the order was made or out of proceedings relating to any other matter considered with that matter), his deposit shall be paid in part or full settlement of the costs or preparation time order—

(a) when an order is made in favour of one party, to that party; and

(b) when orders are made in favour of more than one party, to all of them or any one or more of them as the tribunal or chairman thinks fit, and if to all or more than one, in such proportions as the tribunal or chairman considers appropriate; and if the amount of the deposit exceeds the amount of the costs or preparation time order, the balance shall be refunded to the party who paid it.

Commencement
October 1, 2004.

WASTED COSTS ORDERS AGAINST REPRESENTATIVES

Personal liability of representatives for costs

48.—(1) A tribunal or chairman may make a wasted costs order **4–308** against a party's representative.

(2) In a wasted costs order the tribunal or chairman may:—

(a) disallow, or order the representative of a party to meet the whole or part of any wasted costs of any party, including an order that the representative repay to his client any costs which have already been paid; and

(b) order the representative to pay to the Secretary of State, in whole or in part, any allowances (other than allowances paid to members of tribunals) paid by the Secretary of State under section 5(2) or (3) of the Employment Tribunals Act to any person for the purposes of, or in connection with, that person's attendance at the tribunal by reason of the representative's conduct of the proceedings.

(3) "Wasted costs" means any costs incurred by a party:—

(a) as a result of any improper, unreasonable or negligent act or omission on the part of any representative; or

(b) which, in the light of any such act or omission occurring after they were incurred, the tribunal considers it unreasonable to expect that party to pay.

(4) In this rule "representative" means a party's legal or other representative or any employee of such representative, but it does not include a representative who is not acting in pursuit of profit with regard to those proceedings. A person is considered to be acting in pursuit of profit if he is acting on a conditional fee arrangement.

(5) A wasted costs order may be made in favour of a party whether or not that party is legally represented and such an order may also be made in favour of a representative's own client. A wasted costs order may not be made against a representative where that representative is an employee of a party.

(6) Before making a wasted costs order, the tribunal or chairman shall give the representative a reasonable opportunity to make oral or written representations as to reasons why such an order should

not be made. The tribunal or chairman [may] also have regard to the representative's ability to pay when considering whether it shall make a wasted costs order or how much that order should be.

(7) When a tribunal or chairman makes a wasted costs order, it must specify in the order the amount to be disallowed or paid.

(8) The Secretary shall inform the representative's client in writing:—

    (a) of any proceedings under this rule; or

    (b) of any order made under this rule against the party's representative.

(9) Where a tribunal or chairman makes a wasted costs order it or he shall provide written reasons for doing so if a request is made for written reasons within 14 days of the date of the wasted costs order. This 14 day time limit may not be extended under rule 10. The Secretary shall send a copy of the written reasons to all parties to the proceedings.

Commencement

October 1, 2004. "May" in square brackets substituted with effect from the same date for "shall" by the Employment Tribunals (Constitution and Rules of Procedure) (Amendment) Regulations 2004 (SI 2004 No. 2351).

Rule 48(3)—"Wasted costs"

4–309
The definition of wasted costs here, as in the Employment Appeal Tribunal Rules, is in identical terms to that provided by s.51(7) of the Supreme Court Act 1981, so exercise of the power can be expected to be guided by the practice of the ordinary civil courts: see generally Civil Procedure 2007, 48.7.1–48.7.20.

The courts apply a three-stage test when a wasted costs order is contemplated (*Ridehalgh v Horsefield* [1994] 3 W.L.R. 462; [1994] 3 All E.R. 848, CA). The three stages are:

    (1) Has the legal representative of whom complaint is made acted improperly, unreasonably or negligently?

    (2) If so, did such conduct cause the applicant to incur unnecessary costs?

    (3) If so, is it in all the circumstances just to order the legal representative to compensate the applicant for the whole or any part of the relevant costs?

The EAT has now confirmed that employment tribunals should apply the same three-stage test when considering making an order under this rule (in *Mitchells Solicitors v Tunwerk Information Technologies York Ltd* [2008] UKEAT/0541/07).

For an instance of an exercise of the power to make a wasted costs order, upheld by the EAT, see *Highvogue Ltd v Davies*, unreported, UKEAT/0093/07.

Rule 48(3)—Improper, unreasonable or negligent

4–310
The Court of Appeal in Ridehalgh gave the following guidance on the meaning of these words for the purposes of the wasted costs jurisdiction:

"'"Improper"'" . . . covers, but is not confined to, conduct which would ordinarily be held to justify disbarment, striking off, suspension from practice or other serious professional penalty. It covers any significant breach of a substantial duty imposed by a relevant code of professional conduct. But it is not in our judgment limited to that. Conduct which would be regarded as improper according to the consensus of professional (including judicial) opinion can be fairly stigmatised as such whether or not it violates the letter of a professional code. 'Unreasonable' . . . aptly describes conduct which is vexatious, designed to harass the other side rather than advance the resolution of the case, and it makes no difference that the conduct is the product of excessive zeal and not improper motive. But conduct cannot be described as unreasonable simply because it leads in the event to an unsuccessful result or because other more cautious legal representatives would have acted differently. The acid test is whether the conduct permits of a reasonable explanation. If so, the course adopted may be regarded as optimistic and as reflecting on a practitioner's judgment, but it is not unreasonable. . . '[N]egligent' should be understood in an untechnical way to denote failure to act with the competence reasonably to be expected of ordinary members of the profession. In adopting an untechnical approach to the meaning of negligence in this context, we would however wish firmly to discountenance any suggestion that an applicant for a wasted costs order under this head need prove anything less than he would have to prove in an action for negligence: 'advice, acts or omissions in the course of their professional work which no member of the profession who was reasonably well informed and competent would have given or done or omitted to do'; an error 'such as no reasonably well-informed and competent member of that profession could have made' (Saif Ali v Sydney Mitchell & Co at pages 218 D, 220 D, per Lord Diplock)."

Breach of duty to the court

Moreover, before a wasted costs order can properly be made, there must be an element of breach of duty to the court. See *Ridehalgh* (above): **4–311**

"The court's jurisdiction to make a wasted costs order against a solicitor is founded on a breach of the duty owed by the solicitor to the court to perform his duty as an officer of the court in promoting within his own sphere the cause of justice."

It is not improper, unreasonable or negligent of a lawyer to present a case which he regards as bound to fail provided he does not lend his assistance to proceedings which are an abuse of the process of the court.

Rule 48(4)—"representative"

It remains to be seen how the requirement of something amounting to a breach of the lawyer's duty to the tribunal will be applied in the case of non-lawyer representatives. In practice, the standards of conduct and competence expected by tribunals of such representatives are likely to be somewhat lower than the standards expected of lawyers. **4–312**

Rule 48(4)—"In pursuit of profit"

The words "with regard to those proceedings" make it clear that the intention is to protect those providing genuinely gratuitous services from the risk of wasted costs orders irrespective of whether they themselves are paid by an employer for their time. Hence, partners in solicitors' firms, salaried assistants, employees of advice charities, barristers and unqualified volunteers will all be protected alike provided their involvement in the particular case does not form part of a commercial arrangement with the client. However, it is thought that a person is **4–313**

219

likely to be considered to be acting in pursuit of profit with regard to proceedings if he provides "free" employment tribunal representation as one element of a package of benefits for which, as a whole, his client pays.

Rule 48(6)—The representative's ability to pay

4–314   Compare r.41(2) under which the employment judge or tribunal "may" have regard to the paying party's ability to pay. It seems that before making a wasted costs order the tribunal must make its own inquiries as to the representative's ability to pay if no such information is volunteered. The policy behind this difference of approach is obscure; possibly harmonisation of the two provisions was simply overlooked when the original draft of r.41(2) was changed to read "may".

Rule 48(7)—Amount of a wasted costs order

4–315   Note that there is no mechanism for assessment of wasted costs in the County Court, and no upper limit on the amount that may be specified by the tribunal.

POWERS IN RELATION TO SPECIFIC TYPES OF PROCEEDINGS

Sexual offences and the Register

4–316   **49. In any proceedings appearing to involve allegations of the commission of a sexual offence the tribunal, the chairman or the Secretary shall omit from the Register, or delete from the Register or any judgment, document or record of the proceedings, which is available to the public, any identifying matter which is likely to lead members of the public to identify any person affected by or making such an allegation.**

Definitions

4–317   For "sexual offence" see the Employment Tribunals Act 1996, s.11(6) which defines it as "any offence" to which s.4 of the Sexual Offences (Amendment) Act 1976, the Sexual Offences (Amendment) Act 1992 or s.274(2) of the Criminal Procedure (Scotland) Act 1995 applies (offences under the Sexual Offences Act 1956, Pt 1 of the Criminal Law (Consolidation) (Scotland) Act 1995 and certain other enactments); for "chairman", "register", "Secretary" and "tribunal" see reg.2 of the Employment Tribunals (Constitution and Rules of Procedure) Regulations 2004.

General

4–318   Where cases involve allegations of the commission of a sexual offence the power to ensure that all documents and decisions that prevent the identification of any person affected by or making the allegation derives from s.11(1) of the Employment Tribunals Act 1996. The duty on the employment judge or the Secretary under this provision is mandatory, not discretionary. The allegations of the commission of a sexual offence do not have to be the basis of the cause of action, or to be central to the decision making, the case simply has to involve allegations of the commission of a sexual offence (*X v Stevens (Commissioner Metropolitan Police Service)* [2003] I.R.L.R. 411; [2003] I.C.R. 1031, EAT).

Restricted reporting orders

4–319   **50.—(1) A restricted reporting order may be made in the following types of proceedings:—**

(a) any case which involves allegations of sexual misconduct;

(b) a complaint under section 17A or 25(8) of the Disability Discrimination Act in which evidence of a personal nature is likely to be heard by the tribunal or a chairman.

(2) A party (or where a complaint is made under the Disability Discrimination Act, the complainant) may apply for a restricted reporting order (either temporary or full) in writing to the Employment Tribunal Office, or orally at a hearing, or the tribunal or chairman may make the order on its or his own initiative without any application having been made.

(3) A chairman or tribunal may make a temporary restricted reporting order without holding a hearing or sending a copy of the application to other parties.

(4) Where a temporary restricted reporting order has been made the Secretary shall inform all parties to the proceedings in writing as soon as possible of—

(a) the fact that the order has been made; and

(b) their right to apply to have the temporary restricted reporting order revoked or converted into a full restricted reporting order within 14 days
of the temporary order having been made.

(5) If no application under paragraph (4)(b) is made within the 14 days, the temporary restricted reporting order shall lapse and cease to have any effect on the fifteenth day after the order was made. If such an application is made the temporary restricted reporting order shall continue to have effect until the pre-hearing review or Hearing at which the application is considered.

(6) All parties must be given an opportunity to advance oral argument at a pre-hearing review or a Hearing before a tribunal or chairman decides whether or not to make a full restricted reporting order (whether or not there was previously a temporary restricted reporting order in the proceedings).

(7) Any person may make an application to the chairman or tribunal to have a right to make representations before a full restricted reporting order is made. The chairman or tribunal shall allow such representations to be made where he or it considers that the applicant has a legitimate interest in whether or not the order is made.

(8) Where a tribunal or chairman makes a restricted reporting order—

(a) it shall specify in the order the persons who may not be identified;

(b) a full order shall remain in force until both liability and remedy have been determined in the proceedings unless it is revoked earlier; and

(c) the Secretary shall ensure that a notice of the fact that a restricted reporting order has been made in relation to those proceedings is displayed on the notice board of the employment tribunal with any list of the proceedings taking place before the employment tribunal, and on the door of the room in which the proceedings affected by the order are taking place.

(9) Where a restricted reporting order has been made under this rule and that complaint is being dealt with together with any other proceedings, the tribunal or chairman may order that the restricted reporting order applies also in relation to those other proceedings or a part of them.

(10) A tribunal or chairman may revoke a restricted reporting order at any time.

(11) For the purposes of this rule liability and remedy are determined in the proceedings on the date recorded as being the date on which the judgment disposing of the claim was sent to the parties, and references to a restricted reporting order include references to both a temporary and a full restricted reporting order.

Definitions

4–320   For "restricted reporting order" see the Employment Tribunals Act 1996, s.11(6) which defines it as an order: (a) made in exercise of a power conferred by regulations made by virtue of that section; and (b) prohibiting the publication in Great Britain of identifying matter in a written publication available to the public, or its inclusion in a relevant programme for reception in Great Britain. "Relevant programme" and "written publication" have the same meaning as in the Sexual Offences (Amendment) Act 1992; for "identifying matter", see the Employment Tribunals Act 1996, s.11(6) which defines it as in relation to a person, any matter likely to lead members of the public to identify him as a person affected by, or as the person making, the allegation; for "sexual misconduct" see the Employment Tribunals Act 1996, s.11(6) which defines it as the commission of a sexual offence, sexual harassment or other adverse conduct (of whatever nature) related to sex, and conduct is related to sex whether the relationship with sex lies in the character of the conduct or in its having reference to the sex or sexual orientation of the person at whom the conduct is directed; for "chairman", "Employment Tribunal Office", "Secretary" and "tribunal" see reg.2 of the Employment Tribunals (Constitution and Rules of Procedure) Regulations 2004.

General

4–321   The power to make restricted reporting orders in cases involving allegations of sexual misconduct derives from s.11(1) of the Employment Tribunals Act 1996. The purpose of a restricted reporting order is to allow complaints of sexual misconduct at work or of disability discrimination to be brought, and witnesses to give evidence about instances of harassment, without fear of intimate personal details being publicised (*R (Associated Newspapers) v London (North) Industrial Tribunal* [1998] I.R.L.R. 569, DC). Although a restricted reporting order has the effect of limiting and controlling the actions of persons other than the claimant and respondent before a tribunal that does not make them parties to the case nor confer on them any right beyond a right of audience so as to enable them to apply to be allowed to make representations before a full restricted reporting order is made (*Dallas McMillan (A Firm) (2) A v (1) B (2) F Davidson*, judgment of January 8, 2008, EAT). Breach of a restricted reporting order is an offence for which the perpetrator is liable on summary conviction to a fine not exceeding level five on the standard scale: s.11(2) of the Employment Tribunals Act 1996. A tribunal also has a similar power under s.39 of the Children's and Young Persons Act 1933 to direct that no identifying matter of any child or young person concerned in the proceedings is published in any newspaper.

Para.50(1)

The allegations of sexual misconduct do not have to be the basis of the cause of **4–322** action or to be central to the decision making (*X v Stevens (Commissioner Metropolitan Police Service)*, above). The making of a restricted reporting order is at the discretion of the employment judge or tribunal. The power is not to be exercised auto-matically or at the request of one or both of the parties, but only after consideration of whether it is in the public interest that the press should be deprived of the right to communicate information to the public if it became available (*X v Z Ltd (Restricted Reporting Orders)* [1998] I.C.R. 43, CA). Further a tribunal will err in the exercise of its discretion if it fails to consider both the interests of the victim of the alleged harassment and the interests of the persons against whom the allegations of harassment are being made (*H v (1) Curtis (2) Prospects Care Services Ltd*, judgment of August 18, 1999, EAT). It will also err if it makes a blanket order prohibiting the identification of all likely witnesses and parties to the proceedings without considering on a person to person basis whether it is justified to restrict the general freedom of the press to report (*McAvory v Scottish Daily Record & Sunday Mail Ltd*, judgment of February 22, 2002, EAT). Although the basis of a tribunal's jurisdiction to make a restricted reporting order in situations falling within r.50(1) is statutory, a tribunal is also under an obligation pursuant to s.6 of the Human Rights Act 1998 to act in a way which is compatible with Convention rights, which means balancing the art.8 rights of the individuals involved (right to respect for private and family life) and the art.10 rights of the press (right to freedom of expression). A recent example of the courts conducting such a balancing exercise is *HRH Prince of Wales v Associated Newspapers Ltd* [2006] EWCA Civ. 1776 in which the Court of Appeal prohibited the publication of HRH Prince of Wales' private diaries on the grounds, inter alia, that the interference with his art.8 rights outweighed those of the press under art.10. Furthermore, even in cases which do not fall within the scope of r.50(1) it is likely that a tribunal has jurisdiction to restrain publicity derived from its obligation to give effect to Convention rights (In *Re S (A Child) (Identification: Restrictions on Publication)* [2004] 3 W.L.R. 1129, H.L. at [23]). However, compelling circumstances would be required to justify further exceptions to the principle of open justice (In *Re S (A Child) (Identification: Restrictions on Publication)*, above at [20]).

Cases involving allegations of discrimination or harassment on account of gender reassignment may be thought to fall outside the scope of r.50(1). However the EAT has held that since art.6 of the Equal Treatment Directive (Council Directive 76/207/EEC) obliges the courts and tribunals, being emanations of the State, to ensure that complainants have an effective remedy for discrimination they have suffered, r.50(1) must be read so as to empower tribunals to make restricted reporting orders in cases involving such allegations. Otherwise victims of gender reassignment discrimination would be deterred from asserting their Community law rights (*X v Stevens (Commissioner Metropolitan Police Service)*, above; *Chief Constable of West Yorkshire Police v A* [2000] I.R.L.R. 465).

Para.50(2)

4–323   In cases involving allegations of sexual misconduct an application for a restricted reporting order may be made by either party; in such cases the alleged perpetrator may have as great, if not a greater, interest in such an order being made as the complainant. In cases involving allegations of disability discrimination an application may only be made by the complainant since the intimate personal details which could justify such an order being made would only relate to him or her.

Paras 50(3)—(6)

4–324   A temporary restricted reporting order takes effect initially for 14 days. If no application is made to convert it into a full restricted reporting order it will lapse on the fifteenth day after it was made. If such an order is made then it will continue to have effect until the application is considered at the pre-hearing review or hearing.

Para.50(7) "Any person"

4–325   This provision enables a person who is not a party to the proceedings but has a legitimate interest in whether a full restricted reporting order should be made to make representations to the employment judge or tribunal. Examples of persons who may have such a legitimate interest are journalists and employees about whom allegations of sexual misconduct may be made in the course of the hearing. However only a person who is a party to the case may apply for a restricted reporting order to be revoked under para.50 (10) (*Dallas McMillan (A Firm) (2) A v (1) B (2) F Davidson*, above).

Para.50(8)(a)

4–326   A restricted reporting order cannot specify a body corporate as a person who may not be identified because a body corporate does not come within the words "persons affected by the allegation" in s.11(6) of the Employment Tribunals Act 1996. It was not Parliament's intention to extend reporting restrictions to protect the reputation of corporate respondents (*Leicester University v A* [1999] I.C.R. 701, EAT; *R (Associated Newspapers) v London (North) Industrial Tribunal*, above).

Para.50(8)(c)

4–327   This provision does not require that the notice specify the identity of the persons who may not be identified. This is presumably because this would have the effect that the restricted reporting order is intended to prevent, namely disclosing the identity to the general public of those alleged to be involved in allegations of sexual misconduct. However, journalists attending the hearing will need to be informed of the identity of those whom they may not identify in their reports of the hearing in order to avoid breaching the terms of the restricted the reporting order and rendering themselves, and their publishers, liable to criminal proceedings. One way of doing this is to make copies of the restricted reporting order available to journalists attending the hearing.

Para.50(10)

4–327/1   A person who is not a party to a case in which a restricted reporting order has been made has no right to apply for the order to be revoked (*Dallas McMillan (A Firm) (2) A v (1) B (2) F Davidson*, above). Further there is no requirement to interpret domestic legislation so as to create such a right on the part of the press in order to comply with the right to freedom of expression under art. 10 of the Convention; such an approach would ignore the competing right to privacy of those whom the restricted reporting order is intended to protect (*Dallas McMillan (A Firm) (2) A v (1) B (2) F Davidson*, above).

Proceedings involving the National Insurance Fund

51. The Secretary of State shall be entitled to appear as if she were **4–328** a party and be heard at any hearing in relation to proceedings which may involve a payment out of the National Insurance Fund, and in that event she shall be treated for the purposes of these rules as if she were a party.

General

Proceedings which may involve a payment out of the National Insurance Fund **4–329** are:

(a) those brought under s.166 and s.188 of the Employment Rights Act 1996 in respect of redundancy payments, unpaid wages and other debts owed by an insolvent employer to an employee at the date of insolvency, and

(b) those brought under s.126 of the Pension Schemes Act 1993 in respect of unpaid contributions owed by an insolvent employer to an employee's occupational pension scheme or personal pension scheme at the date of insolvency.

Collective agreements

52. Where a claim includes a complaint under section 6(4A) of the **4–330** Sex Discrimination Act 1986 [relating to a term of a collective agreement, the following persons, whether or not identified in the claim, shall be regarded as the persons against whom a remedy is claimed and shall be treated as respondents for the purposes of these rules, that is to say—

(a) the claimant's employer (or prospective employer); and

(b) every organisation of employers and organisation of workers, and every association of or representative of such organisations, which, if the terms were to be varied voluntarily, would be likely, in the opinion of a chairman, to negotiate the variation; provided that such an organisation or association shall not be treated as a respondent if the chairman, having made such enquiries of the claimant and such other enquiries as he thinks fit, is of the opinion that it is not reasonably practicable to identify the organisation or association.

Definitions

For "chairman" and "Sex Discrimination Act" see reg.2 of the Employment **4–331** Tribunals (Constitution and Rules of Procedure) Regulations 2004. For the meaning of "collective agreement" see s.178 of the Trade Union and Labour Relations Act 1992.

Employment Agencies Act 1973

53. In relation to any claim in respect of an application under **4–332** section 3C of the Employment Agencies Act 1973 for the variation or revocation of a prohibition order, the Secretary of State shall be treated as the respondent in such proceedings for the purposes of these rules. In relation to such an application the claim does not need to include the name and address of the persons against whom the claim is being made.

National security proceedings

4–333   54.—(1) A Minister of the Crown (whether or not he is a party to the proceedings) may, if he considers it expedient in the interests of national security, direct a tribunal or chairman by notice to the Secretary to:—

(a) conduct proceedings in private for all or part of particular Crown employment proceedings;

(b) exclude the claimant from all or part of particular Crown employment proceedings;

(c) exclude the claimant's representative from all or part of particular Crown employment proceedings;

(d) take steps to conceal the identity of a particular witness in particular Crown employment proceedings.

(2) A tribunal or chairman may, if it or he considers it expedient in the interests of national security, by order—

(a) do [in relation to particular proceedings before it] anything which can be required by direction to be done [in relation to particular Crown employment proceedings] under paragraph (1);

(b) order any person to whom any document (including any judgment or record of the proceedings) has been provided for the purposes of the proceedings not to disclose any such document or the content thereof:—

  (i) to any excluded person;

 (ii) in any case in which a direction has been given under paragraph (1)(a) or an order has been made under paragraph "(2)(a) read with paragraph (1)(a), to any person excluded from all or part of the proceedings by virtue of such direction or order; or

(iii) in any case in which a Minister of the Crown has informed the Secretary in accordance with paragraph (3) that he wishes to address the tribunal or chairman with a view to an order being made under paragraph (2)(a) read with paragraph (1)(b) or (c), to any person who may be excluded from all or part of the proceedings by virtue of such an order, if an order is made, at any time before the tribunal or

> chairman decides whether or not to make such an order;

> (c) take steps to keep secret all or part of the reasons for its judgment.

The tribunal or chairman (as the case may be) shall keep under review any order it or he has made under this paragraph.

(3) In any proceedings in which a Minister of the Crown considers that it would be appropriate for a tribunal or chairman to make an order as referred to in paragraph (2), he shall (whether or not he is a party to the proceedings) be entitled to appear before and to address the tribunal or chairman thereon. The Minister shall inform the Secretary by notice that he wishes to address the tribunal or chairman and the Secretary shall copy the notice to the parties.

(4) When exercising its or his functions, a tribunal or chairman shall ensure that information is not disclosed contrary to the interests of national security.

Commencement

October 1, 2004. The words in square brackets in para.54(2)(a) were inserted by SI 2005/1865, regs.2(1), 4(j) as from October 1, 2005.   **4–334**

Definitions

For "national security proceedings" see reg.2 of the Employment Tribunals (Constitution and Rules) Regulations 2004; for "Crown employment proceedings" see s.10(8) of the Employment Tribunals Act 1996, which states that they are proceedings where the employment to which the complaint relates is either: (a) Crown employment, or (b) is connected with the performance of functions on behalf of the Crown; for "Crown employment" see s.38(2) of the Employment Tribunals Act 1996 which defines it as employment under or for the purposes of a government department or any officer or body exercising on behalf of the Crown functions conferred by a statutory body; for "chairman" and "Secretary" and "tribunal" see reg.2 of the Employment Tribunals (Constitution and Rules of Procedure) Regulations 2004.   **4–335**

General

Rule 54 of Sch.1 and Sch.2 of the Employment Tribunals (Constitution and Rules of Procedure) Regulations 2004 lay down a detailed system for dealing with employment tribunal cases that involve questions of national security. They replace the regime that was first introduced in the 2001, Rules and came into force on July 16, 2001. Prior to July 16, 2001, no such regime was necessary because Crown servants, including members of the security and intelligence agencies could be prevented from making claims of unfair dismissal and asserting other employment rights if a Minister of the Crown had issued a certificate that the employment in question required to be excepted from those provisions for the purpose of safeguarding national security. The position changed when that restriction was removed by the Employment Relations Act 1999 so that, except security and intelligence services employees who cannot bring public interest disclosure claims, employees in Crown employment now have a right to pursue all claims in employment tribunals. However, s.10(1) of the Employment Tribunals Act 1996, which similarly came into   **4–336** force on July 16, 2001, provides that claims of unfair dismissal and of victimisation on the grounds of trade union membership must be dismissed where it is shown that the action was taken for the purpose of safeguarding national security. The scope of s.10(1) is not restricted to crown employment but arises in the context of any employment. Further, it is not necessary for the employer to show that the dismissal had the effect of protecting national security, nor what the underlying facts were. It is enough that the dismissal was for the purposes of safeguarding national security (*B v BAA Plc* [2005] I.R.L.R. 927; [2005] I.C.R. 1530). Nevertheless, it is for the employment tribunal and not for the Minister to decide whether the action was in fact taken for that purpose. Moreover an employer seeking to rely on s.10(1) has to show not only that the removal of the employee from the post in question was required for the purposes of national security, but that the steps that were taken by way of dismissal were also required, taking into account the issues that would normally need to be considered in a case of substantial other reason for dismissal, such as whether it was within the range of reasonable responses to dismiss rather than deploy. In this latter respect s.3 of the Human Rights Act 1998 requires a tribunal to interpret s.10(1) so as not to exclude considerations of fairness (*B v BAA Plc*, above).

Since the changes brought about in 2001 increased the jurisdiction of the employment tribunals to hear cases capable of raising sensitive matters involving questions of national security, provision was made to provide for the possibility of making substantial modifications to the normal rules of procedure in order to safeguard national security interests. Section 10 of the Employment Tribunals Act 1996 thus conferred the power to make the orders and directions described in r.54 of Sch.1. The overriding objective of r.54 is to ensure that information is not disclosed contrary to the interests of national security. Two means of achieving this objective are envisaged. First, under r.54(1) a direction may be made by a Minister of the Crown to a tribunal or employment judge, in which case the latter has no discretion in the matter. Secondly, using the procedure described in r.54(3) a Minister of the Crown may request a tribunal or employment judge to make an order under r.54(2). Although r.54(2) appears to provide for the possibility of a tribunal or employment judge making orders of their own volition to protect the interests of national security, it is very difficult to imagine circumstances in which, without the intervention of a Minister of the Crown, an employment judge or tribunal would be aware of facts that would justify such steps being taken.

Proceedings in relation to which a direction is given under para.54(1) or an order is made under para.54(2) are known as national security proceedings: reg.2 of the Employment Tribunals (Constitution and Rules of Procedure) Regulations 2004. National security is not defined but is likely to bear the natural and ordinary meaning of a threat to the interests of the nation as a whole. Further, the House of Lords has held that a risk to national security does not have to represent a direct threat to the United Kingdom nor are the interests of national security limited to actions that can be said to be targeted at the United Kingdom, but include actions the consequences of which would threaten the United Kingdom (*Shafiq Rehman v Secretary of State for the Home Department* [2001] 3 W.L.R. 877). The rules set out in Sch.2 of the Employment Tribunals (Constitution and Rules) Regulations 2004 apply to national security proceedings or proceedings where the right in r.54(3) has been exercised. If there is conflict between the rules set out in Sch.2 and those in any other Schedule to the Employment Tribunals (Constitution and Rules of Procedure) Regulations 2004, the rules in Sch.2 prevail: r.1(2) of Sch.2.

Para.54(1) and (2)

4–337   The measures contemplated in these provisions appear to raise questions of compatibility with the right to a fair trial under art.6(1) of the ECHR. In fact the power to conduct a hearing in private is not problematical. Although there is a right to a public hearing under art.6(1) of the Convention that provision specifically provides that the public and press may be excluded from all or part of a trial in the interests of national security. However, holding a hearing in private where there are no grounds for doing so renders it unlawful (*Storer v British Gas* [2000] I.R.L.R. 495, CA). Nevertheless, where a tribunal failed to remove a "private" sign from the hearing room door immediately after evidence being heard in private on grounds of national security had been concluded, the EAT held the failing was de minimis and did not justify a re-hearing (*EC Magagnin v Chief Constable of the West Yorkshire Police* (2004), EAT/0653/04). Taking the further step of excluding the claimant and/or his representative from a hearing raises more difficult issues. This is particularly so since r.54(2)(b) also provides that a tribunal or employment judge may order that documentary evidence relied upon in the proceedings is not disclosed to any excluded person or, where a Minister of the Crown has informed the Secretary that he wishes to address the tribunal or employment judge in accordance with r.54(3), to any person who may be excluded. On the face of it this procedure denies the claimant the right to know the details of the case against him in contravention of the right under art.6(1). However, r.8 of Sch.2 of the Employment Tribunals (Constitution and Rules of Procedure) Regulations 2004 lays down a mechanism for the appointment of "special advocates" to represent the interests of the claimant in circumstances where his representative is excluded, both he and his representative are excluded, or he is excluded where he does not have a representative. Such a special advocate is entitled to see all the evidence relied on in the proceedings but must not communicate directly with any excluded person on any matter discussed or referred to during any part of the proceedings in which the tribunal or employment judge has sat in private or, in a case where a direction has been made under r.54(1) or an order has been made under r.54(2) following an intervention by a Minister of the Crown under r.54(3), on any matter which forms part of the respondent's written grounds. However, a special advocate may apply for orders from the tribunal or employment judge authorising him to seek instructions on, or otherwise communicate with, an excluded person on these matters. There are both Strasbourg and domestic authorities holding similar such processes to be compatible with art.6(1) of the Convention on the basis that they provide a substantial degree of protection to the individual whilst giving due weight to the interests of national security (see *Chalal v United Kingdom* [1996] 23 E.H.R.R. 413, ECtHR; *Tinnely v McElduff* [1999] 27 E.H.R.R. 249, ECtHR; *R v H* [2004] 2 A.C. 134, HL; *A v Secretary of State for the Home Department* (No. 2) [2005] 1 W.L.R. 414, CA, reversed on a different point in the House of Lords). However, in the recent case of *Secretary of State for the Home Department v MB* [2007] 3 W.L.R. 681 the House of Lords held that although the special advocate procedure was, in any given case, highly likely to safeguard the individual against significant injustice there might be cases where a core, irreducible minimum of procedural protection would not be met and in those cases the relevant procedural rules would have to be read down via the interpretative obligation under s.3 Human Rights Act 1998 so as to comply with art. 6(1) of the Convention. In *A Farooq v Commr of Police of the Metropolis*, judgment of November 20, 2007, EAT, the EAT stated at paras 12 and 25 that there was nothing in the judgment of the House of Lords in *MB* to suggest that the r.54 and Sch.2 procedure in the Employment Tribunal was unlawfull, but that every possible step must be taken to ensure that the procedure is operated as fairly as possible. That case appears to be the first in which a contested hearing has taken place in the Employment Tribunal with a special advocate representing the claimant. The claimant brought claims of race discrimination, religious discrimination and victimisation following his transfer away from firearms supervision and high profile security matters after he failed a security vetting. Taking steps to conceal the identity of a particular witness such as allowing a witness to give evidence from behind a screen that shields him from public view does not mean that the proceedings are not in public and therefore raises no issue with the right to a public hearing under art.6(1) of the Convention. Such a step could therefore probably be taken by an employment judge or tribunal in an exceptional course which merited such an unusual step being taken even if it was not necessary in the interests of national security (*R (A Police Officer of the Northumbria Police Force) (1997) v Her Majesty's Coroner For Newcastle upon Tyne*, judgment of January 19, 1998, QBD).

It is important that a tribunal or employment judge who has made an order under r.54(2) remembers that he is required to keep it under review so that the restriction on the claimant's fair trial rights are no greater than necessary (*A Farooq v Commr of Police of the Metropolis*, above at para.10).

Para.54(4)

4–338   This is the overriding objective of this Rule and should be the basis for any order made by an employment judge or tribunal under these provisions.

Dismissals in connection with industrial action

4–339   **55.—(1) In relation to a complaint under section 111 of the Employment Rights Act 1996 (unfair dismissal: complaints to employment tribunal) that a dismissal is unfair by virtue of section 238A of TULR(C)A (participation in official industrial action) a tribunal or chairman may adjourn the proceedings where civil proceedings have been brought until such time as interim proceedings arising out of the civil proceedings have been concluded.**

(2) In this rule—

> **(a) "civil proceedings" means legal proceedings brought by any person against another person in which it is to be determined whether an act of that other person, which induced the claimant to commit an act, or each of a series of acts, is by virtue of section 219 of TULR(C)A not actionable in tort or in delict; and**
>
> **(b) the interim proceedings shall not be regarded as having concluded until all rights of appeal have been exhausted or the time for presenting any appeal in the course of the interim proceedings has expired.**

Definitions

4–340   For "chairman" and "tribunal" and "TULR(C)A" see reg.2 of the Employment Tribunals (Constitution and Rules of Procedure) Regulations 2004.

General

4–341   This provision was introduced in the 2001 Rules. It provides that a tribunal or employment judge may adjourn a claim of unfair dismissal that is said to be unfair by virtue of s.238A TULR(C)A 2002 until the conclusion of interlocutory civil proceedings in which it is to be determined whether certain acts are immune from tort liabilities under s.219 of TULR(C)A. Section 238A of TULR(C)A, as amended by the Employment Relations Act 2004 gives a striker an initial period of twelve weeks protection from dismissal provided that his action is "protected industrial action" because he has been induced to commit it by actions that are rendered lawful under s.219 by virtue of being done in contemplation or furtherance of a trade dispute. That latter issue is commonly determined in the course of civil proceedings brought by the employer against the union which induced the employee to take the industrial action in question. The proceedings in the employment tribunal may be adjourned until the conclusion of any interim proceedings arising out of the civil proceedings.

Devolution issues

56.—(1) In any proceedings in which a devolution issue within the definition of the term in paragraph 1 of Schedule 6 to the Scotland Act 1998 arises, the Secretary shall as soon as reasonably practicable by notice inform the Advocate General for Scotland and the Lord Advocate thereof (unless they are a party to the proceedings) and shall at the same time—   4–342

> **(a) send a copy of the notice to the parties to the proceedings; and**
>
> **(b) send the Advocate General for Scotland and the Lord Advocate a copy of the claim and the response.**

(2) In any proceedings in which a devolution issue within the definition of the term in paragraph 1 of Schedule 8 to the Government of Wales Act 1998 arises, the Secretary shall as soon as reasonably practicable by notice inform the Attorney General and the National Assembly for Wales thereof (unless they are a party to the proceedings) and shall at the same time—

> **(a) send a copy of the notice to the parties to the proceedings; and**
>
> **(b) send the Attorney General and the National Assembly for Wales a copy of the claim and the response.**

(3) A person to whom notice is given in pursuance of paragraph (1) or (2) may within 14 days of receiving it, by notice to the Secretary, take part as a party in the proceedings, so far as they relate to the devolution issue. The Secretary shall send a copy of the notice to the other parties to the proceedings.

Definitions

For "Secretary" see reg.2 of the Employment Tribunals (Constitution and Rules of Procedure) Regulations 2004.   **4–343**

General

This provision was introduced in the 2001 Rules. It provides for the Secretary of the Office of the Tribunals to give notice to the Advocate General for Scotland and the Lord Advocate, in the case of the Scotland, and the Attorney General and the National Assembly for Wales, in the case of Wales, in any proceedings in which a devolution issue arises so that they may take part as a party in the proceedings, so far as they relate to the devolution issue.   **4–344**

Transfer of proceedings between Scotland and England & Wales

4–345   **57.**—(1) The President (England and Wales) or a Regional Chairman may at any time, with the consent of the President (Scotland), order any proceedings in England and Wales to be transferred to an Employment Tribunal Office in Scotland if it appears to him that the proceedings could be (in accordance with regulation 19), and would more conveniently be, determined in an employment tribunal located in Scotland.

(2) The President (Scotland) or the Vice President may at any time, with the consent of the President (England and Wales), order any proceedings in Scotland to be transferred to an Employment Tribunal Office in England and Wales if it appears to him that the proceedings could be (in accordance with regulation 19), and would more conveniently be, determined in an employment tribunal located in England or Wales.

(3) An order under paragraph (1) or (2) may be made by the President, Vice President or Regional Chairman without any application having been made by a party. A party may apply for an order under paragraph (1) or (2) in accordance with rule 11.

(4) Where proceedings have been transferred under this rule, they shall be treated as if in all respects they had been presented to the Secretary by the claimant.

Definitions

4–346   For "President", "Regional Chairman", "Vice President" and "Secretary" see reg.2 of the Employment Tribunals (Constitution and Rules of Procedure) Regulations 2004.

General

4–347   Regulation 19 of the Employment Tribunals (Constitution and Rules of Procedure) Regulations 2004 specifies the circumstances in which, on the one hand, employment tribunals in England and Wales and, on the other, employment tribunals in Scotland have jurisdiction to deal with proceedings. (These rules are not to be confused with those for determining whether a tribunal has territorial jurisdiction to hear a particular type of claim under a particular statute, see, for example, *Lawson v Serco Ltd* [2006] I.C.R. 250, HL). Sometimes a claim may satisfy the criteria for both jurisdictions and be capable of being properly presented either in England and Wales or in Scotland. In these circumstances r.57 makes provision for a case to be transferred from one country to another if it appears that the proceedings could be (in accordance with reg.19) and would more conveniently be determined in an employment tribunal located in the other country. In England and Wales the decision is that of the President or regional employment judge and in Scotland the decision is that of the President or Vice President, although the consent of the President of the other jurisdiction must be obtained. It must be stressed that the power to transfer between countries can be exercised only if the claim was properly presented in the country of origin. The power cannot be used to transfer a case to the proper country where the claim has been presented in the wrong country. In that case a new claim must be brought in the right country, and the claim presented in the wrong country will be struck out for want of jurisdiction.

Para.57(3)

Unlike the position under the previous rules, there is no requirement under the **4–348** 2004 Rules, where an order for a transfer is made by the President, Vice President (Scotland) or regional employment judge (England and Wales) without any application having been made by a party, for a notice to be sent to the parties giving them an opportunity to show cause why such an order should not be made.

References to the European Court of Justice

58. Where a tribunal or chairman makes an order referring a **4–349 question to the European Court of Justice for a preliminary ruling under Article 234 of the Treaty establishing the European Community, the Secretary shall send a copy of the order to the Registrar of that Court.**

Definitions

For "tribunal", "chairman", and "Secretary" see reg.2 of the Employment **4–350** Tribunals (Constitution and Rules of Procedure) Regulations 2004.

General

References to the European Court of Justice are considered at Ch.14 below. **4–351**

Transfer of proceedings from a court

59. Where proceedings are referred to a tribunal by a court, these **4–352 rules shall apply to them as if the proceedings had been sent to the Secretary by the claimant.**

Definitions

For "tribunal" and "Secretary" see reg.2 of the Employment Tribunals (Constitu- **4–353** tion and Rules of Procedure) Regulations 2004.

GENERAL PROVISIONS

Powers

60.—(1) Subject to the provisions of these rules and any practice **4–354 directions, a tribunal or chairman may regulate its or his own procedure.**

(2) At a Hearing, or a pre-hearing review held in accordance with rule 18(3), a tribunal may make any order which a chairman has power to make under these rules, subject to compliance with any relevant notice or other procedural requirements.

(3) Any function of the Secretary may be performed by a person acting with the authority of the Secretary.

Definitions

For "chairman", "hearing", "Secretary" and "tribunal" see reg.2 of the Employ- **4–355** ment Tribunals (Constitution and Rules of Procedure) Regulations 2004.

General

The power of a tribunal to regulate its own procedure is a wide, residual power **4–356** that enables a tribunal to take steps in its management of cases which are not specifically provided for elsewhere in the Rules of Procedure. However many matters which previously could only be done pursuant to this general power are now specifically addressed in r.10 of the 2004 Rules. Examples of this are the power to permit amendments to the claim form, or to add or substitute a respondent, and the power to order exchange of witness statements (*Cocking v Sandhurst (Stationers) Ltd* [1974] I.C.R. 650, NIRC; *British Newspaper Printing Corporation (North) v Kelly* [1989] I.R.L.R. 222, CA; *Selkent Bus Company Ltd v Moore* [1996] I.C.R. 836, EAT; *Eurobell (Holdings) Ltd v Barker* [1998] I.C.R. 299, EAT; *Marks & Spencer Plc v Martins* [1998] I.C.R. 1005, CA). These matters are now dealt with in r.10(2)(k), (l), (q) and (s). One matter that is not specifically addressed in the Rules but which may be the subject of the powers of a tribunal to regulate its own procedure is to order a hearing to be discontinued and a re-hearing to take place. However this power must be exercised most sparingly and only for a good reason (*Charman v Palmers Scaffolding Ltd* [1970] I.C.R. 335, EAT; *Automobile Proprietary Ltd v Healy* [1979] I.C.R. 809, EAT; *Peter Simper & Co v Cooke* [1984] I.C.R. 6, EAT).

Notices, etc.

4–357   **61.—(1) Any notice given or document sent under these rules shall (unless a chairman or tribunal orders otherwise) be in writing and may be given or sent—**

> **(a) by post;**
>
> **(b) by fax or other means of electronic communication; or**
>
> **(c) by personal delivery.**

(2) Where a notice or document has been given or sent in accordance with paragraph (1), that notice or document shall, unless the contrary is proved, be taken to have been received by the party to whom it is addressed—

> **(a) in the case of a notice or document given or sent by post, on the day on which the notice or document would be delivered in the ordinary course of post;**
>
> **(b) in the case of a notice or document transmitted by fax or other means of electronic communication, on the day on which the notice or document is transmitted;**
>
> **(c) in the case of a notice or document delivered in person, on the day on which the notice or document is delivered.**

(3) All notices and documents required by these rules to be presented to the Secretary or an Employment Tribunal Office, other than a claim, shall be presented at the Employment Tribunal Office as notified by the Secretary to the parties.

(4) All notices and documents required or authorised by these rules to be sent or given to any person listed below may be sent to or delivered at—

> **(a) in the case of a notice or document directed to the Secretary of State in proceedings to which she is not a party and which are brought under section 170 of the Employment Rights Act, the offices of the Redundancy**

Payments Directorate of the Insolvency Service at PO Box 203, 21 Bloomsbury Street, London WC1B 3QW, or such other office as may be notified by the Secretary of State;

(b) in the case of any other notice or document directed to the Secretary of State in proceedings to which she is not a party (or in respect of which she is treated as a party for the purposes of these rules by rule 51), the offices of the Department of Trade and Industry (Employment Relations Directorate) at 1 Victoria Street, London, SW1H 0ET, or such other office as be notified by the Secretary of State;

(c) in the case of a notice or document directed to the Attorney General under rule 56, the Attorney General's Chambers, 9 Buckingham Gate, London, SW1E 7JP;

(d) in the case of a notice or document directed to the National Assembly for Wales under rule 56, the Counsel General to the National Assembly for Wales, Crown Buildings, Cathays Park, Cardiff, CF10 3NQ;

(e) in the case of a notice or document directed to the Advocate General for Scotland under rule 56, the Office of the Solicitor to the Advocate General for Scotland, Victoria Quay, Edinburgh, EH6 6QQ;

(f) in the case of a notice or document directed to the Lord Advocate under rule 56, the Legal Secretariat to the Lord Advocate, 25 Chambers Street, Edinburgh, EH1 1LA;

(g) in the case of a notice or document directed to a court, the office of the clerk of the court;

(h) in the case of a notice or document directed to a party:—

    (i) the address specified in the claim or response to which notices and documents are to be sent, or in a notice under paragraph (5); or

    (ii) if no such address has been specified, or if a notice sent to such an address has been returned, to any other known address or place of business in the United Kingdom or, if the party is a corporate body, the body's registered or principal office in the United Kingdom, or, in any case, such address or place outside the United Kingdom as the President, Vice President or a Regional Chairman may allow;

(i) in the case of a notice or document directed to any person (other than a person specified in the foregoing provisions of this paragraph), his address or place of business in the United Kingdom or, if the person is a corporate body, the body's registered or principal office in the United Kingdom; and a notice or document sent or given to the authorised representative of a party shall be taken to have been sent or given to that party.

(5) A party may at any time by notice to the Employment Tribunal Office and to the other party or parties (and, where appropriate, to the appropriate conciliation officer) change the address to which notices and documents are to be sent or transmitted.

(6) The President, Vice President or a Regional Chairman may order that there shall be substituted service in such manner as he may deem fit in any case he considers appropriate.

(7) In proceedings which may involve a payment out of the National Insurance Fund, the Secretary shall, where appropriate, send copies of all documents and notices to the Secretary of State whether or not she is a party.

(8) Copies of every document sent to the parties under rules 29, 30 or 32 shall be sent by the Secretary:—

(a) in the case of proceedings under the Equal Pay Act, the Sex Discrimination Act or the Sex Discrimination Act 1986, to the Equal Opportunities Commission;

(b) in the case of proceedings under the Race Relations Act, to the Commission for Racial Equality; and

(c) in the case of proceedings under the Disability Discrimination Act, to the Disability Rights Commission.

Definitions

4–358   For "chairman", "Employment Tribunal Office", "President", "Regional Chairman", "tribunal" and "Vice President" see reg.2 of the Employment Tribunals (Constitution and Rules of Procedure) Regulations 2004. Para.61(2).

4–359   Since this provision contains its own rules on time of receipt it should not be necessary to have recourse to those set out in s.7 of the Interpretation Act 1978 which, in any event, only deals with postal delivery and similarly uses the test of delivery in the "ordinary course of post" (normally two working days for first-class delivery).

Para.61(4)(h)

4–360   A notice or document directed to party must be sent to the address specified in the claim or response for that purpose. There is no mechanism for automatically directing service of documents to the human resource departments of large corporations and time limits will continue to run whilst a notice or document takes time internally to reach the appropriate recipient. If an address has not been specified or the notice has been returned, the notice may be sent to any other known address or place of business. The phrase "any other known address or place of business" can cover the respondent's last known place of business, with documents sent there presumed to have been received (*Zietsman (t/a Berkshire Orthodontics) v Stubbington* [2002] I.C.R. 249, EAT). If the party is a corporate body, service can be effected at the body's registered or principal office in the United Kingdom or such address or place outside the United Kingdom as the President,

Vice President or regional employment judge may allow. When a party is known to be serving a substantial term of imprisonment the notice or document should be sent to the prison at which he is incarcerated and not to his home (*Lexi Holdings Plc v Shaid Luqman*, judgment of 22 October 2007, ChD).

Para.61(6)

The President, Vice President or regional employment judge has the power to **4–361** order substituted service in such manner as he may deem fit in any appropriate case. Substituted service is normally effected by placing an advertisement in a local or national newspaper, but this happens only rarely when there is a compelling reason to bring proceedings to the attention of a party who has disappeared. Where a claim form has been served incorrectly an order for substituted service cannot apply retrospectively so as to deem retrospectively that there has been valid service by an alternative method (*Elmes v Hygrade Food Products Ltd* [2001] All E.R. D 158, CA; *Maggs v Marshall* [2005] EWHC 3162 (QB)).

SCHEDULE 2

Regulation 16(2)

The Employment Tribunals (National Security) Rules of Procedure

Application of Schedule 2

4–362   1.—(1) The rules in this Schedule only apply to national security proceedings or proceedings where the right in rule 54(3) of Schedule 1 has been exercised.

(2) The rules in this Schedule modify the rules in Schedule 1 in relation to such proceedings. If there is conflict between the rules contained in this Schedule and those in any other Schedule to these Regulations, the rules in this Schedule shall prevail.

(3) Any reference in this Schedule to rule 54 is a reference to rule 54 in Schedule 1.

Notification of national security proceedings

4–363   2. When proceedings before an employment tribunal become national security proceedings the Secretary shall inform the parties of that fact in writing as soon as practicable.

Responding to a claim

4–364   3.—(1) If before the expiry of the period for entering the response—

(a) a direction of a Minister of the Crown under rule 54(1)(b) (exclusion of claimant) applicable to this stage of the proceedings is given; or

(b) a Minister of the Crown has informed the Secretary in accordance with rule 54(3) that he wishes to address the tribunal or chairman with a view to the tribunal or chairman making an order under rule 54(2) applicable to this stage of the proceedings to exclude the claimant; rule 4(3)(d) (grounds for the response) of Schedule 1 shall not apply and paragraphs (2) and (3) of this rule shall apply instead.

(2) In a case falling within paragraph (1)(b), if the tribunal or chairman decides not to make an order under rule 54(2), the respondent shall within 28 days of the decision present to the Employment Tribunal Office the written grounds on which he resists the claim. On receiving the written grounds the Secretary shall send a copy of them to all other parties and they shall be treated as part of the response.

(3) In a case falling within paragraph (1)(b) where the tribunal or chairman makes the order, or in a case falling within paragraph (1)(a), the respondent shall with 44 days of the direction or order being made, present to the Employment Tribunal Office (and, where applicable, to the special advocate) the written grounds on which he resists the claim and they shall be treated as part of the response.

(4) The time limits in paragraphs (2) and (3) may be extended if it is just and equitable to do so and if an application is presented to the Employment Tribunal Office before the expiry of the relevant time limit. The application must explain why the respondent cannot comply with the time limit.

Serving of documents by the Secretary

4.—(1) The Secretary shall not send a copy of the response or grounds for the response to any person excluded from all or part of the proceedings by virtue of a direction or order given or made under rule 54.

4–365

(2) Where a Minister of the Crown has informed the Secretary in accordance with rule 54(3) that he wishes to address the tribunal or chairman with a view to an order being made under rule 54(2)(a) to exclude the claimant's representative from all or part of the proceedings, the Secretary shall not at any time before the tribunal or chairman has considered the Minister's representations, send a copy of the response or the grounds for the response to any person who may be excluded from all or part of the proceedings by such an order if it were made.

Default judgment

5. Rule 8(1) (default judgments) of Schedule 1 shall apply in relation to the time limit for presenting a response, but it shall not apply in relation to the time limits in paragraphs (2) and (3) of rule 3 in this Schedule.

4–366

Witness orders and disclosure of documents

6.—(1) Where—

4–367

(a) a Minister has issued a direction or the tribunal or a chairman has made an order under rule 54 to exclude a claimant or his representative from all or part of the proceedings; and

(b) a chairman or the tribunal is considering whether to make, or has made, an order described in rule 10(2)(c) or "(d) of Schedule 1 (requiring a person to attend and give evidence or to produce documents) or under rule 8 of Schedule 3 or rule 7 of Schedule 4; a Minister of the Crown (whether or not he is a party to the proceedings) may make an application to the tribunal or chairman objecting to the imposition of a requirement described in rule 10(2)(c) or (d) of Schedule 1 or under Schedules 3 or 4. If such an order has been made the Minister may make an application to vary or set aside the order.

(2) The tribunal or chairman shall hear and determine the Minister's application in private and the Minister shall be entitled to address the tribunal or chairman. The application shall be made by notice to the Secretary and the Secretary shall give notice of the application to all parties.

Case management discussions and pre-hearing reviews

4–368 7.—(1) Rule 14(4) (hearings-general) of Schedule 1 shall be modified in accordance with paragraph (2).

(2) In proceedings in which a special advocate has been appointed in respect of the claimant, if the claimant has been excluded from a case management discussion or a pre-hearing review, at such a hearing the claimant shall not have the right to advance oral argument, but oral argument may be advanced on the claimant's behalf by the special advocate.

Special advocate

4–369 8.—(1) In any proceedings in which there is an excluded person the tribunal or chairman shall inform the Attorney General (or in Scotland, the Advocate General) of the proceedings before it with a view to the Attorney General (or the Advocate General, in Scotland), if he thinks it fit to do so, appointing a special advocate to represent the interests of the claimant in respect of those parts of the proceedings from which—

(a) any representative of his is excluded;

(b) both he and his representative are excluded; or

(c) he is excluded, where he does not have a representative.

(2) A special advocate shall have a general qualification for the purposes of section 71 of the Courts and Legal Services Act 1990 or shall be an advocate or a solicitor admitted in Scotland.

(3) Where the excluded person is the claimant, he shall be permitted to make a statement to the tribunal or chairman before the commencement of the proceedings, or the part of the proceedings, from which he is excluded.

(4) Except in accordance with paragraphs (5) to (7), the special advocate may not communicate directly or indirectly with any person (including an excluded person)—

(a) (except in the case of the tribunal, chairman and the
   - respondent) on any matter contained in the grounds for the response referred to in rule 3(3);

(b) (except in the case of a person who was present) on any matter discussed or referred to during any part of the proceedings in which the tribunal or chairman sat in private in accordance with a direction or an order given or made under rule 54.

(5) The special advocate may apply for orders from the tribunal or chairman authorising him to seek instructions from, or otherwise to communicate with, an excluded person—

(a) on any matter contained in the grounds for the response referred to in rule 3(3); or

(b) on any matter discussed or referred to during any part of the proceedings in which the tribunal or chairman sat in private in accordance with a direction or an order given or made under rule 54.

(6) An application under paragraph (5) shall be made in writing to the Employment Tribunal Office and shall include the title of the proceedings and the grounds for the application.

(7) The Secretary shall notify the Minister of an application under paragraph (5) and the Minister shall be entitled to address the tribunal or chairman on the application.

(8) In these rules and those in Schedule 1, in any case in which a special advocate has been appointed to represent the interests of the claimant in accordance with paragraph (1), any reference to a party shall (save in those references specified in paragraph (9)) include the special advocate.

(9) The following references to "party" or "parties" shall not include the special advocate—

(a) regulation 9(3);

(b) in Schedule 1, rule 2(2)(b), 9, 10(2)(r), 10(3), the first two references in rule 11(4), 11(5), 18(7), 20, 22, 23, 27(3), 27(5), 29(3), 30(6)(f), 33(1), 34(2), all references in rule 38 save that in 38(10), 39, 40, 41, all references in rule 42 save that in rule 42(8), 44 to 48, 51, 54(1), the first reference in rule 54(3), 56(3), 61(3), 61(4)(a) and (b), and 61(7);

(c) in Schedule 4, rule 5(b), 6(5) and 10; and

(d) in Schedule 5, rule 4(b).

General

The appointment of a special advocate to represent the interests of the claimant is discussed in the context of r.54 of the Employment Tribunals (Constitution and Rules of Procedure) Regulations 2004. The exclusion of the special advocate from the reference to party or parties in some of the rules under r.8(9) serves to emphasise that the function of the special advocate is to represent the interests of

4–370

the claimant, rather than to become the claimant's representative. See also *A Farooq*, above, at para.24.

Hearings

4–371   9.—(1) Any hearing of or in connection with a claim shall, subject to any direction of a Minister of the Crown or order of a tribunal or chairman under rule 54 that all or part of the proceedings are to take place in private and subject to rule 16 of Schedule 1, take place in public.

(2) A member of the Council on Tribunals shall not be entitled to attend any hearing taking place in private in his capacity as member where the hearing is taking place in private under a direction of a Minister of the Crown or an order of a tribunal or chairman under rule 54.

(3) Subject to any direction of a Minister of the Crown or order of a tribunal or chairman under rule 54, a party shall be entitled to give evidence, to call witnesses, to question any witnesses and to address the tribunal at a Hearing.

General

4–371/1   There is no reason why the procedure adopted before the Special Immigration Appeal Commission (SIAC) of hearing the claimant's open evidence prior to the closed evidence must be followed in the Employment Tribunal. There is no advantage to the special advocate or to the claimant if the open evidence is heard first. The nature of the open evidence is known and nothing additional is likely to be learnt as a result of hearing the open evidence compared with the advantage of full disclosure to the Tribunal and the special advocate of the closed evidence. However, the special advocate may need to make an application, in the light of the open evidence, for the closed hearing to be reconvened; see *A Farooq*, above. Further, the guidance laid down in *Wong v Igen Ltd (formerly Leeds Careers Guidance)* (2005) 3 All E.R. 812 as regards establishing the existence of discrimination does not require the claimant's open evidence to be given first in order to satisfy the Tribunal that there has been discrimination. *Wong* refers to the need for great care by a Tribunal in sifting and making use of evidence but the order of witnesses can always be subject to practice directions given by the Tribunal; *A Farooq*, above.

Reasons in national security proceedings

4–372   10.—(1) This rule applies to written reasons given under rule 30 of Schedule 1 for a judgment or order made by the tribunal or chairman in national security proceedings.

(2) Before the Secretary sends a copy of the written reasons ("the full written reasons") to any party, or enters them in the Register under rule 32 of Schedule 1, he shall send a copy of the full written reasons to the Minister.

(3) If the Minister considers it expedient in the interests of national security and he has given a direction or the tribunal or a chairman has made an order under rule 54 in those proceedings, the Minister may—

(a) direct the tribunal or chairman that the full written reasons shall not be disclosed to persons specified in the direction, and to prepare a further document ("the edited reasons") setting out the reasons for the judgment or order, but with the omission of such of the information as is specified in the direction;

(b) direct the tribunal or chairman that the full written reasons shall not be disclosed to persons specified in the direction, but that no further document setting out the tribunal or chairman's reasons should be prepared.

(4) Where the Minister has directed the tribunal or chairman in accordance with paragraph 3(a), the edited reasons shall be signed by the chairman and initialled in each place where an omission has been made.

(5) Where a direction has been made under paragraph (3)(a), the Secretary shall—

(a) send a copy of the edited reasons referred to in paragraph (3)(a) to any person specified in the direction and to the persons listed in paragraph (7);

(b) enter the edited reasons in the Register, but omit from the Register the full written reasons; and

(c) send a copy of the full written reasons to the persons listed in paragraph (7).

(6) Where a direction has been made under paragraph (3)(b), the Secretary shall send a copy of the full written reasons to the persons listed in paragraph (7), but he shall not enter the full written reasons in the Register.

(7) The persons to whom full written reasons should be sent in accordance with paragraph (5) or (6) are—

(a) the respondent;

(b) the claimant or the claimant's representative if they were not specified in the direction made under paragraph (3);

(c) if applicable, the special advocate;

(d) where the proceedings were referred to the tribunal by a court, to that court; and

(e) where there are proceedings before a superior court (or in Scotland, an appellate court) relating to the decision in question, to that court.

General

This Rule only applies to written reasons given under r.30 of Sch.1. However **4–373** where oral reasons are given at the time of issuing the judgment or order a tribunal or employment judge must bear in mind the combined effect of r.54(2)(c) and r.54(4) of Sch.1, namely the power to take steps to keep secret all or part of the reasons for its judgment and the overriding objective to ensure that information is not disclosed contrary to the interests of national security. If a employment judge or tribunal is in any doubt whatsoever as to what may be disclosed by way of oral reasons the proper course would be to reserve judgment and follow the procedure set out in this rule.

Correction of written reasons

4–374   **11. Where written reasons (whether "full" or "edited") have been omitted from the Register in accordance with rule 10 and they are corrected by certificate under rule 37 of Schedule 1, the Secretary shall send a copy of the corrected reasons to the same persons who had been sent the reasons in accordance with rule 10.**

Review of judgments or decisions

4–375   **12. In rule 34(3) of Schedule 1 (review of other judgments and decisions), the reference in sub-paragraph (c) to decisions being made in the absence of a party does not include reference to decisions being made in the absence of a party where this is done in accordance with a direction given or an order made under rule 54.**

SCHEDULE 3

Regulation 16(3)(a)

The Employment Tribunals (Levy Appeals) Rules of Procedure

FOR USE ONLY IN PROCEEDINGS ON LEVY APPEALS

Application of Schedule 1

1. Subject to rules 9 and 10 of this Schedule, Schedule 1 shall apply to levy appeals. The rules in this Schedule modify the rules in Schedule 1 in relation to levy appeals. If there is conflict between the rules contained in this Schedule and those in Schedule 1, the rules in this Schedule shall prevail.   **4–376**

Levy appeals, generally

Employment tribunals were created (as industrial tribunals) by s.12 of the Industrial Training Act 1964, for the purpose of hearing appeals against annual assessments to training levy by industrial training boards, created by statutory instrument for the purpose of promoting and providing training within an industry. The tribunal's jurisdiction now derives from s.12(4) of the Industrial Training Act 1982 (the 1982 Act). The levy is raised against all employers whose business wholly or mainly falls within the "scope" [for which see "Board" para.4–383 below] of a training board, subject to any specific exemptions created under s.14 of the 1982 Act or the general exemption for small employers, defined in relation to their total wage bill plus amounts paid to labour-only subcontractors, provided for in the annual Levy Order.   **4–377**

The Rules

These Rules, which have effect by virtue of reg.16(3)(a) of the Employment Tribunal Regulations (see para.3–065) should be cited as The Employment Tribunals (Levy Appeals) Rules of Procedure 2004 (reg.1(1)(c) as amended by SI 2005/1865, reg.2(2)). They replace, unamended in substance, rules of procedure which are largely unchanged since 1964. Provisions governing levy appeals which were formerly within the Employment Tribunals (Levy Appeals) Rules of Procedure 2001 (SI 2001/1171, Sch.4) and its predecessors but which are now to be found in Sch.1 are: attendance of witnesses and discovery [r.10(2)(c) and (d)]; time and place of hearing [r.14(4)]; the hearing and procedure at the hearing [r.16–hearings which may be held in private, and rr.26 and 27 the hearing and its conduct]; devolution issues [r.56]; decision of tribunal [r.28(4)-majority decisions, and rr.29 (form and contents of judgment,), 30, (reasons,), 31 (absence of employment judge), 32 (the Register) and 37 (correction of clerical errors)]; costs [rr.38 to 48, costs, preparation time and wasted costs orders]; miscellaneous powers and applications [rr.10 and 11 generally, and r.60(1), power to regulate own procedure]; notices [r.61]. Rule 9 (below) deals with the provisions of Sch.1 which do not apply to levy appeals, and the commentary on the individual rules highlights differences of practical importance between levy appeal rules and Sch.1 and significant changes in wording from the 2001 Levy Appeal Rules.   **4–378**

Composition of tribunal

Rule 9(1) of the 2001 Rules provided for the appeal to be heard "by a tribunal composed in accordance with s.4(1) and (2) of the (Employment Tribunals Act 1996)", i.e. a full tribunal subject to the ability of the parties to agree in writing to   **4–379** an employment judge sitting alone, or to an employment judge sitting alone if the appeal was no longer contested. This provision is not reproduced in the new Rules but was otiose as the provisions of s.4 applied in any event. As the Respondent Board invariably does not appear at the hearing of an appeal but relies on written representations instead, consent to an employment judge sitting alone must be obtained from them in writing in advance of the hearing.

Conciliation
4–380   ACAS has no power to conciliate in levy appeals (Employment Tribunals Act 1996, s.18).

Further appeals
4–381   The 1982 Act does not provide for a further appeal beyond the employment tribunal and the Act is not listed in s.21 of the Employment Tribunals Act 1996, (Employment Appeal Tribunal). Any appeal against the judgment of the employment tribunal would therefore be by way of judicial review.

Definitions
4–382   **2. In this Schedule and in relation to proceedings to which this Schedule applies—**

"Board" means in relation to an appeal the respondent industrial training board;

"Industrial Training Act" means the Industrial Training Act 1982;

"levy" means a levy imposed under section 11 of the Industrial Training Act;

"levy appeal" means an appeal against an assessment to a levy;

"respondent" means the Board.

"Board"
4–383   There were formerly at least 31 industrial training boards constituted by statutory instrument but only two, the Construction Industry Training Board (CITB) and the Engineering Construction Industry Training Board (ECITB) remain. The activities of the construction industry in respect of which the CITB may exercise levy raising powers (the Board's "scope") are set out in para.1 of Sch.1 to the Industrial Training (Construction Board) Order 1964 (Amendment) Order 1992 (SI 1992/3048) and the exceptions in para.2 of the Schedule. The "scope" of the ECITB is set out in paras 1 and 2 of Sch.1 to the Industrial Training (Engineering Construction Board) Order 1991 (SI 1991/1305).

"levy", amount of
4–384   The amount of the levy is determined by annual statutory instruments made by the Secretary of State pursuant to s.12(6) of the 1982 Act on the recommendation of the respective Boards which normally, but not invariably, come into effect in mid February. The 2007 SIs are 2007/607 for CITB and 2007/609 for ECITB: the 2008 SIs are 2008/534 for CITB and 2008/535 for ECITB.

"levy appeal", tribunal's powers on
4–385   The 1982 Act s.12(5):

"(a) on an appeal under subsection (4), if the appellant satisfies the tribunal that he ought not to have been assessed to the levy or ought to have been assessed in a smaller amount, the tribunal shall rescind or, as the case may be, reduce the assessment but (subject to paragraph (b) below) in any other case it shall confirm it; and (b) if it appears to the tribunal that the appellant ought to have been assessed to the levy in a larger amount, the tribunal may increase the amount accordingly."

Note that while the tribunal is obliged ("shall") to rescind or reduce the assessment if it finds in the appellant's favour, it is not obliged ("may") to increase an assessment.

"levy appeal", burden of proof
The burden is on the appellant to upset the assessment, not on the Board to uphold it.   **4–386**

Notice of Appeal
3. A person wishing to appeal an assessment to a levy (the   **4–387**
appellant) shall do so by sending to the Board two copies of a notice
of appeal which must be substantially in accordance with Form 1 in
the Annex to this Schedule, and they must include the grounds of
their appeal.

Notice of appeal
The form is not mandatory but there appear to be no reported decisions on the   **4–388**
extent to which an appellant may permissibly depart from the form. As the notice is
sent to the Board rather than the tribunal, this issue is only likely to arise in the
context of an opposed application by an appellant to extend the time for appealing
(for which see below). The tribunal has no express power to determine whether a
rejected notice of appeal should have been accepted by the Board which, if it
becomes an issue, therefore appears to be a matter for judicial review. Although the
assessment notice does not include an appeal form, it informs the appellant of the
address from which a form can be obtained. The notice of appeal can only be
submitted by post or delivered by hand as there are currently no facilities to submit
them to the Boards online or by email.

Time for entering appeal
The time limit for entering the appeal is one month from the date of service of   **4–389**
the assessment notice, (art.9 of both of the 2007 Orders) which, unless the contrary
is proved, is in the normal course of post, i.e. two days after posting if by first class
post or four days if by second class post (Interpretation Act 1978, s.7). However, as
the Board may "for good cause" (art.9(2)) allow the appellant to appeal to the
tribunal "at any time within the period of four months from the date of the
assessment notice or within such further period or periods as the Board may allow
before such time as may then be limited for appealing has expired", issues over the
precise date of service are unlikely to arise. If the Board refuses the application for
an extension of time the appellant may apply to the tribunal for an extension,
which, when considering the application shall "have the like powers as the Board
under paragraph (2)". (art.9(3)). The wording of art.9(2) suggests that an
application for an extension of time must be made (and possibly even granted)
before the primary 28 day time limit or any subsequent extension of it has expired.
As the application to the tribunal is governed by art.9 of the 2006 Orders and not
the ETR 2004 the tribunals' discretion to extend time appears to be extremely
wide.

Grounds of appeal

4–390 These are likely to be restricted to challenges to the way the levy has been calculated and claims that the appellant employer's business is out of the "scope" of the Board and therefore not liable to levy. The tribunal has no jurisdiction to determine challenges to the validity of the Levy Order itself and issues over ability to pay are a matter between the appellant and the Board. The tribunal has no power to order an extension of time for payment of the levy.

Action on receipt of appeal

4–391 **4.—(1) Subject to rules 5 and 6, the Board shall, within 21 days of receiving the notice of appeal send the following documents to the Employment Tribunal Office—**

(a) **one copy of the notice of appeal;**

(b) **a copy of the assessment notice and of any notice by the Board allowing further time for appealing;**

(c) **a notice giving the Board's address for service under these rules where that address is different from the address specified in the assessment notice as the address for service of a notice of appeal; and**

(d) **any representations in writing relating to the appeal that the Board wishes to submit to the tribunal.**

(2) Failure to comply with any provision of this rule or rule 5 shall not make the appeal invalid.

Postponement

4–392 This step is postponed if the Board requests further information (r.5(4) and (5) below at para.4–396).

Rule 5

4–393 Request for further information; see below at para.4–396.

Rule 6

4–394 Withdrawal of appeal or assessment; see below at para.4–400.

Non-compliance by Board

4–395 The tribunal has no power to intervene or accept the notice of appeal directly from the appellant if the Board should fail to comply with this requirement. The tribunal does not become part of the appeal process until the notice of appeal and accompanying documents are received from the Board (see r.7 below at para.4–402).

Requests for further information

4–396 **5.—(1) Subject to rule 6, this rule applies when, on receiving the notice of appeal, the Board considers that it requires further information on the appellant's grounds for the appeal and of any facts relevant to those grounds.**

(2) The Board shall send the appellant a notice specifying the further information required by the Board within 21 days of receiving the notice of appeal.

(3) The appellant shall send the Board two copies of the further information within 21 days of receiving the notice requesting the information, or within such further period as the Board may allow.

(4) Subject to paragraph (5), within 21 days of receiving the further information the Board shall send the following documents to the Employment Tribunal Office—

    (a) the documents listed in rule 4(1);

    (b) a copy of the notice requesting further information;

    (c) any further information which has been provided to the Board; and

    (d) any representations in writing regarding such information which the Board wishes to submit to the tribunal.

(5) If further information is not received by the Board within the time limit, the documents listed in sub-paragraphs (a) and (b) of paragraph (4) shall be sent by the Board to the Employment Tribunal Office—

    (a) within 50 days of the receipt of the notice of appeal by the Board; or

    (b) if the Board has allowed a further period of time for delivery of further particulars under paragraph (3), within 7 days of the end of that period.

Role of tribunal

At this stage the tribunal is not involved and the request is not communicated to **4–397** the tribunal. An employment judge has no power to make an order for further information until after the notice of appeal has been sent to the Secretary (r.7 below).

Non-compliance

A failure by the appellant to provide the requested information does not **4–398** invalidate the appeal and the Board is still required to forward the prescribed documents to the tribunal (para.(5)). The Board may then apply for an Order under r.8.

Extensions of time

These are purely at the discretion of the Board and requests for extensions of **4–399** time should be addressed to the Board and not the tribunal which has no role in the process at this stage.

Withdrawal of appeal or assessment

6.—(1) The appellant may withdraw the notice of appeal by notice **4–400** given to the Board at any time and in that event no further action shall be taken in relation to the appeal.

(2) When an assessment is withdrawn by the Board, it shall notify the Employment Tribunal Office and no further action shall be taken in relation to the appeal.

4–401   Although this rule precedes r.7, "Entry of Appeal", it is presumably intended to apply to the withdrawal of either the appeal or the assessment before or after the Board has sent the notice of appeal and accompanying documents to the tribunal. This is apparent from para.(2) which was not in the 2001 Rules and also from the omission from para.(1) of the words "before the entry of the appeal in the Register" which were in the 2001 Rules. Rule 25 of Sch.1 does not apply to such a withdrawal (see r.9 below), and it is not therefore open to the Board to apply for a judgment formally dismissing a withdrawn appeal.

Entry of appeal

4–402   **7.—(1) The Secretary shall as soon as reasonably practicable after receiving from the Board the relevant documents in accordance with rule 4(1), 5(4) or 5(5)—**

    (a) give notice to the appellant and to the Board of the case number of the appeal (which must from then on be referred to in all correspondence relating to the appeal) and of the address to which notices and other communications to the Employment Tribunal Office shall be sent;

    (b) give notice to the appellant of the Board's address for service; and

    (c) send to the appellant a copy of any representations in writing that the Board has submitted to the tribunal under rule 4 or 5.

4–403   This rule has been modified from the 2001 Rules only to reflect the abolition of the Public Register. The Secretary is not empowered to reject the appeal and the Board is not required to enter a response, any written representations by the Board sent to the tribunal under r.4(1)(d) in effect amounting to their response.

Order for further information

4–404   **8.—(1) In any case in which the appellant has not sent to the Board further information which has been requested by the Board in accordance with rule 5, a chairman or tribunal may, on the application of the Board, by notice order the appellant to supply such further information as may be specified in the notice, and the appellant shall send two copies of such information to the Employment Tribunal Office within such time as the chairman or tribunal may direct.**

    (2) As soon as is reasonably practicable after receiving the further information from the appellant, the Secretary shall send a copy of the information to the Board.

    (3) An order made under paragraph (1) shall be treated as an order made under rule 10 of Schedule 1 for the purposes of rule 13 of Schedule 1 (compliance with orders and practice directions).

4–405   The wording of this rule differs from that of its predecessor (Rules of Procedure 2001, r.6) in two significant respects in that it does not contain an express power; (a) for the tribunal to dismiss the appeal if the appellant fails to comply with the notice; and (b) to require the Board to "furnish any particulars relating to the assessment which appear to be requisite for the decision of the appeal." Such provisions are now unnecessary because of the general powers contained in Sch.1, r.12 read with r.10(2)(b) and r.13. Any application for an order by the Board must be in compliance with r.11 of Sch.1 and any order made by the employment judge on his or her own initiative must be in compliance with r.12. There is no reason in principle why an "unless" order under r.13(2) should not be made against the Board as well as the appellant.

Provisions of Schedule 1 which do not apply to levy appeals

9. The following rules in Schedule 1 shall not apply in relation to levy appeals: rules 1 to 9, 16(1)(c), 18(2)(c) and (e), 20 to 25, 33, 34(1)(a), 34(2), 34(4), 38(4), 39, 42(4), 43, 47, 49 to 53, 55, and paragraphs (4)(a), (7) and (8) of rule 61. All references in Schedule 1 to the rules listed in this rule shall have no effect in relation to a levy appeal.   4–406

Rules 1 to 9: bringing and responding to a claim

Rule 16(1)(c): ability to hear evidence in private where the disclosure of information might cause substantial injury to any undertaking of the witness

Rule 18(2)(c): order a deposit to be paid under r.20

Rule 18(2)(e): applications for interim relief

Rule 20: requirement to pay a deposit as a condition for continuing with a claim

Rule 21 to 25: conciliation

Rule 33: review of default judgments

Rule 34(1)(a), 34(2) and (4): review of decisions not to accept claims or responses

Rule 38(4): power to make costs or expenses orders against or in favour of a respondent who has not entered a response

Rule 39: where a costs or expenses order must be made

Rule 42(4): power to make a preparation time order against a respondent who has not entered a response

Rule 43: when a preparation time order must be made

Rule 47: costs, expenses or preparation time orders when a deposit has been taken

Rules 49 to 53: powers in relation to specific types of proceedings

Rule 55: dismissals in connection with industrial action

Rule 61(4)(a): notices and documents sent to the Secretary of State when not a party to the proceedings

Rule 61(7): proceedings involving a payment out of the National Insurance Fund

Rule 61(8): copies of documents to be sent to certain bodies in discrimination cases.

Modification of Schedule 1

10. Schedule 1 shall be further modified in relation to levy appeals as follows—   4–407

    (a) all references in Schedule 1 to a claim or claimant shall be read as references to a levy appeal or to an appellant in a levy appeal respectively and as the context may require; and

    (b) in rule 61 (Notices, etc.) after paragraph 4(i) insert:—

"(j) in the case of a notice of an appeal brought under the Industrial Training Act, the Board's address for service specified in the assessment notice;

(k) in the case of any other document directed to the Board, the Board's address for service;".

SCHEDULE 4

Regulation 16(3)(b)

The Employment Tribunals (Health and Safety—Appeals Against Improvement and Prohibition Notices) Rules of Procedure

1. Application of Schedule 1

Subject to rules 11 and 12 of this Schedule, Schedule 1 shall apply **4–408** to appeals against an improvement notice or a prohibition notice. The rules in this Schedule modify the rules in Schedule 1 in relation to such appeals. If there is conflict between the rules contained in this Schedule and those in Schedule 1, the rules in this Schedule shall prevail.

2. Definitions

In this Schedule and in relation to proceedings to which this **4–409** Schedule applies—

"Health and Safety Act" means the Health and Safety at Work etc Act 1974;

"improvement notice" means a notice under section 21 of the Health and Safety Act;

"inspector" means a person appointed under section 19(1) of the Health and Safety Act;

"prohibition notice" means a notice under section 22 of the Health and Safety Act; and

"respondent" means the inspector who issued the improvement notice or prohibition notice which is the subject of the appeal.

Improvement notice

If an inspector is of the opinion that a person has contravened one or more of the **4–410** relevant statutory provisions of the Health and Safety at Work etc. Act 1974 or has contravened one or more of those provisions in circumstances that makes it likely that the contravention will continue or be repeated, the inspector may serve on him an improvement notice stating that he is of that opinion, specifying the provision or provisions as to which the inspector is of that opinion, giving particulars of the reasons why he is of that opinion, and requiring that person to remedy the contravention: s.21 of the Health and Safety at Work etc Act 1974.

Recipients of improvement notices are entitled to know what was wrong and why it was wrong, and the notice has to be clear and easy to understand. Where a statute provided an option to prescribe how a recipient could comply with a notice, any directions given as to compliance formed part of the notice and, if confusing, could operate to make the notice invalid (*BT Fleet Ltd v Jason Stephen Joseph McKenna* [2005] EWHC 387).

Prohibition notice.

Where an inspector is of the opinion activities identified in the Health and Safety **4–411** at Work etc. Act 1974 will involve a risk of serious personal injury, the inspector may serve on that person a prohibition notice: s.22 of the Health and Safety at Work etc. Act 1974.

A prohibition notice states that the inspector is of the opinion that there is a risk of serious personal injury and other material information required under the Act.

3. Notice of appeal

4–412   A person wishing to appeal an improvement notice or a prohibition notice (the appellant) shall do so by sending to the Employment Tribunal Office ... a notice of appeal which must include the following—

(a) the name and address of the appellant and, if different, an address to which he requires notices and documents relating to the appeal to be sent;

(b) the date of the improvement notice or prohibition notice appealed against and the address of the premises or the place concerned;

(c) the name and address of the respondent;

(d) details of the requirements or directions which are being appealed; and

(e) the grounds for the appeal.

4. Time limit for bringing appeal

4–413   (1) Subject to paragraph (2), the notice of appeal must be sent to the Employment Tribunal Office within 21 days from the date of the service on the appellant of the notice appealed against.

(2) A tribunal may extend the time mentioned above where it is satisfied, on an application made in writing to the Secretary either before or after the expiration of that time, that it is or was not reasonably practicable for an appeal to be brought within that time.

5. Action on receipt of appeal

4–414   On receiving the notice of appeal the Secretary shall—

(a) send a copy of the notice of appeal to the respondent; and

(b) inform the parties in writing of the case number of the appeal (which must from then on be referred to in all correspondence relating to the appeal) and of the address to which notices and other communications to the Employment Tribunal Office shall be sent.

6. Application for a direction suspending the operation of a prohibition notice

4–415   (1) When an appeal is brought against a prohibition notice, an application may be made by the appellant under section 24(3)(b) of the Health and Safety Act for a direction suspending the operation of the prohibition notice until the appeal is determined or withdrawn. The application must be presented to the Employment Tribunal Office in writing and shall include—

(a) the case number of the appeal, or if there is no case number sufficient details to identify the appeal; and

(b) the grounds on which the application is made.

(2) The Secretary shall send a copy of the application to the respondent as soon as practicable after it has been received and shall inform the respondent that he has the opportunity to submit representations in writing if he so wishes, within a specified time but not less than 7 days.

(3) The chairman shall consider the application and any representations submitted by the respondent, and may—

(a) order that the application should not be determined separately from the full hearing of the appeal;

(b) order that the operation of the prohibition notice be suspended until the appeal is determined or withdrawn;

(c) dismiss the appellant's application; or

(d) order that the application be determined at a Hearing (held in accordance with rule 26 of Schedule 1).

(4) The chairman must give reasons for any decision made under paragraph (3) or made following a Hearing ordered under paragraph (3)(d).

(5) A decision made under paragraph (3) or made following a Hearing ordered under paragraph (3)(d) shall be treated as a decision which may be reviewed upon the application of a party under rule 34 of Schedule 1.

7. General power to manage proceedings

(1) The chairman may at any time on the application of a party, **4–416** make an order in relation to any matter which appears to him to be appropriate. Such orders may be those listed in rule 10(2) of Schedule 1 (subject to rule 11 below) or such other orders as he thinks fit. Subject to the case management rules in Schedule 1, orders may be issued as a result of a chairman considering the papers before him in the absence of the parties, or at a hearing (see regulation 2 for the definition of 'hearing').

(2) If the parties agree in writing upon the terms of any decision to be made by the tribunal or chairman, the chairman may, if he thinks fit, decide accordingly.

8. Appointment of an assessor

The President, Vice President or a Regional Chairman may, if he **4–417** thinks fit, appoint in accordance with section 24(4) of the Health and Safety Act a person having special knowledge or experience in relation to the subject matter of the appeal to sit with the tribunal or chairman as an assessor.

9. Right to withdraw proceedings

4–418 (1) An appellant may withdraw all or part of the appeal at any time. This may be done either orally at a hearing or in writing in accordance with paragraph (2).

(2) To withdraw an appeal or part of one in writing the appellant must inform the Employment Tribunal Office in writing of the appeal or the parts of it which are to be withdrawn.

(3) The Secretary shall inform all other parties of the withdrawal. Withdrawal takes effect on the date on which the Employment Tribunal Office (in the case of written notifications) or the tribunal or chairman receives notice of it and where the whole appeal is withdrawn proceedings are brought to an end against the respondent on that date and the tribunal or chairman shall dismiss the appeal.

10. Costs and expenses

4–419 (1) A tribunal or chairman may make an order ("a costs order") that a party ("the paying party") make a payment in respect of the costs incurred by another party ("the receiving party").

(2) For the purposes of paragraph (1) "costs" shall mean fees, charges, disbursements, [or expenses] incurred by or on behalf of a party in relation to the proceedings. In Scotland all references in this Schedule to costs or costs orders shall be read as references to expenses or orders for expenses.

(3) The amount of a costs order against the paying party can be determined in the following ways—

  (a) the tribunal may specify the sum which the party must pay to the receiving party, provided that sum does not exceed £10,000;

  (b) the parties may agree on a sum to be paid by the paying party to the receiving party and if they do so the costs order shall be for the sum so agreed;

  (c) the tribunal may order the paying party to pay the receiving party the whole or a specified part of the costs of the second party with the amount to be paid being determined by way of detailed assessment in a County Court in accordance with the Civil Procedure Rules or, in Scotland, as taxed according to such part of the table of fees prescribed for proceedings in the sheriff court as shall be directed by the order.

(4) The tribunal or chairman shall have regard to the paying party's ability to pay when considering whether it or he shall make a costs order or how much that order should be.

(5) For the avoidance of doubt, the amount of a costs order made under either paragraph (4)(b) or (c) may exceed £10,000.

Wording in square brackets in r.10(2) substituted by SI 2005/1865 as from October 1, 2005.

11. Provisions of Schedule 1 which do not apply to appeals against improvement notices or prohibition notice

4–420 The following rules in Schedule 1 shall not apply in relation to appeals against improvement and prohibition notices: rule 1 to 9, 10(1), 10(2)(g), (i), (k), (l), and (r), 12, 13, 16(1)(c), 18(2)(c) and (e), 18(8), 20 to 25, 29(3), 33, 34(1)(a), 34(2), 38 to 47, 49 to 53, 55, and 61(4)(a), (7) and (8). All references in Schedule 1 to the rules listed in this rule shall have no effect in relation to an appeal against an improvement notice or a prohibition notice.

12. Modification of Schedule 1

4–421 Schedule 1 shall be further modified so that all references in Schedule 1 to a claim shall be read as references to a notice of appeal or to an appeal against an improvement notice or a prohibition notice, as the context may require, and all references to the claimant shall be read as references to the appellant in such an appeal.

Appeal against improvement or prohibition notice

4–422 A person on whom a notice is served may within 21 days of its service appeal to an employment tribunal. On such an appeal the employment tribunal may either cancel or affirm the notice and, if it affirms it, may do so either in its original form or with such modifications as the employment tribunal may in the circumstances think fit.

The relevant statutory provisions

4–423 The relevant statutory provisions are set out in Sch.1 of the Health and Safety at Work Act 1974.

SCHEDULE 5

Regulation 16(3)(C)

The Employment Tribunals (Non-Discrimination Notices Appeals) Rules of Procedure

FOR USE ONLY IN PROCEEDINGS IN AN APPEAL AGAINST A NON-DISCRIMINATION NOTICE

1. Application of Schedule 1

4–424   Subject to rules 5 and 6 of this Schedule, Schedule 1 shall apply to appeals against a non-discrimination notice. The rules in this Schedule modify the rules in Schedule 1 in relation to such appeals. If there is conflict between the rules contained in this Schedule and those in Schedule 1, the rules in this Schedule shall prevail.

Applicable statutory provisions

4–425   The relevant statutory commissions have power to issue non-discrimination notices under the provisions of ss.67–70 of the Sex Discrimination Act 1975 and the Sex Discrimination (Formal Investigations) Regulations 1975 (SI 1975/1993), ss.48–52 of the Race Relations Act 1976 and the Race Relations (Formal Investigations) Regulations 1977 (SI 1977/841), and ss.3–6 of the Disability Rights Commission Act 1999.

2. Definitions

4–426   **In this Schedule and in relation to proceedings to which this Schedule applies—**

"appeal", unless the context requires otherwise, means an appeal referred to in section 68(1)(a) of the Sex Discrimination Act, in section 59(1)(a) of the Race Relations Act or, as the case may be, in paragraph 10(1) and (2)(a) of Schedule 3 to the Disability Rights Commission Act;

"Disability Rights Commission Act" means the Disability Rights Commission Act 1999;

"non-discrimination notice" means a notice under s.67 of the Sex Discrimination Act, under s.58 of the Race Relations Act or, as the case may be, under s.4 of the Disability Rights Commission Act; and

"respondent" means the Equal Opportunities Commission established under section 53 of the Sex Discrimination Act, the Commission for Racial Equality established under section 43 of the Race Relations Act or, as the case may be, the Disability Rights Commission established under section 1 of the Disability Rights Commission Act.

4–427   For "non discrimination notice" see s.67 of the Sex Discrimination Act 1975, see s.58 of the Race Relations Act 1976, and s.4 of the Disability Rights Commission Act 1999.

This Schedule concerns appeals against a non-discrimination notice served by either the Equal Opportunities Commission, the Commission for Racial Equality or the Disability Rights Commission ("the Statutory Commission"). Schedule 5 is the Employment Tribunals (Non-Discrimination Notices Appeals) Rules of Procedure. They replace the previous rules in Sch.6 of the Employment Tribunal Rules of Procedure Regulations 2001. When the material provisions of the Equality Act 2006 are brought into force, these functions will be transferred from the existing Statutory Commissions to the new Commission for Equality and Human Rights (the CEHR). Under s.21 of the Equality Act (not yet brought into force) the CEHR will have the power to issue unlawful act notices. Appeals against such notices will be to the employment tribunal if a claim in respect of the unlawful act could be made to the tribunal, i.e. if the context in which the unlawful act identified in the notice occurred is such that the jurisdiction of the employment tribunal would be engaged under any of the applicable substantive anti-discrimination statutory schemes.

A non-discrimination notice, requires the recipient to discontinue an unlawful discriminatory act. The Statutory Commissions are empowered to issue non-discrimination notices following a formal investigation, if in the course of the formal investigation, the Statutory Commission is satisfied that a person is committing, or has committed, any such unlawful act. In those circumstances, the Statutory Commission may in the prescribed manner serve on that person a non discrimination notice requiring him not to commit any unlawful act(s), and where compliance involves changes in any of his practices or other arrangements, to inform the Statutory Commissions that he has effected those changes and what those changes are. Further the recipient may have to take such steps as may be reasonably required by the notice for the purpose of affording that information to other persons concerned.

The non-discrimination notice procedure is a follows: (1) the Statutory Commissions must first give the person a notice that they are minded to issue a non discrimination notice, specifying the grounds on which they contemplate doing so, and offering an opportunity to make oral or written representations within a period of not less than 28 days in respect of the notice; (2) Take account of the representations made by the recipient; (3) Not later than six weeks after a non discrimination notice is served on any person the recipient may appeal against any requirement of the notice to the employment tribunal so far as the requirement relates to acts which are within the jurisdiction of the employment tribunal; and (4) If the non-discrimination notice becomes final it is entered into a public register. **4–428**

If the non-discrimination notice is appealed, the recipient is entitled to reopen all the issues including the facts found in support of the non-discrimination notice.

The process requires that the Statutory Commission should set out the facts it relies on, and thereafter the recipient should identify the facts it is going to challenge (*Commission for Racial Equality v Amari Plastics Ltd* [1982] I.R.L.R. 252, CA).

If the employment tribunal considers a requirement in respect of which an appeal is brought to be unreasonable because it is based on an incorrect finding(s) of fact or for any other reason, the employment tribunal shall quash the requirement. On quashing a requirement, the employment tribunal may direct that the non discrimination notice shall be treated as if, in place of the requirement quashed, it has contained a requirement in terms specified by the tribunal itself.

3. Notice of Appeal

A person wishing to appeal a non-discrimination notice (the appellant) shall do so by sending to the Employment Tribunal Office . . . a notice of appeal which must be in writing and must include the following— **4–429**

(a) the name and address of the appellant and, if different, an address to which he requires notices and documents relating to the appeal to be sent;
   (b) the date of the non-discrimination notice appealed against;
   (c) the name and address of the respondent;
   (d) details of the requirements which are being appealed; and
   (e) the grounds for the appeal.

4. Action on receipt of appeal

4–430   On receiving the notice of appeal the Secretary shall—

(a) send a copy of the notice of appeal to the respondent; and
   (b) inform the parties in writing of the case number of the appeal (which must from then on be referred to in all correspondence relating to the appeal) and of the address to which notices and other communications to the Employment Tribunal Office shall be sent.

5. Provisions of Schedule 1 which do not apply to appeals against non-discrimination notices

4–431   The following rules in Sch.1 shall not apply in relation to appeals against a non-discrimination notice: r.1–9, 16(1)(c), 18(2)(c) and (e), 20 to 24, 33, 34(1)(a), 34(2), 34(4), 38(4), 39, 42(4), 43, 47, 49 to 53, 55, and paras (4)(a), (7) and (8) of r.61. All references in Sch.1 to the rules listed in this rule shall have no effect in relation to an appeal against a non-discrimination notice.

6. Modification of Schedule 1

4–432   Schedule 1 shall be further modified so that all references in Schedule 1 to a claim shall be read as references to a notice of appeal or to an appeal against a non-discrimination notice, as the context may require, and all references to the claimant shall be read as references to the appellant in such an appeal.

SCHEDULE 6

Regulation 16(4)

The Employment Tribunals (Equal Value) Rules of Procedure

1. General

The rules in this Schedule shall only apply in proceedings involving **4–433**
an equal value claim and they modify and supplement the rules in
Schedule 1. If there is conflict between Schedule 1 and this Schedule,
the provisions of this Schedule shall prevail.

The Schedule only applies to proceedings involving an equal value claim **4–434**
commenced after October 1, 2004. The Employment Tribunals (Constitution and
Rules of Procedure)(Amendment) Regulations 2004 (SI 2004/2351) resulted in
radical changes to the procedural rules concerning these claims. There was a need
to case manage these claims to avoid the delays and to address in a orderly manner
the various stages of an equal value claim (stage 1, stage 2, the appointment of the
expert, written questions to the expert, and the use of the expert's evidence at the
hearing).

The aim of the rules is to give employment tribunals a new case management **4–435**
structure for dealing with equal value claims in an attempt to speed up their
progress. Primarily this is achieved by changing the approach: where previously the
practice was to attempt to dispose of any claim for equal pay based on like work,
now the equal value claim takes priority. That does not prevent the like work claim
being disposed of at the same time but the equal value claim dictates the pace of
the litigation. The Rules now state that if there is a dispute as to whether the work
is of equal value, the tribunal is obliged to conduct what is termed a stage 1 hearing
in accordance with r.4. A tribunal may hold more than one stage 1 or stage 2
hearings in accordance with r.13(2).

2. Interpretation

(1) In this Schedule and in relation to proceedings to which this **4–436**
Schedule applies:

"comparator" means the person of the opposite sex to the
claimant in relation to whom the claimant claims that his
work is of equal value as described in section 1(2)(c) of
the Equal Pay Act;

"Equal Pay Act" means the Equal Pay Act 1970;

"equal value claim" means a claim by a claimant which
rests upon entitlement to the benefit of an equality clause
by virtue of the operation of section 1(2)(c) of the Equal
Pay Act;

"the facts relating to the question" has the meaning in
rule 7(3);

"independent expert" means a member of the panel of
independent experts mentioned in section 2A(4) of the
Equal Pay Act;

261

"indicative timetable" means the indicative timetable set out in the Annex to this Schedule;

"the question" means whether the claimant's work is of equal value to that of the comparator as described in section 1(2)(c) of the Equal Pay Act; and

"report" means a report required by a tribunal to be prepared by an independent expert, in accordance with section 2A(1)(b) of the Equal Pay Act.

(2) A reference in this Schedule to a rule, is a reference to a rule in this Schedule unless otherwise provided.

(3) A reference in this Schedule to "these rules" is a reference to the rules in Schedules 1 and 6 unless otherwise provided.

3. General power to manage proceedings

4–437 (1) In addition to the power to make orders described in rule 10 of Schedule 1, the tribunal or chairman shall have power (subject to rules 4(3) and 7(4)) to make the following orders:

  (a) the standard orders set out in rules 5 or 8, with such addition to, omission or variation of those orders (including specifically variations as to the periods within which actions are to be taken by the parties) as the chairman or tribunal considers is appropriate;

  (b) that no new facts shall be admitted in evidence by the tribunal unless they have been disclosed to all other parties in writing before a date specified by the tribunal (unless it was not reasonably practicable for a party to have done so);

  (c) that the parties may be required to send copies of documents or provide information to the other parties and to the independent expert;

  (d) that the respondent is required to grant the independent expert access to his premises during a period specified by the tribunal or chairman in order for the independent expert to conduct interviews with persons identified as relevant by the independent expert;

  (e) when more than one expert is to give evidence in the proceedings, that those experts present to the tribunal a joint statement of matters which are agreed between them and those matters on which they disagree;

  (f) where proceedings have been joined, that lead claimants be identified.

(2) Any reference in Schedule 1 or 2 to an order made under rule 10 of Schedule 1 shall include reference to an order made in accordance with this Schedule.

Under the old rules the employment tribunal was empowered to appoint an **4–438** expert to provide an evaluation report unless there were "no reasonable grounds" for determining that the claimant and the comparator did work of equal value. The "no reasonable grounds" prohibition no longer applies and an employment tribunal can appoint an expert where it feels it appropriate. A feature of the new rules is the choice the employment tribunal needs to make: whether to appoint an independent expert or to determine the issue itself. Where the employment tribunal determines not to appoint an independent expert, the parties must be allowed to call its own expert evidence which the employment tribunal should consider (*Wood v William Ball Ltd* [1999] I.R.L.R. 773 (the employment tribunal formed the view that it was a waste of public money to appoint an expert as the case was hopeless)). Only in the clearest of cases should the employment tribunal dispense with the assistance of expert evidence.

4. Conduct of stage 1 equal value hearing

(1) When in an equal value claim there is a dispute as to whether **4–439** any work is of equal value as mentioned in section 1(2)(c) of the Equal Pay Act, the tribunal shall conduct a "stage 1 equal value hearing" in accordance with both this rule and the rules applicable to pre-hearing reviews in Schedule 1.

(2) Notwithstanding rule 18(1) and (3) of Schedule 1, a stage 1 equal value hearing shall be conducted by a tribunal composed in accordance with section 4(1) of the Employment Tribunals Act.

(3) At the stage 1 equal value hearing the tribunal shall:

    (a) where section 2A(2) of the Equal Pay Act applies, strike out the claim (or the relevant part of it) if, in accordance with section 2A(2A) of that Act, the tribunal must determine that the work of the claimant and the comparator are not of equal value;

    (b) decide, in accordance with section 2A(1) of the Equal Pay Act, either that:

        (i) the tribunal shall determine the question; or

        (ii) it shall require a member of the panel of independent experts to prepare a report with respect to the question;

    (c) subject to rule 5 and with regard to the indicative timetable, make the standard orders for the stage 1 equal value hearing as set out in rule 5;

    (d) if the tribunal has decided to require an independent expert to prepare a report on the question, require the parties to copy to the independent expert all information which they are required by an order to disclose or agree between each other;

    (e) if the tribunal has decided to require an independent expert to prepare a report on the question, fix a date for the stage 2 equal value hearing, having regard to the indicative timetable;

(f) if the tribunal has not decided to require an independent expert to prepare a report on the question, fix a date for the Hearing, having regard to the indicative timetable;

(g) consider whether any further orders are appropriate.

(4) Before a claim or part of one is struck out under paragraph (3)(a), the Secretary shall send notice to the claimant giving him the opportunity to make representations to the tribunal as to whether the evaluation contained in the study in question falls within paragraph (a) or (b) of section 2A(2A) of the Equal Pay Act. The Secretary shall not be required to send a notice under this paragraph if the claimant has been given an opportunity to make such representations orally to the tribunal as to why such a judgment should not be issued.

(5) The tribunal may, on the application of a party, hear evidence upon and permit the parties to address it upon the issue contained in section 1(3) of the Equal Pay Act (defence of a genuine material factor) before determining whether to require an independent expert to prepare a report under paragraph (3)(b)(ii).

(6) When the Secretary gives notice to the parties of the stage 1 equal value hearing under rule 14(4) of Schedule 1, he shall also give the parties notice of the matters which the tribunal may and shall consider at that hearing which are described in paragraphs (3) and (5) of this rule and he shall give the parties notice of the standard orders in rule 5.

(7) The tribunal's power to strike out the claim or part of it under paragraph (3)(a) is in addition to powers to strike out a claim under rule 18(7) of Schedule 1.

5. Standard orders for stage 1 equal value hearing

4–440   (1) At a stage 1 equal value hearing a tribunal shall, unless it considers it inappropriate to do so and subject to paragraph (2), order that:—

(a) before the end of the period of 14 days after the date of the stage 1 equal value hearing the claimant shall:

(i) disclose in writing to the respondent the name of any comparator, or, if the claimant is not able to name the comparator he shall instead disclose such information as enables the comparator to be identified by the respondent; and

(ii) identify to the respondent in writing the period in relation to which he considers that the claimant's work and that of the comparator are to be compared;

(b) before the end of the period of 28 days after the date of the stage 1 equal value hearing:

      (i)   where the claimant has not disclosed the name of the comparator to the respondent under sub-paragraph (a), if the respondent has been provided with sufficient detail to be able to identify the comparator, he shall disclose in writing the name of the comparator to the claimant;

      (ii) the parties shall provide each other with written job descriptions for the claimant and any comparator;

      (iii) the parties shall identify to each other in writing the facts which they consider to be relevant to the question;

(c) the respondent is required to grant access to the claimant and his representative (if any) to his premises during a period specified by the tribunal or chairman in order for him or them to interview any comparator;

(d) the parties shall before the end of the period of 56 days after the date of the stage 1 equal value hearing present to the tribunal a joint agreed statement in writing of the following matters:

      (i)   job descriptions for the claimant and any comparator;

      (ii) facts which both parties consider are relevant to the question;

      (iii) facts on which the parties disagree (as to the fact or as to the relevance to the question) and a summary of their reasons for disagreeing;

(e) the parties shall, at least 56 days prior to the Hearing, disclose to each other, to any independent or other expert and to the tribunal written statements of any facts on which they intend to rely in evidence at the Hearing; and

(f) the parties shall, at least 28 days prior to the Hearing, present to the tribunal a statement of facts and issues on which the parties are in agreement, a statement of facts and issues on which the parties disagree and a summary of their reasons for disagreeing.

(2) Any of the standard orders for the stage 1 equal value hearing may be added to, varied or omitted as the tribunal considers appropriate.

The additional case management powers contained in Sch.6 provide a prescrip-   **4–441**
tive approach to the case management of equal pay claims. The standard Stage 1 hearing will consider whether there is a valid job evaluation scheme and if there is, the claim will be struck out. If the job evaluation scheme is itself discriminatory or otherwise unsuitable (and should not be relied on) the claim can proceed. At this

hearing the employment tribunal will consider whether to appoint an independent expert. At the Stage 1 hearing the employment tribunal will (unless it is inappropriate to do so) make the orders contained in r.5(1). It is open to the parties to make representation to the expert, and he is obliged to consider any relevant representations made. The expert can also seek further information from the parties. The expert can approach this exercise as he thinks appropriate unless an impermissible consideration which may be discriminatory (such as the number of hours) is being applied (*Leverton v Clwyd CC* [1989] I.C.R. 33).

The independent expert is required to give notice to the Secretary of State in writing, within 14 days of his appointment, unless not practicable to do so, of the date when the report can be expected; in addition progress reports can be asked for.

A summary of the report should be sent to the parties for their comments. The final report should identify any representations made by the parties.

6. Involvement of independent expert in fact finding

4–442   **(1) This rule applies only to proceedings in relation to which the tribunal has decided to require an independent expert to prepare a report on the question.**

(2) In proceedings to which this rule applies a tribunal or chairman may if it or he considers it appropriate at any stage of the proceedings order an independent expert to assist the tribunal in establishing the facts on which the independent expert may rely in preparing his report.

(3) Examples of the circumstances in which the tribunal or chairman may make an order described in paragraph (2) may include:

    (a) a party not being legally represented;

    (b) the parties are unable to reach agreement as required by an order of the tribunal or chairman;

    (c) the tribunal or chairman considers that insufficient information may have been disclosed by a party and this may impair the ability of the independent expert to prepare a report on the question;

    (d) the tribunal or chairman considers that the involvement of the independent expert may promote fuller compliance with orders made by the tribunal or a chairman.

(4) A party to proceedings to which this rule applies may make an application under rule 11 of Schedule 1 for an order under paragraph (2).

7. Conduct of stage 2 equal value hearing

4–443   **(1) This rule applies only to proceedings in relation to which the tribunal has decided to require an independent expert to prepare a report on the question. In such proceedings the tribunal shall conduct a "stage 2 equal value hearing" in accordance with both this rule and the rules applicable to pre-hearing reviews in Schedule 1.**

(2) Notwithstanding rule 18(1) and (3) of Schedule 1, a stage 2 equal value hearing shall be [conducted by a tribunal] composed in accordance with section 4(1) of the Employment Tribunals Act.

(3) At the stage 2 equal value hearing the tribunal shall make a determination of facts on which the parties cannot agree which relate to the question and shall require the independent expert to prepare his report on the basis of facts which have (at any stage of the proceedings) either been agreed between the parties or determined by the tribunal (referred to as "the facts relating to the question").

(4) At the stage 2 equal value hearing the tribunal shall:

(a) subject to rule 8 and having regard to the indicative timetable, make the standard orders for the stage 2 equal value hearing as set out in rule 8;

(b) make any orders which it considers appropriate;

(c) fix a date for the Hearing, having regard to the indicative timetable.

(5) Subject to paragraph (6), the facts relating to the question shall, in relation to the question, be the only facts on which the tribunal shall rely at the Hearing.

(6) At any stage of the proceedings the independent expert may make an application to the tribunal for some or all of the facts relating to the question to be amended, supplemented or omitted.

(7) When the Secretary gives notice to the parties and to the independent expert of the stage 2 equal value hearing under rule 14(4) of Schedule 1, he shall also give the parties notice of the standard orders in rule 8 and draw the attention of the parties to paragraphs (4) and (5) of this rule.

The Stage 2 hearing follows the appointment of an independent expert to **4–444** prepare a report. At this hearing the employment tribunal will make findings of fact regarding issues the parties cannot agree on concerning the questions the independent expert requires to prepare the report. It is usual for most of the relevant facts to be agreed between the parties.

At the subsequent hearing, the employment tribunal will determine where an independent expert has been appointed whether to admit the report in evidence. At this substantive hearing, the employment tribunal will consider the equal value question and if necessary the material factor defence and remedies.

It is not usual for the employer to ask the employment tribunal to consider the material factor defence first before considering whether the work is of equal value. The employment tribunal has a discretion whether to adopt this approach (*McGregor v General Municipal Boilermakers & Allied Trades Union* [1987] I.C.R. 505). Because of the potential to save cost, and having regard to the overriding objective to act justly, this course is often adopted. If the employer fails in making good the material factor defence at this stage, the employer is prohibited from raising it again after the expert's report or determination by the employment tribunal that the claim is of equal value.

8. Standard orders for stage 2 equal value hearing

(1) At a stage 2 equal value hearing a tribunal shall, unless it **4–445** considers it inappropriate to do so and subject to paragraph (2), order that:—

(a) by a date specified by the tribunal (with regard to the indicative timetable) the independent expert shall prepare his report on the question and shall (subject to rule 14) have sent copies of it to the parties and to the tribunal; and

(b) the independent expert shall prepare his report on the question on the basis of the facts relating to the question and no other facts which may or may not relate to the question.

(2) Any of the standard orders for the stage 2 equal value hearing may be added to, varied or omitted as the tribunal considers appropriate.

9. The Hearing

4–446 (1) In proceedings in relation to which an independent expert has prepared a report, unless the tribunal determines that the report is not based on the facts relating to the question, the report of the independent expert shall be admitted in evidence in those proceedings.

(2) If the tribunal does not admit the report of an independent expert in accordance with paragraph (1), it may determine the question itself or require another independent expert to prepare a report on the question.

(3) The tribunal may refuse to admit evidence of facts or hear argument as to issues which have not been disclosed to the other party as required by these rules or any order made under them, unless it was not reasonably practicable for the party to have so complied.

10. Duties and powers of the independent expert

4–447 (1) When a tribunal requires an independent expert to prepare a report with respect to the question or an order is made under rule 6(2), the Secretary shall inform that independent expert of the duties and powers he has under this rule.

(2) The independent expert shall have a duty to the tribunal to:

(a) assist it in furthering the overriding objective in regulation 3;

(b) comply with the requirements of these rules and any orders made by the tribunal or a chairman in relation to the proceedings;

(c) keep the tribunal informed of any delay in complying with any order in the proceedings with the exception of minor or insignificant delays in compliance;

(d) comply with any timetable imposed by the tribunal or chairman in so far as this is reasonably practicable;

(e) inform the tribunal or a chairman on request by it or him of progress in the preparation of the independent expert's report;

(f) prepare a report on the question based on the facts relating to the question and (subject to rule 14) send it to the tribunal and the parties;

(g) make himself available to attend hearings in the proceedings.

(3) The independent expert may make an application for any order or for a hearing to be held as if he were a party to the proceedings.

(4) At any stage of the proceedings the tribunal may, after giving the independent expert the opportunity to make representations, withdraw the requirement on the independent expert to prepare a report. If it does so, the tribunal may itself determine the question, or it may determine that a different independent expert should be required to prepare the report.

(5) When paragraph (4) applies the independent expert who is no longer required to prepare the report shall provide the tribunal with all documentation and work in progress relating to the proceedings by a date specified by the tribunal. Such documentation and work in progress must be in a form which the tribunal is able to use. Such documentation and work in progress may be used in relation to those proceedings by the tribunal or by another independent expert.

(6) When an independent expert has been required to prepare a report in proceedings the Secretary shall give the independent expert notice of all hearings, orders or judgments in those proceedings as if the independent expert were a party to those proceedings and when these rules require a party to provide information to another party, such information shall also be provided to the independent expert.

11. Use of expert evidence

(1) Expert evidence shall be restricted to that which, in the **4–448** opinion of the tribunal, is reasonably required to resolve the proceedings.

(2) An expert shall have a duty to assist the tribunal on matters within his expertise. This duty overrides any obligation to the person from whom he has received instructions or by whom he is paid.

(3) No party may call an expert or put in evidence an expert's report without the permission of the tribunal. No expert report shall be put in evidence unless it has been disclosed to all other parties and any independent expert at least 28 days prior to the Hearing.

(4) In proceedings in which an independent expert has been required to prepare a report on the question, the tribunal shall not admit evidence of another expert on the question unless such evidence is based on the facts relating to the question. Unless the

tribunal considers it inappropriate to do so, any such expert report shall be disclosed to all parties and to the tribunal on the same date on which the independent expert is required to send his report to the parties and to the tribunal.

(5) If an expert (other than an independent expert) does not comply with these rules or an order made by the tribunal or a chairman, the tribunal may order that the evidence of that expert shall not be admitted.

(6) Where two or more parties wish to submit expert evidence on a particular issue, the tribunal may order that the evidence on that issue is to be given by one joint expert only. When such an order has been made, if the parties wishing to instruct the joint expert cannot agree who should be the expert, the tribunal may select the expert.

4–448/1   Rule 11(4) Use of independent experts. The tribunal is not deprived by rule 11(4)of the power to hear evidence from an expert instructed by the parties. The expert could not challenge facts accepted or found, but could challenge the methodology adopted: the system of job evaluation is not a science and is susceptible to different methodologies. (*Middlesborough Borough Council v Surtees (No. 2)* [2008] ICR 349;[2007] I.R.L.R. 981.

12. Written questions to experts

4–449   (1) When any expert (including an independent expert) has pre-pared a report, a party or any other expert (including an independent expert) involved in the proceedings may put written questions about the report to the expert who has prepared the report.

(2) Unless the tribunal or chairman agrees otherwise, written questions under paragraph (1):

  (a) may be put once only;
  (b) must be put within 28 days of the date on which the parties were sent the report;
  (c) must be for the purpose only of clarifying the factual basis of the report;
  (d) must be copied to all other parties and experts involved in the proceedings at the same time as they are sent to the expert who prepared the report.

(3) When written questions have been put to an expert in accord-ance with paragraph (2) he shall answer those questions within 28 days of receiving them.

(4) An expert's answers to questions put in accordance with paragraph (2) shall be treated as part of the expert's report.

(5) Where a party has put a written question in accordance with this rule to an expert instructed by another party and the expert does not answer that question, or does not do so within 28 days, the tribunal may order that the party instructing the expert may not rely on the evidence of that expert.

13. Procedural matters

(1) In proceedings in which an independent expert has been required to prepare a report, the Secretary shall send him notices and inform him of any hearing, application, order or judgment in those proceedings as if he were a party to those proceedings.

(2) For the avoidance of doubt, any requirement in this Schedule to hold a stage 1 or a stage 2 equal value hearing does not preclude holding more than one of each of those types of hearing or other hearings from being held in accordance with Schedule 1.

(3) Any power conferred on a chairman in Schedule 1 may (subject to the provisions of this Schedule) be carried out by a tribunal or a chairman in relation to proceedings to which this Schedule applies.

14. National security proceedings

(1) In equal value cases which are also national security proceedings, if a tribunal has required an independent expert to prepare a report on the question, the independent expert shall send a copy of the report to the tribunal and shall not send it to the parties. In such proceedings if written questions have been put to the independent expert under rule 12, the independent expert shall send any answers to those questions to the tribunal and not to the parties.

(2) Before the Secretary sends to the parties a copy of a report or answers which have been sent to him by the independent expert under paragraph (1), he shall follow the procedure set out in rule 10 of Schedule 2 as if that rule referred to the independent expert's report or answers (as the case may be) instead of written reasons, except that the independent expert's report or answers shall not be entered on the Register.

(3) If the Minister does not give a direction under rule 10(3) of Schedule 2 within the period of 28 days from the date on which the Minister was sent the report or answers to written questions the Secretary shall send a copy of the independent expert's report or answers to written questions (as the case may be) to the parties.

4–450

4–451

CHAPTER 5

EMPLOYMENT APPEAL TRIBUNAL RULES 1993

1993 No. 2854

Contents

Schedule

Citation and commencement.

5–001   **1.—(1) These Rules may be cited as the Employment Appeal Tribunal Rules 1993 and shall come into force on 16th December 1993.**

(2) As from that date the Employment Appeal Tribunal Rules 1980, the Employment Appeal Tribunal (Amendment) Rules 1985 and the Employment Appeal Tribunal (Amendment) Rules 1988 shall be revoked.

Commencement

December 16, 1993

Amendment

Employment Appeal Tribunal (Amendment) Rules 1996, 2001, 2004 and 2005 **5–002**
and the Information and Consultation of Employees Regulations 2004. The
amendments that came into force on July 16, 2001 (SI 2001/1128) and October 1,
2004 (SI 2004/2526) amendments were the most substantial. The most significant
of the 2004 changes were the insertion of the overriding objective at r.2A, the
strengthening of the EAT's power at r.3(7) (see below), the creation of a power to
make a temporary restricted reporting order without a hearing (see para.5–080
below), a thorough overhaul of the power to award costs (see para.5–115 et seq.
below), and the insertion at r.37(4) of a requirement that anything to be done by or
on a particular day must be done by 4pm on that day.

General

By s.30(3) of the Employment Tribunals Act 1996, the Employment Appeal **5–003**
Tribunal has power to regulate its own procedure subject to these rules. The *"Burns*
procedure" whereby the Appeal Tribunal directs the employment tribunal to
provide further reasons for its decision pending an appeal based on inadequacy of
reasons (see para.5–017 below) is an example of an exercise of this power not
clearly referable to any other specific power provided in the Rules.

See generally the Practice Direction (Employment Appeal Tribunal—Procedure)
para.6–001. Where appropriate the EAT will be guided by the Civil Procedure
Rules: PD para.1.8.

Unrepresented parties

The Employment Appeal Tribunal is accustomed to dealing with unrepresented **5–004**
parties, and EAT staff will normally be helpful and informative on matters of
practicality, although they are not able to advise on the law. In some cases either
the Free Representation Unit or the Bar Pro Bono Unit may be able to provide pro
bono representation; for more detail, see the page entitled "getting advice" at
http://www.etclaims.co.uk.

Legal proceedings in Wales

An appeal to the Employment Appeal Tribunal from a Welsh employment **5–005**
tribunal is not a "legal proceeding in Wales" for the purposes of s.22 of the Welsh
Language Act 1993 (*Williams v Cowell t/a The Stables (No.1)* [2000] I.C.R. 85; [2000] 1
W.L.R. 187).

Interpretation

2.—(1) In these rules— **5–006**

**"the 1992 Act" means the Trade Union and Labour Relations
(Consolidation) Act 1992;**
"the 1996 Act" means the Employment Tribunals Act 1996;
**"the 1999 Regulations" means the Transnational Information and
Consultation of Employees Regulations 1999;**
**"the 2004 Regulations" means the European and Public Limited-
Liability Company Regulations 2004;**
**the Information and Consultation Regulations" means the Infor-
mation and Consultation of Employees Regulations 2004;**

"the Appeal Tribunal" means the Employment Appeal Tribunal established under section 87 of the Employment Protection Act 1975 and continued in existence under section 20(1) of the 1996 Act and includes the President, a judge, a member or the Registrar acting on behalf of the Tribunal;

"the CAC" means the Central Arbitration Committee;

"the Certification Officer" means the person appointed to be the Certification Officer under section 254(2) of the 1992 Act;

"costs officer" means any officer of the Appeal Tribunal authorised by the President to assess costs or expenses;

"Crown employment proceedings" has the meaning given by section 10(8) of the 1996 Act;

"document" includes a document delivered by way of electronic communication;

"electronic communication" shall have the meaning given to it by section 15(1) of the Electronic Communications Act 2000;

"excluded person" means, in relation to any proceedings, a person who has been excluded from all or part of the proceedings by virtue of—

(a) a direction of a Minister of the Crown under rule 30A(1)(b) or (c); or

(b) an order of the Appeal Tribunal under rule 30A(2)(a) read with rule 30A(1)(b) or (c);

"judge" means a judge of the Appeal Tribunal nominated under section 22(1)(a) or (b) of the 1996 Act and includes a judge nominated under section 23(2) of, or a judge appointed under section 24(1) of, the 1996 Act to be a temporary additional judge of the Appeal Tribunal;

"legal representative" shall mean a person, including a person who is a party's employee, who—

(a) has a general qualification within the meaning of the Courts and Legal Services Act 1990;

(b) is an advocate or solicitor in Scotland; or

(c) is a member of the Bar of Northern Ireland or a Solicitor of the Supreme Court of Northern Ireland.

"member" means a member of the Appeal Tribunal appointed under section 22(1)(c) of the 1996 Act and includes a member appointed under section 23(3) of the 1996 Act to act temporarily in the place of a member appointed under that section;

"national security proceedings" shall have the meaning given to it in regulation 2 of the Employment Tribunals (Constitution and Rules of Procedure) Regulations 2004;

"the President" means the judge appointed under section 22(3) of the 1996 Act to be President of the Appeal Tribunal and includes a judge nominated under section 23(1) of the 1996 Act to act temporarily in his place;

"the Registrar" means the person appointed to be Registrar of the Appeal Tribunal and includes any officer of the Tribunal authorised by the President to act on behalf of the Registrar;

"the Secretary of Employment Tribunals" means the person acting for the time being as the Secretary of the Central Office of the Employment Tribunals (England and Wales) or, as may be appropriate, of the Central Office of the Employment Tribunals (Scotland);

"special advocate" means a person appointed pursuant to rule 30A(4);

"writing" includes writing delivered by means of electronic communication;

(2) ...

(3) Any reference in these Rules to a person who was the claimant or, as the case may be, the respondent in the proceedings before an employment tribunal includes, where those proceedings are still continuing, a reference to a person who is the claimant or, as the case may be, is the respondent in those proceedings.

Commencement

July 6, 2001

5–007

Amendment

Employment Appeal Tribunal (Amendment) Rules 2001, SI 2001/1128, r.2; Employment Appeal Tribunal (Amendment) Rules 2004, SI 2004/2526, r.2(1); Constitutional Reform Act 2005, s.59(5), Sch.11 Pt 3, para.5.

5–007/1

"General qualification"

A person has a "general qualification" if he has a right of audience in relation to any class of proceedings in any part of the Supreme Court, or all proceedings in county courts or magistrates' courts: s.71(3) of the Courts and Legal Services Act 1990.

5–007/2

"Electronic communication"

The definition in the Electronic Communications Act 2000 is opaque, but its practical significance is that where anything is required to be communicated in writing, "writing" includes writing delivered by means of electronic communication. Faxes and emails are therefore included.

5–008

Overriding Objective

2A.—(1) The overriding objective of these Rules is to enable the Appeal Tribunal to deal with cases justly.

(2) Dealing with a case justly includes, so far as practicable—

5–009

Employment Appeal Tribunal Rules 1993

(a) **ensuring that the parties are on an equal footing;**

(b) **dealing with the case in ways which are proportionate to the importance and complexity of the issues;**

(c) **ensuring that it is dealt with expeditiously and fairly; and**

(d) **saving expense.**

(3) The parties shall assist the Appeal Tribunal to further the overriding objective.

Commencement

5–009/1   Inserted by the Employment Appeal Tribunal (Amendment) Rules 2004, SI 2004/2526, from October 1, 2004.

Definitions

5–010   For "the Appeal Tribunal" see r.2(1) at para.5–006.

General

5–011   The introduction of the overriding objective into the EAT Rules from October 1, 2004 followed its appearance in the Employment Tribunal Rules in 2001. For commentary on its operation there, see above, and for commentary on the very similar (although not identical) overriding objective in the Civil Procedure Rules, see Civil Procedure 2007, 1.3.1–1.3.11.

The EAT has shown some willingness to rely on the introduction of the overriding objective as a justification for departing from earlier authority. In *Williams v Ferrosan Ltd* [2004] I.R.L.R. 607, EAT, Hooper J. said,

> "One of the advantages of the Civil Procedure Rules has been that a rule which, prior to the introduction of the CPR, had become "encrusted" by numerous cases can be looked at afresh."

In *Sodhexo Ltd v D A Gibbons* [2005] I.C.R. 1647, EAT, H.H. J. Peter Clark (sitting alone) exercised the employment tribunal's power to vary its own order, relying on the EAT's jurisdiction conferred by s.35(1) of the Employment Tribunals Act 1996 to exercise any of the powers of the body from which the appeal was brought instead of remitting the question for re-hearing. The judge commented that he must have "due regard to the strictures of the Court of Appeal" in *Bennett v London Borough of Southwark* [2002] I.C.R. 881, where it was said that the EAT could only use the power to substitute its own decision where the decision substituted was incontestably the decision which, properly directed in law, the lower tribunal would have reached (and see also *Morgan v Electrolux Ltd* [1991] I.C.R. 369, CA), but relied on the overriding objective to justify his decision to exercise the employment tribunal's power notwithstanding that the conditions laid down by the Court of Appeal did not obtain.

Institution of appeal

5–012   **3.—(1) Every appeal to the Appeal Tribunal shall, subject to paragraphs (2) and (4), be instituted by serving on the Tribunal the following documents—**

(a) **a notice of appeal in, or substantially in, accordance with Form 1, 1A or 2 in the Schedule to these rules;**

    (b) in the case of an appeal from a judgment of an employment tribunal a copy of any claim and response in the proceedings before the employment tribunal or an explanation as to why either is not included; and

    (c) in the case of an appeal from a judgment of an employment tribunal a copy of the written record of the judgment of the employment tribunal which is subject to appeal and the written reasons for the judgment, or an explanation as to why written reasons are not included;

    (d) in the case of an appeal made pursuant to regulation 38(8) of the 1999 Regulations or regulation 47(6) of the 2004 Regulations or regulation 35(6) of the Information and Consultation Regulations from a declaration or order of the CAC, a copy of that declaration or order; and

    (e) in the case of an appeal from an order of an employment tribunal a copy of the written record of the order of the employment tribunal which is subject to appeal and (if available) the written reasons for the order;

    (f) in the case of an appeal from a decision or order of the Certification Officer a copy of the decision or order of the Certification Officer which is subject to appeal and the written reasons for that decision or order.

(2) In an appeal from a judgment or order of the employment tribunal in relation to national security proceedings where the appellant was the claimant—

    (i) the appellant shall not be required by virtue of paragraph (1)(b) to serve on the Appeal Tribunal a copy of the response if the response was not disclosed to the appellant; and

    (ii) the appellant shall not be required by virtue of paragraph (1)(c) or (e) to serve on the Appeal Tribunal a copy of the written reasons for the judgment or order if the written reasons were not sent to the appellant but if a document containing edited reasons was sent to the appellant, he shall serve a copy of that document on the Appeal Tribunal.

(3) The period within which an appeal to the Appeal Tribunal may be instituted is—

    (a) in the case of an appeal from a judgment of the employment tribunal—

        (i) where the written reasons for the judgment subject to appeal—

(aa) were requested orally at the hearing before the employment tribunal or in writing within 14 days of the date on which the written record of the judgment was sent to the parties; or

(bb) were reserved and given in writing by the employment tribunal 42 days from the date on which the written reasons were sent to the parties;

(ii) in an appeal from a judgment given in relation to national security proceedings, where there is a document containing edited reasons for the judgment subject to appeal, 42 days from the date on which that document was sent to the parties; or

(iii) where the written reasons for the judgment subject to appeal—

(aa) were not requested orally at the hearing before the employment tribunal or in writing within 14 days of the date on which the written record of the judgment was sent to the parties; and

(bb) were not reserved and given in writing by the employment tribunal 42 days from the date on which the written record of the judgment was sent to the parties;

(b) in the case of an appeal from an order of an employment tribunal, 42 days from the date of the order;

(c) in the case of an appeal from a decision of the Certification Officer, 42 days from the date on which the written record of that decision was sent to the appellant;

(d) in the case of an appeal from a declaration or order of the CAC under regulation 38(8) of the 1999 Regulations or regulation 47(6) of the 2004 Regulations or regulation 35(6) of the Information and Consultation Regulations, 42 days from the date on which the written notification of that declaration or order was sent to the appellant.

(4) In the case of a an appeal from a judgment or order of the employment tribunal in relation to national security proceedings, the appellant shall not set out the grounds of appeal in his notice of appeal and shall not append to his notice of appeal the written reasons for the judgment of the tribunal.

(5) In an appeal from the employment tribunal in relation to national security proceedings in relation to which the appellant was

the respondent in the proceedings before the employment tribunal, the appellant shall, within the period described in paragraph (3)(a), provide to the Appeal Tribunal a document setting out the grounds on which the appeal is brought.

(6) In an appeal from the employment tribunal in relation to national security proceedings in relation to which the appellant was the claimant in the proceedings before the employment tribunal—

   (a) the appellant may, within the period described in paragraph 3(a)(ii) or (iii) or paragraph 3(b), whichever is applicable, provide to the Appeal Tribunal a document setting out the grounds on which the appeal is brought; and

   (b) a special advocate appointed in respect of the appellant may, within the period described in paragraph 3(a)(ii) or (iii) or paragraph 3(b), whichever is applicable, or within 21 days of his appointment, whichever is later, provide to the Appeal Tribunal a document setting out the grounds on which the appeal is brought or providing supplementary grounds of appeal.

(7) Where it appears to a judge or the Registrar that a notice of appeal or a document provided under paragraph (5) or (6)—

   (a) discloses no reasonable grounds for bringing the appeal; or

   (b) is an abuse of the Appeal Tribunal's process or is otherwise likely to obstruct the just disposal of proceedings, he shall notify the Appellant or special advocate accordingly informing him of the reasons for his opinion and, subject to paragraphs (8) and (10), no further action shall be taken on the notice of appeal or document provided under paragraph (5) or (6).

(7A) In paragraphs (7) and (10) reference to a notice of appeal or a document provided under paragraph (5) or (6) includes reference to part of a notice of appeal or document provided under paragraph (5) or (6).

(8) Where notification has been given under paragraph (7), the appellant or the special advocate, as the case may be, may serve a fresh notice of appeal, or a fresh document under paragraph (5) or (6), within the time remaining under paragraph (3) or (6) or within 28 days from the date on which the notification given under paragraph (7) was sent to him, whichever is the longer period.

(9) Where the appellant or the special advocate serves a fresh notice of appeal or a fresh document under paragraph (8), a judge or

the Registrar shall consider such fresh notice of appeal or document with regard to jurisdiction as though it were an original notice of appeal lodged pursuant to paragraphs (1) and (3), or as though it were an original document provided pursuant to paragraph (5) or (6), as the case may be.

(10) Where notification has been given under paragraph (7) and within 28 days of the date the notification was sent, an appellant or special advocate expresses dissatisfaction in writing with the reasons given by the judge or Registrar for his opinion, he is entitled to have the matter heard before a judge who shall make a direction as to whether any further action should be taken on the notice of appeal or document under paragraph (5) or (6).

Commencement

5–012/1   Substituted by the Employment Appeal Tribunal (Amendment) Rules 2001, SI 2001/1128, r.218 April 2001.

Definitions

5–013   For "the 1999 Regulations", "the 2004 Regulations", "the Information and Consultation Regulations", "the Appeal Tribunal", "the CAC", "the Certification Officer", "document", "judge", "national security proceedings", "the Registrar", "special advocate", "writing" see r.2(1) at para.5–006.

General

5–014   An appeal lies to the Employment Appeal Tribunal on "any question of law arising from any decision of, or arising in any proceedings before, an employment tribunal": see s.21(1) of the Employment Tribunals Act 1996. There is no requirement for permission to appeal, although in practice r.3(7) (see below) operates in many ways like a permission stage—complete with the right to renew the application at an oral hearing—but with the important difference that dismissal of an appeal under r.3(7) is open to further appeal.

The question what is a question of law fit for the EAT is a difficult one that has exercised the EAT and the Court of Appeal on many occasions. The Court of Appeal has frequently cautioned against too nice an analysis of the decisions of employment tribunals (e.g. in *Retarded Children's Aid Society v Day* [1978] I.C.R. 437; *Hollister v National Farmers Union* [1979] I.C.R. 542; *Meek v Birmingham CC* [1987] I.R.L.R. 251; *Union of Construction, Allied Trades and Technicians v Brain* [1981] I.C.R. 542) in the hope of finding an error of law.

Categories of error: misdirection on the law, perversity

5–015   Cases where the contention on appeal is that there has been a self-misdirection on the law, or misunderstanding or misapplication of the legal rule or test are easily recognised. The circumstances in which the appellate courts can disturb an employment tribunal's findings of primary fact, inferences and exercises of discretion are far more difficult to define.

Perversity

5–016   In *British Telecommunications Plc v Sheridan* [1990] I.R.L.R. 27, para.35, Lord Donaldson M.R. identified two categories of error beside a misdirection as to the applicable law, namely a finding of fact for which there is no evidence, and a decision that is "perverse" in the sense explained by Lord Justice May in *Neale v*

Hereford & Worcester CC [1986] I.C.R. 471 at 483. Lord Justice May's explanation is as follows:

"Deciding these cases is the job of industrial tribunals and when they have not erred in law neither the appeal tribunal nor this court should disturb their decision unless one can say in effect: 'My goodness, that was certainly wrong'."

Findings of fact for which there is no supporting evidence are sometimes treated as a species of perversity, and sometimes as a separate category of error. However it is classified, the limits of this category present no particular difficulties of definition: if the tribunal arrives at a material finding of fact with no foundation in the evidence (or contrary to undisputed evidence), then that is a mistake which the EAT is entitled to correct.

The category of free-standing perversity is the last resort of the disappointed litigant who cannot identify any other error of law, and its limits are much more difficult to define. For both reasons it has received a great deal of appellate attention. Authorities subsequent to *Sheridan* and *Neale* indicate that the cases that fall into this category will be very rare. In *Piggott Brothers & Co Ltd v Jackson* [1992] I.C.R. 85, Lord Donaldson M.R. accepted May L.J.'s formulation, but sounded this note of caution:

"The danger in the approach of May L.J. is that an appellate court can very easily persuade itself that, as it would certainly not have reached the same conclusion, the tribunal which did so was 'certainly wrong.' . . . [T]his is a classic non sequitur. It does not matter whether, with whatever degree of certainty, the appellate court considers that it would have reached a different conclusion. What matters is whether the decision under appeal was a permissible option. To answer that question in the negative in the context of employment law, the appeal tribunal will almost always have to be able to identify a finding of fact which was unsupported by any evidence or a clear self-misdirection in law by the industrial tribunal. If it cannot do this, it should re-examine with the greatest care its preliminary conclusion that the decision under appeal was not a permissible option and has to be characterised as 'perverse'".

In *Crofton v Yeboah* [2002] I.R.L.R. 634, on an appeal on perversity grounds against a number of findings of race discrimination, Mummery L.J. said (at 93)

"Such an appeal ought only to succeed where an overwhelming case is made out that the Employment Tribunal reached a decision which no reasonable tribunal, on a proper appreciation of the evidence and the law, would have reached.

For examples of cases where this exacting standard has been met in relation to factual conclusions, see *Anglian Home Improvements Ltd v Kelly* [2005] ICR 242; *Glasgow School of Art v Talor*, unreported, UKEAT/0011/06; and *Agrico UK Ltd v Ireland*, unreported, UKEAT/0024/05.

Both factual inferences and exercises of discretion, including exercises of discretion as to case management, may be attacked as perverse. To upset a tribunal's (or employment judge's) exercise of discretion, the EAT must find that the tribunal has taken into account some matter which it was improper to take into account, or failed to take into account some matter which it was necessary to take into account, or exercised its discretion in a way so far beyond what any reasonable tribunal could have done that it may be rejected as perverse: Arnold J. in *Bastick v James Lane (Turf Accountants) Ltd* [1979] I.C.R. 778 at 782, approved by Stephenson L.J. in *Carter v Credit*

Change Ltd [1979] I.C.R. 908 at 918. *Bastick* and *Carter* were both unsuccessful challenges to an employment judge's refusal to adjourn; for examples of successful challenges to exercises of case management discretion, see *Exel Management v Lumb* UKEAT/0121/06 and *Mid-Devon DC v Stevenson* UKEAT/0196/07.

Failure adequately to explain reasons

5–017   The employment tribunal has an obligation to give a sufficient account of its findings of fact and reasoning to enable the EAT to judge whether any question of law arises (*Meek v City of Birmingham District Council* [1987] I.R.L.R. 250). This is a distinct head of appeal, but its power has been reduced by the EAT's adoption of a practice of adjourning such appeals and remitting the case to the tribunal for expansion or clarification of the reasons (see *Burns v Royal Mail Group Plc* [2004] I.C.R. 1103, EAT). The practice was approved by the Court of Appeal in *Barke v Seetec Business Technology Centre Ltd* [2005] I.C.R. 1373, subject only to the caution (at 1389, 46) that it is not appropriate where bias was alleged or where "the inadequacy of the reasoning is on its face so fundamental that there is a real risk that supplementary reasons will be reconstructions of proper reasons, rather than the unexpressed actual reasons for the decision".

Failure to resolve key issues of fact

5–018   It is a basis for appeal if the tribunal has failed to resolve any sufficiently material dispute of fact. In *Anya v University of Oxford* [2001] I.C.R. 847, CA, at 860, Sedley L.J. said,

> "[I]t is the job of the tribunal of first instance not simply to set out the relevant evidential issues, as this industrial tribunal conscientiously and lucidly did, but to follow them through to a reasoned conclusion except to the extent that they become otiose; and if they do become otiose, the tribunal needs to say why."

This is not to say that the tribunal must resolve or even allude to every factual dispute between the parties: as Peter Gibson L.J. said in *Miriki v General Council of the Bar* [2002] I.C.R. 505, CA, at 523, distinguishing *Anya*, "It cannot be right that in every case the tribunal must make express findings on every piece of circumstantial evidence, however peripheral, merely because the applicant chooses to make it the subject of complaint". There are similar comments in *High Table v Horst* [1998] I.C.R. 409 at 420, and in *Richard Hemeng v Secretary of State for the Home Department* [2007] EWCA Civ. 640, the Court of Appeal held that an immigration adjudicator's statement that he had fully accepted the evidence of the mother of an applicant for entry clearance, constituted adequate explanation of his decision in the circumstances. It had not been incumbent on him to explain why he had not accepted or relied on a contrary statement of the applicant himself in an interview with the Entry Clearance Officer. For a case, post-*Miriki*, where the tribunal's failure to resolve an evidential issue was held to be fatal to the decision, see *Comfort v Lord Chancellor's Department* [2004] EWCA Civ. 349, CA (unreported).

Bias

5–019   An employment tribunal decision may be set aside for actual or apparent bias. The test is whether a fair-minded and informed observer present at the hearing, not being a party or associated with a party, having considered the facts, would consider that there was a real possibility that the tribunal was biased (*Porter v Magill* [2002] 2 A.C. 357 at 495).

Bias is considered in detail below at 15–013 to 15–023.

Procedural guidance on how bias appeals to the EAT should be approached is set out in the PD at para.11 (see below) and in *Facey v Midas Retail Security Ltd* [2001] I.C.R. 287.

Delay

The Court of Appeal considered the question of delay in promulgation of the **5–020** employment tribunal's decision in *Bangs v Connex South Eastern Ltd* [2005] I.R.L.R. 389, at para.44, Mummery L.J. formulated the test thus:

> "[T]he key question is whether, due to the unreasonable delay, there is a real risk that Connex has in substance been denied or deprived of the article 6 right to a fair trial of the race discrimination claim by Mr Banks and whether it would be unfair or unjust to allow the delayed decision to stand. This test is, on the one hand, less stringent than the perversity ground of appeal, but it is, on the other hand, more stringent than the "unsafe" decision test formulated and applied by the employment appeal tribunal, as it excludes an appeal on fact and insists on the existence of a question of law".

"Less stringent than perversity but more stringent than the 'unsafe' decision test" is an unhelpful formulation. In practice, it must be doubted whether any appeal will ever succeed on grounds of delay unless it would, independently, succeed on grounds of perversity. At any event, there is as yet no EAT case in which an appeal founded on the *Bangs* test has succeeded. The appeal in *Radley v Department for Work and Pensions*, unreported, [2005] UKEAT 0141/05/2806 (June 28, 2005) failed notwithstanding unconscionable delay coupled with the loss of the employment judge's notes at some indeterminate time after the hearing.

Other procedural impropriety

Other procedural improprieties that may invalidate a tribunal's decision include **5–021** sleeping or drunkenness of any member of the tribunal (see *Stansbury v Datapulse* [2004] I.C.R. 523), and failure to hold the hearing in public as required (see *Storer v British Gas Plc* [2000] I.C.R. 603).

Procedural irregularities should be raised in the course of the hearing, but a failure to do so will not necessarily defeat an appeal on this ground. If the problem is raised in the course of the hearing and the parties consent to continue with the hearing, they will not subsequently be able to rely on the procedural irregularity as a ground of appeal unless it is continued or repeated thereafter (*Fordyce v Hammersmith & Fulham Conservative Association* UKEAT/0390/05, January 13, 2006).

Rule 3(1)

An appeal notice not accompanied by the prescribed documents will not be **5–022** regarded as validly lodged: see EAT Practice Statement (2005). The effect of lodging any of the prescribed documents late or not at all will be that the appeal notice is treated as not validly lodged in time (*Kanapathiar v London Borough of Harrow* [2003] I.R.L.R. 571; and see 5–025 below for the strictness with which the rule is enforced). *Kanapathiar* marked a change in practice: previously the EAT's habit, notwithstanding the letter of the rules, was to accept notice of appeal served without the prescribed documents.

Where one or more of the prescribed documents is unavailable during the time for institution of the appeal and an acceptable explanation as to why it is not included is given with an appeal notice, it is thought that the appeal notice will be treated as lodged in time.

Note that "the written record of the judgment" and "the written reasons for the judgment" are separate documents: both must be included (*Jurkowska v Hlmad Ltd* [2008] EWCA Civ. 231, unreported).

Substantially in accordance with Form 1, 1A or 2

The notice of appeal should also comply with the detailed requirements of the **5–023** PD. Note in particular the requirements of para.2 relating to appeals where there has also been an application to the employment tribunal for review and perversity appeals, para.7 relating to notes of evidence and para.8 relating to fresh evidence and new points of law.

Amending a notice of appeal

5–024 A party cannot reserve a right to amend a notice of appeal: PD 2.7. An application to amend, as for other interim applications, should be made in writing to the Registrar: PD 4.1. See further the notes to r.24(5) below.

Rule 3(3)—"42 days from"

5–025 Regulation 15 of the Employment Tribunals (Constitution and Rules of Procedure) Regulations 2004 provides that in the ET Rules, where any act must be done within a certain number of days of or from an event, the day of that event shall not be included in the calculation; para.1.8.1 of the Practice Direction stipulates that the same rule will be applied here. The last day of the limitation period for lodging an appeal is therefore day 42, where day one is the day after the day on which the judgment or written reasons were sent to the parties. Thus if the judgment or written reasons are sent out on a Wednesday, any appeal must be lodged by the Wednesday six weeks later. By para.1.8.3 of the PD, where time expires on a day when the central office of the EAT (or the EAT office in Edinburgh) is closed, time is extended to the next working day. By r.37(1A), any act which is required to be done on or by a particular day must be done by 4pm on that day; anything done after 4pm will be treated as done on the following day.

The time limit is strictly enforced. In *Aziz v Bethnal Green City Challenge Company Ltd* [2000] I.R.L.R. 111 (approving *United Arab Emirates v Abdelghafar* [1995] I.R.L.R. 243) the Court of Appeal endorsed a marked distinction between the practice of the EAT in granting extensions of the generous 42 day period for appealing and the Court of Appeal's own practice in extending its 14 day period for appealing.

Where the notice of appeal is faxed to the EAT, transmission of it together with all the prescribed accompanying documents (see 5–022 above) must be completed by 4pm (*Woodward v Abbey National Plc* [2005] I.C.R. 1702; [2005] I.R.L.R. 782, EAT (Burton P., disapproving his own slightly more generous approach in *Midland Packaging Ltd v Clark* [2005] 2 All E.R. 266)). In *Jurkowska v Hlmad Ltd* [2008] EWCA Civ. 231, exceptionally, the EAT was prepared to extend time by 33 minutes. Solicitors for the appellant had not realised that the tribunal's "judgment" and "reasons" were separate documents, the judgment having been handed to counsel at the conclusion of the hearing, with no copy posted to the solicitors. However, they acted with impressive dispatch to discover and remedy the omission when it was drawn to their attention.

It was said by Burton P. in *Initial Electronic Security Systems Ltd v Avdic* [2005] I.R.L.R. 671, that documents served by email can, absent any indication that transmission has failed, be expected to have arrived within a reasonable time, perhaps up to half an hour, after sending. It is suggested that in any case in which the actual arrival time of an email is critical, its arrival time at the EAT should be equated with the time when it reaches the EAT's email server, whether that is physically located in the EAT building or (as is more likely) elsewhere; otherwise the time that an emailed notice of appeal is deemed delivered will depend on when the EAT staff check their email, because only at that point will it move from an external server to the EAT's computer. See also *Beasley v National Grid Electricity Transmissions* [2007] UKEAT 0626/06/0608, where in the context of the question whether an unfair dismissal claim had been presented in time the EAT upheld the tribunal's ruling that an email sent 88 seconds after midnight on the last day was out of time. It is not clear from the EAT judgment whether it had been established when the email had been delivered to the ETS email server; it may be that this figure was taken from the time the email was recorded as "sent" by the claimant's email program. In *Miller v Community Links Trust*, unreported, EAT/0846/07, following the same logic, the EAT ruled that a claim that had reached the Employment Tribunal Service server at eight seconds past midnight was out of time.

If a tribunal's reasons have been withdrawn and re-promulgated, time runs from the date of the re-promulgated reasons (or at least must be treated as running from that date): *Aziz-Mir v Sainsury's Supermarket Plc* UKEAT/0537/06. *Jurkowska v Hlmad Ltd* [2008] EWCA Civ. 231 is a rare example of an exercise by the EAT of its discretion to extend time.

The date on which written reasons were sent to the parties

"Sent" is to be given its ordinary meaning and is not affected by s.7 of the **5–026** Interpretation Act 1978 (*Gdynia America Shipping Lines (London) Ltd v Chelminski* [2004] I.C.R. 1523; [2004] I.R.L.R. 725, CA).

Rule 3(7)

This version of r.3(7), brought into force with the October 1, 2004 amendments, **5–027** replaced a weaker power to discontinue an appeal only where it appeared to the Registrar that the grounds of appeal did not give the Appeal Tribunal jurisdiction to entertain the appeal. In *Ansar v Lloyds Bank Plc* [2006] I.C.R. 1565 Burton J. observed that an appeal raising allegations of bias or improper conduct could properly be dealt with under r.3(7), normally after operation of the procedure envisaged at para.11 of the PD. The judgment appears to envisage provision not only of an affidavit by the appellant, but also affidavits by other parties and comments by the employment judge and members of the tribunal at this stage; contrast para.11(3) of the PD, which is prefaced by the words "If the appeal is allocated to the PH or FH track, the EAT may take the following steps prior to such a hearing". See further notes to para.11 of the PD.

Rule 3(8)

There is nothing to suggest that an appellant whose fresh notice of appeal is also **5–028** rejected under r.3(7) may not serve a further fresh notice of appeal within 28 days from the date when that notification was sent to him. By r.3(9) the judge or Registrar must consider the fresh notice as though it were an original notice of appeal.

Rule 3(10)

See PD 9.6. There is no prescribed form for the expression of dissatisfaction, nor **5–029** any requirement to give reasons for it at this stage. A skeleton argument will be required ten days before the oral hearing (see PD 13.9.1).

Service of notice of appeal

4.—(1) On receipt of notice under rule 3, the Registrar shall seal **5–030** **the notice with the Appeal Tribunal's seal and shall serve a sealed copy on the appellant and on—**

    (a) every person who, in accordance with rule 5, is a respondent to the appeal; and

    (b) the Secretary of Employment Tribunals in the case of an appeal from an employment tribunal; or

    (c) the Certification Officer in the case of an appeal from any of his decisions; or

Employment Appeal Tribunal Rules 1993

    (d) the Secretary of State in the case of an appeal under Chapter II of Part IV of the 1992 Act or Part XI of the Employment Rights Act 1996 to which he is not a respondent; or

    (e) the Chairman of the CAC in the case of an appeal from the CAC under regulation 38(8) of the 1999 Regulations or regulation 47(6) of the 2004 Regulations [or regulation 35(6) of the Information and Consultation Regulations].

(2) On receipt of a document provided under rule 3(5)—

    (a) the Registrar shall not send the document to a person in respect of whom a Minister of the Crown has informed the Registrar that he wishes to address the Appeal Tribunal in accordance with rule 30A(3) with a view to the Appeal Tribunal making an order applicable to this stage of the proceedings under rule 30A(2)(a) read with 30A(1)(b) or (c) (exclusion of a party or his representative), at any time before the Appeal Tribunal decides whether or not to make such an order; but if it decides not to make such an order, the Registrar shall, subject to sub-paragraph (b), send the document to such a person 14 days after the Appeal Tribunal's decision not to make the order; and

    (b) the Registrar shall not send a copy of the document to an excluded person, but if a special advocate is appointed in respect of such a person, the Registrar shall send a copy of the document to the special advocate.

(3) On receipt of a document provided under rule 3(6)(a) or (b), the Registrar shall not send a copy of the document to an excluded person, but shall send a copy of the document to the respondent.

Definitions

5–031   For "the 1992 Act", "the 1999 Regulations", "the 2004 Regulations", "the Information and Consultation Regulations", "the Appeal Tribunal", "the CAC", "the Certification Officer", "document", "excluded person", "the Registrar", "the Secretary of Employment Tribunals", "special advocate" see r.2(1) at para.5–006.

Respondents to appeals

5–032   5. The respondents to an appeal shall be—

    (a) in the case of an appeal from an employment tribunal or of an appeal made pursuant to section 45D, 56A, 95, 104 or 108C of the 1992 Act from a decision of the Certification Officer, the parties (other than the appellant) to the proceedings before the employment tribunal or the Certification Officer;

(b) in the case of an appeal made pursuant to section 9 or 126 of the 1992 Act from a decision of the Certification Officer, that Officer.

(c) in the case of an appeal made pursuant to regulation 38(8) of the 1999 Regulations or regulation 47(6) of the 2004 Regulations [or regulation 35(6) of the Information and Consultation Regulations] from a declaration or order of the CAC, the parties (other than the appellant) to the proceedings before the CAC.

Definitions

For "the 1992 Act", "the 1999 Regulations", "the 2004 Regulations" "the CAC", **5–033** "the Certification Officer" see r.2 at para.5–006.

Respondent's answer and notice of cross-appeal

6.—(1) The Registrar shall, as soon as practicable, notify every **5–034** respondent of the date appointed by the Appeal Tribunal by which any answer under this rule must be delivered.

(2) A respondent who wishes to resist an appeal shall, subject to paragraph (6), and within the time appointed under paragraph (1) of this rule, deliver to the Appeal Tribunal an answer in writing in, or substantially in, accordance with Form 3 in the Schedule to these Rules, setting out the grounds on which he relies, so, however, that it shall be sufficient for a respondent to an appeal referred to in rule 5(a) or 5(c) who wishes to rely on any ground which is the same as a ground relied on by the employment tribunal, the Certification Officer or the CAC for making the judgment, decision, declaration or order appealed from to state that fact in his answer.

(3) A respondent who wishes to cross-appeal may subject to paragraph (6), do so by including in his answer a statement of the grounds of his cross-appeal, and in that event an appellant who wishes to resist the cross-appeal shall, within a time to be appointed by the Appeal Tribunal, deliver to the Tribunal a reply in writing setting out the grounds on which he relies.

(4) The Registrar shall serve a copy of every answer and reply to a cross-appeal on every party other than the party by whom it was delivered.

(5) Where the respondent does not wish to resist an appeal, the parties may deliver to the Appeal Tribunal an agreed draft of an order allowing the appeal and the Tribunal may, if it thinks it right to do so, make an order allowing the appeal in the terms agreed.

(6) In an appeal from the employment tribunal in relation to national security proceedings, the respondent shall not set out the grounds on which he relies in his answer to an appeal, nor include in his answer a statement of the grounds of any cross-appeal.

(7) In an appeal from the employment tribunal in relation to national security proceedings in relation to which the respondent was not the claimant in the proceedings before the employment tribunal, the respondent shall, within the time appointed under paragraph (1), provide to the Registrar a document, setting out the grounds on which he intends to resist the appeal, and may include in that document a statement of the grounds of any cross-appeal.

(8) In an appeal from the employment tribunal in relation to national security proceedings in relation to which the respondent was the claimant in the proceedings before the employment tribunal—

(a) the respondent may, within the time appointed under paragraph (1) provide to the Registrar a document, setting out the grounds on which he intends to resist the appeal, and may include in that document a statement of the grounds of any cross-appeal; and

(b) a special advocate appointed in respect of the respondent may, within the time appointed under paragraph (1), or within 21 days of his appointment, whichever is the later, provide to the Registrar a document, setting out the grounds, or the supplementary grounds, on which the respondent intends to resist the appeal, and may include in that document a statement of the grounds, or the supplementary grounds, of any cross-appeal.

(9) In, if the respondent, or any special advocate appointed in respect of a respondent, provides in the document containing grounds for resisting an appeal a statement of grounds of cross-appeal and the appellant wishes to resist the cross-appeal—

(a) where the appellant was not the applicant in the proceedings before the employment tribunal, the appellant shall within a time to be appointed by the Appeal Tribunal deliver to the Tribunal a reply in writing setting out the grounds on which he relies; and

(b) where the appellant was the claimant in the proceedings before the employment tribunal, the appellant, or any special advocate appointed in respect of him, may within a time to be appointed by the Appeal Tribunal deliver to the Tribunal a reply in writing setting out the grounds on which the appellant relies.

(10) Any document provided under paragraph (7) or (9) (a) shall be treated by the Registrar in accordance with rule 4(2), as though it were a document received under rule 3(5).

(11) Any document provided under paragraph (8) or (9)(b) shall be treated by the Registrar in accordance with rule 4(3), as though it were a document received under rule 3(6)(a) or (b).

(12) Where it appears to a judge or the Registrar that a statement of grounds of cross-appeal contained in respondent's answer or document provided under paragraph (7) or (8)—

(a) discloses no reasonable grounds for bringing the cross-appeal; or

(b) is an abuse of the Appeal Tribunal's process or is otherwise likely to obstruct the just disposal of proceedings, he shall notify the appellant or special advocate accordingly informing him of the reasons for his opinion and, subject to paragraphs (14) and (16), no further action shall be taken on the statement of grounds of cross-appeal.

(13) In paragraphs (12) and (16) reference to a statement of grounds of cross-appeal includes reference to part of a statement of grounds of cross-appeal.

(14) Where notification has been given under paragraph (12), the respondent or special advocate, as the case may be, may serve a fresh statement of grounds of cross-appeal before the time appointed under paragraph (1) or within 28 days from the date on which the notification given under paragraph (12) was sent to him, whichever is the longer.

(15) Where the respondent or special advocate serves a fresh statement of grounds of cross-appeal, a judge or the Registrar shall consider such statement with regard to jurisdiction as though it was contained in the original Respondent's answer or document provided under (7) or (8).

(16) Where notification has been given under paragraph (12) and within 28 days of the date the notification was sent, a respondent or special advocate expresses dissatisfaction in writing with the reasons given by the judge or Registrar for his opinion, he is entitled to have the matter heard before a judge who shall make a direction as to whether any further action should be taken on the statement of grounds of cross-appeal.

Rule 6(1)—The date appointed by the Appeal Tribunal

In default of appointment, the date is within 14 days of the seal date of the order permitting the appeal to go to a full hearing: PD para.10.1. A respondent who does not lodge an answer may be debarred under r.26 from taking any further part in proceedings. A respondent can apply for an extension of time under r.37. More latitude is likely to be extended to an answer than a notice of appeal, but the principles applying to presentation of an appeal can be expected to apply with full rigour to a cross-appeal.

5–035

Rule 6(5)—Where the respondent does not wish to resist an appeal

5–036   Where both parties agree that the decision of the employment tribunal is wrong, they can apply to the EAT to dispose of the appeal by consent. If the EAT sees fit this may be dealt with by correspondence (*British Publishing Co Ltd v Fraser* [1987] I.C.R. 517, EAT), but the EAT will not reverse the employment tribunal's decision on a point of law unless it is satisfied that it was wrong (*J Sainsbury Plc v Moger* [1994] I.C.R. 800).

Conciliation

5–037   Where it considers that there is a reasonable prospect of disposal of the appeal by consent, the EAT may take any steps it considers appropriate to facilitate conciliation: r.37.

In June 2007 ACAS issued a press release indicating that it would be extending its services to cases referred to it by the EAT. At the same time, the EAT issued a "Conciliation Protocol" (see 5–145 below) setting out the procedure that will be followed in cases considered by a Judge to be suitable for conciliation.

Rules 6(13), 6(15)

5–038   See notes to r.3(8) and 3(10) above at paras 5–028 and 5–029.

Disposal of appeal

5–039   **7.—(1) The Registrar shall, as soon as practicable, give notice of the arrangements made by the Appeal Tribunal for hearing the appeal to—**

    (a) every party to the proceedings; and

    (b) the Secretary of Employment Tribunals in the case of an appeal from an employment tribunal; or

    (c) the Certification Officer in the case of an appeal from one of his decisions; or

    (d) the Secretary of State in the case of an appeal under Part XI of the Employment Rights Act 1996 or Chapter II of Part IV of the 1992 Act to which he is not a respondent; or

    (e) the Chairman of the CAC in the case of an appeal from a declaration or order of, or arising in any proceedings before, the CAC under regulation 38(8) of the 1999 Regulations or regulation 47(6) of the 2004 Regulations or regulation 35(6) of the Information and Consultation Regulations.

(2) Any such notice shall state the date appointed by the Appeal Tribunal by which any interim application must be made.

Definitions

5–040–1   For "the 1992 Act", "the 1999 Regulations", "the 2004 Regulations", "the Information and Consultation Regulations", "the Appeal Tribunal", "the CAC", "the Certification Officer", "the Registrar", "the Secretary of Employment Tribunals" see r.2(1) at para.5–006.

Employment judge's notes of evidence

Where either party considers that a point of law raised by the notice of appeal or **5–042** answer cannot be argued without reference to evidence given (or the fact that particular evidence was not given) before the employment tribunal, it should first seek the agreement of the other party or parties as to the nature of the evidence or lack of evidence. Failing agreement, an application should be made for the employment judge's notes of evidence. This application should be made with the notice of appeal or respondent's answer, with the skeleton argument or written submissions lodged prior to a PH, or in the case of an appeal listed for FH without a PH, within 14 days of the seal date of the order directing that the case is to go to a FH: see PD para.7. See also the notes to r.25 below.

Application to admit documents or oral evidence not before the employment tribunal

An application by either party to put in any document or witness evidence, which **5–043** was not before the employment tribunal, should be lodged with the EAT, with the notice of appeal or respondent's answer. In the case of a document or documents, copies should be lodged with the application and served on the other party together with a statement of the date on which the party first became aware of its existence. In the case of oral evidence, the application should be accompanied by a signed statement incorporating a statement of truth from the relevant witness. The EAT will be guided by the principles set out in *Ladd v Marshall* [1954] 1 W.L.R. 1489. See PD para.8 and the discussion of *Ladd* in Civil Procedure 2008.

Appeals from the Registrar's decision on an interim application

The Registrar's decision may be appealed to a judge. There is no prescribed form **5–044** for an interim appeal, but the appeal must be notified to the EAT within five days (working days: see CPR r.2.8(4)) of the date when the Registrar's decision was sent to the parties: PD 4.3. Thus if the Registrar's decision was sent on Monday 24 July, any appeal must be notified to the EAT by 4pm on Monday 31 July.

Application in respect of exclusion or expulsion from, or unjustifiable discipline by, a trade union

8. Every application under section 67 or 176 of the 1992 Act to the **5–045**
Appeal Tribunal for:

> (a) **an award of compensation for exclusion or expulsion from a trade union; or**
> (b) **one or both of the following, that is to say—**
>> (i) **an award of compensation for unjustifiable discipline;**
>> (ii) **an order that the union pay to the applicant an amount equal to any sum which he has paid in pursuance of any such determination as is mentioned in section 64(2)(b) of the 1992 Act;**

shall be made in writing in, or substantially in, accordance with Form 4 in the Schedule to these Rules and shall be served on the Appeal Tribunal together with a copy of the decision or order declaring that the applicant's complaint against the trade union was well-founded.

Definitions

5–046   For "the 1992 Act", "the Appeal Tribunal", "writing" see r.2(1) at para.5–006.

5–047   9. If on receipt of an application under rule 8(a) it becomes clear that at the time the application was made the applicant had been admitted or re-admitted to membership of the union against which the complaint was made, the Registrar shall forward the application to the Central Office of [Employment Tribunals].

Service of application under rule 8

5–048   10. On receipt of an application under rule 8, the Registrar shall seal it with the Appeal Tribunal's seal and shall serve a sealed copy on the applicant and on the respondent trade union and the Secretary of Industrial Tribunals.

Definitions

5–049   For "the Appeal Tribunal", "member", "the Registrar" see reg.2(1) at para.5–006.

Appearance by respondent trade union

5–050   11.—(1) Subject to paragraph (2) of this rule, a respondent trade union wishing to resist an application under rule 8 shall within 14 days of receiving the sealed copy of the application enter an appearance in, or substantially in, accordance with Form 5 in the Schedule to these Rules and setting out the grounds on which the union relies.

(2) Paragraph (1) above shall not require a respondent trade union to enter an appearance where the application is before the Appeal Tribunal by virtue of having been transferred there by an [employment tribunal] and, prior to that transfer, the respondent had entered an appearance to the proceedings before the [employment tribunal].

Definitions

5–051   For "the Appeal Tribunal" see reg.2(1) at para.5–006.

5–052   12. On receipt of the notice of appearance under rule 11 the Registrar shall serve a copy of it on the applicant.

Definitions

5–053   For "the Registrar" see reg.2(1) at para.5–006.

Application for restriction of proceedings order

5–054   13. Every application to the Appeal Tribunal by the Attorney General or the Lord Advocate under [section 33 of the 1996 Act] for a restriction of proceedings order shall be made in writing in, or substantially in, accordance with Form 6 in the Schedule to these

Rules, accompanied by an affidavit in support, and shall be served on the Tribunal.

Definitions

For "the 1996 Act", "the Appeal Tribunal", "writing" see r.2(1) at para.5–006. **5–055**

Section 33 of the 1996 Act

Section 33 deals with restriction of vexatious proceedings. **5–056**

Service of application under rule 13

14. On receipt of an application under rule 13, the Registrar shall **5–057**
seal it with the Appeal Tribunal's seal and shall serve a sealed copy
on the Attorney General or the Lord Advocate, as the case may be, on
the Secretary of Industrial Tribunals and on the person named in the
application.

Definitions

For "the Appeal Tribunal", "the Registrar" see r.2(1) at para.5–006. **5–058**

Appearance by person named in application under rule 13

15. A person named in an application under rule 13 who wishes to **5–059**
resist the application shall within 14 days of receiving the sealed copy
of the application enter an appearance in, or substantially in,
accordance with Form 7 in the Schedule to these Rules, accompanied
by an affidavit in support.

16. On receipt of the notice of appearance under rule 15 the **5–060**
Registrar shall serve a copy of it on the Attorney General or the Lord
Advocate, as the case may be.

Definitions

For "the Registrar" see r.2(1) at para.5–006. **5–061**

Complaints under regulations 20 and 21 of the 1999 Regulations

[16A. Every complaint under regulation 20 or 21 of the 1999 **5–062**
Regulations shall be made by way of application in writing in, or
substantially in, accordance with Form 4A in the Schedule to these
Rules and shall be served on the Appeal Tribunal.]

Definitions

For "the 1999 Regulations", "the Appeal Tribunal", "writing" see r.2(1) at **5–063**
para.5–006.

Complaint under regulation 20 or 21 of the 1999 Regulations

Complaints about failure to establish a European Works Council or information **5–064**
and consultation procedure or the operation of such a Council or procedure under
the Transnational Information and Consultation of Employees Regulations 1999 (SI
1999/3323).

Applications under regulation 33(6) of the 2004 Regulations

5–065   16AA. Every application under regulation 33(6) of the 2004 Regulations or regulation 22(6) of the Information and Consultation Regulations shall be made by way of application in writing in, or substantially in, accordance with Form 4B in the Schedule to these Rules and shall be served on the Appeal Tribunal together with a copy of the declaration referred to in regulation 33(4) of [the 2004 Regulations or regulation 22(4) of the Information and Consultation Regulations], or an explanation as to why none is included.

Definitions

5–066   For "the 2004 Regulations", "the Information and Consultation Regulations", "the Appeal Tribunal", "writing" see r.2(1) at para.5–006.

Service of application under rule 16A

5–067   16B. On receipt of an application under [rule 16A or 16AA] , the Registrar shall seal it with the Appeal Tribunal's seal and shall serve a sealed copy on the applicant and on the respondent.

Definitions

5–068   For "the Appeal Tribunal", "the Registrar" see reg.2(1) at para.5–006.

Appearance by respondent

5–069   16C. A respondent wishing to resist an application under rule 16A or 16AA shall within 14 days of receiving the sealed copy of the application enter an appearance in, or substantially in, accordance with Form 5A in the Schedule to these Rules and setting out the grounds on which the respondent relies.

5–070   16D. On receipt of the notice of appearance under rule 16C the Registrar shall serve a copy of it on the applicant.

Definitions

5–071   For "the Registrar" see reg.2(1) at para.5–006.

Disposal of application

5–072   17.—(1) The Registrar shall, as soon as practicable, give notice to the parties to an application under rule 8, 13, 16A or 16AA of the arrangements made by the Appeal Tribunal for hearing the application.

(2) Any such notice shall state the date appointed by the Appeal Tribunal by which any interim application must be made.

Joinder of parties

5–073   18. The Appeal Tribunal may, on the application of any person or of its own motion, direct that any person not already a party to the proceedings be added as a party, or that any party to proceedings shall cease to be a party, and in either case may give such consequential directions as it considers necessary.

Interim applications

19.—(1) An interim application may be made to the Appeal Tribunal by giving notice in writing specifying the direction or order sought.

5–074

(2) On receipt of a notice under paragraph (1) of this rule, the Registrar shall serve a copy on every other party to the proceedings who appears to him to be concerned in the matter to which the notice relates and shall notify the applicant and every such party of the arrangements made by the Appeal Tribunal for disposing of the application.

Directions

See PD 4.1–4.3. By r.25 directions can be given by the EAT of its own motion or on the application of a party, but parties are encouraged in the PD to make them at a PH or directions hearing if one is listed.

5–075

Disposal of interim applications

20.—(1) Every interim application made to the Appeal Tribunal shall be considered in the first place by the Registrar who shall have regard to rule 2A (the overriding objective) and, where applicable, to rule 23(5).

5–076

(2) Subject to sub-paragraphs (3) and (4), every interim application shall be disposed of by the Registrar except that any matter which he thinks should properly be decided by the President or a judge shall be referred by him to the President or judge who may dispose of it himself or refer it in whole or part to the Appeal Tribunal as required to be constituted by section 28 of the 1996 Act or refer it back to the Registrar with such directions as he thinks fit.

(3) Every interim application for a restricted reporting order shall be disposed of by the President or a judge or, if he so directs, the application shall be referred to the Appeal Tribunal as required to be constituted by section 28 of the 1996 Act who shall dispose of it.

(4) Every interim application for permission to institute or continue or to make a claim or application in any proceedings before an employment tribunal or the Appeal Tribunal, pursuant to section 33(4) of the 1996 Act, shall be disposed of by the President or a judge, or, if he so directs, the application shall be referred to the Appeal Tribunal as required to be constituted by section 28 of the 1996 Act who shall dispose of it.

Appeals from Registrar

21.—(1) Where an application is disposed of by the Registrar in pursuance of rule 20(2) any party aggrieved by his decision may appeal to a judge and in that case the judge may determine the appeal

5–077

himself or refer it in whole or in part to the Appeal Tribunal as required to be constituted by section 28 of the 1996 Act.

(2) Notice of appeal under paragraph (1) of this rule may be given to the Appeal Tribunal, either orally or in writing, within five days of the decision appealed from and the Registrar shall notify every other party who appears to him to be concerned in the appeal and shall inform every such party and the appellant of the arrangements made by the Tribunal for disposing of the appeal.

Within five days of

5–078   PD 1.8 indicates that the EAT will be guided by the CPR where appropriate, and specifically (at PD 1.8.4) that a time limit of five days will be treated as five working days.

Hearing of interlocutory applications

5–079   22.—(1) The Appeal Tribunal may, subject to any direction of a Minister of the Crown under rule 30A(1) or order of the Appeal Tribunal under rule 30A(2)(a) read with rule 30A(1), and, where applicable, to rule 23(6), sit either in private or in public for the hearing of any interim application.

Rule 30A

5–080   Rule 30A empowers a Minister, in the interests of national security, to direct the EAT to sit in private, to exclude the claimant or his representative from proceedings or to conceal the identity of a witness.

Cases involving allegations of sexual misconduct or the commission of sexual offences

5–081   23.—(1) This rule applies to any proceedings to which section 31 of the 1996 Act applies.

(2) In any such proceedings where the appeal appears to involve allegations of the commission of a sexual offence, the Registrar shall omit from any register kept by the Appeal Tribunal, which is available to the public, or delete from any order, judgment or other document, which is available to the public, any identifying matter which is likely to lead members of the public to identify any person affected by or making such an allegation.

(3) In any proceedings to which this rule applies where the appeal involves allegations of sexual misconduct the Appeal Tribunal may at any time before promulgation of its decision either on the application of a party or of its own motion make a restricted reporting order having effect, if not revoked earlier by the Appeal Tribunal, until the promulgation of its decision.

(4) A restricted reporting order shall specify the persons who may not be identified.

(5) Subject to paragraph (5A) the Appeal Tribunal shall not make a full restricted reporting order unless it has given each party to the

proceedings an opportunity to advance oral argument at a hearing, if they so wish.

(5A) The Appeal Tribunal may make a temporary restricted reporting order without a hearing.

(5B) Where a temporary restricted reporting order has been made the Registrar shall inform the parties to the proceedings in writing as soon as possible of:

(a) the fact that the order has been made; and

(b) their right to apply to have the temporary restricted reporting order revoked or converted into a full restricted reporting order within 14 days of the temporary order being made.

(5C) If no such application is made under subparagraph (5B)(b) within the 14 days, the temporary restricted reporting order shall lapse and cease to have any effect on the fifteenth day after it was made. When such an application is made the temporary restricted reporting order shall continue to have effect until the Hearing at which the application is considered.

(6) Any hearing shall, subject to any direction of a Minister of the Crown under rule 30A(1) or order of the Appeal Tribunal under rule 30A(2)(a) read with rule 30A(1), or unless the Appeal Tribunal decides for any of the reasons mentioned in rule 29(2) to sit in private to hear evidence, be held in public.

(7) The Appeal Tribunal may revoke a restricted reporting order at any time where it thinks fit.

(8) Where the Appeal Tribunal makes a restricted reporting order, the Registrar shall ensure that a notice of that fact is displayed on the notice board of the Appeal Tribunal at the office in which the proceedings in question are being dealt with, on the door of the room in which those proceedings are taking place and with any list of the proceedings taking place before the Appeal Tribunal.

(9) In this rule, "promulgation of its decision" means the date recorded as being the date on which the Appeal Tribunal's order finally disposing of the appeal is sent to the parties.

Register

See PD para.5 at para.6–037.   **5–082**

Allegations of sexual misconduct

In *West Yorkshire Police v A* [2001] I.C.R. 128, EAT, Lindsay P. (sitting alone)   **5–083**
rejected the proposition that a transsexual's complaint of sex discrimination amounted to a complaint of "sexual misconduct" for the purposes of this rule. Rule 23 therefore provided no power to protect her anonymity. See also the notes to r.50(1) of the Employment Tribunals Rules of Procedure at para.4–322.

Analogous powers to protect identity

5–084   However, Lindsay P. also held, in the same judgment that since there was unchallenged and convincing evidence that the risk of publicity identifying her would be sufficient to deter her from enforcing her right to equal treatment, r.23 was inadequate to give effect to the principle of effectiveness under European law (see *Johnston v Chief Constable of the Royal Ulster Constabulary (222/84)* [1987] I.C.R. 83; *Coote v Granada Hospitality Ltd* (Case C-185/97) [1999] I.C.R. 100; *Levez v Jennings (Harlow Pools) Ltd* (Case C-326/96) [1999] I.C.R. 521; *Marshall v Southampton and South West Hampshire Health Authority (Teaching) (No.2)* (Case C-271/91) [1993] I.C.R. 893). In the circumstances, this required a prohibition of indefinite duration on publication of any material sufficient to identify her.

Lindsay P.'s reasoning in *West Yorkshire Police* rested on in part on his conclusion that the EAT had inherent powers as a superior court of record (at paras 28 to 29 of the judgment) in relation to matters incidental to its jurisdiction, and in part on the observation that the respondent in that case was an emanation of the state against which the Equal Treatment Directive was directly enforceable (para.28).

In *X v Stevens* [2003] I.R.L.R. 411, the EAT reconsidered these questions after fuller argument, albeit in the event obiter. The judgment leaves open the question whether the EAT has any inherent powers (para.44). Instead it is held that employment tribunals and the EAT have a similar power, derivable from their own statutory rules as interpreted in the light of the need to give effect to art.6, to make orders protecting the identity of a party on a temporary or permanent basis. The power is available irrespective of whether the respondent to the claim is an emanation of the state. It would seem to follow that the power is available irrespective of whether the right sought to be enforced is of European or purely domestic origin: it is the tribunal's own obligation under s.6 of the Human Rights Act 1998 to give effect to Convention rights, specifically art.6, from which its power to make such orders originates. Restricted reporting orders in disability cases

5–085   **23A.—(1) This rule applies to proceedings to which section 32(1) of the 1996 Act applies.**

(2) In proceedings to which this rule applies the Appeal Tribunal may, on the application of the complainant or of its own motion, make a restricted reporting order having effect, if not revoked earlier by the Appeal Tribunal, until the promulgation of its decision.

(3) Where the Appeal Tribunal makes a restricted reporting order under paragraph (2) of this rule in relation to an appeal which is being dealt with by the Appeal Tribunal together with any other proceedings, the Appeal Tribunal may direct that the order is to apply also in relation to those other proceedings or such part of them as it may direct.

(4) Paragraphs (5) to (9) of rule 23 apply in relation to the making of a restricted reporting order under this rule as they apply in relation to the making of a restricted reporting order under that rule.

Section 32(1) of the 1996 Act

5–086   Section 32(1) applies to proceedings on an appeal against a decision on an application for a restricted reporting order and on an appeal against an interlocutory decision in proceedings in which the employment tribunal has made a restricted reporting order.

Appointment for directions

24.—(1) Where it appears to the Appeal Tribunal that the future **5–087** conduct of any proceedings would thereby be facilitated, the Tribunal may (either of its own motion or on application) at any stage in the proceedings appoint a date for a meeting for directions as to their future conduct and thereupon the following provisions of this rule shall apply.

(2) The Registrar shall give to every party in the proceedings notice of the date appointed under paragraph (1) of this rule and any party applying for directions shall, if practicable, before that date give to the Appeal Tribunal particulars of any direction for which he asks.

(3) The Registrar shall take such steps as may be practicable to inform every party of any directions applied for by any other party.

(4) On the date appointed under paragraph (1) of this rule, the Appeal Tribunal shall consider every application for directions made by any party and any written representations relating to the application submitted to the Tribunal and shall give such directions as it thinks fit for the purpose of securing the just, expeditious and economical disposal of the proceedings, including, where appropriate, directions in pursuance of rule 36, for the purpose of ensuring that the parties are enabled to avail themselves of opportunities for conciliation.

(5) Without prejudice to the generality of paragraph (4) of this rule, the Appeal Tribunal may give such directions as it thinks fit as to—

    (a) the amendment of any notice, answer or other document;

    (b) the admission of any facts or documents;

    (c) the admission in evidence of any documents;

    (d) the mode in which evidence is to be given at the hearing;

    (e) the consolidation of the proceedings with any other proceedings pending before the Tribunal;

    (f) the place and date of the hearing.

(6) An application for further directions or for the variation of any directions already given may be made in accordance with rule 19.

Rule 24(5)(a)—Amendments to the notice of appeal

H.H. Judge Serota considered at some length the power to amend a notice of **5–088** appeal in *Khudados v Leggate* [2005] I.R.L.R. 540, EAT at [83]-[86]. He noted first that the strict principles applied to extensions of time for presenting a notice of appeal set out in *United Arab Emirates v Abdelhgafar* [1995] I.C.R. 65 do not apply in their entirety. Relevant factors were the merits of the amendment; whether the applicant is in breach of the Rules or PD (specifically the requirement at para.2(6) of the PD that an application for permission to amend is to be made as soon as the need for amendment is known); whether there has been a full, honest and acceptable explanation for any delay or failure to comply with the Rules or PD; the extent to which the amendment, if allowed, would cause delay; and the balance of prejudice between the parties, having in mind that a party is not prejudiced in the relevant sense simply in facing an argument by way of appeal that he would not otherwise face; and the public interest in ensuring that the business of the EAT is conducted expeditiously.

Appeal Tribunal's power to give directions

5–089   **25. The Appeal Tribunal may either of its own motion or on application, at any stage of the proceedings, give any party directions as to any steps to be taken by him in relation to the proceedings.**

At any stage of the proceedings

5–090   Parties are encouraged to make any applications at a PH or directions hearing if one is listed: see PD and notes to r.19 at para.5–075.

Default by parties

5–091   **26. If a respondent to any proceedings fails to deliver an answer or, in the case of an application made under section 67 or 176 of the 1992 Act or, section 33 of the 1996 Act, regulation 20 or 21 of the 1999 Regulations, regulation 33 of the 2004 Regulations or regulation 22 of the Information and Consultation Regulations, a notice of appearance within the time appointed under these Rules, or if any party fails to comply with an order or direction of the Appeal Tribunal, the Tribunal may order that he be debarred from taking any further part in the proceedings, or may make such other order as it thinks just.**

Consequences of default

5–092   An extension of time for serving a respondent's answer will in practice be much more likely to be granted than an extension of time for commencing an appeal under r.3. There are no reported cases in which a respondent has been debarred from taking part in an appeal after having served an answer, albeit late. In *Ayobiojo v London & Quadrant Housing Trust* [1995] UKEAT 483; unreported, October 13, 1995, the EAT treated the fact that instructions from the respondent's solicitors to their counsel to draft an answer had been lost by their document exchange service as a satisfactory explanation for a delay of six days notwithstanding that the solicitors had been notified of the deadline.

Attendance of witnesses and production of documents

5–093   **27.—(1) The Appeal Tribunal may, on the application of any party, order any person to attend before the Tribunal as a witness or to produce any document.**
[(1A) Where—

   (a) a Minister has at any stage issued a direction under rule 30A(1)(b) or (c) (exclusion of a party or his representative), or the Appeal Tribunal has at any stage made an

order under rule 30A(2)(a) read with rule 30A(1)(b) or (c); and

(b) the Appeal Tribunal is considering whether to impose, or has imposed, a requirement under paragraph (1) on any person, the Minister (whether or not he is a party to the proceedings) may make an application to the Appeal Tribunal objecting to the imposition of a requirement under paragraph (1) or, where a requirement has been imposed, an application to vary or set aside the requirement, as the case may be. The Appeal Tribunal shall hear and determine the Minister's application in private and the Minister shall be entitled to address the Appeal Tribunal thereon. The application shall be made by notice to the Registrar and the Registrar shall give notice of the application to each party.]

(2) No person to whom an order is directed under paragraph (1) of this rule shall be treated as having failed to obey that order unless at the time at which the order was served on him there was tendered to him a sufficient sum of money to cover his costs of attending before the Appeal Tribunal.

Attendance of witnesses and production of documents

Appeal to the EAT is on a point of law only, so except where necessary for exercise of the EAT's limited original jurisdiction, this power will be exercised rarely. However, if there is a relevant dispute of fact about the manner in which the hearing was conducted before the ET, it is the EAT's function to resolve it (*Stansbury v Datapulse* [2004] I.C.R. 523; [2004] I.R.L.R. 466). This may in some cases properly be done by the EAT under r.3(7) without a hearing (see *Ansar v Lloyds TSB Bank Plc* [2006] ICR 1565). **5–094**

In a suitable case the EAT might entertain an application for an direction that a party discloses its notes of evidence: see, by analogy, *Comfort v Department of Constitutional Affairs* (2005) 102(35) L.S.G. 42. *Comfort* was an appeal against a tribunal's refusal to order disclosure of the respondent's notes of evidence for the purposes of a remitted hearing, rather than a decision on an application to the EAT for disclosure of notes for the purposes of the appeal, but the EAT held that notes of evidence taken by legal advisers for the parties were not the subject of legal professional privilege, and although they were not ordinarily to be made the subject of an order for disclosure, in the particular circumstances of that case parts of the respondent's notes of evidence should be disclosed.

Direction under rule 30A(1)(b) or (c) or 30A(2)(a)

A direction by a Minister excluding a party or his representative in the interests of national security. Rule 27(1A) gives the Minister, whether or not a party to the proceedings, standing to object to an order that any person attend before the tribunal as a witness or produce any document, and requires that the EAT should hear that objection in private. **5–095**

Oaths

28. The Appeal Tribunal may, either of its own motion or on application, require any evidence to be given on oath. **5–096**

5–097   Again, exercise of this power will be rare by reason of the limited nature of the EAT's jurisdiction.

Oral hearings
5–098   **29.—(1) Subject to paragraph (2) of this rule and to any direction of a Minister of the Crown under rule 30A(1)(a) or order of the Appeal Tribunal under rule 30A(2)(a) read with rule 30A(1)(a), an oral hearing at which any proceedings before the Appeal Tribunal are finally disposed of shall take place in public before, where applicable, such members of the Tribunal as (subject to section 28 of the 1996 Act) the President may nominate for the purpose.**

(2) Notwithstanding paragraph (1), the Appeal Tribunal may sit in private for the purpose of hearing evidence from any person which in the opinion of the Tribunal is likely to consist of—

> **(a) information which he could not disclose without contravening a prohibition imposed by or by virtue of any enactment;**
> **(b) information which has been communicated to him in confidence or which he has otherwise obtained in consequence of the confidence reposed in him by another person; or**
> **(c) information the disclosure of which would, for reasons other than its effect on negotiations with respect to any of the matters mentioned in section 178(2) of the 1992 Act, cause substantial injury to any undertaking of his or in which he works.**

Any direction. . . under rule 30A(1)(a)
5–099   A direction by a Minister excluding a party or his representative in the interests of national security.

Rule 29(2)—power to sit in private
5–100   In *XXX v YYY & ZZZ* [2004] I.R.L.R. 137, EAT, Mitting J. pointed out that the employment tribunal's power to sit in private (provided at r.10(3) of the 2001 Rules, now at r.16 of the 2004 Rules) permitted the employment tribunal to sit in private for the purpose of viewing video evidence, the public airing of which would have constituted a breach of a third party's art.8 rights. Although the EAT decision in *XXX* was overruled in part at [2004] I.R.L.R. 471, the CA did not question the conclusion that the power to sit in private could be used in defence of art.8 rights in this way. The EAT's power to sit in private is framed in materially identical terms, so that conclusion must be equally applicable to hearings of the EAT.

Duty of Appeal Tribunal concerning disclosure of information
5–101   **30. When exercising its functions, the Appeal Tribunal shall ensure that information is not disclosed contrary to the interests of national security.**

Proceedings in cases concerning national security

30A.—(1) A Minister of the Crown (whether or not he is a party to the proceedings) may, if he considers it expedient in the interests of national security, direct the Appeal Tribunal by notice to the Registrar to

5–102

(a) sit in private for all or part of particular Crown employment proceedings;

(b) exclude any party who was the claimant in the proceedings before the employment tribunal from all or part of particular Crown employment proceedings;

(c) exclude the representatives of any party who was the claimant in the proceedings before the employment tribunal from all or part of particular Crown employment proceedings;

(d) take steps to conceal the identity of a particular witness in particular Crown employment proceedings.

(2) The Appeal Tribunal may, if it considers it expedient in the interests of national security, by order—

(a) do in relation to particular proceedings before it anything of a kind which the Appeal Tribunal can be required to do [in relation to particular Crown employment proceedings]

by direction under paragraph (1) of this rule;

(b) direct any person to whom any document (including any decision or record of the proceedings) has been provided for the purposes of the proceedings not to disclose any such document or the content thereof—

(i) to any excluded person;

(ii) in any case in which a direction has been given under paragraph (1)(a) or an order has been made under paragraph (2)(a) read with paragraph (1)(a), to any person excluded from all or part of the proceedings by virtue of such direction or order; or

(iii) in any case in which a Minister of the Crown has informed the Registrar in accordance with paragraph (3) that he wishes to address the Appeal Tribunal with a view to the Tribunal making an order under paragraph (2)(a) read with paragraph (1)(b) or (c), to any person who may be excluded from all or part of the proceedings by virtue of such an order, if an order is made, at any time before the Appeal Tribunal decides whether or not to make such an order;

(c) take steps to keep secret all or part of the reasons for any order it makes.

The Appeal Tribunal shall keep under review any order it makes under this paragraph.

(3) In any proceedings in which a Minister of the Crown considers that it would be appropriate for the Appeal Tribunal to make an order as referred to in paragraph (2), he shall (whether or not he is a party to the proceedings) be entitled to appear before and to address the Appeal Tribunal thereon. The Minister shall inform the Registrar by notice that he wishes to address the Appeal Tribunal and the Registrar shall copy the notice to the parties.

(4) In any proceedings in which there is an excluded person, the Appeal Tribunal shall inform the Attorney General or, in the case of an appeal from an employment tribunal in Scotland, the Advocate General for Scotland, of the proceedings before it with a view to the Attorney General (or, as the case may be, the Advocate General), if he thinks it fit to do so, appointing a special advocate to represent the interests of the person who was the applicant in the proceedings before the employment tribunal in respect of those parts of the proceedings from which—

(a) any representative of his is excluded;
(b) both he and his representative are excluded; or
(c) he is excluded, where he does not have a representative.

(5) A special advocate shall have a general qualification within the meaning of section 71 of the Courts and Legal Services Act 1990, or, in the case of an appeal from an employment tribunal in Scotland, shall be—

(a) an advocate; or
(b) a solicitor who has by virtue of section 25A of the Solicitors (Scotland) Act 1980 rights of audience in the Court of Session or the High Court of Justiciary.

(6) Where the excluded person is a party to the proceedings, he shall be permitted to make a statement to the Appeal Tribunal before the commencement of the proceedings, or the part of the proceedings, from which he is excluded.

(7) Except in accordance with paragraphs (8) to (10), the special advocate may not communicate directly or indirectly with any person (including an excluded person)—

(a) (except in the case of the Appeal Tribunal or the party who was the respondent in the proceedings before the employment tribunal) on any matter contained in the documents referred to in rule 3(5), 3(6), 6(7) or 6(8)(b); or

(b) (except in the case of a person who was present) on any matter discussed or referred to during any part of the proceedings in which the Appeal Tribunal sat in private pursuant to a direction of the Minister under paragraph (1)(a) or an order of the Appeal Tribunal under paragraph (2)(a) read with paragraph (1)(a).

(8) The special advocate may apply for directions from the Appeal Tribunal authorising him to seek instructions from, or otherwise to communicate with, an excluded person—

(a) on any matter contained in the documents referred to in rule 3(5), 3(6), 6(7) or 6(8)(b); or

(b) on any matter discussed or referred to during any part of the proceedings in which the Appeal Tribunal sat in private as referred to in paragraph (7)(b).

(9) An application under paragraph (8) shall be made by presenting to the Registrar a notice of application, which shall state the title of the proceedings and set out the grounds of the application.

(10) The Registrar shall notify the Minister of an application for directions under paragraph (8) and the Minister shall be entitled to address the Appeal Tribunal on the application.

(11) In these rules, in any case in which a special advocate has been appointed in respect of a party, any reference to a party shall (save in those references specified in paragraph (12)) include the special advocate.

(12) The references mentioned in paragraph (11) are those in rules 5 and 18, the first and second references in rule 27(1A), paragraphs (1) and (6) of this rule, the first reference in paragraph (3) of this rule, rule 34(1), the reference in item 4 of Form 1, and in item 4 of Form 1A, in the Schedule to these Rules.

Definitions

For "the Appeal Tribunal", "Crown employment proceedings", "document", "excluded person", "the Registrar", "special advocate" see r.2(1) at para.5–006.

5–103

Drawing up, reasons for, and enforcement of orders

31.—(1) Every order of the Appeal Tribunal shall be drawn up by the Registrar and a copy, sealed with the seal of the Tribunal, shall be served by the Registrar on every party to the proceedings to which it relates and—

5–104

    (a) in the case of an order disposing of an appeal from an employment tribunal or of an order under section 33 of the 1996 Act, on the Secretary of the Employment Tribunals;

    (b) in the case of an order disposing of an appeal from the Certification Officer, on that Officer;

    (c) in the case of an order imposing a penalty notice under regulation 20 or 21 of the 1999 Regulations [. . .] regulation 33 of the 2004 Regulations or regulation 22 of the Information and Consultation Regulations, on the Secretary of State; or

    (d) in the case of an order disposing of an appeal from the CAC made under regulation 38(8) of the 1999 Regulations, on the Chairman of the CAC.

(2) Subject to rule 31A, the Appeal Tribunal shall, on the application of any party made within 14 days after the making of an order finally disposing of any proceedings, give its reasons in writing for the order unless it was made after the delivery of a reasoned judgment.

(3) Subject to any order made by the Court of Appeal or Court of Session and to any directions given by the Appeal Tribunal, an appeal from the Tribunal shall not suspend the enforcement of any order made by it.

General

5–105   Section 35(1) of the Employment Tribunals Act 1996 gives the EAT power to exercise any of the powers of the body or officer from whom the appeal was brought, or remit the case to that body or officer. The power to dismiss an appeal that the EAT does not consider well-founded is clearly implicit, although curiously it is nowhere conferred in terms.

Remission to the same or a fresh tribunal

5–106   In *Sinclair Roche & Temperley v Heard* [2004] I.R.L.R. 763, the EAT laid down criteria for the exercise of the discretion to remit a case to the same or a different tribunal under the following six headings:

    (i) *proportionality*
      The cost of a complete re-hearing and the distress for parties and witnesses in giving their evidence a second time are relevant considerations.

    (ii) *passage of time*
      The case must not be remitted to the same tribunal if there is a real risk that it will have forgotten about the case.

    (iii) *bias or partiality*
      The case must not be remitted to the same tribunal where the appeal has succeeded on the basis of bias or misconduct, or where there are other grounds to doubt that the tribunal will approach its task with an open mind.

    (iv) *totally flawed decision*
      The case should not be remitted to the same tribunal where it completely mishandled the first time or where the approach was wholly flawed.

(v) *second bite*
> The EAT should only send a case back to the same tribunal if it is confident that the tribunal would be prepared, if necessary, to come to a different decision

(vi) *tribunal professionalism.*
> These factors should be balanced against assumption that in the absence of clear indications to the contrary tribunals will normally be capable of a professional approach.

Order

A refusal by the EAT to review its own decision dismissing an appeal is not an "order finally disposing of any proceedings," so this rule does not create an obligation to give reasons for refusing a review application (*Persson v Matra Marconi Space UK Ltd, The Times,* December 10, 1996, CA). The Court observed, however, that although there was no obligation, it would be good practice to give brief reasons.

5–107

Consent orders

See the note to r.6(5) at para.5–036.

5–108

Reasons for orders in cases concerning national security

31A.—(1) Paragraphs (1) to (5) of this rule apply to the document setting out the reasons for the Appeal Tribunal's order prepared under rule 31(2) or any reasoned judgment of the Appeal Tribunal as referred to in rule 31(2), in any particular Crown employment proceedings in which a direction of a Minister of the Crown has been given under rule 30A(1)(a), (b) or (c) or an order of the Appeal Tribunal has been made under rule 30A(2)(a) read with rule 30A(1)(a), (b) or (c).

5–109

(2) Before the Appeal Tribunal gives its reasons in writing for any order or delivers any reasoned judgment, the Registrar shall send a copy of the reasons or judgment to the Minister.

(3) If the Minister considers it expedient in the interests of national security, he may—

> (a) direct the Appeal Tribunal that the document containing its reasons for any order or its reasoned judgment shall not be disclosed to any person who was excluded from all or part of the proceedings and to prepare a further document setting out the reasons for its order, or a further reasoned judgment, but with the omission of such reasons as are specified in the direction; or

> (b) direct the Appeal Tribunal that the document containing its reasons for any order or its reasoned judgment shall not be disclosed to any person who was excluded from all or part of the proceedings, but that no further document setting out the Appeal Tribunal's reasons for its order or further reasoned judgment should be prepared.

(4) Where the Minister has directed the Appeal Tribunal in accordance with paragraph (3)(a), the document prepared pursuant to that direction shall be marked in each place where an omission has been made. The document may then be given by the Registrar to the parties.

(5) The Registrar shall send the document prepared pursuant to a direction of the Minister in accordance with paragraph (3)(a) and the full document without the omissions made pursuant to that direction—

    (a) to whichever of the appellant and the respondent was not the [claimant] in the proceedings before the employment tribunal;

    (b) if he was not an excluded person, to the person who was the [claimant] in the proceedings before the employment tribunal and, if he was not an excluded person, to his representative;

    (c) if applicable, to the special advocate; and

    (d) where there are proceedings before a superior court relating to the order in question, to that court.

(6) Where the Appeal Tribunal intends to take steps under rule 30A(2)(c) to keep secret all or part of the reasons for any order it makes, it shall send the full reasons for its order to the persons listed in sub-paragraphs (a) to (d) of paragraph (5), as appropriate.

Registration and proof of awards in respect of exclusion or expulsion from, or unjustifiable discipline by, a trade union

5–110   32.—(1) This rule applies where an application has been made to the Appeal Tribunal under section 67 or 176 of the 1992 Act.

(2) Without prejudice to rule 31, where the Appeal Tribunal makes an order in respect of an application to which this rule applies, and that order—

    (a) makes an award of compensation, or

    (b) is or includes an order of the kind referred to in rule 8(b)(ii), or both, the Registrar shall as soon as may be enter a copy of the order, sealed with the seal of the Tribunal, into a register kept by the Tribunal (in this rule referred to as "the Register")

(3) The production in any proceedings in any court of a document, purporting to be certified by the Registrar to be a true copy of an entry in the Register of an order to which this rule applies shall, unless the contrary is proved, be sufficient evidence of the document and of the facts stated therein.

Review of decisions and correction of errors

33.—(1) The Appeal Tribunal may, either of its own motion or on   **5–111**
application, review any order made by it and may, on such review,
revoke or vary that order on the grounds that—

- (a) the order was wrongly made as the result of an error on
      the part of the Tribunal or its staff;
- (b) a party did not receive proper notice of the proceedings
      leading to the order; or
- (c) the interests of justice require such review.

(2) An application under paragraph (1) above shall be made within
14 days of the date of the order.

(3) A clerical mistake in any order arising from an accidental slip
or omission may at any time be corrected by, or on the authority of, a
judge or member.

(4) The decision to grant or refuse an application for review may
be made by a judge.

Scope of the power

In *Blockleys Plc v Miller* [1992] I.C.R. 749, EAT, Wood J. examined the authorities   **5–112**
on the power of review at some length, concluding that "the power of review
whether in an industrial tribunal or in this Appeal Tribunal must be exercised
within a very narrow margin." Wood J. identified four classes of case that could
justify review:

- (a) where the issue of jurisdiction arises (see *British Midland Airways v Lewis*
      [1978] I.C.R. 782; *Stannard v Wilson* [1983] I.C.R. 652);
- (b) where there has been a fundamental procedural error (see *Trimble v
      Supertravel* [1982] I.C.R. 440);
- (c) cases of fraud appearing very soon after the decision (see *Yorkshire Engineer-
      ing v Burnham* [1974] I.C.R. 77); and
- (d) simple cases of minor error or omissions comparable to the slip rule.

However, in *Williams v Ferrosan Ltd* [2004] I.R.L.R. 607, EAT, Hooper J. relied on
the overriding objective in support of a broader approach to the employment
tribunal's power to review its decisions than that suggested by earlier authority. If
that is right, then the proper approach to the EAT's power to review must be due
for similar reconsideration.

Procedure

For the manner in which the EAT deals with review applications, see para.20 of   **5–113**
the PD.

"Proto-review"

In *Photocorporation (UK) Ltd v Truelove* [2003] UKEAT/0080/03, April 11, 2003,   **5–114**
H.H. Judge McMullen acceded to an application made by the appellant in the
course of the judgment for an opportunity to make submissions on an authority
referred to by the judge but not previously canvassed in argument. Judgment
having been pronounced but no order having been perfected, the EAT heard

Employment Appeal Tribunal
Rules 1993

further argument and reversed its initial decision on the point. H.H. Judge McMullen left it open ("we are in a proto-review situation") whether this was to be regarded as a review under r.33(1), or referable to the overriding objective alone. Since the overriding objective does not itself provide powers, but rather guidance on the manner in which powers are to be exercised, the course taken by the EAT is perhaps better regarded as an exercise of the EAT's power to regulate its own procedure at s.30(3) of the Employment Tribunals Act 1996, as guided by the overriding objective.

COSTS OR EXPENSES

General power to make costs or expenses orders

5–115   **34.—(1) In the circumstances listed in rule 34A the Appeal Tribunal may make an order ("a costs order") that a party or a special advocate, ("the paying party") make a payment in respect of the costs incurred by another party or a special advocate ("the receiving party").**

(2) For the purposes of these Rules "costs" includes fees, charges, disbursements and expenses incurred by or on behalf of a party or special advocate in relation to the proceedings, including the reimbursement allowed to a litigant in person under rule 34D. In Scotland, all references to costs or costs orders (except in the expression "wasted costs") shall be read as references to expenses or orders for expenses.

(3) A costs order may be made against or in favour of a respondent who has not had an answer accepted in the proceedings in relation to the conduct of any part which he has taken in the proceedings.

(4) A party or special advocate may apply to the Appeal Tribunal for a costs order to be made at any time during the proceedings. An application may also be made at the end of a hearing, or in writing to the Registrar within 14 days of the date on which the order of the Appeal Tribunal finally disposing of the proceedings was sent to the parties.

(5) No costs order shall be made unless the Registrar has sent notice to the party or special advocate against whom the order may be made giving him the opportunity to give reasons why the order should not be made. This paragraph shall not be taken to require the Registrar to send notice to the party or special advocate if the party or special advocate has been given an opportunity to give reasons orally to the Appeal Tribunal as to why the order should not be made.

(6) Where the Appeal Tribunal makes a costs order it shall provide written reasons for doing so if a request for written reasons is made within 21 days of the date of the costs order. The Registrar shall send a copy of the written reasons to all the parties to the proceedings

Costs incurred by another party

5–116   Only a party may recover costs. In *Walsall Metropolitan BC v Sidhu* [1980] I.C.R. 519 the EAT refused to award costs under the 1976 Rules, although the circumstances otherwise justified an award, because the respondent was backed by the

Commission for Racial Equality and had not herself incurred any. The CRE had incurred costs, but was not a party. It is worth noting the suggestion of Slynn J. (as he then was) at p.523 that the position might be different "if there were a liability on the part of the person assisted to reimburse the Commission for Racial Equality, whether or not that liability were ever enforced."

When a costs or expenses order may be made

34A.—(1) Where it appears to the Appeal Tribunal that any pro- **5–117** **ceedings brought by the paying party were unnecessary, improper, vexatious or misconceived or that there has been unreasonable delay or other unreasonable conduct in the bringing or conducting of proceedings by the paying party, the Appeal Tribunal may make a costs order against the paying party.**

(2) The Appeal Tribunal may in particular make a costs order against the paying party when—

(a) he has not complied with a direction of the Appeal Tribunal;

(b) he has amended its notice of appeal, document provided under rule 3 sub-paragraphs (5) or (6), Respondent's answer or statement of grounds of cross-appeal, or document provided under rule 6 sub-paragraphs (7) or (8); or

(c) he has caused an adjournment of proceedings.

(3) Nothing in paragraph (2) shall restrict the Appeal Tribunal's discretion to award costs under paragraph (1).

General

Costs orders remain exceptional in the EAT. The main changes (similar to **5–118** changes made at the same time to the employment tribunals' costs powers) brought in by the October 1, 2004 amendments are the power to make a wasted costs order against a party's representative, the power to make a costs award in favour of a litigant in person, and the power to take the paying party's means into account when assessing costs.

Procedure

For detailed provisions on the procedure to be followed in relation to a costs **5–119** application, see PD para.19.

Costs of a preliminary hearing

Costs can be awarded at a preliminary hearing (*Ravelin v Bournemouth City Council*, **5–120** *The Times*, July 19, 1986, EAT). Provision in the PD of December 9, 2004 for the submission by a respondent of concise written submissions directed to showing that there is no reasonable prospect of success for all or any of the grounds of appeal increases the likelihood that respondents to appeals will have incurred some costs by this stage.

Misconceived

For the purposes of the costs power of the employment tribunals, the word is **5–121** partially defined at reg.2(1) of the Employment Tribunals (Constitution and Rules of Procedure) Regulations 2004: "'misconceived' includes having no reasonable prospect of success." Although there is no equivalent definition for the purposes of these rules, it is presumably intended to have the same meaning here. Use of the word "includes" suggests that there may be appeals which have a reasonable prospect of success, but are nevertheless misconceived. An example might be an appeal which, while technically well-founded, is incapable of producing any benefit for the appellant.

The initial judicial sift carried out by the EAT means that appeals that are misconceived or which it is otherwise unreasonable to bring will rarely reach the stage of a full inter partes hearing. In *Iron & Steel Trades Confederation v ASW Ltd* [2004] I.R.L.R. 926 Burton J. disapproved an earlier suggestion that costs would never be awarded on the grounds of unreasonable conduct in bringing an appeal that had survived the initial sift, unless the EAT had been materially misled at that stage, but he accepted that the fact of having been permitted to proceed to a full hearing by a judge was a factor.

Costs of a reference to the ECJ

5–122   The ECJ treats costs incurred on a reference as costs of the proceedings before the national court which made the reference. In employment tribunal litigation, this is capable of having the anomalous consequence that where a reference is made by the employment tribunal or the EAT, the costs of the reference are only recoverable in exceptional circumstances; whereas if the reference is made by the Court of Appeal, costs of the reference follow the event. It was suggested by Browne-Wilkinson J. in *Burton v British Railways Board* [1983] I.C.R. 544, that this might in an appropriate case be dealt with by requiring an undertaking as to the costs of the reference.

The amount of a costs or expenses order

5–123   **34B.—(1) Subject to sub-paragraphs (2) and (3) the amount of a costs order against the paying party can be determined in the following ways:**

> **(a) the Appeal Tribunal may specify the sum which the paying party must pay to the receiving party;**
> **(b) the parties may agree on a sum to be paid by the paying party to the receiving party and if they do so the costs order shall be for the sum agreed; or**
> **(c) the Appeal Tribunal may order the paying party to pay the receiving party the whole or a specified part of the costs of the receiving party with the amount to be paid being determined by way of detailed assessment in the High Court in accordance with the Civil Procedure Rules 1998 or in Scotland the Appeal Tribunal may direct that it be taxed by the Auditor of the Court of Session, from whose decision an appeal shall lie to a judge.**

(2) The Appeal Tribunal may have regard to the paying party's ability to pay when considering the amount of a costs order.

(3) The costs of an assisted person in England and Wales shall be determined by detailed assessment in accordance with the Civil Procedure Rules

Personal liability of representatives for costs

34C.—(1) The Appeal Tribunal may make a wasted costs order **5–124** against a party's representative.

(2) In a wasted costs order the Appeal Tribunal may disallow or order the representative of a party to meet the whole or part of any wasted costs of any party, including an order that the representative repay to his client any costs which have already been paid.

(3) "Wasted costs" means any costs incurred by a party (including the representative's own client and any party who does not have a legal representative):

(a) as a result of any improper, unreasonable or negligent act or omission on the part of any representative; or

(b) which, in the light of any such act or omission occurring after they were incurred, the Appeal Tribunal considers it reasonable to expect that party to pay.

(4) In this rule "representative" means a party's legal or other representative or any employee of such representative, but it does not include a representative who is not acting in pursuit of profit with regard to the proceedings. A person is considered to be acting in pursuit of profit if he is acting on a conditional fee arrangement.

(5) Before making a wasted costs order, the Appeal Tribunal shall give the representative a reasonable opportunity to make oral or written representations as to reasons why such an order should not be made. The Appeal Tribunal may also have regard to the representative's ability to pay when considering whether it shall make a wasted costs order or how much that order should be.

(6) When the Appeal Tribunal makes a wasted costs order, it must specify in the order the amount to be disallowed or paid.

(7) The Registrar shall inform the representative's client in writing—

(a) of any proceedings under this rule; or

(b) of any order made under this rule against the party's representative.

(8) Where the Appeal Tribunal makes a wasted costs order it shall provide written reasons for doing so if a request is made for written reasons within 21 days of the date of the wasted costs order. The Registrar shall send a copy of the written reasons to all parties to the proceedings.]

Wasted costs

The definition of wasted costs here, as in the Employment Tribunals Procedure **5–125** Rules, is in identical terms to that provided by s.51(7) of the Supreme Court Act 1981, so exercise of the power can be expected to be guided by the practice of the ordinary civil courts: see the notes to r.48 of the Employment Tribunals Procedure Rules 2004 and Civil Procedure 2007, 48.7.1–48.7.20.

Litigants in person and party litigants

5–126   34D.—(1) This rule applies where the Appeal Tribunal makes a costs order in favour of a party who is a litigant in person.

(3) The litigant in person shall be allowed—

    (a) costs for the same categories of—

        (i) work; and

        (ii) disbursements, which would have been allowed if the work had been done or the disbursements had been made by a legal representative on the litigant in person's behalf;

    (b) the payments reasonably made by him for legal services relating to the conduct of the proceedings;

    (c) the costs of obtaining expert assistance in assessing the costs claim; and

    (d) other expenses incurred by him in relation to the proceedings.

(4) The amount of costs to be allowed to the litigant in person for any item of work claimed shall be—

    (a) where the litigant in person can prove financial loss, the amount that he can prove he had lost for the time reasonably spent on doing the work; or

    (b) where the litigant in person cannot prove financial loss, an amount for the time which the Tribunal considers reasonably spent on doing the work at the rate of oe25.00 per hour;

(5) For the year commencing 6th April 2006 the hourly rate of £25.00 shall be increased by the sum of £1.00 and for each subsequent year commencing on 6 April, the hourly rate for the previous year shall also be increased by the sum of £1.00.

(6) A litigant in person who is allowed costs for attending at court to conduct his case is not entitled to a witness allowance in respect of such attendance in addition to those costs.

(7) For the purpose of this rule, a litigant in person includes—

    (a) a company or other corporation which is acting without a legal representative; and

    (b) in England and Wales a barrister, solicitor, solicitor's employee or other authorised litigator (as defined in the

Courts and Legal Services Act), who is acting for himself; and

(c) in Scotland, an advocate or solicitor (within the meaning of the Solicitors (Scotland) Act 1980) who is acting for himself.

(8) In the application of this rule to Scotland, references to a litigant in person shall be read as references to a party litigant.

Service of documents

35.—(1) Any notice or other document required or authorised by   5–127
these Rules to be served on, or delivered to, any person may be sent to him by post to his address for service or, where no address or service has been given, to his registered office, principal place of business, head or main office or last known address, as the case may be, and any notice or other document required or authorised to be served on, or delivered to, the Appeal Tribunal may be sent by post or delivered to the Registrar—

(a) in the case of a notice instituting proceedings, at the central office or any other office of the Tribunal; or

(b) in any other case, at the office of the Tribunal in which the proceedings in question are being dealt with in accordance with rule 38(2).

(2) Any notice or other document required or authorised to be served on, or delivered to, an unincorporated body may be sent to its secretary, manager or other similar officer.

(3) Every document served by post shall be assumed, in the absence of evidence to the contrary, to have been delivered in the normal course of post.

(4) The Appeal Tribunal may inform itself in such manner as it thinks fit of the posting of any document by an officer of the Tribunal.

(5) The Appeal Tribunal may direct that service of any document be dispensed with or be effected otherwise than in the manner prescribed by these Rules.

Conciliation

36. Where at any stage of any proceedings it appears to the Appeal   5–128
Tribunal that there is a reasonable prospect of agreement being reached between the parties or of disposal of the appeal or a part of it by consensual means, the Tribunal may take such steps as it thinks fit to enable the parties to avail themselves of any opportunities for conciliation, whether by adjourning any proceedings or otherwise.

Time

5–129   **37.**—**(1)** The time prescribed by these Rules or by order of the Appeal Tribunal for doing any act may be extended (whether it has already expired or not) or abridged, and the date appointed for any purpose may be altered, by order of the Tribunal.

(1A) Where an act is required to be done on or before a particular day it shall be done by 4 pm on that day.

(2) Where the last day for the doing of any act falls on a day on which the appropriate office of the Tribunal is closed and by reason thereof the act cannot be done on that day, it may be done on the next day on which that office is open.

(3) An application for an extension of the time prescribed for the doing of an act, including the institution of an appeal under rule 3, shall be heard and determined as an interim application under rule 20.

(4) An application for an extension of the time prescribed for the institution of an appeal under rule 3 shall not be heard until the notice of appeal has been served on the Appeal Tribunal.

Rule 37(1A)

5–130   Rule 37(1A), inserted from October 1, 2004, was presaged by para.1(9)(b) of the 2002 Practice Direction to the same effect. The interesting question—whether the time for appealing laid down in the EAT Rules of Procedure could validly be shortened by eight hours by way of a Practice Direction—is now academic. Paragraph (1A) is carelessly drafted. Its literal effect as regards anything required to be done "before" a particular day, namely that it may be done at any time up to 4pm on that day, is misleading: what must be intended is that anything required to be done "before" a particular day must be done by 4pm on the previous day.

Tribunal offices and allocation of business

5–131   **38.**—**(1)** The central office and any other office of the Appeal Tribunal shall be open at such times as the President may direct.

(2) Any proceedings before the Tribunal may be dealt with at the central office or at such other office as the President may direct.

Non-compliance with, and waiver of, rules

5–132   **39.**—**(1)** Failure to comply with any requirements of these Rules shall not invalidate any proceedings unless the Appeal Tribunal otherwise directs.

(2) The Tribunal may, if it considers that to do so would lead to the more expeditious or economical disposal of any proceedings or would otherwise be desirable in the interests of justice, dispense with the taking of any step required or authorised by these Rules, or may direct that any such steps be taken in some manner other than that prescribed by these Rules.

(3) The powers of the Tribunal under paragraph (2) extend to authorising the institution of an appeal notwithstanding that the period prescribed in rule 3(2) may not have commenced.

Transitional provisions

40.—(1) Where, prior to 16th December 1993, an employment tribunal **5–133** has given full written reasons for its decision or order, those reasons shall be treated as extended written reasons for the purposes of rule 3(1)(c) and rule 3(2) and for the purposes of Form 1 in the Schedule to these Rules.

(2) Anything validly done under or pursuant to the Employment Appeal Tribunal Rules 1980 shall be treated as having been done validly for the purposes of these Rules, whether or not what was done could have been done under or pursuant to these Rules.

SCHEDULE

FORM 1 *Notice of Appeal from Decision of Employment Tribunal*   **5–134**
Rule 3

1. The appellant is (*name and address of appellant*).

2. Any communication relating to this appeal may be sent to the appellant at (*appellant's address for service, including telephone number if any*).

3. The appellant appeals from   (*here give particulars of the decision of the industrial tribunal from which the appeal is brought including the date*).

4. The parties to the proceedings before the industrial tribunal, other than the appellant, were (*names and addresses of other parties to the proceedings resulting in decision appealed from*).

5. A copy of the industrial tribunal's decision or order and of the extended written reasons for that decision or order are attached to this notice.

6. The grounds upon which this appeal is brought are that the industrial tribunal erred in law in that (*here set out in paragraphs the various grounds of appeal*).

Date
Signed

FORM 1A *Notice of Appeal from the CAC made pursuant to regulation 38(8) of*   **5–135**
the Transnational Information and Consultation of Employees Regulations 1999
Rule 3

1. The appellant is (*name and address of appellant*).

2. Any communication relating to this appeal may be sent to the appellant at (*appellant's address for service, including telephone number if any*).

3. The appellant appeals from (*here give particulars of the decision, declaration or order of the CAC from which the appeal is brought including the date*).

4. The parties to the proceedings before the CAC, other than the appellant, were (*names and addresses of other parties to the proceedings resulting in decision appealed from*).

5. A copy of the CAC's decision, declaration or order appealed from is attached to this notice.

6. The grounds upon which this appeal is brought are that the CAC erred in law in that (*here set out in paragraphs the various grounds of appeal*).

Date
Signed

5–136   FORM 2 *Notice of Appeal from Decision of Certification Officer*
Rule 3

1. The appellant is (*name and address of appellant*).

2. Any communication relating to this appeal may be sent to the appellant at (*appellant's address for service, including telephone number if any*).

3. The appellant appeals from   (*here give particulars of the order or decision of the Certification Officer from which the appeal is brought*).

4. The appellant's grounds of appeal are: (*here state the grounds of appeal*).

5. A copy of the Certification Officer's decision is attached to this notice.

Date
Signed

5–137   FORM 3 *Respondent's Answer*
Rule 6

1. The respondent is (*name and address of respondent*).

2. Any communication relating to this appeal may be sent to the respondent at (*respondent's address for service, including telephone number if any*).

3. The respondent intends to resist the appeal of (*here give the name of appellant*). The grounds on which the respondent will rely are [the grounds relied upon by the industrial tribunal/Certification Officer for making the decision or order appealed from] [and] [the following grounds]: (*here set out any grounds which differ from those relied upon by the industrial tribunal or Certification Officer, as the case may be*).

4. The respondent cross-appeals from   (*here give particulars of the decision appealed from*).

5. The respondent's grounds of appeal are: (*here state the grounds of appeal*).

Date
Signed

5–138   FORM 4 *Application to the Employment Appeal Tribunal for Compensation for Exclusion or Expulsion from a Trade Union or for Compensation or an Order in respect of Unjustifiable Discipline*
Rule 8

1. My name is   My address is

2. Any communication relating to this application may be sent to me at (*state address for service, including telephone number, if any*).

3. My complaint against (*state the name and address of the trade union*) was declared to be well-founded by (*state tribunal*) on (*give date of decision or order*).

4. (*Where the application relates to exclusion or expulsion from a trade union*) I have not been admitted/re-admitted* to membership of the above-named trade union and hereby apply for compensation on the following grounds.

(*Where the application relates to unjustifiable discipline*) The determination infringing my right not to be unjustifiably disciplined has not been revoked./ The trade union has failed to take all the steps necessary for securing the reversal of things done for the purpose of giving effect to the determination.*

(* Delete as appropriate)

Date
Signed

NB—A copy of the decision or order declaring the complaint against the trade union to be well-founded must be enclosed with this application.

FORM 4A *Application under regulation 20 or 21 of the Transnational*   **5–139**
Information and Consultation of Employees Regulations 1999
Rule 16A

1. The applicant is (*name and address of applicant*)

2. Any communication relating to this application may be sent to the applicant at (*state address for service, including telephone number, if any*).

3. The application is made against (*state identity or, where applicable, identities of respondents*) who is/are, or is/are representative of, the central or local management/the European Works Council/one or more information and consultation representatives (*delete what does not apply*).

4. The address(es) of the respondent(s) is/are

5. My complaint against the respondent(s) is that it/they failed to comply with its/their obligations under regulation 20 or 21 of the Transnational Information and Consultation of Employees Regulations 1999 as follows (*give particulars, set out in paragraphs and making reference to the specific provisions in the 1999 Regulations alleged to have been breached*).

Date
Signed

FORM 5 *Notice of Appearance to Application to Employment Appeal Tribunal for*   **5–140**
Compensation for Exclusion or Expulsion from a Trade Union or for Compensation or an Order in respect of Unjustifiable Discipline

Rule 11

1. The respondent trade union is (*name and address of union*).

2. Any communication relating to this application may be sent to the respondent at (*respondent's address for service, including telephone number, if any*).

3. The respondent intends to resist the application of (*here give name of the applicant*). The grounds on which the respondent will rely are as follows:

4. (*Where the application relates to exclusion or expulsion from the trade union, state whether or not the applicant had been admitted or re-admitted to membership on or before the date of application.*)

(*Where the application relates to unjustifiable discipline, state whether—*

(**a**) *the determination infringing the applicant's right not to be unjustifiably disciplined has been revoked; and*

(**b**) *the trade union has taken all the steps necessary for securing the reversal of anything done for the purpose of giving effect to the determination.*)

Date
Signed

Position in union

5–141   FORM 5A *Notice of Appearance to the Employment Appeal Tribunal under regulation 20 or 21 of the Transnational Information and Consultation of Employees Regulations 1999*
Rule 16C

1. The respondent is (*name and address of respondent*)

2. Any communication relating to this application may be sent to the respondent at (*respondent's address for service, including telephone number, if any*)

3. The respondent intends to resist the application of (*here give the name or description of the applicant*)

The grounds on which the respondent will rely are as follows: (*give particulars, set out in paragraphs and making reference to the specific provisions in the Transnational Information and Consultation of Employees Regulations 1999 alleged to have been breached*)

Date
Signed
Position in respondent company or undertaking:

(*Where appropriate give position in respondent central or local management or position held in relation to respondent Works Council*).

5–142   FORM 6 *Application to the Employment Appeal Tribunal Under section 33 of the 1996 Act for a Restriction of Proceedings Order*

Rule 13

1. The applicant is *(the Attorney General/Lord Advocate)*.

2. Any communication relating to this application may be sent to the applicant at *(state address for service, including telephone number)*.

3. The application is for a restriction of proceedings order to be made against *(state the name and address of the person against whom the order is sought)*.

4. An affidavit in support of the application is attached.

Date
Signed

FORM 7 *Notice of Appearance to Application to the Employment Appeal Tribunal* **5–143**
under section 33 of the 1996 Act for a Restriction of Proceedings Order
Rule 15

1. The respondent is *(state name and address of respondent)*.

2. Any communication relating to this application may be sent to the respondent at *(respondent's address for service, including telephone number, if any)*.

3. The respondent intends to resist the application. An affidavit in support is attached to this notice.

Date
Signed

Forms 1, 3 and 8 can be downloaded in pdf format from **5–144**
http:www.employmentappeals.gov.uk.

Employment Appeal Tribunal
Rules 1993

CHAPTER 6

PRACTICE DIRECTION (EMPLOYMENT APPEAL TRIBUNAL— PROCEDURE) 2004

Contents

PD

1 Introduction and objective

1.1 This Practice Direction ("PD") supersedes all previous Practice Directions. It comes into force on 9 December 2004.　**6–001**

1.2 The Employment Appeal Tribunal Rules 1993 (SI 1993/2854) as amended by the Employment Appeal Tribunal (Amendment) Rules 2001 (SI 2001/1128 and 2001/1476) and the Employment Appeal Tribunal (Amendment) Rules 2004 (SI 2004/2526) ("the Rules") apply to all proceedings irrespective of when those proceedings were commenced.　**6–002**

1.3 By s.30(3) of the Employment Tribunals Act 1996 ("ETA 1996") the Employment Appeal Tribunal ("the EAT") has power, subject to the Rules, to regulate its own procedure. In so doing, the EAT regards itself as subject in all its actions to the duties imposed by　**6–003**

Rule 2A. It will seek to apply the overriding objective when it exercises any power given to it by the Rules or interprets any Rule.

6–004 1.4 The overriding objective of this PD is to enable the EAT to deal with cases justly. Dealing with a case justly includes, so far as is practicable:

> 1.4.1 ensuring that the parties are on an equal footing;
> 1.4.2 dealing with the case in ways which are proportionate to the importance and complexity of the issues;
> 1.4.3 ensuring that it is dealt with expeditiously and fairly;
> 1.4.4 saving expense.

6–005 1.5 The parties are required to help the EAT to further the overriding objective.

6–006 1.6 Where the Rules do not otherwise provide, the following procedure will apply to all appeals to the EAT.

6–007 1.7 The provisions of this PD are subject to any specific directions which the EAT may make in any particular case. Otherwise, the directions set out below must be complied with in all appeals from Employment Tribunals. In national security appeals, and appeals from the Certification Officer and the Central Arbitration Committee, the Rules set out the separate procedures to be followed and the EAT will normally give specific directions.

6–008 1.8 Where it is appropriate to the EAT's jurisdiction, procedure, unrestricted rights of representation and restricted costs regime, the EAT is guided by the Civil Procedure Rules. So, for example:

> 1.8.1 For the purpose of serving a valid Notice of Appeal under Rule 3 and para 3 below, when an Employment Tribunal decision is sent to parties on a Wednesday, that day does *not* count and the Notice of Appeal must arrive at the EAT on or before the Wednesday 6 weeks (ie 42 days) later.
> 1.8.2 When a date is given for serving of a document or for doing some other act, the complete document must be received by the EAT or the relevant party by 4.00pm on that date. Any document received after 4.00 pm will be deemed to be lodged on the next working day.
> 1.8.3 Except as provided in 1.8.4 below, all days count, but if a time limit expires on a day when the central office of the EAT, or the EAT office in Edinburgh (as appropriate), is closed, it is extended to the next working day.

1.8.4 **Where the time limit is 5 days (e.g. an appeal against a Registrar's order or direction), Saturdays, Sundays, Christmas Day, Good Friday and Bank Holidays do not count.**

1.9 **In this PD any reference to the date of an order shall mean the date stamped upon the relevant order by the EAT ("the seal date").**   6–009

1.10 **The parties can expect the EAT normally to have read the documents (or the documents indicated in any essential reading list if permission is granted under para 6.3 below for an enlarged appeal bundle) in advance of any hearing.**   6–010

Overriding objective
See para.5–009.   6–011

Time limit of 5 days
The words "or less" from CPR r.28.1(4) are omitted, presumably by oversight. 6–012
There is no sensible basis on which time limits of exactly five days should be treated as under the CPR, but not shorter time limits.

2 Institution of appeal

2.1 **The Notice of Appeal must be, or be substantially, in accord-ance with Form 1 (in the amended form annexed to this Practice Direction) or Forms 1A or 2 of the Schedule to the Rules and must identify the date of the judgment, decision or order being appealed. Copies of the judgment, decision or order appealed against and of the Employment Tribunal's written reasons, together with a copy of the Claim (ET1) and the Response (ET3) must be attached, or if not, a written explanation must be given. A Notice of Appeal without such documentation will not be validly lodged.**   6–013

2.2 **If the appellant has made an application to the Employment Tribunal for a review of its judgment or decision, a copy of such application should accompany the Notice of Appeal together with the judgment and written reasons of the Employment Tribunal in respect of that review application, or a statement, if such be the case, that a judgment is awaited. If any of these documents cannot be included, a written explanation must be given. The appellant should also attach (where they are relevant to the appeal) copies of any orders includ-ing case management orders made by the Employment Tribunal.**   6–014

2.3 **Where written reasons of the Employment Tribunal are not attached to the Notice of Appeal, either (as set out in the written explanation) because a request for written reasons has been refused by the Employment Tribunal or for some other reason, an appellant**   6–015 must, when lodging the Notice of Appeal, apply in writing to the EAT to exercise its discretion to hear the appeal without written reasons or to exercise its power to request written reasons from the Employment Tribunal, setting out the full grounds of that application.

6–016   2.4 The Notice of Appeal must clearly identify the point(s) of law which form(s) the ground(s) of appeal from the judgment, decision or order of the Employment Tribunal to the EAT. It should also state the order which the appellant will ask the EAT to make at the hearing.

6–017   2.5 Rules 3(7)-(10) give a judge or the Registrar power to decide that no further action shall be taken in certain cases where it appears that the Notice of Appeal or any part of it (a) discloses no reasonable grounds for bringing the appeal, or (b) is an abuse of the Employment Appeal Tribunal's process or is otherwise likely to obstruct the just disposal of proceedings. The Rules specify the rights of the appellant and the procedure to be followed. The appellant can request an oral hearing before a judge to challenge the decision. If it appears to the judge or Registrar that a Notice of Appeal or an application gives insufficient grounds of, or lacks clarity in identifying, a point of law, the judge or Registrar may postpone any decision under Rule 3(7) pending the appellant's amplification or clarification of the Notice of Appeal or further information from the Employment Tribunal.

6–018   2.6 Perversity Appeals: an appellant may not state as a ground of appeal simply words to the effect that "the judgment or order was contrary to the evidence," or that "there was no evidence to support the judgment or order", or that "the judgment or order was one which no reasonable Tribunal could have reached and was perverse" unless the Notice of Appeal also sets out full particulars of the matters relied on in support of those general grounds.

6–019   2.7 A party cannot reserve a right to amend, alter or add, to a Notice of Appeal or a respondent's Answer. Any application for leave to amend must be made as soon as practicable and must be accompanied by a draft of the amended Notice of Appeal or amended Answer which makes clear the precise amendments for which permission is sought.

6–020   2.8 A respondent to the appeal who wishes to resist the appeal and/or to cross-appeal, but who has not delivered a respondent's Answer as directed by the Registrar, or otherwise ordered, may be precluded from taking part in the appeal unless permission is granted to serve an Answer out of time.

2.9 Where an application is made for leave to institute or continue relevant proceedings by a person who has been made the subject of a Restriction of Proceedings Order pursuant to s.33 of ETA 1996, that application will be considered on paper by a judge, who may make an order granting, refusing or otherwise dealing with such application on paper.

6–021

General

See generally the notes to r.3 of the EAT rules at para.5–012 *et seq.* above.

6–022

3 Time for instituting appeals

3.1 The time within which an appeal must be instituted depends on whether the appeal is against a judgment or against an order or decision of the Employment Tribunal.

6–023

3.2 If the appeal is against an order or decision, the appeal must be instituted within 42 days of the date of the order or decision. The EAT will treat a Tribunal's refusal to make an order or decision as itself constituting an order or decision. The date of an order or decision is the date when the order or decision was sent to the parties, which is normally recorded on or in the order or decision.

6–024

3.3 If the appeal is against a judgment, the appeal must be instituted within 42 days from the date on which the written record of the judgment was sent to the parties. However in three situations the time for appealing against a judgment will be 42 days from the date when written reasons were sent to the parties. This will be the case *only* if (1) written reasons were requested orally at the hearing before the Tribunal or (2) written reasons were requested in writing within 14 days of the date on which the written record of the judgment was sent to the parties or (3) the Tribunal itself reserved its reasons and gave them subsequently in writing: such exception will *not* apply if the request to the Tribunal for written reasons is made out of time (whether or not such request is granted). The date of the written record and of the written reasons is the date when they are sent to the parties, which is normally recorded on or in the written record and the written reasons.

6–025

3.4 The time limit referred to in paras 3.1 to 3.3 above apply *even though* the question of remedy and assessment of compensation by the Employment Tribunal has been adjourned or has not been dealt with and *even though* an application has been made to the Employment Tribunal for a review.

6–026

3.5 An application for an extension of time for appealing cannot be considered until a Notice of Appeal in accordance with para 2(1) above has been lodged with the EAT.

6–027

6–028   3.6 Any application for an extension of time for appealing must be made as an interim application to the Registrar, who will normally determine the application after inviting and considering written representations from each side. An interim appeal lies from the Registrar's decision to a judge. Such an appeal must be notified to the EAT within 5 days of the date when the Registrar's decision was sent to the parties. [See para 4.3 below.]

6–029   3.7 In determining whether to extend the time for appealing, particular attention will be paid to whether any good excuse for the delay has been shown and to the guidance contained in the decisions of the EAT and the Court of Appeal, as summarised in *United Arab Emirates v Abdelghafar* [1995] ICR 65 and *Aziz v Bethnal Green City Challenge Co Ltd* [2000] IRLR 111.

6–030   3.8 It is not usually a good reason for late lodgment of a Notice of Appeal that an application for litigation support from public funds has been made, but not yet determined; or that support is being sought from, but has not yet been provided by, some other body, such as a trade union, employers' association or one of the equality Commissions.

6–031   3.9 In any case of doubt or difficulty, a Notice of Appeal should be lodged in time and an application made to the Registrar for directions.

General
6–032   See generally the notes to r.3 of the EAT rules at para.5–013 above.

4   Interim applications
6–033   4.1 Interim applications should be made in writing (no particular form is required) and will be initially referred to the Registrar who after considering the papers may deal with the case or refer it to a judge. The judge may dispose of it himself or refer it to a full EAT hearing. Parties are encouraged to make any such applications at a Preliminary Hearing ("PH") or an Appointment for Directions if one is ordered (see paras 9.7–9.18 and 11.2 below).

6–034   4.2 Unless otherwise ordered, any application for extension of time will be considered and determined as though it were an interim application to the Registrar, who will normally determine the application after inviting and considering written representations from each side.

6–035   4.3 An interim appeal lies from the Registrar's decision to a judge. Such an appeal must be notified to the EAT within 5 days of the date when the Registrar's decision was sent to the parties.

Amendment

For notes on amending a notice of appeal to the Court of Appeal, equally applicable to amendment of grounds of appeal to the EAT, see para.8–095. **6–036**

5 The right to inspect the register and certain documents and to take copies

5.1 Any document lodged in the Central Office of the EAT in London or in the EAT office in Edinburgh in any proceedings before the EAT shall be sealed with the seal of the EAT showing the date (and time, if received after 4.00 pm) on which the document was lodged. **6–037**

5.2 Particulars of the date of delivery at the Central Office of the EAT or in the EAT office in Edinburgh of any document for filing or lodgment together with the time, if received after 4.00 pm, the date of the document and the title of the appeal of which the document forms part of the record shall be entered in the Register of Cases kept in the Central Office and in Edinburgh or in the file which forms part of the Register of Cases. **6–038**

5.3 Any person shall be entitled during office hours by appointment to inspect and request a copy of any of the following documents filed or lodged in the Central Office or the EAT office in Edinburgh, namely: **6–039**

5.3.1 any Notice of Appeal or respondent's Answer or any copy thereof;

5.3.2 any judgment or order given or made in court or any copy of such judgment or order;
    and

5.3.3 with the permission of the EAT, which may be granted on an application, any other document.

5.4 A copying charge per page will be payable for those documents mentioned in para 5.3 above. **6–040**

5.5 Nothing in this Direction shall be taken as preventing any party to an appeal from inspecting and requesting a copy of any document filed or lodged in the Central Office or the EAT office in Edinburgh before the commencement of the appeal, but made with a view to its commencement. **6–041**

6 Papers for use at the hearing.

6.1 It is the responsibility of the parties or their advisers (see paras 6.5 and 6.6 below) to prepare a core bundle of papers for use at any hearing. Ultimate responsibility lies with the appellant, following **6–042** consultation with other parties. The bundle must include only those exhibits (*productions* in Scotland) and documents used before the Employment Tribunal which are considered to be necessary for the appeal. It is the duty of the parties or their advisers to ensure that only those documents are included which are (a) relevant to the point(s) of law raised in the appeal and (b) likely to be referred to at the hearing.

6–043   6.2 The documents in the core bundle should be numbered by item, then paginated continuously and indexed, in the following order:

    6.2.1 Judgment, decision or order appealed from and written reasons

    6.2.2 Sealed Notice of Appeal

    6.2.3 Respondent's Answer if a Full Hearing ("FH"), respondent's Submissions if a PH

    6.2.4 ET1 Claim (and any Additional Information or Written Answers)

    6.2.5 ET3 Response (and any Additional Information or Written Answers)

    6.2.6 Questionnaire and Replies (discrimination and equal pay cases)

    6.2.7 Relevant orders, judgments and written reasons of the Employment Tribunal

    6.2.8 Relevant orders and judgments of the EAT

    6.2.9 Affidavits and Employment Tribunal comments (where ordered)

    6.2.10 Any documents agreed or ordered pursuant to para 7 below.

6–044   6.3 Other documents relevant to the particular hearing (for example the relevant particulars or contract of employment and any relevant procedures) referred to at the Employment Tribunal may follow in the core bundle, if the total pages do not exceed 100. No bundle containing more than 100 pages should be agreed or lodged without the permission of the Registrar or order of a judge which will not be granted without the provision of an essential reading list as soon as practicable thereafter. If permitted or ordered, further pages should follow, with consecutive pagination, in an additional bundle or bundles if appropriate.

6–045   6.4 All documents must be legible and unmarked.

6–046   6.5 PH cases (see para 9.5.2 below), Appeals from Registrar's Order, Rule 3(10) hearings, Appointments for Directions: the appellant must prepare and lodge 4 copies (2 copies if judge sitting alone) of the bundle as soon as possible after service of the Notice of Appeal and no later than 21 days from the seal date of the relevant order unless otherwise directed.

6.6 FH cases (see para 9.5.3 below): the parties must co-operate in agreeing a bundle of papers for the hearing. By no later than 35 days from the seal date of the relevant order, unless otherwise directed, the appellant is responsible for ensuring that 4 copies (2 copies if judge sitting alone) of a bundle agreed by the parties is lodged at the EAT. The EAT will not retain bundles from a case heard at a PH. **6–047**

6.7 Warned List and Fast Track FH cases: the bundles should be lodged as soon as possible and (unless the hearing date is within 7 days) in any event within 7 days after the parties have been notified that the case is expedited or in the Warned List. **6–048**

6.8 In the event of disagreement between the parties or difficulty in preparing the bundles, the Registrar may give appropriate directions, whether on application in writing (on notice) by one or more of the parties or of his/her own initiative. **6–049**

6.5 "the relevant order"

The order directing that the case is to be listed for a PH, r.3(10) hearing, or appointment for directions as the case may be. Although this paragraph asks that bundles should be lodged as soon as possible after service of the notice of appeal, it is respectfully suggested that the more practical course is to wait for the EAT to give directions so that it is known when bundles are prepared for what kind of hearing they are needed and how many copies are required. **6–050**

7 Evidence before the employment tribunal

7.1 An appellant who considers that a point of law raised in the Notice of Appeal cannot be argued without reference to evidence given (or not given) at the Employment Tribunal, the nature or substance of which does not, or does not sufficiently, appear from the written reasons, must ordinarily submit an application with the Notice of Appeal. The application is for the nature of such evidence (or lack of it) to be admitted, or if necessary for the relevant parts of the Chairman's notes of evidence to be produced. If such application is not so made, then it should be made: **6–051**

> 7.1.1 if a PH is ordered, in the skeleton or written submissions lodged prior to such PH; or
>
> 7.1.2 if the case is listed for FH without a PH, then within 14 days of the seal date of the order so providing.

Any such application by a respondent to an appeal, must, if not made earlier, accompany the respondent's Answer.

6–052   7.2 The application must explain why such a matter is considered necessary in order to argue the point of law raised in the Notice of Appeal or respondent's Answer. The application must identify:

    7.2.1 the issue(s) in the Notice of Appeal or respondent's Answer to which the matter is relevant;

    7.2.2 the names of the witnesses whose evidence is considered relevant, alternatively the nature of the evidence the absence of which is considered relevant;

    7.2.3 (if applicable) the part of the hearing when the evidence was given;

    7.2.4 the gist of the evidence (or absence of evidence) alleged to be relevant; and

    7.2.5 (if the party has a record), saying so and by whom and when it was made, or producing an extract from a witness statement given in writing at the hearing.

6–053   7.3 The application will be considered on the papers, or if appropriate at a PH, by the Registrar or a judge. The Registrar or a judge may give directions for written representations (if they have not already been lodged), or may determine the application, but will ordinarily make an order requiring the party who seeks to raise such a matter to give notice to the other party(ies) to the appeal/cross-appeal. The notice will require the other party(ies) to co-operate in agreeing, within 21 days (unless a shorter period is ordered), a statement or note of the relevant evidence, alternatively a statement that there was no such evidence. All parties are required to use their best endeavours to agree such a statement or note.

6–054   7.4 In the absence of such agreement within 21 days (or such shorter period as may be ordered) of the requirement, any party may make an application within 7 days thereafter to the EAT, for directions. The party must enclose all relevant correspondence and give notice to the other parties. The directions may include: the resolution of the disagreement on the papers or at a hearing; the administration by one party to the others of, or a request to the Chairman to respond to, a questionnaire; or, if the EAT is satisfied that such notes are necessary, a request that the Chairman produce his/her notes of evidence either in whole or in part.

6–055   7.5 If the EAT requests any documents from the Chairman, it will supply copies to the parties upon receipt.

6–056   7.6 In an appeal from an Employment Tribunal which ordered its proceedings to be tape recorded, the EAT will apply the principles above to any application for a transcript.

7.7 A note of evidence is not to be produced and supplied to the **6–057**
parties to enable the parties to embark on a "fishing expedition" to
establish grounds or additional grounds of appeal or because they
have not kept their own notes of the evidence. If an application for
such a note is found by the EAT to have been unreasonably made or
if there is unreasonable lack of co-operation in agreeing a relevant
note or statement, the party behaving unreasonably is at risk of
being ordered to pay costs.

Notes of evidence

Paragraph 7.1 is unhappily drafted. It is not clear why the EAT needs to be **6–058**
troubled at this stage with an application for evidence given to the tribunal or the
lack thereof to be admitted: that is a matter for the respondent. It is only if the
parties cannot agree what evidence was or was not given that it will be necessary to
apply to the EAT for a direction that the employment judge's notes be produced.
Possibly (although the result could have been more simply achieved) the intention
is to focus the appellant's mind on the question whether notes of evidence will be
needed at an early stage, so as to facilitate agreement and obviate the need for the
employment judge's notes.

It is suggested that the most convenient course is to include in the notice of
appeal an invitation to the respondent to agree the necessary evidence by a date
short of the deadlines given at 7.1.1 and 7.1.2 and to send a copy of the notice of
appeal to the respondent, drawing its attention specifically to that invitation, at the
same time as it is filed at the EAT. If the parties fail to reach agreement on the
relevant evidence, the appellant can apply to the EAT by letter for a direction for
the employment judge's notes.

A party's notes of the evidence before the employment tribunal are not
privileged: see para.5–094 above.

8 Fresh evidence and new points of law

8.1 Where an application is made by a party to an appeal to put in, **6–059**
at the hearing of the appeal, any document which was not before the
Employment Tribunal, and which has not been agreed in writing by
the other parties, the application and a copy of the documents sought
to be admitted should be lodged at the EAT with the Notice of Appeal
or the respondent's Answer, as appropriate. The application and copy
should be served on the other parties. The same principle applies to
any oral evidence not given at the Employment Tribunal which is
sought to be adduced on the appeal. The nature and substance of
such evidence together with the date when the party first became
aware of its existence must be disclosed in a document, where
appropriate a witness statement from the relevant witness with
signed statement of truth, which must be similarly lodged and served.

8.2 In exercising its discretion to admit any fresh evidence or new **6–060**
document, the EAT will apply the principles set out in *Ladd v*
Marshall **[1954] 1 WLR 1489, having regard to the overriding objec-**
tive, ie:

EAT, Practice Direction

    8.2.1 the evidence could not have been obtained with reasonable diligence for use at the Employment Tribunal hearing;

    8.2.2 it is relevant and would probably have had an important influence on the hearing;

    8.2.3 it is apparently credible.

Accordingly the evidence and representations in support of the application must address these principles.

6–061   **8.3** A party wishing to resist the application must, within 14 days of its being sent, submit any representations in response to the EAT and other parties.

6–062   **8.4** The application will be considered by the Registrar or a judge on the papers (or, if appropriate, at a PH) who may determine the issue or give directions for a hearing or may seek comments from the Chairman. A copy of any comments received from the Chairman will be sent to all parties.

6–063   **8.5** If a respondent intends to contend at the FH that the appellant has raised a point which was not argued below, the respondent shall so state:

    8.5.1 if a PH has been ordered, in writing to the EAT and all parties, within 14 days of receiving the Notice of Appeal;

    8.5.2 if the case is listed for a FH without a PH, in a respondent's Answer.

In the event of dispute the Chairman should be asked for his/her comments as to whether a particular legal argument was deployed.

New evidence

6–064   See notes to r.7 of the EAT Rules at para.5–042 *et seq.*

New point of law

6–065   The EAT will not as a rule entertain as a ground of appeal a point that was not argued before the employment tribunal. The authorities on the precise limits of this rule are in a confused state. *Kumchyk v Derby City Council* [1978] I.C.R. 1116, EAT, in which a stringent version of this rule is stated, is regularly cited in the EAT. Although *Kumchyk* is referred to with approval by the Court of Appeal in *Mensah v East Hertfordshire NHS Trust* [1998] I.R.L.R. 531; *Jones v Governing Body of Burdett Coutts School* [1999] I.C.R. 38; and *Divine-Bortey v London Borough of Brent* [1998] I.C.R. 886, it should be noted, that the Court of Appeal cast some doubt on the reasoning in *Hellyer Brothers v McLeod* [1987] I.C.R. 526 at 564 E-H. See also *B v London Borough of Harrow and the Special Educational Needs Tribunal* [1998] EWCA Civ 508, where *Kumchyk* was robustly distinguished (notwithstanding that the consequence was remittal for further evidence and fact-finding) on the basis that *B*, the party seeking to argue a new point, had not had legal representation or the support of a trade union at first instance. In *Glennie v Independent Magazines Ltd* [1999] I.R.L.R. 719, CA, Brooke L.J., commenting on the decision of the EAT in *House v Emerson Electric Industrial Controls* [1980] I.C.R. 795, said at para.12:

"Without challenging the facts found by the Industrial Tribunal, the appellants sought to rely on the Interpretation Act for the first time in their appeal in order to argue that the Industrial Tribunal had been wrong in law to decline jurisdiction. It is hardly surprising that the Employment Appeal Tribunal allowed this point of law to be argued for the first time before them. If the Industrial Tribunal was wrong in law to decline jurisdiction on the facts before it, it was clearly the duty of the Employment Appeal Tribunal to put it right".

More recently, however, in *Leicestershire CC v Unison* [2006] I.R.L.R. 810 the Court of Appeal (relying on *Jones*) concluded that new points should be entertained as an appeal only in exceptional circumstances.

Two significant exceptions to the rule as stated *Kumchyk* are to be found in the decisions of the EAT in *Langston v Cranfield University* EAT/647/96, January 12, 1998 and *Atos Origin v Haddock* [2005] I.R.L.R. 20. In the former, H.H. Judge Clark identified a category of principle "so well-established that an industrial tribunal may be expected to consider it as a matter of course" in relation to which the failure to take the point expressly before the tribunal will not prejudice a party on appeal. In the latter, a respondent that had not entered an appearance before the employment tribunal (and had therefore argued no points at all at first instance) was permitted to appeal on the question of remedy. In *Lipscombe v Forestry Commission* UKEAT/0191/06, September 28, 2006, the EAT permitted a litigant in person suffering from "a mildly severe stress disorder" to reframe his argument on appeal to include a contention not raised before the employment tribunal. However, on the facts of that case, that step did not require consideration of any further evidence.

In *Secretary of State for Health v Rance* [2007] I.R.L.R. 665 (part of the *Preston v Wolverhampton Healthcare NHS Trust* (No. 3) [2004] I.C.R. 993 litigation), H.H. Judge McMullen reviews the authorities on when the EAT will be prepared to entertain a new point of law or permit a concession to be withdrawn, and sets out at [50] of his judgment the following principles:

"(1) There is a discretion to allow a new point of law to be argued in the EAT. It is tightly regulated by authorities; Jones paragraph 20. (2) The discretion covers new points and the re-opening of conceded points; ibid. (3) The discretion is exercised only in exceptional circumstances; ibid (4) It would be even more exceptional to exercise the discretion where fresh issues of fact would have to be investigated; ibid. (5) Where the new point relates to jurisdiction, this is not a trump card requiring the point to be taken; Barber v Thames Television plc [1991] IRLR 236 EAT Knox J and members at paragraph 38; approved in Jones. It remains discretionary. (6) The discretion may be exercised in any of the following circumstances which are given as examples: (a) It would be unjust to allow the other party to get away with some deception or unfair conduct which meant that the point was not taken below: Kumchyk v Derby City Council [1978] ICR 1116, EAT Arnold J and members at 1123 (b) The point can be taken if the EAT is in possession of all the material necessary to dispose of the matter fairly without recourse to a further hearing. Wilson v Liverpool Corporation [1971] 1 WLR 302, 307, per Widgery LJ. (c) The new point enables the EAT plainly to say from existing material that the Employment Tribunal judgment was a nullity, for that is a consideration of overwhelming strength; House v Emerson Electric Industrial Controls [1980] ICR 795 at 800, EAT Talbot J and members, followed and applied in Barber at paragraph 38. In such a case it is the EAT's duty to put right the law on the facts available to the EAT; Glennie paragraph 12 citing House. (d) The EAT can see a glaring injustice in refusing to allow an unrepresented party to rely on evidence which could have been adduced at the Employment Tribunal; Glennie paragraph (e) The EAT can see an obvious knock-out point; Glennie, paragraph (f) The issue is a discrete one of pure law requiring no further factual enquiry; Glennie para 17 per Laws LJ. (g) It is of particular public importance for a legal point to be decided provided no further factual investigation and no further evaluation by the specialist Tribunal is required; Laws LJ in Leicestershire para 21. (7) The discretion is not to be exercised where by way of example; (a) What is relied upon is a chance of establishing lack of jurisdiction by calling fresh evidence; Barber para 20 as interpreted in Glennie para 15. (b) The issue arises as a result of lack of skill by a represented party, for that is not a sufficient reason; Jones para 20. (c) The point was not taken below as a result of a tactical decision by a representative or a party; Kumchyk at page 1123, approved in Glennie at para 15. (d) All the material is before the EAT but what is required is an evaluation and an assessment of this material and application of the law to it by the specialist first instance Tribunal; Leicestershire para 21. (e) A represented party has fought and lost a jurisdictional issue and now seeks a new hearing; Glennie para 15. That applies whether the jurisdictional issue is the same as that originally canvassed (normal retiring age as in Barber) or is a different way of establishing jurisdiction from that originally canvassed (associated employers and transfer of undertakings as in Russell v Elmdom Freight Terminal Ltd [1989] ICR 629 EAT Knox J and members). See the analysis in Glennie at paras 13 and 14 of these two cases. (f) What is relied upon is the high value of the case; Leicestershire para 21."

Additional factors which H.H. Judge McMullen considered relevant in *Rance* itself were:

(i)   the short time (in the context of protracted litigation) since the concession in question had been made;

(ii) the fact that the concession had been wrongly made in respect of 120 individual cases out of some 11,000 related cases being dealt with under protocols directed by the employment tribunal; and

(iii) the fact that the matter had been dealt with by the employment tribunal by way of a judgment on the papers without a contested hearing.

Unfortunately, there is no attempt in the judgment to reconcile the sometimes contradictory "principles" listed. In particular, para.6(c) appears to open the door to new arguments or the re-opening of conceded points wherever it is clear from the material before the EAT that the employment tribunal's decision was wrong (the words "a nullity" add nothing); whereas 7(b) and (c) appear much more restrictive. The rule is perhaps still most accurately stated, "The EAT will allow new points of law to be argued when it feels like it".

9   Case tracks and directions: the sift of appeals

6–066   **9.1 Consistent with the overriding objective, the EAT will seek to give directions for case management so that the case can be dealt with quickly, or better considered, and in the most effective and just way.**

6–067   **9.2 Applications and directions for case management will usually be dealt with on the papers ("the sift") by a judge, or by the Registrar with an appeal to a judge. Any party seeking directions** must serve a copy on all parties. Directions may be given at any stage, before or after the registration of a Notice of Appeal. An order made will contain a time for compliance, which must be observed or be the subject of an application by any party to vary or discharge it, or to seek an extension of time. Otherwise, failure to comply with an order in time or at all may result in the EAT exercising its power under Rule 26 to strike out the appeal, cross-appeal or respondent's Answer or debar the party from taking any further part in the proceedings or to make any other order it thinks fit, including an award of costs.

9.3 Any application to vary or discharge an order, or to seek an **6–068** extension of time, must be lodged at the EAT and served on the other parties within the time fixed for compliance. Such other parties must, if opposing the application and within 14 days (or such shorter period as may be ordered) of receiving it, submit their representations to the EAT and the other parties.

9.4 An application to amend a Notice of Appeal or respondent's **6–069** Answer must include the text of the original document with any changes clearly marked and identifiable, for example with deletions struck through in red and the text of the amendment either written or underlined in red. Any subsequent amendments will have to be in a different identifiable colour.

9.5 Notices of Appeal are sifted by a judge or the Registrar so as to **6–070** determine the most effective case management of the appeal. The sift will result in a decision as to which track the appeal will occupy, and directions will be given. There are 4 tracks:

    9.5.1 Rule 3(7) cases [see para 9.6 below].
    9.5.2 Preliminary Hearing (PH) cases [see paras 9.7–9.18 below].
    9.5.3 Full Hearing (FH) cases [see para 9.19 below].
    9.5.4 Fast Track Full Hearing (FTFH) cases [see paras 9.20–9.21 below].

The judge or Registrar may also stay (or *sist* in Scotland) the appeal for a period, normally 21 days pending the making or the conclusion of an application by the appellant to the Employment Tribunal (if necessary out of time) for a review or pending the response by the Employment Tribunal to an invitation from the judge or Registrar to clarify, supplement or give its written reasons.

Rule 3(7) cases (9.5.1)

9.6 The judge or Registrar, having considered the Notice of Appeal **6–071** and, if appropriate, having obtained any additional information, may decide that it or any of the grounds contained in it disclose no reasonable grounds for bringing the appeal or are an abuse of the process or otherwise likely to obstruct the just disposal of the proceedings. Reasons will be sent and within 28 days the appellant may submit a fresh Notice of Appeal for further consideration or request an oral hearing before a judge. At that hearing the judge may confirm the earlier decision or order that the appeal proceeds to a Preliminary or Full Hearing. A hearing under Rule 3(10), including judgment and any directions, will normally last not more than one hour. A judge or Registrar may also follow the Rule 3(7) procedure, of his or her own initiative, or on application, at any later stage of the proceedings, if appropriate.

Preliminary Hearing cases (9.5.2)

6–072 9.7 The purpose of a PH is to determine whether:

> 9.7.1 the grounds in the Notice of Appeal raise a point of law which gives the appeal a reasonable prospect of success at a FH; or
>
> 9.7.2 for some other compelling reason the appeal should be heard eg that the appellant seeks a declaration of incompatibility under the Human Rights Act 1998; or to argue that a decision binding on the EAT should be considered by a higher court.

6–073 9.8 Prior to the PH there will be automatic directions. These include sending the Notice of Appeal to the respondent(s) to the appeal. The direction may order or in any event will enable the respondent(s) to lodge and serve, within 14 days of the seal date of the order (unless otherwise directed), concise written submissions in response to the Notice of Appeal, dedicated to showing that there is no reasonable prospect of success for all or any grounds of any appeal. Such submissions will be considered at the PH.

6–074 9.9 If the respondent to the appeal intends to serve a cross-appeal this must be accompanied by written submissions and must be lodged and served within 14 days of service of the Notice of Appeal. The respondent to the appeal must make clear whether it is intended to advance the cross-appeal:

> 9.9.1 in any event (an unconditional cross-appeal); or
>
> 9.9.2 only if the Appellant succeeds (a conditional cross-appeal).

In either case the respondent is entitled to attend the PH, which will also amount to a PH of the cross-appeal, and make submissions.

9.10 All parties will be notified of the date fixed for the PH. In the **6–075** normal case, unless ordered otherwise, only the appellant and/or a representative should attend to make submissions to the EAT on the issue whether the Notice of Appeal raises a point of law with a reasonable prospect of success:

9.10.1 Except where the respondent to the appeal makes a cross-appeal, or the EAT orders a hearing with all parties present, the respondent to the appeal is not required to attend the hearing and is not usually permitted to take part in it. But any written submissions as referred to in (8) above will be considered at the PH.

9.10.2 If the appellant does not attend, the appeal may nevertheless be dealt with as above on written submissions, and be wholly or in part dismissed or allowed to proceed.

9.11 The PH, including judgment and directions, will normally last **6–076** no more than one hour.

9.12 The sift procedure will be applied to cross-appeals as well as **6–077** appeals. If an appeal has been assigned to the FH track, without a PH, and the respondent includes a cross-appeal in the respondent's Answer, the respondent must immediately apply to the EAT in writing on notice to the appellant for directions on the papers as to whether the EAT considers that there should be a PH of the cross-appeal.

9.13 If satisfied that the appeal (and/or the cross-appeal) should **6–078** be heard at a FH on all or some of the grounds of appeal, the EAT will give directions relating to, for example, a time estimate, any application for fresh evidence, a procedure in respect of matters of evidence before the Employment Tribunal not sufficiently appearing from the written reasons, the exchange and lodging of skeleton arguments and an appellant's Chronology, and bundles of documents and authorities.

9.14 Permission to amend a Notice of Appeal (or cross-appeal) may **6–079** be granted:

9.14.1 If the proposed amendment is produced at the hearing, then, if such amendment has not previously been notified to the other parties, and the appeal (or cross-appeal) might not have been permitted to proceed but for the amendment, the opposing party(ies) will have the opportunity to apply on notice to vary or discharge the permission to proceed, and for consequential directions as to the hearing or disposal of the appeal or cross-appeal.

9.14.2 If a draft amendment is not available at the PH, an application for permission to amend, in writing on notice to the other party(ies) in accordance with para 9.4 above, will be permitted to be made within 14 days. Where, but for such proposed amendment, the appeal (or cross-appeal) may not have been permitted to proceed to a FH, provision may be made in the order on the PH for the appeal (or cross-appeal) to be dismissed if the application for permission to amend is not made. Where such an application is made and refused, provision will be made for any party to have liberty to apply, in writing on notice to the other party(ies), as to the hearing or disposal of the appeal.

6–080   9.15 If not satisfied that the appeal, or any particular ground of it, should go forward to a FH, the EAT at the PH will dismiss the appeal, wholly or in part, and give a judgment setting out the reasons for doing so.

6–081   9.16 If an appeal is permitted to go forward to an FH on all grounds, a reasoned judgment will not normally be given.

6–082   9.17 Parties who become aware that a similar point is raised in other proceedings at an Employment Tribunal or the EAT are encouraged to co-operate in bringing this to the attention of the Registrar so that consideration can be given to the most expedient way of dealing with the cases, in particular to the possibility of having two or more appeals heard together.

6–083   9.18 If an appeal is permitted to go forward to an FH, a listing category will be assigned ie: P (recommended to be heard in the President's list);

A (complex, and raising point(s) of law of public importance);

B (medium level);

C (involving legal principles which are well settled).

Full Hearing cases (9.5.3)

6–084   9.19 If a judge or the Registrar decides to list the case for an FH without a PH s/he will consider appropriate directions, relating for example to amendment, further information, any application for fresh evidence, a procedure in respect of matters of evidence at the Employment Tribunal not sufficiently appearing from the written reasons, allegations of bias, apparent bias or improper conduct, provisions for skeleton arguments, appellant's Chronology and bundles of documents and of authorities, time estimates and listing category (as set out in para 9.18 above). Fast Track Full Hearing cases (9.5.4)

9.20 FH cases are normally heard in the order in which they are **6–085** received. However, there are times when it is expedient to hear an appeal as soon as it can be fitted into the list. Appeals placed in this Fast Track, at the discretion of a judge or the Registrar, will normally fall into the following cases:

9.20.1 appeals where the parties have made a reasoned case on the merits for an expedited hearing;

9.20.2 appeals against interim orders or decisions of an Employment Tribunal, particularly those which involve the taking of a step in the proceedings within a specified period, for example adjournments, further information, amendments, disclosure, witness orders;

9.20.3 appeals on the outcome of which other applications to the Employment Tribunal or the EAT or the civil courts depend;

9.20.4 appeals in which a reference to the European Court of Justice (ECJ), or a declaration of incompatibility under the Human Rights Act 1998, is sought;

9.20.5 appeals involving reinstatement, re-engagement, interim relief or a recommendation for action (discrimination cases).

9.21 Category C cases estimated to take two hours or less may also **6–086** be allocated to the Fast Track.

Rule 3(7) cases

See notes to r.3(7) and 3(10) at paras 5–027 and 5–029. **6–087**

Amendment

For notes on amending a notice of appeal to the Court of Appeal, equally **6–088** applicable to amendment of grounds of appeal to the EAT, see para.8–095.

10   Respondent's answer and directions

10.1 After the sift stage or a PH, at which a decision is made to **6–089** permit the appeal to go forward to an FH, the EAT will send the Notice of Appeal, with any amendments which have been permitted, and any submissions or skeleton argument lodged by the appellant, to all parties who are respondents to the appeal. Within 14 days of the seal date of the order (unless otherwise directed), respondents must lodge at the EAT and serve on the other parties a respondent's Answer. If it contains a cross-appeal, the appellant must within 14 days of service (unless otherwise directed), lodge and serve a Reply.

6–090   10.2 After lodgment and service of the respondent's Answer and of any Reply to a cross-appeal, the Registrar may, where necessary, invite applications from the parties in writing, on notice to all other parties, for directions, and may give any appropriate directions on the papers or may fix a day when the parties should attend on an Appointment for Directions.

6–091   10.3 A judge may at any time, upon consideration of the papers or at a hearing, make an order requiring or recommending consideration by the parties or any of them of compromise, conciliation, mediation or, in particular, reference to ACAS.

11   Complaints about the conduct of the employment tribunal hearing

6–092   11.1 An appellant who intends to complain about the conduct of the Employment Tribunal (for example bias, apparent bias or improper conduct by the Chairman or lay members or any procedural irregularity at the hearing) must include in the Notice of Appeal full particulars of each complaint made.

6–093   11.2 An appeal which is wholly or in part based on such a complaint will be sifted by a judge or the Registrar as set out in para 9.5 above and this may result in a decision as to the appropriate track which the appeal will occupy. At the sift stage or before, the judge or Registrar may postpone a decision as to track, and direct that the appellant or a representative provide an affidavit setting out full particulars of all allegations of bias or misconduct relied upon. At the sift stage the Registrar may enquire of the party making the complaint whether it is intended to proceed with it.

6–094   11.3 If the appeal is allocated to the PH or FH track, the EAT may take the following steps prior to such hearing within a time-limit set out in the relevant order:

> 11.3.1   require the appellant or a representative to provide, if not already provided, an affidavit as set out in para 11.2 above;
>
> 11.3.2   require any party to give an affidavit or to obtain a witness statement from any person who has represented any of the parties at the Tribunal hearing, and any other person present at the Tribunal hearing or a relevant part

of it, giving their account of the events set out in the affidavit of the appellant or the appellant's representative. For the above purpose, the EAT will provide copies of any affidavits received from or on behalf of the appellant to any other person from whom an account is sought;

11.3.3 seek comments, upon all affidavits or witness statements received, from the Chairman of the Employment Tribunal from which the appeal is brought and may seek such comments from the lay members of the Tribunal. For the above purpose, copies of all relevant documents will be provided by the EAT to the Chairman and, if appropriate, the lay members; such documents will include any affidavits and witness statements received, the Notice of Appeal and other relevant documents.

11.3.4 the EAT will on receipt supply to the parties copies of all affidavits, statements and comments received.

11.4 A respondent who intends to make such a complaint must include such particulars as set out in paras 11.1 and 11.2 above: **6–095**

11.4.1 (in the event of a PH being ordered in respect of the appellant's appeal, in accordance with para 9.5.2 above) in the cross-appeal referred to in para 9.9 above, or, in the absence of a cross-appeal, in written submissions, as referred to in para 9.8 above;

11.4.2 (in the event of no PH being ordered, in accordance with para 9.5.3 above) in his respondent's Answer. A similar procedure will then be followed as in para 11.3 above.

11.5 In every case which is permitted to go forward to an FH the EAT will give appropriate directions, ordinarily on the papers after notice to the appellant and respondent, as to the procedure to be adopted at, and material to be provided to, the FH; but such directions may be given at the sift stage or at a PH. **6–096**

11.6 Parties should note the following: **6–097**

11.6.1 The EAT will not permit complaints of the kind mentioned above to be raised or developed at the hearing of the appeal unless this procedure has been followed.

11.6.2 The EAT recognises that Chairmen and Employment Tribunals are themselves obliged to observe the overriding objective and are given wide powers and duties of case management (see Employment Tribunal (Constitu-

EAT, Practice Direction

tion and Rules of Procedure) Regulations 2004 (SI No 1861), so appeals in respect of their conduct of Employment Tribunals, which is in exercise of those powers and duties, are the less likely to succeed.

11.6.3 Unsuccessful pursuit of an allegation of bias or improper conduct, particularly in respect of case management decisions, may put the party raising it at risk of an order for costs.

Costs

6–098   The EAT's power to make a costs order is defined and circumscribed by r.34A at para.5–117. The PD is not capable of varying the circumstances in which the EAT may award costs; 11.6.2 merely operates as a warning that a party who unsuccessfully pursues an allegation of bias or improper conduct may be particularly likely to meet the conditions set out at r.34A.

12 Listing of appeals

6–099   12.1 Estimate of Length of Hearing: the lay members of the EAT are part-time members. They attend when available on pre-arranged dates. They do not sit for continuous periods. Consequently appeals which run beyond their estimated length have to be adjourned part-heard (often with substantial delay) until a day on which the judge and members are all available. To avoid inconvenience to the parties and to the EAT, and to avoid additional delay and costs suffered as a result of adjournment of part-heard appeals, all parties are required to ensure that the estimates of length of hearing (allowing for the fact that the parties can expect the EAT to have pre-read the papers and for the giving of a judgment) are accurate when first given. Any change in such estimate, or disagreement with an estimate made by the EAT on a sift or at a PH, is to be notified immediately to the Listing Officer.

6–100   12.2 If the EAT concludes that the hearing is likely to exceed the estimate, or if for other reasons the hearing may not be concluded within the time available, it may seek to avoid such adjournment by placing the parties under appropriate time limits in order to complete the presentation of the submissions within the estimated or available time.

6–101   12.3 Subject to para 12.6 below a date will be fixed for a PH as soon as practicable after the sift (referred to in para 9.5 above) and for an FH as soon as practicable after the sift if no PH is ordered, or otherwise after the PH.

6–102   12.4 The Listing Officer will normally consult the parties on dates, and will accommodate reasonable requests if practicable, but is not bound to do so. Once the date is fixed, the appeal will be set down in the list. A party finding that the date which has been fixed causes serious difficulties may apply to the Listing Officer for it to be changed, having first notified all other parties entitled to appear on the date of their application and the reasons for it.

12.5 Parties receiving such an application must, as soon as poss- 6–103
ible and within 7 days, notify the Listing Officer of their views.

12.6 In addition to this fixed date procedure, a list ("the warned 6–104
list") may be drawn up. Cases will be placed in such warned list at the discretion of the Listing Officer or may be so placed by the direction of a judge or the Registrar. These will ordinarily be short cases, or cases where expedition has been ordered. Parties or their representatives will be notified that their case has been included in this list, and as much notice as possible will be given of the intention to list a case for hearing, when representations by way of objection from the parties will be considered by the Listing Officer and if necessary on appeal to the Registrar or a judge. The parties may apply on notice to all other parties for a fixed date for hearing.

12.7 Other cases may be put in the list by the Listing Officer with 6–105
the consent of the parties at shorter notice: for example, where other cases have been settled or withdrawn or where it appears that they will take less time than originally estimated. Parties who wish their cases to be taken as soon as possible and at short notice should notify the Listing Officer. Representations by way of objection may be made by the parties to the Listing Officer and if necessary by appeal to a judge or the Registrar.

12.8 Each week an up-to-date list for the following week will be 6–106
prepared, including any changes which have been made, in particular specifying cases which by then have been given fixed dates. The list appears on the EAT website.

EAT website

The address is *http://www.employmentappeals.gov.uk*. 6–107

13 Skeleton arguments

(This part of the Practice Direction does not apply to an appeal 6–108
heard in Scotland, unless otherwise directed in relation to that appeal by the EAT in Edinburgh)

13.1 Skeleton arguments must be provided by all parties in all 6–109
hearings, unless the EAT is notified by a party or representative in writing that the Notice of Appeal or respondent's Answer or relevant application contains the full argument, or the EAT otherwise directs

in a particular case. It is the practice of the EAT for all the members to read the papers in advance. A well-structured skeleton argument helps the members and the parties to focus on the point(s) of law required to be decided and so make the oral hearing more effective.

6–110　13.2 The skeleton argument should be concise and should identify and summarise the point(s) of law, the steps in the legal argument and the statutory provisions and authorities to be relied upon, identifying them by name, page and paragraph and stating the legal proposition sought to be derived from them. It is not, however, the purpose of the skeleton argument to argue the case on paper in detail. The parties can be referred to by name or as they appeared at the Employment Tribunal ie claimant (C) and respondent (R).

6–111　13.3 The skeleton argument should state the form of order which the party will ask the EAT to make at the hearing: for example, in the case of an appellant, whether the EAT will be asked to remit the whole or part of the case to the same or to a different Employment Tribunal, or whether the EAT will be asked to substitute a different decision for that of the Employment Tribunal.

6–112　13.4 The appellant's skeleton argument must be accompanied by a Chronology of events relevant to the appeal which, if possible, should be agreed by the parties. That will normally be taken as an uncontroversial document, unless corrected by another party or the EAT.

6–113　13.5 Unless impracticable, the skeleton argument should be prepared using the pagination in the index to the appeal bundle. In a case where a note of the evidence at the Employment Tribunal has been produced, the skeleton argument should identify the parts of the record to which that party wishes to refer.

6–114　13.6 Represented parties should give the instructions necessary for their representative to comply with this procedure within the time limits.

6–115　13.7 The fact that settlement negotiations are in progress in relation to the appeal does not excuse delay in lodging and exchanging skeleton arguments.

6–116　13.8 A skeleton argument may be lodged by the appellant with the Notice of Appeal or by the respondent with the respondent's Answer.

6–117　13.9 Skeleton arguments must (if not already so lodged):

　　　13.9.1 be lodged at the EAT not less than 10 days (unless otherwise ordered) before the date fixed for the PH, appeal against Registrar's Order, Rule 3 (10) hearing or Appointment for Directions; or, if the hearing is fixed at less than 7 days' notice, as soon as possible after the hearing date has been notified. In the event that the hearing has been ordered to be heard with all parties present, the skeleton arguments must also then be exchanged between the parties;

13.9.2 be lodged at the EAT, *and* exchanged between the parties, not less than 21 days before the FH;

13.9.3 in the case of warned list and fast track FH cases be lodged at the EAT and exchanged between the parties as soon as possible and (unless the hearing date is less than 7 days later) in any event within 7 days after the parties have been notified that the case is expedited or in the warned list.

13.10 Failure to follow this procedure may lead to an adjournment **6–118** of an appeal or to dismissal for non-compliance with the PD, and to an award of costs. The party in default may also be required to attend before the EAT to explain their failure. It will always mean that the defaulting party must immediately despatch any delayed skeleton argument to the EAT by hand or by fax or by email to *londoneat@ETs.gsi.gov.uk* or, as appropriate, *edinburgheat@ETs.gsi.gov.uk* and (unless notified by the EAT to the contrary) bring to the hearing sufficient copies (a minimum of 6) of the skeleton argument and any authorities referred to. The EAT staff will not be responsible for supplying or copying these on the morning of the hearing.

Purpose of the skeleton argument

Paragraph 13.2 asserts that it is not the purpose of the skeleton argument to **6–119** argue the case on paper in detail, but the EAT itself does not always proceed as if that is so. It is not suggested that this guidance should be ignored, but neither is it prudent to take it quite at face value. Judicial views formed in the course of pre-reading can be difficult to shift in oral argument.

Reference to the parties

Reference to "appellant" and "respondent" (as the parties appear before the **6–120** EAT) is implicitly discouraged. This is because if the appeal is brought by the respondent to the original claim, the respondent becomes the appellant and the claimant becomes the respondent. Referring to the parties to the appeal as "appellant" and "respondent" can therefore lead to ambiguity and confusion.

Form of order

For commentary on the circumstances in which the EAT will substitute a **6–121** different decision for that of the employment tribunal see para.5–011. As to the decision whether any remittal should be to the same or a different tribunal, see para.5–106.

EAT, Practice Direction

Time limits for skeleton arguments

6–122   Where the skeleton argument is unavoidably delayed, the clerk responsible for the case at the EAT (whose initials are the two letters at the end of the EAT case number) is likely to be a helpful source of guidance as to the time by which skeletons can be lodged without real inconvenience to the EAT.

14   Citation of authorities

General

6–123   **14.1 It is undesirable for parties to cite the same case from different sets of reports. The parties should, if practicable, agree which report will be used at the hearing. Where the Employment Tribunal has cited from a report it may be convenient to cite from the same report.**

6–124   **14.2 It is the responsibility of a party wishing to cite any authority to provide photocopies for the use of each member of the Tribunal and photocopies or at least a list for the other parties. All authorities should be bundled, indexed and incorporated in an agreed bundle.**

6–125   **14.3 Parties are advised not to cite an unnecessary number of authorities either in skeleton arguments or in oral argument at the hearing. It is of assistance to the EAT if parties could highlight or sideline passages relied on within the bundle of authorities.**

6–126   **14.4 It is unnecessary for a party citing a case in oral argument to read it in full to the EAT. Whenever a case is cited in a skeleton argument or in an oral argument it is helpful if the legal proposition for which it is cited is stated. References need only be made to the relevant passages in the report. If the formulation of the legal proposition based on the authority cited is not in dispute, further examination of the authority will often be unnecessary.**

6–127   **14.5 For decisions of the ECJ, the official report should be used where possible.**

PH cases

6–128   **14.6 If it is thought necessary to cite any authority at a PH, appeal against Registrar's Order, Rule 3 (10) hearing or Appointment for Directions, 3 copies should be provided for the EAT (one copy if a judge is sitting alone): and additional copies for any other parties notified. All authorities should be bundled, indexed and incorporated in one agreed bundle.**

FH cases

6–129   **14.7 The parties must co-operate in agreeing a list of authorities and must jointly or severally lodge a list and 3 bundles of copies (one copy if judge sitting alone) of such authorities at the EAT not less than 7 days before the FH, unless otherwise ordered.**

This guidance is strongly reminiscent of that provided by CPR 52 PD (see para.8–156), and similar comments (see para.8–172) apply. See also *Sage (UK) Ltd v G Bacco* UKEAT/0597/06, in which H.H.J. Clark made a practice statement to the effect that a party relying on a reported case should provide a photocopy of the report and include the correct citation in its list of authorities. Transcripts of judgments should only be used where no report was available.

6–130

15   Disposal of appeals by consent

15.1 An appellant who wishes to abandon or withdraw an appeal should notify the other parties and the EAT immediately. If a settlement is reached, the parties should inform the EAT as soon as possible. The appellant should submit to the EAT a letter signed by or on behalf of the appellant and signed also by or on behalf of the respondent, asking the EAT for permission to withdraw the appeal and to make a consent order in the form of an attached draft signed by or for both parties dismissing the appeal, together with any other agreed order.

6–131

15.2 If the other parties do not agree to the proposed order the EAT should be informed. Written submissions should be lodged at the EAT and served on the parties. Any outstanding issue may be determined on the papers by the EAT, particularly if it relates to costs, but the EAT may fix an oral hearing to determine the outstanding matters in dispute between the parties.

6–132

15.3 If the parties reach an agreement that the appeal should be allowed by consent, and that an order made by the Employment Tribunal should be reversed or varied or the matter remitted to the Employment Tribunal on the ground that the decision contains an error of law, it is usually necessary for the matter to be heard by the EAT to determine whether there is a good reason for making the proposed order. On notification by the parties, the EAT will decide whether the appeal can be dealt with on the papers or by a hearing at which one or more parties or their representatives should attend to argue the case for allowing the appeal and making the order that the parties wish the EAT to make.

6–133

15.4 If the application for permission to withdraw an appeal is made close to the hearing date the EAT may require the attendance of the Appellant and/or a representative to explain the reasons for delay in making a decision not to pursue the appeal.

6–134

16   Appellant's failure to present a response

16.1 If the appellant in a case did not present a Response (ET3) to the Employment Tribunal and did not apply to the Employment Tribunal for an extension of time for doing so, or applied for such an

6–135

extension and was refused, the Notice of Appeal must include particulars directed to the following issues, namely whether:

16.1.1 there is a good excuse for failing to present a Response (ET3) and (if that be the case) for failing to apply for such an extension of time; and

16.1.2 there is a reasonably arguable defence to the Claim (ET1).

6–136 16.2 In order to satisfy the EAT on these issues, the appellant must lodge at the EAT, together with the Notice of Appeal, a witness statement explaining in detail the circumstances in which there has been a failure to serve a Response (ET3) in time or apply for such an extension of time, the reason for that failure and the facts and matters relied upon for contesting the Claim (ET1) on the merits. There should be exhibited to the witness statement all relevant documents and a completed draft Response (ET3).

New point of law

6–137 A respondent that did not present a response to the employment tribunal is not thereby precluded from appealing, notwithstanding that any argument it may raise must necessarily be raised for the first time on appeal (see *Atos Origin v Haddock* [2005] I.R.L.R. 20 and para.6–065).

17 Hearings

6–138 17.1 Where consent is to be obtained from the parties pursuant to s28(3) of the ETA 1996 to an appeal commencing or continuing to be heard by a judge together with only one lay member, the parties must, prior to the commencement or continuation of such hearing in front of a two-member court, themselves or by their representatives each sign a form containing the name of the one member remaining, and stating whether the member is a person falling within s28(1)(a) or (b) of the ETA 1996.

6–139 17.2 Video and Telephone Hearings. Facilities can be arranged for the purpose of holding short PHs or short Appointments for Directions by video or telephone link, upon the application (in writing) of an appellant or respondent who, or whose representative, has a relevant disability (supported by appropriate medical evidence). Such facilities will only be made available for a hearing at which the party or, if more than one party will take part, both or all parties is or are legally represented. An application that a hearing should be so held will be determined by a judge or the Registrar, and must be made well in advance of the date intended for the hearing, so that arrangements may be made. So far as concerns video conferencing facilities, they may not always be available, dependent on the location of the parties: as for telephone hearings or, especially, telephone conferencing facilities, consideration may need to be given as to payment by a party or parties of any additional expenditure resulting.

18 Handing down of judgments

(England and Wales)

18.1 When the EAT reserves judgment to a later date, the parties **6–140** will be notified of the date when it is ready to be handed down. It is not necessary for a party or representative to attend unless it is intended to make an application, either for costs or for permission to appeal to the Court of Appeal (see paras 19 and 21 below), in which case notice of that fact, and, in the case of an intended application for costs, notice of the matters set out in para 19.3 below, should be given to the other party(ies) and to the EAT 48 hours before the date.

18.2 Copies of the judgment will be available to the parties or their **6–141** representatives on the morning on which it is handed down or, if so directed by a judge, earlier to the parties' representatives in draft subject to terms as to confidentiality. Where a draft judgment has been provided in advance, any intended application for permission to appeal referred to in para 18.1 above must be accompanied by a draft Notice of Appeal.

18.3 The judgment will be pronounced without being read aloud, **6–142** by the judge who presided or by another judge, on behalf of the EAT. The judge may deal with any application or may refer it to the judge and/or the Tribunal who heard the appeal, whether to deal with on the papers or at a further oral hearing on notice.

18.4 Transcripts of unreserved judgments at a PH, appeal against **6–143** Registrar's Order, Appointment for Directions and Rule 3(10) hearing will not (save as below) be produced and provided to the parties:

18.4.1 Where an appeal, or any ground of appeal, is dismissed in the presence of the appellant, no transcript of the judgment is produced unless, within 14 days of the seal date of the order, either party applies to the EAT for a transcript, or the EAT of its own initiative directs that a judgment be transcribed (in circumstances such as those set out in para 18.5.2 below).

18.4.2 Where an appeal or any ground of appeal is dismissed in the absence of the appellant, a transcript will be supplied to the appellant.

18.4.3 Where an appeal is allowed to go forward to a PH or an FH, a judgment will not normally be delivered, but, if it is, the judge may order it to be transcribed, in which case a transcript is provided to the parties.

6–144   18.5 Transcripts of unreserved judgments at an FH. Where judgment is delivered at the hearing, no transcript will be produced and provided to the parties unless:

18.5.1 either party applies for it to the EAT within 14 days of that hearing; or

18.5.2 the EAT of its own initiative directs that the judgment be transcribed, eg where it is considered that a point of general importance arises or that the matter is to be remitted to, or otherwise continued before, the Employment Tribunal.

6–145   18.6 Where judgment at either a PH or an FH is reserved, and later handed down in writing, a copy is provided to all parties, and to recognised law reporters.

(Scotland)

6–146   18.7 Judgments are normally reserved in Scotland and will be handed down as soon as practicable thereafter on a provisional basis to both parties who will thereafter have a period of 14 days to make any representations with regard to expenses, leave to appeal or any other relevant matter. At the expiry of that period or after such representations have been dealt with, whichever shall be the later, an order will be issued to conform to the original judgment.

EAT Website

6–147   18.8 All FH judgments which are transcribed or handed down will be posted on the EAT website.

Draft judgments

6–148   See para.8–174.

19   Costs (Expenses in Scotland)

6–149   19.1 In this PD "costs" includes legal costs, expenses, allowances paid by the Secretary of State and payment in respect of time spent in preparing a case. Such costs may relate to interim applications or hearings or to a PH or FH.

6–150   19.2 An application for costs must be made either during or at the end of a relevant hearing, or in writing to the Registrar within 14 days of the seal date of the relevant order of the EAT or, in the case of a reserved judgment, as provided for in paragraph 18.1 above.

19.3 The party seeking the order must state the legal ground on 6–151 which the application is based and the facts on which it is based and, by a schedule or otherwise, show how the costs have been incurred. If the application is made in respect of only part of the proceedings, particulars must be given showing how the costs have been incurred on that specific part. If the party against whom the order is sought wishes the EAT to have regard to means and/or an alleged inability to pay, a witness statement giving particulars and exhibiting any documents must be served on the other party(ies) and lodged with the EAT: further directions may be required to be given by the EAT in such case.

19.4 Such application may be resolved by the EAT on the papers, 6–152 provided that the opportunity has been given for representations in writing by all relevant parties, or the EAT may refer the matter for an oral hearing, and may assess the costs either on the papers or at an oral hearing, or refer the matter for detailed assessment.

19.5 Wasted Costs. An application for a wasted costs order must be 6–153 made in writing, setting out the nature of the case upon which the application is based and the best particulars of the costs sought to be recovered. Such application must be lodged with the EAT and served upon the party(ies) sought to be charged: further directions may be required to be given by the EAT in such case.

19.6 Where the EAT makes any costs order it shall provide written 6–154 reasons for so doing so if such order is made by decision on the papers. If such order is made at a hearing, then written reasons will be provided if a request is made at the hearing or within 21 days of the seal date of the costs order. The Registrar shall send a copy of the written reasons to all the parties to the proceedings.

20 Review

Where an application is made for a review of a judgment or order 6–155 of the EAT, it can be considered on paper by a judge who may, if he or she heard the original appeal or made the original order alone, without lay members, make such order, granting, refusing, adjourning or otherwise dealing with such application, as he or she may think fit. If the original judgment or order was made by the judge together with lay members, then the judge may, pursuant to Rule 33, consider and refuse such application for review on the papers. If the judge does not refuse such application, he or she may make any relevant further order, but would not grant such application without notice to the opposing party and reference to the lay members, for consideration with them, either on paper or in open court.

21 Appeals from the EAT

Appeals heard in England and Wales

6–156   21.1 An application to the EAT for permission to appeal to the Court of Appeal must be made (unless the EAT otherwise orders) at the hearing or when a reserved judgment is handed down as provided in paras 18.1 and 18.2 above. If not made then, or if refused, or unless the EAT otherwise orders, any such applications must be made to the Court of Appeal within 14 days of the sealed order. An application for an extension of time for permission to appeal may be entertained by the EAT where a case is made out to the satisfaction of a judge or Registrar that there is a need to delay until after a transcript is received (expedited if appropriate). Applications for an extension of time for permission to appeal should however normally be made to the Court of Appeal.

6–157   21.2 The party seeking permission must state the point of law to be advanced and the grounds.

Appeals heard in Scotland

6–158   21.3 An application to the EAT for permission to appeal to the Court of Session must be made within 42 days of the date of the hearing where judgment is delivered at that hearing: if judgment is reserved, within 42 days of the date the transcript was sent to parties.

6–159   21.4 The party seeking permission must state the point of law to be advanced and the grounds.

THE HONOURABLE MR JUSTICE BURTON

PRESIDENT

Dated: 9 December 2004

Application for permission to appeal to the Court of Appeal

6–160   See para.7–019.

FORM 1

Notice of appeal from decision of employment tribunal

1 The Appellant is (*name and address of the Appellant*):-   **6–161**

2 Any communication relating to this appeal may be sent to the Appellant at (*Appellant's address for service, including telephone number if any*):-

3 The Appellant appeals from (*here give particulars of the judgment, decision or order of the Employment Tribunal from which the appeal is brought including the location of the Employment Tribunal and the date*):-

4 The parties to the proceedings before the Employment Tribunal, other than the Appellant, were (*names and addresses of other parties to the proceedings resulting in judgment, decision or order appealed from*):-

5 Copies of: the written record of the Employment Tribunal's judgment, decision or order and the Written Reasons of the Employment Tribunal the Claim (ET1) and Response (ET3) or an explanation as to why any of these documents are not included are attached to this notice. [If relevant.] [If the Appellant has made an application to the Employment Tribunal for a review of its judgment or decision, a copy of such application, together with the judgment and Written Reasons of the Employment Tribunal in respect of that review application, or a statement by or on behalf of the Appellant, if such be the case, that a judgment is awaited, is attached to this Notice. If any of these documents exist but cannot be included, then a written explanation must be given.]

6. The grounds upon which this appeal is brought are that the Employment Tribunal erred in law in that
(*here set out in paragraphs the various grounds of appeal*):-

Signed ....

Date: ....

N.B. The details entered on your Notice of Appeal must be legible and suitable for photocopying. The use of black ink or typescript is recommended

EAT, Practice Direction

CHAPTER 7

CIVIL PROCEDURE RULES PART 52

Contents
RULES

General

For commentary on the historical background to the far-reaching reforms of the **7–001** civil appeals process that came into force on May 2, 2000, see *Civil Procedure 2007*, 52.0.2–52.0.8.

Jurisdiction

The Court of Appeal is a statutory body whose constitution and general powers **7–002** are governed by ss.1–3, 15–18 and 53–58 of the Supreme Court Act 1981. By s.37 of the Employment Tribunals Act 1996 appeal lies to the Court of Appeal (or in proceedings in Scotland, to the Court of Session) from the EAT on any question of law. For commentary on the various categories of error of law, see paras 5–015—5–021.

Nature of appeal

In general, an appeal lies against the EAT's order, not against its reasoning. For **7–003** example, in *Lake v Lake* [1955] P. 336; [1955] 3 W.L.R. 145, the husband's petition for divorce on grounds of cruelty and adultery was dismissed on the ground that adultery had been condoned; the wife sought to appeal the finding that she had committed adultery. The Court of Appeal held that no appeal lay against the lower court's reasoning in the absence of a challenge to the order.

An important exception to this rule was made by the Court of Appeal in *Curtis v London Rent Assessment Committee* [1998] 3 W.L.R. 1427; [1999] Q.B. 92. A landlord had appealed the decision of a rent assessment committee, making a number of complaints about the manner in which it had approached its decision. He had won his appeal, with an order remitting the case to the committee for re-hearing, on only one of these grounds. When he sought to appeal further, the Court of Appeal held that if he was correct in saying that the judge's rulings on the substantive issues were wrong or were such as to mislead a new committee, the judge's order had not given him all he was entitled to. It must equally be open to an appellant who has won a remitted hearing on his appeal to the EAT to appeal further if he contends that the basis on which he has won his appeal is apt to mislead the tribunal on the rehearing.

Points not argued below

7–004   The Court of Appeal's approach to points not argued below is stated by Widgery L.J. in *Wilson v Liverpool Corp* [1971] 1 W.L.R. 302 at 307: "[I]f a point is not taken in the court of trial, it cannot be taken in the appeal court unless that court is in possession of all the material necessary to enable it to dispose of the matter finally, without injustice to the other party, and without recourse to a further hearing below." Widgery L.J. continued: "I recognise, as does Lord Denning M.R., that being a rule of practice this rule contains an element of discretion. There may well be cases in which justice demands that a different view be taken owing to the special circumstances of the case. . . ".

Civil Procedure 2007 quotes (at para.52.8.2) the more discouraging remarks of May L.J. in *Jones v MBNA International Bank*, unreported, June 30, 2000 at para.52. See however the analysis of Peter Gibson L.J. (with whom May L.J. agreed) at paras 38–40: since the Court of Appeal in *Jones* was persuaded that it was not in possession of all the material necessary to enable it to dispose of the matter finally, the decision that case is wholly consistent with the rule as stated in *Wilson*, and May L.J.'s remarks, to whatever extent they would seem to suggest a stricter rule, are obiter. See also *Hellyer Brothers Ltd v McLeod* [1987] I.C.R. 526, where the approach of the EAT (see para.6–065) is described as "more stringent" than that of the Court of Appeal.

Overriding objective

7–005   Part 1.2 of the Civil Procedure Rules requires the court to give effect to the overriding objective when it exercises any power or interprets any rule. The overriding objective is stated at Pt 1.1, in terms slightly more elaborate than those in which it appears in the Employment Tribunals (Constitution and Rules of Procedure) Regulations 2004, as follows:

7–006   "(1) These Rules are a new procedural code with the overriding objective of enabling the court to deal with cases justly.

    (2) Dealing with a case justly includes, so far as is practicable—

        (a) ensuring that the parties are on an equal footing;
        (b) saving expense;
        (c) dealing with the case in ways which are proportionate—

            (i) to the amount of money involved;
            (ii) to the importance of the case;
            (iii) to the complexity of the issues; and
            (iv) to the financial position of each party;

        (d) ensuring that it is dealt with expeditiously and fairly; and
        (e) allotting to it an appropriate share of the court's resources, while taking into account the need to allot resources to other cases."

Court of Appeal material on the internet

7–007   The Court Service website includes a section dedicated to the Court of Appeal. Navigating to it from the homepage of the Court Service at *www.hmcourtsservice.gov.uk* is less straightforward than might be hoped, but the address "*www.civilappeals.gov.uk*" typed into a browser redirects to the correct site, and googling "civil appeals" will also reach it. The site provides access to court forms, (which, at the time of writing can be edited and printed, but not saved,) daily cause lists, forms, guidance notes, selected judgments from 1996 and other useful information. Note that on the homepage of this section there are two links called "forms and guidance." The one of the left hand side of the page directs the user to a search form; the other, on the right hand side, under the heading "further information," provides a more user-friendly list of direct links to forms and guidance notes specific to the Court of Appeal.

All significant judgments from August 1999 and all substantive judgments from January 2003 (new judgments appearing within three days of handing down) are published on the website of the British and Irish Legal Information Institute at *www.bailii.org*.

Unrepresented parties

Similar comments apply as to unrepresented parties in the EAT (para.5–004), **7–008** except that for appeals to the Court of Appeal the Royal Courts of Justice CAB is a further source of free advice.

Scope and interpretation

52.1—(1) The rules in this Part apply to appeals to—   **7–009**

    (a) **the civil division of the Court of Appeal;**

    (b) **the High Court; and**

    (c) **a county court.**

(2) [This Part does not apply to an appeal in detailed assessment proceedings against a decision of an authorised court officer.]

[. . .]

(Rules 47.20 to 47.23 deal with appeals against a decision of an authorised court officer in detailed assessment proceedings)

(3) In this Part—

    (a) **"appeal" includes an appeal by way of case stated;**

    (b) **"appeal court" means the court to which an appeal is made;**

    (c) **"lower court" means the court, tribunal or other person or body from whose decision an appeal is brought;**

    (d) **"appellant" means a person who brings or seeks to bring an appeal;**

    (e) **"respondent" means—**

        (i) **a person other than the appellant who was a party to the proceedings in the lower court and who is affected by the appeal; and**

        (ii) **a person who is permitted by the appeal court to be a party to the appeal; and**

    (f) **"appeal notice" means an appellant's or respondent's notice.**

(4) This Part is subject to any rule, enactment or practice direction which sets out special provisions with regard to any particular category of appeal.

Definitions

7-010   By CPR r.2.3(1) "court officer" means a member of the court staff.

7-011   The definitions given at 52.1(3) reflect the applicability of Pt 52 to a variety of appeals to the High Court or the county courts as well as to the Court of Appeal. This commentary is concerned only with appeals from the Employment Appeal Tribunal to the Court of Appeal, so for these purposes "appeal court" means the Court of Appeal and "lower court" means the Employment Appeal Tribunal.

Parties to comply with the practice direction

7-012   **52.2 All parties to an appeal must comply with the relevant practice direction.**

Status of practice directions

7-013   Practice directions, previously an exercise of the inherent power of the courts to regulate their own procedure, are governed by s.5 of the Civil Procedure Act 1997, as amended with effect from April 3, 2006. However, there is nothing in the new statutory power to make practice directions that reduce the force of Hale L.J.'s observations on practice directions in *Re C (Legal Aid: Preparation of a Bill of Costs)* [2001] 1 F.L.R. 602 at para.21: "Practice Directions are not made by statutory instrument. They are not laid before Parliament or subject to either the negative or positive resolution procedures in Parliament. They go through no democratic process at all, although if approved by the Lord Chancellor he will bear ministerial responsibility for them to Parliament." In *Godwin v Swindon BC* [2002] 1 W.L.R. 997; [2002] 4 All E.R. 641, May L.J. said "Practice Directions are subordinate to the Rules. They are, in my view, at best a weak aid to the interpretation of the rules themselves."

7-014   The latter remark should not of course be understood as meaning that the only or best use to be made of practice directions is as a weak aid to the construction of the rules themselves, but merely that, viewed specifically as an aid to the construction of the rules, the assistance they provide is weak. Their proper function is to regulate practice within the rules and to fill gaps left by the rules (see *R. (on the application of Terence Patrick Ewing) v Department of Constitutional Affairs* [2006] 2 All E.R. 993 and the cases there cited).

Permission

7-015   **52.3—(1) An appellant or respondent requires permission to appeal—**

          (a) where the appeal is from a decision of a judge in a county court or the High Court, except where the appeal is against—

               (i) a committal order;

               (ii) a refusal to grant habeas corpus; or

               (iii) a secure accommodation order made under section 25 of the Children Act 1989 (c.41) or

          (b) as provided by the relevant practice direction.

(Other enactments may provide that permission is required for particular appeals)

(2) An application for permission to appeal may be made—

    (a) to the lower court at the hearing at which the decision to be appealed was made; or

    (b) to the appeal court in an appeal notice.

(Rule 52.4 sets out the time limits for filing an appellant's notice at the appeal court. Rule 52.5 sets out the time limits for filing a respondent's notice at the appeal court. Any application for permission to appeal to the appeal court must be made in the appeal notice (see rules 52.4(1) and 52.5(3))

(Rule 52.13(1) provides that permission is required from the Court of Appeal for all appeals to that court from a decision of a county court or the High Court which was itself made on appeal)

(3) Where the lower court refuses an application for permission to appeal, a further application for permission to appeal may be made to the appeal court.

(4) Subject to paragraph (4A), where the appeal court, without a hearing, refuses permission to appeal, the person seeking permission may request the decision to be reconsidered at a hearing.

(4A) Where the Court of Appeal refuses permission to appeal without a hearing, it may, if it considers that the application is totally without merit, make an order that the person seeking permission may not request the decision to be reconsidered at a hearing. The court may not make such an order in family proceedings.

('Family proceedings' is defined by section 32 of the Matrimonial and Family Proceedings Act 1984)

(4B) Rule 3.3(5) will not apply to an order that the person seeking permission may not request the decision to be reconsidered at a hearing made under paragraph (4A).

(5) A request under paragraph (4) must be filed within seven days after service of the notice that permission has been refused.

(6) Permission to appeal may be given only where—

    (a) the court considers that the appeal would have a real prospect of success; or

    (b) there is some other compelling reason why the appeal should be heard.

(7) An order giving permission may—

    (a) limit the issues to be heard; and

    (b) be made subject to conditions.

(Rule 3.1(3) also provides that the court may make an order subject to conditions)

(Rule 25.15 provides for the court to order security for costs of an appeal)

Definitions

7–016   "Judge" means, unless the context otherwise requires, a judge, Master or district judge or a person authorised to act as such: CPR r.2.3(1).

Permission to appeal from the EAT

7–017   By s.37(1) of the Employment Tribunals Act 1996, appeal lies to the Court of Appeal or in the case of proceedings in Scotland to the Court of Session from any decision or order of the EAT with the permission of the EAT or of the relevant appeal court.

Vexatious litigants

7–018   There is no appeal from a decision of the EAT refusing leave for the institution or continuance, or for the making of an application in, proceedings by a person who is the subject of an order restricting vexatious proceedings under s.33 of the ETA 1996: s.37(3).

Application for permission

7–019   Paragraph 21.1 of the EAT PD (see para.6–156) provides that an application to the EAT for permission to appeal to the Court of Appeal "must" be made (unless the EAT otherwise orders) at the hearing or when a reserved judgment is handed down. The practice direction to Pt 52 provides at para.4.6 that an application for permission to appeal "should" be made orally at the hearing at which the decision to be appealed against is made. Rule 52.3(2), however, simply provide that permission may be requested either to the lower court at the hearing at which the decision was made or the appeal court. Practice directions are subordinate to the rules themselves, as noted above at para.7–013, so a dissatisfied party may without sanction apply to the Court of Appeal for permission to appeal without first applying to the EAT.

There are usually good reasons, as pointed out in *Civil Procedure 2007*, para.52.3.4, for making an initial application to the EAT:

> "(a) The judge below is fully seized of the matter and so the application will take minimal time. Indeed the judge may have already decided that the case raises questions fit for appeal. (b) An application at this stage involves neither party in additional costs. (c) No harm is done if the application fails. The litigant enjoys two bites at the cherry. (d) No harm is done if the application succeeds, but the litigant subsequently decides not to appeal. (e) If the application succeeds and the litigant subsequently decides to appeal, he avoids the expensive and time-consuming permission stage in the appeal court." It was said in *Re T (a Child)* [2002] EWCA Civ 1736 [13] by Thorpe L.J. that this guidance should be followed "in the vast majority of cases."

Two contrary observations may be made, however. The first is that where the judgment of the lower court is reserved, then unless there is some other reason why advocates need attend when it is handed down, the application will not be cost-free. The second is unintentionally underlined by Thorpe L.J. in the same paragraph: "The judge thereby has an opportunity to give on the requisite form his or her reasons for rejecting the application, the statement of which may be of some value to this court if the permission application is subsequently renewed." The applicant may legitimately make a tactical choice to deprive the Court of Appeal of that assistance if he does not consider it likely to be to his advantage. See also the notes on conditional permission to appeal at para.7–030 below.

If an application for permission is not made to the EAT when judgment is handed down, then unless the proposing appellant has requested an adjournment of the hearing for the purpose of an application for permission in accordance with PD 4.3B, the EAT has no power to hear a subsequent permission application: any application must now be made to the Court of Appeal. See *Balmoral Group v Borealis (UK) Ltd* [2006] EWHC 2228.

Refusal of permission

Article 6 of the European Convention of Human Rights requires that refusal of **7–020** permission must be adequately reasoned (*Hyams v Plender* [2001] 1 W.L.R. 32 at para.17).

52.3(4)—Where permission is refused without a hearing

The Court of Appeal has a discretion whether to deal with an application initially **7–021** on paper or to list it for an oral permission hearing, but where it is refused without an oral hearing the unsuccessful applicant may request an oral hearing. Although the Rules do not in terms provide that the request must be granted, PD 4.13 refers to the applicant's "right to have [the decision] reconsidered at an oral hearing," and *Jolly v Jay* [2002] EWCA Civ 277 and *Bulled v Khayat* [2002] EWCA Civ 804, holding that no oral hearing need be held where the Court of Appeal plainly lacks jurisdiction, proceed on the assumption that an oral hearing was otherwise an entitlement. Paragraph 52.3(4A) now modifies that position slightly.

52.3(4A)—"totally without merit"

This is wider than the class of appeals for which the Court of Appeal plainly lacks **7–022** jurisdiction discussed in *Jolly v Jay* and *Bulled v Khayat* (above). The mechanism chosen to exclude unmeritorious applications from the right of an oral permission hearing is to allow the court to prohibit the person seeking permission from requesting the decision to be reconsidered at a hearing. It must be implicit that if such a request is made in the teeth of an order prohibiting it, it need not be granted.

52.3(4B)

Rule 3.3(5) provides that where an order is made without hearing the parties or **7–023** giving them an opportunity to make representations, they may apply to have it set aside, varied or stayed and must be told of that right.

Request for oral permission hearing must be filed within 7 days

By CPR r.2.8, "days" means clear days, so if notice of refusal of permission is **7–024** served on Monday November 20, the request for an oral permission hearing must be filed by 16.00 on Monday November 27.

"Real prospect of success"

"Real" means that the prospect of success must be realistic rather than fanciful **7–025** (*Tanfern Ltd v Cameron MacDonald (Practice Note)* [2000] 1 W.L.R. 1311).

In *Cooke v Secretary of State for Social Security* (2001) EWCA Civ 734; (2002) 3 All E.R. 279, Hale L.J. expressed the view that although appeal from a decision of the Social Security Commissioners is not a second appeal for the purposes of 52.13 (see para.7–074 below), the policy behind the more restrictive permission regime for second appeals was equally applicable to such an appeal, and consequently (at para.17) "a robust attitude to the prospect of success criterion ought to be adopted in these cases." Hale L.J. expressly confined her remarks to the particular tribunal structure under consideration, but remarked at para.18 that similar arguments might be expected to arise in relation to appeals from the EAT and other specialist tribunals. In relation to the EAT, it is suggested that the argument has little force: the characterisation of social security law as a "highly specialised area of law which many lawyers—indeed, I would suspect most lawyers—rarely encounter in practice" is not applicable to employment law.

"Some other compelling reason"

7–026   In *Smith v Cosworth Casting Processes Ltd* [1997] 1 W.L.R. 1538, Lord Woolf said "There can be many reasons for granting leave even if the court is not satisfied that the appeal has any prospect of success. For example, the issue may be one which the court considers should in the public interest be examined by this court or, to be more specific, this court may take the view that the case raises an issue where the law requires clarifying." In principle it is easy to see how this may be so: the judge who considers the application may take the view that the point is one on which, despite confusion at the level of the court below, there is in reality only one tenable position. Nevertheless, cases where the Court of Appeal finds a sufficiently compelling reason to allow an appeal to with no real prospect of success proceed must be expected to be rare. For an example see *R. (on the application of Yvonne Watts) v Bedford Primary Care Trust* [2003] EWHC 2401, Admin.

Permission "may be given"

7–027   Note that 52.3(6) does not require permission to be given in every case where the court considers that the appeal would have a real prospect of success: the court has a discretion. This must be expected to operate differently in relation to 52.3(6)(a) and (b), however: while there are many factors which could lead a court to refuse permission for an appeal which it considers has a real prospect of success, it is difficult if not impossible to imagine how a court could rationally refuse permission when it considers that there is some compelling reason why the appeal should be heard.

Appeal from a case management decision

7–028   See PD 4.4, 4.5 for the additional factors that may be taken into account in deciding whether to give permission for an appeal from a case management decision.

Limitation of the issues to be heard

7–029   The obvious use of this power is to limit the grounds of appeal to those which have a real prospect of success. Where the permission application has been dealt with on paper and permission has been given limited to certain grounds, the appellant may, subject to the time limit at 52.3(5), request an oral hearing of the permission application in respect of the remaining grounds: see PD 4.20. However, where limited permission has been given at an oral permission hearing, the court cannot consider grounds not included in the permission. The effect of the rules and the PD is that while a refusal of permission on the papers can be revisited either at an oral permission hearing or, where limited permission has been given on the papers, at the substantive hearing, if permission has been granted on one or more grounds but refused on other grounds after an oral hearing, an application to re-open those other grounds cannot be entertained (*James v Baily Gibson* [2002] EWCA Civ 1690).

Conditional permission

7–030   Where conditions are attached to permission to appeal, they seem most often to be conditions relating to costs, or to payment of or security for the amount ordered to be paid by the court below (see for example *Ungi v Liverpool City Council* [2004]

EWCA Civ 161). In *Lloyd Jones v T Mobile (UK) Ltd, The Times,* September 10, 2003; [2003] 49 E.G. 130, CA, Brooke L.J. commented at paras 26–28 on the power, treating it in effect as a special case of the general power at CPR r.3.1(3)(a) to attach conditions to any order. He said at para.28: "I mention these matters because this new power to make conditional orders gives courts a greater flexibility to make orders that are both proportionate and just than used to be the case when the court's powers were limited to saying 'yes' or 'no' in response to applications of this kind."

Part of the justification in the *T Mobile* case for making permission to appeal conditional was that the appellant was a large corporation that considered the point at issue sufficiently important for its wider business to incur substantial costs, whereas the respondents were individual objectors. With this reasoning available, the power to attach conditions to permission to appeal is capable of taking on a considerable significance in the context of appeals from the EAT, where (partly because costs do not normally follow the event there) impecunious litigants often appear, represented cheaply, *pro bono,* or not at all, against substantial employers that have reasons going well beyond the issues in the individual case to wish to secure authoritative rulings on questions of employment law. Contrast the much more restrictive approach to pre-emptive costs orders (e.g. *R. v Lord Chancellor Ex p. Child Poverty Action Group* [1999] 1 W.L.R. 347, [1998] 2 All E.R. 755); *R (on the application of Corner House Research) v Secretary of State for Trade & Industry,* unreported, [2004] EWHC 3011 (Admin.).

It is unclear whether the Employment Appeal Tribunal itself has power to attach conditions to a grant of permission to appeal; the EAT Rules and PD are silent on the question. A party seeking a condition might sensibly oppose the grant of permission by the EAT on that basis. It should also ensure that it makes written or oral representations at the time of the permission application, since an application to add conditions at a later date under r.52.9 will encounter the need to show a "compelling reason": see para.7–064 below.

Challenging a permission decision

There is no further appeal against a refusal of permission by the Court of Appeal after an oral hearing. Where permission is given, an application may in rare circumstances be made to set it aside: see r.52.9 and the following commentary at para.7–059.   **7–031**

Appellant's notice

52.4—(1) Where the appellant seeks permission from the appeal court it must be requested in the appellant's notice.   **7–032**

(2) The appellant must file the appellant's notice at the appeal court within—

> **(a) such period as may be directed by the lower court (which may be longer or shorter than the period referred to in sub-paragraph (b)); or**
>
> **(b) where the court makes no such direction, 21 days after the date of the decision of the lower court that the appellant wishes to appeal.**

(3) Unless the appeal court orders otherwise, an appellant's notice must be served on each respondent—

(a) **as soon as practicable; and**

(b) **in any event not later than 7 days,**

after it is filed.

The appellant's notice

7–033   CPR r.4 requires that the forms set out in PD 4 must be used in the cases to which they apply. The form for an appellant's notice is N161, available from the Court Service website (see para.7–007) in PDF format. Note that the form can be completed electronically and printed, but not saved.

Fees

7–034   Fees are listed on form 200, available at *www.civilappeals.gov.uk* (see para.7–007 for help with navigating the site.) Where the appellant in the appeal notice seeks permission and/or an extension of time for appealing, the fee payable on filing the appellant's notice is £200; a further £400 will have to be paid, if permission is granted, on filing the appeal questionnaire. Where permission has been granted by the EAT, the fee is £400, but no fee will be payable on filing the appellant's questionnaire.

Date from which time runs

7–035   Under this rule, time for appealing runs from the date of the decision, not the date on which the order was sealed: if the plain words of the rule needed confirmation, they got it in *Sayers v Clarke Walker* [2002] EWCA Civ 645. For the purposes of appeals from the EAT, however, some confusion is introduced by the EAT PD, which states at para.21.1 "such applications must be made to the Court of Appeal within 14 days of the sealed order." Arguably, this takes effect as a direction within 52.4(4)(1)(a) for the purposes of all further appeals from the EAT; also arguably, however, what 52.4(1)(a) confers is a power to vary the standard period for appealing on a case by case basis rather than a power to give a general direction varying the time for appealing in all cases from a particular court. The safer course must be to treat the EAT PD as misleading and either seek a specific direction as to time for appealing or file the appeal notice within 21 days of the date when the EAT decision was handed down.

"Within 21 days after"

7–036   By CPR r.2.8, "days" means clear days. So, for example if the decision is handed down on Wednesday November 15, the notice of appeal must be filed by Wednesday December 6.

Time of day for filing

7–037   There is no general provision equivalent to r.37(1A) of the EAT rules as to the time of day by which things to be done on a particular day must be done. An appeal notice may be sent by post or DX, or delivered personally to the court; because it requires to be accompanied by a fee, it may not (subject to PD 52, para.15.1A, as to which see para.8.170 below) be faxed or emailed: PD 5, para.5.3(9)(a) and PD 5B para.3.2. An appeal notice delivered personally must be taken to the Civil Appeals Office (room E307). Fees in the form of a cheque or postal order are acceptable at the Civil Appeals Office, but if the fee is to be paid in cash or by banker's draft, it must be paid at the Fees Room (E01) before the appeal notice is lodged at the Civil Appeals Office. Both offices close for the payment of fees at 16.00, so this must be regarded as the deadline for the filing of an appeal notice. Rooms E01 and E307 are located, some distance apart, in a particularly confusing part of the Royal Courts of Justice on the Strand, so ample time should be allowed for finding them, queuing if necessary, paying the fee and filing the necessary documents. For detailed guidance on filing an appellant's notice, see Form 202 "How to Appeal to the Court of Appeal," available at the Court Service website (see para.7–007).

Skeleton arguments and other documents accompanying the appeal notice

For the documents that must accompany the appeal notice, see PD 5.6, 5.6A and **7–038** 5.7; for guidance on skeleton arguments see PD 5.9; and for detailed guidance on the preparation of appeal bundles see form 204 (see para.7–007 above). For guidance on supplementary skeletons see PD 15.11A.

Service on respondents

For general rules about service, see CPR Pt 6 and its practice directions. **7–039**

Bundles of authorities

It is the duty of the appellant's advocate to agree and file with the court a bundle **7–040** of photocopies of the authorities to relied upon by either side: see PD 15.11 (at para.8–157) for detailed guidance.

Respondent's notice

52.5—(1) A respondent may file and serve a respondent's notice. **7–041**

(2) A respondent who—

    (a) is seeking permission to appeal from the appeal court; or

    (b) wishes to ask the appeal court to uphold the order of the lower court for reasons different from or additional to those given by the lower court, must file a respondent's notice.

(3) Where the respondent seeks permission from the appeal court it must be requested in the respondent's notice.

(4) A respondent's notice must be filed within—

    (a) such period as may be directed by the lower court; or

    (b) where the court makes no such direction, 14 days after the date in paragraph (5).

(5) The date referred to in paragraph (4) is—

    (a) the date the respondent is served with the appellant's notice where—

        (i) permission to appeal was given by the lower court; or

        (ii) permission to appeal is not required;

    (b) the date the respondent is served with notification that the appeal court has given the appellant permission to appeal; or

    (c) the date the respondent is served with notification that the application for permission to appeal and the appeal itself are to be heard together.

  (6) Unless the appeal court orders otherwise a respondent's notice must be served on the appellant and any other respondent—

    (a) as soon as practicable; and

    (b) in any event not later than 7 days, after it is filed.

"A respondent may file and serve a respondent's notice"

7–042   This rule read on its own would suggest that a respondent who does not wish to cross-appeal or ask the Court of Appeal to uphold the decision on grounds other than those given by the EAT need do nothing at this stage. However, by PD 15.6 a respondent must inform the Civil Appeals Office and the appellant in writing whether he intends to file a respondents notice within 21 days of receiving notification either that permission to appeal has been granted or that the permission application is to be heard together with the appeal. For comment on the importance of this see *Mlauzi v Secretary of State for the Home Department* [2005] EWCA Civ 128.

Within 14 days

7–043   By CPR r.2.8, "days" means clear days.

Form

7–044   The form for the respondent's notice is N162 (see para.7–007 above).

Where the respondent seeks permission

7–045   That is, for a cross-appeal.

Time for filing of the respondent's notice

7–046   The effect of 52.5(4) and (5) is that as soon as the respondent has received the appeal notice and knows that the appeal will proceed, it has 14 days to decide how it wishes to respond and to draft and file its respondent's notice including any cross-appeal.

"Such period as may be directed by the lower court"

7–047   Where the other party has sought permission to appeal from the EAT, the respondent should consider whether it can meet the 14 day time limit for filing its respondent's notice. If there is real doubt that it can, it should apply to the EAT for a longer period whether or not the potential appellant's permission application has been granted. An application to the EAT will be the cheaper and more convenient course, but if the respondent realises only after the hearing at which the permission application was made to the EAT that it will require extra time to file its respondent's notice, it may apply subsequently to the Court of Appeal for an extension of time: see CPR r.3.1(2)(a) and PD 7.5 at para.8–110 below.

Respondent's skeleton

7–048   A respondent that files a respondent's notice and wishes to address arguments to the Court of Appeal must, if represented, file and serve on the appellant and any other respondents a skeleton argument with its respondent's notice or within 14 days thereafter: see PD 7.6–7.8 at paras 8–112—8–116 below. An unrepresented respondent is encouraged to file a skeleton argument, but need not do so. If the respondent's skeleton is not filed with the respondent's notice, it must be served on the appellant and any other respondent at the same time as it is filed at court: PD 7.7B. A certificate of service must be filed: see CPR r.6.10. The reason for requiring the respondent's skeleton at this stage is apparently "to assist with case management decisions" (see *Philosophy Inc v Ferretti Studios SRL* [2003] R.P.C. 15; [2002] EWCA Civ 921, para.30).

A respondent that has not filed and served a respondent's notice is not thereby barred from addressing arguments to the court. A represented respondent that wishes to be heard must file and serve a skeleton argument at least seven days before the hearing of the appeal: PD 7.7(1), (2); an unrepresented respondent that wishes to be heard is encouraged, but not obliged, to do the same.

Content of skeleton

A respondent's skeleton must conform to the requirements of PD 5.10 and 5.11: **7–049** PD 7.8.

Other documents accompanying the respondent's notice

The appellant should have included all documents relevant to the appeal in the **7–050** appeal bundle, but if the respondent considers that relevant documents have been omitted it should either agree amendments to the appeal bundle with the appellant, or, failing agreement, prepare and file copies of a supplemental bundle: see PD 7.11, 7.12.

Service on the appellant

For general rules about service, see CPR Pt 6. **7–051**

Variation of time

52.6—(1) An application to vary the time limit for filing an appeal **7–052** **notice must be made to the appeal court.**

(2) The parties may not agree to extend any date or time limit set by—

> **(a) these Rules;**
> **(b) the relevant practice direction; or**
> **(c) an order of the appeal court or the lower court.**

(Rule 3.1(2)(a) provides that the court may extend or shorten the time for compliance with any rule, practice direction or court order (even if an application for extension is made after the time for compliance has expired))

(Rule 3.1(2)(b) provides that the court may adjourn or bring forward a hearing)

Considerations relevant to an application to extend time

The court will consider the matters listed as relevant to an application for relief **7–053** for any sanction imposed for failure to comply with a rule, practice direction or order listed at CPR r.3.9 (*Sayers v Clarke Walker* [2002] 1 W.L.R. 3095; [2002] EWCA Civ 645 at para.21). Rule 3.9 lists: "all the circumstances including (a) the interests of the administration of justice; (b) whether the application for relief has been made promptly; (c) whether the failure to comply was intentional; (d) whether there is a good explanation for the failure; (e) the extent to which the party in default has complied with other rules, practice directions, court orders and any relevant pre-action protocol; (f) whether the failure to comply was caused by the party or his legal representative; (g) whether the trial date or the likely trial date can still be met if relief is granted; (h) the effect which the failure to comply had on each party; and (i) the effect which the granting of relief would have on each party." If the arguments for granting or refusing an extension of time are otherwise balanced, the court will consider the merits of the appeal.

If the application to extend time is made before time has expired, it is not an application for relief from a sanction for non-compliance with the rules, so r.3.9 does not apply (*Robert v Momentum Services Ltd* [2003] EWCA Civ 299; [2003] 2 All E.R. 74).

Short-warned list

7–054   See PD 15.9 for arrangements for appeals which the court considers may be prepared for hearing on short notice by an advocate other than the one originally instructed.

Stay

7–055   52.7—**Unless—**

(a) **the appeal court or the lower court orders otherwise; or**

(b) **the appeal is from the Asylum and Immigration Appeal Tribunal,**

an appeal shall not operate as a stay of any order or decision of the lower court.

Definitions

7–056   "Stay" is explained in the glossary appended to the CPR: "A stay imposes a halt on proceedings, apart from taking any steps allowed by the Rules or the terms of the stay. Proceedings can be continued if a stay is lifted."

Stay

7–057   The normal rule is for no stay (Potter L.J., *Leicester Circuits Ltd v Coates Brothers Plc* [2002] EWCA Civ 474, para.13, cited in *Bell Electric Ltd v Aweco Appliance Systems GmbH & Co KG* [2002] EWCA Civ 1501 at para.24). The approach to the exercise of discretion was described by Clarke L.J. in *Hammond Suddard Solicitors v Agrichem International Holdings Ltd* [2002] EWCA Civ 2065 at para.22:

> "Whether the court should exercise its discretion to grant a stay will depend upon all the circumstances of the case, but the essential question is whether there is a risk of injustice to one or both parties if it grants or refuses a stay. In particular, if a stay is refused what are the risks of an appeal being stifled? If a stay is granted and the appeal fails, what are the risks that the respondent will be unable to enforce the judgment? On the other hand, if a stay is refused and the appeal succeeds, and the judgment is enforced in the meantime, what are the risks [*sic*] of the appellant being able to recover any monies paid from the respondent?"

A stay may be made subject to conditions; see, for example *Contract Facilities v Estate of Rees (deceased)* [2003] EWCA 465.

Amendment of appeal notice

52.8 An appeal notice may not be amended without the permission of the appeal court.   7–058

See para.8–095.   7–059

Striking out appeal notices and setting aside or imposing conditions on permission to appeal

52.9—(1) The appeal court may—   7–060

(a) **strike out the whole or part of an appeal notice;**

(b) **set aside permission to appeal in whole or in part;**

(c) **impose or vary conditions upon which an appeal may be brought.**

(2) The court will only exercise its powers under paragraph (1) where there is a compelling reason for doing so.

(3) Where a party was present at the hearing at which permission was given he may not subsequently apply for an order that the court exercise its powers under sub-paragraphs (1)(b) or (1)(c).

Definitions

"Striking out" and "set aside" are explained in the glossary appended to the CPR, respectively: "the court ordering written material to be deleted so that it may no longer be relied upon" and "cancelling a judgment or order or a step taken by a party in the proceedings."   7–061

Striking out the appeal notice

On the rare occasions when this power is used, it will normally be as a sanction for failure to comply with orders: see, for example *Carr v Bower Cotton* [2002] EWCA Civ 789 at para.36 and *Taiga v Taiga* [2004] EWCA Civ 1399. An application to strike out an appeal for abuse of process was made to the Court of Appeal with odd results in *Madarassy v Nomura International Plc* [2006] EWCA Civ 371. The court "remitted" the application to the High Court on the grounds that the Court of Appeal itself "does not normally hear oral evidence and decide facts" (para.27); but Bean J., dealing with the application in the High Court ([2006] EWHC 748, QB), considered that he lacked jurisdiction to decide the application. He therefore heard evidence and made findings of fact relevant to the application before referring the matter back to the Court of Appeal.   7–062

Setting aside permission to appeal

The requirement for a compelling reason for the exercise of this power serves as a warning that the court will not look kindly on optimistic or speculative applications. In *Barings Bank Plc (in liquidation) v Coopers & Lybrand* [2002] EWCA Civ 1155, Laws L.J. said   7–063

"The rule is there to cater for the rare case in which the lord justice granting permission to appeal has actually been misled. If he has, the court's process has been abused and that is of course a special situation. There may also be cases where, as Longmore LJ indicated in Nathan v Smilovitch [2002] EWDCA Civ 759, some decisive authority or statute has been overlooked by the lord justice granting permission. But where such a state of affairs is asserted, the learning in question must in my view be plainly and unarguably decisive of the issue. If there is anything to argue about, an application to set aside the grant of permission will be misconceived."

Conditions

7–064   Compare r.52.3(7)(b), which imposes no requirement for "compelling reasons" before a condition may be attached to the initial grant of permission.

52.9(3)

7–065   The main significance of this prohibition is that a respondent that seeks a condition is well advised to do so at the permission application (see para.7–030 above); but if it is not ready to do so then, (for example because it has yet to marshal the necessary evidence), it should not attend.

Kuwait Airways Corp v Iraqi Airways Co [2005] EWCA Civ 934 at paras 73–81 is cited by *Civil Procedure 2007* (at para.52.9.5) for the propositions that r.52.9(3), despite its unequivocal terms, should not be construed so as to bar an appellant from challenging a condition which would prevent him from obtaining access to the court; and although it refers to "a party", it does not apply to an appellant. At the time of writing, no case with this citation is to be found on either the Court Service or British and Irish Legal Information websites.

Appeal court's powers

7–066   **52.10—(1) In relation to an appeal the appeal court has all the powers of the lower court.**

(Rule 52.1(4) provides that this Part is subject to any enactment that sets out special provisions with regard to any particular category of appeal—where such an enactment gives a statutory power to a tribunal, person or other body it may be the case that the appeal court may not exercise that power on an appeal)

(2) The appeal court has power to—

(a) affirm, set aside or vary any order or judgment made or given by the lower court;

(b) refer any claim or issue for determination by the lower court;

(c) order a new trial or hearing;

(d) make orders for the payment of interest;

(e) make a costs order.

(3) In an appeal from a claim tried with a jury the Court of Appeal may, instead of ordering a new trial—

(a) make an order for damages or

(b) vary an award of damages made by the jury.

(4) The appeal court may exercise its powers in relation to the whole or part of an order of the lower court.

(Part 3 contains general rules about the court's case management powers)

(5) If the appeal court—

(a) refuses an application for permission to appeal;
(b) strikes out an appellant's notice; or
(c) dismisses an appeal,

and it considers that the application, the appellant's notice or the appeal is totally without merit, the provisions of paragraph (6) must be complied with.

(6) Where paragraph (5) applies—

(a) the court's order must record the fact that it considers the application, the appellant's notice or the appeal to be totally without merit; and
(b) the court must at the same time consider whether it is appropriate to make a civil restraint order.

Definitions

By CPR r.2.3(1), "Civil restraint order" means an order restraining a party—(a) from making any further applications in current proceedings (a limited civil restraint order); (b) from issuing certain claims or making certain applications in specified courts (an extended civil restraint order); or (c) from issuing any claim or making any application in specified courts (a general civil restraint order).

"Damages" are explained in the glossary appended to the CPR: "a sum of money awarded by the court as compensation to the claimant."

7–067

The powers of the lower court

By s.35(1) of the Employment Tribunals Act 1996, the EAT may exercise any of the powers of the body or officer from which the first appeal was brought. It would seem, therefore, that the effect of 52.10(1) must be to confer on the Court of Appeal all the powers of the employment tribunal. The intention behind the qualification in parentheses at 52.10(1) is obscure, but it is clear that it does not inhibit the Court of Appeal from either remitting a case to the employment tribunal or imposing its own order in a suitable case.

7–068

Power to order a new hearing

The Court of Appeal will normally deal with an appeal on its merits, with the result either that it upholds the judgment of the EAT or, where it allows the appeal, that it sets aside the EAT's judgment and either restores the order of the employment tribunal, orders a re-hearing by the employment tribunal or make its own order finally disposing of the matter. Only rarely will it remit a case for re-hearing by the EAT (*Lambe v 186K Ltd* [2005] I.C.R. 307; [2004] EWCA Civ 104 at para.83). Examples of the circumstances in which it will do so include a successful appeal against the EAT's judgment that it lacked jurisdiction to hear the appeal (*Grady v Prison Service* [2003] All E.R. 745, CA), an appeal against the EAT's decision at a preliminary hearing to permit only some of the appellant's grounds of appeal to go to a full hearing (*Vincent v MJ Gallagher Contractors Ltd* [2003] I.C.R. 1244, CA), and an appeal in which the Court of Appeal had at the permission stage identified

7–069

arguable grounds of appeal which had not been put before the EAT (*Sukul-Lennard v Croydon Primary Care Trust, The Times*, July 22, 2003).

Nature of the Court of Appeal's function

7–070   The Court of Appeal has repeatedly emphasised that its function in hearing appeals from the EAT is to consider the correctness of the employment tribunal's decision, not the EAT's (see *Vento v Chief Constable of West Yorkshire Police (No.2)* [2002] EWCA Civ 1871; [2003] I.R.L.R 102, para.25 and the cases there cited). However, in *Gover v Propertycare Ltd* [2006] I.C.R. 1073 at para.8, Buxton L.J. commented (obiter):

> "I would be less than frank if I did not express some reserve about that guidance. . . [T]his court's jurisdiction to hear this appeal, coming as it does from a statutory tribunal, is only to be found in section 37(1) of the Employment Tribunals Act 1996, which provides for an appeal from the EAT on a question of law only. I do not see how we can in any realistic sense be hearing an appeal from the EAT if we are only concerned with whether the ET was right. As to the business of this court, the assumption that we in effect repeat the exercise already performed by the expert EAT of reviewing the decision of the ET tends in practice to impose on this court an exercise that is inappropriate both in its nature and in its extent."

It is suggested that the earlier authorities are correct. The key to Buxton L.J.'s anxieties may be at para.9 of the judgment: "It was suggested [by Counsel for the appellants] that failure to take the point before the EAT was irrelevant because our task was to review the ET." This is a *non sequitur*, but it is as much an error to throw out the premise with the conclusion as the baby with the bathwater. Appeal only lies to the EAT, as to the Court of Appeal, on a point of law (see para.5–014 *et seq.* above). If Buxton L.J. was right, a distinction must somehow be formulated between two classes of error of law: those fit for the Court of Appeal, and those fit for the EAT only. The prospect is an unattractive one, although one that Buxton L.J. appeared still to be willing to countenance in his subsequent judgment in *Balfour Beatty v Wilcox* [2007] I.R.L.R. 63, CA.

Hearing of appeals

7–071   **52.11—(1) Every appeal will be limited to a review of the decision of the lower court unless—**

> **(a) a practice direction makes different provision for a particular category of appeal; or**
>
> **(b) the court considers that in the circumstances of an individual appeal it would be in the interests of justice to hold a re-hearing.**

(2) Unless it orders otherwise, the appeal court will not receive—

> **(a) oral evidence; or**
>
> **(b) evidence which was not before the lower court.**

(3) The appeal court will allow an appeal where the decision of the lower court was—

(a) **wrong; or**

(b) **unjust because of a serious procedural or other irregularity in the proceedings in the lower court.**

(4) The appeal court may draw any inference of fact which it considers justified on the evidence.

(5) At the hearing of the appeal a party may not rely on a matter not contained in his appeal notice unless the appeal court gives permission.

Review or re-hearing

No relevant practice direction makes provision for appeals from the EAT to the Court of Appeal to be dealt with by way of re-hearing. Part 52 applies (by 52.1) to appeals to the High Court and to a county court as well as to the Court of Appeal, and the provisions of 52.11(1) are far more readily applicable to the former category of appeal. The power to hold a re-hearing will rarely if ever arise in relation to an appeal to the Court of Appeal. **7–072**

New evidence

The pre-CPR guidelines as to the exercise of the power to hear evidence not before the tribunal below laid down by the Court of Appeal in *Ladd v Marshall* [1954] 3 All E.R. 745 remain applicable under 52.11 (*R. (Iran) v SSHD* [2005] EWCA Civ 982 at paras 34–37). The *Ladd v Marshall* criteria are: (1) that the evidence could not have been obtained with reasonable diligence for use before the tribunal below; (2) the new evidence must be such that, if given, it would probably have had an important influence on the result of the case (though it need not be decisive); and (3) the new evidence must be apparently credible although it need not be incontrovertible. See also *Hertfordshire Investments Ltd v Bubb* [2000] 1 W.L.R. 2318 at 2325. **7–073**

For a convincing demonstration (in the context of a strike out application) of the Court of Appeal's reluctance to hear oral evidence, see *Madarassy v Nomura International Plc* [2006] EWCA Civ 371, and para.7–062 above.

Non-disclosure of Part 36 offers and payments

52.12—(1) The fact that a Part 36 offer or payment into court has been made must not be disclosed to any judge of the appeal court who is to hear or determine— **7–073/1**

(a) **an application for permission to appeal; or**

(b) **an appeal,**

until all questions (other than costs) have been determined. (2) Paragraph (1) does not apply if the Part 36 offer or payment into court is relevant to the substance of the appeal.

(3) Paragraph (1) does not prevent disclosure in any application in the appeal proceedings if disclosure of the fact that a Part 36 offer or payment into court has been made is properly relevant to the matter to be decided.

(Rule 36.3 has the effect that a Part 36 offer made in proceedings at first instance will not have consequences in any appeal proceed-

ings. Therefore, a fresh Part 36 offer needs to be made in appeal proceedings. However, rule 52.12 applies to a Part 36 offer whether made in the original proceedings or in the appeal.)

Part 36 offers and payments

7–073/2   Although the Pt 36 procedure is not available before the employment tribunal or the EAT, there is no reason why a party to an appeal to the Court of Appeal should not make a Pt 36 offer at that stage in proceedings: see r.36.3(2)(b).

Statutory appeals—court's power to hear any person

7–073/3   **52.12A—(1) In a statutory appeal, any person may apply for permission—**

      (a) to file evidence; or

      (b) to make representations at the appeal hearing.

(2) An application under paragraph (1) must be made promptly.

Amendment

7–073/4   Rule 52.12A was inserted with effect from October 1, 2007 by the Civil Procedure Amendment Rules 2007, and makes express the Court's power to hear representations from a person wishing to intervene in proceedings to which he or it is not a party, and from an unqualified representative of a party or other person. See also PD52, paras 17.7—17.9 (para.8–175 below).

Second appeals to the court

7–074   **52.13—(1) Permission is required from the Court of Appeal for any appeal to that court from a decision of a county court or the High Court which was itself made on appeal.**

(2) The Court of Appeal will not give permission unless it considers that—

      (a) the appeal would raise an important point of principle or practice; or

      (b) there is some other compelling reason for the Court of Appeal to hear it.

Second appeals

7–075   Appeal from the EAT to the Court of Appeal is not a "second appeal" for these purposes; but see para.7–025 above.

(Editorial Note: the remainder of Pt 52 has no application to appeals from the Employment Appeal Tribunal, and is not reproduced in this work).

CHAPTER 8

Civil Procedure Rules Part 52, Practice Direction—Appeals

Contents

379

PRACTICE DIRECTION—APPEALS

This Practice Direction Supplements CPR Part 52

CONTENTS OF THIS PRACTICE DIRECTION

8–001   **1.1 This Practice Direction is divided into four sections:**

- **Section I—General provisions about appeals**
- **Section II—General provisions about statutory appeals and appeals by way of case stated**
- **Section III—Provisions about specific appeals**
- **Section IV—Provisions about reopening appeals**

SECTION 1   GENERAL PROVISIONS ABOUT APPEALS

8–002   **2.1 This practice direction applies to all appeals to which Part 52 applies except where specific provision is made for appeals to the Court of Appeal.**

8–003   **2.2 For the purpose only of appeals to the Court of Appeal from cases in family proceedings this Practice Direction will apply with such modifications as may be required.**

Routes of Appeal

2A.1 The court or judge to which an appeal is to be made (subject **8–004**
to obtaining any necessary permission) is set out in the tables below:

> Table 1 addresses appeals in cases other than insolvency proceed-
> ings and those cases to which Table 3 applies;
> Table 2 addresses insolvency proceedings; and
> Table 3 addresses certain family cases to which CPR Pt 52 may
> apply.

The tables do not include so-called "leap frog" appeals either to the
Court of Appeal pursuant to section 57 of the Access to Justice Act
1999 or to the House of Lords pursuant to section 13 of the
Administration of Justice Act 1969.
(An interactive routes of appeal guide can be found on the Court of
Appeal's website at *www.hmcourts-service.gov.uk/infoabout/coa—civil/
routes—app/index.htm*)

Table 1
*(Editorial Note: This table identifies the destination of appeals. It is unnecessary to reproduce it
in this work, since all appeals from the EAT lie to the Court of Appeal.)*

Table 2: *Insolvency proceedings*
(Editorial Note: this table is not reproduced since it is outside the scope of this work.)

2A.2 A "final decision" is a decision of a court that would finally **8–005**
determine (subject to any possible appeal or detailed assessment of
costs) the entire proceedings whichever way the court decided the
issues before it. Decisions made on an application to strike-out or
for summary judgment are not final decisions for the purpose of
determining the appropriate route of appeal (Art. 1 Access to Justice
Act 1999 (Destination of Appeals) Order 2000). Accordingly:

> (1) a case management decision;
> (2) the grant or refusal of interim relief;
> (3) a summary judgment;
> (4) a striking out,

are not final decisions for this purpose.

2A.3 A decision of a court is to be treated as a final decision for **8–006**
routes of appeal purposes where it:

    (1) is made at the conclusion of part of a hearing or trial which has been split into parts; and

    (2) would, if it had been made at the conclusion of that hearing or trial, have been a final decision.

Accordingly, a judgment on liability at the end of a split trial is a "final decision" for this purpose and the judgment at the conclusion of the assessment of damages following a judgment on liability is also a "final decision" for this purpose.

8–007   2A.4 An order made:

    (1) on a summary or detailed assessment of costs; or

    (2) on an application to enforce a final decision, is not a "final decision" and any appeal from such an order will follow the routes of appeal set out in the tables above.

(Section 16(1) of the Supreme Court Act 1981 (as amended); section 77(1) of the County Courts Act 1984 (as amended); and the Access to Justice Act 1999 (Destination of Appeals) Order 2000 set out the provisions governing routes of appeal).

8–008   2A.5—(1) Where an applicant attempts to file an appellant's notice and the appeal court does not have jurisdiction to issue the notice, a court officer may notify the applicant in writing that the appeal court does not have jurisdiction in respect of the notice.

    (2) Before notifying a person under paragraph (1) the court officer must confer—

    (a) with a judge of the appeal court; or,

    (b) where the Court of Appeal, Civil Division is the appeal court, with a court officer who exercises the jurisdiction of that Court under rule 52.16.

(3) Where a court officer in the Court of Appeal, Civil Division notifies a person under paragraph (1), rule 52.16(5) shall not apply.

Amendment

8–008/1   In *Scribes West v Anstalt* (No.1) [2004] EWCA Civ. 835, the Court of Appeal announced and explained substantial amendments to the practice direction, effective from June 30, 2004.

Destination of appeals

8–009   Paragraph 2A of the practice direction restates and supplements the provisions of the Access to Justice Act 1999 (Destination of Appeals) Order 2000. See *Civil Procedure 2007*.

Status of practice direction

8–010   See para.7–013.

Routes of appeal

Appeal from the EAT is always to the Court of Appeal. There is no applicable **8–011** provision for "leap frog" appeals. Because the EAT is not bound by its own previous decisions, there is limited need for such a procedure. A party wishing to challenge EAT authority of long or distinguished pedigree, or seeking a declaration of incompatibility with the Human Rights Act 1998 (which the EAT lacks jurisdiction to grant: see Human Rights Act 1998, s.4(5) and para.15–005), might sensibly seek to save costs by inviting the EAT to list the case for a preliminary hearing in order to consider whether to dismiss the appeal as having, at that level, no reasonable prospect of success, and deal with any application for permission to appeal.

GROUNDS FOR APPEAL

3.1 Rule 52.11(3)(a) and (b) sets out the circumstances in which 8–012 the appeal court will allow an appeal.

3.2 The grounds of appeal should— 8–013

    (1) **Set out clearly the reasons why rule 52.11(3)(a) or (b) is said to apply; and**
    (2) **specify, in respect of each ground, whether the ground raises an appeal on a point of law or is an appeal against a finding of fact.**

Appeal on a point of law or against a finding of fact

Appeal from the EAT to the Court of Appeal lies only on a point of law: **8–014** Employment Tribunals Act 1996, s.37 (see paras 2–089 and 2–090).

PERMISSION TO APPEAL

4.1 Rule 52.3 sets out the circumstances when permission to appeal 8–015 is required.

4.2 The permission of— 8–016

    (1) **the Court of Appeal; or**
    (2) **where the lower court's rules allow, the lower court, is required for all appeals to the Court of Appeal except as provided for by statute or rule 52.3.**

(The requirement of permission to appeal may be imposed by a practice direction—see rule 52.3(b).)

4.3 Where the lower court is not required to give permission to 8–017 appeal, it may give an indication of its opinion as to whether permission should be given.
(Rule 52.1(3)(c) defines "lower court".)

8–018   4.3A—(1) This paragraph applies where a party applies for permission to appeal against a decision at the hearing at which the decision was made.

(2) Where this paragraph applies, the judge making the decision shall state—

(a) whether or not the judgment or order is final;

(b) whether an appeal lies from the judgment or order and, if so, to which appeal court;

(c) whether the court gives permission to appeal; and

(d) if not, the appropriate appeal court to which any further application for permission may be made.

(Rule 40.2(4) contains requirements as to the contents of the judgment or order in these circumstances.)

8–019   4.3B Where no application for permission to appeal has been made in accordance with rule 52.3(2)(a) but a party requests further time to make such an application, the court may adjourn the hearing to give that party the opportunity to do so.

Appeals from case management decisions
8–020   4.4 Case management decisions include decisions made under rule 3.1(2) and decisions about:

(1) disclosure

(2) filing of witness statements or experts reports

(3) directions about the timetable of the claim

(4) adding a party to a claim

(5) security for costs.

8–021   4.5 Where the application is for permission to appeal from a case management decision, the court dealing with the application may take into account whether:

(1) the issue is of insufficient significance to justify the costs of an appeal;

(2) the procedural consequences of an appeal (e.g. loss of trial date) outweigh the significance of the case management decision;

(3) it would be more convenient to determine the issue at or after trial.

Court to which permission to appeal application should be made
8–022   4.6 An application for permission should be made orally at the hearing at which the decision to be appealed against is made.

4.7 Where: 8–023

    (a) no application for permission to appeal is made at the hearing; or

    (b) the lower court refuses permission to appeal,

an application for permission to appeal may be made to the appeal court in accordance with rules 52.3(2) and (3).

4.8 There is no appeal from a decision of the appeal court to allow   8–024
or refuse permission to appeal to that court (although where the
appeal court, without a hearing, refuses permission to appeal, the
person seeking permission may request that decision to be reconsidered at a hearing). See section 54(4) of the Access to Justice Act
and rule 52.3(2), (3), (4) and (5).

Second appeals

4.9 An application for permission to appeal from a decision of the   8–025
High Court or a county court which was itself made on appeal must
be made to the Court of Appeal.

Appeal from the EAT to the Court of Appeal is not a second appeal for these   8–026
purposes: see para.7–025.

4.10 If permission to appeal is granted the appeal will be heard by   8–027
the Court of Appeal.

Consideration of permission without a hearing

4.11 Applications for permission to appeal may be considered by   8–028
the appeal court without a hearing.

4.12 If permission is granted without a hearing the parties will be   8–029
notified of that decision and the procedure in paragraphs 6.1 to 6.6
will then apply.

4.13 If permission is refused without a hearing the parties will be   8–030
notified of that decision with the reasons for it. The decision is
subject to the appellant's right to have it reconsidered at an oral
hearing. This may be before the same judge.

4.14 A request for the decision to be reconsidered at an oral   8–031
hearing must be filed at the appeal court within 7 days after service
of the notice that permission has been refused. A copy of the request
must be served by the appellant on the respondent at the same time.

Permission hearing

4.14A—(1) This paragraph applies where an appellant, who is   8–032
represented, makes a request for a decision to be reconsidered at an
oral hearing.

(2) The appellant's advocate must, at least 4 days before the hearing, in a brief written statement—

    (a) inform the court and the respondent of the points which he proposes to raise at the hearing;

    (b) set out his reasons why permission should be granted notwithstanding the reasons given for the refusal of permission; and

    (c) confirm, where applicable, that the requirements of paragraph 4.17 have been complied with (appellant in receipt of services funded by the Legal Services Commission).

8–033   4.15 Notice of a permission hearing will be given to the respondent but he is not required to attend unless the court requests him to do so.

8–034   4.16 If the court requests the respondent's attendance at the permission hearing, the appellant must supply the respondent with a copy of the appeal bundle (see paragraph 5.6A) within 7 days of being notified of the request, or such other period as the court may direct. The costs of providing that bundle shall be borne by the appellant initially, but will form part of the costs of the permission application.

Appellants in receipt of services funded by the Legal Services Commission applying for permission to appeal

8–035   4.17 Where the appellant is in receipt of services funded by the Legal Services Commission (or legally aided) and permission to appeal has been refused by the appeal court without a hearing, the appellant must send a copy of the reasons the appeal court gave for refusing permission to the relevant office of the Legal Services Commission as soon as it has been received from the court. The court will require confirmation that this has been done if a hearing is requested to re-consider the question of permission.

Limited permission

8–036   4.18 Where a court under rule 52.3(7) gives permission to appeal on some issues only, it will—

    (1) refuse permission on any remaining issues; or

    (2) reserve the question of permission to appeal on any remaining issues to the court hearing the appeal.

8–037   4.19 If the court reserves the question of permission under paragraph 4.18(2), the appellant must, within 14 days after service of the court's order, inform the appeal court and the respondent in writing whether he intends to pursue the reserved issues. If the appellant does intend to pursue the reserved issues, the parties must include in any time estimate for the appeal hearing, their time estimate for the reserved issues.

4.20 If the appeal court refuses permission to appeal on the remaining issues without a hearing and the applicant wishes to have that decision reconsidered at an oral hearing, the time limit in rule 52.3(5) shall apply. Any application for an extension of this time limit should be made promptly. The court hearing the appeal on the issues for which permission has been granted will not normally grant, at the appeal hearing, an application to extend the time limit in rule 52.3(5) for the remaining issues. **8–038**

4.21 If the appeal court refuses permission to appeal on remaining issues at or after an oral hearing, the application for permission to appeal on those issues cannot be renewed at the appeal hearing. See section 54(4) of the Access to Justice Act 1999. **8–039**

Respondent's costs of permission applications

4.22 In most cases, applications for permission to appeal will be determined without the court requesting— **8–040**
(1) submissions from, or
(2) if there is an oral hearing, attendance by the respondent.

4.23 Where the court does not request submissions from or attendance by the respondent, costs will not normally be allowed to a respondent who volunteers submissions or attendance. **8–041**

4.24 Where the court does request— **8–042**
(1) submissions from; or
(2) attendance by the respondent, the court will normally allow the respondent his costs if permission is refused.

Permission to appeal

Permission is always required for an appeal from the EAT to the Court of Appeal. The EAT can give permission, and the application for permission should normally be made first to the EAT: see para.7–019. **8–043**

The cost/benefit ratio

The specific power in Pt 52 to take into account whether the issue is of insufficient significance to justify the costs of an appeal from a case management decision might be taken to preclude (*expressio unius est exclusio alterius*) that factor from the court's consideration in any substantive appeal. Appearing in the Practice Direction, however, it should not be taken to restrict the court's discretion in that way: see generally para.7–013 on the status of the PD. **8–044**

See paras 6–156, 7–019.

Decision of appeal court on permission to appeal to that court

Although the EAT's r.3(7) procedure is in some ways parallel to a permission stage, a crucial difference is that failure at this stage is capable of challenge by way of appeal to the Court of Appeal. **8–045**

Within 7 days

8–046   "Days" means clear days; see e.g. para.7–024.

Unrepresented respondents

8–047   In general, parties who are not represented will do well to comply with instructions directed to parties who are represented if they are able to.

The time limit in r.52.3(5)

8–048   Seven days after service of notice that permission has been refused.

Respondent's costs of a permission hearing

8–049   Paragraphs 4.22–4.24 echo the guidance on the interpretation of the PD as it then stood given by Brooke L.J. in *Jolly v Jay* [2002] EWCA Civ 277 at para.47:

> "Where an application for permission is to be determined on paper, any submission from the respondent must be in writing. Even in the event of an oral hearing a respondent should consider whether he can make his submission equally well in writing, particularly as he may not be allowed the costs of his attendance at the hearing".

APPELLANT'S NOTICE

8–050   **5.1 An appellant's notice must be filed and served in all cases. Where an application for permission to appeal is made to the appeal court it must be applied for in the appellant's notice.**

Human Rights

8–051   **5.1A—(1) This paragraph applies where the appellant seeks—**

> **(a) to rely on any issue under the Human Rights Act 1998; or**
> **(b) a remedy available under that Act, for the first time in an appeal.**

(2) The appellant must include in his appeal notice the information required by paragraph 15.1 of the practice direction supplementing Part 16.

(3) Paragraph 15.2 of the practice direction supplementing Part 16 applies as if references to a statement of case were to the appeal notice.

8–052   **5.1B CPR rule 19.4A and the practice direction supplementing it shall apply as if references to the case management conference were to the application for permission to appeal.**

(The practice direction to Part 19 provides for notice to be given and parties joined in certain circumstances to which this paragraph applies).

Extension of time for filing appellant's notice

8–053   **5.2 Where the time for filing an appellant's notice has expired, the appellant must—**

    (a) file the appellant's notice; and

    (b) include in that appellant's notice an application for an extension of time.

The appellant's notice should state the reason for the delay and the steps taken prior to the application being made.

5.3 Where the appellant's notice includes an application for an **8–054** extension of time and permission to appeal has been given or is not required the respondent has the right to be heard on that application. He must be served with a copy of the appeal bundle (see paragraph 5.6A). However, a respondent who unreasonably opposes an extension of time runs the risk of being ordered to pay the appellant's costs of that application.

5.4 If an extension of time is given following such an application **8–055** the procedure at paragraphs 6.1 to 6.6 applies.

Applications

5.5 Notice of an application to be made to the appeal court for a **8–056** remedy incidental to the appeal (*e.g.* an interim remedy under rule 25.1 or an order for security for costs) may be included in the appeal notice or in a Part 23 application notice.

(Rule 25.15 deals with security for costs of an appeal)

(Paragraph 11 of this practice direction contains other provisions relating to applications)

Documents

5.6—(1) This paragraph applies to every case except where the **8–057** appeal—

    (a) relates to a claim allocated to the small claims track; and

    (b) is being heard in a county court or the High Court.

(Paragraph 5.8 applies where this paragraph does not apply)

(2) The appellant must file the following documents together with an appeal bundle (see paragraph 5.6A) with his appellant's notice—

    (a) two additional copies of the appellant's notice for the appeal court; and

    (b) one copy of the appellant's notice for each of the respondents;

    (c) one copy of his skeleton argument for each copy of the appellant's notice that is filed (see paragraph 5.9);

    (d) a sealed copy of the order being appealed;

(e) a copy of any order giving or refusing permission to appeal, together with a copy of the judge's reasons for allowing or refusing permission to appeal;

(f) any witness statements or affidavits in support of any application included in the appellant's notice;

(g) a copy of the order allocating a case to a track (if any).

8–058   5.6A—(1) An appellant must include in his appeal bundle the following documents:

(a) a sealed copy of the appellant's notice;

(b) a sealed copy of the order being appealed;

(c) a copy of any order giving or refusing permission to appeal, together with a copy of the judge's reasons for allowing or refusing permission to appeal;

(d) any affidavit or witness statement filed in support of any application included in the appellant's notice;

(e) a copy of his skeleton argument;

(f) a transcript or note of judgment (see paragraph 5.12), and in cases where permission to appeal was given by the lower court or is not required those parts of any transcript of evidence which are directly relevant to any question at issue on the appeal;

(g) the claim form and statements of case (where relevant to the subject of the appeal);

(h) any application notice (or case management documentation) relevant to the subject of the appeal;

(i) in cases where the decision appealed was itself made on appeal (eg from district judge to circuit judge), the first order, the reasons given and the appellant's notice used to appeal from that order;

(j) in the case of judicial review or a statutory appeal, the original decision which was the subject of the application to the lower court;

(k) in cases where the appeal is from a Tribunal, a copy of the Tribunal's reasons for the decision, a copy of the decision reviewed by the Tribunal and the reasons for the original decision and any document filed with the Tribunal setting out the grounds of appeal from that decision;

(l) any other documents which the appellant reasonably considers necessary to enable the appeal court to reach its decision on the hearing of the application or appeal; and

(m) such other documents as the court may direct.

(2) All documents that are extraneous to the issues to be considered on the application or the appeal must be excluded. The appeal bundle may include affidavits, witness statements, summaries, experts' reports and exhibits but only where these are directly relevant to the subject matter of the appeal.

(3) Where the appellant is represented, the appeal bundle must contain a certificate signed by his solicitor, counsel or other representative to the effect that he has read and understood paragraph (2) above and that the composition of the appeal bundle complies with it.

5.7 Where it is not possible to file all the above documents, the appellant must indicate which documents have not yet been filed and the reasons why they are not currently available. The appellant must then provide a reasonable estimate of when the missing document or documents can be filed and file them as soon as reasonably practicable.

8–059

5.8 (Editorial Note: this part of the Practice Direction concerns small claims track appeals, and is not reproduced in this work.)

8–060

Skeleton arguments

5.9—(1) The appellant's notice must, subject to (2) and (3) below, be accompanied by a skeleton argument. Alternatively the skeleton argument may be included in the appellant's notice. Where the skeleton argument is so included it will not form part of the notice for the purposes of rule 52.8.

8–061

(2) Where it is impracticable for the appellant's skeleton argument to accompany the appellant's notice it must be filed and served on all respondents within 14 days of filing the notice.

(3) An appellant who is not represented need not file a skeleton argument but is encouraged to do so since this will be helpful to the court.

Content of skeleton arguments

5.10—(1) A skeleton argument must contain a numbered list of the points which the party wishes to make. These should both define and confine the areas of controversy. Each point should be stated as concisely as the nature of the case allows.

8–062

(2) A numbered point must be followed by a reference to any document on which the party wishes to rely.

(3) A skeleton argument must state, in respect of each authority cited—

    (a) the proposition of law that the authority demonstrates; and

(b) the parts of the authority (identified by page or paragraph references) that support the proposition.

(4) If more than one authority is cited in support of a given proposition, the skeleton argument must briefly state the reason for taking that course.

(5) The statement referred to in sub-paragraph (4) should not materially add to the length of the skeleton argument but should be sufficient to demonstrate, in the context of the argument—

(a) the relevance of the authority or authorities to that argument; and

(b) that the citation is necessary for a proper presentation of that argument.

(6) The cost of preparing a skeleton argument which—

(a) does not comply with the requirements set out in this paragraph; or

(b) was not filed within the time limits provided by this Practice Direction (or any further time granted by the court),

will not be allowed on assessment except to the extent that the court otherwise directs.

8–063 5.11 The appellant should consider what other information the appeal court will need. This may include a list of persons who feature in the case or glossaries of technical terms. A chronology of relevant events will be necessary in most appeals.

Suitable record of the judgment
8–064 5.12 Where the judgment to be appealed has been officially recorded by the court, an approved transcript of that record should accompany the appellant's notice. Photocopies will not be accepted for this purpose. However, where there is no officially recorded judgment, the following documents will be acceptable:

Written judgments

8–065 (1) Where the judgment was made in writing a copy of that judgment endorsed with the judge's signature.

Note of judgment

8–066 (2) When judgment was not officially recorded or made in writing a note of the judgment (agreed between the appellant's and respondent's advocates) should be submitted for approval to the judge whose decision is being appealed. If the parties cannot agree on a single note of the judgment, both versions should be provided to that judge with an explanatory letter. For the purpose of an application for permission to appeal the note need not be approved by the respondent or the lower court judge.

Advocates' notes of judgments where the appellant is unrepresented

(3) When the appellant was unrepresented in the lower court it is the duty of any advocate for the respondent to make his/her note of judgment promptly available, free of charge to the appellant where there is no officially recorded judgment or if the court so directs. Where the appellant was represented in the lower court it is the duty of his/her own former advocate to make his/her note available in these circumstances. The appellant should submit the note of judgment to the appeal court. **8–067**

Reasons for judgment in Tribunal cases

(4) A sealed copy of the Tribunal's reasons for the decision. **8–068**

5.13 An appellant may not be able to obtain an official transcript or other suitable record of the lower court's decision within the time within which the appellant's notice must be filed. In such cases the appellant's notice must still be completed to the best of the appellant's ability on the basis of the documentation available. However it may be amended subsequently with the permission of the appeal court. **8–069**

Advocates' notes of judgments

5.14 Advocates' brief (or, where appropriate, refresher) fee includes: **8–070**

(1) remuneration for taking a note of the judgment of the court;
(2) having the note transcribed accurately;
(3) attempting to agree the note with the other side if represented;
(4) submitting the note to the judge for approval where appropriate;
(5) revising it if so requested by the judge;
(6) providing any copies required for the appeal court, instructing solicitors and lay client; and
(7) providing a copy of his note to an unrepresented appellant.

Transcripts or notes of evidence

5.15 When the evidence is relevant to the appeal an official transcript of the relevant evidence must be obtained. Transcripts or notes of evidence are generally not needed for the purpose of determining an application for permission to appeal. **8–071**

Notes of evidence

8–072   5.16 If evidence relevant to the appeal was not officially recorded, a typed version of the judge's notes of evidence must be obtained.

Transcripts at public expense

8–073   5.17 Where the lower court or the appeal court is satisfied that—

(1) an unrepresented appellant; or

(2) an appellant whose legal representation is provided free of charge to the appellant and not funded by the Community Legal Service; is in such poor financial circumstances that the cost of a transcript would be an excessive burden the court may certify that the cost of obtaining one official transcript should be borne at public expense.

8–074   5.18 In the case of a request for an official transcript of evidence or proceedings to be paid for at public expense, the court must also be satisfied that there are reasonable grounds for appeal. Whenever possible a request for a transcript at public expense should be made to the lower court when asking for permission to appeal.

Transcripts of judgments at public expense

8–075   Paragraph 5.17 of the practice direction relates principally to transcripts of judgments. In *Perotti v Westminster* [2005] EWCA Civ 581 the Court of Appeal upheld an order that P's application for a transcript at public expense should not be considered until after he had furnished detailed grounds of appeal. In some cases this is an appropriate course, in order to prevent the fruitless expenditure of public funds.

Filing and service of appellant's notice

8–076   5.19 Rule 52.4 sets out the procedure and time limits for filing and serving an appellant's notice. The appellant must file the appellant's notice at the appeal court within such period as may be directed by the lower court which should not normally exceed 28 days or, where the lower court directs no such period, within 14 days of the date of the decision that the appellant wishes to appeal.

(Rule 52.15 sets out the time limit for filing an application for permission to appeal against the refusal of the High Court to grant permission to apply for judicial review)

8–077   5.20 Where the lower court judge announces his decision and reserves the reasons for his judgment or order until a later date, he should, in the exercise of powers under rule 52.4(2)(a) , fix a period for filing the appellant's notice at the appeal court that takes this into account.

8–078   5.21 (1) Except where the appeal court orders otherwise a sealed copy of the appellant's notice, including any skeleton arguments must be served on all respondents in accordance with the timetable prescribed by rule 52.4(3) except where this requirement is modified by paragraph 5.9(2) in which case the skeleton argument should be served as soon as it is filed.

(2) The appellant must, as soon as practicable, file a certificate of service of the documents referred to in paragraph (1).

5.22 Unless the court otherwise directs a respondent need not take any action when served with an appellant's notice until such time as notification is given to him that permission to appeal has been given. **8–079**

5.23 The court may dispense with the requirement for service of the notice on a respondent. Any application notice seeking an order under rule 6.9 to dispense with service should set out the reasons relied on and be verified by a statement of truth. **8–080**

5.24—(1) Where the appellant is applying for permission to appeal in his appellant's notice, he must serve on the respondents his appellant's notice and skeleton argument (but not the appeal bundle), unless the appeal court directs otherwise. **8–081**

(2) Where permission to appeal—

(a) has been given by the lower court; or
(b) is not required, the appellant must serve the appeal bundle on the respondents with the appellant's notice.

Amendment of appeal notice

5.25 An appeal notice may be amended with permission. Such an application to amend and any application in opposition will normally be dealt with at the hearing unless that course would cause unnecessary expense or delay in which case a request should be made for the application to amend to be heard in advance. **8–082**

Remedies under the Human Rights Act

See generally Ch.15. **8–083**

Application to extend time

For the considerations relevant to the exercise of the discretion to extend time, see notes to CPR r.52.6 above at para.7–053. **8–084**

Documents to be filed

The drafting of para.5.6 and 5.6A is reminiscent of nothing so much as the "rules of cricket as explained to a foreigner" so often reproduced on tea-towels. The requirement to include in the appeal bundle a sealed copy of the appellant's notice, in particular, appears paradoxical: the appellant's notice will not acquire the court's seal until the court has had hold of it, that is, until it has been filed. **8–085**

What parties or their representatives actually need to take to the Civil Appeals Office is the following:

(1) an appeal bundle, comprising the documents listed at 5.6A(1)(a) to (m) (with the reservation that inevitably, when the bundle is compiled, the appellant's notice will not be sealed);

(2) the following separate loose documents (a) one copy of the appellant's notice per respondent, plus two more for the court; (b) the same number of copies of the appellant's skeleton argument (if it has been practicable to prepare one in time: see para.5.9); (c) a sealed copy of the order being appealed; (d) a copy of any order made by the EAT giving or refusing permission to appeal, together with reasons for that decision; (e) any witness statements or affidavits in support of any application included in the appellant's notice.

When these documents are taken to the Civil Appeals Office, court staff will apply the court's seal to the copy of the appellant's notice in the appeal bundle: thus the bundle that is left behind at the Civil Appeals Office will comply with 5.6A(1)(a) notwithstanding that it did not do so when it left the solicitor's office.

Additional copies of the bundle

8–086   The appellant must of course retain a copy of the appeal bundle. If permission is granted, the court will in due course require further copies of the appeal bundle. There is no set time for lodging additional copies of the bundle at the court: the Civil Appeals Office will give instructions in each case.

Rule 52.8

8–087   A skeleton argument, whether or not it forms part of the appeal notice, may be amended without leave of the court.

Unrepresented appellants

8–088   See para.7–008 above.

Citation of authorities

8–089   See also PD 15.11 and the following notes at para.8–157.

Other information

8–090   The decision whether to provide a list of persons (often referred to as a "cast list"), glossary or chronology is left to the advocates or unrepresented parties' discretion.

Note of the judgment

8–091   In the EAT extempore judgments are invariably tape-recorded, and a transcript made available if requested by either party within 14 days of the hearing: see EAT PD 18.5 at para.6–144. Advocates' notes of the judgment will therefore only be needed if the equipment malfunctions or the tape is lost.

Notes of evidence

8–092   If notes of evidence are relevant to the appeal, they will normally have been agreed or obtained for the purposes of the appeal to the EAT.

Transcripts of evidence at public expense

8–093   Where the EAT directs the employment judge to produce notes of evidence given to the employment tribunal, a typed version is produced without charge to the appellant.

Transcripts of judgments at public expense

Again, this provision is inapplicable to appeals from the EAT, which produces **8–094** transcripts of judgments on request and without charge.

Amendment

The principles governing amendment of statements of case (which definition **8–095** includes an appeal notice) under CPR r.17 are consistent across the board (see *Thurrock BC v Secretary of State for the Environment, Transport and the Regions, The Times*, December 20, 2000, CA). In *Cobbold v Greenwich LBC*, unreported, August 9, 1999, CA, Peter Gibson L.J. said, after referring to the overriding objective, "Amendments in general ought to be allowed so that the real dispute between the parties can be adjudicated upon provided that any prejudice to the other party caused by the amendment can be compensated for in costs, and the public interest in the administration of justice is not significantly harmed." The merits of the amendment and the date at which it is sought are also relevant; see further the notes to CPR r.17 in *Civil Procedure 2007*, paras 17.3.4–17.3.7.

Application for permission to amend

The Practice Direction to CPR r.17 is short; the relevant parts are as follows: **8–096**

1.1 The application may be dealt with at a hearing or, if r.23.8 applies, without a hearing.

1.2 When making an application to amend a statement of case, the applicant should file with the court: (1) the application notice, and (2) a copy of the statement of case with the proposed amendments.

1.3 Where permission to amend has been given, the applicant should within 14 days of the date of the order, or within such other period as the court may direct, file with the court the amended statement of case.

1.4 If the substance of the statement of case is changed by reason of the amendment, the statement of case should be re-verified by a statement of truth.

1.5 A copy of the order and the amended statement of case should be served on every party to the proceedings, unless the court orders otherwise.

2.1 The amended statement of case and the court copy of it should be endorsed as follows: where the court's permission was required: (1) Amended [Particulars of *Claim or as may be*] by Order of [Master ....][District Judge .... *or as may be*] dated .... (2) ....

2.2 The statement of case in its amended form need not show the original text. However, where the court thinks it desirable for both the original text and the amendments to be shown, the court may direct that the amendments should be shown either: (1) by coloured amendments, either manuscript or computer generated, or (2) by use of a numerical code in a monochrome computer generated document.

2.3 Where colour is used, the text to be deleted should be struck through in colour and any text replacing it should be inserted or underlined in the same colour.

2.4 The order of colours to be used for successive amendments is: (1) red, (2) green, (3) violet and (4) yellow.

8–097   6.1 This paragraph sets out the procedure where:

(1) permission to appeal is given by the appeal court; or

(2) the appellant's notice is filed in the appeal court and—

    (a) permission was given by the lower court; or

    (b) permission is not required.

8–098   6.2 If the appeal court gives permission to appeal, the appeal bundle must be served on each of the respondents within 7 days of receiving the order giving permission to appeal.
(Part 6 (service of documents) provides rules on service.)

8–099   6.3 The appeal court will send the parties—

(1) notification of—

    (a) the date of the hearing or the period of time (the 'listing window') during which the appeal is likely to be heard; and

    (b) in the Court of Appeal, the date by which the appeal will be heard (the 'hear by date');

(2) where permission is granted by the appeal court a copy of the order giving permission to appeal; and

(3) any other directions given by the court.

8–100   6.3A—(1) Where the appeal court grants permission to appeal, the appellant must add the following documents to the appeal bundle—

    (a) the respondent's notice and skeleton argument (if any);

    (b) those parts of the transcripts of evidence which are directly relevant to any question at issue on the appeal;

    (c) the order granting permission to appeal and, where permission to appeal was granted at an oral hearing, the transcript (or note) of any judgment which was given; and

    (d) any document which the appellant and respondent have agreed to add to the appeal bundle in accordance with paragraph 7.11.

(2) Where permission to appeal has been refused on a particular issue, the appellant must remove from the appeal bundle all documents that are relevant only to that issue.

Appeal Questionnaire in the Court of Appeal

8–101   6.4 The Court of Appeal will send an Appeal Questionnaire to the appellant when it notifies him of the matters referred to in paragraph 6.3.

6.5 The appellant must complete and file the Appeal Questionnaire 8–102
within 14 days of the date of the letter of notification of the matters
in paragraph 6.3. The Appeal Questionnaire must contain:

(1) **if the appellant is legally represented, the advocate's time**
estimate for the hearing of the appeal;

(2) **where a transcript of evidence is relevant to the appeal,**
confirmation as to what parts of a transcript of evidence
have been ordered where this is not already in the bundle
of documents;

(3) **confirmation that copies of the appeal bundle are being**
prepared and will be held ready for the use of the Court
of Appeal and an undertaking that they will be supplied to
the court on request. For the purpose of these bundles
photocopies of the transcripts will be accepted;

(4) **confirmation that copies of the Appeal Questionnaire and**
the appeal bundle have been served on the respondents
and the date of that service.

Time estimates

6.6 The time estimate included in an Appeal Questionnaire must 8–103
be that of the advocate who will argue the appeal. It should exclude
the time required by the court to give judgment. If the respondent
disagrees with the time estimate, the respondent must inform the
court within 7 days of receipt of the Appeal Questionnaire. In the
absence of such notification the respondent will be deemed to have
accepted the estimate proposed on behalf of the appellant.

Adding and removing documents

Documents to be added to bundles already lodged with the court should be 8–104
provided hole-punched and without staples, bearing appropriate page numbers and
accompanied by a revised index: see 15.4(10) below at para.8–147. There is no
guidance in the PD on removing documents, but it is suggested that the sensible
course is to provide a page bearing the words "page [x] is missing" or "pages [x] to
[y] are missing" to replace each of the documents to be discarded, together with a
revised index, both under cover of a letter indicating which pages are to be
discarded. If amendments are to be made after copies of the bundle have been
served on the respondents to the appeal, their bundles should be revised in the
same manner.

Unrepresented appellants

It is suggested that time estimates are an exception to the general proposition 8–105
that unrepresented appellants should if possible comply voluntarily with requirements placed on represented parties: unrepresented parties will rarely be in a
position to provide the court with a helpful time estimate.

<small>RESPONDENT</small>

7.1 A respondent who wishes to ask the appeal court to vary the 8–106
order of the lower court in any way must appeal and permission will
be required on the same basis as for an appellant.

(Paragraph 3.2 applies to grounds of appeal by a respondent.)

8–107   7.2 A respondent who wishes only to request that the appeal court upholds the judgment or order of the lower court whether for the reasons given in the lower court or otherwise does not make an appeal and does not therefore require permission to appeal in accordance with rule 52.3(1).

(Paragraph 7.6 requires a respondent to file a skeleton argument where he wishes to address the appeal court)

8–108   7.3—(1) A respondent who wishes to appeal or who wishes to ask the appeal court to uphold the order of the lower court for reasons different from or additional to those given by the lower court must file a respondent's notice.

(2) If the respondent does not file a respondent's notice, he will not be entitled, except with the permission of the court, to rely on any reason not relied on in the lower court.

8–109   7.3A Paragraphs 5.1A, 5.1B and 5.2 of this practice direction (Human Rights and extension for time for filing appellant's notice) also apply to a respondent and a respondent's notice.

Time limits
8–110   7.4 The time limits for filing a respondent's notice are set out in rule 52.5(4) and (5).

8–111   7.5 Where an extension of time is required the extension must be requested in the respondent's notice and the reasons why the respondent failed to act within the specified time must be included.

8–112   7.6 Except where paragraph 7.7A applies, the respondent must file a skeleton argument for the court in all cases where he proposes to address arguments to the court. The respondent's skeleton argument may be included within a respondent's notice. Where a skeleton argument is included within a respondent's notice it will not form part of the notice for the purposes of rule 52.8.

8–113   7.7—(1) A respondent who—

    (a) files a respondent's notice; but
    (b) does not include his skeleton argument within that notice, must file and serve his skeleton argument within 14 days of filing the notice.

(2) A respondent who does not file a respondent's notice but who files a skeleton argument must file and serve that skeleton argument at least 7 days before the appeal hearing.

(Rule 52.5(4) sets out the period for filing and serving a respondent's notice)

7.7A—(1) Where the appeal relates to a claim allocated to the **8–114** small claims track and is being heard in a county court or the High Court, the respondent may file a skeleton argument but is not required to do so.

(2) A respondent who is not represented need not file a skeleton argument but is encouraged to do so in order to assist the court.

7.7B The respondent must— **8–115**
(1) serve his skeleton argument on—

    (a) the appellant; and
    (b) any other respondent, at the same time as he files it at the court; and

(2) file a certificate of service.

Content of skeleton arguments

7.8 A respondent's skeleton argument must conform to the dir- **8–116** ections at paragraphs 5.10 and 5.11 with any necessary modifications. It should, where appropriate, answer the arguments set out in the appellant's skeleton argument.

Applications within respondent's notices

7.9 A respondent may include an application within a respondent's **8–117** notice in accordance with paragraph 5.5 above.

Filing respondent's notices and skeleton arguments

7.10—(1) The respondent must file the following documents with **8–118** his respondent's notice in every case:

    (a) two additional copies of the respondent's notice for the appeal court; and
    (b) one copy each for the appellant and any other respondents.

(2) The respondent may file a skeleton argument with his respondent's notice and—

    (a) where he does so he must file two copies; and
    (b) where he does not do so he must comply with paragraph 7.7.

7.11 If the respondent wishes to rely on any documents which he **8–119** reasonably considers necessary to enable the appeal court to reach its decision on the appeal in addition to those filed by the appellant, he must make every effort to agree amendments to the appeal bundle with the appellant.

8–120　7.12—(1) If the representatives for the parties are unable to reach agreement, the respondent may prepare a supplemental bundle.

(2) If the respondent prepares a supplemental bundle he must file it, together with the requisite number of copies for the appeal court, at the appeal court—

> (a) with the respondent's notice; or
> (b) if a respondent's notice is not filed, within 21 days after he is served with the appeal bundle.

8–121　7.13 The respondent must serve—
(1) the respondent's notice;
(2) his skeleton argument (if any); and
(3) the supplemental bundle (if any), on—

> (a) the appellant; and
> (b) any other respondent, at the same time as he files them at the court.

[*deleted paragraphs 8–11*]

Disposing of applications or appeals by consent

Dismissal of Applications or Appeals by Consent

8–122　12.1 These paragraphs do not apply where—

(1) any party to the proceedings is a child or protected party; or
(2) the appeal or application is to the Court of Appeal from a decision of the Court of Protection.

8–123　12.2 Where an appellant does not wish to pursue an application or an appeal, he may request the appeal court for an order that his application or appeal be dismissed. Such a request must contain a statement that the appellant is not a child or protected party and that the appeal or application is not from a decision of the Court of Protection. If such a request is granted it will usually be on the basis that the appellant pays the costs of the application or appeal.

8–124　12.3 If the appellant wishes to have the application or appeal dismissed without costs, his request must be accompanied by a consent signed by the respondent or his legal representative stating—

(1) that the respondent is not a child or protected party and that the appeal or application is not from a decision of the Court of Protection; and

(2) that he consents to the dismissal of the application or appeal without costs.

12.4 Where a settlement has been reached disposing of the application or appeal, the parties may make a joint request to the court stating that— **8–125**

(1) none of them is a child or protected party; and

(2) the appeal or application is not from a decision of the Court of Protection, and asking that the application or appeal be dismissed by consent. If the request is granted the application or appeal will be dismissed.

('Child' and 'protected party' have the same meaning as in rule 21.1(2).)

Allowing unopposed appeals or applications on paper

13.1 The appeal court will not normally make an order allowing an appeal unless satisfied that the decision of the lower court was wrong, but the appeal court may set aside or vary the order of the lower court with consent and without determining the merits of the appeal, if it is satisfied that there are good and sufficient reasons for doing so. Where the appeal court is requested by all parties to allow an application or an appeal the court may consider the request on the papers. The request should state that none of the parties is a child or protected party and that the application or appeal is not from a decision of the Court of Protection and set out the relevant history of the proceedings and the matters relied on as justifying the proposed order and be accompanied by a copy of the proposed order. **8–126**

Procedure for consent orders and agreements to pay periodical payments involving a child or protected party or in applications or appeals to the Court of Appeal from a decision of the Court of Protection

13.2 Where one of the parties is a child or protected party or the application or appeal is to the Court of Appeal from a decision of the Court of Protection— **8–127**

(1) a settlement relating to an appeal or application; [. . .]

(2) in a personal injury claim for damages for future pecuniary loss, an agreement reached at the appeal stage to pay periodical payments; or

(3) a request by an appellant for an order that his application or appeal be dismissed with or without the consent of the respondent, requires the court's approval.

Child

8–128   13.3 In cases involving a child a copy of the proposed order signed by the parties' solicitors should be sent to the appeal court, together with an opinion from the advocate acting on behalf of the child.

Protected party

8–129   13.4 Where a party is a protected party the same procedure will be adopted, but the documents filed should also include any relevant reports prepared for the Court of Protection.

Periodical payments

8–130   13.5 Where periodical payments for future pecuniary loss have been negotiated in a personal injury case which is under appeal, the documents filed should include those which would be required in the case of a personal injury claim for damages for future pecuniary loss dealt with at first instance. Details can be found in the Practice Direction which supplements Part 21.

Amendment

8–130/1   References in paras 12 and 13 to the Court of Protection inserted, and references to "patient" replaced by references to a "protected party," with effect October 1, 2007.

Summary Assessment of Costs

8–131   14.1 Costs are likely to be assessed by way of summary assessment at the following hearings:

(1) contested directions hearings;
(2) applications for permission to appeal at which the respondent is present;
(3) dismissal list hearings in the Court of Appeal at which the respondent is present;
(4) appeals from case management decisions; and
(5) appeals listed for one day or less.

8–132   14.2 Parties attending any of the hearings referred to in paragraph 14.1 should be prepared to deal with the summary assessment.

Other Special Provisions Regarding the Court of Appeal

Filing of documents

8–133   15.1—(1) The documents relevant to proceedings in the Court of Appeal, Civil Division must be filed in the Civil Appeals Office Registry, Room E307, Royal Courts of Justice, Strand, London, WC2A 2LL.

(2) The Civil Appeals Office will not serve documents and where service is required by the CPR or this practice direction it must be effected by the parties.

15.1A—(1) A party may file by email—   **8–134**

    (a) an appellant's notice;

    (b) a respondent's notice;

    (c) an application notice,

in the Court of Appeal, Civil Division, using the email account specified in the "Guidelines for filing by Email" which appear on the Court of Appeal, Civil Division website at *www.civilappeals.gov.uk*.

(2) A party may only file a notice in accordance with paragraph (1) where he is permitted to do so by the "Guidelines for filing by Email".

Core bundles

15.2 In cases where the appeal bundle comprises more than 500   **8–135** pages, exclusive of transcripts, the appellant's solicitors must, after consultation with the respondent's solicitors, also prepare and file with the court, in addition to copies of the appeal bundle (as amended in accordance with paragraph 7.11) the requisite number of copies of a core bundle.

15.3—(1) The core bundle must be filed within 28 days of receipt   **8–136** of the order giving permission to appeal or, where permission to appeal was granted by the lower court or is not required, within 28 days of the date of service of the appellant's notice on the respondent.

(2) The core bundle—

    (a) must contain the documents which are central to the appeal; and

    (b) must not exceed 150 pages.

Preparation of bundles

15.4 The provisions of this paragraph apply to the preparation of   **8–137** appeal bundles, supplemental respondents' bundles where the parties are unable to agree amendments to the appeal bundle, and core bundles.

(1) Rejection of bundles

Where documents are copied unnecessarily or bundled   **8–138** incompletely, costs may be disallowed. Where the provisions of this Practice Direction as to the preparation or delivery of bundles are not followed the bundle may be rejected by the court or be made the subject of a special costs order.

(2) Avoidance of duplication

8–139   No more than one copy of any document should be included unless there is a good reason for doing otherwise (such as the use of a separate core bundle—see paragraph 15.2).

(3) Pagination

8–140   (a) Bundles must be paginated, each page being numbered individually and consecutively. The pagination used at trial must also be indicated. Letters and other documents should normally be included in chronological order. (An exception to consecutive page numbering arises in the case of core bundles where it may be preferable to retain the original numbering).
(b) Page numbers should be inserted in bold figures at the bottom of the page and in a form that can be clearly distinguished from any other pagination on the document.

(4) Format and presentation

8–141   (a) Where possible the documents should be in A4 format. Where a document has to be read across rather than down the page, it should be so placed in the bundle as to ensure that the text starts nearest the spine.
(b) Where any marking or writing in colour on a document is important, the document must be copied in colour or marked up correctly in colour.
(c) Documents which are not easily legible should be transcribed and the transcription marked and placed adjacent to the document transcribed.
(d) Documents in a foreign language should be translated and the translation marked and placed adjacent to the document translated. The translation should be agreed or, if it cannot be agreed, each party's proposed translation should be included.
(e) The size of any bundle should be tailored to its contents. A large lever arch file should not be used for just a few pages nor should files of whatever size be overloaded.
(f) Where it will assist the Court of Appeal, different sections of the file may be separated by cardboard or other tabbed dividers so long as these are clearly indexed. Where, for example, a document is awaited when the appeal bundle is filed, a single sheet of paper can be inserted after a divider, indicating the nature of the document

awaited. For example, 'Transcript of evidence of Mr J Smith (to follow)'.

(5) Binding

(a) All documents, with the exception of transcripts, must be   8–142
bound together. This may be in a lever arch file, ring binder or
plastic folder. Plastic sleeves containing loose documents must not
be used. Binders and files must be strong enough to withstand heavy
use.

(b) Large documents such as plans should be placed in an easily
accessible file. Large documents which will need to be opened up
frequently should be inserted in a file larger than A4 size.

(6) Indices and labels

(a) An index must be included at the front of the bundle listing all   8–143
the documents and providing the page references for each. In the
case of documents such as letters, invoices or bank statements, they
may be given a general description.

(b) Where the bundles consist of more than one file, an index to
all the files should be included in the first file and an index included
for each file. Indices should, if possible, be on a single sheet. The full
name of the case should not be inserted on the index if this would
waste space. Documents should be identified briefly but properly.

(7) Identification

(a) Every bundle must be clearly identified, on the spine and on   8–144
the front cover, with the name of the case and the Court of Appeal's
reference. Where the bundle consists of more than one file, each file
must be numbered on the spine, the front cover and the inside of the
front cover.

(b) Outer labels should use large lettering eg 'Appeal Bundle A' or
'Core Bundle'. The full title of the appeal and solicitors' names and
addresses should be omitted. A label should be used on the front as
well as on the spine.

(8) Staples etc.

All staples, heavy metal clips etc, must be removed.   8–145

(9) Statements of case

(a) Statements of case should be assembled in 'chapter' form - i.e   8–146
claim followed by particulars of claim, followed by further information, irrespective of date.

(b) Redundant documents, eg particulars of claim overtaken by amendments, requests for further information recited in the answers given, should generally be excluded.

(10)   New documents

8–147   (a) Before a new document is introduced into bundles which have already been delivered to the court, steps should be taken to ensure that it carries an appropriate bundle/page number so that it can be added to the court documents. It should not be stapled and it should be prepared with punch holes for immediate inclusion in the binders in use.

(b) If it is expected that a large number of miscellaneous new documents will from time to time be introduced, there should be a special tabbed empty loose-leaf file for that purpose. An index should be produced for this file, updated as necessary.

8–148   (11) Inter-solicitor correspondence. Since inter-solicitor correspondence is unlikely to be required for the purposes of an appeal, only those letters which will need to be referred to should be copied.

8–149   (12) Sanctions for non-compliance. If the appellant fails to comply with the requirements as to the provision of bundles of documents, the application or appeal will be referred for consideration to be given as to why it should not be dismissed for failure to so comply.

Master in the Court of Appeal, Civil Division
8–150   15.5 When the Head of the Civil Appeals Office acts in a judicial capacity pursuant to rule 52.16, he shall be known as Master. Other eligible officers may also be designated by the Master of the Rolls to exercise judicial authority under rule 52.16 and shall then be known as Deputy Masters.

Respondent to notify Civil Appeals Office whether he intends to file respondent's notice
8–151   15.6 A respondent must, no later than 21 days after the date he is served with notification that—
(1) permission to appeal has been granted; or
(2) the application for permission to appeal and the appeal are to be heard together, inform the Civil Appeals Office and the appellant in writing whether—

   (a) he proposes to file a respondent's notice appealing the order or seeking to uphold the order for reasons different from, or additional to, those given by the lower court; or

(b) he proposes to rely on the reasons given by the lower court for its decision.

(Paragraph 15.11B requires all documents needed for an appeal hearing, including a respondent's skeleton argument, to be filed at least 7 days before the hearing)

Listing and hear-by dates

15.7 The management of the list will be dealt with by the listing officer under the direction of the Master.   **8–152**

15.8 The Civil Appeals List of the Court of Appeal is divided as follows: **8–153**

The applications list—applications for permission to appeal and other applications.

The appeals list—appeals where permission to appeal has been given or where an appeal lies without permission being required where a hearing date is fixed in advance. (Appeals in this list which require special listing arrangements will be assigned to the special fixtures list)

The expedited list—appeals or applications where the Court of Appeal has directed an expedited hearing. The current practice of the Court of Appeal is summarised in *Unilever plc v Chefaro Proprietaries Ltd* (Practice Note) [1995] 1 W.L.R. 243.

The stand-out list—Appeals or applications which, for good reason, are not at present ready to proceed and have been stood out by judicial direction.

The second fixtures list—[see paragraph 15.9A(1) below].

The second fixtures list—if an appeal is designated as a 'second fixture' it means that a hearing date is arranged in advance on the express basis that the list is fully booked for the period in question and therefore the case will be heard only if a suitable gap occurs in the list.

The short-warned list—appeals which the court considers may be prepared for the hearing by an advocate other than the one originally instructed with a half day's notice, or such other period as the court may direct.

Special provisions relating to the short-warned list

15.9—(1) Where an appeal is assigned to the short-warned list, the Civil Appeals Office will notify the parties' solicitors in writing. The court may abridge the time for filing any outstanding bundles in an appeal assigned to this list.   **8–154**

(2) The solicitors for the parties must notify their advocate and their client as soon as the Civil Appeals Office notifies them that the appeal has been assigned to the short-warned list.

(3) The appellant may apply in writing for the appeal to be removed from the short-warned list within 14 days of notification of its assignment. The application will be decided by a Lord Justice, or the Master, and will only be granted for the most compelling reasons.

(4) The Civil Appeals Listing Officer may place an appeal from the short-warned list 'on call' from a given date and will inform the parties' advocates accordingly.

(5) An appeal which is 'on call' may be listed for hearing on half a day's notice or such longer period as the court may direct.

(6) Once an appeal is listed for hearing from the short warned list it becomes the immediate professional duty of the advocate instructed in the appeal, if he is unable to appear at the hearing, to take all practicable measures to ensure that his lay client is represented at the hearing by an advocate who is fully instructed and able to argue the appeal.

Special provisions relating to the special fixtures list

8–155   15.9A—(1) The special fixtures list is a sub-division of the appeals list and is used to deal with appeals that may require special listing arrangements, such as the need to list a number of cases before the same constitution, in a particular order, during a particular period or at a given location.

(2) The Civil Appeals Office will notify the parties' representatives, or the parties if acting in person, of the particular arrangements that will apply. The notice—

> (a) will give details of the specific period during which a case is scheduled to be heard; and
> (b) may give directions in relation to the filing of any outstanding documents.

(3) The listing officer will notify the parties' representatives of the precise hearing date as soon as practicable. While every effort will be made to accommodate the availability of counsel, the requirements of the court will prevail.

Requests for directions

8–156   5.10 To ensure that all requests for directions are centrally monitored and correctly allocated, all requests for directions or rulings (whether relating to listing or any other matters) should be made to the Civil Appeals Office. Those seeking directions or rulings must not approach the supervising Lord Justice either directly, or via his or her clerk.

Bundles of authorities

8–157   15.11(1) Once the parties have been notified of the date fixed for the hearing, the appellant's advocate must, after consultation with his opponent, file a bundle containing photocopies of the authorities upon which each side will rely at the hearing.

(2) The bundle of authorities should, in general—

    (a) have the relevant passages of the authorities marked;

    (b) not include authorities for propositions not in dispute; and

    (c) not contain more than 10 authorities unless the scale of the appeal warrants more extensive citation.

(3) The bundle of authorities must be filed—

    (a) at least 7 days before the hearing; or

    (b) where the period of notice of the hearing is less than 7 days, immediately.

(4) If, through some oversight, a party intends, during the hearing, to refer to other authorities the parties may agree a second agreed bundle. The appellant's advocate must file this bundle at least 48 hours before the hearing commences.

(5) A bundle of authorities must bear a certification by the advocates responsible for arguing the case that the requirements of sub-paragraphs (3) to (5) of paragraph 5.10 have been complied with in respect of each authority included.

Supplementary skeleton arguments

15.11A—(1) A supplementary skeleton argument on which the **8–158** appellant wishes to rely must be filed at least 14 days before the hearing.

(2) A supplementary skeleton argument on which the respondent wishes to rely must be filed at least 7 days before the hearing.

(3) All supplementary skeleton arguments must comply with the requirements set out in paragraph 5.10.

(4) At the hearing the court may refuse to hear argument from a party not contained in a skeleton argument filed within the relevant time limit set out in this paragraph.

Papers for the appeal hearing

15.11B—(1) All the documents which are needed for the appeal **8–159** hearing must be filed at least 7 days before the hearing. Where a document has not been filed 10 days before the hearing a reminder will be sent by the Civil Appeals Office.

(2) Any party who fails to comply with the provisions of paragraph (1) may be required to attend before the Presiding Lord Justice to seek permission to proceed with, or to oppose, the appeal.

Disposal of bundles of documents

15.11C—(1) Where the court has determined a case, the official **8–160** transcriber will retain one set of papers. The Civil Appeals Office will destroy any remaining sets of papers not collected within 21 days of—

(a) where one or more parties attend the hearing, the date of the court's decision;

(b) where there is no attendance, the date of the notification of court's decision.

(2) The parties should ensure that bundles of papers supplied to the court do not contain original documents (other than transcripts). The parties must ensure that they—

(a) bring any necessary original documents to the hearing; and

(b) retrieve any original documents handed up to the court before leaving the court.

(3) The court will retain application bundles where permission to appeal has been granted. Where permission is refused the arrangements in sub-paragraph (1) will apply.

(4) Where a single Lord Justice has refused permission to appeal on paper, application bundles will not be destroyed until after the time limit for seeking a hearing has expired.

Availability of reserved judgments before hand down

8–161 15.12 This section applies where the presiding Lord Justice is satisfied that the result of the appeal will attract no special degree of confidentiality or sensitivity.

8–162 15.13 A copy of the written judgment will be made available to the parties' legal advisers by 4 p.m. on the second working day before judgment is due to be pronounced or such other period as the court may direct. This can be shown, in confidence, to the parties but only for the purpose of obtaining instructions and on the strict understanding that the judgment, or its effect, is not to be disclosed to any other person. A working day is any day on which the Civil Appeals Office is open for business.

8–163 15.14 The appeal will be listed for judgment in the cause list and the judgment handed down at the appropriate time.

Attendance of advocates on the handing down of a reserved judgment

8–164 15.15 Where any consequential orders are agreed, the parties' advocates need not attend on the handing down of a reserved judgment. Where an advocate does attend the court may, if it considers such attendance unnecessary, disallow the costs of the attendance. If the parties do not indicate that they intend to attend, the judgment may be handed down by a single member of the court.

Agreed orders following judgment

15.16—(1) The parties must, in respect of any draft agreed orders— **8–165**

    (a) fax a copy to the clerk to the presiding Lord Justice; and

    (b) file four copies in the Civil Appeals Office, no later than 12 noon on the working day before the judgment is handed down.

15.17 A copy of a draft order must bear the Court of Appeal case reference, the date the judgment is to be handed down and the name of the presiding Lord Justice. **8–166**

Corrections to the draft judgment

15.18 Any proposed correction to the draft judgment should be sent to the clerk to the judge who prepared the draft with a copy to any other party. **8–167**

Application for leave to appeal

15.19 Where a party wishes to apply for leave to appeal to the House of Lords under section 1 of the Administration of Justice (Appeals) Act 1934 the court may deal with the application on the basis of written submissions. **8–168**

15.20 A party must, in relation to his submission— **8–169**

    (a) fax a copy to the clerk to the presiding Lord Justice; and

    (b) file four copies in the Civil Appeals Office, no later than 12 noon on the working day before the judgment is handed down.

15.21 A copy of a submission must bear the Court of Appeal case reference, the date the judgment is to be handed down and the name of the presiding Lord Justice. **8–170**

Filing by email

The guidelines can be found on the Court Service Website at *http://www.hmcourts-service.gov.uk/cms/7735.htm*. Service by email is only available to those represented by solicitors, and must be accompanied by an undertaking to pay any applicable fee as soon as practicable and in any event no later than seven days from the day when the email is sent, and a statement that the named sender is authorised to give undertakings on behalf of the firm of solicitors concerned. The notice will be rejected if it is larger than 20 pages in length or two megabytes or contains "material color content." It would seem that the intention must be to permit the filing of the appeal notice itself by email, with the documents listed at 5.6 (see para.8–057 above) to follow in hard copy thereafter; but in the absence of any confirmation of that either in the guidelines or the PD, it will take a solicitor with strong nerves to rely on that supposition. **8–171**

In the circumstances, and until the guidance is clarified, it is suggested that any attempt to file a notice of appeal by email is ill-advised.

Marking the relevant passages

8–172   In *Haggis v DPP* [2003] EWHC 2481, at [33], Latham L.J. said: "I draw particular attention to the need to mark in the authorities the passages on which the advocates wish to rely. It is also very helpful if the page number can be mentioned in the skeleton argument, although that is not specified in the practice direction. The reason for this is that the judges wish to be able to pre-read whenever they reasonably can. If they are simply referred to a case which may have 20 or 25 pages in it, it is unlikely that they are going to be enthusiastic about reading all 25 pages in order to run to earth, if they spot it, the principle on which the advocate seeks to rely." In *Harvey Shopfitters v Adi Ltd* [2003] EWCA Civ 1757, at [21], Latham L.J. modified this by saying that strict attention need not be paid to the duty to mark relevant passages if—but only if—the precise passages the court should read have been identified in the skeleton arguments.

Number of authorities

8–173   Paragraphs 15.11(2)(b) and (c) are the latest of a number of attempts to inhibit the tendency of advocates to cite excessive volumes of case law. Although they are still widely ignored, often without sanction or even comment, significant breach can cause the court great inconvenience and corresponding annoyance (see, for example, the comments of Munby J. in *Governor of the Bank of Scotland v Henry Butcher & Co* [2003] EWCA Civ 67; [2006] 2 All E.R. 610, at [77]). Note too the potential costs sanction against a non-compliant party.

These strictures can place advocates in some difficulty: where conscientious efforts have been made to keep the citation of authorities to the minimum necessary to the appeal in obedience to the PD, the court itself may take a different view of what is necessary and require argument on authorities that have been considered but excluded from the bundle. This probably explains the widespread temptation to err on the side of completeness. It is suggested that the better course is to seek to agree a bundle of authorities that includes only the minimum authorities that the advocates consider necessary, but to attend the hearing with sufficient copies of any other relevant authorities that it is reasonably anticipated the court might wish to discuss.

Comments on draft judgments before hand down

8–174   The purpose of circulating judgments in draft is to enable formal or typographical amendments to be made; it is not an occasion for making new submissions on matters of substance which ought to have been made during the appeal itself (*Robinson v Fernsby* [2003] EWCA Civ 1820, at [95]). Nevertheless, a judge has discretion to alter his draft judgment before it is handed down, and a judge cannot be required to hand down for the first time a judgment which he believes to be wrong: *Robinson* [98]. In the same case, at [120], Peter Gibson L.J. said,

"With one possible qualification it is in my judgment incontrovertible that until the order of a judge has been sealed he retains the ability to recall the order he has made even if he has given reasons for that order by a judgment handed down or orally delivered. . . Such judicial tergiversation is in general not to be encouraged, but circumstances may arise in which it is necessary for a judge to have the courage to recall his order. If. . . the judge realises that he has made an error, how can he be true to his judicial oath other than by correcting that error so long as it lies within his power to do so? No doubt that will happen only in exceptional circumstances, but I have serious misgivings about elevating that correct description of the circumstances when that occurs as exceptional into some sort of criterion for what is required for the recalling of an order before it is sealed."

In principle, these remarks leave an advocate who believes that a draft judgment betrays a material oversight or misunderstanding in some difficulty. If the judgment appears to contain a material oversight or misunderstanding, then the decision whether to seek to persuade the judge to alter the draft before it is handed down can, it is suggested, only sensibly depend on whether there seems to be a realistic prospect of persuading the judge that he is mistaken. If the matter has been fully argued, there will be no reason to expect further written submissions to carry the day. In any event, the occasions on which serious consideration need be given to whether the Court of Appeal can be persuaded to tergiversation can be expected to be vanishingly rare.

(Paras 16 and 17.1—17.6 are outside the scope of this work and are not reproduced.)

Rule 52.12A Statutory appeals—court's power to hear any person

17.7 Where all the parties consent, the court may deal with an application under rule 52.12A without a hearing. **8–175**

17.8 Where the court gives permission for a person to file evidence or to make representations at the appeal hearing, it may do so on conditions and may give case management directions.

17.9 An application for permission must be made by letter to the relevant court office, identifying the appeal, explaining who the applicant is and indicating why and in what form the applicant wants to participate in the hearing.

17.10 If the applicant is seeking a prospective order as to costs, the letter must say what kind of order and on what grounds.

17.11 Applications to intervene must be made at the earliest reasonable opportunity, since it will usually be essential not to delay the hearing.

(Editorial Note: the remainder of the Practice Direction has no application to appeals from the Employment Appeal Tribunal, and is not reproduced in this work.)

PART 2

ISSUES IN EMPLOYMENT LITIGATION PRACTICE

CHAPTER 9

Limitation

Contents
Sect.

Editorial introduction

The limitation periods which are applicable to claims brought in an employment **9–001** tribunal fall into four broad categories:

(1) limitation periods subject to extension where an employment tribunal is satisfied that it was not reasonably practicable for the complaint to be presented before the end of the period. For example, the provisions governing the time limit for bringing a claim for unfair dismissal under the Employment Rights Act 1996;
(2) limitation periods subject to extension where an employment tribunal considers that in all the circumstances it is just and equitable to do so. Examples of this category include discrimination claims;
(3) limitation periods which are subject to extension only in narrowly pre-scribed circumstances such as where there has been concealment or where the claimant has been under a disability. This applies to claims under the Equal Pay Act 1970; and
(4) claims where no limitation period is specified.

Each of the four categories is dealt with below by reference to the principal provisions to which it applies. A comprehensive table of the time limits and extension provisions for all of the relevant statutory provisions is at para.9–039.

The circumstances in which the time for bringing a claim is extended by operation of the Employment Act 2002 (Dispute Resolution) Regulations 2004, reg.15, is considered separately. However it should be noted that where the employer completes the statutory procedure just before the end of the orignal time limit so that there is no automatic extension under reg.15 an employment tribunal may grant an extension under the "reasonably practicable" provisions (see *Ashcroft v Haberdashers Aske's Boys School* [2007] UKEAT/151/07 and *Royal Bank of Scotland v Bevan* [2007] UKEAT440/07).

(1) Claims Governed by "Not Reasonably Practicable" Provisions

9–002   Unsurprisingly the provisions dealing with complaints of unfair dismissal have been the subject of the most judicial scrutiny. Other provisions which are in the same terms are not set out below save insofar as there is a distinction between the governing legal principles (see for example s.11 of the Employment Rights Act 1996). For a full list of the claims governed by these provisions see para.9–039.

EMPLOYMENT RIGHTS ACT 1996

111. Complaints to employment tribunal

9–003   **(1) A complaint may be presented to an [employment tribunal] against an employer by any person that he was unfairly dismissed by the employer.**

(2) Subject to subsection (3), an [employment tribunal] shall not consider a complaint under this section unless it is presented to the tribunal—

(a) **before the end of the period of three months beginning with the effective date of termination, or**

(b) **within such further period as the tribunal considers reasonable in a case where it is satisfied that it was not reasonably practicable for the complaint to be presented before the end of that period of three months.**

(3) Where a dismissal is with notice, an [employment tribunal] shall consider a complaint under this section if it is presented after the notice is given but before the effective date of termination.

(4) In relation to a complaint which is presented as mentioned in subsection (3), the provisions of this Act, so far as they relate to unfair dismissal, have effect as if—

(a) **references to a complaint by a person that he was unfairly dismissed by his employer included references to a complaint by a person that his employer has given him notice in such circumstances that he will be unfairly dismissed when the notice expires,**

(b) **references to reinstatement included references to the withdrawal of the notice by the employer,**

(c) **references to the effective date of termination included references to the date which would be the effective date of termination on the expiry of the notice, and**

(d) **references to an employee ceasing to be employed included references to an employee having been given notice of dismissal.**

"Presented to the tribunal"

The presentation of complaints is considered in detail elsewhere in the commen- **9–004**
tary on the rules. The position is summarised below.

A claim form is presented in time if it arrives at the employment tribunal before
midnight on the last date of the three month limitation period (*Post Office v Moore*
[1981] I.C.R. 623, EAT).

Complaint presented by post

The leading case addressing the principles governing the presentation of a **9–005**
complaint sent by post is *Sealy v Consignia* Plc [2002] I.C.R. 1193. The principles—
now reflected in r.61(2) of the 2004 Tribunal Rules—were reviewed by Brooke L.J.
and are summarised below. It should be noted that whilst the Court of Appeal has
subsequently held that *Consignia* is wrongly decided insofar as it states the position
under the CPR, *Consignia* remains an accurate and binding statement of the law as
regards the Employment Tribunal Rules (see *Coldridge v HM Prison Service* [2005]
I.C.R. para.7 recent points xxii EAT):

(1) a complaint is "presented" when it arrives at the Central Office of
Employment Tribunals or an Office of the Tribunals ("the Office");
(2) if a claimant shows by way of evidence that it was impossible to present a
complaint—for example, because the tribunal office was locked and did not
have a letter-box—it may be possible to argue that it was not reasonably
practicable for the complaint to have been presented on time;
(3) if the claim form is sent by post presentation will be assumed to have been
effected unless the contrary is proved at the time when the letter would be
delivered in the ordinary course of post;
(4) if the claim form is sent by first-class post, it is legitimate to adapt CPR
r.6.7 and conclude that in the ordinary course of post, it will be delivered on
the second day following postage (excluding days when post is not normally
delivered i.e. Sundays and Bank holidays) (this principle is now reflected in
r.61(2) of the 2004 Tribunal Rules);
(5) if the claim form does not arrive at the time when it would be expected to
arrive in the ordinary course of post, but is unexpectedly delayed, a tribunal
may conclude that it was not reasonably practicable for the complaint to be
presented on time;
(6) if a form is date-stamped on a Monday by a tribunal, office so as to be
outside a three-month period which ends on the Saturday or Sunday, it will
be open to a tribunal to find as a fact that it was posted by first class post
not later than the Thursday and arrived on the Saturday, alternatively to
extend time as a matter of discretion if satisfied that the letter was posted
by first class post not later than the Thursday;
(7) this regime does not allow for any unusual subjective expectation, whether
based on inside knowledge of the postal system or on lay experience of what
happens in practice, to the effect that a letter posted by first class post may
arrive earlier than the second day (excluding Sundays etc.: see (2) above)
after it is posted. The "normal and expected" result of posting a letter must
be objectively, not subjectively, assessed and it is that the letter will arrive
at its destination in the ordinary course of post;
(8) if the claimant takes a chance and the letter containing the claim form
happens to arrive at the office on the day after it was posted, and therefore
within the permitted three-month period, it will have been presented in
time and the rule in *Godwin v Swindon BC* [2002] 1 W.L.R. 997, in relation

to the deemed date of service of documents does not apply in employment tribunal cases.

The unexplained failure of an application to reach the employment tribunal is not sufficient to satisfy the test in s.111(2) unless all reasonable steps were taken to confirm that the application had been duly received (see *Capital Foods Retails Ltd v Corrigan* [1993] I.R.L.R. 430). It is a matter of ordinary and prudent practice to employ some system of checking that replies which might reasonably have been expected have been received, and that the conduct of business is taking its normal course.

Complaints presented by email

9–006　　The principles set out in *Consignia* were applied to electronic communications by the Employment Appeal Tribunal in *Initial Electronic Security Systems Ltd v Avdic* [2005] I.R.L.R. 671. The Employment Appeal Tribunal held that the reasonable expectation of the sender of an electronic mail communication is that, in the absence of any indication to the contrary, it will be delivered and will arrive within a very short time after transmission, normally 30 or 60 minutes.

Complaint presented during notice and prior to subsequent summary dismissal

9–007　　In *Patel v Nagesan* [1995] I.R.L.R. 370, the Court of Appeal held that an employment tribunal did have jurisdiction to consider an employee's complaint of unfair dismissal which had been lodged whilst she was under notice of dismissal, notwithstanding that she was subsequently summarily dismissed. An employment tribunal's jurisdiction to consider a complaint of unfair dismissal which is presented after an employee has been given notice of termination, but before that termination takes effect, is unaffected by a subsequent summary dismissal.

"Shall not consider a complaint"

9–008　　It is well-established that the time limit for unfair dismissal claims is jurisdictional and not procedural. It follows that an employment tribunal is precluded from entertaining a complaint which is out of time (*Westward Circuits Ltd v Read* [1973] I.C.R. 301, NIRC per Sir John Donaldson). The practical effect of a jurisdictional time limit is that the parties cannot waive the time limit; neither is a party estopped from taking the point late in the proceedings. In *Rogers v Bodfari (Transport) Ltd* [1973] I.C.R. 325, the NIRC upheld the dismissal by an employment tribunal of a complaint on the grounds that it was out of time, notwithstanding the fact that the time point was taken for the first time at an adjourned hearing to consider the question of remedy. The jurisdictional nature of the time limit was confirmed by the Court of Appeal in *Dedman v British Building and Engineering Appliances Ltd* [1974] I.C.R. 53.

Whilst the time limit in s.111 of the Employment Rights Act (dealing with unfair dismissal) is jurisdictional it has been held that the time limit in s.11(4) of the Employment Rights Act (statement of initial employment particulars), which requires a complaint in respect of failure to provide particulars to be made within a three month period from the date of cessation of employment, is merely procedural. In *Grimes v Sutton LBC* [1973] I.C.R. 240 the NIRC held that words of the predecessor to s.11—which provided that an employment tribunal "shall not entertain a reference . . . unless . . ."—amounted to a procedural provision introduced for the benefit of the employer, to protect him from the embarrassment of stale references. The result was that it was open to the parties to waive the time limit in s.11. It is submitted that it is unsatisfactory to construe the phrase "shall not consider" as having a different meaning in s.11 of the Employment Rights Act to the meaning it has in s.111. If and when the appellate courts have an opportunity to consider the current versions of s.11 and s.111, they are likely to be construed consistently, and both time limits to be considered as jurisdictional.

Calculation of the period—"three months beginning with"

Month means calendar month (Interpretation Act 1978, Sch.1). **9–009**

The period beginning with the Effective Date of Termination ("EDT") includes the EDT as part of the period of three months (see *Hammond v Haigh Castle & Co Ltd* [1973] I.C.R. 148 following *Trow v Ind Coope (West Midlands) Ltd* [1967] 2 Q.B. 899, CA).

The proper method of calculating the period of three months within which a complaint of unfair dismissal must be presented was explained by the Employment Appeal Tribunal in *Pruden v Cunard Ellerman*, [1993] I.R.L.R. 317, as follows (i) find the effective date of termination; (ii) take the day and the date before the ETD; and (iii) then go forward three months. If there is no corresponding date in the relevant month, the last day of the month is taken. For example, if the ETD is the 31st of the month, the three-month period would expire on the 30th of the third month following, save if that happened to be February, in which case it would expire on the 29th or 28th of February.

Effect of an internal appeal

The fact that an internal appeal has been pursued will not affect the date from **9–010** which time runs, unless the contract can be read as saving the contract of employment in all the circumstances pending the conclusion of the appeal. Thus, time will not be extended if the effect of the contract of employment is that an employee who has been dismissed is reinstated with full back pay in the event that the appeal succeeds, but if the appeal fails he is deprived of his right to work and from remuneration from the date of dismissal (*Savage v J Sainsbury Ltd* [1981] I.C.R. 1, CA).

Addition of a new respondent by amendment

An application to amend a claim form to add an additional respondent is treated **9–011** as a question of discretion, and is not determined by the application of the time-bar rules. There is no time limit as such, where a claimant seeks to add or substitute a respondent to an application which has been lodged timeously. The question as to whether or not the amendment should be allowed is one of the exercise of discretion in the whole circumstances of the case (*Gillick v BP Chemicals Ltd* [1993] I.R.L.R. 437, EAT and *Drinkwater Sabey Ltd v Burnett* [1995] I.C.R. 328, EAT). See also *Linbourne v Constable* [1993] I.C.R. 698, where an amendment to correct the name of the respondent was allowed at the appeal stage in circumstances where the true Respondent had known throughout the proceedings that it was the Claimant's employer, and that there was a claim against it and all of the relevant matters had been thoroughly investigated before the employment tribunal.

"a series of similar acts"

Under the whistleblowing provisions of the ERA, an employee may present a **9–011A** complaint to an employment tribunal that he has been subjected to a detriment in contravention of s.47B. By s.48(3) an employment tribunal shall not (subject to the escape provisions) consider a complaint unless it is presented before the end of the period of three months beginning with the date of the act or failure to act to which the complaint relates or, where that act or failure is part of a series of similar acts or failures, the last of them. Provisions of this nature appear in other contexts: see for example the Part-Time Workers (Prevention of Less Favourable Treatment) Regulations 2000, reg.8(2).

In order to determine whether the acts are part of a series, some evidence is needed to determine what link, if any, there is between the acts in the three-month period and the acts outside the three-month period. It is necessary to look at all the circumstances surrounding the acts. Were they all committed by fellow employees? If not, what connection (if any) was there between the alleged perpetrators? Were their actions organised or concerted in some way? It would also be relevant to inquire why they did what is alleged. "Motive" is not a helpful departure from the legislative language according to which the determining factor is whether the act was done "on the ground" that the employee had made a protected disclosure (see *Arthur v London Eastern Railway Ltd* [2007] I.R.L.R. 58, CA at para.35).

"not reasonably practicable"

9–012   The words "not reasonably practicable" have been given a liberal interpretation by the courts. The starting point for an employment tribunal applying the "not reasonably practicable" test remains the dicta of Lord Denning in *Dedman v British Building and Engineering Appliances Ltd* [1974] I.C.R. 53, where he held that: "the words 'not practicable' should be given a liberal interpretation, as a strict construction would give rise to an injustice which Parliament cannot have intended".

In *Palmer v Southend-on-Sea BC* [1984] I.C.R. 372 the Court of Appeal held (at para.34) that the correct approach is "to ask colloquially and untrammelled by too much legal logic—'was it reasonably feasible to present the complaint to the [Employment] Tribunal within the relevant three months?'".

In *Wall's Meat Co Ltd v Khan* [1979] I.C.R. 52, the Court of Appeal applied the test set out in *Dedman*. Lord Denning explained the test as follows:

"Had the man just cause or excuse for not presenting his complaint within the prescribed time? Ignorance of his rights—or ignorance of the time limit—is not just cause or excuse, unless it appears that he or his advisers could not reasonably be expected to have been aware of them. If he or his advisers could reasonably have been so expected, it was his or their fault, and he must take the consequences."

Per Brandon L.J.:

"The performance of an act, in this case the presentation of a complaint, is not reasonably practicable if there is some impediment which reasonably prevents, or interferes with, or inhibits, such performance. The impediment may be physical, for instance the illness of the complainant or a postal strike; or the impediment may be mental, namely, the state of mind of the complainant in the form of ignorance of, or mistaken belief with regard to, essential matters. Such states of mind can, however, only be regarded as impediments making it not reasonably practicable to present a complaint within the period of three months, if the ignorance on the one hand, or the mistaken belief on the other, is itself reasonable. Either state of mind will, further, not be reasonable if it arises from the fault of the complainant in not making such inquiries as he should reasonably in all the circumstances have made, or from the fault of his solicitors or other professional advisers in not giving him such information as they should reasonably in all the circumstances have given him."

The Court of Appeal set out the following principles in *Wall's Meat Co Ltd* (per Brandon L.J. at p.61):

"An Employment Tribunal could and should be satisfied that it was not reasonably practicable for his complaint to be presented within the period if an employee was reasonably ignorant of either: (a) his right to make a complaint of unfair dismissal at all; (b) how to make it; or (c) that it was necessary for him to make it within a period of three months from the date of dismissal. Provided always that the ignorance in each case is reasonable there is no difference between ignorance of (a) the existence of the right, or (b) the proper way to exercise it, or (c) the proper time within which to exercise it. However in practice there is a great deal of difference in the ease or difficulty with which a finding that the relevant ignorance is reasonable may be made. Thus, where a person is reasonably ignorant of the existence of the right at all, he can hardly be found to have been acting unreasonably in not making inquiries as to how, and within what period, he should exercise it. By contrast, if he does know of the existence of the right, it may in many cases at least, though not necessarily all, be difficult for him to satisfy an [employment] tribunal that he behaved reasonably in not making such inquiries."

Relevance of the part of the limitation period during which any disability applies

In *Schultz v Esso Petroleum* [1999] I.C.R. 1202, the Court of Appeal held that an **9–013** employment tribunal had erred in holding that it was reasonably practicable for a Claimant to present his complaint within the three-month limitation period in circumstances in which, although he had been too ill to give instructions to his solicitors during the final six weeks of that period, he had been sufficiently well to do so for the first seven weeks. In assessing whether or not something could or should have been done within the limitation period, while looking at the period as a whole, attention will in the ordinary way focus upon the closing rather than the early stages. Thus, in cases where illness is relied upon, a period of disabling illness should not be given similar weight regardless of in what part of the period of limitation it falls. The approach should vary according to whether the illness falls in the earlier weeks or in the far more critical weeks leading up to expiry of the limitation period.

Effect of advice from a "skilled adviser"

In *Dedman*, Lord Denning dealt with the position of a Claimant who has skilled **9–014** advisers (at p.361):

"But what is the position if he goes to skilled advisers and they make a mistake? The English court has taken the view that the man must abide by their mistake. . . I think that was right. If a man engages skilled advisers to act for him—and they mistake the time limit and present it too late—he is out. His remedy is against them."

In *London International College v Sen* [1993] I.R.L.R. 333, the Court of Appeal held that the cases—insofar as they suggest that a prospective complainant who consults a solicitor or a trade union official or similar adviser can no longer say that it was not reasonably practicable for him to comply with the time limit even if the adviser advised wrongly—are not purporting to lay down a rule of law to govern what is essentially a question of fact. A prospective complainant does not lose for all time his right to rely on the "not reasonably practicable" defence once he consults a solicitor who is potentially liable for wrong advice if—as was the case in Sen—he distrusts that advice and immediately proceeds to obtain further advice from a body such as an employment tribunal which may not be so liable.

Effect of advice from the CAB

In *Marks & Spencer Plc v Williams-Ryan* [2005] I.C.R. 1293, the Court of Appeal, **9–015** following, *Wall's Meat Co Ltd* (above), declined to interfere with the decision of an employment tribunal that it was not reasonably practicable to present the complaint in time, in circumstances where the information given by the employer to the employee was insufficient and misleading, and the employee had reasonably understood that she had to wait for the outcome of her internal appeal before presenting a complaint. The Claimant had received limited advice from the CAB which made no mention of her right to complain to an employment tribunal. The Court of Appeal considered that the principle in *Dedman* (that a claimant must abide by the mistake of his skilled advisers) did not necessarily extend to advice from the CAB. It may well depend on who it was who gave the advice and in what circumstances. Certainly, the mere fact of seeking advice from a CAB cannot, as a matter of law, rule out the possibility of demonstrating that it was not reasonably practicable to make a timely application to an employment tribunal. See further *Royal Bank of Scotland Plc v Theobald* UKEAT/0444/06.

Effect of advice from the staff of the office of employment tribunals

9–016   The Employment Appeal Tribunal held in *Jean Sorelle Ltd v Rybak* [1991] I.C.R. 127, that advice from an employee of the office of employment tribunals falls into a different category to advice obtained by a claimant from someone asked to advise in the prosecution of his tribunal claim. It was open to an employment tribunal to find as a fact that it was not reasonably practicable for the claimant to have presented her complaint in time, notwithstanding the fact that the claimant had received advice from a member of staff at the office of employment tribunals.

Effect of continuing negotiations/relationship between the parties

9–017   The fact that negotiations are taking place does not mean that it is not reasonably practicable to lodge a complaint. In *Times Newspapers Ltd v O'Regan* [1977] I.R.L.R. 101, the Employment Appeal Tribunal held that an employment tribunal had erred in law in finding that it was not reasonably practicable for an employee to make her complaint of unfair dismissal within the requisite three-month time period on grounds of her belief that the three-month time period ran from the end of negotiations between her union and the employer. Similarly, in *Birmingham Optical Group Plc v Johnson* [1995] I.C.R. 459, the EAT held that where a former employee continued in a commercial relationship with the former employer and abstained from issuing proceedings for unfair dismissal with a view to preserving the relationship it did not follow that it was "not reasonably practicable" to present a complaint on time. In *London Underground v Noel* [1999] I.R.L.R. 621, the Court of Appeal held that an offer of re-employment in a new job with the same employer with a significant cut in salary did not make it reasonably impracticable to present a complaint of unfair dismissal within the time limit.

Amendment to an existing claim to add a new ground

9–018   In *Marley (UK) Ltd v Anderson* [1996] I.C.R. 728, the Court of Appeal held that the question of whether or not it is reasonably practicable to bring a complaint depends upon an awareness of the specific grounds for complaint. Notwithstanding a finding that the employee's complaint of unfair dismissal on the initial ground put forward was time-barred an employment tribunal was entitled to go on to hold that it did have jurisdiction to consider the complaint on a different ground, which had subsequently come to light and was raised by amendment to the existing claim, within a reasonable period after acquiring the relevant knowledge (see also *James W Cook & Co (Wivenhoe) Ltd v Tipper* [1990] I.R.L.R. 386, CA).

Effect of a subsequent explanation of the existing law

9–019   The words "reasonably practicable", when read in conjunction with a "reasonable" period thereafter, point to some temporary impediment or hindrance. A declaration by the House of Lords to the effect that the threshold provisions in the predecessor to the Employment Rights Act 1996 were indirectly discriminatory could not be taken into account as a ground for arguing that it was not "reasonably practicable" before the date of the declaration to present a claim within the time limit. It would be contrary to the principle of legal certainty to allow past transactions to be re-opened and limitation periods to be circumvented because the existing law at the relevant time had not yet been explained or had not been fully understood (*Biggs v Somerset CC* [1996] I.C.R. 364, CA, per Neill L.J. at paras 23–24).

The facts which must be proven

The Court of Appeal held in *Machine Tool Industry Research Association v Simpson* [1988] I.C.R. 558, that the exercise to be performed is a study of the subjective state of mind of the employee as at the stage that he decides that there is a case to bring before an employment tribunal. It is not necessary for the claimant to establish, as facts, the matters which caused a genuine frame of mind, and reasonably so caused it, to form a decision to present a complaint.   **9–020**

Where a claimant seeks to invoke the power that the tribunal has to allow a late claim to proceed, on the basis that it has be presented within a reasonable time after the expiry of the three month period it is incumbent on the claimant to give a full and frank explaination of how and why the delay occurred, particularly the delay once what was erroneously throught to have been an obstacle has been removed (*Royal Bank of Scotland v Theobald* UKEAT/0444/06).

Effect of a short delay

The fact that the delay in lodging the claim may be extremely short does not mean that time will be extended. The limits are strictly applied. Thus in *JR Beasley v National Grid Electricity Transmissions* UKEAT/0626/06 the Employment Appeal Tribunal upheld the decision of a tribunal that it did not have jurisdiction to hear a claim presented 88 seconds out of time. Similarly in *D Millar v Community Links Trust Ltd* UKEAT/0486/07, the Employment Appeal Tribunal uphled the decision of a tribunal that it did not have jurisdication in respect of a claim presented nine seconds out of time.   **9–020/1**

Appeals

The appellate courts are slow to interfere with the exercise of an employment tribunal's discretion. A constant thread running throughout the cases is that whether or not it is reasonably practicable to present the complaint in time is pre-eminently an issue of fact for the employment tribunal, and that it is seldom that an appeal from its decision will lie (see *Palmer* above per May L.L.J. at 385C).   **9–021**

(2) Claims Governed by "Just and Equitable" Provisions

The "just and equitable" extension, which applies to discrimination claims, is considered by reference to the Sex Discrimination Act 1975. For a full list of the claims falling within this category see para.9–039.   **9–022**

SEX DISCRIMINATION ACT 1975

63. Jurisdiction of Employment Tribunals

(1) A complaint by any person ("the complainant") that another person ("the respondent")   **9–023**

    (a) has committed an act of discrimination or harassment against the complainant which is unlawful by virtue of [Part II or section 35A or 35B], or

(b) is by virtue of section 41 or 42 to be treated as having committed such an act of discrimination or harassment against the complainant, may be presented to an employment tribunal

(2) Subsection (1) does not apply to a complaint under section 13(1) of an act in respect of which an appeal, or proceedings in the nature of an appeal, may be brought under any enactment

76. Period within which proceedings to be brought

9–024
(1) An employment tribunal shall not consider a complaint under section 63, unless it is presented to the tribunal before the end of—

(a) the period of three months beginning when the act complained of was done; or

(b) in a case to which section 85(9A) applies, the period of six months so beginning.

(2) A county court or a sheriff court shall not consider a claim under section 66 unless proceedings in respect of the claim are instituted before the end of

(a) the period of six months beginning when the act complained of was done; or

(b) in a case to which section 66(5) applies, the period of eight months so beginning.

(2A) Where in England and Wales—

(a) proceedings or prospective proceedings under section 66 relate to the act or omission of a qualifying institution, and

(b) the dispute concerned is referred as a complaint under the student complaints scheme before the end of the period of six months mentioned in subsection (2)(a),

the period allowed by subsection (2)(a) shall be extended by two months.

(2B) In subsection (2A)—
"qualifying institution" has the meaning given by section 11 of the Higher Education Act 2004;
"the student complaints scheme" means a scheme for the review of qualifying complaints, as defined by section 12 of that Act, that is provided by the designated operator, as defined by section 13(5)(b) of that Act."

(3) An employment tribunal, county court or sheriff court shall not consider an application under section 72(2)(a) unless it is made before the end of the period of six months beginning when the act to which it relates was done; and a county court or sheriff court shall not consider an application under section 72(4) unless it is made before the end of the period of five years so beginning.

(4) An employment tribunal shall not consider a complaint under section 73(1) unless it is presented to the tribunal before the end of the period of six months beginning when the act complained of was done.

(5) A court or tribunal may nevertheless consider any such complaint, claim or application which is out of time if, in all the circumstances of the case, it considers that it is just and equitable to do so.

(6) For the purposes of this section—

(a) where the inclusion of any term in a contract renders the making of the contract an unlawful act that act shall be treated as extending throughout the duration of the contract, and

(b) any act extending over a period shall be treated as done at the end of that period, and

(c) a deliberate omission shall be treated as done when the person in question decided upon it,

and in the absence of evidence establishing the contrary a person shall be taken for the purposes of this section to decide upon an omission when he does an act inconsistent with doing the omitted act or, if he has done no such inconsistent act, when the period expires within which he might reasonably have been expected to do the omitted act if it was to be done.

"presented to the tribunal"

The position in relation to the presentation of complaints is summarised above. **9–025**

"shall not consider"

The time limit under the Sex Discrimination Act 1975 is jurisdictional and not **9–026**
procedural. Thus an employment tribunal is precluded from entertaining a complaint which is out of time (*Westward Circuits Ltd v Read* [1973] I.C.R. 301, NIRC). The practical effect is that the parties cannot waive the time limit neither is a party estopped from taking the point at any stage of the proceedings.

"beginning when the act complained of was done"

Time runs from the date the act complained of is done. In *Mensah v Royal College* **9–027**
of Midwives, unreported, (1995) UKEAT 124/94 the EAT held (Mummery P. at para.6):

"It is not correct to say that the time under Section 68(1) only runs from the date when knowledge is acquired, for example, of a comparable person of a different race or colour who has received more favourable treatment . . . An act occurs when it is done, not when you acquire knowledge of the means of proving that the act done was discriminatory. Knowledge is a factor relevant to the discretion to extend time. It is not a pre-condition of the commission of an act which can be relied on as an act of discrimination."

In *Coutts & Co Plc v Cure* [2005] I.C.R. 1099, the claimants brought a complaint under the fixed-term Employees (Prevention of Less Favourable Treatment) Regulations 2002, alleging that they had been less favourably treated in relation to a bonus paid in 2002. The EAT accepted that the employees were not precluded from making a claim notwithstanding the fact that the employer had announced in 2001 that the bonus was not to be paid since the 2001 announcement was insufficiently detailed.

In *Virdi v Commissioner of Police of the Metropolis* [2007] I.R.L.R. 24, the Employment Appeal Tribunal confirmed that an act is "done" when it is completed and that an act is complete for the limitation purposes when a decision is taken rather than when it is communicated.

Where the act complained of is the giving of notice an employment tribunal is entitled to take the view that time runs from the date the dismissal takes effect, which will be the date of the expiry of any period of notice (*Gloucester Working Men's Club and Institute v James* [1986] I.C.R. 603).

"act extending over a period"

The distinction between acts extending over a period and acts whose con- **9–028**
sequences extend over a period is an important one. In the case of "acts extending over a period" time will run from the end of the period; in the case of "acts whose

consequences extend over a period" time will run from the date of the act. It has long been established that s.76(6)(b) is concerned with continuing acts and not with the continuing consequences of acts (see *Amies v Inner London Education Authority* [1977] I.C.R. 308 approved in *Barclays Bank v Kapur* [1991] I.C.R. 208, HL(E) and *Sougrin v Haringey Health Authority* [1992] I.C.R. 650, CA). Thus in *Amies* the failure to appoint a teacher to a particular post was held to be a one-off act with continuing consequences and not an act extending over a period. In *Kapur* the House of Lords held (per Lord Griffiths at 215);

> "if [an employer] continued to pay lower wages to the coloured employees it would be a continuing act lasting throughout the period of a coloured employee's employment within the meaning of subsection [6(b)]. A man works not only for his current wage but also for his pension and to require him to work on less favourable terms as to pension is as much a continuing act as to require him to work for lower current wages".

In *Sougrin* where the "act complained of" was that the employer had refused to upgrade the employee while upgrading her comparator (and not that there operated a policy or rule not to upgrade black nurses) the discriminatory act was a one-off event, occurring at the latest on the dismissal of employee's appeal.

In *Owusu v London Fire & Civil Defence Authority* [1995] I.R.L.R. 574 the Employment Appeal Tribunal held that the employer's failure to re-grade the Claimant and its failure to allow him to act up over a two year period were capable of amounting to continuing acts. An act extends over a period of time if it takes the form of some policy, rule or practice, in accordance with which decisions are taken from time to time. A succession of specific instances can indicate the existence of a practice, which, in turn, can constitute a continuing act extending over a period. Per Mummery J. at para.23:

> "a succession of specific instances could indicate the existence of a practice, which in turn could constitute an act extending over a period which is a continuing act".

The distinction between continuing acts and the continuing consequences of acts is not always straightforward as is demonstrated by *Cast v Croydon College* [1998] I.C.R. 500. In *Cast* the Court of Appeal held that: (1) a further decision following the repetition of an earlier request may constitute an act of discrimination for the purposes of s.63(1) and s.76(1) of the Sex Discrimination Act 1975, whether or not it was made on the same facts as before, if it resulted from a further consideration of the matter and was not merely a reference back to an earlier decision; and (2) where the complaint relates to several decisions which are said to be discriminatory that may indicate the existence of a discriminatory policy and therefore constitute "an act extending over a period".

In *Hendricks v Metropolitan Police Commissioner* [2003] I.R.L.R. 96, the Court of Appeal held that an employment tribunal had been entitled to find that it had jurisdiction to entertain the Claimant's allegations of race and sex discrimination on the basis that they amounted to "an act extending over a period" notwithstanding that she had been off work sick for the 12 months prior to her tribunal complaint. Per Mummery L.J. at para.52:

> "The concepts of policy, rule, practice, scheme or regime in the authorities were given as examples of when an act extends over a period. They should not be treated as a complete and constricting statement of the indicia of 'an act

extending over a period'... the focus should be on the substance of the complaints that the [employer] was responsible for an ongoing situation or a continuing state of affairs in which female [employees] were treated less favourably. The question is whether that is 'an act extending over a period' as distinct from a succession of unconnected or isolated specific acts, for which time would begin to run from the date when each specific act was committed."

In *Robertson v Bexley Community Centre* [2003] I.R.L.R. 434, the Court of Appeal took a more restrictive view of an "act extending over a period" holding that it must be shown that the employer had a practice, policy rule or regime governing the act said to constitute it.

The tension between *Hendricks* and *Robertson* was touched upon but not resolved by the Court of Appeal in *Lyfar v Brighton and Sussex University Hospitals Trust* [2006] EWCA Civ. 1548. In *Lyfar*, it was agreed between Counsel that the meaning given to "an act extending over a period" in Hendricks was a correct one. The Court of Appeal in *Lyfar* held that in the light of the agreement it was unnecessary to discuss *Robertson* other than to say Robertson could be read as limiting "an act extending over a period" to such matters as "policy, rule, practice, scheme or regime" (per Hooper L.J. at para.16).

In *Tyagi v BBC World Service* [2001] I.R.L.R. 465, the Court of Appeal held that the reference in *Amies* to continuing discrimination related to a potential complaint by an employee denied access to opportunities for promotion. A general discriminatory practice which is not an act in respect of a particular applicant because he is not employed by the employer or because there is no job on offer is policed only by the Commission for Racial Equality, in accordance with s.28 of the RRA.

"when the person . . . decided upon it"

In *Swithland Motors Plc v Clarke* [1994] I.C.R. 231, the EAT held that "decided" **9–029** means "decided at a time and in circumstances when [the employer] was in a position to implement that decision", and not "decided on the hypothetical basis that he will implement the decision when and if circumstances arise in which he is able to do so." Thus the employer in *Swithland* could not argue that an application was out of time on the basis that it took the decision to dismiss while it was still in negotiations with the receiver and prior to becoming the employer of the relevant employee.

Consideration of a complaint out of time where it is "just and equitable to do so"

It has long since been established that these words give an employment tribunal **9–030** a wide discretion to do what it thinks is just and equitable in all the circumstances (see *Hutchison v Westward Television Ltd* [1977] I.R.L.R. 69, EAT).

As a matter of good practice when considering whether or not to extend time under this provision, an employment tribunal should adopt as a checklist the factors mentioned in s.33 of the Limitation Act 1980 (*British Coal v Keeble* [1997] I.R.L.R. 336, EAT). Under s.33 of the Limitation Act the court enjoys a broad discretion to extend the limitation period of three years in cases of personal injury and is required to consider the prejudice which each party would suffer as the result of the decision to be made and also to have regard to all the circumstances of the case including: (a) the length of and reasons for the delay; (b) the extent to which the cogency of the evidence is likely to be affected by the delay; (c) the extent to which the party sued had cooperated with any requests for information; (d) the promptness with which the plaintiff acted once he or she knew of the facts giving rise to the cause of action; (e) the steps taken by the plaintiff to obtain appropriate professional advice once he or she knew of the possibility of taking action.

Limitation

It should be noted that it will not be an error of law if an employment tribunal fails to go through the matters listed in s.33(3) of the 1980 Act provided that no significant factor has been left out of account by the employment tribunal in exercising its discretion (*London Borough of Southwark v Afolabi* [2003] I.R.L.R. 220, CA).

In *Robertson v Bexley Community Centre* [2003] I.R.L.R. 434, the Court of Appeal held (per Auld L.J.) that

"It is also of importance to note that the time limits are exercised strictly in employment and industrial cases. When tribunals consider their discretion to consider a claim out of time on just and equitable grounds there is no presumption that they should do so unless they can justify failure to exercise the discretion. Quite the reverse. A tribunal cannot hear a complaint unless the applicant convinces it that it is just and equitable to extend time. So, the exercise of discretion is the exception rather than the rule".

Notwithstanding the above, a review of the authorities suggests that in practice employment tribunals and the appellate courts have adopted a liberal approach to the extension of time. *Robertson* is perhaps best explained as an example of the reluctance on the part of the appellate courts to interfere with exercise of the wide discretion the statute affords an employment tribunal. Thus in *Afolabi* (above) the Court of Appeal, whilst noting the brevity of the time limits in employment cases, declined to interfere with the decision of an employment tribunal that it was just and equitable to extend time for nine years. The Court of Appeal considered that whilst such a case was "wholly exceptional" it was a decision which was open to the employment tribunal on the basis of its findings of fact.

Effect of advice

9–031   It is important to emphasise that the authorities relating to the extension of time under the "not reasonably practicable" provisions governing unfair dismissal are of no application here. Thus in considering whether it is just and equitable to extend time an employment tribunal may take account of the failure by a legal adviser to enter proceedings in time. The raison d'etre for this approach is that the legal adviser's failure should not be visited upon the claimant for otherwise the defendant would be in receipt of a windfall (see *Chohan v Derby Law Centre* [2004] I.R.L.R. 685, EAT).

Effect of a change in the law

9–032   In considering whether it is just and equitable to extend time, an employment tribunal may take into account the fact that a claimant and her legal advisors were reasonably unaware of the claimant's rights pending a decision of the European Court of Justice (see *Mills and Crown Prosecution Service v Marshall* [1998] I.R.L.R. 494, EAT, and *Foster v South Glamorgan Health Authority* [1988] I.C.R. 526, EAT).

Effect of use of internal procedures

9–033   There is no general rule that so long as there is an unexhausted internal procedure, then delay to await its outcome necessarily furnishes an acceptable reason for delaying the presentation of a complaint so as to lead to an extension of time on "just and equitable" grounds. When delay on account of an incomplete internal appeal is relied upon as a reason for delaying an complaint or failing to present it in time that fact may be considered by the employment tribunal and put into the balance when the justice and equity of the matter is considered (see *Robinson v Post Office* [2000] I.R.L.R. 804, EAT).

(3) Claims Where Time may be Extended Only in Narrowly Prescribed Circumstances

Equal Pay Act 1970

2. Disputes as to, and enforcement of, requirement of equal treatment

(1) Any claim in respect of the contravention of a term modified or **9–034** included by virtue of an equality clause, including a claim for arrears of remuneration or damages in respect of the contravention, may be presented by way of a complaint to an employment tribunal.

(1A) Where a dispute arises in relation to the effect of an equality clause the employer may apply to an employment tribunal for an order declaring the rights of the employer and the employee in relation to the matter in question.

(2) Where it appears to the Secretary of State that there may be a question whether the employer of any women is or has been contravening a term modified or included by virtue of their equality clauses, but that it is not reasonable to expect them to take steps to have the question determined, the question may be referred by him as respects all or any of them to an employment tribunal and shall be dealt with as if the reference were of a claim by the women or woman against the employer.

(3) Where it appears to the court in which any proceedings are pending that a claim or counterclaim in respect of the operation of an equality clause could more conveniently be disposed of separately by an employment tribunal, the court may direct that the claim or counterclaim shall be struck out; and (without prejudice to the foregoing) where in proceedings before any court a question arises as to the operation of an equality clause, the court may on the application of any party to the proceedings or otherwise refer that question, or direct it to be referred by a party to the proceedings, to an employment tribunal for determination by the tribunal, and may stay or sist the proceedings in the meantime.

(4) No determination may be made by an employment tribunal in the following proceedings—

(a) on a complaint under subsection (1) above,
(b) on an application under subsection (1A) above, or
(c) on a reference under subsection (2) above, unless the proceedings are instituted on or before the qualifying date (determined in accordance with section 2ZA below).

(5) A woman shall not be entitled, in proceedings brought in respect of a contravention of a term modified or included by virtue of an equality clause (including proceedings before an employment

tribunal), to be awarded any payment by way of arrears of remuneration or damages—

    (a) in proceedings in England and Wales, in respect of a time earlier than the arrears date (determined in accordance with section 2ZB below), and

    (b) in proceedings in Scotland, in respect of a time before the period determined in accordance with section 2ZC below.

(5A) In this section "employer", in relation to the holder of an office or post to which section 1 above applies by virtue of subsection (6A) of that section, shall be construed in accordance with that subsection.

"Qualifying date" under section 2(4)

9–035   2ZA.—(1) This section applies for the purpose of determining the qualifying date, in relation to proceedings in respect of a woman's employment, for the purposes of section 2(4) above.

    (2) In this section—

"concealment case" means a case where—

    (a) the employer deliberately concealed from the woman any fact (referred to in this section as a "qualifying fact")—

        (i) which is relevant to the contravention to which the proceedings relate, and

        (ii) without knowledge of which the woman could not reasonably have been expected to institute the proceedings, and

    (b) the woman did not discover the qualifying fact (or could not with reasonable diligence have discovered it) until after—

        (i) the last day on which she was employed in the employment, or

        (ii) the day on which the stable employment relationship between her and the employer ended, (as the case may be);

"disability case" means a case where the woman was under a disability at any time during the six months after—

    (a) the last day on which she was employed in the employment,

    (b) the day on which the stable employment relationship between her and the employer ended, or

   (c) the day on which she discovered (or could with reason-
       able diligence have discovered) the qualifying fact delib-
       erately concealed from her by the employer (if that day
       falls after the day referred to in paragraph (a) or (b)
       above, as the case may be), (as the case may be);

"stable employment case" means a case where the proceedings
relate to a period during which a stable employment relationship
subsists between the woman and the employer, notwithstanding that
the period includes any time after the ending of a contract of
employment when no further contract of employment is in force;
"standard case" means a case which is not—

   (a) a stable employment case,
   (b) a concealment case,
   (c) a disability case, or
   (d) both a concealment and a disability case.

(3) In a standard case, the qualifying date is the date falling six
months after the last day on which the woman was employed in the
employment.
(4) In a case which is a stable employment case (but not also a
concealment or a disability case or both), the qualifying date is the
date falling six months after the day on which the stable employment
relationship ended.
(5) In a case which is a concealment case (but not also a disability
case), the qualifying date is the date falling six months after the day
on which the woman discovered the qualifying fact in question (or
could with reasonable diligence have discovered it).
(6) In a case which is a disability case (but not also a concealment
case), the qualifying date is the date falling six months after the day
on which the woman ceased to be under a disability.
(7) In a case which is both a concealment and a disability case, the
qualifying date is the later of the dates referred to in subsections (5)
and (6) above.

"presented to the tribunal"

The position in relation to the presentation of complaints is summarised above. **9–036**
   The time limit for bringing a claim under the Equal Pay Act 1970 is six months.
In contrast to most claims in an employment tribunal (for example unfair dismissal
or discrimination claims) the time limits for equal pay claims are strict and the
escape provisions are narrowly circumscribed. An equal pay claim must be brought
within the qualifying date (s.2ZA). The period is ordinarily six months and is
subject to extension only where there has been concealment or in a disability case.
   Where there is a TUPE transfer the time for bringing a claim runs from the date
of transfer (*Powerhouse Retail Ltd v Burroughs* [2006] I.R.L.R. 381 H.L., considered in
Unison v Allen [2007] I.R.L.R. 975 EAT).

Ordinarily any award made by an employment tribunal may be backdated to cover arrears up to six years before the day on which the proceedings were instituted. In a "concealment" or "disability" case arrears can be backdated to the date of the breach of the equality clause (s.2ZB).

(4) Claims Where no Limitation Period is Specified

9–037   No limitation prior is specified in respect of claims under s.177 of the Employment Rights Act (i.e. claims for payments equivalent to redundancy payments in respect of public sector employees). The Employment Appeal Tribunal has held that in the absence of any limitation period such claims are subject to the ordinary six-year limitation period for actions for breach of contract found in the Limitation Act 1980 (see *Greenwich Health Authority v Skinner and Ward* [1989] I.C.R. 220).

Use of pre-hearing reviews to determine whether or not a complaint is in time

9–038   It will sometimes save time and costs for an employment tribunal to determine whether or not the complaint is in time at a pre-hearing review under the provisions of r.18 of the 2004 Employment Tribunals Rules, (which replaced the previous r.6 under the 2001 Rules, under which tribunals had power to determine the entitlement of a party to bring proceedings.). In *Munir v Jang Publications Ltd* [1989] I.C.R. 1, CA, it was held that there are many occasions on which it is a convenient course to have a preliminary issue decided in advance of the main hearing of a complaint where it is felt that the decision on the preliminary issue will shorten the main hearing. If that is so, it can save time for the employment tribunal and help listing to have a preliminary issue decided. An obvious instance is where there is an issue entirely separate from the disputes on the merits of the complaint as, for instance, whether the complaint was lodged in due time or not. Note that on the facts of *Munir* the issue of whether the Tribunal had jurisdiction necessarily involved hearing substantial evidence which would trespass on the question of whether the employer had acted reasonably or unreasonably and the Court of Appeal considered, with the benefit of hindsight, that there should not have been a preliminary hearing. See further *National Union of Teachers v Governing Body of St Mary's Church of England (Aided) Junior School* [1995] I.C.R. 317 where Mummery J. held:

> "It is not in dispute that an [employment tribunal] has power to order the trial of a preliminary issue or question. Care must, however, be taken in acceding to such a procedure, even if all the parties favour it. In deciding whether or not to order the trial of a preliminary question or issue of law, industrial tribunals would be well advised to follow the guidance in Decisions on R.S.C., Ord.33, r.3. Under that rule the court may order any question or issue, whether of fact or law, or partly of law to be tried before the trial of the matter. There are, however, dangers in taking what looks at first sight to be a short cut but turns out in fact to be productive of more delay and costs than if the dispute had been tried in its entirety and the questions of law then decided in the context of the facts found. The isolation of what appears to be a discrete issue for preliminary determination may have the unfortunate effect of isolating a question for argument and decision which is inextricably bound up with all the other aspects of the legal and factual dispute."

For the successor to RSC Ord.33, r.3 under the CPR see CPR r.3.1(2)(i). Where the claimant is contending that the alleged acts of discrimination extended over a period of time it will be rare for the tribunal to determine the issue of whether the claim is out of time as a discrete issue at a pre-hearing review.

9–039

Statutory Provision	Complaint	Time Limit	Normal extension provision	Application of Dispute Regulations
Disability Discrimination Act 1995	act of discrimination	three months beginning with date of the act complained of (Sch.3, Pt I para.3(1))	just and equitable (Sch.3, Pt 1, para.3(2))	three month extension (reg.15)
Disability Rights Commission Act 1999	appeal against non-discrimination notice	six weeks beginning on day after date of service (Sch.3, Pt I, para.10(1))	none	not applicable
Employment Equality (Age) Regulations 2006 ("Age Regs")	act of discrimination	three months beginning with date of act complained of (reg.42(1))	just and equitable (reg.42(3))	three month extension (reg.15)
Age Regs	failure to notify employee of right to request postponement of retirement date	three months beginning with last date for compliance or first day on which employee knew or should have known intended date of retirement (Sch.6, para.11(2)(a))	not reasonably practicable (sch 6, para.11(2)(b))	not applicable
Age Regs	denial of right to be accompanied	three months beginning with date of failure or threat (Sch.6, para.12(2)(a))	not reasonably practicable (Sch.6, para.12(2)(b))	not applicable
Employment Equality (Religion or Belief) Regulations 2003	act of discrimination	three months beginning with date of act complained of (armed services 6 months) (reg.34(1))	just and equitable (reg.34(3))	three month extension (reg.15)
Employment Equality (Sexual Orientation) Regulations 2003	act of discrimination	three months beginning with date of act complained of (armed forces six months) (reg.34(1))	just and equitable (reg.34(3))	three month extension (reg.15)
Employment Relations Act 1999	compliance with right to be accompanied at hearing	three months beginning with date of failure or threat (s.11(2)(a))	not reasonably practicable (s.11(2)(b))	not applicable

Statutory Provision	Complaint	Time Limit	Normal extension provision	Application of Dispute Regulations
Employment Tribunals Extension of Jurisdiction (England and Wales) Order 1994 ("Extension of Jurisdiction Order")	employee's breach of contract claim	three months beginning with EDT or last working day (art.7(a) and (b)) (note a claim before the EDT is premature, *Capek v Lincolnshire Council* [2000] I.R.L.R. 590, CA	not reasonably practicable (art.7(c))	three month extension (reg.15)
Extension of Jurisdiction Order	employer's breach of contract claim	six weeks beginning with the day on which originating application received (art.8(c)(i))	not reasonably practicable (art.8(c)(ii))	not applicable
Employment Rights Act 1996 ("ERA")	statement initial employment particulars/ changes/ itemised pay (ss.1, 4 and 8)	three months beginning with date on which employment ceased s.11(4)(a))	not reasonably practicable (s.11(4)(b))	not applicable
ERA	unauthorised deductions (s.13)	three months beginning with date of payment of wages from which deduction made or date when payment received (s.23(2))	not reasonably practicable (s.23(4))	three month extension (reg.15)
ERA	guarantee payments	three months beginning with date when guarantee payment due (s.34(2)(a))	not reasonably practicable (s.34(2)(b))	not applicable
ERA	detriment in employment	three months beginning with date of act or failure (s.48(3)(a))	not reasonably practicable (s.48(3)(b))	three month extension (reg.15)
ERA	failure to allow time off for public duties/ looking for work	three months from failure (s.51(2)(a)/ s.54(2)(a))	not reasonably practicable (s.51(2)(b)/ s.54(2)(b))	not applicable

438

Statutory Provision	Complaint	Time Limit	Normal extension provision	Application of Dispute Regulations
ERA	time off for ante-natal care	three months beginning with date of appointment (s.57(2)(a))	not reasonably practicable (s.57(2)(b))	not applicable
ERA	time off for dependants	three months beginning with date of refusal (s.57B(2)(a))	not reasonably practicable (s.57B(2)(b))	not applicable
ERA	time off for pension scheme trustees	three months beginning with date when failure occurred (s.60(2)(a))	not reasonably practicable (s.60(2)(b))	not applicable
ERA	time off for employee representatives or young person for study or training	three months beginning with day on which time off taken or should have been permitted (s.63(2)(a)/ s.63C(2)(a))	not reasonably practicable (s.63(2)(b)/ s.63C(2)(b))	not applicable
ERA	remuneration on suspension on medical or maternity grounds	three months beginning with first day of suspension (s.70(2)(a))	not reasonably practicable (s.70(2)(b))	not applicable
ERA	parental leave	three months beginning with date of matters complained of (s.80(2)(a))	not reasonably practicable (s.80(2)(b))	not applicable
ERA	flexible working	three months beginning with relevant date (s.80H(5)(a))	not reasonably practicable (s.80H(5)(b))	not applicable
ERA	unfair dismissal	three months beginning with EDT s.111(2)(a)	not reasonably practicable (s.111(2)(b))	three month (reg.15)
ERA	written reasons for dismissal	three months beginning with EDT s.93(3)	not reasonably practicable	not applicable
ERA	interim relief	seven days immediately following EDT (whether before on or after that date) (s.128(2))	none	not applicable

439

Statutory Provision	Complaint	Time Limit	Normal extension provision	Application of Dispute Regulations
ERA	redundancy payments	six months beginning with relevant date (s.164(1))	in six months following period referred to in s.164(1), just and equitable (s164(2))	three month extension (reg.15)
Equal Pay Act 1970	breach of equality clause	six months after the last day of employment (s.2ZA(3))	time limit disapplied in cases of concealment, stable employment or disability (s.2ZA(2)).	three month extension (reg.15)
European Public Limited-Liability Company Regulations 2004	time off for members of special negotiating body etc	Three months beginning with date when time off taken or should have been permitted (reg.41(2)(a))	not reasonably practicable (reg.41(2)(b))	not applicable
European Public Limited-Liability Company Regulations 2004	detriment claims	three months beginning with date of act (reg.45(3)) and s.48(2) to (5) of ERA)	not reasonably practicable	not applicable
Fixed-term Employees (Prevention of Less Favourable Treatment) Regulations 2002	less favourable treatment relating to fixed-term employees	three months beginning with last date of less favourable treatment or date on which other individuals informed of vacancy (reg.7(2))	just and equitable (reg.7(3))	not applicable
Flexible Working (Procedural Requirements) Regulations 2002	right to be accompanied	three months beginning with failure or threat (reg.15(2)(a))	not reasonably practicable (reg.15(2)(b))	not applicable
Health and Safety (Consultation with Employees) Regulations 1996	time off for safety representatives	three months of date on which failure occurred (Sch.2, para.3)	not reasonably practicable (Sch.2, para.3)	not applicable

440

Statutory Provision	Complaint	Time Limit	Normal extension provision	Application of Dispute Regulations
Information and Consultation of Employees Regulations 2004	time off for representatives	three months beginning with date when time off was taken or should have been permitted (reg.29(2)(a))	not reasonably practicable (reg.29(2)(b))	not applicable
National Minimum Wage Act 1998 ("NMWA")	access to records	three months following end of 14 days from receipt of production notice (s.11(3))	not reasonably practicable	not applicable
NMWA	detriment claims	three months beginning with act or failure (s.24(2))	not reasonably practicable	three month extension (reg.15)
NMWA	appeal against enforcement notice or penalty notice	four weeks following date of service of notice (s.19(4) and s.22(1))	none	not applicable
Part-Time Workers (Prevention of Less Favourable Treatment) Regulations 2000	less favourable treatment relating to part-time workers	three months beginning with last date of less favourable treatment or detriment (six months for armed forces) reg.8(2)	just and equitable (reg.8(3))	not applicable
Pension Schemes Act 1993	unpaid contributions of insolvent employer	three months beginning with date of communication of decision of Secretary of State (s.126(2))	not reasonably practicable (s.126(2))	not applicable
Race Relations Act 1976 ("RRA")	act of racial discrimination	three months beginning with date of act complained of (s.68(1)) (six months armed services)	just and equitable (s.68(1))	three month extension (reg.15)
RRA	complaint by CRE	six months beginning when act to which it relates was done (s.64(4))	just and equitable (s.64(6))	not applicable

441

Statutory Provision	Complaint	Time Limit	Normal extension provision	Application of Dispute Regulations
Road Transport (Working Time) Regulations 2005	appeal against notice	21 days from date of service (Sch.2, para.6(2)	none	not applicable
Sex Discrimination Act 1975 ("SDA")	act of sex discrimination	three months beginning with date of act (s.76(1)) (six months armed forces)	just and equitable (s.76(5))	three month extension (reg.15)
SDA	complaint by EOC	six months beginning when act to which it relates was done (s.76(3))	just and equitable	not applicable
Trade Union and Labour Relations (Consolidation) Act 1992 (TULR(C)A)	disciplining trade union member	three months beginning with date of infringement (s.66(2))	not reasonably practicable or delay attributable to reasonable attempt to appeal	not applicable
TULR(C)A	compensation for disciplining trade union member	not before the end of four weeks beginning with date of declaration or later than six months after that date (s.67(3))	none	not applicable
TULR(C)A	deduction of unauthorised subscriptions	three months beginning with date of payment of wages from which deduction or last of deductions made (s.68A(1)(a))	not reasonably practicable (s.68A(1)(b))	not applicable
TULR(C)A	failure to comply with collective bargaining obligations	three months beginning with date of alleged failure (s.70C(2)(a))	not reasonably practicable (s.70C(2)(b))	not applicable
TULR(C)A	wrongful deduction of political fund contribution	three months beginning with date of payment s.87(2)	not reasonably practicable	not applicable

Statutory Provision	Complaint	Time Limit	Normal extension provision	Application of Dispute Regulations
TULR(C)A	failure to comply with tribunal order under s.87(5)	not before the end of four weeks beginning with date of order or later than six months after that date (s.87(6))	none	not applicable
TULR(C)A	refusal of employment or service of employment agency	three months beginning with date of conduct to which complaint relates (s.139(1)(a))	not reasonably practicable (s.139(1)(b))	not applicable
TULR(C)A	inducements relating to union membership or activities or collective bargaining	three months beginning with date of offer or last in a series of offers (s.145C(a))	not reasonably practicable (s.145C(b))	three month extension (reg.15)
TULR(C)A	detriment in relation to union membership and activities	three months beginning with last act or failure (s.147(1)(a))	not reasonably practicable (s.147(1)(b))	three month extension (reg.15)
TULR(C)A	interim relief (unfair dismissal)	seven days following EDT (s.161(2))	none	not applicable
TULR(C)A	time off for union duties	within three months of the date when the failure occurred (s.171(a))	not reasonably practicable (s.171(b))	not applicable
TULR(C)A	Exclusion or expulsion from union	before the end of six months beginning with date of exclusion or expulsion (s.175(a))	not reasonably practicable (s.175(b))	not applicable
TULR(C)A	compensation for exclusion	not before the end of four weeks beginning with date of declaration or later than six months after that date s.176(3)	none	not applicable

443

Limitation

Statutory Provision	Complaint	Time Limit	Normal extension provision	Application of Dispute Regulations
TULR(C)A	redundancy consultation	three months beginning with date on which dismissal takes effect s.189(5)	not reasonably practicable	not applicable
TULR(C)A	claim under protective award	three months beginning with date of failure to pay (s.192(2)(a))	not reasonably practicable (s.192(2)(b))	not applicable
TULR(C)A	unfair dismissal	six months beginning with date of dismissal (s.239(2)(a))	not reasonably practicable (s.239(2)(b))	not applicable
TULR(C)A	detriment short of dismissal	three months beginning with date of act or failure (Sch. A1, para.157(1)(a))	not reasonably practicable (Sch.A1, para.157(1)(b))	three month extension (reg.15)
Transfer of Undertakings (Protection of Employment) Regulations 2006 ("TUPE")	failure to notify	three months beginning with date of relevant transfer (reg.12(2)(a))	not reasonably practicable (reg.12(2)(b))	not applicable
TUPE	failure to inform or consult	three months beginning with completion of transfer (reg.15(12)(a)). A complaint may be presented before the transfer (see *South Durham Health Authority v UNISON* [1995] I.C.R. 495)	not reasonably practicable	not applicable
Working Time Regulations 1998	refusal to allow exercise of rights or make payments	three months beginning with date when exercise of right should have been permitted or payment should have been made (six months for members of armed forces) (reg.30(2)(a))	not reasonably practicable (reg.30(2)(b))	three month extension (reg.15)

CHAPTER 10

EMPLOYMENT ACT 2002

Contents

PART 3

DISPUTE RESOLUTION ETC.

STATUTORY PROCEDURES

Interpretation of this Section

In this section:

10–001

"DRR" means the Employment Act 2002 (Dispute Resolution) Regulations 2004 (SI 2004/752)

"DDP" means the Statutory Dismissal and Disciplinary Procedure under EA Sch.2, Pt 1

"EA" means the Employment Act 2002

"GP" means the Statutory Grievance Procedure under EA Sch.2, Pt 2

"General Requirements" means the General Requirements applicable to both the DDP and GP under EA Sch.2, Pt 3

"Step 1 letter" means the written statement of grievance required to be sent to the employer by paras 6 or 9 of the GP

29 Statutory dispute resolution procedures

10–002　(1) **Schedule 2 (which sets out the statutory dispute resolution procedures) shall have effect.**

(2) **The Secretary of State may by order—**

(a) **amend Schedule 2;**

(b) **make provision for the Schedule to apply, with or without modifications, as if—**

(i) **any individual of a description specified in the order who would not otherwise be an employee for the purposes of the Schedule were an employee for those purposes; and**

(ii) **a person of a description specified in the order were, in the case of any such individual, the individual's employer for those purposes.**

(3) **Before making an order under this section, the Secretary of State must consult the Advisory, Conciliation and Arbitration Service.**

Commencement

10–003　Subss.(2) and (3) April 27, 2003.

Subs.(1) October 1, 2004.

Modifications

10–004　Modified in relation to governing bodies of schools with delegated budgets by:

(1) art.3 of and the Schedule to the Education (Modification of Enactments Relating to Employment) (England) Order 2003 (SI 2003/1964) with effect from September 1, 2003; and

(2) art.3 of and the Schedule to the Education (Modification of Enactments Relating to Employment) (Wales) Order 2006 (SI 2006/1073) (which applies only to Wales) with effect from May 12, 2006.

Orders

10–005　As of April 25, 2008, no Orders have been made under this section.

30 Contracts of employment

10–006　(1) **Every contract of employment shall have effect to require the employer and employee to comply, in relation to any matter to which a statutory procedure applies, with the requirements of the procedure.**

446

(2) Subsection (1) shall have effect notwithstanding any agreement to the contrary, but does not affect so much of an agreement to follow a particular procedure as requires the employer or employee to comply with a requirement which is additional to, and not inconsistent with, the requirements of the statutory procedure.

(3) The Secretary of State may for the purpose of this section by regulations make provision about the application of the statutory procedures.

(4) In this section, "contract of employment" has the same meaning as in the Employment Rights Act 1996 (c.18).

Commencement

Subs.(3) April 27, 2003. The remainder of the section is yet to be brought into effect. **10–007**

Modifications

See s.29 above at para.10–004. **10–008**

Non-completion of procedure: whether breach of contract

The failure to bring s.30 into effect robs the dispute resolution procedures of **10–009** much of their effectiveness in cases which do not result in dismissal or give rise to complaints of actionable detriment or discrimination. Until s.30 is brought into effect, the failure by an employer to observe the DDP when taking relevant disciplinary action against an employee (for the definition of which see reg.2 DRR at para.11–002) is not a breach of contract, although of course the disciplinary action taken, such as suspension without pay, may be. Nor would a failure to observe procedure in a non-dismissal case itself entitle the employee to resign and complain of constructive unfair dismissal, although, again, the disciplinary action taken may do so. It may be possible for the employee to rely on the employer's failure to comply with the applicable statutory procedure in support of a complaint that the implied term of mutual trust and confidence has been breached.

31 Non-completion of statutory procedure: adjustment of awards

(1) This section applies to proceedings before an employment **10–010** tribunal relating to a claim under any of the jurisdictions listed in Schedule 3 by an employee.

(2) If, in the case of proceedings to which this section applies, it appears to the employment tribunal that—

> (a) the claim to which the proceedings relate concerns a matter to which one of the statutory procedures applies,
> (b) the statutory procedure was not completed before the proceedings were begun, and
> (c) the non-completion of the statutory procedure was wholly or mainly attributable to failure by the employee—
>
>> (i) to comply with a requirement of the procedure, or
>> (ii) to exercise a right of appeal under it,

it must, subject to subsection (4), reduce any award which it makes to the employee by 10 per cent, and may, if it considers it just and equitable in all the circumstances to do so, reduce it by a further amount, but not so as to make a total reduction of more than 50 per cent.

(3) If, in the case of proceedings to which this section applies, it appears to the employment tribunal that—

(a) the claim to which the proceedings relate concerns a matter to which one of the statutory procedures applies,

(b) the statutory procedure was not completed before the proceedings were begun, and

(c) the non-completion of the statutory procedure was wholly or mainly attributable to failure by the employer to comply with a requirement of the procedure,

it must, subject to subsection (4), increase any award which it makes to the employee by 10 per cent and may, if it considers it just and equitable in all the circumstances to do so, increase it by a further amount, but not so as to make a total increase of more than 50 per cent.

(4) The duty under subsection (2) or (3) to make a reduction or increase of 10 per cent does not apply if there are exceptional circumstances which would make a reduction or increase of that percentage unjust or inequitable, in which case the tribunal may make no reduction or increase or a reduction or increase of such lesser percentage as it considers just and equitable in all the circumstances.

(5) Where an award falls to be adjusted under this section and under section 38 the adjustment under this section shall be made before the adjustment under that section.

(6) The Secretary of State may for the purposes of this section by regulations—

(a) make provision about the application of the statutory procedures;

(b) make provision about when a statutory procedure is to be taken to be completed;

(c) make provision about what constitutes compliance with a requirement of a statutory procedure;

(d) make provision about circumstances in which a person is to be treated as not subject to, or as having complied with, such a requirement;

(e) make provision for a statutory procedure to have effect in such circumstances as may be specified by the regulations with such modifications as may be so specified;

    (f) make provision about when an employee is required to exercise a right of appeal under a statutory procedure.

(7) The Secretary of State may by order—

    (a) amend Schedule 3 for the purpose of—

        (i) adding a jurisdiction to the list in that Schedule, or

        (ii) removing a jurisdiction from that list;

    (b) make provision, in relation to a jurisdiction listed in Schedule 3, for this section not to apply to proceedings relating to claims of a description specified in the order;

    (c) make provision for this section to apply, with or without modifications, as if—

        (i) any individual of a description specified in the order who would not otherwise be an employee for the purposes of this section were an employee for those purposes, and

        (ii) a person of a description specified in the order were, in the case of any such individual, the individual's employer for those purposes.

Commencement

Subss.(6) and (7) April 27, 2003.   **10–011**
Subss.(1) to (4) October 1, 2004 subject to transitional provisions.

Transitional Provisions

The section does not apply in relation to a grievance where the employee has **10–012** presented a complaint to the employment tribunal about that grievance prior to October 1, 2004: art.3 of the Employment Act 2002 (Commencement No. 6 and Transitional Provisions) Order 2004 (SI 2004/1717).

Modifications

See s.29 above at para.10–004.   **10–013**

Regulations

See the Employment Act 2002 (Dispute Resolution) Regulations 2004 (SI **10–014** 2004/752) (DRR) at Ch.11.

Orders

See the Employment Act 2002 (Amendment of Schs 3,4, and 5) Order 2007 (SI **10–015** 2007/30). For amendments and additions to the Schedule by primary and other secondary legislation see the commentary to Sch.3 (see para.10–085).

Subsections (2) and (3)—Non-completion of a statutory procedure

Generally

". . . what must be guarded against is, once the procedure has been enacted, that **10–016** it can create its own hostage to fortune and, in fact, introduce an entirely and, we are satisfied, unintended result of creating undue technicality and over sophistication . . . It is not . . . the intention of the legislation either that employees should be barred [from bringing proceedings] or that employers should unwittingly find themselves liable for automatic unfair dismissal. These are sanctions which should very rarely be used: the purpose of the legislation is quite other . . ." (*Shergold v Fieldway Medical Centre* [2006] I.R.L.R. 76; [2006] I.C.R. 304, EAT at [27] and [28]).

It is important to recognise that although it is always the claimant who brings employment tribunal proceedings and who raises a written grievance, and always the employer who commences the DDP, either the employer or the employee may be responsible for the non-completion of the applicable procedure whether it is the GP or DDP which is being followed. This is because in both instances the obligations to attend meetings and to conduct them in accordance with the general requirements are mutual.

What amounts to non-completion

10–017   For what does and does not amount to a written statement of grievance (Step 1 letter) see paras 10–067 to 10–069.

For the timing of the Step 1 letter see para.10–070.

For the Dismissal and Disciplinary Procedure (DDP) see the commentary to Sch.2, Pt 1 below (paras 10–054 to 10–058).

For the General Requirements see the commentary to Sch.2, Pt 3 below, at para.10–078.

Non-compliance and non-completion: relationship between

10–018   For the correlation between a party's failure to comply with a requirement of a procedure, whether that party has in consequence failed to complete that procedure and whether that failure is attributable to that party, see the commentary to regs 11 and 12 DRR at paras 11–053 and 11–057.

Appeal against finding of non-completion

10–019   Whether a statutory procedure has been complied with is a question of mixed fact and law: see *Alexander v Bridgen Enterprises Ltd* [2006] I.R.L.R. 422; [2006] I.C.R. 1277, EAT; and *Martin v Class Security Installations Ltd* UKEAT/01880/06, doubting the view to the contrary stated in *Commotion Ltd v Rutty* [2006] I.R.L.R. 171; [2006] I.C.R. 290, EAT.

Duty of the tribunal to consider whether statutory procedures have been followed

10–020   Subsection (4) confirms that the words "If . . . it appears to the tribunal . . . the tribunal must. . ." in s.31(2) and (3), impose a duty on the tribunal to consider the question of non-completion of the procedure, whether or not the issue is expressly pleaded or directly raised by either party, although it would be a breach of the rules of natural justice for the tribunal to determine that there had been non-completion of the procedure which was attributable to a party without giving at least that party the opportunity to address them and, if satisfied that there had been non-completion, without giving both parties the opportunity to address them on what the consequences should be. In *Venniri v Autodex Ltd* UKEAT/0436/07 at [34], it was held that whether there has been non-completion of the procedure and if so whether it is wholly or mainly attributable to the fault of the employer, are matters which the tribunal should have in mind in every unfair dismissal case. It is not necessary for the claimant to raise the issue explicitly.

Failure by employer

For cases where the employer did not personally cause the non-compliance see the commentary to reg.12(3) and (4) DRR (see para.11–059).   **10–021**

Failure by employee

Where the employee complains in writing to his employer that he has been issued with a warning wrongly and in breach of contract, the employee's failure to attend a meeting which would be an appeal against the warning is not a breach of the grievance procedure as the meeting was not a Step 2 meeting for that purpose. Whether the meeting to which the claimant was invited is "to discuss the grievance" or for some other purpose is a question of fact (*Galaxy Showers Ltd v Wilson* [2006] I.R.L.R. 83, EAT). It would seem to follow that if the employee was not in breach of the grievance procedure, the employer was in breach in failing to call the employee to a Step 2 meeting.   **10–022**

Completion of a statutory procedure: appeals

Employee's failure to appeal

Although the procedures themselves do not do so, s.32(1)(c)(i) effectively imposes an obligation on the employee to exercise any right of appeal under the applicable procedure as a condition of pursuing the matter to an employment tribunal without the risk of a reduction to their compensatory award. The provisions of reg.11(3) DRR excuse an employee's failure to appeal in the limited circumstances which they describe (for a discussion of which see paras 11–054 and 11–055) but an honest, even reasonably held, belief that because of the employer's handling of the matter thus far an appeal would be futile, does not (although it would be a matter material to the Tribunal's discretion as to the extent of any percentage reduction, see also the commentary to subs.(4) below).   **10–023**

Multiple stage procedures

Neither of the procedures addresses the status of second and subsequent appeals. Both contemplate only one appeal after which ". . .the employer must inform the employee of his final decision": Sch.2 Pt 1 paras 3(5) and 5(4) and Pt 2 para.8(4). Where a further appeal is allowed, the decision of the first appeal is not of course final and the great majority of public sector employers and many larger private employers do permit at least one further appeal in both dismissal and grievance cases. It must be remembered that both procedures are only intended to be the irreducible minimum below which, in the case of the DDP, a dismissal will be automatically unfair. It would therefore be surprising if it was intended that an existing procedure which went beyond the minimum (both in content and the way in which it was applied in the circumstances of an individual case) would be subject to the statutory regime. Although the point is not settled, the better view is that   **10–024** second and subsequent appeals are not subject to the statutory procedures, in particular to the General Requirements. However, it might nonetheless be prudent for employers to act as though they were, as the delays in some areas of the public sector in particular in hearing second stage and subsequent appeals are notoriously long and the possibility that in due course tribunals will conclude that such delays make, or contribute to making, dismissals unfair under s.98(4) ERA (as opposed to s.98A which would not be engaged if the view that second stage appeals are outwith the procedure is correct) must be borne in mind. If second and subsequent appeals are outwith the procedure, the employee need only wait until the conclusion of the first appeal before presenting their tribunal claim as the statutory procedure will then have been completed.

Non-completion of a statutory procedure: adjustments to compensation

Generally

10–025   In *Metrobus Ltd v Cook* UKEAT/0490/06, the EAT upheld an uplift of 40 per cent imposed by the tribunal for a "blatant" disregard of the DDP by a large employer. In *Cex Ltd v Lewis* UKEAT/0031/07, the EAT declined to set out general principles by which tribunals should approach the question of reducing or increasing awards. Upholding the decision of a tribunal to uplift by only ten per cent because the employer's failure to comply with the standard DDP arose from ignorance of its existence rather than a wilful disregard of it, EAT said that the structure of the subsection is that the tribunal has a broad discretion on the basis of what they regard as just and equitable in the circumstances of each individual case.

> "The tribunal's decision as to whether the adjustment should or should not be more that the minimum ten per cent and, if so, how much more is not confined by statute beyond the words 'if it considers it just and equitable in all the circumstances to do so.' Nor has the tribunal's discretion been confined by authority. Parliament has not specified any particular consideration to which the tribunal . . . must have regard. The tribunal must reach their decision on the facts of each case and on the basis of their assessment, judgment and discretion. . . We agree. . . that there is a parallel—albeit an inexact parallel— between this jurisdiction and the tribunal's jurisdiction to find whether, in unfair dismissal, the employee has been guilty of contributory fault in which the tribunal exercise a discretion with which an Appellate Court should be reluctant to interfere: see Hollier v Plysu . . . There is a further parallel with the tribunal's discretion in considering a Polkey [Polkey v A E Dayton Services Ltd [1988] I.C.R. 142 HL] issue." *Cex* at [49].

In *Hollier v Plysu* [1983] I.R.L.R. 260 CA, it was held that the assessment of the degree of contribution was to be approached on the basis of "broad common sense" and was "obviously a matter of impression, opinion and discretion." As with reductions for contributory fault, the tribunal is obliged to give reasons for the percentage reduction or increase which it decides upon under s.31. Although the decision to uplift or reduce compensation in any particular case will largely turn on its own facts, some general principles can be suggested.

Employer at fault

10–026   The uplift to the compensation is designed to punish the employer for the act of non-compliance, not to attempt to compensate the employee for any loss flowing from it (*Metrobus Ltd v Cook* UKEAT/0490/06). The degree of the employer's culpability is therefore likely to be of central importance. However, ultimately, the extent of any uplift is a matter within the discretion of a tribunal, having regard to all material circumstances. For example, a small employer genuinely unaware of his obligations may be thought less culpable, even in circumstances of complete failure, and in consequence an uplift less than the maximum appropriate.

The statutory provisions do not require the tribunal to start at an uplift of 50 per cent and work downwards in accordance with evidence of mitigation provided by the respondent. To do so would be to seriously miss the purpose and wording of the section which provides a discretion. The matters to be considered by the tribunal "are unlimited". In *Butler v G.R. Carr (Essex) Ltd* UKEAT/0128/07, the EAT upheld an uplift of 30 per cent for a significant and serious breach of the procedure (none of Steps 1,2 or 3 complied with), but which was not wilful. In such a case the tribunal was right to place the award in the top bracket of the range 10–50 per cent but exactly where to place it ". . . must be a matter for the discretion, exercised justly and equitably, of the employment tribunal." The question is one of fact [31] to [43].

It should be noted that in unfair dismissal claims the uplift cannot increase the award beyond the statutory maximum.

10–026/1

In *Aptuit (Edinburgh) Ltd v Kennedy* UKEATS/0057/06, it was held that in exercising its discretion to uplift an award, the only circumstances which the tribunal may take into account are those surrounding the failure to complete the statutory procedure. Whether the employer has acted unfairly towards the claimant generally, and the employer's size and administrative resources, are not relevant considerations: [47]. It is submitted that this puts an unwarranted gloss on the statutory language which gives the tribunal the discretion to adjust the award upwards from ten percent "if it considers it just and equitable in all the circumstances to do so" (emphasis added). Determining the reason for the employer's (or in the case of s.31(2), the employee's) failure to comply with the requirements of the applicable statutory procedure would seem to be an essential pre-requisite to the exercise of the discretion and all of the matters said to be irrelevant in *Aptuit* seem, at least potentially, relevant to that question. See also the commentary at 10–025 above.

Employee at fault

10–027

As the tribunal is under a duty to reduce by at least 10 per cent, punitive considerations also apply, but the factors are likely to be significantly different from those affecting the employer. In the absence of a requirement to include the procedures in an employee's written terms and conditions of employment, an unrepresented employee is much more likely to be, and to reasonably be, unaware of their obligations under the procedure than their employer. Even though the employer is required to inform the employee of their right to appeal, there is no obligation to warn them of the consequences of failing to do so. Nor is there any obligation to warn them of the consequences of failing to attend a meeting or to conduct themselves during it in accordance with the General Requirements. Given the inability to commence proceedings where the Step 1 grievance letter has not been sent, the employee can never be in complete non-compliance with the grievance procedure, although after sending the Step 1 letter a refusal, as opposed to a failure, to take any further part in the process might be considered its equivalent. It could also be said that the failure to utilise the appeal stage or even to attend a meeting might be a failure to mitigate loss, but it is suggested that an increase in the percentage reduction to reflect this would require some evidence that a possibility of avoiding dismissal or of having the grievance rectified has actually been lost.

Basic award for unfair dismissal

10–028   The basic award in an unfair dismissal claim is excluded from the effect of s.31 by virtue of s.124A ERA (inserted into the 1996 Act by s.39 EA). As s.120(1A) ERA when read with s.98A(1) only provides for a minimum basic award in cases where the statutory dismissal and disciplinary procedure applies, there is no provision for uplifting or reducing the basic award in a constructive unfair dismissal claim.

SUBSECTION (4)—EXCEPTIONAL CIRCUMSTANCES

10–029   Although the tribunal is given a discretion to do what is "just and equitable", the precondition to the exercise of that discretion is the existence of "exceptional circumstances". There is no authority on what might or might not amount to exceptional circumstances. Given that reg.11(3) DRR provides for limited circumstances in which the procedures are either treated as not applying or as having been completed, and subs.(4) can only apply where the procedure has not been completed (and therefore, ex hypothesi, the circumstances described in reg.11(3) have not arisen) it must be presumed that the circumstances envisaged by subs.(4) are less "exceptional" than those envisaged by reg.11(3). In particular as reg.11(3)(c) applies where it is not practicable (or possibly not reasonably practicable; see the commentary to reg.11(3)) to commence or to continue to comply with the procedure, it must be the case that s.32(4) contemplates circumstances which, whilst being exceptional, do not render it not (reasonably) practicable to continue to comply with the procedure. Such a circumstance is not easy to envisage but it may include a case where, although the tribunal has found that a communication from the claimant was a Step 1 letter, the respondent honestly and reasonably did not believe it to be so; or a situation such as that in *Galaxy Showers Ltd v Wilson* (for the facts of which see the commentary to subss.(2) and (3)—non-completion of a statutory procedure: employee by—at para.10–022) where the employer may have honestly believed that they were acting in compliance with their duty to call a meeting under the GP.

10–029/1   Where it would clearly be pointless for the employers to hold a meeting, e.g. because the circumstances are such that a meeting could not resolve the grievance, this would amount to an exceptional circumstance making it unjust and inequitable to increase any award: *Bainbridge v Redcar & Cleveland BC* [2007] I.R.L.R. 494 EAT, where the respondents had decided not to call the claimants to a Step 2 meeting. The claimants were represented by a solicitor on the basis of a contingency fee agreement which required them to pay their own costs if they settled the claims independently of the solicitor. The statements of grievance had been written by the solicitor and indicated that the claimants would only deal with the respondent through him. But under the respondent's grievance procedure the claimant's were not entitled to be represented by a solicitor. A prior attempt to mediate the claims had failed and the Step 1 letters were said to be merely part of the litigation process and not genuinely intended to be part of an alternative method of resolving the dispute.

Subsection (5)

10–030   Section 38 (failure to give statement of employment particulars) requires the tribunal (absent exceptional circumstances) to award either two and four weeks pay if a claimant who has succeeded in a claim brought under one of the jurisdictions in

Sch.5 (which is identical to Sch.3) has not been issued with a written statement of the main terms of their employment under s.1(1) or 4(1) of the Employment Rights Act 1996. Section 32(5) prevents that award from being uplifted or reduced for non-compliance with a statutory procedure.

32 Complaints about grievances

(1) This section applies to the jurisdictions listed in Schedule 4.　　10–031

(2) An employee shall not present a complaint to an employment tribunal under a jurisdiction to which this section applies if—

(a) it concerns a matter in relation to which the requirement in paragraph 6 or 9 of Schedule 2 applies, and
(b) the requirement has not been complied with.

(3) An employee shall not present a complaint to an employment tribunal under a jurisdiction to which this section applies if—

(a) it concerns a matter in relation to which the requirement in paragraph 6 or 9 of Schedule 2 has been complied with, and
(b) less than 28 days have passed since the day on which the requirement was complied with.

(4) An employee shall not present a complaint to an employment tribunal under a jurisdiction to which this section applies if—

(a) it concerns a matter in relation to which the requirement in paragraph 6 or 9 of Schedule 2 has been complied with, and
(b) the day on which the requirement was complied with was more than one month after the end of the original time limit for making the complaint.

(5) In such circumstances as the Secretary of State may specify by regulations, an employment tribunal may direct that subsection (4) shall not apply in relation to a particular matter.

(6) An employment tribunal shall be prevented from considering a complaint presented in breach of subsections (2) to (4), but only if—

(a) the breach is apparent to the tribunal from the information supplied to it by the employee in connection with the bringing of the proceedings, or
(b) the tribunal is satisfied of the breach as a result of his employer raising the issue of compliance with those provisions in accordance with regulations under section 7 of the Employment Tribunals Act 1996 (c.17) (employment tribunal procedure regulations).

(7) The Secretary of State may for the purposes of this section by regulations—

(a) make provision about the application of the procedures set out in Part 2 of Schedule 2;

(b) make provision about what constitutes compliance with paragraph 6 or 9 of that Schedule;

(c) make provision about circumstances in which a person is to be treated as having complied with paragraph 6 or 9 of that Schedule;

(d) make provision for paragraph 6 or 9 of that Schedule to have effect in such circumstances as may be specified by the regulations with such modifications as may be so specified.

(8) The Secretary of State may by order—

(a) amend, repeal or replace any of subsections (2) to (4);

(b) amend Schedule 4;

(c) make provision for this section to apply, with or without modifications, as if—

(i) any individual of a description specified in the order who would not otherwise be an employee for the purposes of this section were an employee for those purposes, and

(ii) a person of a description specified in the order were, in the case of any such individual, the individual's employer for those purposes.

(9) Before making an order under subsection (8)(a), the Secretary of State must consult the Advisory, Conciliation and Arbitration Service.

(10) In its application to orders under subsection (8)(a), section 51(1)(b) includes power to amend this section.

Commencement

10–032   Subss.(7)–(10) April 27, 2003.
Subss.(1)–(6) October 1, 2004 subject to transitional provisions.

Transitional Provisions

10–033   The section does not apply in relation to a grievance where the employee has presented a complaint to the employment tribunal about that grievance prior to October 1, 2004: art.3 of the Employment Act 2002 (Commencement No. 6 and Transitional Provisions) Order 2004 (SI 2004/1717).

Modifications

10–034   See s.29 above at para.10–004.

Regulations

10–035   Subs.(7): see the Employment Act 2002 (Dispute Resolution) Regulations 2004 (SI 2004/752) (DRR) at Ch.11.

Subs.(5): no Regulations have been made under subs.(5) as of February 28, 2007.

Orders

No Orders have been made under subs.(8) amending subss.(2) to (4) as of April **10–036**
25, 2008. Amendments to Sch.4 are to be made by the Employment Act 2002
(Amendment of Schs 3, 4, and 5) Order 2007 (SI 2007/30) with effect from April 6,
2007. For amendments and additions to Sch.4 by primary and other secondary
legislation see the commentary to Sch.4.

General

The practical effect of this section is to require an employee to comply with **10–037**
statutory grievance obligations before resorting to tribunal proceedings. Although
this requirement, on its face applies to all jurisdictions listed in Sch.4, the practical
reach of this requirement also depends on the provisions of the DRR (in particular,
reg.6) which flesh out the precise circumstances in which the grievance procedures
apply.

Subsection (2)—"Employee"

"Employee" has the same meaning as in s.230(1) of the Employment Rights Act **10–038**
1996 (EA, s.40), that is someone who works under a contract of service or
apprenticeship. Thus external job applicants, office holders such as police con-
stables, workers (as defined by s.230(2) ERA) and claimants who fall only within the
extended definition of "employment" applicable in discrimination cases (e.g. s.82
Sex Discrimination Act 1975, s.78 Race Relations Act 1976 etc), are not required to
comply with the grievance procedure.

Equal pay claims

Where a claimant seeks to rely in a claim form on comparators not named in the **10–038/1**
Step 1 letter, the question for the tribunal is whether there is a material difference
between the comparators identified in the Step 1 letter and those identified in the
claim form. If there is, s.32(2) will prevent the claimant from relying on the new
comparators: *The Highland Council v TGWU(1) UNISON(2)* [2008]I.R.L.R. 273 EAT.
However, the suggestion at [34] (obiter) that s.32 would not operate as an absolute
bar where a claimant sought to introduce materially different comparators by way
of amendment after proceedings had been commenced, but the fact that materially
different comparators were being introduced was merely a factor which the tribunal
would have to take into account when considering the application to amend, seems
doubtful.

Subsection (3)—Waiting 28 days

While proceedings may not be commenced until the claimant has waited 28 days **10–039**
after sending the written statement of grievance, it is important to remember that
even after the 28 days have expired the employee may be penalised for commencing
proceedings if the statutory procedure has not been completed, and the employee is
responsible for its non-completion (see s.31(2)(b)).

The CPR provides guidance on the counting of time when there is doubt as to the **10–039/1**
meaning of a provision and there is no specifically applicable ET rule. Thus 28 days
by analogy with CPR 2.8 means 28 clear days. Therefore where a grievance was
raised on October 1, the claim cannot be presented until October 30: *Basingstoke
Press Ltd v Clarke* [2007] I.R.L.R. 588 EAT; [2007] I.C.R. 1284.

In *Brock v Minerva Dental Ltd* [2007] I.C.R. 917, it was suggested obiter that where
a claim is originally presented as one to which the SGP does not apply, such as a
complaint of unfair dismissal under s.95(1)(a) ERA, and the claimant subsequently

seeks to add or substitute a complaint of constructive unfair dismissal by way of amendment, s.32(3) is only complied with if the original claim had been presented to the tribunal more than 28 days after the Step 1 letter raising the grievance for the purpose of the constructive unfair dismissal claim. This must be doubtful. The better view appears to be that the application to amend to add the complaint of constructive unfair dismissal cannot be made until after the expiration of 28 days from the sending of the Step 1 letter and that the date of the original claim is irrelevant (and see *Mackay v Hanna t/a Blakes Newsagents* at para.10–041 below).

Subsection (4)—Meaning of "original time limit"

10–040   The effect of s.32(4) seemed to be to provide an absolute cut off point after which the right to raise a grievance and in consequence the right to complain to an employment tribunal, was lost.

However, in *Spillet v Tesco Stores Ltd* [2006] I.R.L.R. 248; [2006] I.C.R. 643, EAT it was held that "original time limit" in s.32(4) had a different meaning from "normal time limit" in reg.15(1) DRR (which by reg.15(5) means the primary time limit) and meant the primary time limit including any extension permitted by a tribunal pursuant to its discretion to permit a claim presented late to proceed. This conclusion does, however appear at odds with the following statement by Alan Johnson during the second reading of the Bill (Hansard February 12, 2002 Column 81, not referred to by the EAT):

> "We want to ensure, however, that the grievance is quickly brought to the employer's attention during any extended period. That should ensure that recollection of the events surrounding the grievance remains fresh. We therefore stipulate in subsection (4) that the step 1 action must have been completed within a period of no more than one month after the normal period for making applications to tribunals has ended. For most jurisdictions the normal period for bringing complaints is three months. For those jurisdictions the third criterion [i.e. subs. (4)] means that the step 1 action needs to be taken within 4 months of the event that gave rise to the grievance."

The sending of a Step 1 letter after the primary limitation period (the normal time limit: DRR reg.15(1) and (5)) has expired does not trigger an automatic extension of time, even if it is subsequently held that it was not reasonably practicable for it to have been sent earlier or it is just and equitable to extend the time, as reg.15(3) applies only to s.32(2) and (3). It is for the claimant who wishes to claim that despite their failure to send the Step 1 letter to their employer within four months of the act complained of it is just and equitable to extend the time to allow them to do so, or that it was not reasonably practicable to do so, to raise the issue either in the claim form or on an application to review a decision to reject the claim, and then to satisfy the tribunal at a pre-hearing review that, for one of those reasons, the grievance was raised in time. However, the sending of a step 1 letter is a much less formal step than commencing tribunal proceedings and by no means every ground on which the late submission of a claim might be excused, is likely to excuse the late submission of a Step 1 letter. The issue of whether it is just and equitable to allow the claimant to send the Step 1 letter after the four month period had expired should therefore be addressed by the tribunal first. If answered in the negative, the claimant will not be entitled to bring the proceedings. The decision in *Spillett* still places an obligation on the claimant to act timeously, but only in the sense that the Step 1 letter must be sent within one month of the end of the period by which it was just and equitable to extend time or from when it ceased to be reasonably practicable to send it. Even if the Step 1 letter is held to have been sent in time, the claimant may still have to show that it is also just and equitable to allow them to bring the tribunal proceedings, particularly if there has been considerable additional delay after sending the Step 1 letter.

Subsection (6)—Effect of non-compliance with pre-acceptance procedure

In *Bradford v Pratt* [2007] I.R.L.R. 192, the EAT expressed its concern that the provisions of the EA are capable of producing harsh results, and suggested that a better solution might lay in a requirement for tribunals to stay proceedings commenced before statutory dispute resolution procedures had been followed, pending completion of the required steps, rather than a requirement that removed jurisdiction in such situations. However, in *Hounslow LBC v Miller* UKEAT/0645/06 it was held that a claim form presented prematurely cannot be accepted and stayed under r.1(8) of the Rules of procedure. The claim must be rejected.

10–041

Following *Prakash v Wolverhampton CC* UKEAT/0140/06, where a claim is partially rejected for non-compliance with the requirement to wait 28 days, the rejected claims can be added to the original claim by way of amendment once the 28 day period has expired: *Mackay v Hanna t/a Blakes Newsagents* UKEAT/0181/07 (unopposed appeal).

In *Holc-Gale v Makers Ltd* [2006] I.C.R. 462, the EAT held that the employer was permitted to raise the issue of non-compliance with the requirement to send a Step 1 letter even though in its grounds of response it had been conceded that a Step 1 letter had been sent. Section 32(6) was a matter going to the jurisdiction of the tribunal to hear the claim. The decisions in *Exel Management v Lumb* UKEAT/0232/06 and *Bradford MDC v Pratt* (above) are to the same effect. However, it seems that s. 32(6) is not an absolute jurisdictional bar. "Curiously, although s.32 provides that the employee "shall not present a complaint," if he does so it is not necessarily outwith the jurisdiction of the tribunal to hear it"; *South Kent College v Hall* UKEAT/0087/07 per Elias P. at [10]. "In my view, once the issue of procedural compliance has arisen in a way envisaged by s. 32(6) then the tribunal simply has no jurisdiction to hear a claim. . . " (emphasis added); *Hounslow LBC v Miller* (above) per Elias P. at [24]. It therefore seems necessarily to follow that the tribunal does have jurisdiction to hear a claim where the grievance procedure has not been complied with unless the issue of non-compliance is raised as envisaged by subs. (6)(a) or (b).

10–041/1

Thus, where a claim form had been properly accepted on the basis of the information provided by the claimant, it was not open to the respondent to allege for the first time on appeal that the tribunal had no jurisdiction to hear the claim when they had not raised the issue of non-compliance in their response and had not applied to amend: *Chickerova v Holovachuk* UKEAT/0016/07 (and to the same effect DMC *Business Machines Plc v Plummer* UKEAT/0381/06 at [25] obiter. But see to the contrary *Basingstoke Press Ltd v Clarke* [2007] I.R.L.R. 588 EAT; [2007] I.C.R. 1284, where the claim form was accepted despite having been presented one day prematurely, in which it was assumed without argument (the claimant being unrepresented and the point not being identified as an issue in the appeal) that the sub-section does create an absolute jurisdictional bar which it was open for a respondent who had not entered a response and was barred from defending the claim under r.9, to take on appeal.

An employer who ticks the "No" box on the prescribed response form in answer to the question whether the claimant has raised the subject matter of the claim as a grievance, has done enough to engage s.32(6)(b) even if the point is not taken up in the grounds of resistance to the claim: *South Kent College v Hall* (above). It is unclear whether s.36(2)(a) applies only up to the point at which the claim form is accepted by the Secretary, or whether the tribunal is prevented from hearing a claim where the claim form was wrongly accepted, the respondent does not take the point, but the error is detected subsequently by the tribunal itself. It is submitted that a decision by a tribunal that is has no jurisdiction to hear a claim by virtue of s.32(6)(a) where the claim has been incorrectly accepted by the Secretary, but the error was only discovered after is was no longer possible for the claimant to raise a valid grievance, would be incompatible with the claimant's rights under art.6(1) ECHR, and in consequence the tribunal would be in breach of s.6(1) of the Human Rights Act 1998. The fact that the claimant would appear to have a good prospect of having the primary time limit extended so as to permit a resubmitted claim to proceed, would not appear to be an answer to the point as this could not be guaranteed.

Following *Chickerova* and *DMC Business Machines*, it would be imprudent to assume that a late application to amend a response to allege non-compliance with the SGP is likely to be granted. The usual considerations for determining whether to grant an application to amend a claim or response would seem to apply, paramount among which would be the prejudice a claimant would suffer if the application was made so late that a valid grievance could no longer be raised. The reason why the respondent has delayed taking the point is likely to be of equal importance.

10–041/2   As a quasi-jurisdictional provision, s.32(6) encompasses a rule preventing premature claims (where it applies by reason of a failure to comply with either s.32(2) or 32(3)), and a rule that prevents "late claims" (where it applies by reason of the application of s.32(4)). If jurisdiction is lacking because the claim is premature, it remains open to the employee (subject to applicable time limits, including the automatic extension of the primary time limit in certain circumstances provided for in reg.15(3) DRR—see paras 11–065 to 11–070—and the discretions available to tribunals to extend the primary time permitted for the presentation of a claim, for which see Ch.9 generally) to raise the same claim again in new proceedings. The fact that the first set of proceedings was dismissed on jurisdictional grounds will not give rise to any issue estoppel: see *Excel Management v Lumb* (above).

33 Consequential adjustment of time limits

10–042   **(1) The Secretary of State may, in relation to a jurisdiction listed in Schedule 3 or 4, by regulations make provision about the time limit for beginning proceedings in respect of a claim concerning a matter to which a statutory procedure applies.**

(2) Regulations under this section may, in particular—

   (a) make provision extending, or authorising the extension of, the time for beginning proceedings,

   (b) make provision about the exercise of a discretion to extend the time for beginning proceedings, or

   (c) make provision treating proceedings begun out of time as begun within time.

Commencement

10–043   April 27, 2003.

Regulations

10–044   See reg.15 (DRR) at Ch.11.

Automatic extensions of time

10–045   Regulation 15 DRR defines the circumstances in which the time for bringing employment tribunal proceedings will be automatically extended. The Regulations do not make provisions about the exercise of discretion to extend time, which remains subject to the usual rules (see Ch.9).

SCHEDULE 2

STATUTORY DISPUTE RESOLUTION PROCEDURES

PART 1

DISMISSAL AND DISCIPLINARY PROCEDURES

CHAPTER 1

STANDARD PROCEDURE

Step 1: statement of grounds for action and invitation to meeting

(1) The employer must set out in writing the employee's alleged **10–046** conduct or characteristics, or other circumstances, which lead him to contemplate dismissing or taking disciplinary action against the employee.

(2) The employer must send the statement or a copy of it to the employee and invite the employee to attend a meeting to discuss the matter.

Step 2: meeting

2(1) The meeting must take place before action is taken, except in **10–047** the case where the disciplinary action consists of suspension.

(2) The meeting must not take place unless—

    (a) the employer has informed the employee what the basis was for including in the statement under paragraph 1(1) the ground or grounds given in it, and

    (b) the employee has had a reasonable opportunity to consider his response to that information.

(3) The employee must take all reasonable steps to attend the meeting.

(4) After the meeting, the employer must inform the employee of his decision and notify him of the right to appeal against the decision if he is not satisfied with it.

Step 3: appeal

3(1) If the employee does wish to appeal, he must inform the **10–048** employer.

(2) If the employee informs the employer of his wish to appeal, the employer must invite him to attend a further meeting.

(3) The employee must take all reasonable steps to attend the meeting.

(4) The appeal meeting need not take place before the dismissal or disciplinary action takes effect.

(5) After the appeal meeting, the employer must inform the employee of his final decision.

CHAPTER 2

MODIFIED PROCEDURE

Step 1: statement of grounds for action

10–049   **4 The employer must—**

    (a) set out in writing—

        (i) the employee's alleged misconduct which has led to the dismissal,

        (ii) what the basis was for thinking at the time of the dismissal that the employee was guilty of the alleged misconduct, and

        (iii) the employee's right to appeal against dismissal, and

    (b) send the statement or a copy of it to the employee.

Step 2: appeal

10–050   5(1) If the employee does wish to appeal, he must inform the employer.

     (2) If the employee informs the employer of his wish to appeal, the employer must invite him to attend a meeting.

     (3) The employee must take all reasonable steps to attend the meeting.

     (4) After the appeal meeting, the employer must inform the employee of his final decision.

Commencement

10–051   October 1, 2004 subject to transitional provisions.

Transitional provisions

10–052   The Schedule does not apply in relation to a grievance where the employee has presented a complaint to the employment tribunal about that grievance prior to October 1, 2004: art.3 of the Employment Act 2002 (Commencement No. 6 and Transitional Provisions) Order 2004 (SI 2004/1717).

Modifications

10–053   See s.29 at para.10–004.

The Standard DDP

Step 1

Statement of grounds for disciplinary action

10–054   To achieve the purpose of preventing a matter going to the employment tribunal by providing the possibility for differences to be resolved at an early stage, the information to be provided to the employee "must be at least sufficient to enable the employee to give a considered and informed response to the proposal to dismiss" (*Alexander (1) and Hatherley (2) v Brigden Enterprises Ltd* [2006] I.R.L.R. 422; [2006] I.C.R. 1277, EAT at [34]).

The employer merely has to set out in writing the grounds which lead him to contemplate dismissing or taking relevant disciplinary action against the employee, together with an invitation to a meeting. The statement need do no more than state the issue in broad terms. The employee needs to be told that he is at risk of dismissal and why. In a conduct case this will require the misconduct in issue to be identified. In a capability or redundancy case it may require nothing more than saying "lack of capability" or "redundancy". The approach should be consistent with that adopted in *Canary Wharf Management Ltd v Edebi* [2006] I.R.L.R. 416; [2006] I.C.R. 719, EAT, in respect of grievances: *Alexander v Brigden Enterprises Ltd* at [38].

> "The purpose of these procedures is to ensure that there is a proper and fair opportunity for the parties to seek to address any disciplinary issues and other matters which may lead to dismissal. . . . It is not to create unnecessary technical hurdles for either employer or employee. . . . Shifts in the focus of the case will not lead to an obligation on the employer to write a fresh [step 1 letter] on each occasion."

Thus: "There is very little difference between the original complaint which was unauthorised absence, and misuse of company time" which was expressed to be the reason for dismissal. However, where a quite distinct act of misconduct emerges as a result of the investigatory or disciplinary process, the employer must serve a fresh Step 1 letter (*Silman v I.C.T.S. (UK) Ltd* UKEAT/0630/05 at para.22). Similarly if new information emerges during the disciplinary process which materially changes the basis on which the employer is proceeding, a fresh Step 1 letter should be sent. In *Premier Foods Plc v Garner* UKEAT/0389/06 the claimant appealed against a written warning. The respondent's procedure allowed for a disciplinary sanction to be increased on appeal, a fact of which the claimant was reminded in writing. During the appeal, fresh evidence emerged which led to the claimant being dismissed. *Held*, even though Steps 1 and 2 of the DDP had been complied with in respect of the original warning, the DDP was re-engaged by the realisation that the claimant's culpability was greater than first thought and in consequence dismissal had become the appropriate sanction. A new Step 1 letter should have been sent to the claimant and the letter reminding her that the sanction could be increased on appeal was not sufficient.

The general approach to the construction and application of all of the procedures is likely to be similar. Therefore authorities concerning whether an employee has complied with Step 1 of the standard GP have "relevance and . . . resonance" when determining whether an employer has complied with Step 1 of the DDP. Where the complaint is that neither Step 1 nor Step 2(2)(a) have been complied with, it would be an error of law for the tribunal to consider generally whether the purpose of the procedure had been complied with, or whether there had been compliance with the procedure as a whole, without considering whether there had been compliance with Step 1 separately from compliance with Step 2. In considering whether a letter complied with Step 1 the tribunal is entitled to consider the context in which it was issued, e.g. that it followed an investigatory meeting at which the employers concerns were fully explained to the employee (*Draper v Mears Ltd* [2006] I.R.L.R. 869).

The respondent was held to be in non-compliance with the procedure where they had been alerted to the fact that the Step 1 letter had been sent to an address at which the claimant was no longer living and that the claimant had not received it, a replacement letter was not sent and the claimant was given an oral explanation for the meeting which did not mention the possibility of dismissal (*Sweeny v Indesit Co*, unreported, April 12, 2006, ET).

A letter sent to an employee inviting her to an investigatory meeting which specified the matters of concern and warned that dismissal was a possibility, satisfied the requirements of Step 1. It was therefore not a breach of the DDP when the employee's invitation to attend the subsequent disciplinary hearing (which was largely for the purpose of announcing the employer's decision to dismiss) was made orally. ". . . It is necessary to look beneath the parties' own labels and focus on whether the substantive requirements of the statute, which are in simple and non-technical terms, were or were not met (YMCA *Training v Stewart* [2007] I.R.L.R. 185, EAT). "The temptation to bring in by the back door the full panoply of 'ordinary' unfair dismissal when interpreting and applying the requirements of [the DDP] must be resisted. [15].

There is no requirement for the Step 1 letter to expressly state that the employer is contemplating dismissal or other disciplinary action provided the threat of such action is implicit. In *Homeserve Emergency Services Ltd v Dixon* UKEAT/0127/07, the claimant had been caught red-handed doing a job for his own benefit in his employer's time and using his employer's materials, which he had admitted and did not allege that he did not understand what the subsequent disciplinary hearing was about. The tribunal was therefore wrong to raise the question of whether Step 1 had been complied with. Moreover, there was no breach of Step 2 when the claimant was given no further details of the reason for calling the disciplinary hearing until the meeting itself: *YMCA* followed.

Step 2

Informing the employee

10–055   There is no requirement for the information to be provided to the employee in writing, nor for it to be provided after the Step 1 letter has been sent. Thus an investigatory meeting held prior to the issuing of a Step 1 letter at which the employers concerns are explained fully to the employee can amount to compliance with para.2(2)(a) of the Schedule (*Draper v Mears Ltd* [2006] I.R.L.R. 869, EAT). However, the respondent was in breach of Step 2(2) when it did not give the claimant the management's statement of case against her or the investigation report, until after the disciplinary hearing had commenced, the claimant not having been interviewed as part of the investigation: *Bowen v Millbank Estate Management Organisation* UKEAT/0032/07

In *Alexander (1) and Hatherley (2) v Bridgen Enterprises Ltd* [2006] I.R.L.R. 422; [2006] I.C.R. 1277, EAT, it was held that in a redundancy case the employer must explain why he is contemplating dismissing the individual employee and not merely why it is necessary to make redundancies. This includes not only the criteria used but the employee's own marks or assessment although not those of others in the pool. For the purpose of deciding whether Step 2 of the DDP has been complied with, the tribunal is not concerned with the reasonableness of the selection criteria. However, in *Davies v Farnborough College of Technology* [2008] I.R.L.R. 14, the EAT held that *Alexander* did not mean that if marks are not expressly disclosed, there must automatically have been a breach of the procedure. It is not necessary in every case to give the employee their marks. On the facts of any given case, an employer must give sufficient information in relation to how the criteria were applied to allow the employee both to understand and to challenge their selection. Depending on the circumstances, this may mean that giving the employee their marks may either be not necessary or not sufficient.

Although *Alexander* was a redundancy case, it gives helpful guidance on the kind of information the employee should have in advance of the Step 2 meeting irrespective of the grounds of dismissal. That the issue is one of compliance with process, not of reasonableness is clearly applicable to all cases.

The statutory procedure merely provides a basic minimum standard. It requires only that sufficient material to enable the employee to put her side of the story be disclosed in advance of the meeting. Thus where the allegation against an employee was of fraudulent accounting, the basis of which was spelled out in the Step 1 letter, the employers did not breach Step 2(2)(a) by producing the invoices, which were the evidence in support of the allegations, at the meeting. There is no requirement under the statutory procedure for employers to produce in advance all the evidence on which they intend to rely at the meeting: *Ingram v Bristol Street Parts* UKEAT/0601/06 at [21] to [23].

The obiter remarks of Underhill J. in *YMCA Training v Stewart* [2007] I.R.L.R. 185 EAT at [16], that the fact that the employer announces his decision during the meeting itself rather than after the meeting does not amount to non-compliance with Step 2(4), were correct and would be followed: *Dugdale Plc v Cartlidge* UKEAT/0508/06 at [21].

Step 2(4)—appeal

There is no requirement for the right to an appeal to be stated in writing, nor for **10–055/1** the employer to "offer" an appeal. The only requirement is for the fact that the employee has the right to appeal to be communicated to the employee: *Aptuit (Edinburgh) Ltd v Kennedy* UKEATS/0057/06. An employer's failure to give an employee sufficient information about why he was at risk of redundancy in advance of the Step 2 meeting which put the employer in breach of the procedure could not be cured by giving the employee the missing information prior to the appeal hearing: *Davies v Farnborough College of Technology* UKEAT/0137/07.

Failure to attend a meeting

For the consequences of the failure of an employee or their representatives to **10–056** attend the hearing and the employer's obligation to rearrange the meeting, see reg.13 DRR and commentary at para.11–061.

Step 3

Failure to appeal—consequences of

For the consequences of an employee's failure to appeal against the employer's **10–057** decision, see s.31(2) and commentary at para.10–023.

Reinstatement following appeal

If the employee is reinstated following the appeal, reg.2(f) of the Employment **10–058** Protection (Continuity of Employment) Regulations 1996 (SI 1996/3147) (which is added by reg.17(e) DRR) has the effect of restoring the employee's continuity of employment if "a decision is taken arising out of the use of a statutory dispute resolution procedure". The effect is clear if the disciplinary process which is followed exactly mirrors the statutory procedure, and the position should be the same even if the process does not exactly mirror the statutory provisions. The statutory procedure is only the irreducible minimum below which a dismissal will be automatically unfair and few larger employers will therefore expressly follow it. The better view is that reg.2(f) of the 1996 Regulations assumes that all disciplinary procedures have the statutory procedure subsumed into them and that all reinstatements as the result of a successful appeal where the employer first contemplated dismissing the employee after October 1, 2004 (see reg.18 DRR—the transitional provisions—at para.11–074) will automatically preserve continuity, even if only achieved at a second or subsequent level of appeal.

The modified procedure

When applicable

10–059   See reg.3(2) DRR and commentary at para.11–009. The modified procedure does not apply where the claimant was dismissed by his line manager the day after he allegedly verbally abused and was insubordinate to, the line manager in a telephone conversation. Dismissal was not "at the time the employer became aware of the conduct or immediately after it": *O'Neil v Wooldridge Ecotech Ltd* UKEAT/0282/07.

Consequences of failure to appeal

10–060   For the consequences of an employee's failure to appeal against the employer's decision, see s.31(2) and commentary at para.10–023.

PART 2

GRIEVANCE PROCEDURES

CHAPTER 1

STANDARD PROCEDURE

Step 1: statement of grievance

10–061   **6 The employee must set out the grievance in writing and send the statement or a copy of it to the employer.**

Step 2: meeting

10–062   **7(1) The employer must invite the employee to attend a meeting to discuss the grievance.**
            (2) The meeting must not take place unless—

> **(a) the employee has informed the employer what the basis for the grievance was when he made the statement under paragraph 6, and**
> **(b) the employer has had a reasonable opportunity to consider his response to that information.**

(3) The employee must take all reasonable steps to attend the meeting.

(4) After the meeting, the employer must inform the employee of his decision as to his response to the grievance and notify him of the right to appeal against the decision if he is not satisfied with it.

Step 3: appeal

8(1) If the employee does wish to appeal, he must inform the employer. **10–063**

(2) If the employee informs the employer of his wish to appeal, the employer must invite him to attend a further meeting.

(3) The employee must take all reasonable steps to attend the meeting.

(4) After the appeal meeting, the employer must inform the employee of his final decision.

CHAPTER 2

MODIFIED PROCEDURE

Step 1: statement of grievance

9 The employee must— **10–064**

    (a) set out in writing—

        (i) the grievance, and
        (ii) the basis for it, and

    (b) send the statement or a copy of it to the employer.

Step 2: response

10 The employer must set out his response in writing and send the statement or a copy of it to the employee. **10–065**

The Standard GP

Raising a grievance: the Step 1 letter

Meaning of grievance

For the definition of "grievance" see reg.2 DRR. For these purposes "action" **10–066** taken by an employer should be understood as including action taken by other employees for whose actions the employer is liable, either at common law or under any statutory provision (see, for example, s.41 of the Sex Discrimination Act 1975). There is no requirement for the claimant to send a written statement of grievance to the fellow employee as the statutory procedures have no application to disputes between employees. "Action" can include the employer's handling of an earlier grievance (*Mudchute Association v Petheridge* UKEAT/0569/05).

467

General principles

10–067   There are several reported and unreported cases on what does and does not amount to a Step 1 letter. The leading authority is *Canary Wharf Management Ltd v Edebi* [2006] I.R.L.R. 416; [2006] I.C.R. 719, EAT, which, considering and approving five of the earlier decisions, held that a resignation letter from an employee which complained about his working conditions and the effect they were having on his health did raise a grievance for a constructive unfair dismissal claim but not a disability discrimination claim as there was no allegation of less favourable treatment or a failure to make adjustments. It was merely a generalised complaint about the adverse consequences to his health of the employer's conduct. From the judgment the following principles emerge: "

> . . .the objective of the statute can be fairly met if the employers, on a fair reading of the statement and having regard to the particular context in which it is made, can be expected to appreciate that the relevant complaint is being made" [25]
>
> "If the statement cannot in context fairly be read even in a non-technical and unsophisticated way as raising the grievance which is the subject matter of the tribunal complaint, then the tribunal cannot hear the claim. There is no over-riding interest of justice which can be invoked to save it" [31]
>
> ". . .a direct analogy with the procedural rules and the construction of claim forms in particular [as in *Richardson v U Mole* [2005] I.R.L.R. 668, EAT] is not appropriate here." [37]

The grievance must raise the same complaint as the employee is seeking to have determined by the employment tribunal and it must be extant when proceedings are brought. It is sufficient that the complaint is identified and it is not necessary to set out the basis of the complaint, (but see below under "different requirements of standard and modified procedure" for a criticism of this aspect of the decision) nor is it necessary to actively invoke the grievance procedure or to say that the employee expects the complaint to be dealt with. "The paragraph is satisfied simply if the complaint is made" [2]. There is no maximum time limit prior to the lodging of the claim in which the grievance must have been raised.

See also *Shergold v Fieldway Medical Centre* [2006] I.R.L.R. 76; [2006] I.C.R. 304, EAT—the grievance must relate to the subsequent claim, and the claim must relate to the earlier grievance, but that does not mean that the wording of the two must be anywhere near identical. Provided the general nature of the grievance was substantially the same as the subject matter of the claim, its different description of events or a difference by way of precise ingredients or particulars, does not affect the statutory compliance. Thus a failure to mention in the grievance letter the event which was the "last straw" in a subsequent constructive unfair dismissal claim did not affect the validity of the grievance. However, not only must the grievance have the same factual basis as the subsequent claim, it must have the same legal basis. In *Noskiw v Royal Mail Group Plc*, unreported, March 7, 2005, ET (cited with approval in *Shergold*) a grievance which complained of differential treatment in matters of pay and attributed the reason to a number of causes (none of which could have given rise to tribunal proceedings) which did not include disability discrimination, was not a Step 1 letter for subsequent proceedings which did attribute the differential treatment to disability discrimination.

Form of the statement of grievance

10–068   The following are examples of communications from employees and their representatives which have been held to be written statements of grievance within paras 6 or 9 of the grievance procedure.

Commotion Ltd v Rutty [2006] I.R.L.R. 171; [2006] I.C.R. 290, EAT: a formal written application for flexible working under s.80F of the Employment Rights Act 1996 after having an informal request rejected where the complaint was that the claimant had been constructively unfairly dismissed because of the rejection of her application.

Shergold v Fieldway Medical Centre [2006] I.R.L.R. 76; [2006] I.C.R. 304, EAT: a resignation letter (also *Canary Wharf Management Ltd v Edebi* [2006] I.R.L.R. 416; [2006] I.C.R. 719, EAT).

Mark Warner Ltd v Aspland [2006] I.R.L.R. 87, EAT: correspondence between solicitors (including without prejudice correspondence: *Arnold Clark Automobiles Ltd v Stewart (1) Barnetts Motor Group (2)* UKEAT/0052/05). The normal rules of agency apply.

O'Connell v BBC, unreported, September 27, 2005, ET: claimant had sent a series of emails which she did not think had raised a formal grievance but which clearly made a series of complaints.

Munden-Edge v Esporta Health & Fitness Ltd, unreported, December 29, 2005, ET: notes of an exit interview signed by the claimant.

Chard v Telewest Communications Plc (ET 1401078/05) a letter by the claimant's chiropractor to the respondent emphasising that adjustments were required to the claimant's role.

Shergold v Fieldway Medical Centre [2006] I.R.L.R. 76; [2006] I.C.R. 304, EAT [27] and [28] quoted at para.10–016 and see also *Lipscombe v Forestry Commission* UKEAT/0191/06: a resignation letter.

Kennedy Scott Ltd v Francis UKEAT/204/07: the claimant raised complaints of his treatment in an email and orally but did not allege discrimination. He was advised to see his line manager who would record details of his grievance. At the interview with the line manager the claimant made allegations of racist bullying. *Held*: the line manager's notes of the interview amounted to the Step 1 written statement of grievance. The focus is on substance not technicality. The line manager (who was not acting as the claimant's agent) and the claimant had been working together to put something in writing. The purpose of the exercise was to enable the claimant "to draw up some document evidencing of his grievance" in conjunction with his line manager. The fact that at least part of the purpose of the meeting had been to try and resolve the grievance was not material: [46] to [50]. This case may turn on its own facts which included that the claimant was told that the line manager would make a record of his grievance and the claimant observed her making a note of what he said.

Cummings v Compass Group UK and Ireland Ltd t/a Scolarest UKEAT/0625/06: a written statement of grievance submitted by the claimant's solicitors which mistakenly gave her name as Cummings (a mistake repeated on the claim form) rather than her correct name which was Cowings, was a valid Step 1 statement.

Serco Group Ltd v Wild UKEAT/0519/06: A letter which did not cite a male comparator or mention equal pay but complained about the claimant's level of pay in comparison with another job title, was held to be a Step 1 letter for an equal pay claim. It was necessary to read the letter in the context of an earlier conversation in which the claimant had expressly complained that she was paid less than men doing similar roles which, she had asserted, was against the law. However, and unsurprisingly, "context" does not include events after a document, not obviously a Step 1 letter, came into existence; *Dick Lovett Ltd v Evans* UKEAT/0211/07.

Gibbs t/a Jarlands Financial Services v Harris UKEAT/0023/07. Where some complaints on a claim form are accepted and some rejected because no written statement of grievance had been sent to the respondent, the sending of the claim form to the respondent by the Secretary pursuant to r.2(2)(a) does not amount to the sending of a written statement of grievance in respect of the rejected claims. The claimant must send an independent Step 1 statement.

Alitalia Airport SPA v Akrif UKEAT/0546/07. Union representatives lodged a collective age discrimination grievance under reg.9 DRR. Three union members not named in the grievance were among a larger group who later sent individual age discrimination questionnaires to the respondent. The questionnaires were identical pro formas issued by the union which showed that the three shared precisely the same grievance as those named in the reg.9 collective grievance. They had therefore impliedly asked the union representatives to act as their agents and in consequence the reg.9 grievance could stand as their individual grievances under para.6 of Sch.2 EA. "It would be futile to require the same grievance to be lodged again" [55].

Disabled employees

10–068/1 See the ACAS Code of Practice on Disciplinary and Grievance Procedures at para.75: ". . . Under the Disability Discrimination Act 1995 employers are required to make reasonable adjustments which may include assisting employees to formulate a written grievance if they are unable to do so themselves because of a disability."

What cannot amount to a statement of grievance

10–069 A questionnaire sent to the respondent under one of the statutory discrimination jurisdictions, other than age discrimination (see the commentary to reg.14 DRR at para.11–062; and see *Holc-Gale v Makers Ltd* [2006] I.C.R. 462). However, in principle there is no reason why a statutory grievance could not be "created" by a covering letter with the questionnaire stating that the matters complained of in the questionnaire are also a grievance. The anomaly of the age discrimination questionnaire is to be rectified by the Employment Equality (Age) (Consequential Amendments) Regulations 2007 which it is anticipated will come into force on April 6, 2007.

Timing of statement of grievance

10–070 "The statute does not require any particular timescale in respect of the complaint" (*Galaxy Showers Ltd v Wilson* [2006] I.R.L.R. 83, EAT); also obiter the "unreality" of requiring an employee who has submitted a grievance and then resigned when it has not been resolved, to submit a further grievance before commencing proceedings "is in most cases readily apparent." However in *Mudchute Association v Petheridge* UKEAT/0569/05, it was held that where a claimant raises a grievance which the employer rejects and then raises a further grievance relating to the way in which that grievance was handled, the second grievance stands alone for the purposes of determining whether the Regulations apply and in particular whether reg.15 has triggered an automatic extension of time. It seems to follow that if part of the reason for the employee's resignation is the handling of the first grievance a further grievance must be raised.

> "There is no maximum time limit prior to the lodging of the claim to the tribunal in which the grievance must have been raised. . . . That is not to say, however, that the act of raising a complaint months or years prior to lodging the tribunal claim will necessarily constitute the appropriate raising of the grievance. The grievance must be extant" (*Canary Wharf Management Ltd v Edebi* [2006] I.R.L.R. 416; [2006] I.C.R. 719, EAT).

"Extant" presumably means "not wholly resolved" which in a discrimination claim could include the employer's refusal to pay compensation for injury to the employee's feelings even if the subject matter of the complaint has been resolved. Following *Hart v English Heritage* [2006] I.R.L.R. 915; [2006] I.C.R. 655, EAT if the employee delays so long after raising their grievance before commencing proceedings that even the time limit as automatically extended by reg.15(3) has expired, the right to bring proceedings in respect of the subject matter of the grievance is lost (subject of course to the possibility that the tribunal will extend the time limit on the grounds that is just and equitable to do so) and cannot be revived by raising the grievance again.

Where the claimant raises a grievance about a continuing act of discrimination **10–070/1** e.g. in a disability case the employer's failure to find alternative employment in pursuance of their duty to make reasonable adjustments, there is no requirement for the claimant to raise a second or subsequent grievance if that failure continues. In such cases the tribunal should not restrict its examination of the employer's actions to the period preceding the grievance letter but should consider the whole period up to the presentation of the claim: *Smith v Network Rail Infrastructure Ltd* UKEAT/0047/07 at [29] and [30].

Timing of statement of grievance: equal pay claims

Note the uniquely long limitation period which applies to equal pay claims (in a **10–071** standard case, six months from the ending of the contract of employment in respect of which the complaint is made, which may be many years after the breach of the equality clause has been remedied). If the breach of the equality clause ended prior to October 1, 2004 the claimant was not obliged to raise a written grievance at all. If the breach began before October 1, 2004 and has not been resolved, if the employee "raised a grievance . . . with the employer. . ." prior to October 1, 2004 the statutory grievance procedure does not apply (see the transitional arrangements in reg.18 DRR at para.11–074). There is no express requirement in reg.18 for the pre-October 1, 2004 grievance to have been raised in writing. If the breach of the equality clause began before October 1, 2004 and has not been resolved but the employee did not raise a grievance prior to that date, or the breach did not occur until after that date, the statutory grievance procedure applies and the employee must send a Step 1 letter to the employer. However, having done so, unless the whole of the breach of the equality clause is rectified, i.e. by compensating the claimant for past loss as well as increasing her earnings for the future, the claimant may rely on that Step 1 letter to bring employment tribunal proceedings at any time in the future until the end of the period of six months beginning with the ending of the contract of employment in question. On whether the grievance is still "extant" see *Canary Wharf Management Ltd* at para.10–070 above.

Different requirements of standard and modified procedure

In *Shergold v Fieldway Medical Centre* [2006] I.R.L.R. 76; [2006] I.C.R. 304, EAT it **10–072** was suggested that there was an important difference between the wording of Step 1 of the standard GP and that of Step 1 in the modified procedure in that the modified procedure requires the employee to set out the basis for the grievance. This view was endorsed in *Canary Wharf Management Ltd* and in *City of Bradford MDC v Pratt* UKEAT/0391/06. However, the validity of this distinction is doubtful. Although Step 1 of the modified procedure expressly requires that the employee must set out in writing the grievance "and the basis for it", whilst the standard procedure merely requires that the grievance be set out in writing, Step 2 of the standard procedure provides that the Step 2 meeting "must not take place unless— (a) the employee has informed the employer what the basis for the grievances was when he made the statement under paragraph 6. . ." and does not expressly provide for it to be done at any later stage. In Shergold the EAT treated the provision by the employee of the basis for the grievance to the employer as an interim step between Steps 1 and 2 of the standard procedure. This appears to be an unduly technical reading of the requirements under paras 6 and 7. A better view would be simply that para.7(2)(a) exists only to deal with instances where the statement of the grievance under para.6 is, on its face insufficiently detailed to explain the complaint that is being made, not as an separate "implied" stage in the procedure itself. This conclusion would also avoid the problems which would otherwise arise as to whether the employee has sufficiently complied with the procedure to allow him to commence proceedings.

Step 2

Failure to attend a meeting

10–073   For the consequences of the failure of an employee or their representatives to attend the hearing and the employer's obligation to rearrange the meeting, see reg.13 DRR and commentary at para.11–060. Consequences of failure to appeal

10–074   For the consequences of an employee's failure to appeal against the employer's decision, see s.31(2) and commentary at para.10–023.

PART 3

GENERAL REQUIREMENTS

Introductory

10–075   11 The following requirements apply to each of the procedures set out above (so far as applicable).

Timetable

10–076   12 Each step and action under the procedure must be taken without unreasonable delay.

Meetings

10–077   13(1) Timing and location of meetings must be reasonable.
     (2) Meetings must be conducted in a manner that enables both employer and employee to explain their cases.
     (3) In the case of appeal meetings which are not the first meeting, the employer should, as far as is reasonably practicable, be represented by a more senior manager than attended the first meeting (unless the most senior manager attended that meeting).

General requirements—timing of meetings

10–077/1   It was not reasonable, and therefore a breach of para.13(1), for an employer to schedule an appeal meeting for December 29 when notice of it was only sent by post on December 20. Even if the letter had been delivered by December 28, the first working day after Christmas, (the actual date of delivery was not known because the claimant was away over the Christmas period), the claimant would have had only 24 hours to prepare: *Sovereign Business Integration Plc v Trybus* UKEAT/0107/07 [24].

Unreasonable delay—meaning of

"Inordinate delay" need not be "unreasonable delay" if, e.g. the employer's **10–078** procedure required that an appeal be heard by particular councillors who had not been available. The question whether in the circumstances the delay was unreasonable was remitted to the tribunal for determination: *Patel v Leicester City Council* UKEAT/0368/06.

An unexplained delay of three months in convening an appeal hearing would be unreasonable. A delay of three and a half months caused by the unavailability of the claimant's representative and the need for compliance with "the very important procedures operated within the Civil Service" was not unreasonable: *Khan (1) King (2) v The Home Office* UKEAT/0250/06.

Meetings—the application of the without prejudice rule

The principles for excluding without prejudice communications from considera- **10–078/1** tion by a court apply equally to employment tribunals: *Independent Research Services v Catterall* [1993] I.C.R. 1 EAT.

The public policy underlying the without prejudice rule is that parties should be encouraged so far as possible to settle their disputes without resort to litigation and should not be discouraged by the knowledge that anything that is said in the course of such negotiations may be used to their prejudice in subsequent proceedings: per Oliver L.J. *Cutts v Head* [1984] Ch 90 at 306. There therefore seems no reason in principle why discussions in the context of the statutory procedures should be exempt from the rule. Privilege may attach to both oral and written communications under the rule before litigation is either commenced or threatened. ". . . the crucial consideration would be whether in the course of negotiations the parties contemplated or might reasonably have contemplated litigation if they could not agree." *Framlington Group Ltd v Barneston* [2007] I.R.L.R. 598 CA at [34]; [2007] I.C.R. 1439. But whether the mere act of raising a grievance means that the parties to an employment relationship are necessarily in dispute for the purpose of the rule is unclear. A grievance may be upheld or dismissed for reasons which the employee finds acceptable, in which case the parties never reach the stage where they could properly be said to be "in dispute": *BNP Paribas v Mezzotero* [2004] I.R.L.R. 508 EAT at [28] per Cox J.

". . . the ambit of the rule should not be extended any further than is necessary in the circumstances of any particular case to promote the public policy interest underlying it. The critical question for the court . . . is where to draw the line between serving that interest and wrongly preventing one or other party from putting his case at its best. It is undoubtedly a highly case sensitive issue . . . the dividing line may not always be clear:" *Framlington Group Ltd v Barneston* at [33].

It is suggested that, given the public policy underpinning the dispute resolution procedures, a respondent would not be permitted to invoke the "without prejudice" rule in order to defeat a contention that a meeting or an appeal had been conducted in breach of the general requirements, or that the relevant statutory procedure had otherwise not been complied with. Any attempt to do so would seem to amount to an abuse of the rule and thus fall within one of the established exceptions to it: *Independent Research Services v Catterall* at [6B].

In *BNP Paribas* (which concerned events before the statutory grievance procedure was introduced) it was held, obiter, that the abuse exception to the rule applied to enable the tribunal to hear evidence about a meeting, held to discuss a grievance of sex discrimination, which the employer had expressly said was without prejudice but during which the claimant alleged the employers had committed acts of discrimination and victimisation in respect of which she sought a remedy from the tribunal.

For waiver of privilege in respect of earlier without prejudice negotiations caused by the way in which a subsequent grievance meeting was conducted, see *Brunel University v Vaseghi* [2007] I.R.L.R. 592, CA.

PART 4

SUPPLEMENTARY

Status of meetings

10–079   14 A meeting held for the purposes of this Schedule is a hearing for the purposes of section 13(4) and (5) of the Employment Relations Act 1999 (c.26) (definition of "disciplinary hearing" and "grievance hearing" in relation to the right to be accompanied under section 10 of that Act).

10–079/1   Although para.14 provides that a meeting held for the purposes of the Schedule is a hearing which attracts the right to be accompanied created by the Employment Relations Act 1999, a failure to state in either the Step 1 letter under the DDP or a letter inviting the employee to a meeting under the SGP that they have the right, is not a breach of the applicable statutory procedure as neither procedure requires that the right to be accompanied be spelled out.

Scope of grievance procedures

10–080   15(1) The procedures set out in Part 2 are only applicable to matters raised by an employee with his employer as a grievance.
    (2) Accordingly, those procedures are only applicable to the kind of disclosure dealt with in Part 4A of the Employment Rights Act 1996 (c.18) (protected disclosures of information) if information is disclosed by an employee to his employer in circumstances where—

      (a) the information relates to a matter which the employee could raise as a grievance with his employer, and
      (b) it is the intention of the employee that the disclosure should constitute the raising of the matter with his employer as a grievance.

Para.15—"Whistle blowing" claims and the grievance procedure

10–081   The effect of para.15 is that the employee's act of making a protected disclosure to the employer does not of itself also constitute the raising of a grievance. To serve both purposes, the subject matter of the disclosure must be capable of being raised as a grievance, i.e. it must relate to one of the tribunals' jurisdictions listed in Sch.4, and the employee must intend that it should serve both purposes. Because a protected disclosure is not automatically a grievance, it will clearly be necessary for the employer to be able to distinguish between a protected disclosure which is not also raised as a grievance and one which is. The case law on what amounts to a grievance (for which see the commentary at paras 10–066—10–069) may therefore need to be modified in this context, in particular it would seem to be necessary for the employee to make it clear in the document making the disclosure that she was not only reporting the matter to her employer but also looking to them to resolve it. However, no further formality is likely to be required (see in particular *Canary Wharf Management Ltd*). The DTI Guidance on para.15 (at para.57), that it "effectively gives the employee the right to choose whether to raise a concern as a grievance or as a protected disclosure" is misleading to the extent that it implies that it cannot be raised as both. Paragraph 15 means only that it need not be raised as both. Paragraph 15 is only applicable to claims under s.48 ERA in respect of s.47B—protected disclosures—and has no general application (*Thorpe (1) and Soleil Investments Ltd (2) v Poat (1) and Lake* (2) [2006] All E.R. (D) 30 (Jan)).

SCHEDULE 3

TRIBUNAL JURISDICTIONS TO WHICH SECTION 31 APPLIES

Section 2 of the Equal Pay Act 1970 (c.41) (equality clauses)   10–082
Section 63 of the Sex Discrimination Act 1975 (c.65) (discrimination in the employment field)
Section 54 of the Race Relations Act 1976 (c.74) (discrimination in the employment field)
Section 145A of the Trade Union and Labour Relations (Consolidation) Act 1992 (inducements relating to union membership or activities) [1]
Section 145B of that Act (inducements relating to collective bargaining) [1]
Section 146 of that Act (detriment in relation to union membership and activities) [1]
Paragraph 156 of Schedule A1 to that Act (detriment in relation to union recognition rights)
Section 17A of the Disability Discrimination Act 1995 (c.50) (discrimination in the employment field) [2]
Section 23 of the Employment Rights Act 1996 (c.18) (unauthorised deductions and payments)
Section 48 of that Act (detriment in employment)
Section 111 of that Act (unfair dismissal)
Section 163 of that Act (redundancy payments)
Section 24 of the National Minimum Wage Act 1998 (c.39) (detriment in relation to national minimum wage) [3 The Employment Tribunal Extension of Jurisdiction (England and Wales) Order 1994 (SI 1994/1623) (breach of employment contract and termination)
The Employment Tribunal Extension of Jurisdiction (Scotland) Order 1994 (SI 1994/1624) (corresponding provision for Scotland)
Regulation 30 of the Working Time Regulations 1998 (SI 1998/1833) (breach of regulations)
Regulation 32 of the Transnational Information and Consultation of Employees Regulations 1999 (SI 1999/3323) (detriment relating to European Works Councils)

Regulation 28 of the Employment Equality (Religion or Belief) Regulations 2003 (discrimination in the employment field) [4]

Regulation 28 of the Employment Equality (Sexual Orientation) Regulations 2003 (discrimination in the employment field) [5]

Regulation 36 of the Employment Equality (Age) Regulations 2006 (discrimination in the employment field) [6]

Regulation 45 of the European Public Limited-Liability Company Regulations 2004 (SI 2004/2326) (detriment in employment) [7]

Regulation 33 of the Information and Consultation of Employees Regulations 2004 (SI 2004/3426) (detriment in employment) [7]

Paragraph 8 of the Schedule to the Occupational and Personal Pension Schemes (Consultation by Employers and Miscellaneous Amendment) Regulations 2006 (SI 2006/349) (detriment in employment) [7]

SCHEDULE 4

TRIBUNAL JURISDICTIONS TO WHICH SECTION 32 APPLIES

10–083   Section 2 of the Equal Pay Act 1970 (c.41) (equality clauses)

Section 63 of the Sex Discrimination Act 1975 (c.65) (discrimination in the employment field)

Section 54 of the Race Relations Act 1976 (c.74) (discrimination in the employment field)

Section 145A of the Trade Union and Labour Relations (Consolidation) Act 1992 (inducements relating to union membership or activities) [1]

Section 145B of that Act (inducements relating to collective bargaining) [1]

Section 146 of that Act (detriment in relation to union membership and activities) [1]

Paragraph 156 of Schedule A1 to that Act (detriment in relation to union recognition rights)

Section 17A of the Disability Discrimination Act 1995 (c.50) (discrimination in the employment field) [2]

Section 23 of the Employment Rights Act 1996 (c.18) (unauthorised deductions and payments)

Section 48 of that Act (detriment in employment)

Section 111 of that Act (unfair dismissal)

Section 163 of that Act (redundancy payments)

Section 24 of the National Minimum Wage Act 1998 (c.39) (detriment in relation to national minimum wage) [3]

Regulation 30 of the Working Time Regulations 1998 (SI 1998/1833) (breach of regulations)

Regulation 32 of the Transnational Information and Consultation of Employees Regulations 1999 (SI 1999/3323) (detriment relating to European Works Councils)

Regulation 28 of the Employment Equality (Religion or Belief) Regulations 2003 (discrimination in the employment field) [4]

Regulation 28 of the Employment Equality (Sexual Orientation) Regulations 2003 (discrimination in the employment field) [5]

Regulation 36 of the Employment Equality (Age) Regulations 2006 (discrimination in the employment field) [6]

Regulation 45 of the European Public Limited-Liability Company Regulations 2004 (SI 2004/2326) (detriment in employment) [7]

Regulation 33 of the Information and Consultation of Employees Regulations 2004 (SI 2004/3426) (detriment in employment) [7]

Regulation 17 and Schedule to the Occupational and Personal Pension Schemes (Consultation by Employers and Miscellaneous Amendment) Regulations 2006 (SI 2006/349) (detriment in employment) [7]

Commencement of Schs 3 and 4

October 1, 2004 unless otherwise stated below under "Amendments".   **10–084**

Amendments to Schs 3 and 4

[1] Substituted by s.57(1) of and Sch.1, para.43 to the Employment Relations   **10–085**
     Act 2004, but the substituted provisions do not apply where the act or
     failure to act to which the complaint relates was done before October 1,
     2004, or where the act or failure to act is part of a series and the first act or
     failure in the series was done before that date. For this purpose an act
     extending over a period is done on the last day of that period and a failure
     to act shall be treated as done when it was decided upon: Employment
     Relations Act 2004 (Commencement No. 1 and Transitional Provisions)
     Order 2004 (SI 2004/2566), art.6.
[2] Section 17A was substituted for s.8 of the 1995 Act by the Disability
     Discrimination Act 1995 (Amendment) Regulations 2003 (SI 2003/1673)
     regs 3(2), and 31(3).
[3] Schedule 3 to the Tax Credits Act 1999 (detriment in relation to tax
     credits) was repealed by the Tax Credits Act 2002 s.60 and Sch.6, as from
     April 8, 2003 subject to the savings and transitional provisions in arts 3 and
     5 of the Tax Credits Act 2002 (Commencement No. 4, Transitional
     Provisions and Savings) Order 2003 (SI 2003/962).
[4] Inserted by the Employment Equality (Sexual Orientation) Regulations
     2003 (SI 2003/1661) reg.39 and Sch.5 para.4(a) with effect from December
     1, 2003.
[5] Inserted by the Employment Equality (Religion or Belief) Regulations 2003
     (SI 2003/1660) reg.39(2) and Sch.5 para.4(a) as from December 2, 2003.
[6] Inserted by the Employment Equality (Age) Regulations 2006 (SI
     2006/1031) Sch.8, Pt. 2 para.36 with effect from October 1, 2006.
[7] Inserted by the Employment Act 2002 (Amendment of Schedules 3, 4 and 5)
     Order 2007 (SI 2007/30) with effect from April 6, 2007.

CHAPTER 11

EMPLOYMENT ACT 2002 (DISPUTE RESOLUTION) REGULATIONS 2004

2004 No. 752

Contents

REG.

Citation and commencement

1. These Regulations may be cited as the Employment Act 2002   **11–001**
(Dispute Resolution) Regulations 2004 and shall come into force on
1st October 2004.

Interpretation

2.—(1) In these Regulations—   **11–002**

"the 1992 Act" means the Trade Union and Labour Relations
(Consolidation) Act 1992;

"the 1996 Act" means the Employment Rights Act 1996;

"the 1999 Act" means the Employment Relations Act 1999;

"the 2002 Act" means the Employment Act 2002;

"action" means any act or omission;

"applicable statutory procedure" means the statutory procedure
that applies in relation to a particular case by virtue of these
Regulations;

"collective agreement" has the meaning given to it by section 178(1) of the 1992 Act;

"dismissal and disciplinary procedures" means the statutory procedures set out in Part 1 of Schedule 2;

"dismissed" has the meaning given to it in section 95(1)(a) and (b) of the 1996 Act;

"employers' association" has the meaning given to it by section 122 of the 1992 Act;

"grievance" means a complaint by an employee about action which his employer has taken or is contemplating taking in relation to him;

"grievance procedures" means the statutory procedures set out in Part 2 of Schedule 2;

"independent trade union" has the meaning given to it by section 5 of the 1992 Act;

"modified dismissal procedure" means the procedure set out in Chapter 2 of Part 1 of Schedule 2;

"modified grievance procedure" means the procedure set out in Chapter 2 of Part 2 of Schedule 2;

"non-completion" of a statutory procedure includes non-commencement of such a procedure except where the term is used in relation to the non-completion of an identified requirement of a procedure or to circumstances where a procedure has already been commenced;

"party" means the employer or the employee;

"relevant disciplinary action" means action, short of dismissal, which the employer asserts to be based wholly or mainly on the employee's conduct or capability, other than suspension on full pay or the issuing of warnings (whether oral or written);

"standard dismissal and disciplinary procedure" means the procedure set out in Chapter 1 of Part 1 of Schedule 2;

"standard grievance procedure" means the procedure set out in Chapter 1 of Part 2 of Schedule 2; and a reference to a Schedule is a reference to a Schedule to the 2002 Act.

(2) In determining whether a meeting or written communication fulfils a requirement of Schedule 2, it is irrelevant whether the meeting or communication deals with any other matter (including a different matter required to be dealt with in a meeting or communication intended to fulfil a requirement of Schedule 2).

Application of dismissal and disciplinary procedures

11–003   3.—(1) Subject to paragraph (2) and regulation 4, the standard dismissal and disciplinary procedure applies when an employer contemplates dismissing or taking relevant disciplinary action against an employee.

(2) Subject to regulation 4, the modified dismissal procedure applies in relation to a dismissal where—

(a) the employer dismissed the employee by reason of his conduct without notice,

(b) the dismissal occurred at the time the employer became aware of the conduct or immediately thereafter,

(c) the employer was entitled, in the circumstances, to dismiss the employee by reason of his conduct without notice or any payment in lieu of notice, and

(d) it was reasonable for the employer, in the circumstances, to dismiss the employee before enquiring into the circumstances in which the conduct took place,

but neither of the dismissal and disciplinary procedures applies in relation to such a dismissal where the employee presents a complaint relating to the dismissal to an employment tribunal at a time when the employer has not complied with paragraph 4 of Schedule 2.

Para.(1)

"contemplates dismissing"

The statutory dismissal and disciplinary procedure applies only if the employer **11–004** first contemplated dismissing the employee or taking relevant disciplinary action after October 1, 2004 (reg.18(a)). When an employer first "contemplates" dismissal is a subjective issue wholly for the employer. There is no requirement for the employer's thoughts to be communicated to the employee (*Madhewoo v NHS Direct* UKEAT/0030/06).

Relevance of reason for dismissal

Unless the reason for dismissal falls within reg.4—(dismissals to which the **11–005** dismissal and disciplinary procedures do not apply)—the reason for the contemplated dismissal or relevant disciplinary action is irrelevant. The procedure applies equally to dismissals for serious misconduct as it does to individual redundancies.

Relevance of employee's length of service

The employer is not excused from compliance with the procedure because the **11–006** employee does not have sufficient qualifying service to complain of unfair dismissal. However, in the absence of discrimination, because s.30 of the Employment Act 2002 (EA), which has the effect of incorporating the statutory procedures into individual contracts of employment has not been brought into effect, the employee would appear to be without a remedy if the employer does not follow the procedure. Although s.98A of the Employment Rights Act 1996 provides that dismissal in breach of the statutory procedure is automatically unfair, such a dismissal is not one for which by virtue of s.108(3) of the Act no minimum qualifying service is required.

"relevant disciplinary action"

11–007   See reg.2 (above) for the definition. Suspension on full pay and oral and written warnings are excluded from the definition. However, it may nonetheless have a surprisingly wide application to such things as suspension without pay (whether permitted under the contract of employment or not), reduction in duties, disciplinary transfers and demotions and even extension of a probationary period. Even if the employer only contemplates issuing a warning he would be well advised to follow the statutory procedure from the outset to avoid having to abort the process and begin again if something emerges which makes dismissal a possible outcome.

Consequences of non-compliance with the procedure

11–008   See commentary on ss.30 and 31 EA.

Para.(2)—Modified Procedure

11–009   The modified procedure (EA Sch.2, Pt 1 Chs 2, paras 4 and 5) does not require the employer to meet the employee before dismissing them, the Step one letter being both the statement of the disciplinary offence and the explanation of the employer's basis for thinking that the employee was guilty of it, and assumes that an earlier, summary dismissal has taken place. The DRR do not affect the substantive position as to when summary dismissal is lawful. Regulation 3(2)(c) however provides that the modified procedure only applies if the employer "was entitled" to dismiss without notice or payment in lieu of notice which requires the employer, as in a wrongful dismissal claim, to prove on the balance of probabilities that the employee did in fact commit the act complained of. Regulation 3(2)(d) is the most restricting element, as circumstances in which it can be reasonable for the employer to dismiss before enquiring into them (which given the differences between the standard and modified procedures means enquiring of the employee) are likely to be extremely limited given that in most if not all instances it will be open to (and reasonable for) the employer to suspend the employee on full pay pending completion of the standard procedure. Note also that the relevant issue here is whether it was reasonable to dismiss without an "enquiry into the circumstances in which the conduct took place", not whether the decision to dismiss was substantively a fair decision. The modified procedure is most likely to be applicable only in obvious cases of flagrant acts of gross misconduct. Whether reg.3(2)(d) means that for the modified procedure to be applicable the employer must not speak to the employee at all before deciding to dismiss, is unclear. It would not however appear to be against the spirit of the modified procedure for the employer to speak to the employee perhaps briefly before deciding which procedure to follow.

   In *O'Neill v Wooldridge Ecotech Ltd* UKEAT/0282/07, it was held that it was not open to a tribunal to find that the modified procedure had been complied with where a manager, before deciding to dismiss, consulted with colleagues about what he regarded as an act of insubordination by the claimant directed towards himself and waited 24 hours before dismissing. The manager had failed to act "at the time the employer became aware of the conduct or immediately thereafter."

When not applicable

11–010   If the employee commences tribunal proceedings before the employer has sent the written statement required by para.4 of Sch.2, neither of the statutory procedures applies. This does not have the effect of allowing the employer to escape liability for a failure to follow a statutory disciplinary procedure if in the circumstances of the dismissal the modified procedure was not the applicable procedure, as the proviso applies only to "such a dismissal", i.e. one to which the modified procedure applies.

Dismissals to which the dismissal and disciplinary procedures do not apply

4.—(1) Neither of the dismissal and disciplinary procedures 11–011
applies in relation to the dismissal of an employee where—

(a) all the employees of a description or in a category to which the employee belongs are dismissed, provided that the employer offers to re-engage all the employees so dismissed either before or upon the termination of their contracts;

(b) the dismissal is one of a number of dismissals in respect of which the duty in section 188 of the 1992 Act (duty of employer to consult representatives when proposing to dismiss as redundant a certain number of employees) applies;

(c) at the time of the employee's dismissal he is taking part in—

    (i) an unofficial strike or other unofficial industrial action, or

    (ii) a strike or other industrial action (being neither unofficial industrial action nor protected industrial action),
    unless the circumstances of the dismissal are such that, by virtue of section 238(2) of the 1992 Act, an employment tribunal is entitled to determine whether the dismissal was fair or unfair;

(d) the reason (or, if more than one, the principal reason) for the dismissal is that the employee took protected industrial action and the dismissal would be regarded, by virtue of section 238A(2) of the 1992 Act, as unfair for the purposes of Part 10 of the 1996 Act;

(e) the employer's business suddenly ceases to function, because of an event unforeseen by the employer, with the result that it is impractical for him to employ any employees;

(f) the reason (or, if more than one (sic) principal reason) for the dismissal is that the employee could not continue to work in the position which he held without contravention (either on his part or on that of his employer) of a duty or restriction imposed by or under any enactment;

(g) the employee is one to whom a dismissal procedures agreement designated by an order under section 110 of the 1996 Act applies at the date of dismissal, or

(h) **the reason (or, if more than one, the principle reason) for the dismissal is retirement of the employee (to be determined in accordance with section 98ZA to 98 ZF of the 1996 Act).**

(2) **For the purposes of paragraph (1)—**

"unofficial" shall be construed in accordance with subsections (2) to (4) of section 237 of the 1992 Act;
"strike" has the meaning given to it by section 246 of the 1992 Act;
"protected industrial action" shall be construed in accordance with section 238A(1) of the 1992 Act;

and an employer shall be regarded as offering to re-engage an employee if that employer, a successor of that employer or an associated employer of that employer offers to re-engage the employee, either in the job which he held immediately before the date of dismissal or in a different job which would be suitable in his case.

Commencement
11–012   Paragraph (1)(h) was inserted by the Employment Equality (Age) Regulations 2006 (SI 2006/1031) Sch.8, Pt 2 para.64, with effect from October 1, 2006.

Para.(1)

Effect of disapplication of the statutory procedures

11–013   The disapplication of the statutory dismissal and disciplinary procedures has no impact upon an employer's general duty to act reasonably. Its most important effects are to prevent the employer from being at risk of a finding of automatically unfair dismissal under s.98A(1) of the Employment Rights Act 1996 (ERA) and the consequent uplift of compensation under s.31(3) of the Employment Act 2002.

Para.(1)(a)
11–014   See the definition of "re-engage" at para.(2). An offer of re-engagement can be made by the employer, an associated employer, or a successor of the original employer. Note in particular that an offer of re-engagement is either to the same "job" or a different but suitable "job". What is a job is not further defined. However the better view is that the job comprises those duties which the employee is required to do from day to day, rather than the specific terms on which those duties are performed. As such 3(1)(a) will apply where the employer's intention is to change the terms and conditions of a group of employees by dismissing them and offering them revised terms. Regulation 3(1)(a) does not require that the dismissals shall have been expressly for this purpose or that the offer of re-engagement be made simultaneously with the dismissal.

Para.(1)(b)—Collective redundancies
11–015   It is important to recognise the limited protection which this sub-paragraph affords to employers. They are merely absolved from complying with the obligation to send a Step 1 letter under the statutory dismissal procedure to the individual

employees affected, this being replaced by the duty to provide certain information in writing to representatives of those employees under s.188(4) of the 1992 Act. However, if in the circumstances of a particular case the reasonable employer would also consult with employees individually, the employer must still so consult, in which case the employer must hold what amounts to the Stage 2 meeting and if required the Stage 3 appeal, albeit without the need to comply with the General Requirements, although a failure to do so may still be of significance in the context of whether the dismissal was fair for the purposes of s.98(4) of the Employment Rights Act 1996.

Para.(1)(c)—Industrial action dismissals

This sub-paragraph hides a trap for employers. Section 238(2) of the 1992 Act **11–016** prevents a tribunal from determining the fairness of the complainant's dismissal unless one or more relevant employees (as defined in s.238(3)) of the same employer was not dismissed or that a relevant employee has been offered re-engagement within three months of their dismissal and the complainant has not been offered re-engagement. The disapplication of the statutory dismissal and disciplinary procedure will therefore be revoked retrospectively if a relevant employee has been offered re-engagement and the complainant has not. The paragraph does not apply to dismissals while the employer is conducting or instituting a lock out to which the statutory procedure would appear to apply despite the employee's inability to complain to a tribunal unless s.238(2) applies.

For the meaning of "unofficial" see s.237(2) to (4) of the 1992 Act.

For the meaning of "strike" see s.246 of the 1992 Act.

For the meaning of "protected industrial action" see s.238A(1) of the 1992 Act.

Para.(1)(d)—Protected industrial action--meaning of

"For the purposes of this section an employee takes protected industrial action if **11–017** he commits an act which, or a series of acts each of which, he is induced to commit by an act which by virtue of section 219 is not actionable in tort": TULR(C)A s.238A(1)

Section 219 (protection from certain tort liabilities of acts done in furtherance of a trade dispute) is subject to ss.222–225 (action excluded from protection), s.236 (the requirement for a trade union to hold a ballot before taking industrial action) and to s.234A (requirement to give notice of the action to the employer). "Trade dispute" is defined in s.218.

Para.(1)(e)—Unforeseen events

Regulation 4(1)(e) is presumably intended to apply only to circumstances in **11–018** which the event which causes the business to close is unexpected, unavoidable and sudden, thus putting it beyond the employers power to comply with the procedure.

Para.(1)(f)—Contravention of a statutory duty or restriction—ERA s.98(2)(d)

Again, it is important to recognise the very limited protection which this sub- **11–019** paragraph affords employers and to remember that the disapplication of the statutory procedure by reg.4 has no effect on the employer's general duty to act reasonably. The reason for excluding such dismissals is unclear as they are not exempt from the general test of fairness in s.98(4) ERA and to dismiss such an employee without consultation with a view, e.g. to exploring whether there may be ways round the problem, is likely to be held to be unfair (*Sutcliffe and Eaton Ltd v Pinney* [1977] I.R.L.R. 349, EAT). The employer must also be correct in his belief that the continued employment of the employee would in fact contravene a

EA (DR) Regs 2004

statutory duty or restriction as an erroneous, albeit honestly held, belief that that is the case is insufficient (*Bouchaala v Trusthouse Forte Hotels Ltd* [1980] I.C.R. 721, EAT). Although such a belief may amount to some other substantial reason for dismissing the employee and be fair (Bouchaala) the reason for the dismissal would not then be contravention of a statutory duty or restriction and therefore the statutory dismissal and disciplinary procedure would not be disapplied by reg.4(1)(f). The prudent course for an employer would therefore be to follow the procedure despite para.(1)(f).

Circumstances in which parties are treated as complying with the dismissal and disciplinary procedures

11–020   5.—(1) Where—

(a) either of the dismissal and disciplinary procedures is the applicable statutory procedure in relation to a dismissal,

(b) the employee presents an application for interim relief to an employment tribunal pursuant to section 128 of the 1996 Act (interim relief pending determination of complaint) in relation to his dismissal, and

(c) at the time the application is presented, the requirements of paragraphs 1 and 2 or, as the case may be, paragraph 4 of Schedule 2 have been complied with but the requirements of paragraph 3 or 5 of Schedule 2 have not,

the parties shall be treated as having complied with the requirements of paragraph 3 or 5 of Schedule 2.

(2) Where either of the dismissal and disciplinary procedures is the applicable statutory procedure in relation to the dismissal of an employee or to relevant disciplinary action taken against an employee but—

(a) at the time of the dismissal or the taking of the action an appropriate procedure exists,

(b) the employee is entitled to appeal under that procedure against his dismissal or the relevant disciplinary action taken against him instead of appealing to his employer, and

(c) the employee has appealed under that procedure,

the parties shall be treated as having complied with the requirements of paragraph 3 or 5 of Schedule 2.

(3) For the purposes of paragraph (2) a procedure is appropriate if it—

(a) gives the employee an effective right of appeal against dismissal or disciplinary action taken against him, and

(b) operates by virtue of a collective agreement made between two or more employers or an employers' association and one or more independent trade unions.

Para.(1)—Deemed compliance with the procedure--interim relief

11–021

An application for interim relief can be made in the following types of unfair dismissal complaints where the claimant claims to have been dismissed for performing or proposing to perform the duties of their office:

- under s.100(1)(a) or (b) ERA where the claimant is either a designated health and safety officer or a health and safety representative;
- under s.101A(1)(d) ERA where the claimant is a representative of members of the workforce for the purposes of Sch.1 to the Working Time Regulations 1998 (SI 1998/1833) or a candidate for election as such;
- under s.102(1) ERA where the claimant is a trustee of a relevant occupational pension scheme which relates to his employment;
- under s.103 ERA where the claimant is an employee representative or a candidate for election as such for the purposes of the collective redundancy provisions of the Trade Union and Labour Relations (Consolidation) Act 1992 (TULR(C)A) (Ch.II of Pt IV) or the Transfer of Undertakings (Protection of Employment) Regulations 2006 (SI 2006/246).

An application for interim relief can also be made if the reason for the dismissal is said to be that the employee has made a protected disclosure: ERA s.103A (for the meaning of "protected disclosure" see ERA s.43A) or on grounds related to union membership or activities: TULR(C)A s.161(1) (for the meaning of "grounds related to union membership or activities" see s.152 TULR(C)A).

The procedure is only deemed to have been complied with if the claimant has been dismissed in compliance with either the standard or modified dismissal and disciplinary procedures but presents a complaint of unfair dismissal coupled with an application for interim relief either without informing the employer that he wishes to appeal or before the appeal process is complete.

Paras (2) and (3)

11–022

These provisions are intended to apply to industry wide procedure agreements or collective agreements covering more than one employer in which the appeal lies either to an external organisation or some one other than the employee's employer. For the statutory procedures to be deemed complete the dismissal must have been in compliance with either the standard or modified procedures prior to the appeal stage.

Application of the grievance procedures

11–023

6.—(1) The grievance procedures apply, in accordance with the paragraphs (2) to (7) of this regulation, in relation to any grievance about action by the employer that could form the basis of a complaint by an employee to an employment tribunal under a jurisdiction listed in Schedule 3 or 4, or could do so if the action took place.

(2) Subject to paragraphs (3) to (7), the standard grievance procedure applies in relation to any such grievance.

(3) Subject to paragraphs (4) to (7), the modified grievance procedure applies in relation to a grievance where—

(a) **the employee has ceased to be employed by the employer;**
(b) **the employer—**

>   >   (i) was unaware of the grievance before the employ-
>   >   ment ceased, or
>   >
>   >   (ii) was so aware but the standard grievance procedure
>   >   was not commenced or was not completed before
>   >   the last day of the employee's employment; and
>   >
>   > (c) the parties have agreed in writing in relation to the
>   > grievance, whether before, on or after that day, but after
>   > the employer became aware of the grievance, that the
>   > modified procedure should apply.
>
> (4) Neither of the grievance procedures applies where—
>
>   > (a) the employee has ceased to be employed by the employer;
>   > (b) neither procedure has been commenced; and
>   > (c) since the employee ceased to be employed it has ceased to
>   > be reasonably practicable for him to comply with para-
>   > graph 6 or 9 of Schedule 2.
>
> (5) Neither of the grievance procedures applies where the griev-
> ance is that the employer has dismissed or is contemplating dismiss-
> ing the employee.
>
> (6) Neither of the grievance procedures applies where the griev-
> ance is that the employer has taken or is contemplating taking
> relevant disciplinary action against the employee unless one of the
> reasons for the grievance is a reason mentioned in regulation 7(1).
>
> (7) Neither of the grievance procedures applies where regulation
> 11(1) applies.

Para.(1)—". . . action by the employer"

11–024   The words "about action by the employer" are tautological and unnecessary given the definition of grievance in reg.2 but do not displace that definition. The drafting is "poor and, on a literal approach, leads to a non-sensical result" (*Hart v English Heritage* [2006] I.R.L.R. 915; [2006] I.C.R. 655, EAT at [19]). The words "or could do so if the action took place" refer to the words "or is contemplating taking in relation to him" in the definition of "grievance".

The actions of a claimant's fellow employee for whom the employer is vicariously liable are "action by the employer" for this purpose and the claimant is required to raise a grievance with the employer before bringing a claim to the tribunal. There is, however, no requirement to send a written statement of grievance to the fellow employee as the statutory procedures do not apply to disputes between employees (*Bissett v Martins (1) Castlehill Housing Association (2)* UKEAT/0022/06). In *Odoemelam v The Whittington Hospital NHS Trust* UKEAT/0016/06, it was held that although the first reason given in *Bissett* for holding that the Regulations do not apply to claims against fellow employees was clearly wrong and the second and third reasons "not compelling", the overall conclusion was correct ". . . since I do not see how employee's acts for which they are directly liable should be regarded as those of their employer simply because in addition their employer is vicariously liable for them": per Keith J. at [26].

Breach of contract claims and the grievance procedure

11–025   Regulation 6(1) applies the grievance procedure to action by the employer that could form the basis of a complaint to the tribunal "under a jurisdiction listed in Schedule 3 or 4. . ."

Schedules 3 and 4 to the Employment Act 2002 (EA) are not identical since the tribunal's jurisdiction in breach of contract claims (Employment Tribunals Extension of Jurisdiction (England and Wales) (SI 1994/1623) (see Ch.13) appears only in Sch.3 which is the tribunal's jurisdictions to which s.31 EA "Non-completion of statutory procedure; adjustment of awards" applies. Because the Extension of Jurisdiction Order does not appear in Sch.4 the pre-acceptance procedure in s.32(2) to (4) does not apply to breach of contract claims and it is therefore unnecessary (as a precondition to presenting a claim) for a claimant either to send a grievance letter to their employer or, if they have done so, to wait 28 days before presenting their claim to the tribunal.

Para.(2)—Standard grievance procedure

The standard grievance procedure is set out at Ch.1 paras 6 to 8 of Pt 2 of Sch.2 **11–026** EA (see para.10–061) and is subject to the General Requirements in Pt 3.

Para.(3)—Modified grievance procedure

The modified grievance procedure is set out at Ch.2 paras 9 and 10 of Pt 2 of **11–027** Sch.2 EA (see para.10–064) and is subject to the General Requirements in Pt 3.

The modified procedure only becomes available after the employee's employment has ended and then only if both the employer and employee agree in writing that it should apply. A grievance commenced but not completed under the standard procedure can be concluded under the modified procedure.

Para.(4)—Not reasonably practicable to comply

The material question is whether it is reasonably practicable for the employee to **11–028** commence the grievance process.

In principle there is no reason why "reasonably practicable" as used here should not be construed to the same effect as it is in other contexts--i.e. as synonymous with "reasonably feasible" (see *Palmer v Southend-on Sea BC* [1984] I.C.R. 372). The presence of the qualification of "reasonableness" has, in other contexts been identified as requiring a tribunal to address the issue "against the background of the surrounding circumstances and the aim to be achieved" (see *Schultz v Esso Petroleum Ltd* [1999] I.R.L.R. 488). Merely because raising a grievance would be futile does not mean that it is not reasonably practicable to raise it. Thus the fact that the employer has made it clear in advance that the employee will not be paid what he claims to be owed will not suffice.

This provision may in practice add little to the scope of the exception provided by reg.11(3)(c). However the fact that reg.11(3)(c) is subject to a test of "practicability" rather than "reasonable practicability" strongly suggests that reg.11(3)(c) is the provision of last resort, and that in most instances the requirements of reg.6 will be applied.

Para.(5)—"Dismissed"--Meaning of for the purposes of the statutory procedures

The definition of dismissal at reg.2 excludes s.95(1)(c) of the 1996 Act, **11–029** constructive dismissal. As s.111 of the 1996 Act (unfair dismissal) appears in Sch.4 to the 2002 Act (tribunal jurisdictions to which s.32—the pre-acceptance provisions of the Act--applies) reg.6(5) has the effect of making constructive dismissal complaints subject to the statutory grievance procedure.

Grievances about dismissals

A grievance about the basis on which a claimant had been selected for **11–030** redundancy could not trigger the automatic extension of time provisions under reg.15(3), as by virtue of reg.6(5) only the statutory dismissal and disciplinary procedure can apply where there has been a dismissal even if the grievance relates to a matter which, absent a dismissal would give the claimant grounds to raise a claim in the employment tribunal (*Hart v English Heritage* [2006] I.C.R. 655; [2006] I.R.L.R. 915, EAT). Thus, if the claimant claims that their dismissal is also an act of discrimination the statutory grievance procedure does not apply. In such a case although the claimant is not required to raise a grievance with their employer before commencing proceedings, he is subject to the more limited automatic extension of time provisions which apply under reg.15(2). This is also the case when because of insufficient continuity of employment the claimant cannot complain of unfair dismissal and the only complaint which can be brought is one of discrimination. Similarly, the GP does not apply where the employee's complaint is not that his dismissal was an act of disability discrimination but that the manner in which the employer conducted the investigation, the disciplinary hearing and the appeal were a continuing act of disability discrimination because of a failure to make reasonable adjustments. The essence of the employee's complaint remained that his employer had dismissed or was contemplating dismissing him (*DCA (formerly North Wales Magistrates Courts Committee) v Jones* UKEAT/0333/06). And see also *Lawrence v HM Prison Service* [2007] I.R.L.R. 468 Eat to the same effect.

The distinction may, however, not be clear cut in all instances, e.g. the reason for the dismissal may be that the claimant has struck her manager but did so only after suffering months of sexual harassment, or the claimant is dismissed for capability reasons but complains that they are only in that position because of the employer's prolonged breach of their statutory obligation to make reasonable adjustments under s.4A of the Disability Discrimination Act 1995. In such cases if the claimant is seeking a remedy from the tribunal for events which predate the commencement of the statutory dismissal procedure as well as for the dismissal itself, it would appear to be necessary for them to first comply with the grievance procedure in respect of that part of their claim and, if there are time limit problems in connection with the unfair dismissal claim, to commence separate proceedings and seek to consolidate them after the second claim has been presented.

The statutory grievance procedure does not apply to a complaint that a disciplinary investigation and an appeal against the subsequent dismissal were racially discriminatory, even if no allegation of discrimination was made prior to the commencement of tribunal proceedings: *Otaiku v Rotherham Primary Care NHS Trust* UKEAT/0253/07.

Wrongful dismissal claims

11–031   A complaint of wrongful dismissal, i.e. that the claimant has been dismissed without or with less than the minimum statutory notice (Employment Rights Act 1996 s.86(1)), or the claimant's contractual notice, is a complaint about dismissal, not a complaint that the employer has failed to pay notice pay. Regulation 6(5) therefore applies and the statutory grievance procedures do not apply to the claim (*London Borough of Lambeth v Corlett* [2007] I.C.R. 88, EAT).

"contemplated" dismissals

11–032   The aim of this provision is to avoid the duplication of procedures which would otherwise be the case if an employee was required to issue a grievance (or suffer the consequences set out in ss.31 and 32 EA) in relation to a matter which is already the subject of disciplinary proceedings in which the employer is contemplating dismissing the employee. As such, it is the converse of reg.3(1).

Applying *Junk v Kuhnel* (Case C–188/03) [2005] I.R.L.R. 310 ECJ, an employer is "contemplating dismissal" only when they commence disciplinary action against an employee with a warning that dismissal may follow in the event that the disciplinary charge is found to be proven. A warning of a "disciplinary sanction" is not sufficient: *Brock v Minerva Dental Ltd* [2007] I.C.R. 917 EAT at [51]. Although it is submitted that this interpretation of reg.6(5) is correct, as to have held otherwise would make this difficult provision almost unworkable in practice, it conflicts with *Madhewoo v NHS Direct* UKEAT/0030/06 (which was not drawn to the court's attention in *Brock*), which held that the words "contemplated dismissal" in reg.18(a) (transitional arrangements) implied no requirement for the employer's thoughts to be communicated to the employee.

Constructive dismissal is not dismissal for the purposes of reg.6(5) by virtue of reg.2. Thus the statutory grievance procedure applies even where the employee resigns to avoid dismissal and complains that the employer's handling of the disciplinary procedure amounted to a fundamental breach of contract: *Pinkus v Crime Reduction Initiative* UKEAT/0528/06.

An employer cannot be said to have been contemplating dismissal if the stage in the disciplinary process which has been reached cannot result in dismissal, even if the letter inviting the employee to the disciplinary hearing points out that should the employer subsequently invoke a later stage of the procedure dismissal was the likely outcome: *South Kent College v Hall* UKEAT/0087/07 at [35] to [40]. Obiter, it is not the case that reg. 6(5) can never apply where the claimant relies on a constructive dismissal. "Insofar as *Pinkus* suggests otherwise we respectfully disagree:" at [34].

Para.(6)

This too is a provision designed to prevent a situation in which relevant disciplinary action would in all cases require the employee to "cross-appeal" by raising a grievance. The exception (provided by reg.7(1) was probably designed to cover the situation where the employee objects to the possibility (or actuality) of relevant disciplinary action on the basis that it is being taken for a reason other than the stated reason. The one problem with in this analysis is that "unlawful discrimination" is defined in reg.7 to include all forms of discrimination claims (not simply claims of direct discrimination).

11–033

Note, however, the limitations of this exception which arise from the definition of "relevant disciplinary action". In particular, giving a warning or proposing to give a warning on grounds of capability or conduct is not "relevant disciplinary action". Such actions attract the full force of the grievance procedures.

Circumstances in which parties are treated as complying with the grievance procedures

7.—(1) Where the grievance is that the employer has taken or is contemplating taking relevant disciplinary action against the employee and one of the reasons for the grievance is—

11–034

    (a) that the relevant disciplinary action amounted to or, if it took place, would amount to unlawful discrimination, or

    (b) that the grounds on which the employer took the action or is contemplating taking it were or are unrelated to the grounds on which he asserted that he took the action or is asserting that he is contemplating taking it,

the standard grievance procedure or, as the case may be, modified grievance procedure shall apply but the parties shall be treated as having complied with the applicable procedure if the employee complies with the requirement in paragraph "(2).

(2) **The requirement is that the employee must set out the grievance in a written statement and send the statement or a copy of it to the employer—**

(a) **where either of the dismissal and disciplinary procedures is being followed, before the meeting referred to in paragraph 3 or 5 (appeals under the dismissal and disciplinary procedures) of Schedule 2, or**

(b) **where neither of those procedures is being followed, before presenting any complaint arising out of the grievance to an employment tribunal.**

(3) **In paragraph (1)(a) "unlawful discrimination" means an act or omission in respect of which a right of complaint lies to an employment tribunal under any of the following tribunal jurisdictions (specified in Schedules 3 and 4)—**

section 2 of the Equal Pay Act 1970;

section 63 of the Sex Discrimination Act 1975;

section 54 of the Race Relations Act 1976;

section 17A of the Disability Discrimination Act 1995;

regulation 28 of the Employment Equality (Religion or Belief) Regulations 2003;

regulation 28 of the Employment Equality (Sexual Orientation) Regulations 2003.

General

11–035   The sending of the written statement of grievance is enough for both parties to be treated as having complied with the procedure. The underlying purpose of the statutory scheme is maintained by the requirement that the written statement is to be provided prior to the appeal hearing in the relevant disciplinary process (unless the employer is not following a disciplinary process). However, query whether sending the statement avoids the pre-claim 28 day waiting requirement of s.32(3) of the Employment Act 2002 (EA). This requirement is not itself part of the grievance procedure and therefore would appear to apply, even though the parties are deemed to have completed the grievance procedure.

Circumstances in which reg.7 applies

11–036   If the circumstances described in paras (1)(a) and (b) apply, reg.7 applies only if the employer takes or contemplates taking "relevant disciplinary action" against the employee (i.e. action short of dismissal on the basis of conduct or capability, but not suspension with pay, or any form of warning). It will therefore apply only in a small number of cases.

Para.(1)—"relevant disciplinary action"--meaning of

11–037   See the definition in reg.2 and the commentary to reg.3(1) above.

Para.(1)(a)—"unlawful discrimination"

11–038   See reg.7(3) for what comprises "unlawful discrimination" for this purpose. Discrimination on grounds of age will come within the scope of the regulation on the enactment of the Employment Equality (Age) (Consequential Amendments)

Regulations 2007. The anticipated date in force is April 6, 2007. Until those regulations are in force, discrimination on grounds of age is not within the scope of reg.7(3).

Para.(1)(b)—real grounds unrelated to stated grounds

This is a widely drawn provision, but should be read in conjunction with reg.6(1) which limits the application of the grievance procedures to action that could form the basis of a claim under any of the jurisdictions listed in Sch.3 or 4 of the EA 2002. Thus the "actual" grounds alleged for the employer's action should be capable of founding one or more such claims. Note that the application of this provision turns on what is the substance of the grievance (not on whether the employer is in fact acting or proposing to act for an ulterior purpose). **11–039**

Regulation 7(1)(b) covers cases of quasi-discrimination e.g. action short of dismissal amounting to a detriment (but excluding suspension on full pay and the giving of a formal verbal or written warning which are not 'relevant disciplinary action by virtue of reg.2) taken against an employee for trade union activity or membership related reasons or for "whistle blowing": *Brocklebank v Tile Depot Trading Ltd* UKEAT/0012/07.

Collective agreement

Para.(2)

Although the paragraph refers to either of the disciplinary procedures being followed, the modified procedure, which only applies to summary dismissal, can never apply to relevant disciplinary action. **11–040**

8.—(1) Where— **11–041**

    (a) the standard grievance procedure is the applicable statutory procedure,

    (b) the employee has ceased to be employed by the employer,

    (c) paragraph 6 of Schedule 2 has been complied with (whether before or after the end of his employment); and

    (d) since the end of his employment it has ceased to be reasonably practicable for the employee, or his employer, to "comply with the requirements of paragraph 7 or 8 of Schedule 2,

the parties shall be treated, subject to paragraph (2), as having complied with such of those paragraphs of Schedule 2 as have not been complied with.

(2) In a case where paragraph (1) applies and the requirements of paragraphs 7(1) to (3) of Schedule 2 have been complied with but the requirement in paragraph 7(4) of Schedule 2 has not, the employer shall be treated as having failed to comply with paragraph 7(4) unless he informs the employee in writing of his decision as to his response to the grievance.

Deemed compliance with the grievance procedure

This provision covers situations where standard grievance procedures are interrupted by dismissal or resignation, and situations in which the grievance has been commenced (under the standard procedure) only after dismissal or resignation. If, **11–042**

EA (DR) Regs 2004

following the end of employment completion of the procedure ceases to be "reasonably practicable", the parties are deemed to have complied with the procedure. In principle there is no reason why "reasonably practicable" as used here should not be construed to the same effect as it is in other contexts—i.e. as synonymous with "reasonably feasible" (see *Palmer v Southend-on-Sea BC* [1984] I.C.R. 372). The presence of the qualification of "reasonableness" has, in other contexts been identified as requiring a tribunal to address the issue "against the background of the surrounding circumstances and the aim to be achieved" (see *Schultz v Esso Petroleum Ltd* [1999] I.R.L.R. 488).

An exception is provided by reg.8(2). If all that remains necessary to complete Step 2 of the procedure is the communication of the employer's decision, the employer must provide his decision in writing. However, there is room for confusion between this requirement and the provisions of reg.11(3)(c) which (read in conjunction with reg.11(2)) deems any part-completed procedure as completed where it is "not practicable . . . to . . . comply with the subsequent requirement within a reasonable period". Quite apart from the fact that reg.11(3) turns on "practicability" rather than "reasonable practicability", when will reg.11(3)(c) apply so as to oust the requirement under reg.8(2) in situations where the requirements of reg.8(1) are satisfied? Since in practice it is difficult to see when it will not be "practicable" for an employer to inform an employee of the outcome of his grievance, the requirements of reg.8(2) will probably override the saving provision under reg.11(3) in most instances.

11–043   **9.—(1) Where either of the grievance procedures is the applicable statutory procedure, the parties shall be treated as having complied with the requirements of the procedure if a person who is an appropriate representative of the employee having the grievance has—**

> **(a) written to the employer setting out the grievance; and**
>
> **(b) specified in writing to the employer (whether in setting out the grievance or otherwise) the names of at least two employees, of whom one is the employee having the grievance, as being the employees on behalf of whom he is raising the grievance.**

(2) For the purposes of paragraph (1), a person is an appropriate representative if, at the time he writes to the employer setting out the grievance, he is—

> **(a) an official of an independent trade union recognised by the employer for the purposes of collective bargaining in respect of a description of employees that includes the employee having the grievance, or**
>
> **(b) an employee of the employer who is an employee representative elected or appointed by employees consisting of or including employees of the same description as the employee having the grievance and who, having regard to the purposes for which and method by which he was elected or appointed, has the authority to represent employees of that description under an established pro-**

cedure for resolving grievances agreed between employee representatives and the employer.

(3) For the purposes of paragraph (2)(a) the terms "official", "recognised" and "collective bargaining" have the meanings given to them by, respectively, sections 119, 178(3) and 178(1) of the 1992 Act.

Para.(1)

Regulation 9 applies only to grievances affecting a group of employees in which case all of the employees in the group will either have the same grievance or will be affected by the outcome of the grievance. The concept of "the employee having the grievance" is therefore somewhat artificial and could mean any member of the group. Sub-para.(b) requires that the names of all employees on whose behalf the claim is brought must be disclosed to the employer and only those employees will be able to bring subsequent employment tribunal proceedings on the basis of the collective written statement of grievance.

Sending the collective written statement of grievance is enough for both parties to be treated as having complied with the procedure. Although this seems to be in conflict with the whole purpose of the dispute resolution provisions, the industrial relations realities are likely to mean that the requirements of the collective procedure will be followed instead, but the deemed compliance with the statutory procedure is not made conditional upon that actually happening. By virtue of reg.15(4)(b) the collective grievance is the Step 1 letter for all of the employees on whose behalf the grievance was raised both for the purpose of s.32(2) (pre-acceptance of the claim) and reg.15(3) (automatic extension of time) and it is deemed to have been sent on the date on which the written statement of grievance under para.(1)(a) was sent to the employer or if later, the date on which the representative complied with para.(1)(b).

Regulation 9 does not supplant para.6 of Sch.2 EA, but provides an alternative means of complying with it. Therefore s.32(3) applies and a complaint pursuant to a reg.9 grievance cannot be presented to the tribunal until 28 days have elapsed: *Alitalia Airport SPA v Akrif* UKEAT/0546/07 at [34]. Only those employees whose names have been notified to the employer in writing under para.(1)(b) are entitled to rely on the collective grievance for the purposes of s.32(2) and (3). Quare whether employees can be indirectly named e.g. "all the union members in the paint shop": Alitalia Airport SPA at [40] to [42].

11–044

—burden of proof

If the employees state in their claim form to the tribunal that the proceedings have been brought following a grievance raised on their behalf under reg.9, unless the employers deny that that is the case the point is not in issue and the claimants would not be required to show that reg.9, applies. If the employers do allege that the collective grievance did not comply with reg.9 this will amount to a claim under s.32(6)(b) of the Employment Act 2002 that s.32(2) has not been complied with and the proceedings should not have been accepted by the tribunal. It will then be for the claimants to establish compliance. Such disputes are most likely to involve a challenge to the status of the person acting on behalf of the employees.

11–045

Para.(2)(a)—"recognised" trade union--meaning of

Whether a union is recognised is a mixed question of fact and law (*National Union of Gold, Silver & Allied Trades v Albury Brothers Ltd* [1977] I.R.L.R. 173; [1978] I.C.R. 62, EAT) and may be inferred from a course of dealing (*National Union of Tailors and Garment Workers v Charles Ingram & Co Ltd* [1977] I.R.L.R. 147; [1977] I.C.R. 530,

11–046

EAT). While it will normally be necessary to show that the employer has dealt with the union over a period of time, the definition of "recognition" in s.178(3) of the Trade Union and Labour Relations (Consolidation) Act 1992 (TULR(C)A) includes the phrase "to any extent" so that an employer who has not previously had dealings with a union but who accepts and responds to a grievance presented by a union official will be held to have recognised the union to that extent, provided of course that the subject matter of the grievance falls within one of the areas listed in s.178(2) of the Act.

Para.(2)(b)—"Employee representative"

11–047   Employee representative is not specifically defined, however, the wording of sub-para.(b) is similar to that in s.188(1B)(b)(i) of TULR(C)A (employee representatives for the purposes of consultation about collective redundancies) and reg.13(3)(b)(i) of the Transfer of Undertakings (Protection of Employment) Regulations 2006 (TUPE) (SI 2006/246). The representative need not be one of the employees affected by the grievance and no formalities are prescribed for either their election or appointment. There is no provision in reg.9 which corresponds to s.188(1B)(b)(ii) of TULR(C)A or reg.13(3)(b)(ii) of TUPE providing for the election of employee representatives for the purpose of raising the specific grievance. This, together with the reference to "an established procedure for resolving grievances", strongly implies that para.(2)(b) applies only to established employee representatives and not to one elected ad hoc.

Para.(3)—Definitions

11–048   "'official' means—

(a) an officer of the union or of a branch or section of the union, or
(b) a person elected or appointed in accordance with the rules of the union to be a representative of its members or of some of them

and includes a person so elected or appointed who is an employee of the same employer as the members or one or more of the members whom he is to represent: TULR(C)A s.119.

'recognised' means "the recognition of the union by an employer, or two or more associated employers, to any extent, for the purposes of collective bargaining. . .": TULR(C)A s.178(3).

'collective bargaining' means negotiations relating to or connected with one or more of the matters set out in TULR(C)A s.178(2).

11–049   **10. Where either of the grievance procedures is the applicable statutory procedure but—**

(a) **at the time the employee raises his grievance there is a procedure in operation, under a collective agreement made between two or more employers or an employers' association and one or more independent trade unions, that provides for employees of the employer to raise grievances about the behaviour of the employer and have them considered, and**

(b) **the employee is entitled to raise his grievance under that procedure and does so,**

the parties shall be treated as having complied with the applicable statutory procedure.

Collective agreements

Regulation 10 is concerned with the grievance of an individual employee raised **11–050** by that employee under a collective agreement. There is one unstated but nonetheless fundamental difference between regs 9 and 10. Whereas the collective grievance under reg.9 must be in writing, the employee's grievance under reg.10 must be raised "under that procedure", i.e. in accordance with whatever procedure is stated in the collective agreement. Although it is still necessary for the substance of the grievance to correspond to the claim subsequently made before the tribunal, ascertaining whether this is in fact so may be a subject of difficulty if an agreed procedure permits grievances to be raised orally. The raising of the grievance by the employee is enough for both parties to be treated as having complied with the procedure. It is not a condition for the deemed compliance with the statutory procedure that the requirements of the collective agreement are in fact followed by the employer. If the employee raises the grievance in writing the date of the grievance will be the date on which Step 1 of the statutory grievance procedure will be deemed to have been complied with for the purposes of s.32(2) to (4) of the Employment Act 2002 (EA) (acceptance of the claim) and reg.15(3) of these Regulations (automatic extension of time).

Regulation 10 envisages an agreement made between collective parties— employers and trade unions—which itself sets out a grievance procedure which can be invoked by employees externally of a particular employer. It does not cover, for example, an employer's internal grievance procedure made pursuant to but not forming part of, a national collective agreement such as the 1997 Implementation Agreement in the local government sector: *Bainbridge v Redcar & Cleveland BC* [2007] I.R.L.R. 494 EAT at [72] and [73].

Collective agreement

Collective agreement has the same meaning as in s.178(1) of the Trade Union **11–051** and Labour Relations (Consolidation) Act 1992: see reg.2(1).

General circumstances in which the statutory procedures do not apply or are treated as being complied with

11.—(1) Where the circumstances specified in paragraph (3) apply 11–052 and in consequence the employer or employee does not commence the procedure that would otherwise be the applicable statutory procedure (by complying with paragraph 1, 4, 6 or 9 of Schedule 2), the procedure does not apply.

(2) Where the applicable statutory procedure has been commenced, but the circumstances specified in paragraph (3) apply and in consequence a party does not comply with a subsequent requirement of the procedure, the parties shall be treated as having complied with the procedure.

(3) The circumstances referred to in paragraphs (1) and (2) are that—

> **(a) the party has reasonable grounds to believe that commencing the procedure or complying with the subsequent requirement would result in a significant threat to himself, his property, any other person or the property of any other person;**

    (b) **the party has been subjected to harassment and has reasonable grounds to believe that commencing the procedure or complying with the subsequent requirement would result in his being subjected to further harassment; or**

    (c) **it is not practicable for the party to commence the procedure or comply with the subsequent requirement within a reasonable period.**

(4) **In paragraph (3)(b), "harassment" means conduct which has the purpose or effect of—**

    (a) **violating the person's dignity, or**

    (b) **creating an intimidating, hostile, degrading, humiliating or offensive environment for him,**

but conduct shall only be regarded as having that purpose or effect if, having regard to all the circumstances, including in particular the perception of the person who was the subject of the conduct, it should reasonably be considered as having that purpose or effect.

Paras (1) and (2)

11–053   Regulation 11 prescribes three circumstances which excuse a party either from commencing the procedure (para.(1)) or if having commenced it, from further compliance (para.(2)) by providing that the procedure shall be treated as having been complied with. However the effect of reg.11(3)(a) and (b) must be read in light of the provisions of reg.12(3) and (4): if the procedure cannot be commenced or completed as the case may be because of the behaviour of one of the parties, that party shall be treated as having failed to comply with a requirement of the procedure. Where it applies, reg.11 does not operate to avoid the requirement to wait 28 days before commencing proceedings imposed by s.32(3) EA if the step required under either para.6 or 9 of Sch.2 to the EA has been taken.

    It is not sufficient to excuse a claimant (or a respondent) from compliance with the procedure for them merely to assert that one of the para.(3) reasons applies. Whether any/all of the requirements within reg.1(3) are satisfied will be a question of fact for the tribunal. Given the possible consequences of failing to comply with statutory procedures, both employers and employees should regard reg.11 as a provision of last rather than first resort.

Para.(3)(a) and 3(b)—Threats and harassment

11–054   Although each provision may appear widely framed, it is important to note that the relevant belief: (a) must be based on reasonable grounds; and (b) must be that either commencing or continuing the procedure would result in a relevant threat or act of harassment. It should, however, be noted that there is no requirement that the other party to the procedure must be the source of the threat or act of harassment.

    A threat must be a "significant threat". Understandably, this notion is not further defined. In principle a threat could be a "significant threat" either by reference to an assessment of the likelihood that it will be carried out, or by reference to an assessment of the possible harm that would follow if it was carried out, or by reference to an assessment of both, undertaken in the round. DTI

Guidance suggests that a relevant threat must be a threat of violence either to person or property. However, the paragraph as drafted contains no such limitation, and there is no reason in principle why "threat" should be read in this constrained way.

It would be wrong to assume that merely because the subject of the claimant's grievance is that they have been the victim of harassment they are thereby excused from compliance with the grievance procedure, in particular that they are excused from commencing the procedure. Past harassment could, however be evidence in support of the reasonableness of a belief that commencing or continuing a procedure would result in further harassment.

Para.(3)(c)—"not practicable" to comply "within a reasonable period"

This provision has a wider ambit than either reg.6 or reg.8 (since its application   **11–055**
is not limited to situations in which employment has ended).

"Practicable" means no more than "feasible". But where it is clearly pointless for the employers to hold a meeting e.g. because the surrounding circumstances are such that a meeting could not resolve the grievance, this would amount to exceptional circumstances making it unjust and inequitable to increase any subsequent award: *Bainbridge* (above) at [84] to [91] the facts of which suggest that the pointlessness threshold is something akin to practical impossibility (see the commentary to s.31(4) EA above).

Failure to comply with the statutory procedures

12.—(1) If either party fails to comply with a requirement of an   **11–056**
applicable statutory procedure, including a general requirement contained in Part 3 of Schedule 2, then, subject to paragraph (2), the non-completion of the procedure shall be attributable to that party and neither party shall be under any obligation to comply with any further requirement of the procedure.

(2) Except as mentioned in paragraph (4), where the parties are to be treated as complying with the applicable statutory procedure, or any requirement of it, there is no failure to comply with the procedure or requirement.

(3) Notwithstanding that if regulation 11(1) applies the procedure that would otherwise be the applicable statutory procedure does not apply, where that regulation applies because the circumstances in sub-paragraph (a) or (b) of regulation 11(3) apply and it was the behaviour of one of the parties that resulted in those circumstances applying, that party shall be treated as if—

(a) the procedure had applied, and

(b) there had been a failure to comply with a requirement of the procedure that was attributable to him.

(4) In a case where regulation 11(2) applies in relation to a requirement of the applicable statutory procedure because the circumstances in sub-paragraph (a) or (b) of regulation 11(3) apply, and it was the behaviour of one of the parties that resulted in those circumstances applying, the fact that the requirement was not complied with shall be treated as being a failure, attributable to that party, to comply with a requirement of the procedure.

EA (DR) Regs 2004

Para.(1)—Non-compliance with a requirement of a procedure

11–057   This provision identifies non-completion of a procedure with a failure to comply with any requirement of an applicable statutory procedure (i.e. any of the matters set out in Pts 1–3 of Sch.2, EA. See *Patel v Leicester CC* UKEAT/0368/06 at [31] and [32].

Regulation 12 operates a "guillotine" procedure at each stage of the three steps of the standard procedures. Therefore where the employer had failed to comply with Step 2(2)(a) of the DDP, the employee's subsequent failure to attend the adjourned disciplinary meeting was irrelevant to the question whether the employer was in breach of the procedure and the dismissal was automatically unfair: *Bowen v Millbank Estate Management Organisation* UKEAT/0032/07 at [15].

Para.(2)—Treated as complying

11–058   For the circumstances in which the parties are treated as complying with the procedures (as distinct from the circumstances in which the procedures do not apply) see regs 5, 7, 8, 9, 10, 11(2) and 13(4).

Paras (3) and (4)—Vicarious liability of corporate "parties"

11–059   It seems reasonably clear that employers should be responsible for the actions of their employees which cause the circumstances in reg.11(3)(a) or (b) to arise. As such, common law principles of vicarious liability should be applied.

Failure to attend a meeting

11–060   **13.—(1) Without prejudice to regulation 11(2) and (3)(c), if it is not reasonably practicable for--**

> **(a) the employee, or, if he is exercising his right under section 10 of the 1999 Act (right to be accompanied), his companion; or**
>
> **(c) the employer,**

to attend a meeting organised in accordance with the applicable statutory procedure for a reason which was not foreseeable when the meeting was arranged, the employee or, as the case may be, employer shall not be treated as having failed to comply with that requirement of the procedure.

(2) In the circumstances set out in paragraph (1), the employer shall continue to be under the duty in the applicable statutory procedure to invite the employee to attend a meeting and, where the employee is exercising his rights under section 10 of the 1999 Act and the employee proposes an alternative time under subsection (4) of that section, the employer shall be under a duty to invite the employee to attend a meeting at that time.

(3) The duty to invite the employee to attend a meeting referred to in paragraph (2) shall cease if the employer has invited the employee to attend two meetings and paragraph (1) applied in relation to each of them.

(4) Where the duty in paragraph (2) has ceased as a result of paragraph (3), the parties shall be treated as having complied with the applicable statutory procedure.

Regulation 13 applies equally to the statutory dismissal and disciplinary procedures and the grievance procedures. Note that by reason of para.14 of Sch.2 to the EA a meeting held for the purposes of either of the procedures is a hearing for the purposes of s.13(4) and (5) of the Employment Relations Act 1999 (cf. *London Underground Ltd v Ferenc-Batchelor* [2003] I.R.L.R 252: I.C.R. 656, EAT, an investigatory meeting which cannot lead to the imposition of a sanction is not a disciplinary meeting for the purposes of s.10 of the Employment Relations Act 1999 (ERA)).

This provision adds a gloss to the general provisions concerning the right to be accompanied to hearings provided under s.10 of the ERA. Section 10 itself contains provision for hearings to be scheduled so as to permit the employee's "companion" to attend. Under reg.13 if attendance at a meeting becomes "not reasonably practicable" by reason of events occurring after the date for the meeting has been set, failure to attend is not counted as non-compliance with a statutory procedure. If this occurs the employer's duty to invite the employee to a meeting continues (in accordance with the requirements of paras 12 and 13 of Sch.2 to the EA). The timing of the rearranged meeting may be determined by the employee if he suggests a time that meets the requirements of s.10(5) of the ERA. If the employee fails to attend two meetings, and in each instance that failure is explained on the basis of reg.13(1), the employer's obligation to invite the employee to a meeting comes to an end, and the parties are deemed to have complied with the relevant statutory procedure. Where the meeting does not take place for a reason which does not meet the requirements of reg.13(1), the party whose fault has led to the cancellation will be treated as having failed to comply with this requirement of the applicable procedure and hence responsible for the non-completion of the procedure.

The language of reg.13 does not fit well with a case where the employee does not receive the notice of the appeal meeting, although it is not impossible to describe their resulting non-attendance at the meeting as "impracticable". But where the employer has given the claimant unreasonably short notice of the appeal or has used some evidently unreliable means of communicating the date and time of the appeal, it cannot really be said that the impracticability of the employee's attendance was "not foreseeable when the meeting was arranged" it being all too foreseeable that the notice would not be received. That being so, if the employer fails to call a second meeting they are not in breach of reg.13(2) although they are likely to be in breach of para.13 of Sch.2 EA 2002, the General Requirements: *Sovereign Business Integration Plc v Trybus* UKEAT/0107/07. Although the claimant in Trybus never informed the employer that he had not received the letter in time to attend the appeal hearing prior to making his claim to the tribunal, the position would appear to be the same if he had done so.

Although the point was not taken in *Trybus* (for the facts of which see para.10–078/1 above) this interpretation of the word "unforeseeable", although undoubtedly correct, appears to have the unfortunate consequence of putting the employee who does not attend the meeting of which he is unaware, in breach of the procedure in the case of a Step 2 meeting and therefore at risk of having his compensation reduced under s.31(2)(c)(i) EA 2002 or, in the case of an appeal, having it reduced under s.31(2)(c)(ii) EA 2002. This clearly cannot have been intended and no doubt a tribunal would be quick to regard this as an exceptional circumstance justifying no reduction in the claimant's award. Contrast the obligation on employers to reconvene disciplinary meetings where the employee is exercising her statutory right to be accompanied under s.10 ERA, subs.(4) of which requires the employer to rearrange the meeting if the employee's chosen companion ". . . will not be available at the time proposed for the hearing by the employer." It is therefore likely that, following *Trybus*, there will be cases where the employer is not under an obligation to call a second meeting under reg.13(2) but is under such an obligation

EA (DR) Regs 2004

under s.10 ERA, and the employee is technically in breach of the statutory procedure for not attending the first meeting (although there would appear to be no breach of the procedure if the employee but not his chosen companion was able to attend the original meeting).

Questions to obtain information not to constitute statement of grievance

11–062   14.—(1) Where a person aggrieved questions a respondent under any of the provisions set out in paragraph (2), those questions shall not constitute a statement of grievance under paragraph 6 or 9 of Schedule 2.

(2) The provisions referred to in paragraph (1) are—

section 7B of the Equal Pay Act 1970;
section 74 of the Sex Discrimination Act 1975;
section 65 of the Race Relations Act 1976;
section 56 of the Disability Discrimination Act 1995;
regulation 33 of the Employment Equality (Religion or Belief) Regulations 2003;
regulation 33 of the Employment Equality (Sexual Orientation) Regulations 2003.

Para.(2)—Statutory questionnaires

11–063   Since the Regulations exclude the discrimination questionnaires from the statutory definition of grievance, a distinction cannot be drawn between the statements made by a claimant in that part of the form where the claimant explains why they believe they have been discriminated against and the questions to the employer which then follow. A questionnaire under one of the listed provisions cannot be a grievance for this purpose (*Holc-Gale v Makers UK Ltd* [2006] I.R.L.R. 179; [2006] I.C.R. 462, EAT).

However, since there is no requirement that a grievance be contained in a single document there would appear to be no reason in principle why a covering letter sent with a statutory questionnaire that stated that some or all of the matters within the questionnaire constituted a grievance, could not trigger the application of the grievance procedures.

Age discrimination questionnaires

11–064   The Employment Equality (Age) Regulations 2006 (SI 2006/1031) do not amend reg.14(2). The failure to amend para.(2) appears to be an oversight rather than the result of policy. However, until reg.14(2) is amended to include references to age discrimination questionnaires if such a questionnaire explains the nature of the employee's grievance, there seems to be no reason why it could not fulfil the dual purpose of being the Step 1 statement of grievance and the statutory questionnaire. It is anticipated that this omission with be removed by the provisions of the Employment Equality (Age) (Consequential Amendments) Regulations 2007. These are expected to be in force with effect from April 6, 2007.

Extension of time limits

11–065   15.—(1) Where a complaint is presented to an employment tribunal under a jurisdiction listed in Schedule 3 or 4 and—

(a) either of the dismissal and disciplinary procedures is the applicable statutory procedure and the circumstances specified in paragraph (2) apply; or

(b) either of the grievance procedures is the applicable statutory procedure and the circumstances specified in paragraph (3) apply;

the normal time limit for presenting the complaint is extended for a period of three months beginning with the day after the day on which it would otherwise have expired.

(2) The circumstances referred to in paragraph (1)(a) are that the employee presents a complaint to the tribunal after the expiry of the normal time limit for presenting the complaint but had reasonable grounds for believing, when that time limit expired, that a dismissal or disciplinary procedure, whether statutory or otherwise (including an appropriate procedure for the purposes of regulation 5(2)), was being followed in respect of matters that consisted of or included the substance of the tribunal complaint.

(3) The circumstances referred to in paragraph (1)(b) are that the employee presents a complaint to the tribunal—

(a) within the normal time limit for presenting the complaint but in circumstances in which section 32(2) or (3) of the 2002 Act does not permit him to do so; or

(b) after the expiry of the normal time limit for presenting the complaint, having complied with paragraph 6 or 9 of Schedule 2 in relation to his grievance within that normal time limit.

(4) For the purposes of paragraph (3) and section 32 of the 2002 Act the following acts shall be treated, in a case to which the specified regulation applies, as constituting compliance with paragraph 6 or 9 of Schedule 2—

(a) in a case to which regulation 7(1) applies, compliance by the employee with the requirement in regulation 7(2);

(b) in a case to which regulation 9(1) applies, compliance by the appropriate representative with the requirement in sub-paragraph (a) or (b) of that regulation, whichever is the later; and

(c) in a case to which regulation 10 applies, the raising of his grievance by the employee in accordance with the procedure referred to in that regulation.

(5) In this regulation "the normal time limit" means—

(a) subject to sub-paragraph (b), the period within which a complaint under the relevant jurisdiction must be presented if there is to be no need for the tribunal, in order to be entitled to consider it to—

(i) exercise any discretion, or

(ii) make any determination as to whether it is required to consider the complaint, that the tribunal would have to exercise or make in order to consider a complaint presented outside that period; and

(b) in relation to claims brought under the Equal Pay Act 1970, the period ending on the date on or before which proceedings must be instituted in accordance with section 2(4) of that Act.

Para.(1)—"normal time limit"

11–066   A letter of grievance sent to the employer before the time for commencing tribunal proceedings has begun to run, e.g. before the employee gives notice of resignation in a constructive unfair dismissal claim, complies with para.6 of Sch.2 and therefore the automatic extension of time applies. The requirement created by para.(3)(b) is only that paras 6 or 9 be complied with before the normal time limit expires (*H.M. Prison Service v Barua* [2007] I.R.L.R. 4, EAT; [2007] I.C.R. 671 and *Lewisham LBC v Colbourne*, unreported, December 12, 2006, EAT).

". . . extended for a period of three months"

11–067   In *Singh t/a Rainbow International v Taylor* UKEAT/0183/06 it was held that the phrase ". . .extended for a period of three months beginning with the day after the day on which it would otherwise have expired" had the effect of extending the normal time limit by three months plus one day. Thus where the normal time limit in an unfair dismissal claim expired on September 19, the day after that being the 20th the three month period beginning with that date expired on December 20, not December 19. It has long been settled (*Hammond v Haigh Castle & Co Ltd* [1973] I.R.L.R. 91; (1973) 8 I.T.R. 199, NIRC) that the three month period which begins with the effective date of termination ends not on the three month anniversary of that date but the day before it, the three month anniversary being three months plus a day. The reasoning and conclusion in *Singh* appear doubtful particularly because it overlooks reg.15(1) which reflects the approach in Hammond and it would be prudent to work on the premise that the automatic extension produces the overall result that time expires six months from the effective date of termination, not six months plus one day. The time limit in grievance cases where the primary time limit is also three months would be similarly extended. This paragraph was cited with approval in *Joshi v Manchester CC* UKEAT/0235/07 which held that the reasoning in *Singh* is wrong. The judgments of the Court of Appeal in *Zoan v Rouamba* [2001] W.L.R. 1509 and *Trow v Ind Coope (West Midlands) Ltd* [1967] 2 Q.B. 899 offer a binding construction on the words "beginning with", as in reg.15(1(b), when calculating when a time limit expires.

Para.(1)(b)—Grievance procedure--when not applicable

11–068   When the substance of the complaint is about dismissal the grievance procedure is not applicable and therefore cannot trigger an extension of time. Thus a grievance about the basis on which the employee had been selected for redundancy did not trigger an automatic extension of time as by virtue of reg.6(5) only the dismissal procedure could apply, even if the grievance relates to matters which, absent a dismissal, would give the claimant grounds for a claim to the tribunal (*Hart v English Heritage* [2006] I.C.R. 655; [2006] I.R.L.R. 915, EAT). The grievance procedure is also not applicable to disputes between employees and there is therefore no requirement for a prospective claimant to send a written statement of grievance to a fellow employee for whose discriminatory acts the employer is liable, even if the claimant intends to name the fellow employee as a respondent in tribunal proceedings. If the claimant subsequently names their fellow employee as a respondent to the proceedings, reg.15 DRR does not automatically extend the time limit in respect of the claim against the employee and the proceedings against the fellow employee must therefore be commenced within the applicable primary limitation period (*Bissett v Martins and Castlehill Housing Association Ltd* UKEATS/0022/06).

Bissett was doubted in *Lambeth LBC v Corlett* [2007] I.C.R.88 EAT (per H.H. Judge Clark), but followed as to the result although not the reasoning in *Odoemelam v The Whittington Hospital NHS Trust* UKEAT/0016/06 per Keith J. at [26].

Para.(2)—Dismissal cases

It is important to note that the procedure which the employee reasonably believes to be being followed need not be the statutory procedure. This resolves the problem of second and further stages of appeal in this context (for second and further stage appeals in the context of whether there has been non-compliance with a statutory procedure, see the commentary to s.31(3) of the Employment Act 2002 at para.10–024). Nor is it necessary for the appeal procedure to be actually being followed; the only issue is whether the employee reasonably believed that it was being followed. Whether the employee's belief was reasonable is a matter for the tribunal. Thus in *Piscitelli v Zilli Fish Ltd* UKEAT/0638/95, a solicitor's letter seeking a cash settlement of a potential unfair dismissal claim rather than reinstatement or re-engagement, did not raise an internal appeal and the employee was not therefore reasonable in believing that an internal appeal procedure was underway and so there could be no automatic extension of time.

11–069

A complaint of wrongful dismissal, i.e. dismissal without or with less than the minimum statutory notice (Employment Rights Act 1996, s.86(1)) or the claimant's contractual notice, is a complaint about dismissal, not a complaint about failure to pay notice pay. Therefore reg.15(2) and not reg.15(3) applies. An internal appeal by the claimant against dismissal includes the substance of a wrongful dismissal claim as well as an unfair dismissal claim. Thus the reg.15(1) extension of time will also apply to any anticipated claim to the tribunal (*London Borough of Lambeth v Corlett* [2007] I.C.R. 88).

The issue for the tribunal is not whether the claimant presented his claim with reasonable diligence but whether when he did so he had reasonable grounds for believing that a procedure--not necessarily the statutory procedure—was still being followed: *Arnold Clark Automobiles Ltd v Glass* UKEAT/0095/06.

The fact that the employee submits his appeal very late does not by itself prevent reg.15(2) from being engaged. An employee who, on the advice of solicitors that it was necessary to do so before commencing proceedings, lodged an appeal against dismissal on the 87th day after dismissal, not having previously been informed by his employer that he had the right to appeal, had a reasonable belief that an appeal procedure was being followed when the three month limitation period expired the following day: *Codemasters Software Company Ltd v Wong* UKEAT/0639/06.

The relevant question is not whether the claimant had in fact lodged a formal appeal, but whether she believed on reasonable grounds that there was an ongoing procedure to enable her to challenge her dismissal: *Harris v Towergate London Market Ltd* UKEAT/0090/07. The claimant was made redundant and did not appeal. Later she heard comments suggesting she had been improperly selected and asked for a meeting at which she was represented by her union. Her concerns were raised and the union representative asked to be given certain information to enable a decision to be made whether to take the case to tribunal. On receipt of the information the claimant raised a written grievance which the respondent rejected on the ground that the SGP did not apply and that she had not appealed her original dismissal. This process spanned the date on which the primary time limit expired. Held: the time limit was automatically extended under reg.15(2).

Where a claimant received notification of the outcome of his appeal against dismissal only five hours before the time limit for commencing proceedings expired, reg.15(2) was not engaged but it was open to the tribunal to find that it had not been reasonably practicable to commence proceedings within the three month period: *Royal Bank of Scotland v Bevan* UKEAT/0440/07. See also to the same effect *Ashcroft v Haberdasher's Aske's Boys School* UKEAT/0151/07 which held that the 2004 Regulations created a new scenario which displaces the reasoning in cases such as *Palmer v Southend-on-Sea BC* [1984] I.R.L.R. 117 CA which had held that the pendency of an internal appeal was not a factor which could be taken into account when determining whether it had been reasonably practicable to submit a claim in time.

Para.(3)—Grievance cases

11–070
Where a claimant raises a grievance which the employer rejects and then raises a further grievance relating to the way in which that grievance was handled to the extent that the second grievance raises new issues, it is a fresh grievance for the purpose of reg.15(3), and to that extent the second grievance stands alone for the purposes of determining whether the Regulations apply and in particular whether reg.15 has triggered an automatic extension of time (*Mudchute Association v Petheridge* UKEAT/0569/05). Merely repeating a complaint already made does not amount to a fresh grievance (*Hart v English Heritage* [2006] I.C.R. 655; [2006] I.R.L.R. 915 at EAT [14] and [15]).

As the statutory grievance procedures do not apply to complaints between employees, if the claimant names a fellow employee as a respondent to a discrimination claim, reg.15.(3) cannot operate to extend the time limit for commencing proceedings against the fellow employee (*Bissett v Martins (1) Castlehill Housing Association Ltd (2)* UKEATS/0022/06).

Bissett doubted in *Lambeth LBC v Corlett* [2007] I.C.R. 88 EAT per (H.H.Judge Clark), but followed as to the result although not the reasoning in *Odoemelam v The Whittington Hospital NHS Trust* UKEAT/0016/06 per Keith J. at [26].

Non-dismissal breach of contract claims

11–070/1 In *Mowells v Vox Displays Ltd* UKEAT/0122/07 in which the claimants appeal was allowed by consent, the issue in the appeal being whether a written grievance sent by the claimant had extended the time for presenting the claim by virtue of reg.15(3) it was held that the SGP applies to non-dismissal breach of contract claims by virtue of s.31 of and Sch.3 to the EA 2002 and reg.6(1) DRR. In consequence the written grievance had been a Step 1 letter for the purposes of the SGP and time was extended. It is submitted that both the reasoning and conclusion are doubtful. The reasoning contains a clear error of law—that neither breach of contract nor unauthorised deduction of wages claims are in Sch.4 EA whereas the latter are, although nothing appears to turn on the error. The assumption that art.7(ba) of the Employment Tribunals Extension of jurisdiction (England and wales) Order 1994 [para.13–011] supports the conclusion is also questionable as the article is only engaged where time is extended by virtue of reg.15 and does not itself extend time. As art.7(ba) is not redundant if it has no application to non-dismissal breach of contract claims (it is clearly applicable in dismissal breach of contract claims because of regs 6(5) and 15(2) DRR as the DDP applies to such cases), it is not possible to draw any conclusions from its mere existence in connection with whether the SGP applies to such claims.

National security

16. **Where it would not be possible to comply with an applicable statutory procedure without disclosing information the disclosure of which would be contrary to the interests of national security, nothing in these Regulations requires either party to comply with that procedure.**   11–071

National security proceedings

The application of reg.16 is not limited to national security proceedings, i.e. proceedings in respect of which a Minister of the Crown has issued a notice to the Secretary of the Tribunal under r.54(1) of the Employment Tribunals Rules of Procedure 2004 in respect of Crown employment proceedings, or to proceedings in which a Minister of the Crown is entitled to apply to the tribunal to make certain orders under r.54(3). In principle it will apply to any situation in which compliance with a statutory procedure required disclosure of information, when such disclosure would be contrary to the interests of national security. However, it is likely to be an exception that will be narrowly construed: see and compare *B v BAA* [2005] I.R.L.R. 927. In particular, it is likely that an employer/ employee will be required to comply with the applicable procedure to the full extent possible while avoiding any disclosure that would be contrary to the interests of national security.   11–072

Amendments to secondary legislation

17. [*Amends the Sex Discrimination (Questions and Replies) Order 1975, the Race Relations (Questions and Replies) Order 1977, the Employment Tribunals Extension of Jurisdiction (England and Wales) Order 1994, the Employment Tribunals Extension of Jurisdiction (Scotland) Order 1994, Employment Protection (Continuity of Employment) Regulations 1996, the Working Time Regulations 1998, the Employment Equality (Religion or Belief) Regulations 2003, and the Employment Equality (Sexual Orientation) Regulations 2003*]   11–073

Transitional Provisions

18. **These Regulations shall apply—**   11–074

    (a) **in relation to dismissal and relevant disciplinary action, where the employer first contemplates dismissing or taking such action against the employee after these Regulations come into force; and**

    (b) **in relation to grievances, where the action about which the employee complains occurs or continues after these Regulations come into force,**

but shall not apply in relation to a grievance where the action
continues after these Regulations come into force if the employee
has raised a grievance about the action with the employer before they
come into force.

"contemplates dismissing"

11–075   The statutory dismissal and disciplinary procedure applies only if the employer
first contemplated dismissing the employee or taking relevant disciplinary action
after October 1, 2004. When an employer first "contemplates" dismissal is a
subjective issue wholly for the employer. There is no requirement for the
employer's thoughts to be communicated to the employee (*Madhewoo v NHS Direct*
UKEAT/0030/06).

Grievances

11–076   Merely repeating a complaint already made does not amount to a fresh
grievance. Thus where an employee had raised a grievance before October 1, 2004,
repeating the grievance after that date did not trigger an automatic extension
under reg.15 in virtue of reg.18(b) (*Hart v English Heritage* [2006] I.C.R. 655; [2006]
I.R.L.R 915, EAT at [14] and [15]).

If the cause of action itself has ended, the action does not continue merely
because the employee continues to have the right to bring a claim to the tribunal.

In an equal pay claim where the breach of the equality clause had ended prior to
October 1, 2004, the Regulations do not apply and there is no requirement for the
claimant to raise a grievance: *Bainbridge v Redcar & Cleveland BC* [2007] IR.L.R. 494
EAT at [97] to [99].

CHAPTER 12

THE TERRITORIAL JURISDICTION OF EMPLOYMENT TRIBUNALS

Contents

Territorial Jurisdiction

509

12–001 The territorial scope of an employment tribunal's jurisdiction over statutory and common law claims will differ according to the cause of action in play. Thus, the test which fails to be applied in considering whether or not an employment tribunal has jurisdiction to hear an unfair dismissal claim is very different to the test that applies if the tribunal is concerned solely with a contractual claim for wrongful dismissal. However, the different tests are not wholly distinct. For example, where there is both an unfair dismissal claim and a wrongful dismissal claim the question of whether or not the employment tribunal has jurisdiction to hear the unfair dismissal claim will be a factor which falls to be taken into account in considering whether or not the tribunal should also deal with the breach of contract claim for wrongful dismissal.

The differing principles governing territorial jurisdiction are considered in relation to six broad categories of claim:

(1) unfair dismissal claims;
(2) claims under the Employment Rights Act other than unfair dismissal claims;
(3) discrimination claims;
(4) claims brought under the transfer of undertakings legislation;
(5) claims brought under the working time regulations; and
(6) contractual claims.

In addition to the question of territorial jurisdiction it is necessary to consider the question of the allocation of a claim as between the employment tribunals of England and Wales and the employment tribunals of Scotland.

1 Unfair Dismissal Claims

12–002 Prior to October 25, 1999, employees who ordinarily worked outside Great Britain were excluded from various rights under the Employment Rights Act 1996 (ERA)—including the right to make an unfair dismissal claim—by virtue of s.196. Section 196 of the ERA was repealed by ERA 1999, leaving ERA 1996 silent as to its territorial scope.

Following the repeal of s.196 the right not to be unfairly dismissed is subject to implied territorial restrictions. The scope of those territorial restrictions are signposted in the leading case, *Lawson v Serco* Ltd [2006] I.C.R. 250, HL, which set out the following principles:

12–003 (1) **Principles, not rules**: the territorial extent of the right under s.94(1) is governed by principles, not rules. The question as to whether a case comes within the territorial ambit of s.94(1) is a matter of law not discretion.

(2) **General principle is employment in Great Britain**: the general principle   **12–004**
is that s.94(1) will apply if the employee was working in Great Britain at the time
that he was dismissed. The terms of the contract and the prior history of the
contractual relationship may be relevant but ordinarily the question should be
simply whether the employee is working in Great Britain at the time when he is
dismissed (*Serco*, per Lord Hoffmann at para.27).

(3) **The touchstone for jurisdiction in respect of peripatetic employees is**   **12–005**
their base: With the exception of mariners (for whom express provision is made)
where an employee is peripatetic, e.g. airline pilots, international management
consultants, salesmen; he will come within the territorial scope of s.94(1) if his base
is in Great Britain. In *Serco*, Lord Hoffmann cited with approval the dicta of Lord
Denning MR in *Todd v British Midland Airways Ltd* [1978] I.C.R. 959 at 964:

> "A man's base is the place where he should be regarded as ordinarily working,
> even though he may spend days, weeks or months working overseas. I would only
> make this suggestion. I do not think that the terms of the contract help much in
> these cases. As a rule, there is no term in the contract about exactly where he is
> to work. You have to go by the conduct of the parties and the way they have been
> operating the contract. You have to find at the material time where the man is
> based."

For a recent example of the application for the Serco principles to an ordinary
unfair dismisal claim see *Bleuse v MBT Transport Ltd* UKEAT/0339/07 where Elias P.
upheld the decision of an employment tribunal that an employee who whose base
was outside the UK could not bring an ordinary unfair dismissal claim. Note the
different approach the Employment Appeal Tribunal took to the working time
claim in that case (see para.12–034 below).

(4) **Employees working abroad ("expatriate employees") are covered in**   **12–006**
exceptional circumstances: It is very unlikely that an employee who works abroad
will come within the scope of s.94(1) unless he was working for an employer based
in Great Britain. But, employment will not attract British law merely on account of
British ownership. The fact that the employee also happens to be British or even
that he was recruited in Britain should not in itself be sufficient to take the case out
of the general rule that the place of employment is decisive. Lord Hoffmann gave
two examples of unusual circumstances bringing an employee within the territorial
scope of s.94(1). The first was of an employee posted abroad by a British employer
for the purposes of a business carried on in Britain. Such an employee is not
working for a business conducted in a foreign country which belongs to British
owners or is a branch of a British business, but as a representative of a business
conducted at home. Lord Hoffmann stated that a foreign correspondent on the staff
of a British newspaper would probably fall within this first category. The second
example is an expatriate employee of a British employer who is operating within
what amounts for practical purposes to an extra-territorial British enclave in a
foreign country such as a military base. At this stage it is not clear precisely what
will amount to an "enclave". However, it would appear that a British Embassy will
not constitute an enclave (*Serco* at paras 37–39).

(5) **Question of fact not law**: At this relatively early stage of the development   **12–007**
of the law the question of territorial jurisdiction should be treated (for reasons of
policy) as one of law rather than fact with a view to facilitating the development of
the law by the appellate courts.

For an example of the application of *Serco* principles to particular facts see: *Burke v British Council*; *ADT Fire & Security Plc v Speyer*; *Cameron v Navy & Air Force Institutes* UKEAT/0125/06.

2 CLAIMS UNDER THE **ERA** OTHER THAN UNFAIR DISMISSAL CLAIMS

12–008   In *Serco*, Lord Hoffmann held (at para.14) "There is no reason why all of the various rights included in the 1996 Act should have the same territorial scope". Thus the sort connection required to found jurisdiction in respect of the rights afforded under ERA 1996 other than the right not to be unfairly dismissed, (e.g. the right to an itemised pay statement (ss.8–10), wages protection (Pt II) and maternity rights (Pt VIII)) may well be different to that required under s.94(1). In considering the territorial scope of ERA provisions other than s.94 an employment tribunal should have regard to the following: (i) whether or not the case falls within the "legislative grasp or intendment" of the relevant provision (see *Clark v Oceanic Contractors Inc* [1983] 2 A.C. 130); and (ii) the principle that provisions of the ERA must be construed consistently with the rights afforded under the Posting of Workers Directive (96/71/EC) and set out below.

The Posting of Workers Directive (96/71/EC)

12–009   A "posted worker" is a worker who, for a limited period, carries out his work in the territory of a Member State other than the State in which he normally works. The effect of the Posting of Worker Directive is to ensure that workers who are posted to other Member States on a temporary basis enjoy minimum levels of protection in relation to their employment such as maximum work periods, periods of paid holiday and health and safety protection.

THE POSTING OF WORKERS DIRECTIVE

Article 1—Scope

12–010   **1 This Directive shall apply to undertakings established in a Member State which, in the framework of the transnational provision of services, post workers, in accordance with paragraph 3, to the territory of a Member State.**

2 This Directive shall not apply to merchant navy undertakings as regards seagoing personnel.

3 This Directive shall apply to the extent that the undertakings referred to in paragraph 1 take one of the following transnational measures:

> (a) **post workers to the territory of a Member State on their account and under their direction, under a contract concluded between the undertaking making the posting and the party for whom the services are intended, operating in that Member State, provided there is an employment relationship between the undertaking making the posting and the worker during the period of posting; or**
>
> (b) **post workers to an establishment or to an undertaking owned by the group in the territory of a Member State,**

provided there is an employment relationship between the undertaking making the posting and the worker during the period of posting; or

(c) being a temporary employment undertaking or placement agency, hire out a worker to a user undertaking established or operating in the territory of a Member State, provided there is an employment relationship between the temporary employment undertaking or placement agency and the worker during the period of posting.

4 Undertakings established in a non-member State must not be given more favourable treatment than undertakings established in a Member State.

Article 2—Definition

1 For the purposes of this Directive, 'posted worker' means a worker who, for a limited period, carries out his work in the territory of a Member State other than the State in which he normally works.   **12–011**

2 For the purposes of this Directive, the definition of a worker is that which applies in the law of the Member State to whose territory the worker is posted.

Article 3—Terms and conditions of employment

1 Member States shall ensure that, whatever the law applicable to the employment relationship, the undertakings referred to in Article 1(1) guarantee workers posted to their territory the terms and conditions of employment covering the following matters which, in the Member State where the work is carried out, are laid down: **12–012**

- by law, regulation or administrative provision, and/or
- by collective agreements or arbitration awards which have been declared universally applicable within the meaning of paragraph 8, insofar as they concern the activities referred to in the Annex:

    (a) maximum work periods and minimum rest periods;
    (b) minimum paid annual holidays;
    (c) the minimum rates of pay, including overtime rates; this point does not apply to supplementary occupational retirement pension schemes;
    (d) the conditions of hiring-out of workers, in particular the supply of workers by temporary employment undertakings;
    (e) health, safety and hygiene at work;
    (f) protective measures with regard to the terms and conditions of employment of pregnant women or women who have recently given birth, of children and of young people;

513

(g) equality of treatment between men and women and other provisions on non-discrimination.

For the purposes of this Directive, the concept of minimum rates of pay referred to in paragraph 1(c) is defined by the national law and/or practice of the Member State to whose territory the worker is posted.

2 In the case of initial assembly and/or first installation of goods where this is an integral part of a contract for the supply of goods and necessary for taking the goods supplied into use and carried out by the skilled and/or specialist workers of the supplying undertaking, the first subparagraph of paragraph 1(b) and (c) shall not apply, if the period of posting does not exceed eight days.

This provision shall not apply to activities in the field of building work listed in the Annex.

3 Member States may, after consulting employers and labour, in accordance with the traditions and practices of each Member State, decide not to apply the first subparagraph of paragraph 1(c) in the cases referred to in Article 1(3)(a) and (b) when the length of the posting does not exceed one month.

4 Member States may, in accordance with national laws and/or practices, provide that exemptions may be made from the first subparagraph of paragraph 1(c) in the cases referred to in Article 1(3)(a) and (b) and from a decision by a Member State within the meaning of paragraph 3 of this Article, by means of collective agreements within the meaning of paragraph 8 of this Article, concerning one or more sectors of activity, where the length of the posting does not exceed one month.

5 Member States may provide for exemptions to be granted from the first subparagraph of paragraph 1(b) and (c) in the cases referred to in Article 1(3)(a) and (b) on the grounds that the amount of work to be done is not significant.

Member States availing themselves of the option referred to in the first subparagraph shall lay down the criteria which
the work to be performed must meet in order to be considered as 'non-significant'.

6 The length of the posting shall be calculated on the basis of a reference period of one year from the beginning of the posting.

For the purpose of such calculations, account shall be taken of any previous periods for which the post has been filled by a posted worker.

7 Paragraphs 1 to 6 shall not prevent application of terms and conditions of employment which are more favourable to workers.

Allowances specific to the posting shall be considered to be part of the minimum wage, unless they are paid in reimbursement of expenditure actually incurred on account of the posting, such as expenditure on travel, board and lodging.

8 'Collective agreements or arbitration awards which have been declared universally applicable' means collective agreements or arbitration awards which must be observed by all undertakings in the geographical area and in the profession or industry concerned.

In the absence of a system for declaring collective agreements or arbitration awards to be of universal application within the meaning of the first subparagraph, Member States may, if they so decide, base themselves on:

- collective agreements or arbitration awards which are generally applicable to all similar undertakings in the geographical area and in the profession or industry concerned, and/or
- collective agreements which have been concluded by the most representative employers' and labour organizations at national level and which are applied throughout national territory,

provided that their application to the undertakings referred to in Article 1(1) ensures equality of treatment on matters listed in the first subparagraph of paragraph 1 of this Article between those undertakings and the other undertakings referred to in this subparagraph which are in a similar position.

Equality of treatment, within the meaning of this Article, shall be deemed to exist where national undertakings in a similar position:

- are subject, in the place in question or in the sector concerned, to the same obligations as posting undertakings as regards the matters listed in the first subparagraph of paragraph 1, and
- are required to fulfil such obligations with the same effects.

9 Member States may provide that the undertakings referred to in Article 1(1) must guarantee workers referred to in Article 1(3)(c) the terms and conditions which apply to temporary workers in the Member State where the work is carried out.

10 This Directive shall not preclude the application by Member States, in compliance with the Treaty, to national undertakings and to the undertakings of other States, on a basis of equality of treatment, of:

- terms and conditions of employment on matters other than those referred to in the first subparagraph of paragraph 1 in the case of public policy provisions,

- terms and conditions of employment laid down in the collective agreements or arbitration awards within the meaning of paragraph 8 and concerning activities other than those referred to in the Annex.

Article 4—Cooperation on information

12–013   1 For the purposes of implementing this Directive, Member States shall, in accordance with national legislation and/or practice, designate one or more liaison offices or one or more competent national bodies.

2 Member States shall make provision for co-operation between the public authorities which, in accordance with national legislation, are responsible for monitoring the terms and conditions of employment referred to in Article 3. Such cooperation shall in particular consist in replying to reasoned requests from those authorities for information on the transnational hiring-out of workers, including manifest abuses or possible cases of unlawful transnational activities.

The Commission and the public authorities referred to in the first subparagraph shall co-operate closely in order to examine any difficulties which might arise in the application of Article 3(10).

Mutual administrative assistance shall be provided free of charge.

3 Each Member State shall take the appropriate measures to make the information on the terms and conditions of employment referred to in Article 3 generally available.

4 Each Member State shall notify the other Member States and the Commission of the liaison offices and/or competent bodies referred to in paragraph 1.

Article 5—Measures

12–014   Member States shall take appropriate measures in the event of failure to comply with this Directive.

They shall in particular ensure that adequate procedures are available to workers and/or their representatives for the enforcement of obligations under this Directive.

Article 6—Jurisdiction

12–015   In order to enforce the right to the terms and conditions of employment guaranteed in Article 3, judicial proceedings may be instituted in the Member State in whose territory the worker is or was posted, without prejudice, where applicable, to the right, under existing international conventions on jurisdiction, to institute proceedings in another State.

Article 7—Implementation

Member States shall adopt the laws, regulations and administrative provisions necessary to comply with this Directive by 16 December 1999 at the latest. They shall forthwith inform the Commission thereof.

When Member States adopt these provisions, they shall contain a reference to this Directive or shall be accompanied by such reference on the occasion of their official publication. The methods of making such reference shall be laid down by Member States.

12–016

Article 8—Commission review

By 16 December 2001 at the latest, the Commission shall review the operation of this Directive with a view to proposing the necessary amendments to the Council where appropriate.

12–017

3 DISCRIMINATION CLAIMS

Introduction

The domestic discrimination provisions provide that protection against discrimination is afforded in relation to employment if that employment is "at an establishment in Great Britain". The tests for territorial applicability under the various discrimination Acts are largely identical. There are, however, minor variations in these tests in the contexts of: offshore energy exploration and exploitation; and employment on aircraft and hovercraft: see Sex Discrimination Act 1975, s.1; Race Relations Act 1976, s.8; Disability Discrimination Act 1995, s.68; Employment Equality (Religion or Belief) Regulations 2003, reg.9; Employment Equality (Sexual Orientation) Regulations 2003, reg.9; and Employment Equality (Age) Regulations 2006, reg.10.

12–018

It is convenient to consider the test in the discrimination provisions by reference to the formulae used in the Sex Discrimination Act 1975 (ss.6(1) and 10) which is the same under the Equal Pay Act 1970, s.1(1); the Race Relations Act 1976, s.4(1); the Disability Discrimination Act 1995, s.4(6); the Employment Equality (Religion or Belief) Regulations 2003, reg.6(1); the Employment Equality (Sexual Orientation) Regulations 2003, reg.6(1); and the Employment Equality (Age) Regulations 2006, reg.7(1).

SEX DISCRIMINATION ACT 1975

6. Discrimination against applicants and employees

(1) It is unlawful for a person, in relation to employment by him at an establishment in Great Britain, to discriminate against a woman—

12–019

    (a) in the arrangements he makes for the purpose of determining who should be offered that employment, or

    (b) in the terms on which he offers her that employment, or

    (c) by refusing or deliberately omitting to offer her that employment.

(2) It is unlawful for a person, in the case of a woman employed by him at an establishment in Great Britain, to discriminate against her—

   (a) in the way he affords her access to opportunities for promotion, transfer or training, or to any other benefits, facilities or services or by refusing or deliberately omitting to afford her access to them, or

   (b) by dismissing her, or subjecting her to any other detriment.

10 Meaning of employment at establishment in Great Britain.

12–020   (1) For the purposes of this Part and section 1 of the Equal Pay Act 1970 ("the relevant purposes"), employment is to be regarded as being at an establishment in Great Britain if—

   (a) the employee does his work wholly or partly in Great Britain, or

   (b) the employee does his work wholly outside Great Britain and subsection (1A) applies.

(1A) This subsection applies if—

   (a) the employer has a place of business at an establishment in Great Britain,

   (b) the work is for the purposes of the business carried on at that establishment, and

   (c) the employee is ordinarily resident in Great Britain—

      (i) at the time when he applies for or is offered the employment, or

     (ii) at any time during the course of the employment.

(2) The reference to "employment" in subsection (1) includes—

   (a) employment on board a ship, only if the ship is registered at a port of registry in Great Britain, and

   (b) employment on aircraft or hovercraft, only if the aircraft or hovercraft is registered in the United Kingdom and operated by a person who has his principal place of business, or is ordinarily resident, in Great Britain.

(3) In the case of employment on board a ship registered at a port of registry in Great Britain (except where the employee does his work wholly outside Great Britain and subsection (1A) does not apply) the ship shall for the relevant purposes be deemed to be the establishment.

(4) Where work is not done at an establishment it shall be treated for the relevant purposes as done at the establishment from which it is done or (where it is not done from any establishment) at the establishment with which it has the closest connection.

(5) In relation to employment concerned with exploration of the sea bed or subsoil or the exploitation of their natural resources, Her

Majesty may by Order in Council provide that subsections (1) and (3) shall have effect as if—

(a) the reference to Great Britain in each of paragraphs (a) and (b) of subsection (1), and

(b) each of the references to Great Britain in subsections (1A) to (3)

included any area for the time being designated under section 1(7) of the Continental Shelf Act 1964, except an area or part of an area in which the law of Northern Ireland applies.

(6) An Order in Council under subsection (5) may provide that, in relation to employment to which the Order applies, this Part and section 1 of the Equal Pay Act 1970 are to have effect with such modifications as are specified in the Order.

(7) An Order in Council under subsection (5) shall be of no effect unless a draft of the Order was laid before and approved by each House of Parliament.

(8) Subsections (1) to (4) or, where an Order in Council under subsection (5) is in force, those subsections as modified by the Order, apply for the purposes of determining whether contract work, within the meaning given by section 9, is at an establishment in Great Britain, but so apply with the following modifications—

(a) a reference to employment is to be read as a reference to work to which section 9 applies, and

(b) "employee" and "employer" shall be read (respectively) as "contract worker" and "principal", with "contract worker" and "principal" having the meaning given by section 9.

The effect of section 6

Employment is to be regarded as being "at an establishment in Great Britain" in **12–021** two distinct sets of circumstances. First, where the employee does his work wholly or partly in Great Britain and secondly, where the employer has a place of business at an establishment in Great Britain, the work is for the purposes of the business carried on at that establishment and the employee is ordinarily resident in Great Britain at the material time.

"Great Britain"

Great Britain includes UK territorial waters adjacent to Great Britain: SDA **12–022** 1975, s.82(1); RRA 1976, s.78(1); DDA 1995, s.68(1); RBR 2003, reg.2(3); SOR 2003, reg.2(3); AR 2006, reg.2(2).

"Work wholly or partly in Great Britain"

Employment is to be regarded as being at an establishment in Great Britain **12–023** where an employee "does his work wholly or partly in Great Britain": SDA 1975, s.10(1)(a); RRA 1976, s.8(1)(a); DDA 1995, s.68(2)(a); RBR 2003, reg.9(1)(a); SOR 2003, reg.9(1)(a); AR 2006, reg.10(1)(a).

In determining whether or not an employee works wholly or partly in Great Britain the relevant period is the whole period of the employment, and not merely the period during which discrimination is alleged to have occurred (see *Saggar v Ministry of Defence* [2005] I.C.R. 1073, CA). In *Saggar*, Mummery L.J. held (at 1082F): ". . .the whole period of the employment relationship, not just the limited period during which the discrimination is alleged to have occurred, is the yardstick by which it is determined whether, at the time of the alleged discrimination, the employee wholly or mainly did his work outside Great Britain." In *Saggar*, the Court of Appeal was concerned with a predecessor of the current statutory rule which defined the protection in negative terms, i.e. it provided that an employee was not protected if he did his work "wholly or mainly outside Great Britain". Although the current statutory rule is cast in positive terms (an employee is protected if he did his work "wholly or partly in Great Britain") the principle in *Saggar* remains applicable the relevant period is therefore the whole period of employment and not just the period when the discrimination is alleged to have occurred.

The Employment Appeal Tribunal in *Saggar* (Burton J. presiding) also dealt with the conjoined case of *Ministry of Defence v Gandiya* [2004] I.C.R. 1708. In *Gandiya* the Employment Appeal Tribunal was concerned with another predecessor of the current statutory rule which provided that an employee was excluded from protection if he did his work "wholly outside Great Britain". The Employment Appeal Tribunal held that the de minimis principle applied to the word "wholly". Thus in *Gandiya* a one-day working visit to Great Britain was held not be sufficient to bring such an employee within an employment tribunal's jurisdiction. It seems unlikely that matters which were considered to be "de minimis" under the old rules will now be sufficient to constitute employment which is "wholly or partly" in Great Britain within the meaning of the new rules. It is therefore submitted that the outcome in the *Gandiya* case would be the same if it were decided under the new rules.

"does his work"

12–024 The Court of Appeal has held that the words "does his work" mean does or is to do" (*Deria v General Council of British Shipping* [1986] I.C.R. 172, which concerned the use of the words in s.8(1) of the Race Relations Act). Thus the discrimination provisions cover employment where the employee does "or is to do" his work wholly outside Great Britain. The Court of Appeal held that such a "contemplation" approach is preferable to an "actuality" approach. The effect is that if discrimination takes place during recruitment the issue for the employment tribunal is: as at the time of the recruitment process where did the parties contemplate that the intended place of work would be. Thus where a claimant is refused employment in circumstances where at the relevant time the parties contemplated employment outside Great Britain, it is irrelevant that the employee may—contrary to expectations—end up working in Great Britain.

"work outside Great Britain"

12–025 Where the claimant works wholly outside Great Britain, his employment is nevertheless to be regarded as being at an establishment in Great Britain if:

   (a) the employer has a place of business at an establishment in Great Britain;
   (b) the work is for the purposes of the business carried on at that establishment; and
   (c) the employee is ordinarily resident in Great Britain—

> (i) at the time when he applies for or is offered the employment, or
>
> (ii) at any time during the course of the employment.

See: SDA 1975, s.10(1)(b) and (1A); RRA 1976, s.8(1)(b) and (1A); DDA 1995, s.68(2)(b) and (2A); RBR 2003, reg.9(1)(b) and (2); SOR 2003, reg.9(1)(b) and (2); AR 2006, reg.10(1)(b) and (2).

In *Williams v University of Nottingham* [2007] I.R.L.R. 660 the Employment Appeal Tribunal held that the approach outlined in *Serco* is equally applicable to the strikingly similar statutory lanugage of the DDA. The Employment Appeal Tribuanl emphasised that in considering the question of jurisdiction the focus should be on where the relevant work is performed in practice rather than where contractually it could be required to be performed.

Specific cases

Mariners

Employment on board a ship is to be regarded as being at an establishment in Great Britain only if the ship is registered at a port of registry in Great Britain. **12–026**

Employment on an aircraft or hovercraft

Employment on board an aircraft or hovercraft is to be regarded as being at an establishment in Great Britain only if the aircraft or hovercraft is registered in the UK and operated by a person who has his principal place of business, or is ordinarily resident, in Great Britain. **12–027**

Energy exploration

In relation to employment concerned with exploration of the sea bed or subsoil or the exploitation of their natural resources the SDA (s.10(5)) and RRA (s.8(5)) make provision for Orders so that the references to Great Britain under the SDA, RRA and EqPA shall include any area for the time being designated under s.1(7) of the Continental Shelf Act 1964, except an area or part of an area in which the law of Northern Ireland applies. The Orders made under this provision are the Race Relations (Offshore Employment) Order 1987 (SI 1987/929) and the Sex Discrimination and Equal Pay (Offshore Employment) Order 1987 (SI 1987/930). **12–028**

Employment on the Continental Shelf

The Employment Equality (Sexual Orientation) Regulations 2003 and Employment Equality (Religion or Belief) Regulations 2003 deem employment on the continental shelf to be employment at an establishment in Great Britain if it is: (a) in an area designation under s.1(7) of the Continental Shelf Act 1964 or: (b) is an area within the Frigg Gas Field and the employer is a company registered under the Companies Act 1985 or an overseas company which has an established place of business in Great Britain (RBR 2003, reg.9(4) and (5) and SOR 2003, reg.9(4) and (5)). **12–029**

4 THE TRANSFER OF UNDERTAKINGS (PROTECTION OF EMPLOYMENT) REGULATIONS 2006 (SI 2006/246) (TUPE)

3 A relevant transfer

(1) These Regulations apply to— **12–030**

   (a) a transfer of an undertaking, business or part of an undertaking or business situated immediately before the transfer in the United Kingdom to another person where there is a transfer of an economic entity which retains its identity;

   (b) a service provision change, that is a situation in which—

      (i) activities cease to be carried out by a person ('a client') on his own behalf and are carried out instead by another person on the client's behalf ('a contractor');

     (ii) activities cease to be carried out by a contractor on a client's behalf (whether or not those activities had previously been carried out by the client on his own behalf) and are carried out instead by another person ('a subsequent contractor') on the client's behalf; or

    (iii) activities cease to be carried out by a contractor or a subsequent contractor on a client's behalf (whether or not those activities had previously been carried out by the client on his own behalf) and are carried out instead by the client on his own behalf,

and in which the conditions set out in paragraph (3) are satisfied.

(2) In this regulation 'economic entity' means an organised grouping of resources which has the objective of pursuing an economic activity, whether or not that activity is central or ancillary.

(3) The conditions referred to in paragraph (1)(b) are that—

   (a) immediately before the service provision change—

      (i) there is an organised grouping of employees situated in Great Britain which has as its principal purpose the carrying out of the activities concerned on behalf of the client;

     (ii) the client intends that the activities will, following the service provision change, be carried out by the transferee other than in connection with a single specific event or task of short-term duration; and

   (b) the activities concerned do not consist wholly or mainly of the supply of goods for the client's use.

(4) Subject to paragraph (1), these Regulations apply to—

   (a) public and private undertakings engaged in economic activities whether or not they are operating for gain;

(b) a transfer or service provision change howsoever effected notwithstanding—

    (i) that the transfer of an undertaking, business or part of an undertaking or business is governed or effected by the "law of a country or territory outside the United Kingdom or that the service provision change is governed or effected by the law of a country or territory outside Great Britain;

    (ii) that the employment of persons employed in the undertaking, business or part transferred or, in the case of a service provision change, persons employed in the organised grouping of employees, is governed by any such law;

(c) a transfer of an undertaking, business or part of an undertaking or business (which may also be a service provision change) where persons employed in the undertaking, business or part transferred ordinarily work outside the United Kingdom.

(5) An administrative reorganisation of public administrative authorities or the transfer of administrative functions between public administrative authorities is not a relevant transfer.

(6) A relevant transfer—

(a) may be effected by a series of two or more transactions; and

(b) may take place whether or not any property is transferred to the transferee by the transferor.

(7) Where, in consequence (whether directly or indirectly) of the transfer of an undertaking, business or part of an undertaking or business which was situated immediately before the transfer in the United Kingdom, a ship within the meaning of the Merchant Shipping Act 1995 registered in the United Kingdom ceases to be so registered, these Regulations shall not affect the right conferred by section 29 of that Act (right of seamen to be discharged when ship ceases to be registered in the United Kingdom) on a seaman employed in the ship.

TUPE 2006 applies to "relevant transfers". Relevant transfers are either **12–031** "transfers of undertakings" or "service provision changes".

Effect of Regulation 3

In order for there to be a transfer of an undertaking to which the Regulations **12–032** apply, the undertaking, business or part thereof concerned must be situated in the UK immediately before the transfer (reg.3(1)(a)). As long as this condition is met, a transfer will fall within the territorial scope of the Regulations even if the employees in the undertaking, business or part thereof ordinarily work outside the UK (reg.3(4)(c)). So, for example if there is a transfer of sales department of a UK business, the fact that the sales staff spend the majority of their working week outside the UK will not prevent the Regulations applying to the transfer, so long as the undertaking itself (comprising premises, assets, fixtures & fittings, goodwill as well as employees) is situated in the UK. (See the DTI Guidance, "Employment Rights on the Transfer of an Undertaking: A Guide to the 2006 TUPE Regulations for Employees, Employers and Representatives", p.12.)

In order for there to be a "service provision change" to which the Regulations apply, there must, immediately before the service provision change, be an organised grouping of employees situated in Great Britain (regs 3(1)(b), (3)(a)(i)).

In either type of case, a relevant transfer will not fall outside the scope of the Regulations by virtue of being governed or effected by foreign law, or by virtue of the employees' employment being governed by foreign law (reg.(3(4)(b)).

No extension to the Continental Shelf

12–033   The Regulations do not follow the normal pattern of extension to the Continental Shelf (*Addison v Denholm Ship Management (UK) Ltd* [1997] I.C.R. 770, EAT).

5 CLAIMS UNDER THE WORKING TIME REGULATIONS

12–033/1   Claims under the Working Time Regulations fall outwith the *Serco* principle. In *Bleuse v MBT Transport Ltd* UKEAT/0339/07, Elias P. accepted that since the Working Time Regulations transpose the Working Time Directive into domestic law and since that Directive gives rise to directly effective rights the principle of harmonious construction requires an effective remedy. The Employment Appeal Tribunal therefore held that (at [44]):

> "the implied limitation that might otherwise be deemed appropriate must be modified so as to ensure that directly effective rights can be enforced by the English courts. That is so even if on an application of the *Serco* principles, the base would not be in Great Britain."

6 CONTRACTUAL CLAIMS

12–034   The jurisdiction of an employment tribunal to entertain claims for breach of a contract of employment (or connected contract) stems from s.3 of the Employment Tribunals Act 1996. By art.3(a) of the Employment Tribunals Extension of Jurisdiction (England and Wales) Order 1994, made under the predecessor to s.3(2) of the Employment Tribunals Act 1996, proceedings may be brought before an employment tribunal in respect of a claim to which s.3(2) applies and which a court in England and Wales would under the law for the time being in force have jurisdiction to hear and determine.

The effect of the Employment Tribunals Extension of Jurisdiction (England and Wales) Order 1994 is that the territorial jurisdiction of an employment tribunal to consider a breach of contract claim arising out of a contract of employment mirrors that of the civil courts and the same principles apply (*Dickie v Cathay Pacific Airways Ltd* [2004] I.C.R. 1733, EAT). The rules governing the territorial jurisdiction of the courts are complex. For a more detailed examination of the relevant provisions of the CPR refer to the *White Book* (2007). Further consideration of the principles and the authorities can be found in Briggs Rees, Civil Jurisdiction and Judgments (4th edn, LLP, 2005), and Dicey and Morris, Conflict of Laws (14th edn, Sweet & Maxwell 2006).

The Judgments Regulation

The starting point when considering whether or not an employment tribunal has **12–035** territorial jurisdiction to consider a breach of contract claim is (Council Regulation (EC) 44/2001) "the Judgments Regulation". The Judgments Regulation came into force on March 1, 2002 and is the fundamental provision governing all proceedings instituted in the civil courts. If the claim lies outside the domain of the Judgments Regulation, the traditional common law rules of jurisdiction set out in CPR Pt 6 will apply.

JUDGMENTS REGULATION (COUNCIL REGULATION (EC) 44/2001)

Article 18

1. In matters relating to individual contracts of employment, **12–036** jurisdiction shall be determined by this Section, without prejudice to Article 4 and point 5 of Article 5.

2. Where an employee enters into an individual contract of employment with an employer who is not domiciled in a Member State but has a branch, agency or other establishment in one of the Members States, the employer shall, in disputes arising out of the operations of the branch, agency or establishment, be deemed to be domiciled in that Member State.

Article 19

An employer domiciled in a Member State may be sued **12–037**

1. in the courts of the Member State where he is domiciled; or
2. in another Member State:
   (a) in the courts for the place where the employee habitually carries out his work or in the courts for the last place where he did so, or
   (b) if the employee does not or did not habitually carry out his work in any one country, in the courts for the place where the business which engaged the employee is or was situated

Article 20

1. An employer may bring proceedings only in the courts of the **12–038** Member State in which the employee is domiciled.

2. The provisions of this Section shall not affect the right to bring a counter-claim in the court in which, in accordance with this Section, the original claim is pending.

Article 21

The provisions of this Section may be departed from only by an **12–039** agreement on jurisdiction:

1. which is entered into after the dispute has arisen; or

2. which allows the employee to bring proceedings in courts other than those indicated in this Section.

Effect of Judgments Regulation:

12–040

1. The basic rule is that a person domiciled in a Member State should, whatever their nationality, be sued in the court of that Member State. However, a person domiciled in a Member State may be sued in the courts of another Member State so far as permitted by the Regulation.
2. An employee may bring proceedings against an employer domiciled in a Member State:

    (1) in the courts of the Member State; or
    (2) in another Member State in the courts for the place where the employee habitually carries out his work or last carried out his work; or
    (3) in the courts for the place where the business which engaged the employee is or was situated if the employee does not or did not habitually carry out his work in any one country.
3. An employer may bring proceedings only in the courts of the Member State in which the employee is domiciled.
4. Where the employer is not domiciled in a Member State:

    (1) jurisdiction may be claimed over the defendant on the basis of the traditional jurisdictional rules of the court set out in CPR Pt 6 (considered below);
    (2) a defendant employer may nevertheless be treated as domiciled in a Member State in which it has a branch, agency or other establishment where the dispute arises out the operations that branch, agency or other establishment.
5. Any court which is seised of a claim in respect of which it has jurisdiction under the Regulations has jurisdiction to hear a counter-claim.
6. An agreement as to choice of court is not effective unless entered into after the dispute has arisen or it allows the employee to bring proceedings in courts other than those indicated in s.5 of the Regulations.
7. Where a defendant enters an appearance the court will have jurisdiction save where the appearance was entered to contest the jurisdiction.
8. Where the Posting of Workers Directive applies jurisdiction will be governed by the provisions of that Directive.

In *Samengo-Turner v Marsh & McLennan Co Inc* [2007] EWCA Civ. 723 (2007) CLC 104 the Court of Appeal held that where group companines have an economic interest in an employment contract and the enforcement of its terms those companies should be subject to the same jurisdictional restaints as the employing company. Thus a holding company was to be treated as the employer for the purposes of the allocation of jurisdiction under s.5 of the Judgments Regulation.

Member States

12–041

The Regulation is directly effective in all Member States save for Denmark which is covered by the Brussels Convention. Gibraltar counts as part of the UK for the purposes of the Regulation, whilst the Isle of Man and the Channel Islands are outside the territorial scope of the Regulation.

Domicile

12–042

Article 59 of the Judgments Regulation provides that in order to determine whether a party is domiciled in the Member State whose courts are seised of a matter, the court shall apply its internal law. If a party is not domiciled in the

Member State whose courts are seised of the matter, then in order to determine whether the party is domiciled in another Member State, the court shall apply the law of the Member State.

The domestic rules governing the domicile are found in the Civil Jurisdiction and Judgments Act 1982, Pt V. Section 41 of the Civil Jurisdiction and Judgments Act governs the domicile of individuals and s.42 governs the domicile and seat of corporation of associations.

CIVIL JURISDICTION AND JUDGMENTS ACT 1982

41 Domicile of individuals

(1) Subject to Article 52 (which contains provisions for determin- **12–043** ing whether a party is domiciled in a Contracting State), the following provisions of this section determine, for the purposes of the 1968 Convention [the Lugano Convention] and this Act, whether an individual is domiciled in the United Kingdom or in a particular part of, or place in, the United Kingdom or in a state other than a Contracting State.

(2) An individual is domiciled in the United Kingdom if and only if—

    (a) he is resident in the United Kingdom; and

    (b) the nature and circumstances of his residence indicate that he has a substantial connection with the United Kingdom.

(3) Subject to subsection (5), an individual is domiciled in a particular part of the United Kingdom if and only if—

    (a) he is resident in that part; and

    (b) the nature and circumstances of his residence indicate that he has a substantial connection with that part.

(4) An individual is domiciled in a particular place in the United Kingdom if and only if he—

    (a) is domiciled in the part of the United Kingdom in which that place is situated; and

    (b) is resident in that place.

(5) An individual who is domiciled in the United Kingdom but in whose case the requirements of subsection (3)(b) are not satisfied in relation to any particular part of the United Kingdom shall be treated as domiciled in the part of the United Kingdom in which he is resident.

(6) In the case of an individual who—

    (a) is resident in the United Kingdom, or in a particular part of the United Kingdom; and

    (b) has been so resident for the last three months or more,

the requirements of subsection (2)(b) or, as the case may be, subsection (3)(b) shall be presumed to be fulfilled unless the contrary is proved.

(7) An individual is domiciled in a state other than a Contracting State if and only if—

(a) he is resident in that state; and
(b) the nature and circumstances of his residence indicate that he has a substantial connection with that state.

42   Domicile and seat of corporation or association

12–044 (1) For the purposes of this Act the seat of a corporation or association (as determined by this section) shall be treated as its domicile.

(2) The following provisions of this section determine where a corporation or association has its seat—

(a) for the purpose of Article 53 (which for the purposes of the 1968 Convention [or, as the case may be, the Lugano Convention] equates the domicile of such a body with its seat); and
(b) for the purposes of this Act other than the provisions mentioned in section 43(1)(b) and (c).

(3) A corporation or association has its seat in the United Kingdom if and only if—

(a) it was incorporated or formed under the law of a part of the United Kingdom and has its registered office or some other official address in the United Kingdom; or
(b) its central management and control is exercised in the United Kingdom.

(4) A corporation or association has its seat in a particular part of the United Kingdom if and only if it has its seat in the United Kingdom and—

(a) it has its registered office or some other official address in that part; or
(b) its central management and control is exercised in that part; or
(c) it has a place of business in that part.

(5) A corporation or association has its seat in a particular place in the United Kingdom if and only if it has its seat in the part of the United Kingdom in which that place is situated and—

(a) it has its registered office or some other official address in that place; or

    (b) **its central management and control is exercised in that place; or**

    (c) **it has a place of business in that place.**

(6) **Subject to subsection (7), a corporation or association has its seat in a state other than the United Kingdom if and only if—**

    (a) **it was incorporated or formed under the law of that state and has its registered office or some other official address there; or**

    (b) **its central management and control is exercised in that state.**

(7) **A corporation or association shall not be regarded as having its seat in a Contracting State other than the United Kingdom if it is shown that the courts of that state would not regard it as having its seat there.**

(8) **In this section—**

"business" includes any activity carried on by a corporation or association, and "place of business" shall be construed accordingly;

"official address", in relation to a corporation or association, means an address which it is required by law to register, notify or maintain for the purpose of receiving notices or other communications.

Burden and Standard of Proof required to establish jurisdiction

In the civil courts, the burden is on the claimant to show that there is a good **12–045** arguable case that the court has jurisdiction (see *Carnoustie Universal SA v International Transport Workers Federation* [2002] EWHC 1624; and Konkola *Copper Mines Plc v Caromin* [2005] EWHC 898 Comm, and [2006] EWCA 5). Given that the territorial jurisdiction of an employment tribunal in contractual claims mirrors that of the courts it is submitted that the same burden and standard of proof applies in employment tribunals.

"habitually carries out his work"

The European Court of Justice has held that in the place where an employee **12–046** performs his obligations to employer "A" can be regarded as the place where the employee habitually carries out his work for the purposes of a dispute with employer "B" in circumstances where: (i) the employee's obligations to A under the contract of employment are suspended; and (ii) employer B has an interest in the performance of the employee's services to employer A (see *G Pugliese v Finmeccanica SpA* (Case C-437/00) [2003] I.L.Pr. 21).

The effect of the common law rules governing jurisdiction in employment tribunal proceedings

Where the claim lies outside the domain of the Judgments Regulation, or in **12–047** circumstances where the Regulation itself provides that the traditional rules of jurisdiction apply, then whether or not an employment tribunal has jurisdiction will be governed by the traditional common law rules found in CPR Pt 6. The common law rules are rooted in the concept of service on the defendant. If the defendant is present in the jurisdiction service may be made as of right. If the defendant is outside the jurisdiction the permission of the court may required to effect service out of the jurisdiction.

The principles governing the service out of the jurisdiction where the permission of court is required have yet to be considered by the appellate courts in the context of employment tribunal proceedings. The service provisions of the Employment Tribunals Rules of Procedure 2004, r.61(4) are very different to the rules that apply in the High Court (see CPR r.6.20).

12–048 **61(4) All notices and documents required by these rules to be sent or given to any person listed below may be sent to or delivered at—**

(h) in the case of a notice or document directed to a party—

(i) the address specified in the claim or response to which notices and documents are to be sent, or in a notice under paragraph (5); or

(ii) if no such address has been specified, or if a notice sent to such an address has been returned, to any other known address or place of business in the United Kingdom or, if the party is a corporate body, the body's registered or principal office in the United Kingdom, or, in any case, such address or place outside the United Kingdom as the President, Vice President or a Regional Chairman may allow;

12–049 It is submitted that in considering whether to allow service under r.61(4) provisions, an employment tribunal should have regard to the provisions of CPR r.6.19 and r.6.20 and that service abroad should be allowed under r.61(4) in the circumstances where the High Court would also permit service.

Civil Procedure Rules

Service out of the jurisdiction where the permission of the court is not required (CPR 6.19)

12–050 **6.19—(1) A claim form may be served on a defendant out of the jurisdiction where each claim included in the claim form made against the defendant to be served is a claim which the court has power to determine under the 1982 Act and—**

(a) no proceedings between the parties concerning the same claim are pending in the courts of any other part of the United Kingdom or any other Convention territory; and

(b) (i) the defendant is domiciled in the United Kingdom or in any Convention territory;

(ii) Article 16 of Schedule 1 or 3C to the 1982 Act, or paragraph 11 of Schedule 4 to that Act, refers to the proceedings; or

      (iii) the defendant is a party to an agreement conferring jurisdiction to which Article 17 of Schedule 1 or 3C to the 1982 Act, or paragraph 12 of Schedule 4 to that Act, refers.

(1A) A claim form may be served on a defendant out of the jurisdiction where each claim included in the claim form made against the defendant to be served is a claim which the court has power to determine under the Judgments Regulation and—

    (a) no proceedings between the parties concerning the same claim are pending in the courts of any other part of the United Kingdom or any other Regulation State; and

    (b)   (i) the defendant is domiciled in the United Kingdom or in any Regulation State;

        (ii) Article 22 of the Judgments Regulation refers to the proceedings; or

       (iii) the defendant is a party to an agreement conferring jurisdiction to which Article 23 of the Judgments Regulation refers.

(2) A claim form may be served on a defendant out of the jurisdiction where each claim included in the claim form made against the defendant to be served is a claim which, under any other enactment, the court has power to determine, although—

    (a) the person against whom the claim is made is not within the jurisdiction; or

    (b) the facts giving rise to the claim did not occur within the jurisdiction.

(3) Where a claim form is to be served out of the jurisdiction under this rule, it must contain a statement of the grounds on which the claimant is entitled to serve it out of the jurisdiction.

Service out of the jurisdiction where the permission of the court is required under the CPR

6.20 In any proceedings to which rule 6.19 does not apply, a claim form may be served out of the jurisdiction with the permission of the court if—   **12–051**

"General Grounds"

(1) a claim is made for a remedy against a person domiciled within the jurisdiction.

(2) a claim is made for an injunction ordering (GL) the defendant to do or refrain from doing an act within the jurisdiction.

(3) a claim is made against someone on whom the claim form has been or will be served (otherwise than in reliance on this paragraph) and—

   (a) **there is between the claimant and that person a real issue which it is reasonable for the court to try; and"**

   (b) **the claimant wishes to serve the claim form on another person who is a necessary or proper party to that claim.**

(3A) a claim is a Part 20 claim and the person to be served is a necessary or proper party to the claim against the Part 20 claimant.

  Claims for interim remedies

(4) a claim is made for an interim remedy under section 25(1) of the 1982 Act(5).

  Claims in relation to contracts

(5) a claim is made in respect of a contract where the contract—

   (a) **was made within the jurisdiction;**

   (b) **was made by or through an agent trading or residing within the jurisdiction;**

   (c) **is governed by English law; or**

   (d) **contains a term to the effect that the court shall have jurisdiction to determine any claim in respect of the contract.**

(6) a claim is made in respect of a breach of contract committed within the jurisdiction.

(7) a claim is made for a declaration that no contract exists where, if the contract was found to exist, it would comply with the conditions set out in paragraph (5). . .

The principles governing permission to serve out

12–052   The principles governing the grant of permission to serve out in the High Court are found in *Seaconsar Far East Ltd v Markazi Jomhouri Islam Iran* [1994] 1 A.C. 438 and *Spiliada Maritime Corp v Consulex Ltd*, sub nom. *The Spiliada* [1987] A.C. 460:

(1) the claimant must show that each claim made satisfies at least one of the sub-paragraphs of r.6.20;

(2) the claimant must show a serious issue to be tried which is the same as showing a reasonable prospect of success (*De Molestina v Ponton* [2002] 1 Lloyd's Rep. 271);

(3) the court has a discretion and must consider the question of in which forum the case could most appropriately be tried (forum conveniens);

(4) the application of the principle of forum conveniens where permission is sought to serve out of the jurisdiction will ordinarily be the same as those that govern the application of the forum non conveniens principle where a stay is sought. The criteria are set out in *Spiliada* (followed by the Court of Appeal in the context of employment tribunal proceedings in *Crofts v Cathay Pacific Airways Ltd* [2005] EWCA Civ. 599). In summary:

   (i) the burden is on the claimant to show that England and Wales is the most appropriate forum for the trial;

   (ii) the appropriate forum for the trial of the action is the forum in which the case may most suitably be tried for the interests of all the parties and the ends of justice;

(iii) the court must consider what is the "natural forum" being "that with which the action had the most real and substantial connection taking into account factors including expense, convenience of witness and the law governing the contract";

(iv) ordinary procedural advantages will normally be irrelevant;

(v) if the court concludes that there is another forum which is more suitable than England and Wales it will normally refuse permission unless justice requires that permission should nevertheless be granted;

(vi) where a party seeks to establish a fact or matter for the purpose of persuading the court to exercise its discretion in its favour the burden is on the party asserting the fact or matter.

Staying proceedings—forum non conveniens

Where proceedings have been properly commenced within the jurisdiction, an **12–053** employment tribunal may nevertheless stay them on the grounds of forum non conveniens if it considers that England and Wales is not the appropriate forum for the trial of the action. Ordinarily, the principles which govern an application to stay proceedings on the grounds of forum non-conveniens are the converse of the forum conveniens principles set out above. However, where the respondent is served as of right within the jurisdiction the balance will weigh more heavily in favour of the claimant if he would otherwise lose the benefit of the limitation period (see *Spiliada Maritime Corp v Cansulex Ltd* [1987] A.C. 460).

In *Crofts v Cathay Pacific Airways Ltd* [2005] I.C.R. 1749, HL, Lord Phillips of Worth Matravers, MR described the task of the employment tribunal as follows:

"In essence the task of the court is to consider whether England or the foreign jurisdiction is clearly the more appropriate forum. The pilots' claims for breach of contract are advanced against Hong Kong employers under contracts of employment governed by Hong Kong law, in respect of which the Hong Kong Labour Tribunal has jurisdiction. That Tribunal is already seized of a number of claims from pilots, including Veta and CPA pilots. On the face of it Hong Kong is clearly the more appropriate forum for the breach of contract claims. Had ERA claims been proceeding before the ET, there would have been a strong case for arguing that this factor made the ET the more appropriate forum for the parallel claims for breach of contract. As I have concluded that no ERA claims lie, it follows that I would stay all breach of contract claims."

See also *Shekar v Satyam Computer Services Ltd* [2005] I.C.R. 737, EAT.

The allocation of jurisdiction as between Scotland and England and Wales

The allocation of jurisdiction as between tribunals in Scotland and tribunals in **12–054** England and Wales is governed by the Employment Tribunals (Constitution and Rules of Procedure) Regulations 2004, reg.19.

EMPLOYMENT TRIBUNALS (CONSTITUTION AND RULES OF PROCEDURE) REGULATIONS 2004

19 Jurisdiction of tribunals in Scotland and in England & Wales

(1) An employment tribunal in England or Wales shall only have 12–055 jurisdiction to deal with proceedings (referred to as "English and Welsh proceedings") where—

Territorial Jurisdiction

(a) the respondent or one of the respondents resides or carries on business in England and Wales;

(b) had the remedy been by way of action in the county court, the cause of action would have arisen wholly or partly in England and Wales;

(c) the proceedings are to determine a question which has been referred to the tribunal by a court in England and Wales; or

(d) in the case of proceedings to which Schedule 3, 4 or 5 applies, the proceedings relate to matters arising in England and Wales

(2) An employment tribunal in Scotland shall only have jurisdiction to deal with proceedings (referred to as "Scottish Proceedings") where—

(a) the respondent or one of the respondents resides or carries on business in Scotland;

(b) the proceedings relate to a contract of employment the place of execution or performance of which is in Scotland;

(c) the proceedings are to determine a question which has been referred to the tribunal by a sheriff in Scotland; or

(d) in the case of proceedings to which Schedule 3, 4, or 5 applies, the proceedings relate to matters arising in Scotland."

"resides or carries on business in England and Wales"

12–056   In *Odeco (UK) Inc v Peacham* [1979] I.C.R. 823, EAT, a company was held to reside in England in circumstances where its registered office was in England and notwithstanding the fact that it had its operational base in Scotland. A company registered abroad may still "reside" in England where a majority of the directors and the shareholders controlling the company reside in England (see *Jackson v Ghost Ltd* [2003] I.R.L.R. 824 EAT).

"the place of execution or performance"

12–057   In *Prescription Pricing Authority v Ferguson* [2005] I.R.L.R. 464, the Court of Session held that these words in reg.19(2)(b) meant that the place of performance of the contract should be "wholly or, at least, substantially" in Scotland.

CHAPTER 13

EMPLOYMENT TRIBUNALS EXTENSION OF JURISDICTION (ENGLAND AND WALES) ORDER 1994

1994 No 1623

Contents

Art.

Citation, commencement and interpretation

1.—(1) This Order may be cited as the Employment Tribunals 13–001 Extension of Jurisdiction (England and Wales) Order 1994 and comes into force on the first day after it is made.

(2) In this Order—

"contract claim" means a claim in respect of which proceedings may be brought before an employment tribunal by virtue of article 3 or 4; and

"the 1978 Act" means the Employment Protection (Consolidation) Act 1978.

Provision for the appropriate Minister to confer jurisdiction on the employment **13–002** tribunals to resolve contract disputes had existed under s.131 of the EP(C)A 1978 and later under TURERA 1993, but, following the recommendation of Lord Browne-Wilkinson in *Delaney v Staples* [1992] 2 W.L.R. 451 that the jurisdiction be conferred, the power to extend the jurisdiction was exercised in July 1994. The tribunal was given power to award damages for breach of contract up to £25,000. At that time the tribunal's power to award compensation for unfair dismissal was capped at £11,000 and the jurisdiction in respect of breach of contract claims was substantial by comparison. Whilst the cap in respect of unfair dismissal claims has been increased, and is now increased year on year in line with inflation, and whilst the cap in respect of discrimination claims was removed altogether in 1995, the cap for contract claims has not increased at all. The jurisdiction is further limited in that it can only be invoked where the claim arises or is outstanding on termination (art.3), and it only relates to certain types of claim, set out in art.5. The restriction that only claims outstanding or arising on termination can be made to an employment tribunal means that breach of contract claims cannot be resolved by the tribunal during the currency of the employment relationship, even if the tribunal is seized of another claim at the same time, such as a discrimination claim.

The tribunal may consider claims with a foreign element, and in an appropriate case consider the forum doctrine and order a stay. However, the fact that a tribunal has jurisdiction to hear an unfair dismissal claim is not relevant to the question of whether it has jurisdiction to hear a contract claim (*Dickie v Cathay Pacific Airways Ltd* [2004] I.C.R. 1733, EAT). The tribunal has jurisdiction to hear contractual claims in respect of the dismissals of employees where they work around the world provided the employer is based in the UK (*Crofts v Cathay Pacific Airways Ltd* [2005] EWCA Civ 599).

Transitional provision

13–003   **2. This Order does not enable proceedings in respect of a contract claim to be brought before an employment tribunal unless—**

> **(a) the effective date of termination (as defined in section 55(4) of the 1978 Act) in respect of the contract giving rise to the claim, or**
>
> **(b) where there is no effective date of termination, the last day upon which the employee works in the employment which has terminated,**

occurs on or after the day on which the Order comes into force.

Extension of jurisdiction

13–004   **3. Proceedings may be brought before an [employment tribunal] in respect of a claim of an employee for the recovery of damages or any other sum (other than a claim for damages, or for a sum due, in respect of personal injuries) if—**

> **(a) the claim is one to which section 131(2) of the 1978 Act applies and which a court in England and Wales would under the law for the time being in force have jurisdiction to hear and determine;**
>
> **(b) the claim is not one to which article 5 applies; and**
>
> **(c) the claim arises or is outstanding on the termination of the employee's employment.**

13–005   See *Coors Brewers v Adcock* [2007] EWCA Civ 19 as to the distinction between claims under the contractual jurisdiction and those under Pt II of the Employment Rights Act 1996 (unlawful deduction from wages). The latter must be a claim for a specific sum. The former can be as well, but also extends to claims for unliquidated damages.

A compromise agreement entered between employer and employee is a contract "connected with employment". The combined effect of s.3 of the Employment Tribunals Act 1996 and art.3 is that the tribunal has jurisdiction over a claim of breach of a compromise agreement by the employer where the breach occurred before the termination of employment (*Rock-It Cargo Ltd v Green* [1997] I.R.L.R. 581). Contrast the position in *RS Johnstone v Miller Bros & FP Butler Ltd* [2002] I.C.R.

744 where the breach of the compromise agreement occurred after termination of employment, in which event the Tribunal had no jurisdiction to determine the question.

In *Sarker v South Tees Acute Hospital NHS Trust* [1997] I.C.R. 673 an offer of employment was made to the claimant, but subsequently withdrawn before the claimant commenced work. The trust sought to argue that there was no contract *of* employment, only a contract *for* employment. The argument was rejected and the Tribunal held that there had been a termination, that an employee who had entered a contract of employment, even though work had not commenced, was an employee for the purpose of the Order, and that the Tribunal had jurisdiction to determine the claim.

4. Proceedings may be brought before an employment tribunal in respect of a claim of an employer for the recovery of damages or any other sum (other than a claim for damages, or for a sum due, in respect of personal injuries) if—   **13–006**

> **(a) the claim is one to which section 131(2) of the 1978 Act applies and which a court in England and Wales would under the law for the time being in force have jurisdiction to hear and determine;**
>
> **(b) the claim is not one to which article 5 applies;**
>
> **(c) the claim arises or is outstanding on the termination of the employment of the employee against whom it is made; and**
>
> **(d) proceedings in respect of a claim of that employee have been brought before an employment tribunal by virtue of this Order.**

The tribunal may only hear an employer's claim for breach of contract where the employee has bought a claim by virtue of this order. However, the tribunal may hear an employer's counterclaim even if the employee's original claim is struck out as being out of time (*Anjali Patel v RCMS Ltd* [1999] I.R.L.R. 161). Similarly the fact that an employee's claim settles before the employer's counterclaim is issued does not operate as a bar to the employer's counterclaim provided the same is issued within the specified time limits (*Axios Systems Ltd v Paul Murphy* 2002, EAT (Scotland), unreported, December 1, 1999). The tribunal's power under art.4 is limited to the power to award damages for breach of contract. The tribunal does not have the power to grant any form of specific relief (*Millat Housing Association v Nijhar*, EAT, unreported, February 21, 1999) (no power to order the return of goods).   **13–007**

5. This article applies to a claim for breach of a contractual term of any of the following descriptions—   **13–008**

> **(a) a term requiring the employer to provide living accommodation for the employee;**
>
> **(b) a term imposing an obligation on the employer or the employee in connection with the provision of living accommodation;**

(c) a term relating to intellectual property;

(d) a term imposing an obligation of confidence;

(e) a term which is a covenant in restraint of trade.

In this article, "intellectual property" includes copyright, rights in performances, moral rights, design right, registered designs, patents and trade marks.

13–009   This Regulation identifies the types of contractual claims that are outside the scope of the tribunal's jurisdiction. The exclusion is framed by reference to the nature of the term that is to be enforced. Thus claims based on other terms within a contract that includes "excluded" terms, remain within the tribunal's jurisdiction.

Manner in which proceedings may be brought

13–010   6. Proceedings on a contract claim may be brought before an employment tribunal by presenting a complaint to an employment tribunal.

Time within which proceedings may be brought

13–011   7. An employment tribunal shall not entertain a complaint in respect of an employee's contract claim unless it is presented—

(a) within the period of three months beginning with the effective date of termination of the contract giving rise to the claim, or

(b) where there is no effective date of termination, within the period of three months beginning with the last day upon which the employee worked in the employment which has terminated,

(ba) where the period within which a complaint must be presented in accordance with paragraph (a) or (b) is extended by regulation 15 of the Employment Act 2002 (Dispute Resolution) Regulations 2004, the period within which the complaint must be presented shall be the extended period rather than the period in paragraph (a) or (b), or

(c) where the tribunal is satisfied that it was not reasonably practicable for the complaint to be presented within whichever of those periods is applicable, within such further period as the tribunal considers reasonable.

13–012   The statutory grievance procedure applies to a breach of contract claim brought under the Employment Tribunal Extension of Jurisdiction Order—with the exception of course of a claim for wrongful dismissal. The lodging of a grievance letter will extend the primary limitation period for such a claim by three months. *MJ Mowels v Vox Displays* 2007 UKEAT 0122/07. The approach to limitation is cast in the same terms as the comparable provisions for claims of unfair dismissal. As to the principles that apply, see the section on limitation at Ch.9.

8. An employment tribunal shall not entertain a complaint in **13–013**
respect of an employer's contract claim unless—

(a) it is presented at a time when there is before the tribunal a complaint in respect of a contract claim of a particular employee which has not been settled or withdrawn;

(b) it arises out of a contract with that employee; and

(c) it is presented—

    (i) within the period of six weeks beginning with the day, or if more than one the last of the days, on which the employer (or other person who is the respondent party to the employee's contract claim) received from the tribunal a copy of an originating application in respect of a contract claim of that employee; or

    (ii) where the tribunal is satisfied that it was not reasonably practicable for the complaint to be presented within that period, within such further period as the tribunal considers reasonable.

The President of the Employment Tribunals Scotland issued a Practice Direction, **13–014**
PD No 3, on 14 December 2006 governing the practice in Scotland of the
management of respondents' counterclaims. Under the practice direction the
amount of counterclaim must be specified at the time it is raised if this is
reasonably practicable. On receipt of notice of the counterclaim the claimant must
indicate to the tribunal whether the counterclaim is resisted, and if so the grounds
of resistance, within 28 days. The Practice Direction does not govern practice in the
English tribunals.

As regards whether an employer's counterclaim may be brought where the
employee's claim has been settled or withdrawn, see *Anjali Patel v RCMS Ltd*, above.

Death and bankruptcy

9.—(1) Where proceedings in respect of a contract claim have **13–015**
been brought before an employment tribunal and an employee or
employer party to them dies before their conclusion, the proceedings
shall not abate by reason of the death and the tribunal may, if it
thinks it necessary in order to ensure that all matters in dispute may
be effectually and completely determined and adjudicated upon,
order the personal representatives of the deceased party, or other
persons whom the tribunal considers appropriate, to be made parties
and the proceedings to be carried on as if they had been substituted
for the deceased party.

(2) Where proceedings in respect of a contract claim have been
brought before an employment tribunal and the employee or
employer who is the applicant party to them becomes bankrupt
before their conclusion, the proceedings shall not abate by reason of

the bankruptcy and the tribunal may, if it thinks it necessary in order to ensure that all matters in dispute may be effectually and completely adjudicated upon, order the person in whom the interest of the bankrupt party has vested to be made a party and the proceedings to be carried on as if he had been substituted for the bankrupt party.

Limit on payment to be ordered

13–016   10. An employment tribunal shall not in proceedings in respect of a contract claim, or in respect of a number of contract claims relating to the same contract, order the payment of an amount exceeding £25,000.

13–017   It is not possible to issue proceedings in the employment tribunal for breach of contract limiting the value of the claim to £25,000 and simultaneously (or for that matter, subsequently) issue proceedings in the High Court or county court in respect of the same cause of action for the balance of the claim in excess of £25,000 (*Roderick Fraser v Hlmad Ltd* [2006] I.R.L.R. 687). Where there is only one cause of action, and it has been judicially determined, there is merger of the cause of action with the final judgment. Following the merger the cause of action is extinguished and cannot be litigated further.

It is not necessarily an abuse of process to commence and then withdraw a breach of contract claim commenced in the tribunal, whilst preserving other claims, in order that the contract claim could be litigated in the High Court (*Anne-Marie Verdin v Harrods Ltd* [2006] I.C.R. 396). Where a party wishes to withdraw a contract claim under r.25 of the Employment Tribunal Rules of Procedure 2004 the tribunal employment judge should consider whether the party's intention was to abandon the claim or to bring the claim elsewhere, and depending on the answer whether that would be an abuse of process—see also *Ako v Rothschild Asset Management Ltd* [2002] 2 All E.R. 693 and *Sajid v Sussex Muslim Society* [2002] I.R.L.R. 113.

CHAPTER 14

EU Law Claims in the Employment Tribunal

Contents
Sect.

The legislative context for the introduction of EU law into UK law.

European Communities Act 1972

2—(1) All such rights, powers, liabilities, obligations and restric-   **14–001**
tions from time to time created or arising by or under the Treaties,
and all such remedies and procedures from time to time provided for
by or under the Treaties, as in accordance with the Treaties are
without further enactment to be given legal effect or used in the
United Kingdom shall be recognised and available in law, and be
enforced, allowed and followed accordingly; and the expression
"enforceable Community right" and similar expressions shall be read
as referring to one to which this subsection applies.

(2) Subject to Schedule 2 to this Act, at any time after its passing
Her Majesty may by Order in Council, and any designated Minister
or department may by regulations, make provision—

(a) for the purpose of implementing any Community obligation of the United Kingdom, or enabling any such obligation to be implemented, or of enabling any rights enjoyed
or to be enjoyed by the United Kingdom under or by
virtue of the Treaties to be exercised; or

(b) for the purpose of dealing with matters arising out of or
related to any such obligation or rights or the coming
into force, or the operation from time to time, of subsection (1) above;

and in the exercise of any statutory power or duty, including any
power to give directions or to legislate by means of orders, rules,
regulations or other subordinate instrument, the person entrusted
with the power or duty may have regard to the objects of the
Communities and to any such obligation or rights as aforesaid.

In this subsection "designated Minister or department" means such Minister of the Crown or government department as may from time to time be designated by Order in Council in relation to any matter or for any purpose, but subject to such restrictions or conditions (if any) as may be specified by the Order in Council.

European Community law Within the UK

14–002   The European Communities Act 1972 was enacted in order to give effect to Community law within the United Kingdom from the accession of the United Kingdom to the European Community on 1 January 1973. The adoption of legislation was necessary because under English constitutional law international treaties (such as those establishing the European Community) do not take effect within the domestic legal system until Parliament enacts legislation to that purpose.

The treaties referred to in s.2(1) are defined in s.1(2). Essentially they are the treaties creating the European Communities, Euratom and the European Coal and Steel Community, together with the treaties governing the accession of the United Kingdom and other new Member States. The Treaty that created the European Community is generally known as the Treaty of Rome or the EC Treaty. It was made in 1957 but was substantially amended by the Single European Act 1986, the Treaty of Maastricht of 1991 (which came into force on 1 October 1993), the Treaty of Amsterdam of 1997 (which came into force on 1 May 1999) and the Treaty of Nice of 2001 (which came into force on 2 February 2003). The EC Treaty established the European Community with legal personality and created the Community institutions, namely the European Parliament, the Council of Ministers, the Commission, the Court of Auditors and the European Court of Justice (which is referred to below as the European Court). It confers legislative, executive and judicial powers in prescribed fields upon those institutions including the power to make secondary legislation, stipulating which type of measures the Council or Commission is empowered to adopt in a particular area of Community competence.

Treaty rights

14–003   The EC Treaty is also a direct source of rights for individuals. Although this was not stipulated in the treaty itself, the early case-law of the European Court established that the rights and obligations created under the Treaty (and secondary legislation) are capable of penetrating the national legal systems of the Member States and of being enforced by and against private individuals. This means that although the relevant rights originate as international treaty obligations between sovereign states they do not only have effect at international level but are enforceable in the domestic courts of the Member States (Case 26/62 *Van Gend en Loos v Nederlandse Adminstratie der Belastingen* [1963] E.C.R. 1, ECJ).

Secondary legislation

14–004   Secondary legislation made under the EC Treaty takes the form of regulations, directives, decisions and recommendations. Article 249(2) of the EC Treaty provides that regulations are binding in their entirety and are directly applicable in all the Member States without the need for implementing measures. Indeed Member States are normally prohibited from enacting domestic legislation to implement regulations so that the Community source of the rights in question is not concealed (Case 94/77 *Fratelli Zerbone v Amminstrazione delle Finanze Dello Stato* [1978] E.C.R. 99, ECJ). In fact regulations have had little impact on employment law and the vast majority of EC employment law is derived from the relevant provisions of the EC Treaty and from numerous directives.

In contrast to regulations, directives are binding as to the result to be achieved but leave to the national authorities "the form and choice of methods" as regards implementation: Art.249(3). Accordingly, directives do require implementing measures to be taken by the national authorities, although, in practice, the discretion afforded to Member States as regards implementation is limited. In the United Kingdom directives are sometimes given effect through the adoption of primary legislation. However, s.2(2) of the European Communities Act 1972 enables Community obligations to be enacted in domestic law pursuant to statutory instrument and, in order to save Parliamentary time, many directives are given effect in the United Kingdom in this way.

A directive will almost invariably specify a time by which the Member States to which it is addressed must implement the directive into national law. Once the directive has been implemented correctly, the national implementing measure is the source of rights for individuals concerned. Indeed, if there is a sufficient remedy given by domestic law, it is unnecessary and impermissible to explore the same complaint under the equivalent provisions in a directive (*Blaik v Post Office* [1994] I.R.L.R. 280, EAT). Accordingly, it is only if there is a disparity between the two sources of rights that it becomes necessary to consider whether the provisions in EC law are directly enforceable by the complainant against the respondent. In addition to situations of incomplete or incorrect implementation, the underlying directive may also be of relevance where it is necessary to resolve ambiguity or other problems of interpretation in respect of the domestic implementing measure. When considering the meaning of the underlying Community legislation the relevant provision of Community law must be placed in its context and interpreted in the light of the provisions of Community law as a whole, taking account of the objective being pursued and the state of its evolution at the date at which the provision in question is to be applied (Case 283/81 *CILFIT Srl v Ministry of Health* [1982] E.C.R. 3415, ECJ). This purposive approach to the interpretation of Community law has been repeated on numerous occasions.

The Community institutions may also promulgate recommendations; for example Council Recommendation 86/379/EEC on the employment of disabled people in the Community, and Commission Recommendation 92/131/EEC (and Code of Practice) on the protection of the dignity of women and men at work. Article 249(5) of the EC Treaty provides that recommendations are not legally binding. Therefore they do not themselves confer rights on individuals that may be relied on before the national courts to override inconsistent provisions of domestic law (case 322/88 *Grimaldi v Fond des Maladies Professionelle* [1990] I.R.L.R. 400, ECJ; *Brumfit v Ministry of Defence* [2005] I.R.L.R. 4, EAT). Recommendations are generally adopted when the Community institutions do not have the power to adopt binding acts or when they consider that it is not appropriate to issue more constraining rules. However, recommendations may be taken into account when construing legislation adopted to reflect them or where they are designed to supplement binding Community measures (case 322/88 *Grimaldi v Fond des Maladies Professionelle*, above). The EAT adopted this approach to the recommendation on the protection of the dignity of women and men at work in *Wadman v Carpenter Farrar Partnership* [1993] I.R.L.R. 374, EAT.

Article 249(4) provides that a decision is binding in its entirety upon those to whom it is addressed. Decisions have played no substantial part in the development of EC employment law.

Enforcement of Community Law

Section 2(1) of the European Communities Act 1972 provides that rights and **14–005** obligations derived from the treaties and from secondary Community legislation made under the treaties are capable of being enforced directly in the courts and tribunals of the United Kingdom. Furthermore, enforceable Community rights override any rule of national law with which they conflict. This is known as the principle of supremacy. Accordingly, the courts and tribunals of the United Kingdom must set aside inconsistent domestic laws, including Acts of Parliament, in order to give effect to such rights (*R v Secretary of State for Transport, Ex p Factortame Ltd (No. 2)* [1991] 1 A.C. 603, HL; *Thoburn v Sunderland City Council; Hunt v Hackney LBC; Harman & Dove v Cornwall County Council; Collins v Sutton LBC* [2002] 3 W.L.R. 247, DC). For example, in *Marshall v Southampton and South West Hampshire Health Authority (No. 2)* [1994] 1 A.C. 530; [1994] I.C.R. 242, HL, following a reference to the European Court, the House of Lords held that the statutory limit and non payment of interest on compensation available in the employment tribunal for sex discrimination were incompatible with Council Directive 76/207/EEC (the Equal Treatment Directive). Ms Marshall was able to rely on the provisions of that directive as against her local authority employer to set aside the relevant national provisions. As result of this case, the domestic statutory provisions limiting the amount of compensation available for sex discrimination were removed and a statutory right to interest was enacted.

Direct effect

14–006   Community rights are enforceable in the courts and tribunals of the United Kingdom if they have direct effect. The concept of direct effect is one that has been created by the European Court and is quite complex. Essentially the criteria applied are whether the provision of Community law in question creates an unconditional and sufficiently precise obligation so that the national court may identify the scope and content of the right sought to be enforced without the need for implementing measures (case 8/81, *Becker v Finanzamt Munster-Innenstadt* [1982] E.C.R. 52, ECJ; Cases C-6/90 and 9/90 *Francovich v Italy* [1991] E.C.R. 5357, ECJ). Furthermore, if the provision is subject to a time limit before it comes into force, that time limit must have expired before the provision can be relied upon, although it does not matter if the factual situation relied upon by the individual arose before the deadline for implementation (Cases C-140–141/91 and C-278–279/91 *Suffritti v Istituto Razionale della Previdenza Sociale* (INPS) [1992] E.C.R. I–6337, ECJ; Cases C-87–89/90 *Verholen v Sociale Verzekeringsbank Amsterdam* [1991] E.C.R. I–3757, ECJ). This principle is particularly important in the case of directives where Member States are given a period of time (prescribed by the directive) in order to implement the directive.

Although a directive is not enforceable prior to the deadline given for its implementation it is capable of having some legal effect during that period. In particular during this period a Member State is under an obligation to refrain from taking any measure liable seriously to compromise the attainment of the result prescribed by that directive (case C-129/96 *Inter-Environnement Wallonie* [1997] E.C.R. I–7411, ECJ; case C-144/04 *Mangold v Helm* [2006] I.R.L.R. 143, ECJ). That obligation on the Member States applies as much to the national courts as to other domestic authorities (case C-212/04 *Adeneler v Ellinikos Organismos Galaktos* [2006] I.R.L.R. 716, ECJ). It is immaterial whether or not a domestic measure said to contravene this principle is concerned with the transposition of the directive (case C-14/02 *ATRAL* [2003] E.C.R. I–4431, ECJ; case C-144/04 *Mangold v Helm*, above; case C-212/04 *Adeneler v Ellinikos Organismos Galaktos*, above.) Furthermore, where the directive reflects a principle that is already regarded as a general principle of Community law, the European Court has recently held that it is the responsibility of the national court to provide the legal protection which individuals derive from the rules of Community law in question *prior* to the expiry of the transposition period (case C-144/04 *Mangold v Helm*, above). The implications of this ruling have yet to be worked out but are likely to be far-reaching; the directive in issue in

Mangold was Directive 2000/78, laying down a framework for combating discrimination on grounds of religion or belief, disability, age or sexual orientation, and the principle considered by the European Court to be already part of the general principles of Community law is the prohibition of discrimination on grounds of age.

A similar approach was also taken by the European Court in case C-246/06 *Josefa Valasco Navarro v Fondo de Garantia Salarial (Fogasa)*, judgment January 17, 2008, ECJ. In that case, the European Court confirmed that a directive could not be relied upon to create directly effective rights prior to the deadline given for its transposition, but then held that where national rules purport to cover the subject mater of the directive the lawfulness of such rules is conditional—from the date the directive enters into force—with general principles of Community law and fundamental rights, including the principle of equal treatment.

Horizontal and vertical direct effect

The concept of direct effect is complicated by the distinction between what is **14–007** called horizontal and vertical direct effect. Horizontal direct effect means that the provision can be enforced against all persons, including private individuals; i.e. the provision can impose obligations, as well as rights, on individuals. Vertical direct effect means that the provision can only be enforced against the State or against, what the European Court has termed an "emanation of the State". This means that the provision cannot impose obligations upon individuals.

Where the other conditions for direct effect are satisfied (as regards sufficiently precise and unconditional obligations), treaty provisions and regulations have both horizontal and vertical direct effect (case 43/75 *Defrenne v SABENA* [1976] E.C.R. 455, ECJ; case 36/74 *Walrave and Koch v Association Union Cycliste Internationale* [1974] E.C.R. 1405, ECJ); case C-438/05 *The International Transport Workers Federation & Finnish Seaman's Union v Viking Line ABP and Ou Viking Line Eesti*, judgment of December 11, 2007 (ECJ)).

On the other hand, directives only have vertical direct effect. The reason for this is that directives are addressed to Member States and are not therefore capable of imposing obligations upon individuals. Although directives are supposed to be implemented by national legislation, rather than being relied upon as a direct source of rights, where a Member State has either failed to transpose a directive by its implementation date, or has implemented it incorrectly, the Member State is not able to take advantage of the absence of rights from which the individual would have benefited had the directive been implemented correctly. Hence the individual is entitled to enforce the directive against the Member State (case 152/84 *Marshall v Southampton and South-West Hampshire Area Health Authority* (Teaching) [1986] E.C.R. 723, ECJ). For the purposes of enforcement it is irrelevant whether the body is acting in a private or public capacity.

The principle has been expanded so that it includes not only central government departments but also emanations of the State including local authorities, health authorities, tax authorities, independent bodies responsible for maintaining public order (such as the police), newly privatised industries, and voluntary aided schools (case 152/84 *Marshall v Southampton and South-West Hampshire Area Health Authority* (Teaching), above; case 222/84 *Johnston v Chief Constable of the Royal Ulster Constabulary* [1986] E.C.R. 1651, ECJ; *Griffin v South West Water Service* [1994] I.R.L.R. 15, Ch Div; *National Union of Teachers v Governing Body of St Mary's Church of England (Aided) Junior School* [1997] I.C.R. 334, CA). In *Foster v British Gas plc* [1990] E.C.R. I–3313 the European Court described the test as whether the body in question is subject to the authority or control of the State or has special powers beyond those which result from the normal rules applicable to relations between individuals. The judgment is confusing since in a different passage the European Court described the conditions as cumulative, rather than disjunctive. However it is suggested that it is unlikely that the European Court would apply a rigid, cumulative test in subsequent cases; in general terms the European Court is likely to consider the nature and extent of state control over the body in question in the context of the specific directive that the claimant is seeking to enforce against it.

The European Court recently affirmed this approach in case C-356/05 *Elaine Farrell v Alan Whitty*, Minister of the Environment, judgment of April 19, 2007 (ECJ) although it held that it had been provided with insufficient information to determine whether the body in question, the Motor Insurers' Bureau of Ireland was an emanation of the State for these purposes.

Until recently the European Court had remained consistent and clear in stating that directives could not have horizontal direct effect (case C-91/92 *Faccini Dori v Recreb Srl* [1994] E.C.R. I–3325, ECJ). However, the recent case of C-144/04 *Mangold v Helm*, above, throws some doubt on this principle; the ruling of the European Court appears to have the effect of enabling the claimant to enforce the principle of non-discrimination on grounds of age set out in Directive 2000/78 against his private employer, and hence horizontally. The implications of this ruling have yet to be considered by the courts. In *Adeneler v Ellinikos Organismos Galaktos*, above, the lack of any reference to horizontal direct effect in the Court's discussion of the duty on the national court to interpret national law in accordance, so far as possible, with Community law might suggest that the judgment in *Mangold* was not intended to cast doubt on its previous case-law. Moreover, recently in *Elaine Farrell v Alan Whitty, Minister of the Environment*, (C-356/05) above, and *Carp SNC v Ecorad SRL* (C-80/06), judgment of June 7, 2007 (ECJ), the European Court reaffirmed its traditional position that a directive cannot, of itself, impose obligations on an individual, and cannot therefore be relied upon as such against an individual. Accordingly, even a clear, precise and unconditional provision of a directive seeking to confer rights or impose obligations on individuals cannot, of itself, apply in proceedings exclusively between private parties.

Partial direct effect

14–008   Where a provision of Community law is capable of creating directly enforceable rights in certain circumstances, but further implementing measures are needed to prescribe the intended effect of the measure in all areas where it is contemplated as having effect, it may be regarded as having partial direct effect. In *Defrenne v SABENA*, above, the European Court ruled that Art.119 (now 141) of the EC Treaty, which guarantees equal pay for equal work, had direct effect in respect of overt discrimination which could be identified solely with the aid of the criteria based on equal work and equal pay referred to in that article (see also *Worringham and Humphreys v Lloyds Bank* [1981] E.C.R. 767; [1982] I.R.L.R. 74; [1982] I.C.R. 299, ECJ). However, the article is not directly effective in respect of covert discrimination, where more explicit implementing provisions are required to identify the prohibited conduct. Accordingly, a woman cannot rely on Art.141 where the discrimination alleged arises in respect of two jobs which are not identical but are said to be of equal value; the concept of work for equal value requires further elucidation of the criteria by which equal value is to be assessed (case 157/86 *Murphy v Bord Telecom Eirann* [1988] E.C.R. 673, ECJ). However, Art.141 can be relied upon to bring a claim of indirect discrimination, where a requirement appears to apply equally to men and women but in practice the proportion of one sex who can comply with the requirement is considerably less than the other, and the requirement cannot be objectively justified. In these cases the discrimination can be identified from the facts and Art.141 is directly effective (*Jenkins v Kingsgate (Clothing Productions) Ltd* [1980] I.R.L.R. 6; [1981] E.C.R. 911, ECJ).

A similar approach has been taken in the context of the Equal Treatment Directive (Directive 76/207). Article 3(1), which prohibits discrimination in the conditions including selection criteria for access to jobs, and Art.5(1), which applies the principle of equal treatment to working conditions, including conditions covering dismissal, are directly effective in the national courts (case 152/84 *Marshall v Southampton and South-West Hampshire Area Health Authority* (Teaching), above; case 222/84 *Johnston v Chief Constable of the Royal Ulster Constabulary* [1986] E.C.R. 1651, ECJ). However Art.6, which ensures that Member States shall introduce measures to enable an individual to pursue a claim of unlawful discrimination by judicial process, is partially directly effective in that it confers a directly effective right to an effective judicial remedy but not a right to any particular sanction (case 14/83 *Von Colson and Kamann v Land Nordrhein-Westfalen* [1984] E.C.R. 1891, ECJ; case 222/84 *Johnston v Chief Constable of the Royal Ulster Constabulary*, above).

The right to an effective remedy

Traditionally the European Court has regarded the manner in which national **14–009** courts protect Community rights as a matter of national, and not Community law, on the basis that the EC Treaty is not intended to create new remedies in the national courts to ensure the observance of Community law (case 158/80 *Rewe v Hauptzollamt Kiel* [1981] E.C.R. 1805, ECJ).

This approach is subject to two provisos. The first is that the procedural conditions in which a Community right is exercised, and the substantive remedies which may be obtained in the event of a breach, must not be less favourable than the procedural conditions and substantive remedies which apply to equivalent claims under national law. Similarity depends on whether the purpose, cause of action and essential characteristics of the proceedings are similar (case C-78/98 *Preston v Wolverhampton Healthcare NHS Trust* [2001] 2 W.L.R. 448; [2001] I.R.L.R. 237; [2001] I.C.R. 217, HL). In *Alabaster v Barclays Bank plc and Secretary of State for Social Security (No. 2)* [2005] I.R.L.R. 576 the Court of Appeal held that the claimant was entitled to bring her claim for equal pay in respect of the earnings-related element of her statutory maternity pay under s.1 of the Equal Pay Act 1970 rather than s.13 of the Employment Rights Act 1996 since the latter remedy did not satisfy the EC principle of equality, equivalence and effectiveness.

The second proviso is that the national rules must not make it impossible in practice to exercise the Community rights in question (case 33/76 *Rewe v Landwirtschaftskammer Saarland* [1976] E.C.R. 1989, ECJ; case 45/76 *Comet v Produktschap voor Siergewassen* [1976] E.C.R. 2043, ECJ; case C-246/96 *Magorrian and Cunningham v Eastern Health and Social Services Board* [1997] E.C.R. I–7153, ECJ; case C-472/99 *Clean Car Autoservice GmbH v City of Vienna and Austria* [2001] E.C.R. I–9687, ECJ; and case C-78/98 *Preston v Wolverhampton Healthcare NHS Trust*, above). In *Levez v Jennings* [1998] E.C.R. I–7835; [1999] I.R.L.R. 764; [2000] I.C.R. 58, ECJ the claimant alleged that a provision of the Equal Pay Act 1970, which restricted arrears of remuneration to two years preceding the date on which the proceedings were instituted, was incompatible with Community law. The claimant had been unable to bring her claim during part of the relevant period because her employer had concealed from her the amount of pay earned by her male comparator. The European Court held that in these circumstances to allow the employer to rely on the two year limitation would be manifestly incompatible with the principle of effectiveness and the claimant could rely upon the direct effect of Art.141 of the EC Treaty to set it aside. Similarly, in *Preston v Wolverhampton Healthcare NHS Trust* above, the same rule prevented part-time workers claiming a right to retroactive membership of a pension scheme before two years preceding the commencement of proceedings, and thus prevented the entire service record of those concerned from being taken into account for the purpose of calculating benefits payable after the date of the claim. The claimants were therefore able to set the rule aside on the grounds that it made the exercise of their directly effective Art.141 rights impossible in practice. The provision of the Equal Pay Act 1970 which was at issue was subsequently amended to comply with these judgments.

In more recent cases the European Court has laid greater emphasis on the obligation of the national courts to ensure the full and effective protection of Community law rights. In *Adeneler v Ellinikos Organismos Galaktos*, above, the European Court stated that a measure offering effective and equivalent guarantees for the protection of workers must be capable of being applied in order to punish the prohibited conduct and nullify the breach of Community law. Although in that case the European Court held that it was for the national court to rule on the question of whether the domestic law at issue complied with that requirement it has, on other occasions, decided that rules of national law undermine the effective protection of Community rights and must therefore be set aside (case C-326/96 *Levez v Jennings*, above; case C-78/98 *Preston v Wolverhampton Healthcare NHS Trust* [2000] E.C.R. I–3201, ECJ).

There are, however, limits to the principle of effectiveness. In *Unibet (London) Ltd v Justitiekanslern* (C-432/05) judgment of March 13, 2007 (ECJ), the European Court ruled that the principle of effective judicial protection of an individual's rights under Community law did not require the national legal order of a Member State to provide for the possibility of a free-standing declaration as to whether the national legal provisions were compatible with Community law, provided that other effective legal remedies, which were no less favourable than those governing similar domestic actions, made it possible for such a question of compatibility to be determined as a preliminary issue. Furthermore, it had to be possible, under the legal order of a Member State, to obtain interim relief until the competent court had given a ruling on whether national provisions were compatible with Community law where the grant of such relief was necessary to ensure the full effectiveness of the final judgment. The relevant criteria for the grant of interim relief were those laid down by national law, provided that those criteria were not less favourable than those applying to similar domestic actions, and did not render practically impossible or excessively difficult the interim protection of those rights. Further, in joined cases 222/05–225/05, *Jan Van der Weerd v Minister Van Landbouw, Natuur en Voedselk-waliteit*, judgment of June 7, 2007 (ECJ), the European Court held that the principle of effectiveness did not require the national court of its own motion to raise a plea based on Community law, irrespective of the importance of that provision to the Community legal order, so long as the parties had a genuine opportunity to raise such plea before the national court.

Time limits

14–010   The rights enforced in employment tribunals are domestic rights and Community law is used to set aside incompatible provisions of domestic law, rather than create free-standing Community law claims. Accordingly, where Community law is relied upon the applicable time limits remain those contained in the relevant domestic provisions, subject to compliance with the principles that: (1) they are no more restrictive that those which apply to other analogous domestic law claims (*Preston v Wolverhampton Healthcare NHS Trust*, above; *Alabaster v Barclays Bank plc and Secretary of State for Social Security (No. 2)*, above; *Ben Byrne v (1) Motor Insurers Bureau (2) Secretary of State for Transport* [2007] 3 ALL ER 499; *Local Authorities Mutual Investments Trust v Customs and Excise Commrs* [2004] STC 246,) and (2) they do not make the enforcement of the rights impossible in practice (case 33/76 *Rewe v Land-wirtschaftskammer Saarland*, above; C-128/93 *Fisscher v Voorhuis Hengelo BV* [1994] E.C.R. I–4583, ECJ; C-125/01, *Pflucke v Bundesanstalt v fur arbeit*, above, judgment of September 18, 2003, ECJ).

For several years complications arose as a result of the decision of the European Court that where a Member State has failed to implement a directly effective directive correctly, the time-limit applicable under the analogous domestic law claim will only start to run once the State has rectified that failure (C-208/90 *Emmott v Minister for Social Welfare and the Attorney General* [1991] E.C.R. I–4269, ECJ). Subsequently the question arose as to whether the same principle applied to claims alleging incorrect implementation of Art.141 of the EC Treaty. After some confusion in the EAT the Court of Appeal held that it did not (*Cannon v Barnsley Metropolitan Borough Council* [1992] I.R.L.R. 474; [1992] I.C.R. 698, EAT; *Rankin v British Coal* [1993] I.R.L.R. 69; [1995] I.C.R. 774, EAT; *Biggs v Somerset County Council* [1995] I.R.L.R. 452; [1995] I.C.R. 811, EAT; [1996] I.R.L.R. 203; [1996] I.C.R. 364, CA). Further complications arose when the European Court held that the principle in *Emmott* did not apply to domestic limits on arrears of pay or benefits, since these limits did not prevent the action from being brought but merely restricted the number of years for which benefits could be claimed retrospectively (case C-338/91 *Steenhorst-Neerings v Bestruur van de Bedrijfsvereniging voor Detailhandel, Ambachten en Huisvrouwen* [1993] E.C.R. I–5475, ECJ). This troublesome issue finally disappeared when the European Court held that its decision in *Emmott* was restricted to its own facts (case C-188/95 *Fantask A/S v Industrieministeriet (Ehrvervministeriet)* [1997] E.C.R. I–6783, ECJ). Subsequently in *Secretary of State for Work & Pensions v Walker-Fox, The Times*, December 8, 2005, the Court of Appeal held that the principles enunciated in *Emmott* should be confined to very exceptional circumstances, namely, where in some unconscionable way the state had obstructed the exercise of the individual's judicial remedy or contributed to his failure to exercise it; (see also *Frederick Thomas Poole v HM Treasury* (2006) 2 C.L.C.865). *Fantask* was recently considered by the House of Lords in *Michael Flemming (t/a Bodycraft) v Customs and Excise Commissioners* [2008] 1 WLR 195, in a situation where the legislature had introduced a retrospective time limit without a reasonable transition period for making repayment claims under the Value Added Tax Regulations 1995. The House of Lords held that in such circumstances the retrospective time limit could not be enforced in relation to an accrued right, otherwise there would be a breach of EC law. Where there was no adequate transitional period it was for the courts to fashion the remedy necessary to avoid an infringement of EC law, and the remedy would normally be to disapply the retrospective application of the new time limit, perhaps only for a short period, to claims based on accrued rights.

Interpretation of national legislation

14–011

When interpreting national law there is an obligation on domestic courts and tribunals to interpret, so far as possible, national law in a way that is consistent with Community law. The requirement for national law to be interpreted in conformity with Community law is inherent in the system of the Treaty, since it permits national courts to ensure the full effectiveness of Community law when they determine a dispute before them (see joined cases C-397/01–C-403/01 *Pfeiffer v Deutsches Rotes Kreuz* [2004] E.C.R. I–8835, ECJ; case C-212/04 *Adeneler v Ellinikos Organismos Galaktos*, above). If the Community law in question is based on a directive the obligation applies whether or not the national law was specifically enacted for the purposes of implementing the directive and whether or not the national law was enacted before or after the directive (case C-106/89 *Marleasing SA v La Commercial de Alimentacion* SA [1990] E.C.R. I–4135, ECJ; Case C-160/01 *Mau v Bundesanstalt fur Arbeit* [2003] E.C.R. I–4791, ECJ; joined cases C-397/01–C-403/01 *Pfeiffer v Deutsches Rotes Kreuz*, above). Where a directive is transposed belatedly, the obligation on the national courts to interpret domestic law in conformity with the directive exists only once the period for its transposition has expired (case C-212/04 *Adeneler v Ellinikos Organismos Galaktos*, above). However, applying the principle set out in case C-129/96 *Inter-Environnement Wallonie*, above, the European Court has held that from the date upon which a directive has entered into force the national courts must refrain, as far as possible, from interpreting domestic law in a manner which might seriously compromise, after the period for transposition has expired, the attainment of the objective pursued by the directive (case C-212/04 *Adeneler v Ellinikos Organismos Galaktos*, above).

This obligation goes further than merely requiring that legislation that is capable of bearing a number of meanings be interpreted in a manner consistent with Community law. It requires the courts to depart from normal rules of construction in order to give the domestic law a meaning that accords with Community law. In *Webb v EMO Air Cargo (No. 2)* [1995] 1 W.L.R. 1454; [1995] I.C.R. 1021; [1995] I.R.L.R. 645 the House of Lords were able to bring dismissal on grounds of pregnancy within the comparative language of s.1(1)(a) and s.5(3) of the Sex Discrimination Act 1975 in order to comply with a ruling of the European Court on the scope of the Equal Treatment Directive. (See too *Alabaster v Barclays Bank plc and Secretary of State for Social Security (No. 2)*, above.) In *Litster v Forth Dry Dock and Engineering Co* [1989] 2 W.L.R. 634 the House of Lords read additional words into reg.5(3) of the Transfer of Undertakings (Protection of Employment) Regulations 1981 in order to comply with a ruling of the European Court on the scope of Directive 77/187/EC. More recently, in *X v Stevens (Commissioner Metropolitan Police Service)* [2003] I.R.L.R. 411; [2003] I.C.R. 1031 and *Chief Constable of West Yorkshire Police v A* [2000] I.R.L.R. 465, the EAT held that the predecessor to what is now r.50(1) of Sch.1 of the Employment Tribunals (Constitution and Rules of Procedure) Regulations 2004 must be read so as to empower tribunals to make restricted reporting orders in cases involving allegations of discrimination or harassment on account of gender reassignment in order to comply with Art.6 of Directive 76/207 (the Equal Treatment Directive).

Accordingly, if there is an issue as regards compatibility of domestic law with Community law but the Community right is not enforceable by the claimant against the respondent, that deficiency can often be remedied by a purposive interpretation of the domestic law; if the national law can be construed in a manner compatible with Community law then there is no need to invoke the Community right itself, other than as an aid to construction. However, the obligation is only to construe national law so far as possible to comply with Community law and the national courts are not obliged to distort national legislation or to interpret it "*contra legem*" in order to give effect to Community law (see the Opinion of Advocate General Van Gerven in case C-106/89 *Marleasing SA v La Commercial de Alimentacion SA*, above; case C-212/04 *Adeneler v Ellinikos Organismos Galaktos*, above).

The principle that domestic legislation must be interpreted, so far as possible, in conformity with Community obligations, does not apply to a private law agreement; *Ben Byrne v (1) Motor Insurers Bureau (2) Secretary of State for Transport*, above, applying *White (Brian) v White* (1999) 1 C.M.L.R. 1251.

Damages against the State

14–012   In circumstances where a directive is intended to give rights to individuals but is not properly implemented, those individuals may have a claim for damages against the Member State for breach of its Community law obligations (joined cases C-6/90 and C-9/90 *Francovich v Italy*, above) In this respect it is insufficient for an individual to have an interest in the implementation of the directive; a claimant must identify a right which must necessarily have been granted to the claimant in order to achieve the results required by the directive (*Frederick Thomas Poole v HM Treasury* (2006), above). Further, in order for the claim to succeed the breach must be sufficiently serious. This is determined by factors such as the clarity and precision of the Community law obligation and the breadth of the discretion afforded to the Member States. If the relevant provision was enacted in an area in which a wide discretion is reserved to the Member States then the breach must be manifest and grave. That test is likely to be satisfied where the breach is intentional, where a Member State fails to take account of a decision of the European Court or where it has failed to take any steps to implement the directive prior to the deadline specified for implementation (case C–46/93 *Brasserie du Pecheur SA v Germany* [1996] E.C.R. I–1029, ECJ; case C–178/94 *Dillenkofer v Germany* [1996] E.C.R. I–4845, ECJ; *R v Secretary of State for Transport, Ex parte Factortame (No. 5)* [1999] 3 W.L.R. 1062; [1999] 2 All E.R. 640, HL; Case C–278/05 *Robins and Barnett v Secretary of State for Work and Pensions*, judgment of European Court of Justice, January 25, 2007.) It is not necessary for a claimant to exhaust other domestic remedies before making a claim for *Francovich damages (Spencer v Secretary of State for Work and Pensions* [2007] EWHC 1775 (QB), judgment 27 July 2007 (QBD). However the employment tribunal has no jurisdiction to hear such claims for damages (*Secretary of State for Employment v Mann* [1996] I.R.L.R. 4 EAT; [1997] I.R.L.R. 21; [1997] I.C.R. 209, CA; see below).

Jurisdiction of employment tribunal to hear EC claims

The employment tribunal has no inherent jurisdiction. Its statutory jurisdiction is **14–013** confined to complaints that may be made to it under specific statutes (*Secretary of State for Scotland v Mann* [2001] I.C.R. 1005, EAT; since employment tribunals have no jurisdiction in electoral matters they could not hear complaints of sex discrimination by a candidate in an election to the Scottish Parliament). There is no jurisdiction conferred on them under statute to hear and determine disputes about Community law generally. The Court of Appeal has therefore held that there is no jurisdiction in the tribunal to hear claims based on Community law that have an existence that is separate from domestic law. Accordingly, even if Art.141 (then 119) of the EC Treaty provided a claim for compensation for unfair dismissal, or a right to a redundancy payment, the employment tribunal had no jurisdiction to hear it (*Biggs v Somerset County Council*, above; *Barber v Staffordshire County Council* [1996] I.R.L.R. 209; [1996] I.C.R. 379, CA).

Nevertheless, in the exercise of its jurisdiction the employment tribunal may apply Community law. The application of Community law may have the effect of displacing provisions in domestic law statutes that are incompatible with Community law and thus giving effect in the tribunal to directly effective Community rights. The jurisdictional limit of the employment tribunal therefore has little practical effect on the enforcement of Community law in the employment field. However, one limitation is that as the jurisdiction of the employment tribunal is defined solely by statute it has no jurisdiction to hear and determine claims for damages against the State for failing to implement Community legislation; since there is no UK statute permitting damages claims against the State to be brought in employment tribunals, there is no basis for the exercise of such power (*Secretary of State for Employment v Mann* above, sub nom *Potter v Secretary of State for Employment* [1997] I.R.L.R. 209, CA). In the UK damages claims against the State must be brought in the High Court or County Court.

An employment tribunal has no jurisdiction to hear a claim by a person for employment with a Community institution. Article 236 of the EC Treaty, which gives the European Court jurisdiction "in any dispute between the Community and its servants" confers sole jurisdiction on the European Court, and covers not only claims by existing or former employees, but also claims for employment (*Maidment v EC Commission* [1999] I.C.R. 577, EAT).

Article 234 of the EC Treaty

The Court of Justice shall have jurisdiction to give preliminary **14–014** **rulings concerning:**

(a) the interpretation of this Treaty;

(b) the validity and interpretation of acts of the institutions of the Community and of the ECB;

(c) the interpretation of the statutes of bodies established by an act of the Council, where those statutes so provide.

Where such a question is raised before any court or tribunal of a Member State, that court or tribunal may, if it considers that a decision on the question is necessary to enable it to give judgment, request the Court of Justice to give a ruling thereon.

Where any such question is raised in a case pending before a court or tribunal of a Member State against whose decisions there is no judicial remedy under national law, that court or tribunal shall bring the matter before the Court of Justice.

References to the European Court

14–015   Article 234 of the EC Treaty provides a mechanism by which national courts and tribunals may refer questions of European law for determination by the European Court. A reference is made during the course of proceedings in the national court and obtaining a ruling from the European Court is not, of itself, a remedy but a step in the proceedings that enables the national court to give judgment in the case before it. The ruling given, sometimes called a preliminary ruling, is binding on the national court and, in practice, on all the courts in the European Union (European Communities Act 1972, s.3(1); case 33/76, *Rewe v Landwirtschaftskammer Saarland* [1976] E.C.R. 1989, ECJ). The European Court has given guidance to the national courts on making references: Information Note on References from National Courts for a Preliminary Ruling, Official Journal, 2005/ C 143/01 ("Information Note").

(A supplement to that Information Note now gives guidance to the national court where an urgent preliminary ruling is requested, but since it only applies to references concerning the areas of freedom, security and justice it will not have any application to employment law cases.)

The purpose of the reference procedure is two-fold. First, to guarantee the uniform interpretation and application of European law by ensuring that only one supreme judicial body has jurisdiction to provide definitive guidance as to the meaning of the law (case 6/64, *Costa v ENEL* [1964] E.C.R. 585, ECJ; case 28/67, *Molkerei-Zentrale Westfalen v Hauptzollamt Paderborn* [1968] E.C.R. 143, ECJ). Secondly, to enable parties who would not have standing to challenge the legality of secondary Community legislation directly to bring such issues before the European Court by way of a request for a preliminary ruling. Indeed, if the validity of secondary Community legislation is raised in domestic proceedings then the matter *must* be referred to the European Court because the national courts have no jurisdiction to declare secondary Community legislation invalid (case C-314/85 *Foto-Frost v Hauptzollamt Lubeck-Ost* [1987] E.C.R. 4199, ECJ; Case C-408/95 *Eurotunnel SA v Sea France* [1997] E.C.R. I–6315, ECJ).

A reference to the European Court involves a three-stage process. First, the national court or tribunal must make all the findings of fact necessary to enable the European Court to give a ruling on the case before it. Secondly, on the reference itself, the European Court will give a preliminary ruling on the questions of law that have been referred to it. Finally, after the European Court has made a preliminary ruling, the matter comes back to the national court (the same one that made the reference) and the national court then applies the law as clarified by the European Court to the facts of the case before it.

Nature of question referred

Under Art.234(1) the European Court has jurisdiction to give rulings on the interpretation of the EC Treaty, the validity and interpretation of secondary Community legislation, and also (less commonly) the interpretation of the statutes of bodies established by an act of the Council. The European Court's jurisdiction is therefore limited to giving definitive rulings on questions of law and does not extend to making findings of fact (save in so far as it may declare a particular piece of Community legislation to be invalid). It is the responsibility of the national courts to find the relevant facts and to apply European law, as it has been interpreted by the European Court, to those facts (case 13/68 *Salgoil S.p.A. v Italian Ministry for Foreign Trade* [1968] E.C.R. 453, ECJ; Information Note, above, at para.5).

14–016

Discretion to refer

Article 234(2) confers a discretionary power on a national court or tribunal to refer any question on a matter falling within the scope of the provision to the European Court. A national court or tribunal may refer a question to the European Court as soon as it finds that a ruling on a point of Community law is necessary to enable it to give judgment. The decision to refer is essentially a matter for the discretion of the national court, although Art.234(2) requires that a decision on the question of European law must be necessary to enable the national court to give judgment. It is not necessary that a reference to the European Court will dispose of all the issues between the parties, a reference may be made even if some issues may be outstanding after the European Court has given judgment.

14–017

A number of factors are relevant to the question of whether the national court or tribunal should exercise its discretion to refer. The first is the extent to which the national court can be confident in its judgment on the issue of Community law that has arisen. The UK courts have generally taken a cautious approach and referred matters which are not free from doubt, even where they have formed a clear view themselves as to the likely answers to the questions raised. For example, in *R v Secretary of State for Trade and Industry Ex parte Trade Union Congress* [2000] I.R.L.R. 565 the Divisional Court referred the question of whether the Maternity and Parental Leave Regulations 1999 properly implemented the Parental Leave Directive. Whilst the Divisional Court considered that the arguments on behalf of the TUC were likely to prevail it was not persuaded that the matter was so clear that the point should be decided without guidance from the European Court. It was influenced by the fact that the point at issue concerned a number of other Member States, that proceedings before the European Court had the advantage that representations may be made by the European Commission, the Council and the Member States, and that it would be "inherently undesirable" that it should give a ruling that turned out to be inconsistent with a decision in another Member State or future decision of the European Court.

The second issue is the appropriate point in time at which a reference should be made. A difficult balance has to be struck between ensuring, on the one hand, that a reference to the European Court is really necessary, and that sufficient facts have been found to determine the legal and factual context in which the question of European law arises and, on the other, avoiding unnecessary delay in making the reference. Lower courts and tribunals whose decisions are subject to appeal, such as the employment tribunal and employment appeal tribunal, normally consider that it is more appropriate for the Court of Appeal or House of Lords to take the decision as to whether a reference is necessary and, if so, the questions which need to be referred. However, the difficulty with this approach is that if a reference is in fact found to be necessary this will only have added to the delay and expense incurred in resolving the case: in *Preston v Wolverhampton Healthcare Trust* [2000] I.R.L.R. 506 a reference was not made until the case reached the House of Lords although the uncertainty over the application of Community law had been apparent from a much earlier stage; *cf Jenkins v Kingsgate (Clothing Productions) Ltd*, above, where the reference was made by the EAT. The period of time between making a reference and receiving the judgment of the European Court typically takes 18 months and can often take two years. In these circumstances it may well be less costly and more time efficient for a reference to be made at an earlier stage of the proceedings, as soon as the question of European law that is in issue has been identified and the factual context in which that question arises is clear. The European Court has said that the precise stage at which a reference is to be made is a question for the national court (case 107/76 *Hoffman-La Roche v Centrafarm* [1977] E.C.R. 957; Information Note, above, at paras 18–19).

In *Attridge Law (A Firm) v Coleman* [2007] I.C.R. 654, [2007] I.R.L.R. 88, an appeal from a decision of an employment judge to refer a question to the European Court as regard the proper interpretation of the Equal Treatment Framework Directive 2000/78, failed. The EAT held that a reference was necessary, not solely where, whichever way the point was decided, it was conclusive of the case, but also where it was required to do justice. In that instance the employment judge had been entitled to conclude, in the proper exercise of her discretion, that it was necessary to obtain a ruling of the European Court in order to determine a preliminary issue, namely the proper interpretation of the Directive, before deciding whether the Disability Discrimination Act 1995 should be construed in the way contended by the claimant. By contrast, a recent example of a reference being made at the last stage of the domestic system is *Inland Revenue Commissioners v Stringer*, judgment of House of Lords of December 13, 2006, when questions of the interpretation of Directive 2003/78, on the organisation of working time, concerning the right to annual leave granted by art.7 of the Directive and its relation to employees on sick leave, were not referred to the European Court until the matter reached the House of Lords.

The EAT has held that an employment tribunal errs if it tries to speculate as to the outcome of a reference to the European Court on the same matter in another case; an employment tribunal should stay a claim pending a preliminary ruling by the European Court rather than try to prejudge the European Court's decision: *A Johns v Solend SD Ltd* [2008] I.R.L.R. 88.

Obligation to refer under Article 234(3)

14–018   Article 234(3) imposes a duty to refer on courts or tribunals "against whose decisions there is no judicial remedy under national law". The provision ensures that, save in specified circumstances, all courts of last resort refer questions of European law to the European court and this obligation thus guards against the possibility of a body of case-law developing in a Member State which is at variance with the rest of the Community.

There are three exceptions to the obligation to refer under Art.234(3). First, where the correct application of European law is *acte clair*, that is to say it is so obvious as to leave no scope for any reasonable doubt as to the manner in which the question of European law is to be resolved (case 283/81 *C.I.L.F.I.T. Srl v Ministry of Health* [1982] E.C.R. 3415, ECJ). Secondly, where the question raised is materially identical to a previous question already the subject of a reference (case 28–30/62 *Da Costa en Shaake NV v Nederlandse Belastingadministratie* [1963] E.C.R. 31, ECJ). Thirdly, a court which takes a decision in interlocutory proceedings is not obliged to refer, provided that the decision on the European law point does not bind the court that subsequently hears the main action, and that either party is in a position to ensure that the proceedings in the main action are in fact instituted (case 35–36/82 *Morson and Jhanhan v Netherlands* [1982] E.C.R. 3723, ECJ).

There is considerable case-law identifying which courts fall within the scope of Art.243(3), which is outside the scope of this work. The House of Lords obviously is covered by Art.234(3). It is also clear that the Court of Appeal is not covered by the obligation in circumstances where it grants permission to appeal its decision to the House of Lords (since in those circumstances there is a judicial remedy available against its decision). In circumstances where the Court of Appeal refuses permission to appeal the position is less clear cut; the current position is that the Court of Appeal is not, in those circumstances, to be regarded as a court of last resort because of the possibility of petitioning the House of Lords for permission to appeal (*R v Pharmaceutical Society of Great Britain, Ex p. Association of Pharmaceutical Importers* [1987] 3 C.M.L.R. 951; *R v Licensing Authority, Ex p. Smith Kline & French Laboratories* [1989] 3 C.M.L.R 301). The same reasoning would apply in circumstances where the EAT refuses permission to appeal to the Court of Appeal. Accordingly, the employment tribunal and employment appeal tribunal do not fall within the scope of Art.243(3).

Procedure for making the reference

If an employment tribunal makes a reference the procedure is for the Secretary of the tribunals to send a copy of the tribunal's order making the reference to the Registrar of the European Court (2004 Rules, r.58.) The previous rules had provided that a reference could only be made after the time limit for appealing the employment tribunal's decision had expired, or an appeal had been heard, but the 2004 Rules contain no such restriction as to when the reference may be made. The EAT has no specific rules regarding the making of references but the appropriate procedure for it to follow is set out in RSC Ord.114 (contained in Sch.1 to the Civil Procedure Rules). Paragraph 5(1) of RSC Ord.114 also provides that a copy of the order making the reference must be sent to the Register of the European Court. The address is: Registry of the Court of Justice of the European Communities, L-2925, Luxembourg (telephone +352–4303–1).

14–019

As a matter of good practice, and as set out in r.3 of RSC Ord.114, the order for reference should set out in a judgment a statement of the grounds for reference and separately, in a schedule to the judgment, the request for the preliminary ruling itself. It should be possible to understand the question(s) referred without reference to the statement of the grounds (Information Note at para.24). Further at paras 21–22 the Information Note points out that owing to the need to translate the order for reference it should be drafted simply, clearly and precisely, avoiding superfluous detail; a maximum of about ten pages is usually sufficient to set out in a proper manner the context of the reference and contain all the relevant information to give the Court (and the parties entitled to submit observations) a clear understanding of the factual and legal context of the main proceedings. In particular the order for reference must:

- include a brief account of the subject matter of the dispute and the relevant findings of fact, or, at least, set out the factual situation on which the question referred is based;
- set out the tenor of any applicable national provisions and identify, where necessary, the relevant national case-law, giving in each case precise references;
- identify the Community provisions relevant to the case as accurately as possible;
- explain the reasons which prompted the national court to raise the question of the interpretation of validity of the Community provisions, and the relationship between those provisions and the national provisions applicable to the main proceedings;

EU Law Claims

– include, where appropriate, a summary of the main arguments of the parties.

Finally the referring court may, if it considers itself to be in a position to do so, briefly state its view on the answer to be given to the questions referred (Information Note at para.23). The proceedings will normally be stayed until the European Court has given its judgment.

Once received by the European Court the case is assigned to one of its chambers and to one of the Advocates General (who is not a judge of the Court but has equivalent status). The parties, the European Commission and all the Member States are invited to submit written observations on the matter referred and the case is then set down for a short oral hearing in the language of the referring court. After the conclusion of the hearing the Advocate General produces an Opinion, which is not legally binding but is for the benefit of the judges assigned to hear the case. The parties have no opportunity to comment on the Opinion. The relevant chamber of the Court subsequently produces its judgment and delivers it in open court.

CHAPTER 15

THE APPLICATION OF THE HUMAN RIGHTS ACT 1998 IN THE EMPLOYMENT TRIBUNAL AND FAIR TRIAL RIGHTS

Contents
SECT.

The European Convention on Human Rights

The European Convention on Human Rights ("the Convention") is an inter- **15–001** national treaty which was drawn up in 1950 and came into force in 1953. The Convention sets out, in statements of broad principle, a number of fundamental rights and freedoms. It also established the European Commission of Human Rights and the European Court of Human Rights, both situated in Strasbourg. Under the Convention an individual who has exhausted all available domestic remedies, but has been unable to obtain redress, has the right to bring a direct complaint before the Strasbourg institutions. Until the Eleventh Protocol, which came into force on November 1, 1998, the complainant first presented a petition to the European Commission of Human Rights. If, after investigation, the Commission decided that there was, or may have been a breach of the Convention and that the matter was admissible, the matter was referred, together with the Commission's report, to the European Court of Human Rights. However, the procedures were changed by the Eleventh Protocol which removed the process before the European Commission so that the European Court of Human Rights now decides both whether the application is admissible and whether the complaint is well-founded.

The Government of the UK ratified the Convention in 1950. However, it was not until 1966 that it recognised the jurisdiction of the European Court of Human Rights and accepted the right of an individual in the UK to petition the Court. Furthermore, until the Human Rights Act 1998 came into force on October 2, 2000 the Convention did not have effect as a matter of domestic law but bound only the Government as a matter of international law. Accordingly, a victim of an alleged violation of a Convention right had no direct means of redress in the domestic courts and could only bring his complaint before the Strasbourg institutions. However, the position changed when the Human Rights Act 1998 came into force and "brought rights home" in the sense that it created the necessary legislative structure to enable Convention rights to be enforced by complainants against public authorities directly in the domestic courts of the UK.

The Human Rights Act 1998

The Human Rights Act 1998 received the Royal Assent on November 9, 1998 and **15–002** came into force on October 2, 2000. The Act does not directly incorporate the Convention into domestic law by creating a statutory bill of rights. Section 1 lists those articles of the Convention to which Act applies, and they are set out as Sch.1 to the Act. Section 2 is concerned with the interpretation of Convention rights and provides that a court or tribunal determining a question in connection with a Convention right must take into account relevant judgments, decisions, declarations and opinions of the Commission and Court of Human Rights, and the Committee of Ministers of the Council of Europe, which aims to ensure an interpretation of Convention rights by the domestic courts which is consistent with the Strasbourg institutions. An example of the application of that principle is *X v Y* [2004] I.R.L.R. 625; [2004] I.C.R. 1634 when the Court of Appeal, applying s.2 of the Human Rights Act, took account of the fact that the right to respect for private life under Art.8 of the Convention had been interpreted by the Strasbourg institutions to cover a person's "sexual orientation and sexual life", and the right of a person to establish relationships with others.

Section 6 makes it unlawful for a public authority to act in way which is incompatible with Convention rights, unless it could not have acted differently as a result of a statutory provision; s.7 provides that a person who claims that a public authority has acted, or proposes to act, in a way which is incompatible with a Convention right may, if he is a victim of that act, bring proceedings against the public authority in the appropriate court of tribunal, or rely on the Convention rights concerned in any proceedings. The Act thus incorporates the Convention indirectly whilst preserving and respecting the principle of Parliamentary sovereignty. However, the mechanism of indirect incorporation is greatly strengthened by the enactment in s.3 of a statutory rule of construction which requires that the courts interpret domestic legislation in accordance with the Convention, so far as it is possible to do so, and the provision in s.4 for a "declaration of incompatibility" to be made by (certain defined) courts if legislation cannot be made compatible with the Convention. The Act further provides in s.10 for a fast track remedial mechanism to amend any legislation that is declared to be incompatible.

Since s.6(3)(a) states that courts and tribunals are public authorities within the meaning of s.6(1), the employment tribunal and the EAT are under a specific duty to act in a way which is compatible with Convention rights. This obligation mainly bites in the context of the right under Art.6(1) of the Convention to a fair trial and the corresponding responsibility of the tribunal to ensure that this is satisfied. The s.6(1) obligation may, however, have an impact in other ways and, in particular, may require a tribunal act to take steps in the management of the proceedings so as to protect other Convention rights, such as those under Art.8 of the Convention to respect for privacy and family life. Indeed some case management decisions will require the interests protected by competing Convention rights to be balanced against each other. For example, in deciding whether to make a restricted reporting order a tribunal will have to balance, on the one hand, the right of an individual under Art.8 of the Convention and, on the other, the right of the press to freedom of expression under Art.10 [see the commentary on r.50]. Similarly in deciding whether to hold a hearing, or part of a hearing, in private (under r.16) a tribunal may have to balance rights under Art.8 against the right to a fair trial under Art.6(1). Finally the s.6(1) obligation may also require a tribunal to modify its interpretation of the substantive law. For example, when hearing a claim of unfair dismissal, the Court of Appeal has held that the combined effect of ss.3 and 6(1) of the Human Rights Act is to place an obligation on an employment tribunal to consider whether there has been an unjustified interference with the claimant's Convention rights, whether or not the respondent is a private authority (*X v Y*, above).

Further, when considering whether there is an employment relationship between a minister of the church and the church, the Court of Appeal has held that a tribunal must adopt a different approach to the evidence than it would do in a context in which religious practices and observances are not present in order to comply with art.9; the law should not readily impose a legal relationship on members of a legal community which would be contrary to their religious beliefs (*New Testament Church of God v Sylvester Stewart* [2008] I.R.L.R. 134).

HUMAN RIGHTS ACT 1998

Interpretation of legislation

3.—(1) So far as it is possible to do so, primary legislation and **15–003** subordinate legislation must be read and given effect in a way which is compatible with the Convention rights.

(2) This section—

(a) applies to primary legislation and subordinate legislation whenever enacted;

(b) does not affect the validity, continuing operation or enforcement of any incompatible primary legislation; and

(c) does not affect the validity, continuing operation or enforcement of any incompatible subordinate legislation if (disregarding any possibility of revocation) primary legislation prevents the removal of the incompatibility.

The interpretative obligation under s.3 has been held to have an impact on the **15–004** interpretation of s.98 of the Employment Rights Act 1996. In circumstances where a claim of unfair dismissal is being brought by a claimant against a public body employer this effect is straightforward. If the reason for the dismissal is conduct which falls within the scope of the protection of a Convention right then it is arguable that the public body employer has, by dismissing the claimant, interfered with that right and acted unlawfully contrary to s.6 of the Human Rights Act 1998. When considering whether the dismissal is fair or not under s.98 of the Employment Rights Act the employment tribunal is under a duty pursuant to s.3 of the Human Rights Act to take into account all the matters relevant to an assessment of whether there has been an interference with the claimant's Convention rights by the employer, and those matters advanced by the employer as justification for that interference. If the employment tribunal concludes that the dismissal was in breach of the claimant's Convention rights then it follows that the dismissal was unfair; a public authority employer will not act reasonably under s.98(4) of the Employment Rights Act if it violates an employee's rights guaranteed by the Convention (*Pay v Lancashire Probation Service* [2004] I.R.L.R. 129; [2004] I.C.R. 187, EAT). The EAT has treated, but without argument and without objection from the parties, the employment tribunal's assessment of whether or not a dismissal amounted to a justified interference with a Convention right as a matter of law rather than fact (*Pay v Lancashire Probation Service*, above).

The analysis is more complex when the employer is a private sector employer, since it is not unlawful under s.6 of the Human Rights Act for such an employer to dismiss an employee in breach of his or her Convention rights. Nevertheless the Court of Appeal has held that in these circumstances s.3 of the Act has an "oblique" effect on s.98 of the Employment Rights Act. The fact that s.6(1) of the Human Rights Act makes it unlawful for the tribunal itself to act in a way which is incompatible with a Convention right reinforces the interpretative obligation in s.3 of the Act. This is particularly so where the Court of Human Rights has held that the Convention right in question imposes a positive obligation on the state to secure the enjoyment of that right between private individuals. In these circumstances the Convention right is "blended" with the law of unfair dismissal so that the employment tribunal must in its assessment of the fairness of the dismissal take into account whether there has been an unjustified interference with a Convention right (in *X v Y*, above). Accordingly, in essence the position as between public and private sector employees is harmonised. Provided the Convention right relied upon is one which gives rise to a positive obligation on the state to protect the right from interference by private persons (which includes Arts 8, 9, 10 and 11 of the Convention) employees can invoke Convention rights in support of their claims against private sector employers.

Nevertheless, claims by employees that their dismissals infringed their Convention rights have met with little success. For claims alleging a contravention of the right to respect for private and family life under Art.8 of the Convention see, for example, *Pay v Lancashire Probation Service*, above, (dismissal of a probation officer after employer discovered that the employee was involved in the marketing of sex products and performed in hedonist and fetish clubs); *X v Y*, above, (dismissal of charity officer working with young offenders after he concealed the crime of committing gross indecency in a public toilet); *Jones v University of Warwick* [2003] 1 W.L.R. 954; *McGowan v Scottish Water* [2005] I.R.L.R. 167, EAT, (dismissals by the employer following covert surveillance of the employee's home); *Amwell View School Governors v Doherty* [2007] I.R.L.R. 198 (reliance on covert recording of disciplinary hearing not contrary to Art.8 (although prohibited on public policy grounds); *PM Posh v Cardiff University*, judgment of January 23, 2008, EAT, (dismissal for breach of confidentiality and conflict of interest following employer's search of employee's email account). For claims alleging a contravention of the right to freedom of thought, conscience and religion under Art.9 of the Convention see, for example, *Copsey v WWB Devon Clays* [2005] I.R.L.R. 811; [2005] I.C.R. 1789; CA (dismissal because employee refused to accept a change to a seven-day shift pattern); *New Testament Church of God v Sylvester Stewart*, above, (whether the existence of an employment relationship would be incompatible with art.9. Note that the Employment Equality (Religion or Belief) Regulations 2003 will usually confer much greater protection of religious and other beliefs than Art.9. For claims alleging a contravention of the right to freedom of association under Art.11 of the Convention see, for example, *R (NUJ) v Central Arbitration Committee* [2005] I.R.L.R. 28, EAT, [2006] I.R.L.R. 53, CA (determination in the context of an application for union recognition that a decision by the employer to recognise a union with few members did not infringe the Art.11 rights of the majority of employees who were members of another trade union).

Declaration of incompatibility

15–005   Section 4 of the Human Rights Act provides that a court falling within the scope of that provision may, if it is satisfied that a provision of primary or subordinate legislation is incompatible with a Convention right, make a declaration of that incompatibility. Section 4(5) sets out the courts that have the power to make a declaration of incompatibility. They are (a) the House of Lords; (b) the Judicial Committee of the Privy Council; (c) the Courts-Martial Appeal Court; (d) in Scotland the High Court of Justiciary sitting otherwise than as a trial court or the Court of Session; and (e) in England and Wales or Northern Ireland the High Court or the Court of Appeal. Neither the employment tribunal nor the EAT fall within the scope of s.4 and so do not have the power to make a declaration of incompatibility (see *Whittaker v Watson* [2002] I.C.R. 1244). In *Whittaker v Watson*

Lindsay J. observed that the effect of the legislation was a "little odd", since were he to be sitting alone in the High Court he would, in an appropriate case, be able to make a declaration of incompatibility but sitting in the EAT "assisted by a carefully balanced panel to represent both sides of industry" he could not. Although he thought it right that this odd conclusion should be given some consideration by the legislature no amendment has yet been made to s.4(5).

EUROPEAN CONVENTION

Right to a fair trial

6(1). In the determination of his civil rights and obligations or of any criminal charge against him, everyone is entitled to a fair and public hearing within a reasonable time by an independent and impartial tribunal established by law. Judgment shall be promoted publicly but the press and public may be excluded from all or part of the trial in the interests of morals, public order or national security in a democratic society, where the interests of juveniles or the protection of the private life of the parties so require, or to the extent strictly necessary in the opinion of the court in special circumstances where publicity would prejudice the interests of justice.   **15–006**

The right to a fair hearing

There is a right to a fair hearing as a matter of common law. That is sometimes   **15–007**
referred to in the case law as a matter of "natural justice". Further reg.3 of the Employment Tribunal (Constitution and Rules of Procedure) Regulations 2004 states that the overriding objective of the rules is to enable tribunals to deal with cases justly, which expressly includes ensuring that the case is dealt with fairly. That obligation is now reinforced by Art.6(1) of the European Convention (*Stansbury v (1) Datapulse Plc (2) Troy Holdings International Plc* [2004] I.R.L.R. 466; [2004] I.C.R. 523, CA). The application of Art.6(1) is, however, limited to situations in which some substantive legal right exists, or arguably exists, as a matter of domestic law and in which there arises some impediment of a procedural nature which affects the determination of that right by a court of tribunal. Article 6(1) does not create substantive rights and so cannot be used to challenge the exclusion of certain categories of individuals from rights to which others benefit (*Katie McQuade v Secretary of State for Defence*, judgment of October 7, 2003, Court of Session rejecting a challenge made to the exclusion of members of the armed forces from the right not to be unfairly dismissed; *Matthews v Ministry of Defence* [2003] 1 A.C. 1163; [2003] 2 W.L.R. 435, HL).

In *Jan Jananvagam v Commonwealth Secretariat*, judgment of March 12, 2007, EAT, the appellant appealed against an employment tribunal decision to strike out her claim of post-employment discrimination against the Commonwealth Secretariat, because of the immunity from suit the latter had under the Commonwealth Secretariat Act 1966. The appellant alleged that the Commonwealth Secretariat was a public authority within the meaning of the Human Rights Act 1998 and that its decision to claim immunity from suit deprived her of her right to a fair trial under art.6(1) of the Convention. Langstaff J, held that even if the Commonwealth Secretariat was a public authority, a rule conferring immunity from suit upon such an international organisation, which had a legitimate objective, could not be said generally to constitute a disproportionate breach of art.6(1). In applying the principle of proportionality to the circumstances of a particular case, a material factor was whether the applicants had available to them reasonable alternative means to protect their rights under the Convention. That test was satisfied in the present case.

Opportunity to be heard

15–008   It is a basic principle of fairness that the parties should have the opportunity to address the tribunal upon any issue that is likely to be relevant to the decision. Indeed the lack of formality of tribunal proceedings makes the rules of natural justice particularly important (*Laurie v Holloway* [1994] I.C.R. 32, EAT; *Mahon v Air New Zealand* [1984] A.C. 808, PC). Accordingly, if a new issue arises during the course of a hearing then both parties must have the opportunity to make submissions on the matter; it is therefore not legitimate for a tribunal to identify of its own motion in the course of its deliberations a new head of discrimination and then adjudicate upon it without reference to the parties (*Tarbuck v Sainsbury Supermarkets Ltd* (2006) I.R.L.R. 664, EAT; *Bradford Hospitals NHS Trust v Al-Shabib* [2003] I.R.L.R. 4, EAT; *British Gas Services Ltd v McCaull* [2001] I.R.L.R. 60, EAT). Nor is it legitimate to refuse to adjudicate on a complaint on the ground of the illegality of the contract of employment without sufficiently alerting the parties to that possibility (*Laurie v Holloway*, above). Similarly it is not permissible for a tribunal deciding a claim of unfair dismissal to make a *Polkey* reduction or a finding of contributory fault (under s.123(1) and (6) of the Employment Rights Act 1996) without giving the parties an opportunity to address it on the issue (*Market Force (UK) Ltd v Hunt* [2002] I.R.L.R. 863, EAT; *Slaughter v Brewer & Sons* [1990] I.R.L.R. 426, EAT).

This also means that if the tribunal foresees that it might make a finding of fact which has not been contended for, that the possibility of that finding being made should be raised with the parties during closing submissions. If the tribunal does not realise what its findings of fact are likely to be until after the hearing has finished, it will usually be necessary to give the parties the opportunity to make further submissions, at least in writing (*Judge v Crown* [2005] I.R.L.R. 823, CA). Similarly if a point is to be made by a tribunal criticising a party when it has not been taken by the other party, it has to be made clearly in advance, so that the object of such criticism has an opportunity to deal with it. Accordingly a tribunal erred by making adverse findings relating to a claimant's credit and honesty which were not put to her and were not advanced to the tribunal by the employers (*Doherty v British Midland Airways Ltd* [2006] I.R.L.R. 90, EAT).

There may also be an infringement of the right to be heard if a tribunal dismisses a party's case after insufficient consideration at a pre-hearing review. The EAT held that a employment judge of an employment tribunal erred in effectively deciding substantive issues of unfair dismissal and protected disclosure against the applicant on the papers at a pre-hearing review, without permitting him to advance his case. The factual disputes necessitated a fuller investigation than was possible in a summary procedure with the employment judge sitting alone. Further the serious and fact-sensitive nature of the disputed issues placed the case in that category where the input of lay members in resolving them on the evidence is essential to a just determination of the case: *Hudson v Oxford University*, judgment of EAT of 26 July 2007; and see *Ezsias v North Glamorgan NHS Trust* [2007] I.R.C. 1126.

15–009   Although failure to give the parties an opportunity to address the tribunal on relevant issues will normally lead to the tribunal's decision being set aside on grounds of unfairness, it will not invariably do so. In *Judge v Crown*, above, the Court of Appeal held that the Employment Tribunal Regulations give the employment tribunal a wide discretion on procedural matters which is wide enough to encompass a decision as to the appropriate course to take where the tribunal is minded to make a finding of fact that has not been contended for by the parties; where the legal effect of the finding of fact is obviously and unarguably clear no injustice will be done if the decision is promulgated without giving the parties an opportunity to address the tribunal. However, it may be noted in that case the tribunal's departure from the respective submissions of the parties was relatively modest. A further example is *Eltek (UK) Ltd v Thomson* [2000] I.R.L.R. 689; [2000] I.C.R. 689, EAT in which the tribunal at a preliminary hearing determined that the claimant was not an employee of the respondent but that since she was a contract worker within s.9 of the Sex Discrimination Act 1975 her claim could proceed on that basis. The s.9 claim had not been put forward by the claimant at the preliminary hearing and so the respondent had had no opportunity to deal with it. Stressing the unusual features of the case and that it should not be regarded as any form of precedent, the employer's appeal was dismissed on the basis that the reformulation of the claim was no more than a relabelling exercise and that the matter was only at the stage of a preliminary hearing.

Furthermore, it will not always be a breach of the right to a fair hearing if the tribunal fails to draw the attention of the parties to judicial authorities that are relied upon in its decision; the question is whether the failure was seriously irregular and unfair. In order to satisfy that test the authority must first be shown to be central to the decision and not peripheral to it. If an authority is of little or no importance and serves only to underline, amplify or give greater emphasis to a point that was explicitly or implicitly addressed in the course of the hearing, then no complaint can be made. Nor does it matter that the authority was not mentioned if the point was so clear that a party could not make a useful comment in explanation. Secondly, in addition to establishing the centrality of the authority it must also be shown that a material injustice has resulted. The hearing will not have been unfair if it has caused no substantial prejudice to the party claiming to be aggrieved. The vital question is whether it would have made any different to the outcome if the party had been armed with the authority (*Stanley Cole (Wainfleet) Ltd v Sheridan* [2003] I.R.L.R. 885; [2003] I.C.R. 1449, CA).

Similarly, although it has been held that it is a breach of the rules of fairness to fail to cross-serve final written submissions, (i.e. to serve each party's written submissions on the other party) the subsequent tribunal decision will not be set aside unless it can been shown to have been "seriously irregular and unfair". That test will not be met where the defect is subsequently cured by the tribunal itself in the course of a review of its own decision (*London Borough of Barking & Dagenham v Oguoko* [2000] I.R.L.R. 179), or where the EAT satisfies itself that no material injustice occurred (*J Mayo-Deman v Lewisham College* [2004] EWCA Civ 1277, CA).

A necessary incident of the right to be heard is the duty of the tribunal to be **15–010** alert and to appear to be so. In *Stansbury v Datapulse* [2004] I.R.L.R. 466; [2004] I.C.R. 523 the claimant sought to appeal the decision of the employment tribunal on the grounds that one of the lay members of the tribunal appeared to be drunk and to have fallen asleep during the hearing. The EAT took the view that it was not required to decide issues of fact concerning the behaviour of tribunal members and relied on the fact that the tribunal had reserved its decision and that decision had been unanimous. The Court of Appeal allowed the further appeal, holding that the EAT might have to assume the role of judges of fact when the behaviour of tribunal members was in issue and that the matters relied on by the EAT to uphold the decision were not relevant. It was the duty of each member of the tribunal to be alert and concentrating on the case, and to appear to be so. The allegations in respect of the tribunal member's behaviour had been made out on the balance of probabilities and therefore the requirement that the hearing be seen to be fair was not satisfied. The Court of Appeal added that public confidence in the administration of justice would be damaged were the view to be taken that such behaviour by a member of the tribunal did not matter. A similar view was taken in *Fordyce v Hammersmith & Fulham Conservative Association* [2006] All E.R. (D), EAT in which the EAT said that it was the essence of an employment tribunal decision that it was the decision of all three members, and that if one of the members had been asleep for substantial periods of time that member could not have played a full part in the decision that was made. Further, although counsel had on one occasion pointed out to the employment judge that one of the lay members appeared to have been asleep, and had stated that they were willing to continue with the hearing, that did not amount to a waiver of the right to complain about the fact there were further periods of time, subsequent to that intervention, when the lay member appeared to be asleep. (See also the commentary on reg.9).

In cases involving the interests of national security the Employment Tribunals (Constitution and Rules) Regulations 2004 provide for the possibility of the exclusion of the claimant and/or his representative from the hearing and the use of "closed evidence", that is documentary evidence which has not been disclosed to them and about which they have no opportunity to comment. This procedure infringes the right to be heard and *prima facie* is contrary to Art.6(1) of the Convention. However, when such steps are taken there is a requirement to appoint a "special advocate" to represent the interests of the claimant, and both the Strasbourg and domestic case law dealing with similar systems have regarded the overall protection accorded to the claimant as sufficient to comply with Art.6(1), taking due account of the need to protect the interests of national security. This is referred to in more detail in the commentary on r.54 of Sch.1 and Sch.2 of the Employment Tribunals (Constitution and Rules) Regulations 2004.

A public hearing

15–011   Rules 26(3) and 18(1) of Sch.1 of the Employment Tribunal (Constitution and Rules of Procedure) Regulations 2004 provide, respectively, that hearings and pre-hearing reviews take place in public, subject to the exceptions contained in r.16. Accordingly where a hearing had been held in private, even though no member of the public had sought to attend, the hearing was unlawful (*Storer v British Gas* [2000] I.R.L.R. 495; [2000] I.C.R. 603, CA). The exceptions set out in r.16 are where the evidence or representations is likely to consist of information:

   (i) which could not be disclosed without contravening a prohibition imposed by or by virtue of any enactment;

  (ii) which has been communicated to a witness in confidence, or which he has otherwise obtained in consequence of the confidence placed in him by another person; or

 (iii) the disclosure of which would, for reasons other than its effect on negotiations with respect to any of the matters mentioned in s.178(2) of the Trade Union Law Reform (Consolidation) Act 1992, cause substantial injury to any undertaking of the witness or any undertaking in which he works.

In addition r.54(1)(a) and (2)(a) of Sch.1 and r.9 of Sch.2 of the Employment Tribunal (Constitution and Rules of Procedure) Regulations 2004 make provision for hearings to be conducted in private in the interests of national security.

These exceptions are not only derogations from the requirement in the Rules of Procedure for hearings to be in public but also from the right to a public hearing under Art.6 of the Convention. Accordingly an employment judge or tribunal must take this into account when exercising a discretion under r.16 as to whether to order that a hearing be conducted in private. On the other hand, it may be the case that, as anticipated in Art.6(1), a tribunal has to conduct all or part of a case in private in order to safeguard the Convention rights of a party, witness or member of the public. In such a situation a tribunal can rely upon r.16(i) and the fact that a public hearing would contravene the statutory prohibition in the Human Rights Act against infringement of those rights. In such circumstances a balance has to be struck between the right to a fair and public hearing under Art.6(1) of the Convention and the Convention rights of others. Applying this approach the EAT held it was necessary for a tribunal to play a video recording, which had been adduced as evidence by the employee, in private, in order to safeguard the right to respect for family and private life under Art.8 of the Convention of a child depicted on the recording (*XXX v YYY* [2004] I.R.L.R. 137, EAT). That case concerned a claim of sexual harassment by a nanny employed to look after the child of her former employers. The video recording, which she had made secretly, was said to show the child's father making sexual advances to her. The child was present in much of the footage depicting the conduct. The EAT held that the child's rights under Art.8(1) of the Convention would be infringed if the video was played in public but that both the right of the claimant to a fair hearing and the rights of the child under Art.8 could be securely protected if the video recording was viewed by the employment tribunal in private. In the event, the Court of Appeal held that the video recording should not be adduced in evidence because it was of no probative value: the employers' defence was that the child's father had been involved in a consensual relationship with the nanny and hence the recording was consistent with the account of both parties (*XXX v YYY* [2004] I.R.L.R. 471, CA).

Within a reasonable time

Although Art.6(1) requires that the determination of someone's rights takes place within a reasonable time, it does not lay down what amounts to a reasonable time. The courts have held that the assessment of a reasonable time depends on all the circumstances of the particular case: the nature of the tribunal, its jurisdiction, constitution and procedures, the subject matter of the case, its factual and legal complexity and difficulty, the conduct of the tribunal and of the parties and any other special features of the situation in which delay has occurred (*Bangs v Connex South Eastern Ltd* [2005] I.R.L.R. 389; [2005] 2, All E.R. 316, CA; *Somjee v UK* [2002] I.R.L.R. 886, ECtHR). However, mere delay, even in breach of the reasonable time requirement of Art.6(1), does not in itself constitute a ground of appeal. This would enable appellants to challenge facts found by a tribunal whose decision on the facts could not be characterised as perverse, and circumvent the policy of s.21(1) of the Employment Tribunals Act 1996 confining appeals to questions of law. No question of law arises and no independent ground of appeal exists simply because by virtue of material factual errors and omissions resulting from delay, the decision is "unsafe". In order to succeed in a challenge to the facts found by the tribunal it is necessary to establish that the decision is, as a result of the unreasonable delay, a perverse one either in its overall conclusion or on specific matters of material fact and credibility. However, in exceptional cases unreasonable delay by the tribunal in promulgating its decision can properly be treated as a serious procedural error or material irregularity giving rise to a question of law in the "proceedings before the tribunal". That circumstance falls within s.21(1) which is not confined to questions of law to be found in the substantive decision. Such a case can occur if the appellant establishes that the failure to promulgate the decision within a reasonable time has given rise to a real risk that, due to the delayed decision, the party complaining was deprived of the substance of their right to a fair trial under Art.6(1) (*Bangs v Connex South Eastern Ltd*, above, disapproving *Kwamin v Abbey National Plc* [2004] I.R.L.R. 516; [2004] I.C.R. 841, EAT). Although the Court of Appeal has recognised that this interpretation of s.21(1) is more restrictive of the right of appeal than in an

15–012

ordinary civil case, it has held that it is not incompatible with Art.6(1) (*Bangs v Connex South Eastern Ltd*, above).

Independent and impartial tribunal

15–013   Article 6(1) requires that a tribunal which determines civil rights and obligation must be "independent and impartial".

"Independent" means independent of the executive and also of the parties. In order to determine whether a tribunal can be considered to be independent, regard must be had to factors such the manner of appointment of its members and their term of office, the existence of guarantees against outside pressures and the question of whether the body presents an appearance of independence (*Findlay v UK* (1997) 24 E.H.R.R. 221, ECtHR at para.73). In *Scanfuture UK Ltd v Secretary of State for Trade and Industry* and *Link v Secretary of State for Trade and Industry* [2001] I.R.L.R. 416; [2001] I.C.R. 1096 the EAT held that the employment tribunal was not independent within the meaning of Art.6(1) when it adjudicated on claims against the Secretary of State in respect of debts allegedly owed to claimants by their insolvent former employers because its lay members were appointed by the Secretary of State, who was a party to the proceedings. At the relevant time the Department of Trade and Industry had a large role in the appointment of lay members, in the fixing of their lengths of appointment, in their possible re-appointment, in their possible removal and in their remuneration. Furthermore, the breach of Art.6(1) was not cured by the possibility of appeal to the EAT since its jurisdiction was limited to questions of law. However, the EAT also held that as a result of recent changes to the powers and practices of the Secretary of State in relation to lay members, there are now in place sufficient guarantees to exclude any legitimate doubt as to the independence and impartiality of the employment tribunal where the Secretary of State is a party to the proceedings. (See also the commentary on reg.9).

"Impartiality" has been described by the Court of Human Rights as having a "subjective" and an "objective" element (*Fey v Austria* ((1993) 16 E.H.R.R. 387, ECtHR at para.28). The subjective element concerns the personal conviction and behaviour of a particular judge in a given case and corresponds to the notion of actual bias. The objective element means not only that the tribunal must be truly independent and free from actual bias but also that it must not appear in the objective sense to lack these qualities. Instances of actual bias are, it is hoped, rare and, in any event, difficult to prove because the law does not countenance the questioning of a judge about the extraneous influences affecting his mind (*Locabail* [2000] I.R.L.R. 99; [2000] 2 W.L.R. 870; [2000] Q.B. 451, CA). The policy of the common law is therefore to protect litigants who can discharge the lesser burden of showing objectively a real risk of bias, without requiring them to show that such bias actually exists.

15–014   The objective test of bias is similar (if not identical) to the notion of "independence" (*Magill v Porter & Magill v Weeks* [2002] 2 W.L.R. 37 at para.88). In *Magill v Porter & Magill v Weeks*, above, the House of Lords approved the modification of the common law test of bias, previously set out in *R v Gough* [1993] A.C. 646 HL, that the Court of Appeal had made in *Medicaments and Related Classes of Goods (No.2), Re* [2001] 1 W.L.R. 700. It thus brought the common law doctrine into line with the Strasbourg jurisprudence. The common law test of bias, which is now no different from that under Art.6(1) of the Convention, was stated by the House of Lords as whether the "fair minded and informed observer, having considered the facts, would conclude that there was a real possibility that the tribunal was biased". See also *R v Abdroikov* [2007] UKHL 37 at paras 26–27 referring to a "real and possible source of unfairness" and *Khan v Kirklees MBC*, judgment of December, 17 2007, CA, at para 17. When considering whether there is a real possibility that a tribunal is or was biased the central issue is whether there are ascertainable facts which may raise doubts as to whether the body lacks impartiality (*Wettstein v Switzerland* (Application No. 33958/96), ECtHR at para.44).

In *Scanfuture UK Ltd v Secretary of State for Trade and Industry* and *Link v Secretary of State for Trade and Industry* the EAT had some difficulty in deciding upon the extent of knowledge to be ascribed to the "informed observer". However, in *Magill v Porter & Magill v Weeks*, above, Lord Steyn considered that it was unnecessary to delve into the characteristics to be attributed to the fair-minded and informed observer and referred to the statement of Kirby J. in *Johnson v Johnson* (2000) 200 C.L.R. 488, 509 at para.53 when he stated that a "reasonable member of the public is neither complacent nor unduly sensitive or suspicious".

Although the adjustment made to the *Gough* test was small it constituted a deliberate shift of emphasis away from passing judgment on the likelihood that the particular tribunal under review was in fact biased towards applying an objective test to the circumstances giving rise to the allegation of bias. In *Lawal v Northern Spirit Ltd* [2003] I.R.L.R. 538; [2003] I.C.R. 856, HL Lord Steyn stated that the small but important shift approved in *Magill v Porter & Magill v Weeks*, above, has at its core the need for "the confidence which must be inspired by the courts in a democratic society" (*Belilos v Switzerland* (1988) 10 E.H.R.R. 466, ECtHR). Applying that test the House of Lords held in *Lawal v Northern Spirit Ltd*, above, that it was incompatible with Art.6(1) for a panel of the EAT to include a lay member with whom Counsel for one of the parties had previously sat in his capacity as a part-time judge.

Disqualification on account of bias

In certain situations the existence of bias is effectively presumed. That is where **15–015** the outcome of the case could realistically affect the judge's interests. "Interests" normally mean the judge's pecuniary or proprietary interests (*Locabail*, above). However, in *R. v Bow Street Metropolitan Stipendiary Magistrate, Ex p. Pinochet Ugarte (No.2)* ([2000] 1 A.C. 119 the House of Lords made it plain that the rule extended to a limited class of non-financial interests such as where the judge is taking an active role as a director or trustee of a charity closely allied to and acting with a party to the litigation. Nevertheless, in *R. v Chief Constable of Merseyside Police Ex p. Bennion* [2001] I.R.L.R. 442; [2002] I.C.R. 856, CA the Court of Appeal allowed an appeal from the Queen's Bench Division to hold that the rule did not apply so as to disqualify a Chief Constable from hearing disciplinary proceedings against a police officer in circumstances where there were pending claims of discrimination brought by that police officer in the employment tribunal for which the Chief Constable was potentially vicariously liable. No allegations were made against the Chief Constable personally in the discrimination claim and his status as a defendant in those proceedings was purely titular. In any case where the judge's interest is said to derive from the interest of a spouse, partner or other family member the link must be so close and direct as to render the interest of that other person, for all practical purposes, indistinguishable from an interest of the judge himself. Further, while the older cases speak of disqualification if the judge has an interest in the outcome of the proceedings "however small", in more recent authorities there has been acceptance of a *de minimis* exception. The test is whether the judge's personal interest is so small as to be incapable of affecting his decision one way or the other. However, if there is any doubt it should be resolved in favour of disqualification (*Locabail*, above at para.10). See also *Jones v DAS Legal Expenses Insurance Co Ltd* [2004] I.R.L.R. 218, below.

In other situations the existence of bias is not presumed and will depend on the facts of the particular case, including the nature of the issue to be decided.

However, if on an assessment of all the relevant circumstances the conclusion is that the principle of judicial impartiality would be breached the judge is automatically disqualified from hearing the case and the question of disqualification is not a discretionary case management decision (*Alexander Morrison v AWG Group Ltd* [2006] 1 W.L.R. 1163).

In *Locabail*, above, the Court of Appeal stated at para.25 that it would be "dangerous and futile" to attempt to define exhaustively the factors which could and could not give rise to a real possibility of bias, but nevertheless gave guidance on the effect of some of the more common circumstances:

The matters which could not properly form the basis for such an objection were as follows: religion, ethnic or national origin, gender, age, class, means or sexual orientation of the judge; the judge's social or educational or service or employment background or history, nor that of any member of the judge's family; the judge's previous political associations; membership of social or sporting or charitable bodies; Masonic associations; previous judicial decisions; extra-curricular utterances (whether in textbooks, lectures, speeches, articles, interviews, reports or responses to consultation papers); previous receipt of instructions to act for or against any party, solicitor, or advocate engaged in a case before him; membership of the same Inn, circuit, local law society or chambers.

By contrast the following matters were thought to be such as might give rise to a real possibility of bias: personal friendship or animosity between the judge and any member of the public involved in the case; if the judge were closely acquainted with any member of the public involved in the case, particularly if the credibility of that individual could be significant in the decision of the case; if in any case where the credibility of any individual were an issue to be decided by the judge, he had in a previous case rejected the evidence of that person in such outspoken terms as to throw doubt on his ability to approach such person's evidence with an open mind on any later occasion; if on any question at issue in the proceedings before him the judge had expressed views, particularly in the course of the hearing, in such extreme and unbalanced terms as to throw doubt on his ability to try the issue with an objective judicial mind; or if, for any other reason, there were real grounds for doubting the ability of the judge to ignore extraneous considerations, prejudices and predilections and bring an objective judgment to bear on the issues before him.

Allegations of bias in the Employment Tribunal

Previous experience of parties/representatives

15–016   In *Lodwick v Southwark LBC* [2004] I.R.L.R. 554; [2004] I.C.R. 884 the Court of Appeal held that in determining the issue of bias the tribunal had applied the wrong test. In that case the claimant realised that the employment judge had presided over an earlier case in which he had acted as a representative for one of the parties. On that occasion the tribunal had criticised his conduct and awarded costs against the party he had represented. In view of that history the claimant had made a request that the employment judge recuse himself. The application was refused on the basis that the employment judge was only one of three members with an equal vote and a fair hearing was possible. The Court of Appeal observed that the employment judge presided over the tribunal and was the only one legally qualified. His position was therefore an important one and any apparent bias on his part was not nullified by the presence of two members who could outvote him. In determining the issue of bias the tribunal ought to have applied the test in *Magill v Porter & Magill v Weeks*. Similarly in *Breeze Benton Solicitors v Weddell* UKEAT/0873/03, the EAT held that the employment judge had been wrong to refuse to recuse himself in circumstances where he had been critical of the employers, awarding costs against them in earlier separate proceedings brought by two other former employees. The earlier proceedings had taken place only 12 months before and the tribunal had on that occasion expressed itself in trenchant terms. Further, there was no scope for weighing the risk of bias against the delay in hearing the case which might have resulted from the employment judge recusing himself. Notably, however, the EAT and Court of Appeal have stressed the fact that mere complaint about the conduct of an employment judge in earlier related proceedings cannot give rise to an automatic decision to recuse. In *Ansar v Lloyds TSB Bank Plc* [2006] EWCA Civ 1462 the Court of Appeal upheld a decision of Burton J. in the EAT in which he found that an employment judge had been right to refuse repeated requests to recuse himself from hearing a pre-hearing review of a victimisation claim in circumstances where the claimant had appealed, alleging bias, the employment judge's earlier decision dismissing his claim of race discrimination. The Court of Appeal held that it was the substance of the allegations made that had to be addressed and analysed, and that the allegations made in this case did not warrant the employment judge recusing himself.

However, an employment judge who concluded at a pre-hearing review that the applicant's claims had no prospect of success, and ordered a deposit to be paid, should not have heard the respondent's subsequent application to strike the claims out; a reasonable and fair-minded observer would have concluded that the an employment judge had a closed mind to the applicant's prospects of success. Furthermore, given the extent of the factual dispute, the decision of the employment judge to strike the claims out was legally perverse as the competing accounts of the claimant's dismissal could not be resolved without a full hearing from both parties: *Ezsias v North Glamorgan NHS Trust* [2007] I.R.C. 1126.

Attitude to parties

In *Turner v Harada Ltd (t/a Chequepoint UK Ltd)*, judgment of April 6, 2001, the **15–017** Court of Appeal held that the test of apparent bias was satisfied in circumstances where immediately before the start of the hearing the employment judge made disparaging comments about the respondent and the frequency of its participation in employment disputes. Similarly in *Simper & Co Ltd v Cooke* [1986] I.R.L.R. 19; [1986] I.C.R. 6 the EAT held that comments made by the employment judge during the cross-examination of the claimant would reasonably have been understood by an impartial onlooker as meaning that he had formed a hostile view of the employers before they had given evidence (it being a claim for constructive dismissal). Further in *Calor Gas Ltd v Bray*, judgment of September 29, 2005, the EAT held that the test of apparent bias was satisfied in circumstances where a tribunal had been overwhelmingly hostile to the employer in a way that went significantly beyond the normal dialogue between the parties, their representatives and the tribunal. In particular the employment judge had frequently interrupted cross-examination and had expressed criticism of the questions put to the witnesses. The impartial observer would have been left with the impression that the employer had not had a fair hearing. By contrast, in *BLP UK Ltd v Marsh*, judgment of January 16, 2003, the Court of Appeal held that the EAT had been entitled to conclude that the behaviour of the employment judge during the hearing did not give rise to a real possibility of bias. Although the employment judge denied acting in the biased manner alleged, namely rolling her eyes, tutting, snorting, shaking her head and directing intimidating looks at witnesses giving evidence, the EAT concluded that some hostility to the employer's witnesses had been shown but that it was natural for a tribunal to form a view as to the strength of a case and the relevance of the points being made. The Court of Appeal found that the EAT had applied the right test and had been entitled to use its own experience in assessing factors the well-informed observer would take into account. It was the duty of the employment tribunal not to let time be wasted and there was nothing unreasonable in the tribunal regarding the employer's case as being difficult. See also *Luis Roberto Demarco Almeida v Opportunity Equity Partners* [2006] UKPC 44 in which the Privy Council held that although the judge had acted improperly in making excessive interventions in the course of a trial, his conduct had not been such as to render the trial unfair and there was not reason to suppose there was a real possibility that he was biased; the interventions had been motivated by the desire to understand the evidence and push the trial forward, rather than by any partiality.

The EAT has also held that a case management discussion it is often necessary for an employment judge to ensure that matters are dealt with expeditiously, that time is not spent unreasonably, and that proper progress is made. It is therefore from time to time necessary for an employment judge to be robust, to abbreviate discussion and to move forward. A reasonable and well-informed observer would not take the view that this amounted to an appearance of bias: *EB v BA*, decision of EAT of June 28, 2007.

Preliminary indication of tribunal's view

15–018   In *Southwark LBC v Jiminez* [2003] I.R.L.R. 477; [2003] I.C.R. 1176, CA the tribunal indicated to the parties before the completion of the evidence that its provisional view was that Southwark's treatment of the claimant had been "appalling" and encouraged the parties to settle the matter. The Court of Appeal held that there had been no impropriety in a tribunal encouraging settlement of proceedings and that there was no reason not to accept the subsequent assertion of the employment judge that the views expressed had been genuinely preliminary. It stated that there was no reason "why a strongly expressed view cannot be a provisional view, leaving it open to the party criticised to persuade the tribunal as to why that view was wrong and why the party's conduct was justified". However, in expressing such a view a tribunal should "leave the parties in no doubt that such expressions of view are only provisional and that the tribunal remain open to persuasion". Similarly in *Eastbourne BC v Amir Hafez*, judgment of January 12, 2005, the EAT held that the tribunal had not showed bias by giving a preliminary indication as to the merits of a case and the possible level of compensation at the end of the first day's hearing. Neither had it done so by the fact that one of the members questioned a witness for the local authority at length. By contrast in *Chris Project v Hutt*, UKEATS/0065/05 the EAT held that the tribunal had appeared biased when, before any evidence was called, the employment judge had commented that the employer "faced an uphill struggle with its case". The comment indicated that there had been a prior consideration of the employer's defence with the view reached that it had no merit. It also put undue pressure on the employer's representative, who had subsequently conceded unfair dismissal, to refrain from advancing the defence

However, the EAT has subsequently taken a more robust line and held that the expression of a preliminary view is customary, and although it is better not to express a strong preliminary view, an employment judge should not excuse himself if he does so: *El Farargy v El Farargy* [2007] EWCA Civ. 1149; *Abegaze v Shrewsbury College of Arts and Technology*, judgment of 4 March 2008, EAT. Furthermore, formation of a preliminary view as to the potential value of the claim, even before any evidence is heard, does not amount to apparent bias, rather it is a normal and pragmatic part of case management: *Abegaze v Shrewsbury College of Arts and Technology*, above. There is no obligation to disclose that view to the parties: *Abegaze v Shrewsbury College of Arts and Technology*, above.

Time alone with one party

In *Colback v ENA Ferguson*, judgment of July 25, 2001, the Court of Appeal held **15–019** that, although unwise, the fact that the two lay members of the employment tribunal had accepted a lift in a taxi with one of the respondents did not create a real risk of bias. Similarly in *Deteh v Commissioner of Police for the Metropolis*, judgment of June 20, 2003, the EAT held that the fact that the respondents and their legal team were permitted to remain in the hearing room at the conclusion of the hearing to pack up their papers did not give rise to an appearance of bias on the part of the employment tribunal.

Links between tribunal member and one party

In *Jones v DAS Legal Expenses Insurance Co Ltd* [2004] I.R.L.R. 218 the Court of **15–020** Appeal held that there was no real possibility of bias in circumstances where the employment judge was married to a barrister occasionally instructed by the respondent insurance company. Similarly in *Williams v Inspector of Taxes* [2000] I.R.L.R. 96, CA it was held that the fact that an employment judge had once worked for the Inland Revenue in a junior capacity 35 years before did not disqualify him from hearing discrimination claims brought against it, and in *Smith v Kvaerner Cementation Foundations Ltd* [2007] 1 W.L.R. 370, CA it was held that the mere fact that the judge (a recorder) was a member of the same set of chambers as one of the barristers appearing in the case did not of itself give rise to an appearance of bias (although the fact that the recorder regarded one of the parties as a "long standing lay client" did mean that absent waiver by the other party, the recorder should not have heard the case). By contrast in *University College of Swansea v Cornelius* [1988] I.C.R. 735 the EAT held that there was an appearance of bias where one of the lay members of the tribunal was the mother-in-law of a professor of the respondent university who had been on the appeal panel which had dismissed the claimant's appeal and who had been a named defendant in an earlier action brought by the claimant against the university. Again in *Halford v Sharples* [1992] I.C.R. 146 the EAT held that there was an appearance of bias in circumstances where an equal opportunities officer in the Greater Manchester police force was due to sit as a lay member on a claim of sex discrimination brought by a senior woman police officer. The claim involved an extensive survey of alleged sex discrimination in the police forces. The lay member had recently interviewed the Deputy Chief Constable and the Assistant Chief Constable of the Greater Manchester force for the purposes of the case and the EAT pointed out that this could cause a direct conflict of evidence between the member and a witness. In addition the lay member's knowledge of the reputations of many of the police officers in the case could "give rise to a potential injustice".

Similarly, an employment tribunal member who had had a senior position in a union that had the same equal pay policy as the defendant union, the lawfulness of which policy was under consideration by the tribunal, and who had connections with individuals involved in the relevant events, should have recused herself as her presence on the panel gave the appearance of bias. The fact that an application that the tribunal member be recused had not been made until the hearing had almost been complete was immaterial and could not justify a failure to intervene: *Hamilton v GMB (Northern Region)* [2007] I.R.L.R. 391.

In *M Khan v Kirkless MBC*, above, the Court of Appeal held that the fact that a claimant had brought proceedings against the employment judge hearing his case in a separate unrelated matter in his capacity as a school governor did not give rise to apparent bias. The claim against the employment judge had been brought four years after the proceedings in the employment tribunal were issued and as a deliberate attempt by the claimant to prevent the employment judge from hearing his case. See, however, *D Da'bell v NSPCC*, decision of 13 February 2008, EAT, where the test of apparent bias was met in circumstances where the claimant had informed the regional employment judge that the employment judge hearing her case was involved in a disciplinary matter, thereby causing the latter anxiety and distress.

Insensitivity

15–021   In *X H Diem (known as Anita Ho) v Crystal Services Plc* [2006] All E.R. (D) 84 (Feb), EAT the employment judge enquired whether the claimant was expanding her claim of race discrimination to include less favourable treatment on the grounds of her colour. He then proceeded to question the claimant at length about her skin colour and made comparisons with his own skin colour. The EAT held that the employment judge's enquires "crossed the line"; a fair minded observer would conclude that the remarks were likely to cause the claimant to feel unsettled, humiliated and embarrassed, and that there was a real possibility of unconscious bias on the part of the employment judge. It stressed that claims of race discrimination require sensitive handling by tribunals and that "high standards of understanding and communication by all judicial officers are rightly expected".

Notably, in *El-Farargy v El-Farargy*, above, the Court of Appeal held that a High Court Judge who made several jokes and comments about a Saudi Sheikh who was a party to the proceedings had also crossed the line. The jokes and comments were not just spoken in colourful language but were mocking and disrespectful of S for either his status as a Sheikh, his nationality, his ethnic origin, his Muslim faith, or some or all of these elements. They would give the appearance to the fair-minded and informed observer that there was a real possibility that the employment judge would carry into his judgment the scorn and contempt the words conveyed.

Impropriety

15–021/1   The fact that a trainee lay member of an employment tribunal was present with the employment judge while the latter deliberated, and the emanation of laughter from his chambers during those deliberations, was insufficient to give rise to an inference of bias or impropriety that would render the decision reached by the employment judge unfair: *Robertson (t/a 18th Golf Theme Bar) v Hendrie*, decision of June 8, 2007, EAT.

Correct approach of tribunal

15–022   When an employment judge becomes aware of any matter which could arguably be said to give the appearance of a real possibility of bias the parties should be informed of the matter in advance of the hearing so that they have the opportunity to consider the matter and whether to apply for the employment judge to recuse himself. When considering any such application the employment judge should take into account the statement of the Court of Appeal in *Locabail*, above, at para.21 that "[a judge] would be as wrong to yield to a tenuous or frivolous objection as he would to ignore an objection of substance". If, however, the employment judge only discovers the problem during the course of the hearing he should nevertheless disclose it then, even if that may require a new hearing to be convened in front of a different tribunal. In *Jones v DAS Legal Expenses Insurance Co Ltd*, above, the Court of Appeal gave the following guidance on the correct approach for a judge or employment judge to take when confronted at a hearing with a possible conflict of interest:

"(i) If there is any real as opposed to fanciful chance of objection being taken by a fair-minded spectator, the first step is to ascertain whether or not another judge is available to hear the matter. The judge should make every effort in the time available to clarify what his interest is which gives rise to this conflict so that the full facts can be placed before the parties.

(ii) Some time should be taken to prepare what-ever explanation is to be given to the parties.

(iii) It is vital that the judge's explanation be mechanically recorded or carefully noted where that facility is not available, so as to avoid any controversy about what was or was not said.

(iv) A full explanation must be given to the parties, detailing exactly what matters are within the judge's knowledge which give rise to a possible conflict of interest and explaining why the problem has only arisen so late in the day. The parties deserve also to be told whether it would be possible to move the case to another judge that day.

(v) The options open to the parties should be explained in detail. Those options are to consent to the judge hearing the matter, the consequence being that the parties will thereafter be likely to be held to have lost their right to object. The other option is to apply to the judge to recuse himself. The parties should be told that it is their right to object, that the court will not take it amiss if the right is exercised and that the judge will decide having heard the submissions. They should be told what will happen next. If the court decides the case can proceed, it will proceed. If on the other hand the judge decides he will have to stand down, the parties should be told in advance of the likely dates on which the matter may be re-listed.

(vi) The parties should always be told that time will be afforded to reflect before electing. That should be made clear even where both parties are represented. If there is a litigant in person the better practice may be to rise for five minutes. The litigant in person can be directed to the Citizens Advice Bureau if that service is available and if he wishes to avail himself of it. If the litigant feels he needs more help, he can be directed to the chief clerk and/or the listing officer."

The Court of Appeal added, however, that the guidance was not a checklist, stating: "Sometimes some of the suggestions may be adopted and sometimes none of them may apply. We wish strongly to disabuse any disgruntled litigant of the idea that he may seize upon this judgment and use it as the mantra for complaint about ill-treatment. Any attempt to do so will receive short shrift." For the requirements for a valid waiver, see also *Smith Kvaerner Cementation Foundations Ltd* [2007] 1 W.L.R. 370, CA.

In *Ansar v Lloyds TSB Bank Plc* [2007] I.R.L.R. 211, the Court of Appeal affirmed that mere complaint about the conduct of the employment judge of an employment tribunal does not give rise to an automatic decision to recuse and that the substance of the allegations have to be addressed and analysed. Clearly the same principle applies to the members of an employment tribunal. However, the EAT has stressed that it is important that if lay members have any concerns at all about whether they should sit on a case or not, they should raise the issue with the employment judge who in turn should explore fully the extent of any potential conflict of interest before hearing, or continuing to hear, the case: *Hamilton v GMB (Northern Region)* [2007] I.R.L.R. 391.

A case in which the approach of the tribunal went badly wrong is *D Da'bell v NSPCC*, decision of February 13, 2008, EAT. In that case, whilst her case was adjourned part-heard, the claimant wrote to the regional employment judge alleging bias on the part of the employment judge concerned and also stating that it appeared that the employment judge had been disciplined by the Solicitors

Disciplinary Tribunal for conduct unbefitting a solicitor. Without hearing from the respondent, the employment judge decided to step down. The respondent subsequently appealed. The parties were subsequently informed of the disciplinary matter by telephone conference by the regional employment judge but since the Lord Chancellor decided not to take any action in respect of the disciplinary matter the employment judge reconsidered his previous decision and decided to resume hearing the case. The claimant appealed this decision. The EAT held that save for one matter the employment judge could have resumed hearing the case without risk of apparent bias, despite the catalogue of procedural errors. However, there would be risk of apparent bias because the claimant had brought the disciplinary matter to the attention of the regional employment judge, which would have caused the employment judge anxiety and distress.

Making an allegation of bias or impermissible conduct

15–023   Complaints of bias may be raised at any stage of the proceedings. However, the EAT has stated that it is normally inappropriate for a dissatisfied litigant to apply in the middle of the case for a rehearing before another tribunal as it is undesirable that the tribunal accused of bias should be asked itself to adjudicate on that matter. The dissatisfied litigant should ordinarily await the decision and then, if appropriate, make his dissatisfaction with the conduct of the case by the tribunal a ground of appeal (*Peter Simper v Cooke*, above; See also El-Farargy v El-Farargy, above). When this course of action is taken the appellant must include in the Notice of Appeal full particulars of each complaint made. The subsequent procedure that must then be followed by the EAT and the parties is set out in detail in s.11 of the EAT Practice Direction.

On the other hand it has been stated that it is normally desirable that complaints about conduct which do not suggest bias, such as tribunal members falling asleep or failing to pay attention, should be raised at the tribunal in the course of the hearing (*Red Bank Manufacturing Co Ltd v Meadows* [1992] I.C.R. 204, EAT; *Stansbury v Datapulse*, above). However, making an objection at the hearing is not to be regarded as a precondition to the matter being permitted to constitute a ground of appeal to the EAT (*Kudrath v Ministry of Defence*, judgment of April 26, 1999, EAT). In *Stansbury v Datapulse*, above, the Court of Appeal stated that it is "unrealistic not to recognise the difficulty, even for legal representatives, in raising with the tribunal a complaint about the behaviour of a tribunal member who, if the complaint is not upheld, may yet be part of the tribunal deciding the case" and held it is appropriate to consider a failure to raise an objection before the tribunal against the test of reasonableness in all the circumstances of the case.

Adjournments

15–024   Rule 10(2)(m) of the Employment Tribunal (Constitution and Rules of Procedure) Regulations 2004 provides that an employment judge may postpone or adjourn any hearing. The grant of an adjournment is a discretionary matter (*Jacobs v Norsalta Ltd* [1977] I.C.R. 189, EAT; *Carter v Credit Charge Ltd* [1979] I.R.L.R. 361, CA). However, some adjournments must be granted if not to do so would amount to a denial of justice. The Court of Appeal has held that in order to comply with the right to a fair trial under Art.6(1) of the Convention a litigant whose presence is needed for the fair trial of a case but who is unable to be present through no fault of his own will usually have to be granted an adjournment, however inconvenient it may be to the tribunal and to the other parties (*Teinaz v London Borough of Wandsworth* [2002] I.R.L.R. 721; [2002] I.C.R. 1471).

However, the tribunal is entitled to be satisfied that the inability of the litigant to be present is genuine and the onus is on the applicant for an adjournment to prove the need for an adjournment. If there is evidence that a litigant has been advised by a qualified person not to attend a hearing on medical grounds, but the tribunal has doubts as to whether the evidence is genuine or sufficient, the tribunal has a discretion to direct that further evidence be promptly provided or to invite the party seeking the adjournment to authorise the legal representatives for the other side to have access to the doctor giving the advice in question. However, if a doctor has advised his patient not to attend the hearing and the patient obeys that advice, it is unfair to describe the patient as choosing not to attend and to treat that as a factor against exercising the discretion to adjourn. Nor can his absence be taken to reinforce the view that he has no genuine reason for not attending (*Teinaz v London Borough of Wandsworth*, above). On the other hand, the fact that a person is certified on medical grounds as not fit to attend work does not automatically entail that that person is not fit to attend a tribunal hearing. Accordingly, where a medical certificate which accompanied the employee's application for an adjournment did not address the question of whether the employee was or was not fit to attend the tribunal hearing the Court of Appeal considered that it was sensible of the employment tribunal to have given the employee a further limited opportunity to make good the deficiencies in the medical evidence and, when the employee failed to comply adequately with that order, the employment tribunal had been entitled to refuse the application for an adjournment (*Andreou v Lord Chancellor's Department* [2002] I.R.L.R. 728). Peter Gibson L.J. commented that in deciding whether to refuse an adjournment, an employment tribunal has to balance a number of factors, including fairness not only to the applicant but also to the respondent. Fairness to other litigants may require that indulgences given to those who have had an opportunity to justify an adjournment but have not taken that opportunity adequately are not extended.

Although there was a strong presumption in favour of adjournment where a principal witness was unavoidably absent, the tribunal still had to decide in each case what course was right to take in the interests of justice: *Vision Information Service (UK) Ltd v Coutinho*, judgment of EAT of August 31, 2007.

Restriction of vexatious proceedings

15–025 Section 33 of the Employment Tribunals Act 1996 provides that on an application made by the Attorney General or the Lord Advocate the EAT may make a restriction of proceedings order if it is satisfied ". . . that a person has habitually and persistently and without any reasonable ground—(a) instituted vexatious proceedings, whether in an employment tribunal or before the Appeal Tribunal, and whether against the same person or against different persons, or (b) made vexatious applications in any proceedings, whether in an employment tribunal or before the Appeal Tribunal". Where a restriction of proceedings order is made, the person concerned cannot, without the leave of the EAT, institute or continue proceedings before an employment tribunal or the EAT, or make an application in connection with such proceedings. Unless an order provides that it will cease to have effect at the end of a specified period, it remains in force indefinitely.

The authorities are clear that s.33 of the Employment Tribunals Act does not conflict with the right to a fair hearing under Art.6(1) of the European Convention. The courts have reasoned that the right under Art.6(1) is not an absolute right; a balance has to be struck between the right of the citizen to use the courts and the rights of others and the courts not to be troubled with wholly unmeritorious claims. In any event, since an order under s.33 provides for access to the employment tribunal system so long as permission is obtained, access to the courts is not prohibited; it is provided for on certain terms. That cannot amount to a breach of Art.6 (*Att-Gen v Wheen* [2001] I.R.L.R. 91, CA; *Att-Gen v Tyrrell*, judgment of September 23, 2003, EAT).

Interference with choice of representatives

15–026   Section 6(1) of the Employment Tribunals Act 1996 gives a party to employment tribunal proceedings an unqualified statutory right to be represented by the person of their choice. Although a tribunal has power under its rules of procedure to control the way a representative conducts the case before it, the tribunal cannot take away the party's right to that representative representing them (*Bache v Essex CC* [2000] I.R.L.R. 251; [2000] I.C.R. 313, CA). In *Dispatch Management Services (UK) Ltd v Douglas* [2002] I.R.L.R. 389, EAT it was argued by the employers that s.6(1) had to be read in conjunction with the need for there to be a fair hearing in accordance with Art.6(1) of the Convention, and it did not render the tribunal powerless to order a party's representative to cease to act where there was a conflict of interest between the party's representative and the opposing party to the litigation. That argument was dismissed by the EAT who held that the principle laid down in *Bache* is not inconsistent with the right to a fair hearing; Art.6(1) does not require s.6(1) to be read and given effect as though it enabled a tribunal to require a party to dispense with his chosen representative.

Disclosure

15–027   Pursuant to r.10(2)(d) of the Employment Tribunal (Constitution and Rules of Procedure) Regulations 2004 an employment judge may require any person in Great Britain to grant such disclosure and inspection of documents or information to a party as might be ordered by a county court (or in Scotland by a sheriff). An application for disclosure may raise issues under Art.6(1) of the Convention. In *Barracks v (1) Coles (2) Commissioner of Police of the Metropolis*, judgment of July 21, 2006, CA; [2006] EWCA Civ 1041 the claimant, a police officer, alleged racial discrimination following her unsuccessful application for a position as a field intelligence officer. The police case was that the claimant had failed a security vetting check but stated they were prohibited by law from explaining why the claimant had failed the vetting and prohibited from disclosing the law that prohibited them from providing that explanation. The employment tribunal made an unless order requiring that the police disclose reasons why the claimant's application was rejected. The EAT set aside the unless order and held that a substantive hearing of the discrimination claim should take place without the disclosure sought by the claimant. It rejected the claimant's argument that any domestic legislation prohibiting the disclosure of relevant evidence was incompatible with her right to a fair hearing under Art.6(1) of the Convention and the right to an effective judicial remedy for breach of a European Community right to equal treatment. The Court of Appeal held that the EAT had been right to set aside the unless order: it was wrong to have made an unless order with which the police could not, on their case, comply without breaking the law since it unjustifiably prevented them from defending the discrimination claim in the normal way. However, it rejected the submission for the police that the ruling of the EAT on the compatibility of the non-disclosure with the claimant's Convention and EC rights should stand. The Court of Appeal decided that it should not rule on that matter ahead of knowing what relevant evidence was available, free of restrictions on disclosure, at the hearing. The issues of the right to a fair hearing and an effective judicial remedy should be argued and decided in full knowledge of the position after all the available evidence had been heard before the employment tribunal.

Strike-Out

15–028   Under r.18 of the Employment Tribunal (Constitution and Rules of Procedure) Regulations 2004 a tribunal may strike out all or part of a claim on certain grounds. One ground is that the tribunal considers that it is no longer possible to have a fair hearing. The EAT has held that once a tribunal, having considered all other possibilities, has concluded that this ground is satisfied, not only is the tribunal entitled to accede to an application to exercise its discretion to strike-out the claim, but it must do so. As a public authority under s.6(3)of the Human Rights Act 1998 it cannot order a hearing to go ahead which it has found to be unfair: *Abegaze v Shrewsbury College of Arts and Technology*, above; cf. *A Bayley v (1) Whitbread Hotel Co Ltd (t/a Marriott Worsley Park Hotel) (2) Whitbread Group Ltd*, judgment of August 16, 2007, EAT. In exceptional circumstances a claim may be struck out on this basis even after judgment on liability has been given in favour of the claimant, but prior to the determination of remedy: *Abegaze v Shrewsbury College of Arts and Technology*, above.

CHAPTER 16

Statutory Questionnaires in Discrimination Claims

Contents
Sect.

SEX DISCRIMINATION ACT 1975

74. Help for aggrieved persons in obtaining information etc

16–001 (1) With a view to helping a person ("the person aggrieved") who considers he may have been discriminated against [or subjected to harassment] in contravention of this Act to decide whether to institute proceedings and, if he does so, to formulate and present his case in the most effective manner, the Secretary of State shall by order prescribe—

(a) forms by which the person aggrieved may question the respondent on his reasons for doing any relevant act, or on any other matter which is or may be relevant;

(b) forms by which the respondent may if he so wishes reply to any questions.

(2) Where the person aggrieved questions the respondent (whether in accordance with an order under subsection (1) or not)—

(a) the question, and any reply by the respondent (whether in accordance with such an order or not) shall, subject to the following provisions of this section, be admissible as evidence in the proceedings;

(b) if it appears to the court or tribunal that the respondent deliberately, and without reasonable excuse omitted to reply within [the period applicable under subsection (2A)] or that his reply is evasive or equivocal, the court or tribunal may draw any inference from that fact that it considers it just and equitable to draw, including an inference that he committed an unlawful act.

(2A) The period applicable for the purposes of subsection (2) (b) is—

(a) eight weeks beginning with the day when the question was served on the respondent, if the question relates to discrimination under—

(i) any provision of Part 2,

(3) The Secretary of State may by order—

(a) prescribe the period within which questions must be duly served in order to be admissible under subsection (2) (a) and

(b) prescribe the manner in which a question, and any reply by the respondent, may be duly served.

(5) This section is without prejudice to any other enactment or rule of law regulating interlocutory and preliminary matters in proceedings before a county court, sheriff court or employment tribunal, and has effect subject to any enactment or rule of law regulating the admissibility of evidence in such proceedings.

(6) In this section "respondent" includes a prospective respondent Wording in square brackets in sub-ss (1) and (2)(b) inserted and sub-s (2A)
added by SI 2005/2467 as from 1 October 2005.

SEX DISCRIMINATION (QUESTIONS AND REPLIES) ORDER 1975

(SI 1975/2048, as amended by SI 1977/844)

Citation and operation

This Order may be cited as the Sex Discrimination (Questions and Replies) Order 1975 and shall come into operation on 29 December 1975.

16–002

2 Interpretation

(1) In this Order "the Act" means the Sex Discrimination Act 1975.

(3) The Interpretation Act 1889 shall apply to the interpretation of this Order as it applies to the interpretation of an Act of Parliament.

16–003

3 Forms for asking and answering questions

The forms respectively set out in Schedules 1 and 2 to this Order or forms to the like effect with such variation as the circumstances may require are, respectively, hereby prescribed as forms—

16–004

(a) by which a person aggrieved may question a respondent as mentioned in subsection (1)(a) of section 74 of the Act;

(b) by which a respondent may if he so wishes reply to such questions as mentioned in subsection (1)(b) of that section.

5 Period for service of questions—tribunal cases

In proceedings before a tribunal, a question shall only be admissible as evidence in pursuance of section 74(2)(a) of the Act—

16–005

(a) where it was served before a complaint had been presented to a tribunal, if it was so served—

(i) within the period of three months beginning when the act complained of was done; or

Statutory Questionnaires

(ii) where the period under section 76 of the Act within which proceedings must be brought is extended by regulation 15 of the Employment Act 2002 (Dispute Resolution) Regulations 2004, within that extended period;

(b) where it was served when a complaint had been presented to a tribunal, either if it was so served within the period of twenty-one days beginning with the day on which the complaint was presented or if it was so served later with leave given, and within a period specified, by a direction of a tribunal.

6 Manner of service of questions and replies

16–006   A question and any reply thereto may be served on the respondent or, as the case may be, on the person aggrieved—

(a) by delivering it to him; or

(b) by sending it by post to him at his usual or last-known residence or place of business; or

(c) where the person to be served is a body corporate or is a trade union or employers' association within the meaning of the Trade Union and Labour Relations Act 1974, by delivering it to the secretary or clerk of the body, union or association at its registered or principal office or by sending it by post to the secretary or clerk at that office; or

(d) where the person to be served is acting by a solicitor, by delivering it at, or by sending it by post to, the solicitor's address for service; or

(e) where the person to be served is the person aggrieved, by delivering the reply, or sending it by post, to him at his address for reply as stated by him in the document containing the questions.

RACE RELATIONS ACT 1976

65.   Help for aggrieved persons in obtaining information etc

16–007   (1) With a view to helping a person ("the person aggrieved") who considers he may have been discriminated against [or subjected to harassment] in contravention of this Act to decide whether to institute proceedings and, if he does so, to formulate and present his case in the most effective manner, the Secretary of State shall by order prescribe—

(a) forms by which the person aggrieved may question the respondent on his reasons for doing any relevant act, or on any other matter which is or may be relevant; and

(b) forms by which the respondent may if he so wishes reply to any questions.

(2) Where the person aggrieved questions the respondent (whether in accordance with an order under subsection (1) or not)—

(a) the question, and any reply by the respondent (whether in accordance with such an order or not) shall, subject to the following provisions of this section, be admissible as evidence in the proceedings;

(b) if it appears to the court or tribunal that the respondent deliberately, and without reasonable excuse, omitted to reply within a reasonable period or, where the question relates to discrimination on grounds of race or ethnic or national origins, or to harassment, the period of eight weeks beginning with the day on which the question was served on him] or that his reply is evasive or equivocal, the court or tribunal may draw any inference from that fact that it considers it just and equitable to draw, including an inference that he committed an unlawful act.

(3) The Secretary of State may by order—

(a) prescribe the period within which questions must be duly served in order to be admissible under subsection (2) (a); and

(b) prescribe the manner in which a question, and any reply by the respondent, may be duly served.

(4) Rules may enable the court entertaining a claim under section 57 to determine, before the date fixed for the hearing of the claim, whether a question or reply is admissible under this section or not.

(4A) In section 19B proceedings, subsection (2) (b) does not apply in relation to a failure to reply, or a particular reply, if the conditions specified in subsection (4B) are satisfied.

(4B) Those conditions are that—

(a) at the time of doing any relevant act, the respondent was carrying out public investigator functions or was a public prosecutor; and

(b) he reasonably believes that a reply or (as the case may be) a different reply would be likely to prejudice any criminal investigation, any decision to institute criminal proceedings or any criminal proceedings or would reveal the reasons behind a decision not to institute or a decision not to continue, criminal proceedings.

(4C) For the purposes of subsections (4A) and (4B)—

"public investigator functions" has the same meaning as in section 57;

"section 19B proceedings" means proceedings in respect of a claim under section 57 which has arisen by virtue of section 19B.

(5) This section is without prejudice to any other enactment or rule of law regulating interlocutory and preliminary matters in proceedings before a county court, sheriff court or employment tribunal, and has effect subject to any enactment or rule of law regulating the admissibility of evidence in such proceedings.

(6) In this section "respondent" includes a prospective respondent and "rules"—

Sub sections (4A)–(4C) and (7) added by s.5 of the Race Relations (Amendment) Act 2000 as from April 2, 2001.

RACE RELATIONS (QUESTIONS AND REPLIES) ORDER 1977

1 CITATION AND OPERATION

16–008   This Order may be cited as the Race Relations (Questions and Replies) Order 1977 and shall come into operation on 13th June 1977.

2 Interpretation

16–009   (1) In this Order "the Act" means the Race Relations Act 1976.

(3) The Interpretation Act 1889 shall apply to the interpretation of this Order as it applies to the interpretation of an Act of Parliament.

3 Forms for asking and answering questions

16–010   The forms respectively set out in Schedules 1 and 2 to this Order or forms to the like effect with such variation as the circumstances may require are, respectively, hereby prescribed as forms—

(a) by which a person aggrieved may question a respondent as mentioned in subsection (1)(a) of section 65 of the Act;

(b) by which a respondent may if he so wishes reply to such questions as mentioned in subsection (1)(b) of that section.

5 Period for service of questions—tribunal cases

16–011   In proceedings before a tribunal, a question shall only be admissible as evidence in pursuance of section 65(2)(a) of the Act—

(a) where it was served before a complaint had been presented to a tribunal, if it was so served—

(i) within the period of three months beginning when the act complained of was done; or

(ii) where the period under section 68 of the Act within which proceedings must be brought is extended by regulation 15 of the Employment Act 2002 (Dispute Resolution) Regulations 2004, within that extended period;

(b) where it was served when a complaint had been presented to a tribunal, either if it was served within the period of twenty-one days beginning with the day on which the complaint was presented or if it was so served later with leave given, and within a period specified, by a direction of a tribunal.

6 Manner of service of questions and replies

A question and any reply thereto may be served on the respondent **16–012** or, as the case may be, on the person aggrieved—

(a) by delivering it to him; or

(b) by sending it by post to him at his usual or last-known residence or place of business; or

(c) where the person to be served is a body corporate or is a trade union or employers' association within the meaning of the Trade Union and Labour Relations Act 1974, by delivering it to the secretary or clerk of the body, union or association at its registered or principal office or by sending it by post to the secretary or clerk at that office; or

(d) where the person to be served is acting by a solicitor, by delivering it at, or by sending it by post to, the solicitor's address for service; or

(e) where the person is the person aggrieved, by delivering the reply, or sending it by post, to him at his address for reply as stated by him in the document containing the questions.

DISABILITY DISCRIMINATION ACT 1995

56. Help for aggrieved persons in obtaining information etc.

(1) For the purposes of this section— **16–013**

(a) a person who considers that he may have been—

> > > (i) discriminated against in contravention of Part 2 or 3, or
> > > (ii) subjected to harassment in contravention of Part 2 or section 21A(2), is referred to as "the person aggrieved"; and
> > (b) a person against whom the person aggrieved may decide to institute, or has instituted, proceedings in respect of such discrimination or harassment is referred to as "the respondent".

(2) With a view to helping the person aggrieved decide whether to institute proceedings and, if he does so, to formulate and present his case in the most effective manner, the Secretary of State shall by order prescribe—

> (a) forms by which the person aggrieved may question the respondent on his reasons for doing any relevant act, or on any other matter which is or may be relevant; and
> (b) forms by which the respondent may if he so wishes reply to any questions.

(3) Where the person aggrieved questions the respondent in accordance with forms prescribed by an order under subsection (2)—

> (a) the question, and any reply by the respondent (whether in accordance with such an order or not), shall be admissible as evidence in any proceedings under Part 2 or 3;
> (b) if it appears to the court or tribunal in any such proceedings—
> > (i) that the respondent deliberately, and without reasonable excuse, omitted to reply within the period of eight weeks beginning with the day on which the question was served on him, or
> > (ii) that the respondent's reply is evasive or equivocal,

it may draw any inference which it considers it just and equitable to draw, including an inference that the respondent committed an unlawful act.

(4) The Secretary of State may by order—

> (a) prescribe the period within which questions must be duly served in order to be admissible under subsection (3)(a); and

(b) prescribe the manner in which a question, and any reply by the respondent, may be duly served.

(5) Rules of court may enable a court entertaining a claim under section 25 to determine, before the date fixed for the hearing of the claim, whether a question or reply is admissible under this section or not.

(8) This section is without prejudice to any other enactment or rule of law regulating interlocutory and preliminary matters in proceedings before a county court, the sheriff or an employment tribunal, and has effect subject to any enactment or rule of law regulating the admissibility of evidence in such proceedings.

EMPLOYMENT EQUALITY (RELIGION OR BELIEF) REGULATIONS 2003

33. Help for persons in obtaining information etc

(1) In accordance with this regulation, a person ("the person aggrieved") who considers he may have been discriminated against, or subjected to harassment, in contravention of these Regulations may serve on the respondent to a complaint presented under regulation 28 (jurisdiction of employment tribunals) or a claim brought under regulation 31 (jurisdiction of county and sheriff courts) questions in the form set out in Schedule 2 or forms to the like effect with such variation as the circumstances require; and the respondent may if he so wishes reply to such questions by way of the form set out in Schedule 3 or forms to the like effect with such variation as the circumstances require.

16–014

(2) Where the person aggrieved questions the respondent (whether in accordance with paragraph (1) or not)—

(a) the questions, and any reply by the respondent (whether in accordance with paragraph (1) or not) shall, subject to the following provisions of this regulation, be admissible as evidence in the proceedings;

(b) if it appears to the court or tribunal that the respondent deliberately, and without reasonable excuse, omitted to reply within eight weeks of service of the questions or that his reply is evasive or equivocal, the court or tribunal may draw any inference from that fact that it considers it just and equitable to draw, including an inference that he committed an unlawful act.

(4) In proceedings before an employment tribunal, a question shall only be admissible as evidence in pursuance of paragraph (2)(a)—

(a) where it was served before a complaint had been presented to a tribunal, if it was so served—

    (i) within the period of three months beginning when the act complained of was done; or

(b) where it was served when a complaint had been presented to the tribunal, either—

    (i) if it was so served within the period of twenty-one days beginning with the day on which the complaint was presented, or

    (ii) if it was so served later with leave given, and within a period specified, by a direction of the tribunal.

(5) A question and any reply thereto may be served on the respondent or, as the case may be, on the person aggrieved—

(a) by delivering it to him;

(b) by sending it by post to him at his usual or last-known residence or place of business;

(c) where the person to be served is a body corporate or is a trade union or employers' association within the meaning of the Trade Union and Labour Relations (Consolidation) Act 1992, by delivering it to the secretary or clerk of the body, union or association at its registered or principal office or by sending it by post to the secretary or clerk at that office;

(d) where the person to be served is acting by a solicitor, by delivering it at, or by sending it by post to, the solicitor's address for service; or

(e) where the person to be served is the person aggrieved, by delivering the reply, or sending it by post, to him at his address for reply as stated by him in the document containing the questions.

(6) This regulation is without prejudice to any other enactment or rule of law regulating interlocutory and preliminary matters in proceedings before a county court, sheriff court or employment tribunal, and has effect subject to any enactment or rule of law regulating the admissibility of evidence in such proceedings.

(7) In this regulation "respondent" includes a prospective respondent.

SCHEDULE 2

QUESTIONNAIRE OF PERSON AGGRIEVED

Regulation 33(1)

To . . . . (*name of person to*　**16–015**
be questioned) of

. . . .
(*address*)

1—(1) I . . . . (*name of questioner*) of . . . .

. . . .

. . . . (*address*)

consider that you may have discriminated against me [subjected me to harassment] contrary to the Employment Equality (Religion or Belief) Regulations 2003.

(2) (*Give date, approximate time and a factual description of the treatment received and of the circumstances leading up to the treatment.*)

(3) I consider that this treatment may have been unlawful [because . . . . .
. . . . (*complete if you wish to give reasons, otherwise delete*)].

2 Do you agree that the statement in paragraph 1(2) above is an accurate description of what happened? If not, in what respect do you disagree or what is your version of what happened?

3 Do you accept that your treatment of me was unlawful discrimination [harassment]?

If not—

(*a*) why not,

(*b*) for what reason did I receive the treatment accorded to me, and

(*c*) how far did considerations of religion or belief affect your treatment of me?

4 (*Any other questions you wish to ask.*)

589

5 My address for any reply you may wish to give to the questions raised above is [that set out in paragraph 1(1) above] [the following address. . . .

. . . .

. . . .].

- . . . .*(signature of questioner)*

- . . . . *(date)*

- *N.B*—By virtue of regulation 33 of the Employment Equality (Religion or Belief) Regulations 2003 this questionnaire and any reply are (subject to the provisions of that regulation) admissible in proceedings under the Regulations. A court or tribunal may draw any such inference as is just and equitable from a failure without reasonable excuse to reply within eight weeks of service of this questionnaire, or from an evasive or equivocal reply, including an inference that the person questioned has committed an unlawful act.

SCHEDULE 3

REPLY BY RESPONDENT

Regulation 33(1)

16–016

To . . . . *(name of questioner)* of

. . . .
(address)

1 I . . . . *(name of person questioned)* of

. . . .
(address)

hereby acknowledge receipt of the questionnaire signed by you and dated
. . . . which was served on me on . . . . *(date)*.

2 [I agree that the statement in paragraph 1(2) of the questionnaire is an accurate description of what happened.]

[I disagree with the statement in paragraph 1(2) of the questionnaire in that. . . . .

. . . .]

3 I accept/dispute that my treatment of you was unlawful discrimination [harassment].

[My reasons for so disputing are . . . .

. . . .

The reason why you received the treatment accorded to you and the answers to the other questions in paragraph 3 of the questionnaire are . .

. . . .]

4 (*Replies to questions in paragraph 4 of the questionnaire.*)

5 I have deleted (in whole or in part) the paragraph(s) numbered . . . . above, since I am unable/unwilling to reply to the relevant questions in the correspondingly numbered paragraph(s) of the questionnaire for the following reasons . . . .]

. . . . (*signature of person questioned*)

. . . . (*date*)

EMPLOYMENT EQUALITY (SEXUAL ORIENTATION) REGULATIONS 2003

33. Help for persons in obtaining information etc

(1) In accordance with this regulation, a person ("the person 16–017 aggrieved") who considers he may have been discriminated against, or subjected to harassment, in contravention of these Regulations may serve on the respondent to a complaint presented under regulation 28 (jurisdiction of employment tribunals) or a claim brought under regulation 31 (jurisdiction of county and sheriff courts) questions in the form set out in Schedule 2 or forms to the like effect with such variation as the circumstances require; and the respondent may if he so wishes reply to such questions by way of the form set out in Schedule 3 or forms to the like effect with such variation as the circumstances require.

(2) Where the person aggrieved questions the respondent (whether in accordance with paragraph (1) or not)—

   (a) the questions, and any reply by the respondent (whether in accordance with paragraph (1) or not) shall, subject to the following provisions of this regulation, be admissible as evidence in the proceedings;

   (b) if it appears to the court or tribunal that the respondent deliberately, and without reasonable excuse, omitted to reply within eight weeks of service of the questions or that his reply is evasive or equivocal, the court or tribunal may draw any inference from that fact that it considers it just and equitable to draw, including an inference that he committed an unlawful act.

(4) In proceedings before an employment tribunal, a question shall only be admissible as evidence in pursuance of paragraph (2)(a)—

   (a) where it was served before a complaint had been presented to a tribunal, if it was so served—

      (i) within the period of three months beginning when the act complained of was done; or

   (b) where it was served when a complaint had been presented to the tribunal, either—

      (i) if it was so served within the period of twenty-one days beginning with the day on which the complaint was presented, or

      (ii) if it was so served later with leave given, and within a period specified, by a direction of the tribunal.

(5) A question and any reply thereto may be served on the respondent or, as the case may be, on the person aggrieved—

   (a) by delivering it to him;

   (b) by sending it by post to him at his usual or last-known residence or place of business;

   (c) where the person to be served is a body corporate or is a trade union or employers' association within the meaning of the Trade Union and Labour Relations (Consolidation) Act 1992 by delivering it to the secretary or clerk of the body, union or association at its registered or principal office or by sending it by post to the secretary or clerk at that office;

   (d) where the person to be served is acting by a solicitor, by delivering it at, or by sending it by post to, the solicitor's address for service; or

   (e) where the person to be served is the person aggrieved, by delivering the reply, or sending it by post, to him at his

address for reply as stated by him in the document containing the questions.

(6) This regulation is without prejudice to any other enactment or rule of law regulating interlocutory and preliminary matters in proceedings before a county court, sheriff court or employment tribunal, and has effect subject to any enactment or rule of law regulating the admissibility of evidence in such proceedings.
(7) In this regulation "respondent" includes a prospective respondent.

SCHEDULE 2

QUESTIONNAIRE OF PERSON AGGRIEVED

Regulation 33(1)

To . . . . (*name of person to be questioned*) of **16–018**
(*address*)

1—(1) I . . . . (*name of questioner*) of . . . .
(*address*) consider that you may have discriminated against me [subjected me to harassment] contrary to the Employment Equality (Sexual Orientation) Regulations 2003.

(2) (*Give date, approximate time and a factual description of the treatment received and of the circumstances leading up to the treatment.*)

(3) I consider that this treatment may have been unlawful [because . . . . .
. . . . (*complete if you wish to give reasons, otherwise delete*)].

2 Do you agree that the statement in paragraph 1(2) above is an accurate description of what happened? If not, in what respect do you disagree or what is your version of what happened?

3 Do you accept that your treatment of me was unlawful discrimination [harassment]?

If not—

(a) why not,

(b) for what reason did I receive the treatment accorded to me, and

(c) how far did considerations of sexual orientation affect your treatment of me?

4 (*Any other questions you wish to ask.*)

5 My address for any reply you may wish to give to the questions raised above is [that set out in paragraph 1(1) above] [the following address   ].

. . . . (*signature of questioner*)

. . . . (*date*)

NB—By virtue of regulation 33 of the Employment Equality (Sexual Orientation) Regulations 2003 this questionnaire and any reply are (subject to the provisions of that regulation) admissible in proceedings under the Regulations. A court or tribunal may draw any such inference as is just and equitable from a failure without reasonable excuse to reply within eight weeks of service of this questionnaire, or from an evasive or equivocal reply, including an inference that the person questioned has committed an unlawful act.

SCHEDULE 3

REPLY BY RESPONDENT

Regulation 33(1)

16–019 To . . . .   (*name of questioner*) of . . . .

. . . . (*address*)

1 I . . . .   (*name of person questioned*) of . . . .
. . . . . . (*address*) hereby acknowledge receipt of the questionnaire signed by you and dated . . . . which was served on me on . . . . (*date*).

2 [I agree that the statement in paragraph 1(2) of the questionnaire is an accurate description of what happened.]

[I disagree with the statement in paragraph 1(2) of the questionnaire in that . . . .]

3 I accept/dispute that my treatment of you was unlawful discrimination [harassment].

[My reasons for so disputing are . . . ; the reason why you received the treatment accorded to you and the answers to the other questions in paragraph 3 of the questionnaire are . . . .]

4 (*Replies to questions in paragraph 4 of the questionnaire*)

5 I have deleted (in whole or in part) the paragraph(s) numbered   above, since I am unable/unwilling to reply to the relevant questions in the correspondingly numbered paragraph(s) of the questionnaire for the following reasons . . . .]

. . . . (*signature of person questioned*)

. . . . (*date*)

Commencement

Sections 74(1) and 81(4) of the Sex Discrimination Act 1975 commencing on December 29, 1975.

Sections 65(1) and 74(3) of the Race Relations Act 1976 commencing on June 13, 1977.

Sections 56(2), (4) and 67(3) of the Disability Discrimination Act 1995 commencing on June 30, 2005.

Section 7B of the Equal Pay Act 1970 commencing on April 6, 2003.

Regulation 33(1) and Schedules 2 and 3 of the Employment Equality (Religion or Belief) Regulations 2003 commencing on December 2, 2003.

Regulation 33(1) and Schedules 2 and 3 of the Employment Equality (Sexual Orientation) Regulations 2003 commencing on December 1, 2003.

16–020

Orders

Sex Discrimination (Questions and Replies) Order 1975 (SI 1975/2048) as amended by s.17 of the Employment Act 2002 (Dispute Resolution) Regulations 2004.

Race Relations (Questions and Replies) Order 1977 (SI 1977/842) as amended by s.17 of the Employment Act 2002 (Dispute Resolution) Regulations 2004.

Disability Discrimination (Questions and Replies) Order 2004 (SI 2004/1168) this Order replaced the Disability Discrimination (Questions and Replies) Order 1996 (SI 1996/2793).

Equal Pay (Questions and Replies) Order 2003 (SI 2003/722).

16–021

General

The questionnaire procedure provides a person who considers that he may have been discriminated against or subjected to harassment to secure information to decide whether to (1) institute proceedings, or (2) continue with a claim; and (3) to assist in the presentation of the claim in the most effective manner.

The questionnaire allows an aggrieved person to request information in the form of interrogatories (questions) if the request is made (1) within three months of the act of discrimination, (2) within 21 days of presenting a complaint or (3) out of time with the leave of the employment tribunal.

The respondent questionnaire needs to be responded to within eight weeks.

Schedule 1 of the Orders provides a prescribed format for the asking of questions and Sch.2 a format for the reply.

The replies are admissible in discrimination proceedings and the employment tribunal may draw such inferences as is just and equitable from (1) a failure without reasonable excuse of just cause to reply within time, (2) from an evasive or (3) an equivocal reply, including an inference that the person questioned has discriminated unlawfully.

The questionnaire procedure operates outside the employment tribunal's rules of procedure. Therefore it is not possible to make an application to the employment

16–022

tribunal if the respondent does not respond or replies evasively. However, an employment tribunal may be entitled to draw an adverse inference at a later date in such cases.

Prescribed format

16–023   It is not necessary to use the prescribed formats provided for in the Orders (*Dattani v Chief Constable of West Mercia* [2005] I.R.L.R. 327, EAT), as the Acts provide that the procedures apply where the person aggrieved questions the respondent whether in accordance with an order, or not. Therefore any request for information howsoever made within time attracts possible risk of adverse interference being drawn at a later date, if the respondent does not reply or where the reply is evasive or equivocal.

One or more questionnaires

16–024   There is nothing to prevent an aggrieved person from serving a further questionnaire as it may prove to be necessary in the light of the answers provided. In *Carrington v Helix Lighting Ltd* [1990] I.R.L.R. 6 it was observed that it is a sensible and necessary part of the procedure that after an initial questionnaire an aggrieved person should be able to seek leave, on notice, to administer a further questionnaire. The fact that such application is made on notice would allow the respondents to argue that any question was unnecessary or too wide or oppressive.

Information to be provided

16–025   The help provided by the Acts is limited to the questioning of the respondent and does not extend to the request for the provision of documentation although it is not unusual for documents to be requested as part of the questionnaire process. If relevant the documentation will need to be provided in due course. A request can be declined if it seeks information which clearly goes beyond the matters which could be relevant in a discrimination case although there is a risk that if later that information proves to be relevant an adverse inference may be drawn. Although the questionnaire procedure is not governed by the employment tribunal's procedure rules and therefore does not embrace the overriding objectives to deal with cases justly including dealing with cases in ways which are proportionate, it is unlikely that an employment tribunal will draw an inference where a request is clearly disproportionate and therefore has not been answered. The respondent in those circumstances should ask the aggrieved person to modify the request.

Confidential or personal information

16–026   The questionnaire invariably asks questions which seek confidential information such as the salary details of other employees which by the nature of the request (the identifying of personal data) will engage the provisions of the Data Protection Act 1998 (DPA). The exemption provided at s.35 of the DPA concerning disclosure for the purpose of or in connection with legal proceedings is subject to the provisions of Sch.2 to the DPA (see s.35, read in conjunction with s.27 of the DPA). Schedule 2 of the Data Protection Act 1998 provides when an employer may process personal information. This is possible (1) where the data subject (the other employee) consents to it. The employment tribunal will expect that the respondent will seek permission of the data subject. To disclose the information without consent of the data subject, the respondent must show that (2) the disclosure (processing) is necessary for compliance with a legal obligation that the respondent is subject to, (3) the disclosure is needed for the administration of justice, or (4) disclosure is necessary for the purposes of legitimate interests pursued by the data controller or by a third party to whom the data is disclosed, except where the processing is unwarranted by reason of prejudice to the rights, freedoms or interests of the data subject. Even where the information is to be disclosed, the respondent is under a legal duty to ensure that the disclosure (processing) of the data is fair and lawful which would engage the common law on breach of confidence.

The guidance note in respect of the equal pay questionnaire seeks to address these problems with the suggestion that "in many cases, employers will be able to answer detailed questions in general terms while still preserving the anonymity and confidence of their worker".

Confidential information was considered in *Science Research Council v Nasse; BL Cars Ltd v Vyas* [1979] I.R.L.R. 465, HL in the context of discrimination claims (trade union and race) where confidential documention was requested. The House of Lords held that there was no presumption against disclosure of confidential documentation and therefore it was necessary for the employment tribunal to consider whether it was necessary for the fair disposal of the case that an order for disclosure should be made and whether the information could be obtained by other means not involving a breach of confidence. The argument that the information contained in confidential documents was protected by public interest immunity was rejected.

The nature of the evidence

In *West Midlands Passenger Transport Executive v Singh* [1988] I.R.L.R. 186, CA (an **16–027** appeal concerning discovery) it was held that an employment tribunal may order discovery of the ethnic origins of applicants both successful and unsuccessful for posts similar to that of the claimant by way of a schedule covering a two-year period. The statistical material ordered to be disclosed was relevant to the aggrieved person's complaint, in that it was logically probative of whether the employers discriminated against him on racial grounds when they denied him promotion.

Drawing of inferences

The employment tribunal is entitled to draw adverse inferences from a failure to **16–028** reply or from an equivocal or evasive answer (*King v Great Britain-China Centre* [1991] I.R.L.R. 513). There is no automatic presumption of discrimination by a failure in answering a questionnaire Although failures of this kind are specified at item (7) of the Barton guidelines as endorsed by *Igen Ltd v Wong* [2005] I.C.R. 931 [at 957B], as matters from which an inference can be drawn, that is only 'in appropriate cases' and the drawing of inferences from such failures, as indeed from anything else, is not a tick box exercise. It is necessary in each case to consider whether in the particular circumstances of that case the failure in question is capable of constituting evidence supporting the inference that the respondent acted discriminatorily in the manner alleged; and if so whether in the light of any explanation provided it does in fact justly that inference. As recognised in *D'Silva v NATFHE* UKEAT/0384/07/LA there will be many cases where it should be clear from the start, or soon becomes evident, that an alleged failure of this kind, however reprehensible, can have no bearing on the reason why the Respondent committed the act complained of.

Time limits

If the questionnaire is served out of time, the employment tribunal can give leave **16–029** for time to be extended. There is no "just and equitable" or "reasonably practicable" test to be applied by the employment tribunal in extending time. Where leave is required, the employment tribunal should take into account all the relevant aspects including prejudice, delay, prolixity, oppression and irrelevance

(Williams v Greater London Citizens Advice Bureaux Service [1989] I.C.R. 545, EAT). A copy of the proposed questionnaire should support any application for time to be extended and the respondent should be afforded the opportunity to make representations prior to a decision being made.

CHAPTER 17

COMPENSATION, REMEDIES AND INTEREST

Contents

Compensation, Remedies
and Interest

17–001   In most instances, the major part of the relief awarded by an employment tribunal is the award for compensatory loss. Compensation and remedies could themselves form the subject of an entire book. This section seeks to identify the basic principles that should inform the way in which compensatory losses should be assessed. As a matter of convenience, this is set out by reference to the specific provisions relating to the law of unfair dismissal. For that reason, this section also considers the calculation of statutory basic awards, and the remedies of reinstatement and re-engagement.

The principles that govern the general assessment of compensatory awards on claims of unfair dismissal, apply equally to the assessment of loss on discrimination claims

EMPLOYMENT RIGHTS ACT 1996

CHAPTER II

REMEDIES FOR UNFAIR DISMISSAL

INTRODUCTORY

111   Complaints to an employment tribunal

   . . .

17–002   (Editorial Note. The meaning and effect of section 111 is considered in the chapter on limitation.)

112   The remedies: orders and compensation

17–003   **(1) This section applies where, on a complaint under section 111, an employment tribunal finds that the grounds of the complaint are well-founded.**

   (2) The tribunal shall—

   (a) explain to the complainant what orders may be made under section 113 and in what circumstances they may be made, and

(b) ask him whether he wishes the tribunal to make such an order.

(3) If the complainant expresses such a wish, the tribunal may make an order under section 113.

(4) If no order is made under section 113, the tribunal shall make an award of compensation for unfair dismissal (calculated in accordance with sections 118 to [126]) to be paid by the employer to the employee.

[(5) Where—

(a) an employee is regarded as unfairly dismissed by virtue of section [98ZG or] 98A(1) (whether or not his dismissal is unfair or regarded as unfair for any other reason), and

(b) an order is made in respect of the employee under section 113,

the employment tribunal shall, subject to subsection (6), also make an award of four weeks' pay to be paid by the employer to the employee.

(6) An employment tribunal shall not be required to make an award under subsection (5) if it considers that such an award would result in injustice to the employer.]

Subsections (5), (6) in square brackets added by s.34 of the Employment Act 2002 **17–004** from October 1, 2004.

Amendments made from October 1, 2006 by the Employment Equality (Age) Regulations 2006.

The duty on the employment tribunal

Subsection (1) requires an employment tribunal to explain what orders maybe **17–005** made under s.113. In *Cowley v Manson Timber Ltd* [1995] I.R.L.R. 153 failure by an employment tribunal to comply with the procedure laid down in s.112 did not make any decision on compensation a nullity (no effect in law). The employment tribunal is clearly under a statutory duty to consider the remedies of reinstatement and re-engagement, to explain to the employee what they mean, and to give the claimant a chance to say whether he wants to be reinstated or re-engaged; and an order made without proper compliance with s.112 is capable of being set aside by the Employment Appeal Tribunal (EAT) if it appears that a failure to comply with that statutory duty leads to the possibility of injustice or unfairness.

ORDERS FOR REINSTATEMENT OR RE-ENGAGEMENT

113 The orders

An order under this section may be— **17–006**

(a) an order for reinstatement (in accordance with section 114), or

as the tribunal may decide.

17–007   Section 113 contemplates that reinstatement or re-engagement would be primary remedies for unfair dismissal, and compensation secondary. Orders for either reinstatement or re-engagement are, however, comparatively rare in practice. That is because in many cases to make such an order would be contrary to the wishes of the individual complainant or the constraints of practicability (both of which have to be taken into account under the statute).

114   Order for reinstatement

17–008   **(1) An order for reinstatement is an order that the employer shall treat the complainant in all respects as if he had not been dismissed.**

(2) On making an order for reinstatement the tribunal shall specify—

   (a)   **any amount payable by the employer in respect of any benefit which the complainant might reasonably be expected to have had but for the dismissal (including arrears of pay) for the period between the date of termination of employment and the date of reinstatement,**

   (b)   **any rights and privileges (including seniority and pension rights) which must be restored to the employee, and**

   (c)   **the date by which the order must be complied with.**

(3) If the complainant would have benefited from an improvement in his terms and conditions of employment had he not been dismissed, an order for reinstatement shall require him to be treated as if he had benefited from that improvement from the date on which he would have done so but for being dismissed.

(4) In calculating for the purposes of subsection (2)(a) any amount payable by the employer, the tribunal shall take into account, so as to reduce the employer's liability, any sums received by the complainant in respect of the period between the date of termination of employment and the date of reinstatement by way of—

   (a)   **wages in lieu of notice or ex gratia payments paid by the employer, or**

   (b)   **remuneration paid in respect of employment with another employer,**

and such other benefits as the tribunal thinks appropriate in the circumstances.

17–009   Reinstatement is defined by s.114 of the Employment Rights Act 1996 as "an order that the employer shall treat the (claimant) in all respects as if he had not been dismissed". The claimant is entitled to recover not only his loss of salary but also loss in respect of all contractual entitlements and other benefits which he would have been received had the claimant been employed during the relevant period including loss of increased salary if promoted. The employment tribunal is required to state clearly what the claimant has lost out on, including any benefits received including promotion, and specify the date by which the order must be complied with.

The employment tribunal is not empowered to reduce the amount payable under a reinstatement order in respect of loss of earnings between termination and re-engagement on the ground that the employee failed to mitigate that loss. An order for reinstatement requires the employer to "treat the complainant in all respects as if he had not been dismissed". There is no discretion to increase or decrease what might otherwise be secured had the dismissal not occurred. This produces an idiosyncratic and undesirable discrepancy between comparable cases where either the employee initially seeks compensation rather than re-employment (used to mean either reinstatement or a re-engagement order) or where the employee obtains a re-employment order which the employer declines to follow, since in both those circumstances any failure by the employee to mitigate his loss will lead to a reduction in the award (*City and Hackney Heath Authority v Crisp* [1990] I.C.R. 95, EAT).

Where alternative employment has been secured, set off applies with the earnings from the other employment to be set off: subs.(4)(b).

115 Order for re-engagement

(1) An order for re-engagement is an order, on such terms as the **17–010** tribunal may decide, that the complainant be engaged by the employer, or by a successor of the employer or by an associated employer, in employment comparable to that from which he was dismissed or other suitable employment.

(2) On making an order for re-engagement the tribunal shall specify the terms on which re-engagement is to take place, including—

    (a) the identity of the employer,

    (b) the nature of the employment,

    (c) the remuneration for the employment,

    (d) any amount payable by the employer in respect of any benefit which the complainant might reasonably be expected to have had but for the dismissal (including arrears of pay) for the period between the date of termination of employment and the date of re-engagement,

    (e) any rights and privileges (including seniority and pension rights) which must be restored to the employee, and

    (f) the date by which the order must be complied with.

(3) In calculating for the purposes of subsection (2)(d) any amount payable by the employer, the tribunal shall take into account, so as to reduce the employer's liability, any sums received by the complainant in respect of the period between the date of termination of employment and the date of re-engagement by way of—

(a) wages in lieu of notice or ex gratia payments paid by the employer, or

(b) remuneration paid in respect of employment with another employer,

and such other benefits as the tribunal thinks appropriate in the circumstances.

116 Choice of order and its terms

17–011   (1) In exercising its discretion under section 113 the tribunal shall first consider whether to make an order for reinstatement and in so doing shall take into account—

(a) whether the complainant wishes to be reinstated,

(b) whether it is practicable for the employer to comply with an order for reinstatement, and

(c) where the complainant caused or contributed to some extent to the dismissal, whether it would be just to order his reinstatement.

(2) If the tribunal decides not to make an order for reinstatement it shall then consider whether to make an order for re-engagement and, if so, on what terms.

(3) In so doing the tribunal shall take into account—

(a) any wish expressed by the complainant as to the nature of the order to be made,

(b) whether it is practicable for the employer (or a successor or an associated employer) to comply with an order for re-engagement, and

(c) where the complainant caused or contributed to some extent to the dismissal, whether it would be just to order his re-engagement and (if so) on what terms.

(4) Except in a case where the tribunal takes into account contributory fault under subsection (3)(c) it shall, if it orders re-engagement, do so on terms which are, so far as is reasonably practicable, as favourable as an order for reinstatement.

(5) Where in any case an employer has engaged a permanent replacement for a dismissed employee, the tribunal shall not take that fact into account in determining, for the purposes of subsection (1)(b) or (3)(b), whether it is practicable to comply with an order for reinstatement or re-engagement.

(6) Subsection (5) does not apply where the employer shows—

(a) that it was not practicable for him to arrange for the dismissed employee's work to be done without engaging a permanent replacement, or

(b) that—

> **(i) he engaged the replacement after the lapse of a reasonable period, without having heard from the dismissed employee that he wished to be reinstated or re-engaged, and**
>
> **(ii) when the employer engaged the replacement it was no longer reasonable for him to arrange for the dismissed employee's work to be done except by a permanent replacement.**

The practicable issue is central to the making of a re-employment order. Before **17–012** an order for re-employment is made, an employment tribunal must make a determination or assessment on the evidence before it whether it is practicable for the employer to comply with such an order. But the determination at this first stage is, of necessity, provisional. The final conclusion as to practicability is made when the employer finds whether he can comply with the order in the period prescribed (stage 2). At stage 2 where a re-employment order is made but the employer does not comply with it and the size of the additional award (dealt with below) is being considered, the burden of proof rests firmly on the employer. The determination that is made at stage 1 is not a final one in the sense that it creates an estoppel or restricts the employer at stage 2 to relying only on facts which have occurred after the re-employment order was made (*Port of London v Payne* [1994] I.C.R. 555). The question of practicability can be argued by the employer at stage 2 under s.117(4) of the Employment Rights Act 1996.

The employment relationship is premised on the existence of mutual trust and confidence. Where there is a breakdown of that relationship, it would not be practicable for a re-employment order to be made. It has been held that an employment tribunal had erred in ordering the employers to re-engage the claimant following its finding that his dismissal was unfair (failure to carry out sufficient investigation into allegations against him, including taking and dealing in drugs at the workplace) as re-engagement was not practical given that the employers genuinely believed in the substance of the allegations (*Wood Group Heavy Industrial Turbines Ltd v Crossan* [1998] I.R.L.R. 680). Recently in *Johnson Matthey Plc v Watters* (EAT 0236–38/06) a mere assertion of a breakdown was not sufficient. What the employment tribunal must do is weigh up all the relevant facts before reaching a determination and not rely on a mere assertion of a breakdown. As was observed by the EAT, trust and confidence would inevitably been dented as a result of tribunal proceedings.

A further basis for not making an order (or defending an application for a re-employment order) is where the employee has caused or contributed to some extent to the dismissal. This is a question of fact for the employment tribunal. Regard must be had by the employment tribunal to its finding of contributory fault in respect of the claimant's conduct pre dismissal when considering whether to make a re-employment order.

117 Enforcement of order and compensation

(1) An employment tribunal shall make an award of compensation, 17–013 to be paid by the employer to the employee, if

> **(a) an order under section 113 is made and the complainant is reinstated or re-engaged, but**

605

(b) the terms of the order are not fully complied with.

(2) Subject to section 124, the amount of the compensation shall be such as the tribunal thinks fit having regard to the loss sustained by the complainant in consequence of the failure to comply fully with the terms of the order.

[(2A) There shall be deducted from any award under subsection (1) the amount of any award made under section 112(5) at the time of the order under section 113.]

(3) Subject to subsections (1) and (2), if an order under section 113 is made but the complainant is not reinstated or re-engaged in accordance with the order, the tribunal shall make—

(a) an award of compensation for unfair dismissal (calculated in accordance with sections 118 to [126]), and

(b) except where this paragraph does not apply, an additional award of compensation of [an amount not less than twenty-six and not more than fifty-two weeks' pay],

to be paid by the employer to the employee.

(4) Subsection (3)(b) does not apply where—

(a) the employer satisfies the tribunal that it was not practicable to comply with the order,

(b)

(5) . . .

(6) . . .

(7) Where in any case an employer has engaged a permanent replacement for a dismissed employee, the tribunal shall not take that fact into account in determining for the purposes of subsection (4)(a) whether it was practicable to comply with the order for reinstatement or re-engagement unless the employer shows that it was not practicable for him to arrange for the dismissed employee's work to be done without engaging a permanent replacement.

(8) Where in any case an employment tribunal finds that the complainant has unreasonably prevented an order under section 113 from being complied with, in making an award of compensation for unfair dismissal . . . it shall take that conduct into account as a failure on the part of the complainant to mitigate his loss.

17–014 Where the employment tribunal has made a re-employment order, the award of compensation for non compliance depends on the nature and extent of the non compliance. Where the claimant returns to work but there is a short fall in the pay due, the employment tribunal will award the short fall in pay. Where there is a refusal to re-employ the employment tribunal will calculate compensation in the normal way but also award additional compensation as a punitive measure (dealt with below). Where the re-employment is on significantly inferior terms to the order made, the employment tribunal may treat the employer's non compliance as a refusal to reinstate at all (*Artisan Press v Srawley and Parker* 1986 I.R.L.R. 126).

The employer is provided a second opportunity (stage 2) to argue that it would not be practicable to re-employ by subs.(4)(a). Stage 1 is provided for by s.116(1)(b) and (3)(b) (see above). The arguments deployed at stage 2 are not limited to matters arising between the stage 1 and stage 2 hearings.

The additional award is provided for by subs.3(b) and is a sum not less than 26 nor more than 52 weeks pay, therefore at present between £8,060 and £16,120. The employment tribunal has a discretion to determine the award and in doing so must act judicially (have regard to the relevant factors such as the employers reason for non compliance) (*Motherwell Railway Club v McQueen* [1989] I.C.R. 418).

Where there is a failure to comply with a re-employment order, recoverable is the actual loss occasioned by the unfair dismissal to the extent necessary "fully to reflect the amount specified". This compensation may exceed the statutory maximum compensation award if necessary in order to meet the requirements under ss.114 and 115 relating to arrears of pay: see s.124(3).

COMPENSATION

118 General

(1) **Where a tribunal makes an award of compensation for unfair dismissal under section 112(4) or 117(3)(a) the award shall consist of—** 17–015

(a) **a basic award (calculated in accordance with sections 119 to 122 and 126), and**

(b) **a compensatory award (calculated in accordance with sections 123, 124, [124A and 126]).**

(2) **. . ..**

(3) **. . ..**

Subsections (2) and (3) concerned the making of a special award where dismissal was for reasons relating to health and safety, working time limitations or acting as a pension fund trustee or employee representative. Since October 1999 the special award was abolished and was replaced by a higher additional award and the significant increase in the statutory ceiling for compensatory awards. **17–016**

119 Basic award

(1) **Subject to the provisions of this section, sections 120 to 122 and section 126, the amount of the basic award shall be calculated by—** 17–017

(a) **determining the period, ending with the effective date of termination, during which the employee has been continuously employed,**

(b) **reckoning backwards from the end of that period the number of years of employment falling within that period, and**

(c) allowing the appropriate amount for each of those years of employment.

(2) In subsection (1)(c) 'the appropriate amount' means—

(a) one and a half weeks' pay for a year of employment in which the employee was not below the age of forty-one,

(b) one week's pay for a year of employment (not within paragraph (a)) in which he was not below the age of twenty-two, and

(c) half a week's pay for a year of employment not within paragraph (a) or (b).

(3) Where twenty years of employment have been reckoned under subsection (1), no account shall be taken under that subsection of any year of employment earlier than those twenty years.

(4) . . .

(5) . . .

(6) . . .

17–018 Subsections (4) and (5) repealed as from October 1, 2006.

Subsection (6) repealed by Sch.4, Pt III, para.23 of the Employment Relations Act 1999 as from December 15, 1999.

The basic award is a payment equivalent to the statutory redundancy payment due if the employee had been dismissed on grounds of redundancy.

Continuous employment is determined under Pt XIV, Ch I of the Employment Rights Act 1996

A week's pay is determined under Pt XIV, Ch II of the Employment Rights Act 1996. The maximum value of a week's pay is set annually. For dismissals where the effective date of termination is on or after February 1, 2007 the maximum amount is £310: see SI 2006/3045. For dismissals where the effective date occurred between February 1, 2006 and January 31, 2007 the maximum amount is £290: see SI 2005/3352.

120 Basic award: minimum in certain cases

17–019 (1) The amount of the basic award (before any reduction under section 122) shall not be less than [£4,200] where the reason (or, if more than one, the principal reason)—

(a) in a redundancy case, for selecting the employee for dismissal, or

(b) otherwise, for the dismissal,

is one of those specified in section 100(1)(a) and (b), [101A(d),] 102(1) or 103.

[(1A) Where—

(a) an employee is regarded as unfairly dismissed by virtue of section [98ZG or] 98A(1) (whether or not his dismissal is unfair or regarded as unfair for any other reason),

(b) an award of compensation falls to be made under section 112(4), and

(c) the amount of the award under section 118(1)(a), before any reduction under section 122(3A) or (4), is less than the amount of four weeks' pay,

the employment tribunal shall, subject to subsection (1B), increase the award under section 118(1)(a) to the amount of four weeks' pay.

(1B) An employment tribunal shall not be required by subsection (1A) to increase the amount of an award if it considers that the increase would result in injustice to the employer.]

(2) . . .

The figure in square brackets in subs.(1) substituted by SI 2006/3045 as from February 1, 2007. Previously, from February 1, 2006, the relevant amount was £4,000, see SI 2005/3352.

Wording in square brackets in subs.(1A)(a) inserted by SI 2006/1031 as from October 1, 2006.

The figure of £4,200 applies where the EDT falls on or after February 1, 2007. For the period February 1, 2005 to January 31, 2006 the figure is £3,800. For the period February 1, 2006 to January 31, 2007 the figure is £4,000.

17–020

121 Basic award of two weeks' pay in certain cases

The amount of the basic award shall be two weeks' pay where the tribunal finds that the reason (or, where there is more than one, the principal reason) for the dismissal of the employee is that he was redundant and the employee—

17–021

(a) by virtue of section 138 is not regarded as dismissed for the purposes of Part XI, or

(b) by virtue of section 141 is not, or (if he were otherwise entitled) would not be, entitled to a redundancy payment.

122 Basic award: reductions

(1) Where the tribunal finds that the complainant has unreasonably refused an offer by the employer which (if accepted) would have the effect of reinstating the complainant in his employment in all respects as if he had not been dismissed, the tribunal shall reduce or further reduce the amount of the basic award to such extent as it considers just and equitable having regard to that finding.

17–022

(2) Where the tribunal considers that any conduct of the complainant before the dismissal (or, where the dismissal was with notice, before the notice was given) was such that it would be just and equitable to reduce or further reduce the amount of the basic award to any extent, the tribunal shall reduce or further reduce that amount accordingly.

(3) Subsection (2) does not apply in a redundancy case unless the reason for selecting the employee for dismissal was one of those

specified in section 100(1)(a) and (b), [101A(d),] 102(1) or 103; and in such a case subsection (2) applies only to so much of the basic award as is payable because of section 120.

[(3A) Where the complainant has been awarded any amount in respect of the dismissal under a designated dismissal procedures agreement, the tribunal shall reduce or further reduce the amount of the basic award to such extent as it considers just and equitable having regard to that award.]

(4) The amount of the basic award shall be reduced or further reduced by the amount of—

(a) any redundancy payment awarded by the tribunal under Part XI in respect of the same dismissal, or

(b) any payment made by the employer to the employee on the ground that the dismissal was by reason of redundancy (whether in pursuance of Part XI or otherwise).

17–023   Subsection (2) concerns the reduction of the basic award on grounds of contributory fault. The reduction need not be in the same percentage as the compensatory award. Importantly, the basic award can not be reduced on the basis that although an unfair dismissal, the dismissal was inevitable even if a fair procedure had been adopted (*Rao v Civil Aviation Authority* 1994 I.R.L.R. 240).

Subsection (4) provides for the set off of the redundancy payment against the basic award but only if the dismissal was on grounds of redundancy. It is not enough that an employer made a payment to an employee which was expressed as being on the grounds of redundancy, even where the employee accepts the grounds of dismissal. The real reason must be that of redundancy for the set off to apply. Section 122 has two limbs: the first provides that

> "the amount of the basic award shall be reduced . . . by the amount of any redundancy payment awarded by the tribunal under Part VI in respect of the same dismissal . . .";

the second limb provides that

> "The amount of the basic award shall be reduced . . . by the amount . . . of any payment made by the employer to the employee on the ground that the dismissal was by reason of redundancy, whether in pursuance of Part VI or otherwise": *Boorman v Allmakes Ltd* [1995] I.R.L.R. 533.

123   Compensatory award

17–024   (1) Subject to the provisions of this section and sections 124, 124A and 126, the amount of the compensatory award shall be such amount as the tribunal considers just and equitable in all the circumstances having regard to the loss sustained by the complainant in consequence of the dismissal in so far as that loss is attributable to action taken by the employer.

(2) The loss referred to in subsection (1) shall be taken to include—

(a) any expenses reasonably incurred by the complainant in consequence of the dismissal, and

(b) subject to subsection (3), loss of any benefit which he might reasonably be expected to have had but for the dismissal.

(3) The loss referred to in subsection (1) shall be taken to include in respect of any loss of—

(a) any entitlement or potential entitlement to a payment on account of dismissal by reason of redundancy (whether in pursuance of Part XI or otherwise), or

(b) any expectation of such a payment, only the loss referable to the amount (if any) by which the amount of that payment would have exceeded the amount of a basic award (apart from any reduction under section 122) in respect of the same dismissal.

(4) In ascertaining the loss referred to in subsection (1) the tribunal shall apply the same rule concerning the duty of a person to mitigate his loss as applies to damages recoverable under the common law of England and Wales or (as the case may be) Scotland.

(5) In determining, for the purposes of subsection (1), how far any loss sustained by the complainant was attributable to action taken by the employer, no account shall be taken of any pressure which by—

(a) calling, organising, procuring or financing a strike or other industrial action, or

(b) threatening to do so,

was exercised on the employer to dismiss the employee; and that question shall be determined as if no such pressure had been exercised.

(6) Where the tribunal finds that the dismissal was to any extent caused or contributed to by any action of the complainant, it shall reduce the amount of the compensatory award by such proportion as it considers just and equitable having regard to that finding.

(7) If the amount of any payment made by the employer to the employee on the ground that the dismissal was by reason of redundancy (whether in pursuance of Part XI or otherwise) exceeds the amount of the basic award which would be payable but for section 122(4), that excess goes to reduce the amount of the compensatory award.

[(8) Where the amount of the compensatory award falls to be calculated for the purposes of an award under section 117(3)(a),

there shall be deducted from the compensatory award any award made under section 112(5) at the time of the order under section 113.]

17–025   Subsection (1): words ", 124A and 126" in square brackets substituted by s.53 and Sch.7 of the Employment Act 2002.
From October 1, 2004
Subsection (8): inserted by s.34 of the Employment Act 2002.
From 1, October 2004

Introduction

17–026   Section 123 requires two considerations in determining the amount of compensation to be awarded. First, whether the loss was occasioned by the dismissal, and secondly if it was, what compensatory award would be just and equitable to make in all the circumstances.
The former consideration is a question of fact and the latter is one of discretion. Where the loss to the claimant is not "caused to a material extent by the dismissal" it is not recoverable (*Dignity Funerals Ltd v Bruce* [2005] I.R.L.R. 189).
The second consideration is rarely addressed by employment tribunals. It empowers the employment tribunal to make a final adjustment to an award after determining the actual loss sustained because it is just and equitable to do so. In *W Devis & Sons Ltd v Atkins* [1977] 3 All E.R. 40 the House of Lords asserted that "It cannot be just and equitable that a sum should be awarded in compensation when in fact the employee has suffered no injustice by being dismissed". This was a case of misconduct discovered after dismissal.
There are three central issues for employment tribunals in determining compensation; (1) the period of time for which the compensatory award should be made, (2) what sums are recoverable and/or set off against this loss and (3) the order in which payments and/or deductions are made. This last issue can have a profound impact on the final compensatory award.

The period of time for which the Compensatory Award should be made

17–027   The approach to the question of the loss sustained as a consequence of the dismissal requires the employment tribunal to consider what would have happened had the unfair dismissal not occurred. This requires, essentially, a determination as to whether the dismissal was procedurally or substantially unfair, a distinction which the appeal courts have said is both unnecessary and unproductive (*Lambe v 186K Ltd* [2005] I.C.R. 307). However, this distinction is routinely applied by employment tribunals for good, practical reasons. Procedural unfairness leads to an award limited to the period of time that it would have taken to go through a fair procedure whereas substantive unfairness gives rise to continuing loss subject to mitigation, causation and remoteness. It is suggested in *King v Eaton Ltd (No.2)* [1999] I.R.L.R. 686 (which was adopted in *Lambe*)

> "that (the assessment of compensation) will be a matter of impression and judgment, so that an Employment Tribunal will have to decide whether the unfair departure from what should have happened was of a kind which makes it possible to say, with more or less confidence, that the failure made no difference, or whether the failure was such that one cannot sensibly reconstruct the world as it might have been".

The observations in *King*, in reality, is an endorsement of the procedural or substantive distinction although couched in different language.

Further, if there has been some intervening event which would mean that the claim should come to an end such as the securing of new (and as well paid employment), the failure to mitigate, the closure of the business, or the subsequent discovery of misconduct, then compensatory period will be treated as at an end.

The first question therefore that the employment tribunal needs to address is whether the dismissal was inevitable, either on the discovery of further information such as theft being discovered shortly after dismissal (which would have caused the employee to have been dismissed, *W Devis & Sons Ltd v Atkins* [1977] I.C.R. 662) or if the employer had followed a fair procedure (a procedural unfairness which would make no difference to the outcome) (*Clarkson International Tools Ltd v Short* [1973] I.C.R. 191). In these circumstances, the employment tribunal will award compensation limited to the time it would have taken to go through the appropriate procedural requirements (*Polkey v A E Dayton Services Ltd* [1988] I.C.R. 142).

If the employment tribunal determine that at some time in the future the claimant would have been dismissed (for example the closure of the business) then the award of compensation would end at this point in time (*James W Cook & Co (Wivenhoe) Ltd v Tipper* [1990] I.C.R. 716).

Alternatively, if there is a degree of uncertainty as to what might have happened had a fair procedure been followed, it is open to the employment tribunal to reduce the award of compensation by a percentage to reflect the chance that the claimant would still have lost his employment (*Polkey v A E Dayton Services Ltd* [1988] I.C.R. 142).

Employment tribunals will usually consider the loss up to the hearing date and then if appropriate for a further period, the future loss period.

Future loss period

Future loss awards are always going to be speculative in nature due to the uncertainty as to what is going to happen. When this loss becomes too remote, the future loss period will end. To reflect the future uncertainty the employment tribunal will invariably apply a percentage reduction to the future loss award. In calculating the salary loss during the future loss period, it is important to reflect any salary increase which is likely to have been awarded if the claimant had remained employed.

17–028

The usual practice adopted by employment tribunals is to deduct between 2.5 per cent and 5 per cent from the future loss award as this is an accelerated payment being made before the loss has been incurred (*Brentwood Bros (Manchester) Ltd v Shepherd* [2003] I.C.R. 1000).

A tribunal may apply a percentage reduction to compensation to reflect the chance that the loss claimed would not in fact have been suffered. For example, the employee might have ceased work at some point in the future for reasons insufficiently proximate to the matters complained of in the proceedings (see for example, *Ministry of Defence v Cannock* [1994] I.R.L.R. 509, EAT). Any such reduction should be determined on the basis of a broad and sensible evaluation of whether (and it so when) the loss-reducing event might occur, not be reference to the question whether the event would have occurred on a balance of probabilities.

The compensatory award period will come to an end when the recovery of loss becomes too speculative and remote. As full credit has to be given for monies earned (alternatively deemed to have been earned had the claimant mitigated his loss) there will come a point in time when there will be no recoverable loss as the reduced compensatory figure subject to a loss of a chance deduction is less than the monies earned. The compensatory award period will end where there is no further loss.

It is open to the employment tribunal to apply a percentage deduction to reflect loss of a chance and also a further deduction for contributory fault. If so, the contributory fault deduction is made after the loss chance deduction has been calculated (*Rao v Civil Aviation Authority* [1994] I.C.R. 495).

Importantly, the employment tribunal must advise the parties that it is considering making a loss chance deduction or deduction for contributory fault and to allow them to make representations on this issue (*Market Force (UK) Ltd v Hunt* [2002] I.R.L.R. 863).

Elements of compensation

17–029   Having determined the appropriate period for the compensatory award s.123 provides that the loss which shall be taken into account includes any expenses reasonably incurred and loss of any benefit which might reasonably expect to have had, but for the dismissal. The loss must be attributable to the action of the employer, if not, it is not recoverable (*Simrad Ltd v Scott* [1997] I.R.L.R. 147).

Salary

17–030   The claimant will be entitled to recover the loss of salary on a net basis but including, if appropriate any increases that he was likely to receive had employment continued.

Benefits

17–031   Non contractual benefits such as bonus payments are recoverable (any benefits which he might reasonably expect) and the amount recoverable is the net and not the gross figure otherwise the claimant would be in a better position than he would have been in had he remained employed (*York Trailer Co Ltd v Sparkes* [1973] I.C.R. 518).

Contractual benefits are recoverable and the employment tribunal will have to attribute a value to these benefits such as a medical cover, life cover, company car, subsidised meals, travel concessions, and subsidised or free accommodation. The assessment of the value is based on what it has cost the claimant to secure the same benefit on the open market.

General

17–032   Pension schemes have undergone radical changes in recent years caused primarily by the funding arrangements and the ever increasing burden on the wages bill. This is particularly true of final salary pension schemes.

The pension loss element of the compensatory award needs careful consideration in the light of these changes. When determining the approach to be adopted, a more forensic and precise approach will be expected and required and this has been particularly so as illustrated by the appellate decisions since the increase in the compensatory award from £10,000 to £50,000 in April 2001. There has been an increased reliance on the use of pension experts in determining this loss. As observed in *Clancy v Cannock Chase Technical College* [2001] I.R.L.R. 331:

> "There will have been many cases where a rough and ready computation sufficed in the past because it could be readily seen that the old lower cap would be exceeded. The far higher cap makes a full and accurate computation now more likely to be needed in more case".

A good starting point for the assessment of pension loss is contained in a booklet entitled "Compensation for loss of pension rights in Employment Tribunals (2003)", a publication produced by three employment judges following consultation with the Government's Actuary Department. This booklet was up-dated following the decision in *Clancy v Cannock Chase Technical College* [2001] I.R.L.R. 331 to deal with the assessment of the loss of pension entitlement under a public sector final salary pension scheme where the employee is both the beneficiary of income benefit as well as a lump sum payment. The 2001 booklet was revised in 2003.

Failure to follow its guidance was originally held to expose a determination on pension loss as being wrong in law, *Tradewinds Airways Ltd v Fletcher* [1981] I.R.L.R. 272 where expert evidence was rejected in favour of the guidance given to tribunals by the Government's Actuarial Department. Subsequently, in *Bingham v Hoboun Engineering Ltd* [1992] I.R.L.R. 298 it was held by the EAT that there was no duty on an employment tribunal to follow the guidelines in the booklet. Recently, further support for deviation from the booklet has been provided by the EAT in *Port of Tilbury (London) Ltd v Birch* [2005] I.R.L.R. 92. The EAT stated that there is no duty on the employment tribunal to follow the guidelines in the booklet. The tribunal's first duty is to consider any credible evidence and submissions put forward by the parties in order to ascertain whether a fair and equitable assessment of the loss of pension rights can be worked out on that basis. If it cannot, the tribunal must explain adequately why not. Where there is little forthcoming from the parties, the booklet may assist the tribunal in determining its assessment. It is interesting to note that a slavish approach to the booklet was not advocated by the authors who stated in 2001 that the recommendations are only guidelines.

"They will become trip-wires if they are blindly applied without considering the facts of each case. Any party is free to canvass any method of assessment which he considers appropriate. We hope that this paper will be found useful as a starting point".

The booklet provides an important starting point.

The EAT has subsequently advised tribunals, although the advice is not mandatory, that a five stage approach to the calculation of pension loss is the logical way to proceed:

- The tribunal should identify all possible benefits that the employee could obtain under the pension scheme
- It should set out the terms of the pension scheme relevant to each benefit
- It should consider in respect of each benefit the advantages and disadvantages of applying the simplified approach, the substantial loss approach or any other approach which the tribunal or parties considers appropriate
- It should explain its reasons for adopting a particular approach and for rejecting any other
- Finally it should set out its conclusions and itemise the loss under each head of the claim (*Greenhoff v Barnsley Metropolitan Borough Council* [2006] EAT/0093).

Approach

The basic distinction in the booklet is between final salary pension schemes and money purchase schemes. Where the loss is potentially considerable or the pension scheme unconventional, there will invariably be the need for expert actuarial evidence to be put before the employment tribunal. **17–033**

Final salary purchase scheme

A final salary pension scheme determines the entitlement by reference to the length of service and the salary when the employment ends. It is not determined by reference to the contributions made. Conventionally the entitlement is assessed as **17–034** being 1/60th of the salary for each year of service. Within the public sector entitlement to payment of a reduced salary prior to retirement is provided for. The employee's contribution is usually fixed as a percentage of salary and the employer pays into the scheme such additional amount that is needed to properly fund the pension scheme. Over time, the employer's contribution has increased considerably resulting in a significant number of final salary pension schemes being closed. A survey by Towers Perrin of 170 companies in November 2006 found that typically the employer's contribution is between 15 per cent and 20 per cent of staff salaries whereas the normal employer contribution to a money purchase scheme is seven per cent. It is not surprising that employers are closing these final salary pension schemes down as being financially unviable. It is now incumbent on employers and scheme trustees to implement a recovery programme overseen by the Pensions Regulator and the Pension Protection Fund to make up any shortfall and to find ways of continuing the scheme although the reality is that a significant number of these schemes will close down. The likely closure of the final salary pension scheme in the future is a matter which is relevant in the computation of pension loss.

With a final salary pension scheme, the employee will be entitled to a deferred pension based on the salary at the date of dismissal calculated by reference to the actual length of service. The Social Security Act 1990 deems the deferred pension as increasing at five per cent per annum or by the annual price rise if lower than five per cent. The assessment of pension loss is based on the difference between the deferred pension which the employee would have had a right to but for the dismissal, less any pension received from new employment. The booklet suggestions that this loss is assessed under three headings:

(1) up to the date of the ET hearing (based on either the employer's contributions or 10 per cent for a contributory scheme and 15 per cent for a non contributory scheme). Actuarial evidence is likely to suggest that these default figures are at least modest but more likely to be misleading.

(2) Loss of future pension rights. Again the employer's contribution is used which is multiplied by the appropriate multiplier. The multiplier is based on a number of contingencies including: how long the employee would have remained employed, the future plans for the former employer's pension scheme, the nature of future pensioned employment, and life expectancy. This is a matter of fact for the employment tribunal which would be assisted by actuarial evidence.

Where the future employment has, or is likely to have, no pension scheme the assessment of loss has to take on board that any future employer will have to make contributions to the State Earned Related Pension Scheme (SERPS) and credit needs to be given for this. The booklet recommends that where the SERPS contribution is not known, a figure of three per cent should be factored in.

(3) Loss of enhancement of accrued rights. The booklet suggests that for those employees in public sector schemes, private sector schemes where the employee is within five years of retiring, or where employment would have ended shortly after the dismissal, there should be no loss attributable under this heading. For other employees, the booklet provides an actuarial table identifying multipliers for the calculation of this loss. The multiplier depends on age, and is based on the normal retirement age. Again this assessment using the table is imprecise and actuarial evidence is likely to be preferred by the employment tribunal under this heading.

Money purchase scheme

17–035 This calculation is less problematic than assessing the loss under a final salary pension scheme. The basis of the calculation is the employer's contribution from the date of dismissal which will be uplifted if the former employer's pension scheme penalises an employee who leaves early. The only controversial issue is the appropriate multiplier to be used. Again the same contingencies as identified above under the final salary pension scheme apply.

Loss of statutory rights

Compensation is awarded in recognition that the right to a statutory redundancy **17–036** payment, notice and the right to claim unfair dismissal are conditional on length of service which will have been lost by virtue of the unfair dismissal. The employment tribunal will usually award a sum equal to half of the claimant's statutory notice entitlement (*Daley v A E Dorsett (Almar Dolls Ltd)* [1981] I.R.L.R. 385). Although this award has been challenged in *SH Muffet Ltd v Head* [1987] I.C.R. 1 it did not overrule the earlier decision but provides the basis for challenging the proper assessment of this loss.

Expenses

Any expenses reasonably incurred in consequence of the dismissal can be **17–037** recovered although this does not include legal expenses (*Nohar v Granitstone (Galloway) Ltd* [1974] I.C.R. 273). This will include the reasonable expenses incurred associated with finding alternative work and can include, in the appropriate case, the recovery of the cost of setting up a business (*Gardiner-Hill v Roland Berger Technics Ltd* [1982] I.R.L.R. 498). If to enhance the opportunities to secure new employment the claimant is required to move home, the costs incurred may be recoverable but this will depend on the factual circumstances as it would be unusual to move in order to secure employment (*Co-operative Wholesale Society Ltd v Squirrell* [1974] 9 I.T.R. 191).

Manner of dismissal

No award analogous to an injury to feelings award can be made in respect of the **17–038** manner of the dismissal (*Dunnachie v Kingston Upon Hull City Council* [2004] I.R.L.R. 727) but if the manner of the dismissal disadvantages the claimant in the market place (for example, ill health caused by the manner of the dismissal) it is likely that the compensatory award will be greater to reflect this.

The order in which payments and/or deductions are made

The sequential steps which the employment tribunal is required to follow is set **17–039** out in *Digital Equipment Co Ltd v Clements (No.2)* [1997] I.R.L.R. 140:

(1) The first task is to ascertain the loss which the claimant sustained in consequence of his dismissal in so far as that loss is attributable to the employer.
(2) Set off against this loss are all "termination" payments (payment in lieu of notice, ex-gratia payments and set off for mitigation or the failure to mitigate).
(3) Any percentage deduction to reflect loss of chance and/or uncertainty that compensation would be recoverable (often referred to as a *Polkey* deduction and dealt with below).
(4) Any reduction for contributory fault, and contractual redundancy payments in excess of the statutory payment, and
(5) then if necessary apply the statutory ceiling.

Having reached a final compensation figure, if appropriate, the employment tribunal has to consider whether the final compensation figure is just and equitable.

At stage 2, where the employer makes contractual payments on termination (payment in lieu of notice or ex-gratia payments) it is deducted at the end of the assessment of the compensatory loss figure. This does not apply to a statutory redundancy payment.

Deductions from the compensatory award

17–040   The claimant must give credit for monies earned in new employment and some social security benefits received. Social security benefits are treated differently depending on the nature of the payment.

There is no set off of income support or job seekers allowance as part of the assessment of the compensatory award. Having worked out the loss, the employment tribunal will notify the Department of Employment who can within 21 days of the conclusion of the hearing or nine days after the decision is sent to the parties serve a recoupment notice on the employer identifying the amount of benefit which needs to be repaid. If served in time, the employer will pay the claimant the compensatory award less the amount on the recoupment notice and this sum is then paid to the Department of Employment.

The treatment of invalidity benefit is uncertain as the appeal courts have never adopted a universal approach as to whether a deduction should be made against the compensatory award and if so how much. No deduction was made in *Hilton International Hotels (UK) Ltd v Faraji* [1994] I.R.L.R. 267, half of the amount paid was deducted in *Rubenstein v McGloughlin* [1996] I.R.L.R. 557 and all was deducted in *Puglia v C James & Co* [1996] I.C.R. 301. In seeking to reach agreement the obvious and most equitable approach would be to give half the credit for invalidity benefit.

Another division of the EAT, recognising the inconsistency in the judgments, has advised resolving that inconsistency by applying *Puglia*, on the basis that if full credit is not taken into account, then the dismissed employee receives a bonus (*Morgans v Alpha Plus Security* [2005] I.R.L.R. 234 EAT).

Contributory fault

17–041   Where the employment tribunal finds that the dismissal was to any extent caused or contributed to by the action of the claimant, it shall reduce the amount of the compensatory award by such proportion as it considers just and equitable having regard to that finding (*Parker Foundry Ltd v Slack* [1992] I.R.L.R. 11).

The first issue is determining the causation issue. What is required is blameworthy conduct on the part of the claimant which contributes to his dismissal (*Nelson v BBC (No.2)* [1979] I.R.L.R. 346). If this is established, the employment tribunal will need to consider the extent of the deduction (applying a percentage deduction) which requires a consideration of what is just and equitable. In such an appropriate case, the deduction can be 100 per cent (*W Devis and Sons Ltd v Atkins* [1977] I.C.R. 662).

As there is a requirement for blameworthy conduct (conduct which is perverse, foolish or unreasonable) it applies almost exclusively to misconduct cases. Rarely in a genuine incompetence case (where the claimant is unable to perform) or in an incapacity case (sickness related dismissal) will contributory fault be applicable (*Sutton and Gates (Luton) Ltd v Boxall* [1979] I.C.R. 67).

The determination of both the causation and the contributory fault issues is a question of fact and degree for the employment tribunal and it is therefore unlikely that a decision which considers both issues will be appealable (*Hollier v Plysu Ltd* [1983] I.R.L.R. 260). If the employment tribunal fails to advise the parties that it is considering making a contributory fault deduction, this will amount to an error of law (*Warrilow v Robert Walker Ltd* [1984] I.R.L.R. 304).

As stated above, where the employment tribunal is making a contributory fault reduction it is required to set off any ex-gratia payments made by the employer first before applying the contributory fault deduction. Where the payment is a contractual redundancy payment in excess of the statutory entitlement, full credit must be given to such a payment to reward good industrial practice and this sum is set off after the contributory fault deduction (*Digital Equipment Co Ltd v Clements (No.2)* [1998] I.R.L.R. 134).

Judgment on the award of compensation

It is incumbent on employment tribunal's to set out the basis of the calculation of the compensatory award with sufficient particularity to ensure that the calculation has been properly made and to ensure that it will be possible to identify any errors of law (*Blackwell v GEC Elliott Process Automation Ltd* [1976] I.R.L.R. 144).

17–042

124   Limit of Compensatory Award etc

(1) The amount of—

17–043

(a) any compensation awarded to a person under section 117(1) and (2), or

(b) a compensatory award to a person calculated in accordance with section 123,

shall not exceed [£60,600].

[(1A) Subsection (1) shall not apply to compensation awarded, or a compensatory award made, to a person in a case where he is regarded as unfairly dismissed by virtue of section 100, 103A, 105(3) or 105(6A).]

(2) . . .

(3) In the case of compensation awarded to a person under section 117(1) and (2), the limit imposed by this section may be exceeded to the extent necessary to enable the award fully to reflect the amount specified as payable under section 114(2)(a) or section 115(2)(d).

(4) Where—

(a) a compensatory award is an award under paragraph (a) of subsection (3) of section 117, and

(b) an additional award falls to be made under paragraph (b) of that subsection,

the limit imposed by this section on the compensatory award may be exceeded to the extent necessary to enable the aggregate of the compensatory and additional awards fully to reflect the amount specified as payable under section 114(2)(a) or section 115(2)(d).

(5) The limit imposed by this section applies to the amount which the employment tribunal would, apart from this section, award in respect of the subject matter of the complainant after taking into account—

(a) any payment made by the respondent to the complainant in respect of that matter, and

(b) any reduction in the amount of the award required by any enactment or rule of law.

Statutory maximum

17-044   The statutory maximum is increased annually in February The present maximum £63,000, applies where the effective date of termination falls on or after February 1, 2008: see SI 2007/3570. For dismissals with an effective date of termination falling within the period February 1, 2006 to January 31, 2007, the applicable maximum is £58,400: see SI 2005/3352.

Subsection (3) deals with a case of non-compliance with an order for reinstatement. The compensatory award includes any amount specified in a reinstatement order in terms of s.114(2)(a) to recompense the employee for the loss of benefits between the date of dismissal and the date of reinstatement. That sum is payable under a reinstatement order which is complied with, and is not a free-standing head to be awarded whether or not the employee is reinstated. Where the order is not complied with, therefore, the employee is entitled to a compensatory award which is calculated by including the loss of benefits for the period between dismissal and the date ordered for reinstatement, any future loss suffered by the employee after the reinstatement date, and the loss of statutory rights. The gross loss so calculated is subject to the limit imposed by s.124(4) which provides that in a case of failure to reinstate, the upper limit on the compensatory award "may be exceeded to the extent necessary to enable the aggregate of the compensatory and additional awards fully to reflect the amount specified as payable" in the reinstatement order under s.114(2)(a). The maximum compensatory award is therefore arrived at by deducting the additional award from the award made under s.114(2)(a). To the compensatory award so limited, the additional award and basic award must be added to arrive at the total compensation payable (*Selfridges Ltd v Malik* [1997] I.R.L.R. 577).

Subsection (5) provides that the statutory maximum is applied at the last stage of the assessment process. Ex gratia payments made by the employer will be deducted first from the compensatory award before the statutory maximum is applied thereby resulting in some cases that a sum in excess of the statutory maximum is paid to the claimant.

124A   Adjustments under the Employment Act 2002

17-045   Where an award of compensation for unfair dismissal falls to be—

    (a) **reduced or increased under section 31 of the Employment Act 2002 (non-completion of statutory procedures), or**

    (b) **increased under section 38 of that Act (failure to give statement of employment particulars),**

the adjustment shall be in the amount awarded under section 118(1)(b) and shall be applied immediately before any reduction under section 123(6) or (7).]

126   Acts which are both unfair dismissal and discrimination

17-046   (1) This section applies where compensation falls to be awarded in respect of any act both under—

    (a) the provisions of this Act relating to unfair dismissal, and

    [(b) any one or more of the following—

        (i) the Sex Discrimination Act 1975

(ii) the Race Relations Act 1976

(iii) the Disability Discrimination Act 1995

(iv) the Employment Equality (Sexual Orientation) Regulations 2003;

(v) the Employment Equality (Religion or Belief) Regulations 2003;

(vi) the Employment Equality (Age) Regulations 2006.].

(2) An employment tribunal shall not award compensation under any one of those . . . Acts [or Regulations] in respect of any loss or other matter which is or has been taken into account under [any other of them] by the tribunal (or another employment tribunal) in awarding compensation on the same or another complaint in respect of that act.

The Employment Rights (Increase of Limits) Order 2006

2006 No. 3045

The Secretary of State, in exercise of the powers conferred on him by section 34 of the Employment Relations Act 1999, makes the following Order:

Citation, commencement and interpretation
1.—(1) This Order may be cited as the Employment Rights (Increase of Limits) Order 2006 and shall come into force on 1st February 2007.   **17–047**

(2) In this Order—

(a) "the 1992 Act" means the Trade Union and Labour Relations (Consolidation) Act 1992;

(b) "the 1996 Act" means the Employment Rights Act 1996; and

(c) "the 1999 Act" means the Employment Relations Act 1999.

Revocation
2. Subject to article 4, the Employment Rights (Increase of Limits) Order 2005 is revoked.   **17–048**

Increase of limits
3. Subject to article 4, each of the limits referred to in the first and second columns of the Table in the Schedule to this Order is increased by the substitution, in place of the old amount specified in the third column, of the new amount specified in the fourth column.   **17–049**

Transitional provisions
4.—(1) The increases provided for in article 3 have effect in any case where the appropriate date falls on or after 1st February 2007.   **17–050**

(2) In a case where the appropriate date falls before 1st February 2007, the limits having effect in relation to the case immediately before 1st February 2007 continue to apply.

(3) In this article "the appropriate date" means—

(a) in the case of an application made under section 67(1) of the 1992 Act (compensation for unjustifiable discipline by a trade union), the date of the determination infringing the applicant's right;

(b) in the case of a complaint presented under section 70C of the 1992 Act (failure by an employer to consult with a trade union on training matters), the date of the alleged failure;

(c) in the case of a complaint presented under section 137(2) of the 1992 Act (refusal of employment on grounds related to union membership) or section 138(2) of that Act (refusal of service of employment agency on grounds related to union membership), the date of the conduct to which the complaint relates, as determined under section 139 of that Act;

(d) in the case of a complaint presented under section 145A of the 1992 Act (inducements relating to trade union membership or activities) or under section 145B of the 1992 Act (inducements relating to collective bargaining), the date of the offer made by the employer that is the subject of the worker's complaint;

(e) in the case of an application made under section 176(2) of the 1992 Act (compensation for exclusion or expulsion from a trade union), the date of the exclusion or expulsion from the union;

(f) in the case of a complaint presented under paragraph 156 of Schedule A1 to the 1992 Act (compensation for a detriment that is the termination of a worker's contract not constituting a contract of employment), the date of the termination;

(g) in the case of a guarantee payment to which an employee is entitled under section 28(1) of the 1996 Act, the day in respect of which the payment is due;

(h) in the case of a complaint presented under section 111 of the 1996 Act (complaints of unfair dismissal), for the purpose of calculating the basic award or compensatory award under section 118(1) of that Act, the effective date of termination as defined by section 97 of that Act;

(i) in the case of an award under section 117(1) or (3) of the 1996 Act, where an employer has failed to comply fully with the terms of an order for reinstatement or re-engagement or has failed to reinstate or re-engage the complainant in accordance with such an order, the date by which the order for reinstatement (specified under section 114(2)(c) of that Act) or, as the case may be, re-engagement (specified under section 115(2)(f) of that Act), should have been complied with;

(j) in the case of entitlement to a redundancy payment by virtue of section 135(1)(a) of the 1996 Act (dismissal by reason of redundancy), the relevant date as defined by section 145 of that Act;

(k) in the case of entitlement to a redundancy payment by virtue of section 135(1)(b) of the 1996 Act (lay-off or short-time), the relevant date as defined by section 153 of that Act;

(l) in the case of entitlement to a payment under section 182 of the 1996 Act (payments by the Secretary of State), the appropriate date as defined by section 185 of that Act;

(m) in the case of a complaint presented under section 24 of the National Minimum Wage Act 1998 (compensation for a detriment that is the termination of a worker's contract or arrangements not constituting a contract of employment), the date of the termination;

(n) in the case of a complaint presented under section 11(1) of the 1999 Act (failure or threatened failure to allow worker to be accompanied at disciplinary or grievance hearing, to allow companion to address hearing or confer with worker, or to postpone hearing), the date of the failure or threat;

(o) in the case of an award made under section 38 of the Employment Act 2002 (duty to give a written statement of initial employment particulars or of particulars of change), the date the proceedings to which section 38 of that Act applies were begun; and

(p) in the case of a complaint under Regulation 15 of the Flexible Working (Procedural Requirements) Regulations 2002 (failure or threatened failure to allow employee to be accompanied at meeting or to postpone meeting), the date of the failure or threat.

SCHEDULE

Article 3

17–051 TABLE OF INCREASE OF LIMITS

	Column 1	*Column 2*	*Column 3*	*Column 4*
	Relevant Statutory provision	*Subject of provision*	*Old Limits*	*New Limits*
1	Section 145E(3) of the 1992 Act	Amount of award for unlawful inducement relating to trade union membership or activities, or for unlawful inducement relating to collective bargaining.	£2,600	£2,700
2	Section 156(1) of the 1992 Act	Minimum amount of basic award of compensation where dismissal is unfair by virtue of section 152(1) or 153 of the 1992 Act.	£4,000	£4,200
3	Section 176(6A) of the 1992 Act	Minimum amount of compensation where individual excluded or expelled from union in contravention of section 174 of the 1992 Act and not admitted or re-admitted by date of tribunal application.	£6,300	£6,600
4	Section 31(1) of the 1996 Act	Limit on amount of guarantee payment payable to an employee in respect of any day.	£18.90	£19.60
5	Section 120(1) of the 1996 Act	Minimum amount of basic award of compensation where dismissal is unfair by virtue of section 100(1)(a) and (b), 101A(d), 102(1) or 103 of the 1996 Act.	£4,000	£4,200
6	Section 124(1) of the 1996 Act	Limit on amount of compensatory award for unfair dismissal.	£58,400	£60,600
7	Paragraphs (a) and (b) of section 186(1) of the 1996 Act	Limit on amount in respect of any one week payable to an employee in respect of a debt to which Part XII of the 1996 Act applies and which is referable to a period of time.	£290	£310
8	Section 227(1) of the 1996 Act	Maximum amount of "a week's pay" for the purpose of calculating a redundancy payment or for various awards including the basic or additional award of compensation for unfair dismissal.	£290	£310

EMPLOYMENT TRIBUNALS (INTEREST ON AWARDS IN DISCRIMINATION CASES) REGULATIONS

1996 No. 2803

1.—(1) These Regulations may be cited as the Employment Tri- **17–052**
bunals (Interest on Awards in Discrimination Cases) Regulations
1996 and shall come into force on 2nd December 1996.

(2) In these Regulations

"the 1970 Act" means the Equal Pay Act 1970;

"the 1975 Act" means the Sex Discrimination Act 1975;

"the 1976 Act" means the Race Relations Act 1976;

"the 1995 Act" means the Disability Discrimination Act 1995 and;

"an award under the relevant legislation" means—

(a) an award under the 1970 Act of arrears of remuneration
or damages, or

(b) an order under section 65(1)(b) of the 1975 Act, section
56(1)(b) of the 1976 Act, section 8(2)(b) of the 1995 Act,
[regulation 30(1)(b) of the Employment Equality (Sexual
Orientation) Regulations 2003] [or regulation 30(1)(b) of
the Employment Equality (Religion or Belief) Regulations
2003] [or regulation 38(1)(b) of the Employment Equality
(Age) Regulations 2006] for payment of compensation,

but does not include an award of costs under rule 12 in Schedule 1 to
the Employment Tribunals (Constitution and Rules of Procedure)
Regulations 1993, or expenses under rule 12 in Schedule 1 to the
Employment Tribunals (Constitution and Rules of Procedure) Regulations 1993, even if the award of costs or expenses is made in the
same proceedings as an award under the 1970 Act or such an order.

(3) The Sex Discrimination and Equal Pay (Remedies) Regulations
1993 and the Race Relations (Interest on Awards) Regulations 1994
are revoked.

Commencement

2 December 1996. **17–053**

Amendment

Words in first square brackets inserted by SI 2003/1661 (Employment Equality **17–054**
(Sexual Orientation) Regulations Sch.5, para.3(b).

Words in second square brackets contained in subs.2 inserted by SI 2003/1661
(Employment Equality (Religion or Belief) Regulations), Sch.5, para.3(b).

Save in respect of those jurisdictions mentioned in subs.2(b) interest in the **17–055**
Employment Tribunal is awarded under the Employment Tribunals (Interest)
Order 1990 and is calculated following the expiry of 42 days beginning with the day
of the decision.

Specific regulations concerning the award of interest on damages for discrimination claims were introduced following the decision of the ECJ in *Marshall v Southampton and South West Hampshire Area Health Authority* [1993] I.C.R. 893. These comprised the Sex Discrimination and Equal Pay (Remedies) Regulations 1993, and the Race Relations (Interest on Awards) Regulations 1994. Both sets of regulations are revoked by reg.(3), and consolidated into the present regulations. The regulations govern all awards under the Equal Pay Act 1970, the Sex Discrimination Act 1975, the Race Relations Act 1976, the Disability Discrimination Act 1995, the Employment Equality (Sexual Orientation) Regulations 2003 and the Employment Equality (Religion or Belief) Regulations 2003, and the Employment Equality (Age) Regulations 2006.

17–056   **2.—(1) Where, at any time after the commencement of these Regulations, an employment tribunal makes an award under the relevant legislation—**

> **(a) it may, subject to the following provisions of these Regulations, include interest on the sums awarded; and**
>
> **(b) it shall consider whether to do so, without the need for any application by a party in the proceedings.**

(2) Nothing in paragraph (1) shall prevent the tribunal from making an award or decision, with regard to interest, in terms which have been agreed between the parties.

17–057   The tribunal is subject to a duty to consider making an award of interest. Failure on the part of the tribunal to do is an error of law (*Fasuyi v Greenwich LBC* (EAT/1078/99)).

A tribunal may award interest without regard to these provisions where the terms have been agreed by the parties

17–058   **3.—(1) Interest shall be calculated as simple interest which accrues from day to day.**

(2) Subject to paragraph (3), the rate of interest to be applied shall be, in England and Wales, the rate from time to time prescribed for the Special Investment Account under rule 27(1) of the Court Funds Rules 1987 and, in Scotland, the rate fixed, for the time being, by the Act of Sederunt (Interest in Sheriff Court Decrees or Extracts) 1975.

(3) Where the rate of interest in paragraph (2) has varied during a period for which interest is to be calculated, the tribunal may, if it so desires in the interests of simplicity, apply such median or average of those rates as seems to it appropriate.

17–059   The rate of interest is the Special Investment Account rate of the Court Funds Office, not the Judgement Act 1838 rate specified under the Employment Tribunals (Interest) Order 1990. The Special Investment Account rate varies from time to time. Presently it is 6 per cent, as opposed to the rate under the Judgements Act

1838 which is presently 8 per cent. The current rate may be obtained from the Court Funds Office whose website *www.hmcourts-service.gov.uk* currently publishes the present but not former rates.

4.—(1) In this regulation and regulations 5 and 6 "day of calcula- **17–060** tion" means the day on which the amount of interest is calculated by the tribunal.

(2) In regulation 6, "mid-point date" means the day which falls half-way through the period mentioned in paragraph (3) or, where the number of days in that period is even, the first day of the second half of the period.

(3) The period referred to in paragraph (2) is the period beginning on the date, in the case of an award under the 1970 Act, of the contravention and, in other cases, of the act of discrimination complained of, and ending on the day of calculation.

5.—No interest shall be included in respect of any sum awarded for **17–061** a loss or matter which will occur after the day of calculation or in respect of any time before the contravention or act of discrimination complained of.

6.—(1) Subject to the following paragraphs of this regulation— **17–062**

(a) in the case of any sum for injury to feelings, interest shall be for the period beginning on the date of the contravention or act of discrimination complained of and ending on the day of calculation;

(b) in the case of all other sums of damages or compensation (other than any sum referred to in regulation 5 and all arrears of remuneration, interest shall be for the period beginning on the mid-point date and ending on the day of calculation.

(2) Where any payment has been made before the day of calculation to the complainant by or on behalf of the respondent in respect of the subject matter of the award, interest in respect of that part of the award covered by the payment shall be calculated as if the references in paragraph (1), and in the definition of "mid-point date" in regulation 4, to the day of calculation were to the date on which the payment was made.

(3) Where the tribunal considers that in the circumstances, whether relating to the case as a whole or to a particular sum in an award, serious injustice would be caused if interest were to be awarded in respect of the period or periods in paragraphs (1) or (2), it may—

(a) calculate interest, or as the case may be interest on the particular sum, for such different period, or

627

> (b) **calculate interest for such different periods in respect of various sums in the award,**
>
> **as it considers appropriate in the circumstances, having regard to the provisions of these Regulations.**

17–063   The regulations provide for different calculations for interest for loss in respect of injury to feelings, and interest on any other losses.

The interest on an award for injury to feelings is calculated from the date of the contravention or act complained of up until the date of calculation at the Special Investment Rate prescribed under r.27 of the Court Funds Rules 1987.

The interest on any other award is calculated for only half that period, starting at the mid point of the period under consideration.

The tribunal has a discretion to award interest for a different period or on a sum less than the whole amount of the award if serious injustice would otherwise be caused. The tribunal does not have power to award a different rate of interest.

The treatment of interest under the regulations is in contrast to the position in the civil courts where usually either no interest is awarded in respect of non-pecuniary loss such as injury to feelings, or it is restricted to two per cent, whilst in the case of pecuniary loss interest would usually be recovered for the entire period of loss in the civil courts, but is only recovered for half the period in the tribunal.

17–064   **7.—(1) The tribunal's written statement of reasons for its decision shall contain a statement of the total amount of any interest awarded under regulation 2 and, unless this amount has been agreed between the parties, either a table showing how it has been calculated or a description of the manner in which it has been calculated.**

(2) The tribunal's written statement of reasons shall include reasons for any decision not to award interest under regulation 2.

17–065   **8.—(1) The Employment Tribunals (Interest) Order 1990 shall apply in relation to an award under the relevant legislation (whether or not including interest under regulation 2) as if references in that Order to the calculation day were references to the day immediately following the relevant decision day (as defined in Article 2(3) of the Order) and accordingly interest shall accrue under the Order from that day onwards (including that day).**

(2) Notwithstanding paragraph (1), no interest shall be payable by virtue of that Order if payment of the full amount of the award (including any interest under regulation 2) is made within 14 days after the relevant decision day.

Definition

17–066   "the relevant legislation", is defined at reg.1(2).

17–067   In the event that the award is paid within 14 days then no further interest shall accrue. However, if it is not paid within 14 days then interest continues to attract to the award, this time under the Employment Tribunals (Interest) Order 1990 from the date of the award.

EMPLOYMENT TRIBUNALS (INTEREST) ORDER 1990

1990 No. 479

This Order came into force on April 1, 1990. Sums of money payable as a result **17–068** of a decision of an employment tribunal, other than under a jurisdiction to which the Employment Tribunals (Interest on Awards in Discrimination Cases) Regulations 1996 apply, carry interest at the rate specified for the time being by s.17 of the Judgments Act 1838, presently 8 per cent, when all or part of a sum payable remains unpaid 42 days after the document containing the tribunal's decision is recorded as having been sent to the parties.

Provisions relating to appeals and reviews have the effect, in general, that interest still accrues on money remaining unpaid 42 days after the document containing the tribunal's decision is recorded as having been sent to the parties, but accrues on the amount as varied if the appeal or review results in a variation. Transitional arrangements provided that for the purposes of the Order, decisions of the kind to which the Order refers, made before April 1, 1990 were deemed to have been made on that day.

The Order places a duty on the Secretary of the Tribunals to inform the parties to proceedings of the effect of this Order when an employment tribunal makes a decision to which this Order attaches.

Art 1

(1) **This Order may be cited as the Employment Tribunals (Inter-** **17–069** **est) Order 1990 and shall come into force on 1st April 1990.**

(2) **Where a relevant decision day or a day to be treated as if it were a relevant decision day would, but for this paragraph of this Article, fall on a day before 1st April 1990, the relevant decision day or day to be treated as if it were that day shall be 1st April 1990.**

Commencement: 1 April 1990

Art 2

In this Order, except in so far as the context otherwise requires— **17–070**

'appellate court' means the Employment Appeal Tribunal, the High Court, the Court of Appeal, the Court of Session or the House of Lords as the case may be;

'the calculation day' in relation to a relevant decision means the day immediately following the expiry of the period of 42 days beginning with the relevant decision day;

'interest' means simple interest which accrues from day to day;

'relevant decision' in relation to a tribunal means any award or other determination of the tribunal by virtue of which one party to proceedings before the tribunal is required to pay a sum of money, excluding a sum representing costs or expenses, to another party to those proceedings;

'Rules of Procedure' means rules having effect in relation to proceedings before a tribunal by virtue of any regulations or order made pursuant to an enactment;

'the stipulated rate of interest' has the meaning assigned to it in Article 4 below;

'tribunal' means in England and Wales an employment tribunal established in pursuance of the Industrial Tribunals (England and Wales) Regulations 1965, amended by S.I. 1967/301, 1970/941 and 1977/1473 and in Scotland an employment tribunal established in pursuance of the Industrial Tribunals (Scotland) Regulations 1965

(2) For the purposes of this Order a sum of money is required to be paid by one party to proceedings to another such party if, and only if, an amount of money required to be so paid is:-

(a) specified in an award or other determination of a tribunal or, as the case may be, in an order or decision of an appellate court; or

(b) otherwise ascertainable solely by reference to the terms of such an award or determination or, as the case may be, solely by reference to the terms of such an order or decision,

but where a tribunal or, as the case may be, appellate court has made a declaration as to entitlement under a contract nothing in this Order shall be taken to provide for interest to be payable on any payment under that contract in respect of which no obligation to make the payment has arisen under that contract before the declaration was made.

(3) In this Order, except in so far as the context otherwise requires, "decision day" means the day signified by the date recording the sending of the document which is sent to the parties recording an award or other determination of a tribunal and "relevant decision day", subject to Article 5, 6 and 7 below, means the day so signified in relation to a relevant decision.

(4) In this Order "party" includes the Secretary of State where he has elected to appear as if he were a party in accordance with a Rule of Procedure entitling him so to elect.

Commencement: 1 April 1990

Art 3

17–071   (1) Subject to paragraphs (2) and (3) of this Article and to Article 11 below, where the whole or any part of a sum of money payable by virtue of a relevant decision of a tribunal remains unpaid on the calculation day the sum of money remaining unpaid on the calculation day shall carry interest at the stipulated rate of interest from the calculation day (including that day).

(2) Where, after the calculation day, a party pays to another party some but not all of such a sum of money remaining unpaid on the calculation day, then beginning with the day on which the payment is made interest shall continue to accrue only on that part of the sum of money which then remains unpaid.

(3) For the purposes of the computation of interest under this Order, there shall be disregarded-

(a) any part of a sum of money which pursuant to the Employment Protection (Recoupment of Unemployment Benefit and Supplementary Benefit) Regulations 1996 has been claimed by the Secretary of State in a recoupment notice; and

(b) any part of a sum of money which the party required to pay the sum of money is required, by virtue of any provision contained in or having effect under any enactment, to deduct and pay over to a public authority in respect of income tax or contributions under Part I of the Social Security Act 1975.

Commencement: 1 April 1990   **17–072**

The tribunal's power to award interest is derived from this section alone. In *Nelson v British Broadcasting Corpn (No 2)* [1980] I.C.R. 110, before the Regulations were in force, the Court of Appeal, *per* Brandon L.J., said, at p.128:

> "A general power to include interest in any sums awarded in respect of claims for any debt or damages is given to courts of record by section 3 of the Law Reform (Miscellaneous Provisions) Act 1934. An industrial tribunal is not, in my judgment, a court of record and the provision to which I have referred does not therefore apply to it. There is no separate or special statutory provision empowering an industrial tribunal to award interest on compensation for unfair dismissal."

The period of time for which interest can be awarded is prescribed by art.3 as running from the day immediaitely following the expiry of 42 days beginning with the decision day.This might be thought to serve an injustice if there were a substantial delay between the date when the loss arose and the decision day, but the article gives no relief for such injustice. However in *Melia v Magna Kansei Limited* [2005] I.C.R. 874 Burton P said at para.28:

> "[the Claimant] is seeking to recover compensation, such as is just and equitable, within section 123 of the 1996 Act, to which we shall refer; and that, particularly in a case where, as here, a deduction of 2.5% per annum is made from a calculation in order to make an allowance for accelerated payment, so there ought to be an increase or premium of 2.5% per annum in respect of what one might loosely call "decelerated" or "delayed" payment; . . . . . .this is, of course, considerably less than the annual rate of interest; it is simple fairness to apply the same rate both ways."

Art 4   **17–073**

The stipulated rate of interest shall be the rate of interest specified in section 17 of the Judgments Act 1838 on the relevant decision day.

Commencement: 1 April 1990.

The rate has been 8 per cent since 1 April 1993 when it was reduced from 15 per   **17–074**
cent by the Judgement Debts (Rate of Interest) Order 1993 (SI 1993/564).

Art 5

Where a tribunal reviews its decision pursuant to the Rules of   **17–075**
Procedure and the effect of the review, or of any re-hearing which takes place as a result of the review, is that a sum of money payable

by one party to another party is confirmed or varied the relevant decision day shall be the decision day of the decision which is the subject of the review.

Commencement: 1 April 1990.

Art 6

17–076   Where an appellate court remits a matter to a tribunal for re-assessment of the sum of money which would have been payable by virtue of a previous relevant decision or by virtue of an order of another appellate court, the relevant decision day shall be the decision day of that previous relevant decision or the day on which the other appellate court promulgated its order, as the case may be.

Commencement: 1 April 1990.

Art 7

17–077   Where, on an appeal from a relevant decision, or on a further appeal arising from a relevant decision an appellate court makes an order which confirms or varies the sum of money which would have been payable by virtue of that relevant decision if there had been no appeal, the relevant decision day shall be the decision day of that relevant decision.

Commencement: 1 April 1990.

Art 8

17–078   (1) This Article applies in relation to any order made by an appellate court on an appeal from a determination of any issue by a tribunal which is not a relevant decision, or on any further appeal arising from such a determination, where the effect of the order is that for the first time in relation to that issue one party to the proceedings is required to pay a sum of money, other than a sum representing costs or expenses, to another party to the proceedings.

(2) Where this Article applies in relation to an order, Articles 3 and 4 above shall apply to the sum of money payable by virtue of the order as if it was a sum of money payable by virtue of a relevant decision and as if the day on which the appellate court promulgated the order was the relevant decision day.

Commencement: 1 April 1990.

Art 9

17–079   Where, on an appeal from an order in relation to which Article 8 applies or on a further appeal arising from such an order, an appellate court makes an order which confirms or varies the sum of money which would have been payable by virtue of the order in relation to which Article 8 applies if there had been no appeal, the day to be treated as the relevant decision day shall be the day on which the order in relation to which Article 8 applies was promulgated.

Commencement: 1 April 1990.

Art 10
Where the Employment Appeal Tribunal reviews an order to which Article 8 above applies, the day to be treated as the relevant decision day shall be the day on which the order reviewed was promulgated.

17–080

Commencement: 1 April 1990.

Art 11
Where a sum of money payable by virtue of a relevant decision is varied under one of the procedures referred to in Articles 5, 6 and 7 above, or a sum of money treated as being so payable by virtue of Article 8 above is varied under one of the procedures referred to in Articles 6, 9 and 10 above, the reference in paragraph (1) of Article 3 above, to a sum of money payable by virtue of a relevant decision shall be treated as if it were a reference to that sum as so varied.

17–081

Commencement: 1 April 1990.

Art 12
(1) Where a decision of a tribunal is a relevant decision and a copy of a document recording that decision is sent to all parties entitled to receive that decision, it shall be the duty of the Secretary of the Central Office of the Employment Tribunals (England and Wales) or the Secretary of the Central Office of the Employment Tribunals (Scotland), as the case may be, to cause a notice containing the matters detailed in paragraph (2) below to accompany that document.

17–082

(2) The notice referred to in paragraph (1) above shall specify the decision day, the stipulated rate of interest and the calculation day in respect of the decision concerned.

(3) The failure to discharge the duty under paragraph (1) above correctly or at all shall have no effect on the liability of one party to pay to another party any sum of money which is payable by virtue of this Order.

Commencement: 1 April 1990.

633

CHAPTER 18

COMPROMISING CLAIMS

Contents

Compromise agreements

There is a general principle that the attempts of employers to contractually bind **18–001** their employees to waive their entitlement to statutory protection are void. This principle is stated at various points of the legislative schemes: at s.288 of the Trade Union and Labour Relations (Consolidation) Act 1992; at s.203 of the Employment Rights Act 1996 in relation to the rights existing under that Act and under the Part-Time Workers (Prevention of Less Favourable Treatment) Regulations 2000 and the Fixed-Term Employees (Prevention of Less Favourable Treatment) Regulations 2002, and under the Employment Relations Act 1999 (see s.14 of that Act); at s.77 of the Sex Discrimination Act 1975 (which also relates to claims under the Equal Pay Act 1970); at s.72 of the Race Relations Act 1976; in Sch.3A to the Disability Discrimination Act 1995; at Sch.4 to the Employment Equality (Religion or Belief) Regulations 2003; at Sch.4 to the Employment Equality (Sexual Orientation) Regulations 2003; and at Sch.5 to the Employment Equality (Age) Regulations 2006.

Also stated in those provisions is the exception to the general principle which permits contracting out if the requirements for statutory compromise agreements are met. For each scheme, the requirements that must be satisfied are the same. For the purposes of exposition, the provisions of s.203 of the Employment Rights Act 1996 are set out below. The commentary to that section is applicable to each of the statutory schemes, unless otherwise indicated below.

Contractual claims

The position in relation to contractual claims commenced in the Employment **18–002** Tribunal under the Extension of Jurisdiction Order is materially different. These claims are common law claims, and the statutory provisions preventing contracting out from statutory rights do not apply. Equally there is no requirement that any compromise satisfy the requirements of form of a statutory compromise agreement (*Lunt v Merseyside TEC Limited* [1999] I.C.R. 17). For a contractual claim, an agreement contained in an enforceable contract is sufficient. As such, the "requirements" are those of the law of contract: offer, acceptance, and consideration. Consideration will be present, regardless of the perceived or actual merits of the claim that is compromised, or those of the defence to it, since in all cases the effect of the compromise will be that the parties avoid the inconvenience of continuing to pursue or defend the claim. A compromise of a contractual claim is also capable of being set aside on the basis of the usual principles applicable to contracts—for example, mistake, misrepresentation, duress, by reason of an absence of legal capacity, or by operation of the *non est factum* doctrine.

635

Tribunal orders

18–003   A further effective method of compromising a claim is for the terms of the agreement to be recorded in an order of the employment tribunal, although this will only usually be an option when the settlement is reached in the course of the hearing.

Once an Order has been made, there is no jurisdiction to set the Order aside absent fraud or misrepresentation (*Times Newspapers Limited v Fitt* [1981] I.C.R. 637). In that case, a consent Order made by a solicitor who did not in fact have actual authority to agree to the terms was not set aside since there was no basis on which the agreement underlying the order could be impeached. On the facts of that case, the solicitor did have apparent authority to compromise the claim. In reaching this view the EAT expressly considered the provisions that prevented contracting out (now at, for example, s.203(1) of the Employment Rights Act 1996), and concluded that despite the fact that the underlying agreement, if considered on its own, would be void, once the Order had been made and perfected (i.e. when it was sent to the parties and entered into the Register), there was no automatic right either to alter the terms of the Order, or to set it aside. Once the case had come before the employment tribunal, the legislative purpose of preventing employees from entering into unwise or bad bargains had been exhausted.

Employers should avoid placing undue pressure upon an employee to compromise a discrimination claim. Of itself, seeking to dissuade an employee from pressing a claim to an adjudication does not give rise to a claim of victimisation, but where the conduct in pressing settlement is by reason that the claimant has insisted on his or her claim then a claim of victimisation may be made out. Each case will turn on its facts. *St Helens Borough Council v Derbyshire* [2007] I.C.R. 841, H.L.

EMPLOYMENT RIGHTS ACT 1996

203   Restrictions on contracting out

18–004   **(1) Any provision in an agreement (whether a contract of employ-ment or not) is void in so far as it purports—**

   (a) to exclude or limit the operation of any provision of this Act, or
   (b) to preclude a person from bringing any proceedings under this Act before an employment tribunal.

   (2)   Subsection (1)—

   (a) does not apply to any provision in a collective agreement excluding rights under section 28 if an order under section 35 is for the time being in force in respect of it,
   (b) does not apply to any provision in a dismissal procedures agreement excluding the right under section 94 if that provision is not to have effect unless an order under section 110 is for the time being in force in respect of it,
   (c) does not apply to any provision in an agreement if an order under section 157 is for the time being in force in respect of it,

(d) ...

(e) does not apply to any agreement to refrain from instituting or continuing proceedings where a conciliation officer has taken action under section 18 of the Employment Tribunals Act 1996, and

(f) does not apply to any agreement to refrain from instituting or continuing any proceedings within the following provisions of section 18(1) of the Employment Tribunals Act 1996 (cases where conciliation available)—

    (i) paragraph (d) (proceedings under this Act),

    [(ii) paragraph (h) (proceedings arising out of the Part-time Workers (Prevention of Less Favourable Treatment) Regulations 2000)],

    [(iii) paragraph (i) (proceedings arising out of the Fixed-term Employees (Prevention of Less Favourable Treatment) Regulations 2002),

    (iv) paragraph (j) (proceedings under those Regulations),

if the conditions regulating compromise agreements under this Act are satisfied in relation to the agreement].

(3) For the purposes of subsection (2)(f) the conditions regulating compromise agreements under this Act are that—

(a) the agreement must be in writing,

(b) the agreement must relate to the particular proceedings,

(c) the employee or worker must have received advice from a relevant independent adviser as to the terms and effect of the proposed agreement and, in particular, its effect on his ability to pursue his rights before an employment tribunal,

(d) there must be in force, when the adviser gives the advice, a contract of insurance, or an indemnity provided for members of a profession or professional body, covering the risk of a claim by the employee or worker in respect of loss arising in consequence of the advice,

(e) the agreement must identify the adviser, and

(f) the agreement must state that the conditions regulating compromise agreements under this Act are satisfied.

(3A) A person is a relevant independent adviser for the purposes of subsection (3)(c)—

(a) if he is a qualified lawyer,

(b) if he is an officer, official, employee or member of an independent trade union who has been certified in writing by the trade union as competent to give advice and as authorised to do so on behalf of the trade union,

(c) if he works at an advice centre (whether as an employee or a volunteer) and has been certified in writing by the centre as competent to give advice and as authorised to do so on behalf of the centre, or

(d) if he is a person of a description specified in an order made by the Secretary of State.

(3B) But a person is not a relevant independent adviser for the purposes of subsection (3)(c) in relation to the employee or worker—

(a) if he is, is employed by or is acting in the matter for the employer or an associated employer,

(b) in the case of a person within subsection (3A)(b) or (c), if the trade union or advice centre is the employer or an associated employer,

(c) in the case of a person within subsection (3A)(c), if the employee or worker makes a payment for the advice received from him, or

(d) in the case of a person of a description specified in an order under subsection (3A)(d), if any condition specified in the order in relation to the giving of advice by persons of that description is not satisfied.

(4) In subsection (3A)(a) "qualified lawyer" means—

(a) as respects England and Wales, a barrister (whether in practice as such or employed to give legal advice), a solicitor who holds a practising certificate, or a person other than a barrister or solicitor who is an authorised advocate or authorised litigator (within the meaning of the Courts and Legal Services Act 1990), and

(b) as respects Scotland, an advocate (whether in practice as such or employed to give legal advice), or a solicitor who holds a practising certificate.

(5) An agreement under which the parties agree to submit a dispute to arbitration—

(a) shall be regarded for the purposes of subsection (2)(e) and (f) as being an agreement to refrain from instituting or continuing proceedings if—

(i) the dispute is covered by a scheme having effect by virtue of an order under section 212A of the Trade

> Union and Labour Relations (Consolidation) Act 1992, and
>
> (ii) the agreement is to submit it to arbitration in accordance with the scheme, but
>
> (b) shall be regarded as neither being nor including such an agreement in any other case.

Words in square brackets at 2(f)(ii) added by SI 2000/1551 Part Time Workers (prevention of less favourable treatment) regs 2000

Words in square brackets at 2(f) (iii) and (iv) added by SI 2002/2034 (Fixed-term Employees (Prevention of Less Favourable Treatment) Regulations), Sch.2(1) Para.3(17)(b).

Commencement

August 22, 1996

18–005

Definitions

"collective agreement" has the meaning given by s.178(1) and (2) of the Trade **18–006** Union and Labour Relations (Consolidation) Act 1992.

"dismissal procedures agreement" means an agreement in writing with respect to procedures relating to dismissal made by or on behalf of one or more independent trade unions and one or more employers or employers' associations.

General

Subsection (1) renders void any provision of an agreement that excludes or limits **18–007** the operation of a provision of the Employment Rights Act, or precludes a person from bringing proceedings under the Act.

The rule, applied purposively, would appear to encompass the situation where a contract of employment provided that there was no intention to create legal relations purely with a view to circumventing the provisions of the Employment Rights Act, *M&P Steelcraft v Ellis* UKEAT/0536/07/LA.

The rule is subject to important exceptions. The two most commonly encountered are those provided by subs.2(e) (an ACAS officer may compromise a dispute under s.18 Employment Tribunals Act 1996); and subs.2(f) (a claim under the Employment Rights Act can be compromised, provided that the requirements of subs.(3) are complied with).

If any issue arises as to the validity of a compromise agreement, the first exercise is to identify the meaning and effect of the terms of the agreement itself. In particular it is important to identify which claims are covered by the express terms of the agreement, in order to assess whether the prohibition at s.203(1) bites at all on the terms of the agreement made, and if it does, the extent to which it bites on those terms (see *University of East London v Hinton* [2005] I.C.R. 1260 *per* Mummery L.J. at [17(3)]).

Compromise agreements

The conditions applicable to statutory compromise agreements are mandatory, **18–008** and an agreement will be void to the extent that those requirements are not satisfied (*Network Appliance v Sutherland* [2001] I.R.L.R. 12).

The requirement under ERA s.203 (3)(f) and its corresponding paragraphs in each of the parallel statutes, is strictly construed. An agreement that does not make

639

reference to the precise legislation regulating the compromise agreement is not effective to bar out subsequent litigation: *Palihakkara v British Telecommunications Plc* UKEAT/0185/06/DM. Employee's breach of Compromise Agreement.

Although it is a requirement that the employee must have received advice on the proposed compromise from an independent adviser, there is no requirement that the agreement must be signed or endorsed by that advisor. In practice employers often require counter signature or endorsement by the advisor to the effect that the conditions concerning the provision of advice and those relating to the "standing of the adviser" are satisfied.

Relate to the particular proceedings

18–009   Subsection (3)(b) requires that the agreement must "relate to the particular proceedings". This does not prevent the effective compromise of claims that have been proposed but not actually issued *Lunt v Merseyside TEC Ltd* [1999] I.C.R. 17, and *University of East London v Hinton* [2005] I.C.R. 1260, *per* Mummery L.J. at [17(5)].

The requirement that a compromise agreement must relate to the "particular proceedings" does not mean that each possible claim must be the subject of a separate compromise agreement (see *Lunt*, above). However, an agreement that merely refers to the settlement "all claims" will not be effective for the purposes of s.203.

In *University of East London v Hinton* [2005] I.C.R. 1260, the Court of Appeal concluded that in order to "relate to the particular proceedings" the agreement must expressly identify the specific statutory provision on which the claim rested or sufficiently describe the legal nature or factual basis of the proceedings such that it is clear which type of claim is being compromised. Thus the proceedings to which the compromise agreement relates must be apparent from the terms of the agreement itself. Further, Smith L.J. stated at [34]: "I would add that I would not regard it as good practice for lawyers to draft a standard form of compromise agreement which lists every form of employment right known to the law. Compromise agreements should be tailored to the individual circumstances of the instant case. Only in that way can the purpose behind this provision be fully satisfied."

In principle, it is possible to use the statutory compromise provisions to compromise future claims of which the employee either does not have knowledge, or could not be expected to have knowledge, but if this is the intention "the terms of [the] agreement must be absolutely plain and unequivocal" (*Hilton UK Hotels Limited v McNaughton* (EATS/0059/04), *per* Smith L.J. at [20]). In such a situation, the key issue is to identify precisely what the employee has agreed to. In the absence of a clear provision, it may well be difficult to conclude that the agreement as drafted has effectively excluded claims of which the employee had no knowledge, or did not believe existed.

Anti-Discrimination legislation: "relate to the particular complaint"

18–010   The relevant provisions of the Sex Discrimination Act 1975, the Race Relations Act 1976, the Disability Discrimination Act 1995, the Employment Equality (Religion or Belief) Regulations 2003, the Employment Equality (Sexual Orientation) Regulations 2003, and the Employment Equality (Age) Regulations 2006, refer to "the particular complaint" rather than the "particular proceedings". However, this difference in language ought not to result in any difference of approach: the principles set out in *Hinton* should be taken to apply equally to provisions drafted in terms of "the particular complaint".

Relevant independent advisor

18–011   There are four classes of advisor,

(1) A solicitor or barrister (whether practicing or employed to give legal advice) or a person who is an authorised advocate or authorised litigator within the meaning of the Courts and Legal Services Act 1990. This first class was extended by the Institute of Legal Executives Order 1998 and to include a fellow of the Institute of Legal Executives certified as a Legal Executive Advocate, however in regard to the categories of Legal Executive see class (4) below.

(2) Officers, officials, employees and members of an independent Trade Union certified by the Union as competent to give such advice and authorised to do so.

(3) Persons working at an advice centre provided that the advice centre is not the employer or an associated employer of the complainant.

(4) Persons of a description specified by an order of the Secretary of State. By the Compromise Agreements (Description of Persons) Order 2004 the class of Fellows of the Institute of Legal Executives was extended to those employed by a solicitors practice, provided the fellow was supervised when giving the advice by a practicing solicitor. By SI 2004/2515 the requirement that a fellow of the Institute of Legal Executives must also be a Legal Executive advocate was removed with effect from October 1, 2004.

Compromise agreements and TUPE

18–012 The rules relating to compromise agreements are quite separate from other legal principles affecting the validity of contractual variations. Thus, if a purported variation is ineffective by reason of the rules preventing changes in terms and conditions that occur by reason of a relevant transfer (see Transfer of Undertakings (Protection of Employment) Regulations 2006 at reg.4), the fact that the variation is made by way of a compromise agreement will be irrelevant. This follows from the fact that, wherever the validity of a compromise agreement is in issue, the first stage should be to consider the provisions of the agreement, without regard to the compromise agreement rules, in order to establish what it is that the agreement alone purports to do, and whether in fact it has effectively achieved that purpose.

However, if as a matter of substance, the agreement is designed not to alter terms and conditions of employment, but rather to compromise a claim that exists (regardless of whether the proceedings have actually been commenced), the agreement will be valid if it otherwise complies with the statutory provisions relating to compromise agreements (see *Solectron Scotland Ltd v Roper* [2004] I.R.L.R. 4, *per* Elias J. at [44]–[48]).

Discrimination claims in the county court

18–013 Under each of the anti-discrimination schemes that allow for county court claims, the validity of agreements to compromise such claims does not depend on satisfaction of the conditions relating to statutory compromise agreements

Claims compromised through the intervention of ACAS

18–014 The provisions of s.203(2)(e) of the Employment Rights Act 1996 specifically refer to the provisions of s.18 of the Employment Tribunals Act 1996 as to the powers and duties of ACAS conciliation officers. If an agreement has been reached after the conciliation officer has "taken action" it will be an effective agreement.

The provisions in other statutes (see, for example, s.77(4)(a) of the Sex Discrimination Act 1975) are less specific in this regard: a compromise is stated to be effective if "the contract is made with the assistance of a conciliation officer". *Clarke v Redcar and Cleveland BC* [2006] I.C.R. 897 considered s.77 of the Sex Discrimination Act 1975, and in particular the circumstances in which it could be said that the assistance of the conciliation officer had been provided. The EAT concluded that relevant assistance would be provided wherever the conciliation officer had taken action pursuant to s.18(2) of the Employment Tribunals Act 1996 "to endeavour to promote a settlement of the proceedings", a phrase which was considered apt to include action taken even before proceedings had been commenced.

As to the responsibilities of the conciliation officer, the EAT concluded that there was no responsibility to ensure that the terms of the settlement were fair to the employee; and no obligation to give legal advice as to the merits of the case. It was sufficient that the conciliation officer had intended and purported to act under s.18 of the Employment Tribunals Act 1996. If the settlement had been reached following such action, it could only be set aside if a tribunal concluded that the conciliation officer had acted in bad faith or had used unfair methods to promote the settlement.

Typically compromise agreements prepared by employers will contain a warranty that the employee is not aware of any repudiatory conduct on his part that would entitle the employer to dismiss him without notice and, in addition, that payment of the compromise sum is conditional upon the truth of the warranty. Where the warranty is shown to be a misrepresentation then payment of the compromise sum may be avoided: *Collidge v Freeport Plc* [2007] EWHC 1216, though rescission is unlikely to be available where its effect would be to retrospectively revive the contract of employment: *Crystal Palace Football Club v Dowie* [2007] I.R.L.R. 682.

Appendix 1

ADDRESSES AND CONTACT DETAILS FOR EMPLOYMENT TRIBUNALS IN ENGLAND, WALES AND SCOTLAND

Aberdeen
Mezzanine Floor
Atholl House
84–88 Guild Street
Aberdeen
AB11 6LT
Phone: 01224 593137
Fax: 01224 593138
email: *aberdeenet@tribunals.gsi.gov.uk*

Ashford
1st Floor
Ashford House
County Square Shopping Centre
Ashford
Kent
TN23 1YB
Phone: 01233 621 346
Fax: 01233 624 423
email: *ashfordet@tribunals.gsi.gov.uk*

Bedford
8–10 Howard Street
Bedford
MK40 3HS
Phone: 01234 351 306
Fax: 01234 352 315
email: *bedfordet@tribunals.gsi.gov.uk*

Birmingham
Phoenix House
1–3 Newhall Street
Birmingham
B3 3NH
Phone: 0121 236 6051
Fax: 0121 236 6029
email:
birminghamet@tribunals.gsi.gov.uk

Bristol
Ground Floor
The Crescent Centre
Temple Back
Bristol
BS1 6EZ
Phone: 0117 929 8261
Fax: 0117 925 3452
email: *bristolet@tribunals.gsi.gov.uk*

Bury St Edmunds
100 Southgate Street
Bury St. Edmunds
IP33 2AQ
Phone: 01284 762 171
Fax: 01284 706 064
email: *buryet@tribunals.gsi.gov.uk*

Cardiff
Caradog House
1–6 St Andrews Place
Cardiff
CF10 3BE
Phone: 02920 678 100
Fax: 02920 225 906
email: *cardiffet@tribunals.gsi.gov.uk*

Dundee
Ground Floor
Block C
Caledonian House,
Greenmarket
Dundee
DD1 4–QX
Phone: 0138 222 1578
Fax: 0138 222 7136
email: *dundeeet@tribunals.gsi.gov.uk*

643

Edinburgh
54–56 Melville Street
Edinburgh
EH3 7HF
Phone: 0131 226 5584
Fax: 0131 220 6847
email: *edinburghet@tribunals.gsi.gov.uk*

Exeter
2nd Floor
Keble House
Southernhay Gardens
Exeter
EX1 1NT
Phone: 01392 279 665
Fax: 01392 430 063
email: *exeteret@tribunals.gsi.gov.uk*

Glasgow
Eagle Building
215 Bothwell Street
Glasgow
G2 7TS
Phone: 0141 204 0730
Fax: 0141 204 0732
email: *glasgowet@tribunals.gsi.gov.uk*

Leeds
4th Floor
City Exchange
11 Albion Street
Leeds
LS1 5ES
Phone: 0113 245 9741
Fax: 0113 242 8843
email: *leedset@tribunals.gsi.gov.uk*

Leicester
5a New Walk
Leicester
LE1 6TE
Phone: 0116 255 0099
Fax: 0116 255 6099
email: *leicesteret@tribunals.gsi.gov.uk*

Liverpool
1st Floor
Cunard Building
Pier Head
Liverpool
L3 1TS
Phone: 0151 236 9397
Fax: 0151 231 1484
email: *liverpoolet@tribunals.gsi.gov.uk*

London Central
Ground Floor
Victory House
30–34 Kingsway
London
WC2B 6EX
Phone: 020 7273 8603
Fax: 020 7273 8686
email:
londoncentralet@tribunals.gsi.gov.uk

London South
Montague Court
101 London Road
West Croydon
CR0 2RF
Phone: 020 8667 9131
Fax: 020 8649 9470
email:
londonsouthet@tribunals.gsi.gov.uk

Manchester
Alexandra House
14–22 The Parsonage
Manchester
M3 2JA
Phone: 0161 833 0581
Fax: 0161 832 0249
email: *manchesteret@tribunals.gsi.gov.uk*

Newcastle
Quayside House
110 Quayside
Newcastle Upon Tyne
NE1 3DX
Phone: 0191 260 6900
Fax: 0191 222 1680
email: *newcastleet@tribunals.gsi.gov.uk*

Nottingham
3rd Floor
Byron House
2a Maid Marian Way
Nottingham
NG1 6HS
Phone: 0115 947 5701
Fax: 0115 950 7612
email: *nottinghamet@tribunals.gsi.gov.uk*

Reading
5th Floor
30–31 Friar Street
Reading
RG1 1DY
Phone: 0118 959 4917
Fax: 0118 956 8066
email: *readinget@tribunals.gsi.gov.uk*

Sheffield
14 East Parade
Sheffield
S1 2ET
Phone: 0114 276 0348
Fax: 0114 276 2551
email: *sheffieldet@tribunals.gsi.gov.uk*

Shrewsbury
Prospect House
Belle Vue Rd
Shrewsbury
SY3 7NR
Phone: 01743 358341
Fax: 01743 244186
email:
shrewsburyetct@tribunals.gsi.gov.uk

Southampton
3rd Floor Duke's Keep
Marsh Lane
Southampton
SO14 3EX
Phone: 023 8071 6400
Fax: 023 8063 5506
email: *southampton@tribunals.gsi.gov.uk*

Stratford
44 The Broadway
Stratford
E15 1XH
Phone: 020 8221 0921
Fax: 020 8221 0398
email: *stratfordet@tribunals.gsi.gov.uk*

Watford
3rd Floor
Radius House
51 Clarendon Road
Watford
WD17 1HU
Phone: 01923 281 750
Fax: 01923 281 781
email: *watfordet@tribunals.gsi.gov.uk*

App–
002

Offices of the Employment Appeal Tribunal

London	**Edinburgh**
Audit House	52 Melville Street
58 Victoria Embankment	Edinburgh
London	EH3 7HF
EC4Y 0DS	Phone: 0131 225 3963
Phone: 020 7273 1041	Fax: 0131 220 6694
Fax: 020 7273 1045	email: *edinburgheat@tribunals.gsi.gov.uk*
email: *londoneat@tribunals.gsi.gov.uk*	

INDEX

LEGAL TAXONOMY
FROM SWEET & MAXWELL

This index has been prepared using Sweet and Maxwell's Legal Taxonomy. Main index entries conform to keywords provided by the Legal Taxonomy except where references to specific documents or non-standard terms (denoted by quotation marks) have been included. These keywords provide a means of identifying similar concepts in other Sweet & Maxwell publications and online services to which keywords from the Legal Taxonomy have been applied. Readers may find some minor differences between terms used in the text and those which appear in the index. Suggestions to *taxonomy@sweetandmaxwell.co.uk*.

(all references are to paragraph number)

663

665

671

673

676